Applied International Trade

Second Edition

Harry P. Bowen

*McColl School of Business,
Queens University of Charlotte, USA*

Abraham Hollander

University of Montreal, Canada

Jean-Marie Viaene

*Erasmus School of Economics,
Erasmus University Rotterdam, The Netherlands
CESifo, Germany, and the Tinbergen Institute,
The Netherlands*

First published 2012 by
PALGRAVE MACMILLAN

Palgrave Macmillan in the UK is an imprint of Macmillan Publishers Limited,
registered in England, company number 785998, of Houndmills, Basingstoke,
Hampshire RG21 6XS.

Palgrave Macmillan in the US is a division of St Martin's Press LLC,
175 Fifth Avenue, New York, NY 10010.

Palgrave Macmillan is the global academic imprint of the above companies
and has companies and representatives throughout the world.

Palgrave® and Macmillan® are registered trademarks in the United States,
the United Kingdom, Europe and other countries.

ISBN 978–0–230–52154–4

This book is printed on paper suitable for recycling and made from fully
managed and sustained forest sources. Logging, pulping and manufacturing
processes are expected to conform to the environmental regulations of the
country of origin.

A catalogue record for this book is available from the British Library.

A catalog record for this book is available from the Library of Congress.

10   9   8   7   6   5   4   3   2   1
21   20   19   18   17   16   15   14   13   12

Printed and bound in China

To: Duoying and Anan
*   Ronit and Hyllah*
*   Anne, Arnaud and Nogol, Charlotte and Siu, and Elodie*

Short contents

Contents

Figures

Tables

Preface to the second edition

International trade continues to be one of the most active fields of research in economics. Developments include the analysis of multinational enterprises when markets are imperfectly competitive, the analysis of international labor migration, the examination of causal links between trade and growth, the role of heterogeneous firms in international trade, the revival of interest in the gravity equation and the emergence of political economy and economic geography as distinctive fields. In large measure, this activity sprang from contemporaneous efforts to confront the predictions of the theory with empirical facts. Assisting the latter activity has been the clarification of methods for conducting formal tests of trade theory as well as significant efforts to broaden the scope and availability of internationally comparable data. These advances in theory and empirical methods have deepened our understanding of the causes determining trade and factor flows, challenged conventional wisdom about the effects of trade policies, and injected new arguments into discussions about the merits of free trade.

This book was written with two objectives in mind. First, to give students, practitioners and researchers a text that encompasses the important theoretical and applied developments in the field and brings to the fore questions left unanswered by traditional trade models that more recent models have sought to address. Second, to provide the student of international trade with a single text that integrates theory, applied analysis and the formal testing of theory.

The design of the book reflects our conviction that linking theory and data during the learning process is key. Throughout the book, theory is interwoven with empirics, the latter stressing methodology as well as results. Positive analysis is followed by a presentation of policy issues. In this regard, the discussion of trade policy instruments is not limited to the derivation of qualitative results; proper attention is also paid to the partial and general equilibrium techniques used to measure the welfare and resource allocation effects of policy interventions. In addition, sprinkled throughout the book are exercises designed to deepen the students' understanding of the material and to cast light on issues glanced over in the body of the text. Each chapter concludes with a list of suggested additional readings intended to complement the material presented.

Organization

The book comprises four parts. Part I (Chapter 1 and 2) provides a map for the remainder of the book. Chapter 1 introduces key concepts and provides background data on patterns of trade and factor flows in order to motivate and orient the reader regarding the central issues addressed by the theory. Chapter 2 introduces the subject of trade policy and includes discussion of the institutional framework for administered protection. Part II (Chapter 3 to 7) covers the main theoretical aspects of the Ricardian and Heckscher-Ohlin models as well as in-depth presentation and discussion of the methodologies used to formally test the theory. Also covered are the effects of policy interventions in the setting of perfectly competitive markets. The latter includes discussion of the applied methods, including general equilibrium modeling, that are used to measure the welfare and other effects of trade policy. Part III (Chapters 8 to 11) presents models of imperfect competition as a means of explaining the volume and composition of trade. Two chapters on positive analysis are followed by a chapter on policy which explores the effects of tariffs, quotas and contingent protection. The final chapter of Part III discusses the multinational firm and the implications of foreign direct investment for the pattern of production and international specialization. Part IV (Chapters 12 to 14) is devoted to three selected topics: regional economic integration, the relationship between exchange rates and trade, and trade and growth. A final Appendix discusses the data common in applied analyses of trade and indicates sources for this data, which today are widely available on the Internet.

Prerequisites

The book is intended as a core text for an advanced undergraduate or graduate course in international trade. Students are assumed to have previously followed an intermediate undergraduate course in microeconomics and an introductory (perhaps intermediate) course in econometrics. The mathematical tools used in this book are basic calculus and linear algebra. A few chapters make use of elementary notions of game theory. Some facility with computer programming or a spreadsheet program is necessary to complete some of the exercises.

Acknowledgments

We acknowledge first and foremost our debt to teachers and colleagues who introduced us to the field and taught us many tricks of the trade: Robert E. Baldwin, Alan V. Deardorff, Wilfred J. Ethier, Herbert Glejser, Lawrence R. Klein, Anne O. Krueger, Edward E. Leamer, Robert Lipsey, Richard C. Marston, Ivor Pearce, and Robert M. Stern. The body of applied and theoretical work undertaken by these individuals and their students continues to forcibly shape the field.

We also extend special thanks to several groups of students who were exposed to successive drafts from lectures conducted at Cyprus, Michigan, Montreal, Munich (CES), Namur and the Tinbergen Institute. Our students are a continuing source of inspiration and friendship, and their numerous reactions led to more lucid exposition and many corrections. We would also like to thank those who helped with research assistance at various stages: Jelle Brouwer, Joel Habets, Haris Munandar, Irena Mikolajun, Wai Yee Pat, and Olga Zelenko.

We are indebted to the Tinbergen Institute and Erasmus University Rotterdam for their constant financial and logistical support at various stages of the project. Harry Bowen acknowledges the support of the McColl School of Business, Queens University of Charlotte and financial support from his position as the W.R. Holland Chair of International Business and Finance at Queens University of Charlotte. He also acknowledges earlier support of the Department of Economics and the Paul Merage School of Business at the University of California Irvine.

We would like to extend special thanks to nine anonymous referees for guidance and insightful comments. We owe a special debt to our co-authors and current and former colleagues who have been most generous in their willingness to read and offer helpful comments on the manuscript:

Robert E. Baldwin   Richard Chisik
Alan V. Deardorff   Harris Dellas
Leonard Dudley   Julian Emami Namini
Wilfred J. Ethier   Giovanni Facchini
Rob Feenstra   Switgard Feuerstein

Joe François   Sanjeev Goyal
James Harrigan   James Levinsohn
Charles van Marrewijk   José Luis Moraga-Gonzalez
Richard Paap   Joe Pelzman
Santanu Roy   Teun Schmidt
Robert M. Stern   Leo Sveikauskas
Frans van der Toorn   Casper de Vries
Laixun Zhao   Itzhak Zilcha

In addition, the past and current members of the International Studies Program of the National Bureau of Economic Research have been significant in shaping ideas and a continuing source of encouragement.

We are indebted to Mrs M.C. Ettekoven, M.T.L. Kruining, A. Mes, and S. Brewer who suffered through too many drafts of the manuscript. Our special posthumous thanks go to the late Mrs A. Bogaards-Kok (Anna) who has been with us since the first hour and somehow remained cheerful despite the numerous obstacles.

At Palgrave Macmillan, we are most grateful to Stephen Rutt for his support and remarkable patience at the start of this project. We have continued to benefit considerably from the efficiency, sharp deadlines and valuable encouragement from our editors Aléta Bezuidenhout and Jaime Marshall. We also thank Elizabeth Stone for her excellent editorial work.

Harry P. Bowen (Charlotte)
Abraham Hollander (Montreal)
Jean-Marie Viaene (Rotterdam)

Glossary

AGE	applied general equilibrium
AMS	aggregate measure of support
ANZCERTA	Australia–New Zealand Closer Economic Relations Trade Agreement
ASEAN	Association of South-East Asian Nations
BTN	Brussels Tariff Nomenclature
CCCN	Customs Cooperation Council Nomenclature
CES	constant elasticity of substitution
CET	common external tariff
CGE	computable general equilibrium
CIF	cost insurance freight
CRS	constant returns to scale
CRS/PC	constant returns to scale and perfect competition
CU	customs union
CUSTA	Canada–US Free Trade Agreement
CV	compensating variation
DCR	domestic content requirement
DPMC	differentiated product-monopolistic competition
DRAM	dynamic random access memory
DSPs	dispute settlement procedures
EAP	economically active population
EC	European Community
EEC	European Economic Community
EFTA	European Free Trade Area
EOS	economies of scale
EPT	exchange rate pass-through
ERP	effective rate of protection
EU	European Union
EV	equivalent variation
FAO	Food and Agriculture Organization
FDI	foreign direct investment
FOB	free on board
FPE	factor price equalization
GATS	General Agreement on Trade in Services
GATT	General Agreement on Tariffs and Trade
GDI	gross domestic investment
GIRS	globally increasing returns to scale
GL	Grubel-Lloyd
GTAP	Global Trade and Analysis Project
H-D	Harrod-Domar

H-O	Heckscher-Ohlin
H-O-S	Heckscher-Ohlin-Samuelson
H-O-V	Heckscher-Ohlin-Vanek
ICPSR	Inter-University Consortium for Political and Social Research
IIAS	intra-industry affiliate sales
IIFDI	intra-industry foreign direct investment
IIT	intra-industry trade
ILO	International Labour Office
IMF	International Monetary Fund
I-O	input–output
IRS	increasing returns to scale
IRS/IP	increasing returns to scale and imperfect (monopolistic) competition
ISCO	International Standard Classification of Occupations
ISIC	International Standard Industrial Classification
ITO	International Trade Organization
LDC	less developed countries
MERCOSUR	Southern Common Market
MFA	Multi-fibre Arrangement
MFN	most favored nations
MITI	Ministry of International Trade and Industry (Japan)
MNE	multinational enterprise
NACE	Nomenclature des Activités de la Communauté Européenne
NAFTA	North American Free Trade Agreement
NTB	non-tariff barrier
ODA	official development aid
OECD	Organisation for Economic Co-operation and Development
OPEC	Organization of Petroleum Exporting Countries
OLI	ownership, location and internalization
PCM	price-cost margin
PPF	production possibility frontier
PPP	purchasing power parity
R&D	research and development
RCA	revealed comparative advantage
RE	Ricardian equilibrium
RTA	regional trade agreement
SAM	social accounting matrix
SDR	special drawing right
SF	specific factor
SIC	Standard Industrial Classification
SITC	Standard International Trade Classification
TFP	total factor productivity
TPRM	trade policy review mechanism
TRIPs	Trade-related Aspects of International Property Rights
UNCTAD	United Nations Council on Trade and Development
UNIDO	United Nations Industrial Development Organization
VER	voluntary export restraint
VRA	voluntary restraint agreement
WE	wage equalization equilibrium
WTO	World Trade Organization

Acknowledgments

The authors and publishers wish to thank the following for permission to use copyright material:

The American Economic Association for **Table 7.2** from H.P. Bowen, E.E. Leamer, and L. Sveikauskas (1987), "Multicountry, Multifactor Tests of the Factor Abundance Theory," *American Economic Review*, 77 (5), 791–809; **Table 7.3** from E.E. Leamer and L. Sveikauskas (1987), "Multicountry, Multifactor Tests of the Factor Abundance Theory," *American Economic Review*, 77 (5), 791–809; **Table 7.4** from H.P. Bowen, E.E. Leamer, and L. Sveikauskas (1987), "Multicountry, Multifactor Tests of the Factor Abundance Theory," *American Economic Review*, 77 (5), 791–809; **Table 7.5** from H.P. Bowen, E.E. Leamer, and L. Sveikauskas (1987), "Multicountry, Multifactor Tests of the Factor Abundance Theory," *American Economic Review*, 77 (5), 791–809; **Table 12.3** from C. Broda, N. Limão, and D.E. Weinstein (2008), "Optimal Tariffs and Market Power: The Evidence," *American Economic Review*, 98 (5), 2032–2065.

Elsevier for **Table 6.1** from J. Brouwer, R. Paap, and J.-M. Viaene (2008), "Trade and FDI Effects of EMU Enlargement," *Journal of International Money and Finance*, 27 (2), 188–208; **Table 9.1** from A.B. Bernard, J.B. Jensen, and P.K. Schott (2006), "Trade Costs, Firms and Productivity," *Journal of Monetary Economics*, 53, 917–937; **Table 12.1** from , J.-M. Viaene (1982), "A Customs Union between Spain and the EEC," *European Economic Review*, 18, 345–368; **Table 13.1** from D.O. Cushman (1988), "US Bilateral Trade Flows and Exchange Risk during the Floating Period," *Journal of International Economics*, 24, 317–330; **Table 13.2** from J. Brouwer, R. Paap, and J.-M. Viaene (2008), "Trade and FDI Effects of EMU Enlargement," *Journal of International Money and Finance*, 27 (2), 188–208; **Table 14.4** from D.T. Coe, E. Helpman, and A.W. Hoffmaister (2009), "International R&D Spillovers and Institutions," *European Economic Review*, 53, 723–741.

European Central Bank for **Table 4.5** from M. Andersson, A. Gieseck, B. Pierluigi, and N. Vidalis (2008), "Wage Growth Dispersion across the Euro Area Countries: Some Stylised Facts," Occasional Paper Series No. 90, European Central Bank (Frankfurt: European Central Bank).

Harvard University Press for **Table 11.8** from N. Nunn and D. Trefler (2008), "The Boundaries of the Multinational Firm: an Empirical Analysis," in E. Helpman, D. Marin, and T. Verdier (Eds), *The Organization of Firms in a Global Economy* (Cambridge, MA: Harvard University Press).

Huisman **for Figure 14.3** from F. Huisman (2010), "The Middle East: Measuring Economic Integration and Labor Migration," MSc thesis, Erasmus University Rotterdam.

The Institute for International Economics for **Table 4.4** from W. Leontief (1954), "Domestic Production and Foreign Trade: the American Position Re- examined," *Economica Internazionale*, 7, 3–32.

John Wiley & Sons for **Table 3.3** from G.D.A. MacDougall (1951), "British and American Exports: A Study Suggested by the Theory of Comparative Costs, Part I," *Economic Journal*, 61, 487–521.

Kiel Institute for the World Economy for **Table 12.2** from A. Jacquemin and A. Sapir (1988), "European or World Integration?" *Weltwirtschaftliches Archiv*, 124 (1), 127–138; **Table 12.6** from H.P. Bowen, H. Munandar, and J.-M. Viaene (2010), "How Integrated is the World Economy?" *Review of World Economics* (*Weltwirtschaftliches Archiv*), 146 (3), 389–414.

The Massachusets Institute of Technology for **Table 3.4** from J. McGilvray and D. Simpson (1973), "The Commodity Structure of Anglo-Irish Trade," *Review of Economics and Statistics*, 55, 451–458; **Table 6.2** from K.-Y. Wong (1988), "International Factor Mobility and the Volume of Trade: An Empirical Study," in R.C. Feenstra (Ed.), *Empirical Methods for International Trade* (Cambridge, MA: MIT Press), 231–250.

The Organisation for Economic Co-operation and Development (OECD) for **Table 1.11** from OECD (2002), OECD Economic Outlook, 2002 (1), 309–320, Table VI.1; **Table 12.5** based on data from Table II.1, C. Corporate and capital income taxes, OECD Tax Database, www.oecd.org/ctp/taxdatabase (accessed December 2011).

Princeton University Press for **Table 10.2** from R.C. Feenstra (2003), *Advanced International Trade: Theory and Evidence* (Princeton: Princeton University Press).

Taylor & Francis for **Table 6.4** from S.P. Magee (1980), "Three Simple Tests of the Stolper-Samuelson Theorem," in P. Oppenheimer (Ed.), *Issues in International Economics* (London: Oriel Press), 138–153; **Table 6.5** from S.P. Magee (1980), "Three Simple Tests of the Stolper-Samuelson Theorem," in P. Oppenheimer (Ed.), *Issues in International Economics* (London: Oriel Press), 138–153.

University of Chicago Press for **Table 7.1** from E.E. Leamer (1980), "The Leontief Paradox Reconsidered," *Journal of Political Economy*, 88 (3), 495–503.

US Department of Commerce (USDC) for **Table 1.15** from USDC (2010), *Survey of Current Business* (Washington, DC: US Government Printing Office), July, 20–35.

US International Trade Commission (USITC) for **Table 5.1** from USITC (1989), *The Economic Effects of Significant U.S. Import Restraints*, USITC Publication 2222 (Washington, DC: US International Trade Commission), October.

Wiley for **Table 1.10** from D. Greenaway and C. Milner (1983), "On the Measurement of Intra-industry Trade," *The Economic Journal*, 93, 900–908; **Table 1.13** from T. Straubhaar (1988), "International Labour Migration with A Common Market: Some Aspects of EC Experience," *Journal of Common Market Studies*, 27(1), 45–62; **Table 2.4** from B. Balassa (1965), "Tariff Protection In Industrial Countries: An Evaluation," *Journal of Political Economy*, 73 (6): 573–594; **Table 2.5** from B. Balassa B. and C. Balassa (1984), "Industrial Protection in the Developed Countries," *The World Economy*, 7, 179–196.

The World Trade Organization (WTO) (www.wto.org) for **Table 1.1** from WTO (2010), International Trade Statistics (Geneva: WTO), http://www.wto.org/english/res_e/statis_e/its2010_e/its10_world_trade_dev_e.htm; **Table 1.4** from WTO (1995), International Trade, Trends and Statistics (Geneva: WTO) and WTO. (2010), International Trade Statistics (Geneva: WTO), http://www.wto.org/english/res_e/statis_e/its2010_e/its10_world_trade_dev_e.htm; **Table 2.1 from** GATT (1994), *The Results of the Uruguay Round of Multilateral Trade Negotiations*, Geneva (November); **Table 2.10** from WTO (2006), *World Trade Report* (Geneva: WTO); **Table 2.11** from WTO (2007), *World Trade Report* (Geneva: WTO).

Every effort has been made to trace all the copyright holders, but if any have been inadvertently overlooked the publishers will be pleased to make the necessary arrangements at the first opportunity.

I

The trading world: patterns and policy

1

The structure of international trade and factor flows

International trade is one of the fastest growing areas of research and theoretical discovery in economics. This growth stems from changes that began in the early 1970s, including the movement of countries to floating exchange rates, oil price shocks, widespread trade liberalization and rapid increases in trade and growth. Thus began the era of globalization, with rising trade volumes, the rapid emergence of industrializing countries such as Brazil, China and South Korea, and the increasing internationalization and global market orientation of firms in the most advanced industrialized nations that had previously focused on domestic markets. These changes have placed international trade issues high on the agenda of academic economists and policymakers as the growing economic links between nations have created benefits for all countries. Contributing to the growth of academic inquiry within the field of international trade is an ever increasing desire to match theory with data, with the former increasingly directed toward reconciling itself with the realities of the latter. In recognition of the interplay between theory and data, this chapter first introduces the main themes of international trade theory and then presents data on the evolving patterns of trade and international factor movements. The data are intended to highlight empirical regularities and to introduce the reader to the data and measures commonly used in applied analyses of international trade.

1.1 A preview of trade theory

The theory of international trade is fundamentally an extension and application of microeconomic theories of production and exchange to the study of economic transactions between agents in different countries. International trade theory utilizes and enriches the fundamental paradigms of profit and utility maximization to explain why countries trade, what goods they will export and import, how trade affects resource allocation within and between countries, and whether individual countries benefit from international trade. Two characteristics that distinguish theoretical analyses of international trade from those of traditional microeconomics are its predominant use of general equilibrium analysis and a focus on the role of the nation-state as a facilitator or inhibitor of economic transactions. The latter brings into consideration the question of the benefits, if any, a country receives from international trade and how economic policies toward trade may either increase or decrease these benefits.

Do countries gain from trade?

This is one of the key questions addressed by the theory of international trade, and its answer is a recurrent theme throughout this book. The essence of how trade can benefit a nation was eloquently stated by Adam Smith (1776) in his attack on mercantilist doctrine. Specifically, Smith noted that international trade benefits a nation by extending its opportunities for consumption beyond those available to it in isolation:

> The importation of gold and silver is not the principal, much less the sole benefit which a nation derives from its foreign trade. Between whatever places foreign trade is carried on, they all of them derive two distinct benefits from it. It carries out that surplus part of the produce of their land and labour for which there is no demand among them, and it brings back in turn for it something else for which there is a demand. It gives a value to their superfluities, by exchanging them for something else, which may satisfy a part of their wants, and increase their enjoyments. By means of it, the narrowness of the home market does not hinder the division of labor in any particular branch of art or manufacture from being carried to the highest perfection. By opening a more extensive market for whatever part of the produce of their labour may exceed the home consumption, it encourages them to improve its productive powers, and to augment its annual produce to the utmost, and thereby to increase the real revenue and wealth of the society.
>
> (Smith, 1776: 326)

David Ricardo (1817) recast and amplified Smith's observation on the benefits of trade into the now famous *principle of comparative advantage*. A country is said to have a comparative advantage in a good if its pre-trade relative price of that good is lower than that of a potential trading partner. In its modern form, comparative advantage reflects differences in opportunity costs between countries. Ricardo used his principle of comparative advantage to demonstrate the potential for all countries to gain from engaging in trade. In doing so, Ricardo also indirectly enunciated a theory of the composition of a country's trade: a country will export those goods in which it has a comparative advantage and import those goods in which it has a comparative disadvantage. Since a country benefits from trade when its trade pattern reflects its comparative advantage, it is crucial to understand what determines comparative advantage and how it can change over time.

What determines comparative advantage?

Theories of trade based on the principle comparative advantage are effectively theories of relative price determination. Since "supply and demand" determine price, these theories derive their predictions about differences in pre-trade relative price across countries, and hence the pattern of trade that will result from these differences, from the fundamental determinants of supply and demand. Figure 1.1 provides a stylized schematic of the supply and demand elements underlying the determination of relative prices.

Chapters 3 and 4 develop the theoretical arguments of the two most prominent theories of trade based on comparative advantage: the Ricardian theory and the Heckscher-Ohlin-Samuelson (H-O-S) theory. With reference to Figure 1.1, these theories assume perfectly competitive markets and homogeneous goods and focus on supply side determinants of relative prices, namely factor prices and technology. The Ricardian theory explains comparative

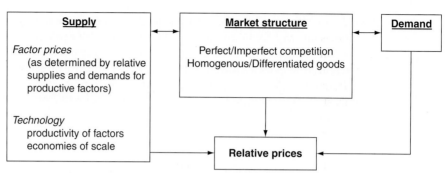

Figure 1.1   Determinants of relative prices: a stylized view

advantage in terms of supply cost differences that arise from differences in technology (factor productivities) across countries. In contrast, the H-O-S theory assumes technologies are the same across countries and so instead ascribes comparative advantage to supply cost differences due to differences in relative factor prices across countries. These relative factor price differences are in turn derived from a more fundamental difference in the relative supplies of productive factors across countries.

As Figure 1.1 indicates, differences in demand can also give rise to relative price differences across countries. However, trade models typically assume away differences in demand as a source of comparative advantage. One reason for ignoring differences in demand is that, if they were the basis of comparative advantage, then a fuller account would require one to state why demands differ – a task perhaps better suited to psychologists than economists.[1]

As Figure 1.1 indicates, another possible supply side explanation for comparative advantage is economies of scale.[2] That is, even if demand and all remaining supply elements are identical across countries, the relative price of a good can still differ between countries due to economies of scale. Since in this case industry size is a determinant of production costs, the goods in which a country has a comparative advantage would be determined by the size of its domestic industries compared with the size of those industries abroad. Chapters 3, 8 and 9 examine economies of scale as a determinant of trade and its implications for the benefits derived from trade.

Market structure and differentiated goods

Reflecting their neoclassical lineage, formal models of the Ricardian and H-O-S theories assume perfectly competitive markets and homogeneous goods. However, as explored in Chapters 8 to 11, relaxing these assumption leads to reasons for trade other than relative price differences between countries, that is, rather than comparative advantages. For example, if goods are differentiated rather than homogeneous and consumers have a preference for variety then trade can arise even if countries are identical in every respect. For example, take the simple case where wine produced in France and wine produced in the United States (US) are imperfect substitutes. It is then easy to imagine trade in "wine" taking place between these countries, even if these countries have identical preferences, technology and factor prices. Tautologically, we might say that France has a comparative advantage in "French" wine while the US has a comparative advantage in "US" wine. However, the source of trade in this case is not relative price differences but rather that consumers in each country, since they have a preference for variety, wish to consume some of each type of wine.[3] Note also a special feature of the trade that results in this case: each country is both an exporter and an importer of "wine." This type of trade is called *intra-industry* trade, as distinguished from *inter-industry* trade, the latter being trade in the goods produced by different industries. Later in this chapter we consider data on the prevalence of intra-industry trade. Chapters 8, 9 and 11 discuss theoretical models and frameworks that predict the existence of intra-industry trade.

Imperfectly competitive market structures can be another source of trade, and gains from trade, independent of comparative advantage. For example, gains from trade can arise within the simplest framework of homogenous goods and Cournot rivalry among firms. This is because the larger market afforded by the opportunity to trade increases rivalry among firms which results in lower product prices and increased output. Models in which competition is imperfect often predict that trade between countries will be intra-industry trade. As discussed in Chapters 8, 9 and 11, further predictions about the nature of trade and the benefits of trade are possible when models combine the assumptions of imperfect competition, economies of scale at the firm level and consumer demand that exhibits a preference for variety.

We now turn to look at data that indicate the nature and significance of international trade flows and their evolution over time. In conducting this examination of the data we will have occasion to consider whether actual trade patterns reflect any of the elements that our brief overview of international trade theory suggests would determine these patterns.

1.2 Patterns of international trade

Globalization

In 2009, the value of world merchandise exports was approximately 12.49 trillion US dollars. As chronicled in Figure 1.2 to Figure 1.4, world trade has grown steadily since the 1950s and this growth has generally exceeded the growth in world output (GDP) with one clear exception: the downturn in 2008 and 2009.[4] During these two years the ratio of world trade to world GDP declined by nearly 30 percent. This "great trade contraction" reflected the

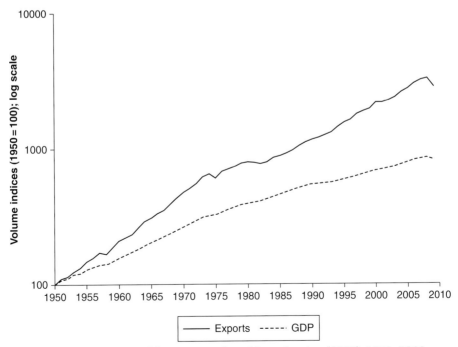

Figure 1.2 The growth in world exports and world production (GDP), 1950–2009
Source: The authors, based on data from WTO (2010).

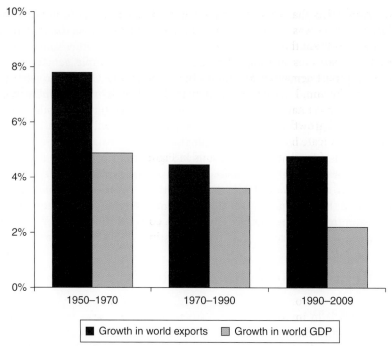

Figure 1.3 Average annual change in world exports and world production for selected sub-periods, 1950–2009

Source: The authors, based on data from WTO (2010).

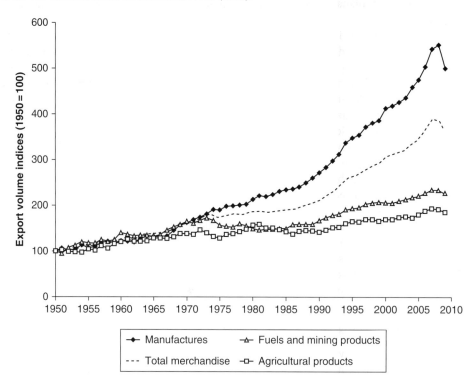

Figure 1.4 Growth in world trade and its major components relative to world output, 1984–2009

Source: The authors, based on data from WTO (2010).

financial crisis that engulfed particularly the US and European economies starting in 2008. Initially, there was great concern that this contraction in world trade reflected the inability of traders to obtain the financing needed to maintain international trade transactions. However, research indicates that most of the contraction can be attributed to a widespread contraction of import demand associated with the onset of recession in most industrialized countries (Eaton, Kortum, Neimanx and Romalis, 2010). By late-2010, world trade had rebounded to almost its pre-financial crisis level. Apart from the downturn in 2008 and 2009, the consistently rapid growth in world trade compared with world output since the 1950s is popularly taken to indicate increasing "globalization."

The data for selected sub-periods in Figure 1.3 indicate that the two decade period from 1970–90 was one of relatively low growth in world trade relative to world output compared with other time periods, with the period from 1990–2009 being a period of particularly high growth in trade relative to the growth in world output.

Figure 1.4 indicates that an important component of globalization has been the growth in trade of manufactured goods. Growth in this aggregate category of goods reflects, but also masks, an important feature of globalization: trade is increasingly in intermediate rather than final goods. The use of intermediate goods sourced abroad is referred to as "vertical specialization trade," and it has been estimated that such trade accounts for 30 percent of the world value of exports (Hummels, Ishii and Yi (2001)). Moreover, a significant portion of the trade in intermediate goods increasingly reflects the exchange of goods among the domestic and foreign-based subsidiaries of multinational companies. Such trade is called *intra-firm trade*, and its rationale and implications are discussed in Chapter 11. The growing importance of intra-firm and intermediate goods trade has been made possible by ongoing advances in telecommunications and lower transport costs. These factors therefore constitute a further explanation for the rapid growth in trade relative to production indicated in Figure 1.2.

As discussed in Chapter 2, another explanation for globalization is the steady reduction in tariffs and other trade barriers since the early 1950s that has been facilitated by the World Trade Organization (WTO) and its flagship General Agreement on Tariffs and Trade (GATT). Still another explanation is the shift since the 1970s in the development strategy of many developing countries, notably in Asia. Broadly speaking, many developing countries began to "liberalize" their trade in the 1970s. This involved reducing levels of protection that shielded domestic industries from import competition while emphasizing export activities as a source of development. Among the most notable examples is China, which opened its economy only in 1979 and has since become a major exporter and importer in the world economy. Last, but not least, has been the accumulation of physical and human capital and transfer of technology,[5] which have increased the capacity for trade and also altered its composition.

Finally, an increasingly important if difficult to measure component of world trade is trade in services. Table 1.1 shows data on the growth in exports of commercial services for four service categories and seven regions. As indicated in Table 1.1, the catch-all category "other commercial services" has been the fastest growing service segment, with North America and Asia being the more important sources of these export flows.

Trade volumes and trade dependence

Changes in the overall volume of trade mask changes in the volume of trade between regions. Table 1.2 lists intra-regional and inter-regional trade as a share of world trade for seven regions in 1979 and 2009. Diagonal entries are intra-regional trade, off-diagonal entries are inter-regional trade. Adding these trade shares across regions reveals that the six trade flows within and between North America, Europe and the Commonwealth of Independent States

Table 1.1 Growth of commercial services exports by category and by region, 1990–2009

	World	North America	South and Central America	Europe	CIS	Africa	Middle East	Asia
Commercial services								
1990–95	8	8	9	...	...	...	...	...
1995–00	5	7	6	...	...	...	...	4
2000–09	9	6	9	10	16	...	...	11
Transportation services								
1990–95	6	4	7	...	...	...	...	11
1995–00	3	3	1	3	...	...	...	3
2000–09	8	4	8	9	13	...	...	8
Travel								
1990–95	9	7	10	...	...	8	...	...
1995–00	3	6	7	2	...	6	...	2
2000–09	7	2	6	7	15	12	...	10
Other commercial services								
1990–95	10	12	10	...	...	...	...	16
1995–00	7	11	9	...	...	...	...	6
2000–09	12	8	13	12	23	...	...	13

Source: Based on WTO (2010, Table III.2).

(CIS, which comprises Russia, Central Asia and the Caucasus), accounted for 48.9 percent of world trade in 1979 and 83.7 percent in 2009. Trade among European countries is by far the largest intra-regional trade flow and reflects primarily the importance of the common market among European Union (EU) member states. Levels of trade between Asian countries are high, but are nonetheless about half that of intra-European trade. Chapter 6 discusses "gravity equation" models that are routinely used to assess empirically the determinants of bilateral trade flows, whether between regions or between individual countries.

Table 1.3 shows average annual compound rates of growth in the value of these regional trade shares between 1979 and 2009.[6] The diagonal terms for North America, Europe, Africa and Asia indicate relatively rapid increases in intra-regional trade, partly reflecting new and renewed implementation of regional agreements that lower intra-regional trade barriers such as the North American Free Trade Agreement (NAFTA) and the Association of South-East Asian Nations (ASEAN); Chapter 12 discusses such regional trade agreements. Only the trade among CIS countries shows a decline between 1979 and 2009, reflecting the breakup of the former USSR and a more market-oriented redirection of the trade of the former communist bloc countries to countries outside the former USSR.

A notable change between 1979 and 2009 is the decline in inter-regional trade between North America and all other regions except Asia. Also notable is that for all regions, inter-regional trade with Asia increased. Conversely, inter-regional trade between CIS countries and all other regions except Africa declined. One fact made evident by these data is that trade

Table 1.2 Regional trade[a] as a percentage of world trade, 1979[b] and 2009

Destination origin	North America	South and C. America	Western Europe	CIS	Africa	Middle East	Asia
North America	12.8 (4.6)						
South and C. America	2.0 (4.0)	2.0 (1.1)					
Europe	5.5 (6.6)	1.4 (2.6)	60.4 (28.8)				
CIS[c]	0.3 (0.5)	0.1 (0.6)	3.2 (4.1)	1.5 (4.3)			
Africa	0.8 (1.9)	0.2 (0.3)	2.6 (5)	0.4 (0.3)	0.7 (0.3)		
Middle East	0.9 (1.9)	0.1 (0.5)	1.9 (5.7)	0.2 (0.5)	0.4 (0.2)	1.8 (0.4)	
Asia	7.9 (6.4)	1.6 (0.9)	8.9 (5)	1.0 (1)	1.6 (0.7)	4.3 (3.8)	30.8 (6.3)

[a] Figures for the trade of origin region A with destination region B is the sum of the value of A's exports to B and the value of B's exports to A divided by world exports plus world imports.
[b] 1979 values are in parentheses.
[c] Central and Eastern Europe and the former USSR (Russian Federation).
Sources: GATT (1990) and WTO (1995, 2010).

Table 1.3 Growth in intra-regional and inter-regional trade, 1999–2009
(average annual rate of growth, in percent)

Destination origin	North America	South and C. America	Europe	CIS	Africa	Middle East	Asia
North America	5.1						
South and C. America	−3.4	3.0					
Europe	−0.9	−3.2	3.7				
CIS	−3.0	−9.4	−1.2	−5.4			
Africa	−4.4	−2.4	−3.3	1.9	4.6		
Middle East	−3.6	−6.6	−5.5	−6.0	3.2	7.5	
Asia	1.1	2.9	2.9	0.0	4.0	0.7	7.9

[a] Russia, Central Asia and the Caucasus.
Source: The authors, based on data from WTO (1995, 2010).

between distinct but "similar" regions tends to be higher, and to grow at higher rates, than trade between "dissimilar" regions.

Table 1.4 provides additional information on trade flows by showing the 20 leading exporters and importers in 1984 and 2009. Over this period, China, Malaysia, Korea, and Spain show the largest increase in rank among exporters; China, Australia, and Mexico show the largest increase in rank among importers. As previously noted, the increased trade of such countries is due, in part, to a change in their development strategy from one of high import

Table 1.4 Leading exporters and importers in world merchandise trade, 1984 and 2009[a]

Exporter	1984		2009		Importer	1984		2009	
	Rank	Share	Value	Share		Rank	Share	Value	Share
1. China	19	1.3	1201.5	9.6	1. United States	1	17.2	1,605.3	12.7
2. Germany	2	10.1	1126.4	9.0	2. China	18	1.3	1,005.7	7.9
3. United States	1	11.5	1056.0	8.5	3. Germany	2	8.7	938.3	7.4
4. Japan	3	8.7	580.7	4.6	4. France	3	6.8	559.8	4.4
5. Netherlands	9	3.4	498.3	4.0	5. Japan	9	3.1	552.0	4.4
6. France	4	5	484.7	3.9	6. United Kingdom	5	5.2	481.7	3.8
7. Italy	8	3.8	405.8	3.2	7. Netherlands	6	4.2	445.5	3.5
8. Belgium	10	2.7	369.9	3.0	8. Italy	10	2.8	412.7	3.3
9. Korea, Republic of	15	1.5	363.5	2.9	9. Hong Kong	12	1.5	352.2	2.8
10. United Kingdom	5	4.8	352.5	2.8	10. Belgium	4	5.2	351.9	2.8
11. Hong Kong	16	1.5	329.4	2.6	11. Canada	13	1.5	329.9	2.6
12. Canada	7	4.6	316.7	2.5	12. Korea, Republic of	8	3.9	323.1	2.5
13. Russian Federation	6	4.7	303.4	2.4	13. Spain	7	4	287.6	2.3
14. Singapore	20	1.2	269.8	2.2	14. Singapore	16	1.4	245.8	1.9
15. Mexico	14	1.5	229.6	1.8	15. Mexico	25	0.8	241.5	1.9
16. Spain	21	1.2	218.5	1.7	16. Russian Federation	15	1.4	191.8	1.5
17. Taipei, Chinese	12	1.6	203.7	1.6	17. Taipei, Chinese	20	1.1	174.4	1.4
18. Switzerland	18	1.3	172.9	1.4	18. Australia	14	1.5	165.5	1.3
19. Malaysia	27	0.8	157.4	1.3	19. Switzerland	19	1.3	155.7	1.2
20. Australia	22	1.2	154.2	1.2	20. Thailand	38	0.5	133.8	1.1
Country above total		72.4	8,795.1	70.4	Country above total		73.4	8,954.2	70.6
World total		100.0	12,490.2	1.2	World total		100.0	12,682.4	100.0

[a] Countries are ordered by their rank in 2009. Shares are world shares, in percent. Values in billions of US dollars.
Source: Adapted from WTO (1995, 2010).

barriers (and hence low export volumes) to one of import liberalization and export promotion. In general, the changes in ranking evident in Table 1.4 attest to the rapid changes in trade that have accompanied globalization.

Two additional facts evident in Table 1.4 are: 1) the largest exporters are also the largest importers and 2) for most countries their trade balance (exports minus imports) is relatively small. The latter situation is not peculiar to 2009 nor is it accidental; it instead most likely reflects the actions of governments that often interpret such imbalances as a source of their internal economic problems.

Trade dependence

Another indicator of a country's involvement in trade is its trade dependence, as measured by the ratio of its exports plus imports to its GDP. Table 1.5 lists the average trade dependence of selected countries over the decades from 1970–79 and 1990–99, and for the years 2000–07. The countries are ranked in descending order of their average trade dependence for the period 2000–07. Note first that the trade dependence of several countries exceeds 200 percent.[7] This most likely reflects that these countries engage primarily in entrepôt (warehouse) trade – that is, they are primarily conduits for the trans-shipment of goods from the country of production to the country of consumption.

Whereas Table 1.4 lists China as the world's largest trader in 2009, Table 1.5 indicates that it ranks relatively low on trade dependence (an average of 58 percent during 2000–07). By comparison, the average trade dependence of Germany is 73 percent while that of Switzerland is 89 percent during the period 2000–07. Whether trade dependence is high or low can reflect a number of factors. For example, low trade dependence may indicate significant restrictions on trade (Somalia) or that non-traded sectors (such as services) are an important source of a country's value added (for example, services account for over 70 percent of US value added). Regardless the level of trade dependence, the revealing aspect of the data in Table 1.4 is the change over time in each country's trade dependence, which generally underscores rising globalization and interdependence. For example, China's average trade dependence rose from 10 percent in 1970–79 to 39 percent in 1990–99 and to 59 percent in 2000–07: a gain of 510 percent between the 1970s and the 2000s.

Trade patterns and revealed comparative advantage

As noted in Section 1.1, a key question addressed by the theory of international trade is what determines the pattern of goods exported and imported, that is, the commodity composition of trade. One explanation has already been suggested – comparative advantage – which in turn derives from differences between countries in the fundamental determinants of supply and demand. But to which of these possible fundamental determinants are trade patterns systematically related? Sorting out which influences are important, or which are the relatively more important, in determining trade patterns is properly the task of empirical tests of trade theory. Chapter 7 considers the issues involved in testing the H-O-S theory, while the empirical merits of other trade theories are discussed in the chapters where they are developed. Here we briefly look at data on the composition of trade and consider what may lie behind observed patterns and to further introduce concepts commonly used in empirical studies of trade.

Revealed comparative advantage

The overriding importance of the theoretical concept of comparative advantage means that its empirical measurement is crucial. However, this theoretical concept relates to patterns of pre-trade relative prices which are not observable. Applied work must therefore devise measures

Table 1.5 Trade dependence of selected countries, 1960–69, 1990–99, 2000–07[a] (in %)

Country	Rank 2000–07	Average 1970–79[b]	Average 1990–99[b]	Average 2000–07[b]	% change		
					1970s to 1990s	1990s to 2000s	1970s to 2000s
Singapore	1	301	338	408	12	21	35
Hong Kong	2	169	264	342	57	30	103
Luxembourg	3	172	204	281	19	37	63
Malaysia	4	84	171	206	104	21	147
Swaziland	7	147	170	173	16	1	18
Belgium	10	106	135	166	28	23	57
Ireland	12	87	133	162	54	22	87
Macao	13	237	145	159	−39	10	−33
Bahrain	14	189	160	158	−16	−1	−17
Iraq	15	108	104	152	−4	46	41
United Arab Emirates	18	112	135	147	21	9	31
Puerto Rico	19	122	130	141	7	8	16
Hungary	20	66	83	140	26	69	112
Panama	21	177	165	139	−7	−16	−21
Vietnam	22	62	81	136	30	68	119
Thailand	24	41	87	134	115	53	230
Netherlands	28	93	113	130	21	16	40
Congo, Republic of	29	86	112	130	30	16	51
Cambodia	31	17	53	128	204	143	640
Bulgaria	33	72	93	128	29	38	79
Jordan	34	90	127	127	41	0	41
Honduras	35	85	108	126	27	17	49
Mongolia	36	55	91	125	65	38	129
Mauritius	38	109	128	124	18	−3	14
Belize	40	92	115	121	24	5	31
Suriname	42	118	124	117	6	−6	−1
Taiwan	44	85	89	116	4	30	36
Afghanistan	49	27	65	107	139	65	295
Vanuatu	50	117	107	106	−9	−1	−9
Philippines	51	46	81	105	77	29	129
Paraguay	56	47	106	102	123	−4	115
Cyprus	57	96	103	102	7	−1	6
Ghana	58	34	59	102	77	71	202
Gambia, The	59	80	105	101	30	−3	26

Mauritania	60	101	83	100	−18	21	−1
Jamaica	61	77	107	99	39	−7	29
Tunisia	62	63	89	99	41	11	57
Namibia	63	156	108	99	−31	−9	−37
Austria	65	61	74	98	21	33	60
Oman	66	101	82	98	−18	19	−3
Costa Rica	67	60	81	96	35	19	61
Gabon	68	107	90	94	−15	4	−12
Denmark	69	61	72	92	17	28	50
Kuwait	70	100	111	90	11	−19	−10
Switzerland	71	63	71	89	13	27	43
Sweden	73	55	68	88	23	29	60
Côte d'Ivoire	74	77	65	87	−16	33	12
Samoa	75	87	95	86	9	−9	−1
Bhutan	76	59	80	85	36	7	45
Botswana	77	107	94	85	−11	−10	−21
Libya	78	93	54	84	−42	56	−9
Guinea-Bissau	79	40	51	82	28	59	102
Nicaragua	80	68	55	81	−19	48	20
Israel	81	71	65	81	−8	24	14
Korea, Republic of	83	56	61	80	10	31	44
Bermuda	84	94	85	78	−10	−8	−17
Saudi Arabia	85	87	66	78	−24	17	−11
Sri Lanka	86	57	74	77	29	5	36
Iceland	87	74	68	77	−9	13	3
Chad	88	50	53	77	6	45	54
Romania	89	26	54	76	105	41	189
Tonga	90	94	78	76	−17	−2	−19
Finland	91	52	60	76	16	26	46
Dominican Republic	92	74	79	75	7	−5	2
Canada	93	46	67	75	45	12	63
Cape Verde	94	96	82	74	−15	−10	−23
Germany	95	37	50	73	36	46	97
Zimbabwe	96	57	70	73	23	4	29
Syria	97	49	65	73	33	11	48
Norway	98	76	72	73	−6	1	−5
El Salvador	99	66	56	71	−15	28	8
Poland	100	49	47	71	−4	51	45
Chile	101	38	57	71	51	24	87

Table 1.5 (Continued)

Country	Rank 2000–07	Average 1970–79[b]	Average 1990–99[b]	Average 2000–07[b]	% change		
					1970s to 1990s	1990s to 2000s	1970s to 2000s
Liberia	102	143	57	70	−60	24	−51
Mozambique	103	18	52	69	194	34	295
Guatemala	104	62	62	68	0	9	9
Madagascar	105	44	48	68	10	40	55
Portugal	106	47	64	67	35	6	43
Senegal	107	54	54	67	0	23	24
Morocco	108	49	53	66	8	24	34
Albania	109	45	53	66	18	25	48
Nigeria	110	36	60	66	67	10	84
Malawi	112	51	52	63	4	20	24
Zambia	113	85	72	63	−15	−13	−26
Turkey	114	14	41	62	196	50	345
New Zealand	115	52	58	61	11	7	18
Mexico	116	20	49	61	139	25	199
Ecuador	117	49	55	61	11	12	24
Laos	118	13	60	61	365	2	373
Lebanon	119	85	77	60	−10	−21	−30
Mali	120	53	53	60	1	13	14
Indonesia	121	42	58	60	38	2	41
Bolivia	122	53	49	58	−8	20	10
China	123	10	39	58	311	48	510
South Africa	124	53	44	58	−18	33	9
Spain	125	28	44	58	55	32	104
Greece	126	37	46	57	26	24	55
Kenya	127	48	50	57	3	14	17
United Kingdom	128	51	53	56	4	6	10
Guinea	129	57	44	55	−24	27	−4
Congo, Dem. Rep.	130	31	42	54	37	28	75
Egypt	131	42	50	54	19	7	28
France	132	37	45	54	23	18	45
Italy	133	39	43	53	10	24	36
Iran	134	75	39	53	−47	34	−30
Sierra Leone	135	52	42	53	−18	25	2
Venezuela	136	46	54	52	17	−4	13
Uruguay	138	34	40	51	21	27	53

Benin	139	85	59	51	−32	−13	−41
Tanzania	140	40	51	48	26	−5	19
Comoros	141	62	57	47	−9	−16	−24
Niger	142	48	43	47	−11	11	−1
Nepal	143	20	50	46	151	−8	129
Cameroon	144	58	39	44	−33	12	−25
Ethiopia	145	20	25	44	26	77	123
Colombia	146	29	35	43	23	22	50
Australia	147	28	38	41	34	10	48
Burundi	148	28	31	41	11	29	43
Uganda	149	27	31	41	13	31	47
Peru	150	44	30	40	−32	32	−9
Bangladesh	151	13	26	39	94	53	198
Sudan	152	31	20	38	−34	88	23
Argentina	153	18	19	38	4	101	110
India	154	10	21	37	106	79	268
Central African Republic	155	62	42	35	−33	−16	−43
Rwanda	156	22	32	34	49	7	59
Pakistan	157	23	29	34	30	16	52
Cuba	159	63	32	30	−48	−8	−52
Brazil	160	10	17	26	58	58	150
United States	161	15	22	26	48	16	71
Japan	162	23	18	25	−20	37	10
Somalia	163	38	3	2	−92	−32	−95

[a]Defined as a country's total exports plus total imports divided by nominal GDP. Ranking among 163 countries.
[b]Unweighted average of annual trade dependence ratios over indicated period.
Source: The authors, based on data from Heston and Summers (1991) and Heston and Summers and Aten (2009).

on the basis of observables that can be used to infer what would have been the pattern of pre-trade prices. Inferring comparative advantage from observed data is called "revealing" comparative advantage. For example, theories of comparative advantage (for example, the H-O-S model) normally predict the pattern of a country's net exports across goods. Applied work therefore uses actual data on a country's net exports to reveal those goods in which the country presumably had a pre-trade comparative advantage.

Table 1.6 illustrates this type of analysis by showing the commodities that are the ten largest net exports and ten largest net imports of selected countries.[8] Also listed for each commodity is the value of another measure of comparative advantage: the revealed comparative advantage (*RCA*) index. The particular *RCA* index shown in Table 1.6 is computed as:[9]

$$RCA = (X_{ij}/X_{wj})/(X_{i\bullet}/X_{w\bullet}) \qquad (1.1)$$

Table 1.6 Ten largest net exports and net imports and RCA indices for selected countries
(based on averages of trade values over the period 2007–09)

Country		Ten largest net exports[a]	RCA	Ten largest net imports[a]	RCA
Brazil	1	281-Iron ore and concentrates	2.293	562-Fertilizers	0.526
	2	222-Oil seeds and oleaginous fruits used for the extraction of soft fixed vegetable oils (excluding flours and meals)	7.204	776-Thermionic, cold cathode or photocathode valves and tubes; diodes, transistors and similar semiconductor devices; integrated circuits, etc.; parts	0.018
	3	12-Meat, other than of bovine animals, and edible offal, fresh, chilled or frozen (except meat and meat offal not suitable for human consumption)	9.443	515-Organo-inorganic compounds, heterocyclic compounds, nucleic acids and their salts	0.214
	4	61-Sugars, molasses, and honey	8.365	334-Petroleum oils and oils from bituminous minerals (other than crude), and products therefrom containing 70% (by Wt) or more of these oils, N.E.S.	0.552
	5	71-Coffee and coffee substitutes	6.520	764-Telecommunications equipment, N.E.S.; and parts, N.E.S., and accessories of apparatus falling within telecommunications, etc.	0.394
	6	81-Feeding stuff for animals (not including unmilled cereals)	14.069	321-Coal, pulverized or not, but not agglomerated	0.000
	7	671-Pig iron and spiegeleisen, sponge iron, iron or steel granules and powders and ferroalloys	20.060	333-Petroleum oils and oils from bituminous minerals, crude	1.338
	8	11-Meat of bovine animals, fresh, chilled or frozen	9.303	542-Medicaments (including veterinary medicaments)	0.165
	9	251-Pulp and waste paper	17.159	874-Measuring, checking, analyzing and controlling instruments and apparatus, N.E.S.	0.164
	10	792-Aircraft and associated equipment; spacecraft (including satellites) and spacecraft launch vehicles; and parts thereof	19.262	714-Engines and motors, nonelectric (other than steam turbines, internal combustion piston engines and power generating machinery); parts thereof, N.E.S.	0.173
China	1	752-Automatic data processing machines and units thereof; magnetic or optical readers; machines transcribing coded media and processing such data, N.E.S.	3.502	776-Thermionic, cold cathode or photocathode valves and tubes; diodes, transistors and similar semiconductor devices; integrated circuits, etc.; parts	1.034

	2	764-Telecommunications equipment, N.E.S.; and parts, N.E.S., and accessories of apparatus falling within telecommunications, etc.	1.552	333-Petroleum oils and oils from bituminous minerals, crude	0.044
	3	845-Articles of apparel, of textile fabrics, whether or not knitted or crocheted, N.E.S.	2.709	281-Iron ore and concentrates	0.001
	4	821-Furniture and parts thereof; bedding, mattresses, mattress supports, cushions and similar stuffed furnishings	3.042	871-Optical instruments and apparatus, N.E.S.	3.695
	5	894-Baby carriages, toys, games and sporting goods	3.430	222-Oil seeds and oleaginous fruits used for the extraction of soft fixed vegetable oils (excluding flours and meals)	0.180
	6	851-Footwear	3.428	682-Copper	0.419
	7	842-Women's or girls' coats, capes, jackets, suits, trousers, dresses, skirts, underwear, etc. of woven textiles (except swimwear and coated etc. apparel)	2.513	728-Machinery and equipment specialized for particular industries, and parts thereof, N.E.S.	0.470
	8	775-Household type electrical and nonelectrical equipment, N.E.S.	3.343	251-Pulp and waste paper	0.027
	9	793-Ships, boats (including hovercraft) and floating structures	2.713	781-Motor cars and other motor vehicles principally designed for the transport of persons (not public transport), including station wagons and racing cars	0.043
	10	763-Sound recorders or reproducers; television image and sound recorders or reproducers	4.102	511-Hydrocarbons, N.E.S. and their halogenated, sulfonated, nitrated or nitrosated derivatives	0.321
Germany	1	781-Motor cars and other motor vehicles principally designed for the transport of persons (not public transport), including station wagons and racing cars	1.663	333-Petroleum oils and oils from bituminous minerals, crude	0.001
	2	728-Machinery and equipment specialized for particular industries, and parts thereof, N.E.S.	2.523	343-Natural gas, whether or not liquefied	0.222
	3	542-Medicaments (including veterinary medicaments)	1.767	752-Automatic data processing machines and units thereof; magnetic or optical readers; machines transcribing coded media and processing such data, N.E.S.	0.504

Table 1.6 (Continued)

Country		Ten largest net exports[a]	RCA	Ten largest net imports[a]	RCA
	4	784-Parts and accessories for tractors, motor cars and other motor vehicles, trucks, public-transport vehicles and road motor vehicles N.E.S.	1.415	57-Fruit and nuts (not including oil nuts), fresh or dried	0.243
	5	772-Electrical apparatus for switching or protecting electrical circuits or for making connections to or in electrical circuits (excluding telephone etc.)	1.795	845-Articles of apparel, of textile fabrics, whether or not knitted or crocheted, N.E.S.	0.456
	6	874-Measuring, checking, analyzing and controlling instruments and apparatus, N.E.S.	1.536	321-Coal, pulverized or not, but not agglomerated	0.012
	7	782-Motor vehicles for the transport of goods and special purpose motor vehicles	1.539	761-TV receivers (including video monitors & projectors) whether or not incorp radiobroadcast receivers or sound or video recording or reproducing apparatus	0.310
	8	743-Pumps (not for liquids), air or gas compressors and fans; ventilating hoods incorporating a fan; centrifuges; filtering etc. apparatus; parts thereof	1.506	54-Vegetables, fresh, chilled, frozen or simply preserved; roots, tubers and other edible vegetable products, N.E.S., fresh or dried	0.258
	9	745-Nonelectrical machinery, tools and mechanical apparatus, and parts thereof, N.E.S.	1.754	931-Special transactions and commodities not classified according to kind	1.640
	10	744-Mechanical handling equipment, and parts thereof, N.E.S.	2.305	281-Iron ore and concentrates	0.000
Japan	1	781-Motor cars and other motor vehicles principally designed for the transport of persons (not public transport), including station wagons and racing cars	2.032	333-Petroleum oils and oils from bituminous minerals, crude	0.000
	2	931-Special transactions and commodities not classified according to kind	1.766	343-Natural gas, whether or not liquefied	0.000
	3	784-Parts and accessories for tractors, motor cars and other motor vehicles, trucks, public-transport vehicles and road motor vehicles N.E.S.	2.236	321-Coal, pulverized or not, but not agglomerated	0.000

	4	776-Thermionic, cold cathode or photocathode valves and tubes; diodes, transistors and similar semiconductor devices; integrated circuits, etc.; parts	2.265	281-Iron ore and concentrates	0.000
	5	793-Ships, boats (including hovercraft) and floating structures	3.124	283-Copper ores and concentrates; copper mattes; cement copper	0.002
	6	728-Machinery and equipment specialized for particular industries, and parts thereof, N.E.S.	2.847	752-Automatic data processing machines and units thereof; magnetic or optical readers; machines transcribing coded media and processing such data, N.E.S.	0.283
	7	778-Electrical machinery and apparatus, N.E.S.	2.014	342-Liquefied propane and butane	0.002
	8	713-Internal combustion piston engines and parts thereof, N.E.S.	1.975	845-Articles of apparel, of textile fabrics, whether or not knitted or crocheted, N.E.S.	0.020
	9	772-Electrical apparatus for switching or protecting electrical circuits or for making connections to or in electrical circuits (excluding telephone etc.)	1.261	334-Petroleum oils and oils from bituminous minerals (other than crude), and products there from containing 70% (by wt) or more of these oils, N.E.S.	0.375
	10	723-Civil engineering and contractors' plant and equipment	3.156	34-Fish, fresh (live or dead), chilled or frozen	0.392
Mexico	1	333-Petroleum oils and oils from bituminous minerals, crude	2.745	334-Petroleum oils and oils from bituminous minerals (other than crude), and products there from containing 70% (by wt) or more of these oils, N.E.S.	0.430
	2	761-TV receivers (including video monitors & projectors) whether or not incorp radiobroadcast receivers or sound or video recording or reproducing apparatus	1.414	776-Thermionic, cold cathode or photocathode valves and tubes; diodes, transistors and similar semiconductor devices; integrated circuits, etc.; parts	0.206
	3	781-Motor cars and other motor vehicles principally designed for the transport of persons (not public transport), including station wagons and racing cars	1.449	931-Special transactions and commodities not classified according to kind	0.532
	4	782-Motor vehicles for the transport of goods and special purpose motor vehicles	2.097	871-Optical instruments and apparatus, N.E.S.	0.097
	5	54-Vegetables, fresh, chilled, frozen or simply preserved; roots, tubers and other edible vegetable products, N.E.S., fresh or dried	3.853	772-Electrical apparatus for switching or protecting electrical circuits or for making connections to or in electrical circuits (excluding telephone etc.)	1.627

Table 1.6 (Continued)

Country		Ten largest net exports[a]	RCA	Ten largest net imports[a]	RCA
	6	773-Equipment for distributing electricity, N.E.S.	4.065	764-Telecommunications equipment, N.E.S.; and parts, N.E.S., and accessories of apparatus falling within telecommunications, etc.	2.019
	7	775-Household type electrical and nonelectrical equipment, N.E.S.	3.390	893-Articles, N.E.S. of plastics	1.121
	8	971-Gold, nonmonetary (excluding gold ores and concentrates)	1.623	759-Parts and accessories suitable for use solely or principally with office machines or automatic data processing machines	0.417
	9	752-Automatic data processing machines and units thereof; magnetic or optical readers; machines transcribing coded media and processing such data, N.E.S.	11.767	343-Natural gas, whether or not liquefied	0.062
	10	872-Instruments and appliances, N.E.S., for medical, surgical, dental or veterinary purposes	2.899	684-Aluminum	0.146
United States	1	792-Aircraft and associated equipment; spacecraft (including satellites) and spacecraft launch vehicles; and parts thereof	2.584	333-Petroleum oils and oils from bituminous minerals, crude	0.032
	2	776-Thermionic, cold cathode or photocathode valves and tubes; diodes, transistors and similar semiconductor devices; integrated circuits, etc.; parts	1.635	781-Motor cars and other motor vehicles principally designed for the transport of persons (not public transport), including station wagons and racing cars	0.811
	3	222-Oil seeds and oleaginous fruits used for the extraction of soft fixed vegetable oils (excluding flours and meals)	1.935	764-Telecommunications equipment, N.E.S.; and parts, N.E.S., and accessories of apparatus falling within telecommunications, etc.	0.851
	4	931-Special transactions and commodities not classified according to kind	2.257	752-Automatic data processing machines and units thereof; magnetic or optical readers; machines transcribing coded media and processing such data, N.E.S.	0.917
	5	723-Civil engineering and contractors' plant and equipment	5.411	334-Petroleum oils and oils from bituminous minerals	0.756
	6	44-Maize (not including sweet corn) unmilled	2.207	761-TV receivers (including video monitors & projectors)	0.359

	7	874-Measuring, checking, analyzing and controlling instruments and apparatus, N.E.S.	1.448	821-Furniture and parts thereof; bedding, mattresses, mattress supports, cushions and similar stuffed furnishings	0.532
	8	971-Gold, nonmonetary (excluding gold ores and concentrates)	3.802	845-Articles of apparel, of textile fabrics, whether or not knitted or crocheted, N.E.S.	0.138
	9	575-Plastics, N.E.S., in primary forms	1.312	894-Baby carriages, toys, games and sporting goods	0.936
	10	41-Wheat (including spelt) and meslin, unmilled	3.162	542-Medicaments (including veterinary medicaments)	0.788

[a]Ranking of net exports values in each of 103 3-digit SITC categories.
[b]n.e.s = not elsewhere specified.
Source: Computed by the authors using 2007–09 trade data taken from United Nations *Comtrade* database (http://comtrade.un.org/).

where X_{ij} denotes the value of country i's exports of commodity j, X_{wj} is the value of world exports of commodity j, $X_{i\bullet}$ is the value of country i's total exports and $X_{w\bullet}$ is the value of total world exports. When the value of (1.1) exceeds (is below) unity, country i is said to have a revealed comparative advantage (comparative disadvantage) in good j. Expression (1.1) is only one of many *RCA* indices that have been devised for applied work.[10] The appropriateness of most *RCA* indices, including expression (1.1), for indicating the theoretical concept of comparative advantage has been questioned in the literature.[11] But despite theoretical concerns, *RCA* indices continue to be used in applied work.

The data in Table 1.6 can be used to infer similarities between the commodities in which a country has an *RCA* and thereby also suggest the characteristics of the country that would give rise to its comparative advantage in the indicated goods. The patterns of *RCA* in Table 1.6 suggest that one possible explanation is differences in factor prices. For example, China's *RCA* lies in computer and telecommunications equipment, footwear and apparel, whereas China's revealed disadvantage is in semiconductor components and raw materials. With respect to its exports of computer and telecommunications equipment, the operations conducted in China are mostly assembly of the components it imports. This hints at the importance of intra-firm trade and trade in intermediate goods. In contrast, Germany's *RCA* lies in categories such as motor vehicles and specialized machinery, whereas Germany's revealed disadvantage is mostly in natural resource products. If the production of motor vehicles and specialized machinery are thought to require mostly physical capital and skilled workers then one might conjecture that Germany's trade pattern reflects that capital and highly skilled labor are relatively cheap in Germany while natural resources and land suitable for growing fruit and nuts is relatively expensive (when the prices of these factors are compared with their prices in other countries). Conversely, the kinds of goods comprising the *RCA* of China suggest that capital and skilled labor are relatively expensive, and unskilled labor relatively cheap, in China.

Whereas the pattern of *RCA* values in Table 1.6 seems to suggest that factor price differences may lie behind some of the observed trade patterns, one can think of other influences. For example, with Figure 1.1 in mind, Germany's *RCA* in automobiles and machinery may instead derive from superior technology, economies of scale or even market power due to patents. As noted, sorting out these various influences is properly the task of empirical tests of trade theory.

Finally, note that the *RCA* index usually exceeds 1 when net exports are positive and is usually less than 1 when net exports are negative (that is, net imports), but this is not always the case (for example, Brazil and Mexico). This points to the concerns raised in the literature about the appropriateness of *RCA* indices as indicators of underlying "true" comparative advantages since traditional comparative advantage models predict the pattern of a country's net exports across goods (industries).

Similarity of trade patterns and country characteristics

If trade patterns are systematically related to comparative advantages derived from differences in supply side characteristics of countries, then countries with similar characteristics should have similar trade patterns. Conversely, countries with similar trade patterns should have similar characteristics. Hence, observing which countries have similar trade patterns may suggest the country characteristics (for example, factor prices) most important in determining trade patterns.

This type of thinking is utilized in Table 1.7 which shows, for each country in Table 1.6, the ten countries whose pattern of net exports across goods is the most similar and the least similar. Here similarity is measured by the correlation between the net export vectors of each pair of countries. For example, Thailand, Hong Kong and Philippines are among the ten countries with trade patterns most similar to China's. Among the countries with trade patterns most dissimilar to China's are Colombia, Canada, and Oman. Which characteristics do these countries share that would imply the similarity or dissimilarity of their trade patterns? Again, factor prices might come to mind or, more directly, unskilled labor. For the US, the countries most similar include France, Spain and Italy; all countries with land suitable for agriculture. Further perusal of these listings suggests other commonalties among the characteristics of the most similar and least similar countries, but there are also a number of puzzling exceptions.

Relative resource supplies

The search for country characteristics that might help to explain trade patterns typifies the search for the determinants of comparative advantage. In this context, it was noted in Section 1.1 that the H-O-S theory of trade focuses on factor price differences, or more directly, differences in relative factor supplies, as the source of comparative advantage across countries. In the H-O-S framework, differences in relative factor supplies are characterized in terms of the "abundance" or "scarcity" of factors. These terms are defined more carefully in Chapter 4, but roughly speaking, a country's abundant factors are cheaper, and its scarce factors more expensive, than are these factors in other countries. The following briefly considers this aspect of countries.

Table 1.8 shows for selected countries and regions in 1970 and 2000 the distribution of physical capital and three categories of labor (human capital) defined by the level of formal education obtained by members of the population.[12] For example, in 1970, China was the location of 5.5 percent of the world's physical capital stock. By 2000, China's share had risen to 15.1 percent. Conversely, China's share of the world's stock of workers with no formal education was 28.2 percent in 1970 and declined to 19.6 percent by 2000.

As discussed in Chapter 7, the ranking of a country's shares of each world resource indicates their relative abundance within the country. For example, the ranking of US resource shares in Table 1.8 indicates that in 1970 and 2000 the US was most abundant in workers who

Table 1.7   Countries whose net trade pattern is most and least similar to that of selected countries (based on averages of net trade values over the period 2007–09)

Rank	Most similar[a]	Least similar	Most similar[a]	Least similar
	to BRAZIL		*to CHINA*	
1	Paraguay	Saudi Arabia	Thailand	Colombia
2	Nicaragua	Bahrain	Hong Kong	Canada
3	Australia	Sudan	Philippines	Oman
4	Uruguay	United Arab Emirates	Hungary	Mauritania
5	Argentina	Kuwait	Republic of Korea	United Arab Emirates
6	Ethiopia	China	Sierra Leone	Azerbaijan
7	Mauritania	Russian Federation	Italy	Ecuador
8	Guyana	Egypt	Poland	Nigeria
9	Malawi	Jordan	Lithuania	Venezuela
10	New Zealand	Ireland	Czech Republic	Kazakhstan
	to GERMANY		*to JAPAN*	
1	Japan	Germany	Colombia	Belgium
2	Czech Republic	Republic of Korea	Algeria	France
3	Spain	Spain	Azerbaijan	Belarus
4	Republic of Korea	Sierra Leone	Ecuador	Bulgaria
5	Belgium	Czech Republic	Nigeria	Italy
6	Sierra Leone	Belgium	United Arab Emirates	Singapore
7	Slovakia	Thailand	Kazakhstan	Lithuania
8	Sweden	Singapore	Norway	Sierra Leone
9	Thailand	France	Russian Federation	Netherlands
10	France	Poland	Oman	United States
	to MEXICO		*to UNITED STATES*	
1	Yemen	Belgium	France	Norway
2	Nigeria	France	Sierra Leone	Yemen
3	Ecuador	Belarus	Spain	Ecuador
4	Azerbaijan	Bulgaria	Italy	Sudan
5	Kazakhstan	Italy	Netherlands	Venezuela
6	Oman	Singapore	Belgium	Kazakhstan
7	Sudan	Lithuania	Lithuania	United Arab Emirates
8	United Arab Emirates	Sierra Leone	Singapore	Oman
9	Venezuela	Netherlands	South Africa	Nigeria
10	Norway	United States	Bulgaria	Azerbaijan

[a] Similarity is measured by the correlation between the net trade vectors of the indicated pair of countries. Most similar countries have the largest positive correlation while least similar countries have the smallest negative correlation.
Sources: The authors, based on 2007–09 trade data taken from United Nations *Comtrade* database (http://comtrade.un.org/).

Table 1.8 Selected country/regional world resource shares (in %), 1970 and 2000[a]

Region/Country	Factor stock	1970	2000	Rank 2000
Advanced Countries (excluding Japan, United States and EU-15)	Secondary education	9.0%	2.2%	3
	Physical capital	7.3%	6.3%	1
	Post secondary education	5.6%	3.6%	2
	No formal education	1.6%	1.2%	4
China	No formal education	28.2%	19.6%	2
	Secondary education	26.4%	30.7%	1
	Post secondary education	5.9%	10.4%	4
	Physical capital	5.5%	15.1%	3
East Asia and the Pacific (excluding Japan and China)	No formal education	6.5%	7.2%	4
	Secondary education	5.5%	10.3%	1
	Post secondary education	5.3%	8.3%	2
	Physical capital	3.1%	8.0%	3
EU-15	Physical capital	25.9%	11.9%	1
	Post secondary education	10.7%	11.7%	2
	Secondary education	10.3%	11.5%	3
	No formal education	1.5%	1.7%	4
Japan	Physical capital	12.0%	13.5%	1
	Post secondary education	6.7%	6.5%	2
	Secondary education	5.0%	3.2%	3
	No formal education	0.2%	0.0%	4
Latin America and the Caribbean	Physical capital	13.7%	11.7%	1
	No formal education	5.8%	5.7%	4
	Post secondary education	4.7%	8.6%	2
	Secondary education	3.6%	6.3%	3
Middle East and North Africa	No formal education	6.0%	5.6%	1
	Secondary education	1.0%	3.3%	2
	Post secondary education	0.9%	2.8%	3
	Physical capital	0.4%	0.4%	4
South Asia	No formal education	40.7%	47.8%	1
	Post secondary education	6.1%	9.5%	3
	Physical capital	4.3%	5.9%	4
	Secondary education	3.8%	14.1%	2
Sub-Saharan Africa	No Formal education	7.8%	10.6%	1
	Physical capital	2.3%	1.0%	3
	Post secondary education	0.9%	1.0%	4
	Secondary education	0.7%	1.1%	2
Transitional economies	Post secondary education	24.4%	10.2%	1
	Secondary education	20.3%	7.9%	2
	No formal education	1.4%	0.5%	3
	Physical capital	0.1%	0.1%	4

United States	Post secondary education	30.5%	27.2%	1
	Physical capital	25.9%	25.8%	2
	Secondary education	16.0%	9.3%	3
	No formal education	0.4%	0.2%	4

[a] Numbers are world share of resource based on a world total for 64 countries. For each region data are sorted by world share in 1970.
[b] Education levels are number of persons aged 15 years or older who completed the indicated level of education.
Source: The authors, using data from Barrow and Lee (2000), Heston and Summers (1991), and Heston, Summers and Aten (2009).

had completed a post-secondary education, followed by physical capital, workers with a secondary education, and finally workers with no formal education. This suggests that the US is abundant in physical capital and labor embodying a high level of human capital. In contrast, China is abundant in labor embodying relatively low levels of human capital and is scarce in physical capital and labor embodying a high level of human capital.

Although the relative abundance of factors within a country can change relatively quickly due to substantial differences across countries in rates of factor accumulation, the factor supply patterns for broad groups of countries change relatively slowly. This is illustrated in Figure 1.5, which shows the structure of factor abundance for advanced versus non-advanced economies in 1970 and 2000 with respect to the four resources listed in Table 1.8. Figure 1.5 indicates that advanced countries are relatively abundant in physical and human capital while non-advanced countries are relatively scarce in these factors and that this difference in the pattern of factor abundance was unchanged between 1970 and 2000.

Trade overlap, intra-industry trade and intra-firm trade

In Section 1.1 it was noted that intra-industry trade, that is, trade between countries in the same or similar product, can arise when goods are differentiated or markets are imperfectly competitive. Efforts to theoretically model the basis for intra-industry trade started in the late 1970s in response to the observation that actual trade data evidenced considerable trade overlap. Trade overlap is defined as the value of matching export and import transactions in a given commodity:

$$TO_{ij} = (X_{ij} + M_{ij}) - |X_{ij} - M_{ij}| \qquad (1.2)$$

where X_{ij} and M_{ij} are the value of country i's exports and imports, respectively, of commodity j either to the world or on a bilateral basis.[13] A common summary measure of the degree of trade overlap is the Grubel-Lloyd (GL) index:[14]

$$GL_{ij} = 100 \left[\frac{TO_{ij}}{X_{ij} + M_{ij}} \right] \qquad (1.3)$$

Values of (1.3) range between 0 (no trade overlap) and 100 (complete trade overlap). Since no level of statistical significance is attached to values of the GL index, what constitutes a high or low level of trade overlap is largely a matter of personal interpretation.

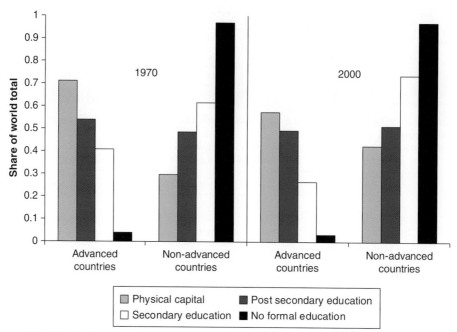

Figure 1.5 Relative factor supplies in advanced and non-advanced countries, 1970 and 2000

Source: The authors, with data from Barrow-Lee (2000), Heston and Summers (1991) and Heston, Summers and Aten (2009).

Trade overlap and categorical aggregation

As discussed in Chapters 8 and 9, there are a number of theoretical models that predict the existence of intra-industry trade. However, the concordance between the industry-based concept of intra-industry trade used in these theoretical models and the amount of trade overlap measured in actual trade data is open to question. For example, measured trade overlap may simply reflect "categorical aggregation" which arises because the system used to classify detailed trade data into a usable number of categories necessarily aggregates dissimilar products into seemingly similar product groups. If trade overlap only reflects categorical aggregation then the theoretical demonstration of intra-industry trade is largely irrelevant for understanding actual trade patterns. A further understanding of this issue is facilitated by considering how actual trade data are collected and categorized.

Countries routinely collect export and import data in order to assemble their national income accounts and as a by-product of collecting taxes levied on their imports and exports. By international agreement, the national agencies responsible for maintaining a country's trade statistics routinely submit these data to supra-national organizations (such as the United Nations or the European Statistical Agency) which maintain the data on a consistent basis. To permit international comparisons, the submitted data are classified according to an internationally agreed system of classification, one of which is the Standard International Trade Classification (SITC).[15] The example in Table 1.9 shows an example of the structure of the SITC system.

As shown in Table 1.9, the SITC system consists of five levels of classification. In this case, the 1-digit *section* 7 is disaggregated into four higher digit groupings (division, group and so on). For present purposes it is important to note that the SITC is a product-based,

Table 1.9 Example of the Standard International Trade Classification (SITC) system

Section 7 – Machinery and transport equipment
Division 79 – Other transport equipment
Group 792 – Aircraft and associated equipment: spacecraft (including satellites) and spacecraft launch vehicles; and parts thereof
Subgroup 792.8 – Aircraft
Item 792.81 – Gliders and hang gliders

not an industry-based, classification. Hence, each SITC category necessarily involves some aggregation of products produced by different industries.

How important is the aggregation in the SITC system for measuring an industry-based concept such as *intra-industry* trade? Table 1.10 considers this question by showing the values of (1.2) computed for the 3-digit SITC *group* "Fixed vegetable oils" and its 4-digit SITC components using United Kingdom (UK) trade data for 1977. The index value at the 3-digit level[16] suggests intra-industry trade is substantial in this "industry." However, the extent of intra-industry trade when measured at the 4-digit level is often small and there is considerable variation. However, the 4-digit values are not zero, and it seems fair to conclude that categorical aggregation is not the only explanation of measured trade overlap.[17]

The extent of trade overlap

Accepting that the theoretical concept of intra-industry trade has an empirical basis, Table 1.11 provides evidence on the extent of trade overlap by showing the value of index (1.3) for a set of selected countries with respect to their trade for three sub-periods 1988–91, 1992–95 and 1996–2000. Also shown is the percentage point change in the index value between the 1988–91 and 1996–2000 periods.

Table 1.11 indicates that the degree of trade overlap varies across countries, even at similar levels of economic development, and that trade overlap has generally risen over time. For example, trade overlap is relatively high for France, Canada, and the Czech Republic but

Table 1.10 Example of the effect of categorical aggregation on measured trade overlap

SITC	Description	Imports[a]	Exports[a]	Grubel-Lloyd Index
421	Fixed vegetable oils	27,308	15,888	74.0[b]
421.2	Soya bean oil	6,648	4,220	78.0
421.3	Cotton seed oil	3,355	24	1.0
421.4	Ground nut oil	8,503	224	5.0
421.5	Olive oil	2,012	410	34.0
421.6	Sunflower seed oil	6,440	8	0.2
421.7	Rape, colza and mustard oils	350	11,002	6.0

[a]Data are for the UK in 1977. All values in millions of British Pounds.
[b]Value is a weighted average of the index values at the 4-digit SITC level.
Source: Based on Greenaway and Milner (1983).

Table 1.11 Index of intra-industry trade in manufactured goods for selected countries, 1988–2000

	1988–91	1992–95	1996–2000	Change
High and increasing intra-industry trade				
Czech Republic	n.a.	66.3	77.4	11.1
Slovak Republic	n.a.	69.8	76	6.2
Mexico	62.5	74.4	73.4	10.9
Hungary	54.9	64.3	72.1	17.2
Germany	67.1	72	72	5
US	63.5	65.3	68.5	5
Poland	56.4	61.7	62.6	6.2
Portugal	52.4	56.3	61.3	8.9
High and stable intra-industry trade				
France	75.9	77.6	77.5	1.6
Canada	73.5	74.7	76.2	2.7
Austria	71.8	74.3	74.2	2.4
UK	70.1	73.1	73.7	3.6
Switzerland	69.8	71.8	72	2.2
Belgium/Luxembourg	77.6	77.7	71.4	−6.2
Spain	68.2	72.1	71.2	3
Netherlands	69.2	70.4	68.9	−0.3
Sweden	64.2	64.6	66.6	2.4
Denmark	61.6	63.4	64.8	3.2
Italy	61.6	64	64.7	3.1
Ireland	58.6	57.2	54.6	−4
Finland	53.8	53.2	53.9	0.1
Low and increasing intra-industry trade				
Korea	41.4	50.6	57.5	16.1
Japan	37.6	40.8	47.6	10
Low and stable intra-industry trade				
New Zealand	37.2	38.4	40.6	3.4
Turkey	36.7	36.2	40	3.3
Norway	40	37.5	37.1	−2.9
Greece	42.8	39.5	36.9	−5.9
Australia	28.6	29.8	29.8	1.2
Iceland	19	19.1	20.1	1.1

Note: Countries are classified as having "high" or "low" level of intra-industry trade according to whether intra-industry trade is above or below 50 percent of total manufacturing trade on average over all periods shown and "increasing" or "stable" according to whether intra-industry trade increases by more than five percentage points between the first and last periods, as shown in the final column.

Source: Organisation for Economic Cooperation and Development (OECD) (2002, Table VI.1).

relatively low for Australia, Greece, and Norway. Trade overlap is generally higher for indus-trialized countries but there are exceptions. Generally, trade overlap has continued to rise over time.

Another aspect of measured trade overlap is that it varies by industry. This is revealed in Table 1.12. As indicated, trade overlap is highest in "basic metals and fabricated metal products," "electrical machinery and apparatus n.e.c.," and "fabricated metal products except machinery and equip.," which are generally differentiated intermediate products. It is lowest in "office accounting and computing machinery" and "wood and products of wood and cork," which are mostly finished products with less product differentiation.

Intra-firm trade

Early studies of trade overlap examined the importance of the phenomena, but recent research has instead turned to investigate whether such trade reflects the flow of trade between related firms located in different countries. This brings into focus the role of the multinational firm and its global network of affiliated companies (foreign subsidiaries). Trade between affiliated companies is called intra-firm trade, and the importance of this trade has increased over time. The growth of such trade reflects the desire of firms to locate parts of their value-chain activities in those locations where they can be undertaken at least cost or in close proximity to customers in foreign markets. Chapter 12 explores these issues.

Figures 1.6 to 1.8 illustrate the importance of intra-firm trade and its evolution by show-ing data on intra-firm trade of US firms and their foreign subsidiaries. Figure 1.6 shows the importance of intra-firm exports and imports in total US exports and imports, respectively. Exports by US firms to their foreign subsidiaries as a percentage of total US exports averaged about 23 percent between 1982 and 2007, but show a decline since the mid-1990s. Imports by US firms from their foreign subsidiaries as a percentage of total US imports averaged about 13 percent between 1982 and 2007.

Figure 1.7 indicates the destination of sales by US foreign subsidiaries between 1997 and 2007. It shows that sales by subsidiaries to their own local markets are declining, whereas sales to other foreign markets (excluding the US market) are increasing. This suggests US sub-sidiaries are increasingly the source of the production of the products sold by US firms in foreign markets.

Finally, Figure 1.8 indicates the importance of purchases by US subsidiaries from affiliated foreign subsidiaries of the same US company – that is, intra-subsidiary trade. As indicated in Figure 1.8, after 1997 the purchases by foreign subsidiaries from related subsidiaries (of the same US parent firm) were rising in importance while purchases by foreign subsidiaries from their US based parent firm are declining in importance. These trends point to the growing importance of the global trade network or global supply chain of multinational firms. While of growing importance, these activities of multinational firms do not invalidate the bases for comparative advantage, and in fact can often reflect that such firms locate subsidiaries outside their home market in order to take advantage of factor cost differences between countries.

1.3 International factor flows

Trade between countries involves not only an exchange of goods but also of factors of production. In this regard, Chapter 6 considers the theoretical and empirical relevance of international labor flows while Chapter 11, which discusses multinational enterprises and

Table 1.12 Index of intra-industry trade by manufacturing industry 1983, 1993, and 2003[a]

Industry	1983	1993	2003	Change 1983–2003
Total Manufacturing	61.7	66.0	69.3	7.5
Basic metals and fabricated metal products	75.9	84.2	83.1	7.2
Electrical machinery and apparatus n.e.c	67.3	72.5	77.7	10.5
Fabricated metal products except machinery and equip.	70.3	77.4	77.2	6.9
Basic metals	69.9	77.0	76.1	6.2
Chemical rubber plastics and fuel products	75.9	75.8	75.7	−0.2
Rubber and plastics products	69.3	74.1	75.0	5.7
Electrical and optical equipment	66.0	69.4	73.3	7.3
Non-ferrous metals	63.7	70.1	73.2	9.5
Machinery and equipment	64.9	68.6	73.1	8.2
Other transport equipment	55.9	69.5	72.2	16.3
Chemicals and chemical products	68.3	69.5	72.2	3.9
Iron and steel	68.4	73.5	71.7	3.3
Food products beverages and tobacco	66.7	68.3	71.1	4.4
Radio television and communication equipment	60.3	65.5	71.0	10.7
Chemicals excluding pharmaceuticals	67.6	68.2	71.0	3.3
Medical precision & optical instruments watches & clocks	57.4	62.5	70.0	12.5
Pulp paper, paper products, printing and publishing	65.1	68.4	70.0	4.9
Machinery and equipment n.e.c.	59.7	63.4	69.5	9.8
Aircraft and spacecraft	49.7	58.2	69.0	19.3
Other non-metallic mineral products	64.0	71.9	68.6	4.6
Manufacturing n.e.c	68.4	69.6	68.2	−0.2
Transport equipment	59.6	63.0	67.7	8.1
Pharmaceuticals	63.6	60.3	66.4	2.8
Textiles textile products leather and footwear	63.9	63.7	65.0	1.1
Coke refined petroleum products and nuclear fuel	54.5	63.9	61.3	6.8
Motor vehicles trailers and semi-trailers	50.8	54.4	60.1	9.4
Building and repairing of ships and boats	45.4	55.4	59.5	14.1
Railroad equipment and transport equip. n.e.c.	48.0	54.7	56.8	8.8
Office accounting and computing machinery	50.7	51.9	52.4	1.7
Wood and products of wood and cork	43.8	50.6	50.7	7.0

Notes: Unweighted averages of the Grubel-Lloyd index across 29 countries. Industries are sorted in descending order of the value of trade overlap in 2003.
Source: The authors, based on data from OECD (2010).

the phenomenon of intra-firm trade, considers trade in capital in the form of financial capital movements as measured by direct investment flows. Below we remark briefly on these international factor flows and consider their relationship to the flow of goods.

Despite evidence to the contrary, trade models routinely assume that factors of production are internationally immobile. As explained in Chapters 3 and 4, this assumption is made

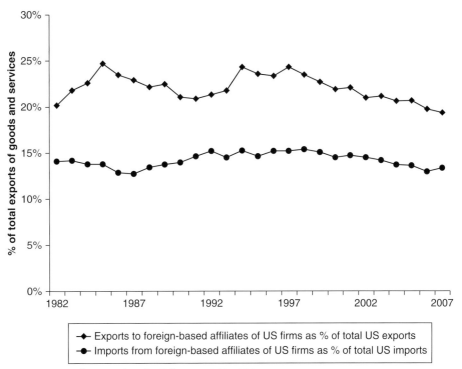

Figure 1.6 Intra-firm trade of US firms, 1982–2007
Notes: Data exclude exports and imports by US subsidiaries of foreign firms.
Source: Wiersema and Bowen (2011, Figure 3).

since, without further assumptions, the pattern of trade in goods would be indeterminate in the sense that there is no way to know if goods, factors or both would move between countries. The indeterminacy of trade patterns when both goods and factors are internationally mobile has interesting implications for the cases in which either goods or factors, but not both, are internationally immobile. For example, in Chapter 4 it is shown that when goods alone are internationally mobile that trade in goods can equalize the returns to factors across countries. Similarly, in Chapter 6 it is shown that when factors alone are mobile that international factor movements can equalize the prices of goods across countries. These theoretical relationships suggest that trade in goods and trade in factors are substitutes. Given this, one would expect an increase in the international mobility of goods caused, for example, by a reduction in trade barriers or in transport costs, to reduce the international flow of factors. The following sections consider this predicted relationship between goods flows and factor flows.

Labor flows

Integrated economic areas such as the European Union (EU) have sought to deregulate their commodity and factor markets by removing trade barriers and formal obstacles to the free movement of factors between member countries. If trade and factor flows are substitutes then, in the context of the EU, one would expect an increase in intra-EU trade to decrease factor movements between EU member countries.

Table 1.13 shows summary data on labor migration and trade flows within the EU between 1958–1980, a time of increasing trade liberalization among EU member states. These data

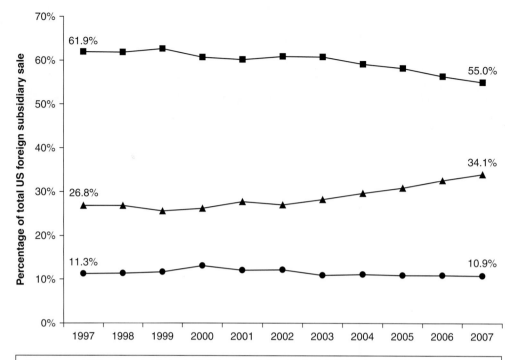

Figure 1.7 Destination of US foreign subsidiary sales, 1997–2007

Notes: Data only for sales of manufactured products by foreign subsidiaries of US firms; data exclude sales to US subsidiaries of foreign firms.

Source: Wiersema and Bowen (2011, Figure 4).

generally corroborate the hypothesis of substitutability between factor flows and commodity flows. However, these average shares mask that the underlying distribution of the annual shares of intra-EU migration in total EU migration is V-shaped, with a trough at 19.3 percent in 1969. The distribution of the annual shares of intra-EU trade in total EU trade has a different pattern, first rising from 29.6 percent in 1958 to 50.1 percent in 1971 and then fluctuating around this value of the remainder of the sample period. As shown in the last column of Table 1.13, the simple correlation between the annual shares of intra-EU migration and intra-EU trade over the 1958–1980 period is −0.553. This negative correlation is consistent with the theoretical prediction that commodity flows tend to substitute for labor flows.[18] Note, however, that the period 1973–80 does not provide evidence of the predicted substitute relationship.

Capital flows

Capital flows, as measured by flows of private investment, are a major part of international exchange. In principle, the determinants of international capital flows can be analyzed using the same framework as that used for the trade in goods, since capital flows represent the exchange of current goods for future goods (that is, lending and borrowing).[19]

Table 1.14 shows data on the net outflow (inflow if negative) of foreign direct investment (FDI) for major world regions averaged over three time periods: 1990–94, 1997–2001 and

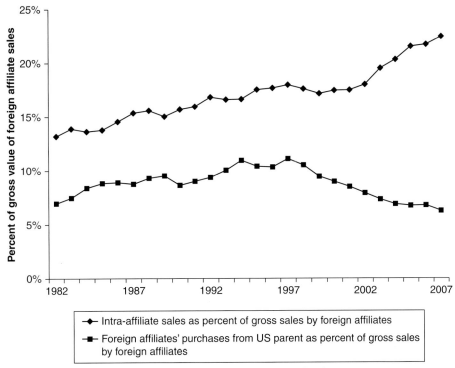

Figure 1.8 Source of intra-firm purchases by US foreign subsidiaries, 1982–2007
Notes: Data are for purchases of products and services by foreign subsidiaries of US firms.
Source: Wiersema and Bowen (2011, Figure 5).

Table 1.13 Labor migration and commodity flows within the European Union (annual averages)

Time Period	Labor Migration as a Share of Total EU Migration		Trade as a Share of Total EU Trade		Correlation of (1) with (3)
	(1) Intra-EC[a]	(2) Extra-EU	(3) Intra-EU	(4) Extra-EU	
1958–73[b]	37.9	62.1	42.1	57.9	−.902
1973–80	42.4	57.6	49.2	50.8	0.089
1958–80	40.1	59.9	44.1	55.9	−.553

[a] Intra-EU refers to the EU-6 or EU-9 countries; extra-EU refers to non-EU countries.
[b] Figures 1958–73 are for the EU-6; Figures 1973–80 are for the EU-9.
Source: Based on Straubhaar (1988).

2005–2009. These data indicate that the main providers of FDI to the world are Europe, North America and Other Developed Countries (for example, Australia, Bermuda, Israel, Japan and New Zealand). All other regions are net recipients of FDI and, among these, the largest recipients in the 2005–2009 period are Africa, East Asia and South and Central America. These regions are among the lowest net recipients of FDI in the period 1990–94. Note that North America (primarily the US) was a net recipient of FDI during the middle period from 1997 to 2001.

Table 1.14 Net outflows of foreign direct investment by country/region, 1990–2009

Region	Net outflow of foreign direct investment (in millions $US)		
	1990–94	1997–2001	2005–2009
Europe	33,251	133,022	246,823
Other developed countries	20,636	15,533	47,291
North America	14,432	−65,835	26,555
Oceania	−345	−350	−1,242
South-East Europe	−176	−1,577	−8,510
Caribbean	171	5,508	−8,535
South Asia	−926	−4,444	−19,350
South-East Asia	−11,026	−14,522	−24,291
CIS	−657	−4,488	−25,071
West Asia	−2,306	−3,064	−38,457
East Asia	−5,177	−41,610	−49,629
Africa	−2,974	−11,206	−50,545
South and Central America	−12,009	−64,319	−60,831

Source: United Nations Conference on Trade and Development (UNCTAD, 2010).

Table 1.15 indicates the regional sources and destinations of US FDI between 2008 and 2009. As indicated in Table 1.15, about 50 percent of all US FDI outflows and almost 85 percent of US inflows are associated with European countries. Extrapolating from the data in

Table 1.15 US outflows and inflows of direct investment by country/region, 2008–09

Region/Country	Outflows	Inflows
	billions $US	billions $US
All Countries	288.4	153.8
Canada	20.6	31.7
Europe	145.0	130.1
Of which:		
Belgium	4.7	15.5
France	4	32.1
Germany	8.6	16.7
Ireland	19.3	6.5
Italy	...	−9.0
Luxembourg	21.3	9.5
Netherlands	44.8	38.8
Spain	...	4.8

Sweden	−10.6	3.1
Switzerland	16.1	24.8
United Kingdom	21.9	−0.5
Latin America and Other Western Hemisphere	87.6	−18.3
Of which:		
Bermuda	31.8	−17.3
Brazil	12.2	. . .
Chile	6.2	. . .
Mexico	8.3	. . .
Netherlands Antilles	4.2	. . .
United Kingdom Islands, Caribbean	12.3	−6.9
Africa	7.6	−0.6
Middle East	5.1	0.4
Asia and Pacific	22.5	10.6
Of which:		
Australia	11.9	5
Japan	. . .	4.5
China	−3.1	. . .
Hong Kong	10.4	. . .
India	2	. . .
Korea, Republic of	4.6	. . .
Singapore	−9.2	. . .

Notes: ". . ." indicates flow not broken out.
Source: US Department of Commerce (2010, Tables C and E).

Table 1.15, the bulk of international investment flows takes place between major industrialized countries, although FDI flows to and from Asia and Latin America are rising. Yet almost three-quarters of all direct investment occurs between developed countries – a figure that mirrors the dominant share of industrial countries in terms of intra-regional trade (see Table 1.2). This suggests, contrary to the theoretical prediction of substitutability, that international trade in financial capital and international trade in goods are complementary.

1.4 Concluding remarks

The past five decades have witnessed an increasing process of globalization and growing interdependence among countries. During this period, the growth of world trade, fueled by large increases in trade of manufactured goods, has exceeded the growth in world output. Trade among established and newly industrialized countries constitutes a significant proportion of the global increase in trade. Intra-regional trade has generally risen faster than inter-regional trade, partly reflecting the implementation of new – and the renewal of existing – regional trade agreements that reduce trade barriers among subsets of countries.

In addition to the changes in regional trade patterns, the composition of trade of individual countries has changed dramatically. For example, the US once accounted for over four-fifths of the exports of manufactured goods but now accounts for less than one-third. Japan, once a major exporter of basic textile products, toys, sporting goods and other light manufactures is now a dominant exporter of automobiles and an importer of its former exports. China, largely closed to trade until 1979, has become the world's largest exporter and importer. The rapid increase in global trade has had dramatic effects on the standard of living in most countries.

Explaining the basis for trade, its patterns within and between countries and its change over time is one goal of international trade theory. Another is to answer the question: "does a country gain from trade?" Trade does permit a nation to extend its opportunities for consumption beyond those available to it in isolation, but whether these extended possibilities also imply a national gain must await further analysis.

In considering the basis for trade, trade theory utilizes the important concept of comparative advantage, which implies a difference in the relative prices of goods across countries. Since relative prices in turn derive from the fundamental determinants of supply and demand, theories of trade based on comparative advantage look to differences in these fundamentals (for example, relative factor supplies or technology) across countries as the basis for trade and its composition. Operating in the framework of perfectly competitive markets and homogeneous goods, these theories predict the emergence of trade as well as the goods that countries will export and import – that is, the *inter-industry* pattern of trade.

Data on the composition of countries' trade and their revealed comparative advantage suggests that countries with similar economic structures do have similar trade patterns. In addition, data on countries' resource supplies indicate persistent differences between the resource structures of advanced and less advanced countries; advanced countries are generally abundant in physical and human capital (that is, highly-skilled labor) when compared with less advanced countries. These differences in relative factor supplies suggest patterns of factor costs that could give rise to comparative advantage and trade. The data also suggest that the resource structures of advanced countries are quite similar.

Comparative advantage as the basis for trade is compelling, but trade can nonetheless emerge for reasons other than relative price differences. If markets are imperfectly competitive or goods differentiated then countries that are in every respect identical may still trade. However, the trade that arises under these circumstances is *intra-industry* rather than *inter-industry* trade. Data on the extent of intra-industry trade, as measured by the amount of trade overlap in a given statistical industry classification, does appear to be an important feature of actual trade flows, particularly among industrialized countries. In this regard, an important and growing component of intra-industry trade flows is trade in intermediate goods and intra-firm trade.

Finally, countries exchange not only goods but also factors of production. The patterns of labor flows within the EU suggest that international movements of goods and factors may exhibit a substitute relationship, but there is also increasing evidence of a complement relationship when non-traded goods sectors are taken into account (Bowen and Wu (2011)). International movements of goods and financial capital tend to be complementary.

Appendix

Aggregate indices of trade overlap

Studies of trade overlap frequently report values of the Grubel-Lloyd (GL) index (1.3) at different levels of aggregation. This appendix discusses the measurement of such indices and issues that arise in this regard.

The literature uses two methods of computing a GL index at higher levels of aggregation. The first simply sums the trade data at lower levels of aggregation and calculates the GL index using these values. In this case, trade overlap for "industry" g is computed as:

$$GL_{ig}^* = 100 \left(1 - \frac{\left| X_{ig}^* - M_{ig}^* \right|}{X_{ig}^* + M_{ig}^*} \right) \tag{1.4}$$

where $X_{ig}^* = \sum_{j \in g} X_{ij}$ and $M_{ig}^* = \sum_{j \in g} M_{ij}$ are the sum of export and import values, respectively, over products that comprise industry g. The second method takes a weighted average of the index GL_{ij} for each commodity within industry g:

$$GL_{ig}^{**} = \sum_{j \in g} \left(\frac{\left| X_{ij} + M_{ij} \right|}{\sum_{j \in g}(X_{ij} + M_{ij})} \right) GL_{ij} = 100 \left(1 - \frac{\sum_{j \in g} \left| X_{ij} - M_{ij} \right|}{X_{ig}^* + M_{ig}^*} \right) \tag{1.5}$$

where the weights are the share of commodity j in the total trade in industry g. The key difference between (1.4) and (1.5) is that the former sums any trade imbalances at the commodity level. If these imbalances are of opposite signs they will tend to cancel out. This is not true of the summations in (1.5). If fact, when computed for the same subset of commodities, (1.5) will tend to be less than (1.4) since $\left| \sum_{j \in g} (X_{ij} - M_{ij}) \right| \leq \sum_{j \in g} \left| X_{ij} - M_{ij} \right|$.

Aggregation of the above industry level indices to obtain an index for the share of intra-industry trade in country i's total trade similarly takes the form of either the weighted or the unweighted average of either GL_{ig}^* or GL_{ig}^{**} over all commodity groups. The weighted averages in each case are:

$$GL_i^* = \sum_g GL_{ig}^* \frac{X_{ig}^* + M_{ig}^*}{\sum_g X_{ig}^* + M_{ig}^*} \tag{1.6}$$

$$GL_i^{**} = 100 \left(1 - \frac{\sum_j \left| X_{ij} - M_{ij} \right|}{X_i + M_i} \right) \tag{1.7}$$

The unweighted averages have the simpler form:

$$Z_i^* = \sum_g GL_{ig}^* / G$$

$$Z_i^{**} = \sum_g GL_{ig}^{**} / G \tag{1.8}$$

where "G" is the number of groups. When trade is balanced ($\sum_j X_{ij} = \sum_j M_{ij}$) these aggregate indices range between 0 and 100.

Table 1.16 Values of unweighted Grubel-Lloyd indices at 1-digit SITC level for United Kingdom and Switzerland, 1977[a]

SITC	United Kingdom				Switzerland			
	(1)	(2)	(3)	(4)	(1)	(2)	(3)	(4)
	Z_i^*	Z_i^{**}	(1) − (2)	(3) ÷ (1)	Z_i^*	Z_i^{**}	(1) − (2)	(3) ÷ (1)
0	35	33	2	.06	24	18	6	.25
1	35	22	13	.37	22	19	3	.14
2	40	35	5	.13	33	32	1	.03
3	58	45	7	.12	9	9	0	0
4	50	26	24	.48	65	40	25	.38
5	69	57	12	.17	60	56	4	.07
6	69	63	6	.09	52	48	4	.08
7	69	64	5	.07	53	48	5	.09
8	80	73	7	.09	63	57	6	.10

[a] Averages computed from Grubel-Lloyd indices computed at the 3-digit SITC level.
Source: UK figures, Greenaway and Milner (1983); Swiss figures, Greenaway (1983).

One indication of the difference produced by these alternative aggregation methods is illustrated in Table 1.16 which reports values of the unweighted indices Z_i^* and Z_i^{**} for Switzerland and the UK. As expected, trade overlap is smaller using the unweighted averages of GL_{ig}^{**}. Comparing the two measures, the difference in their values (column 3) is relatively small at all SITC levels except SITC 4.

Note that regardless which measure is used, the results in Table 1.16 indicate higher than average levels of trade overlap occur in SITCs 5 to 8 (manufactures and consumer goods) than in SITCs 0 to 4 (foodstuffs and raw or unfinished materials). Moreover, except for SITC 4, trade overlap is higher for the UK than for Switzerland.

Trade imbalance corrections

Aggregate indices of trade overlap range between 0 and 100 when trade is balanced but are biased downward if the country has an overall trade imbalance. The greater the trade imbalance the greater will be the share, on average, of net trade in a commodity and hence the smaller the share of intra-industry trade. To correct for this bias, Grubel and Lloyd proposed the following modified index:

$$GL_i^B = 100 \frac{\sum_j (X_{ij} + M_{ij}) - \sum_j |X_{ij} + M_{ij}|}{\sum_j (X_{ij} + M_{ij}) - |\sum_j (X_{ij} - M_{ij})|} \tag{1.9}$$

This can be written in the reduced form:

$$GL_i^B = \frac{GL_i^*}{(1 - b_i)}$$

where GL_i^* is defined in (1.6) and b_i is country i's trade imbalance as a fraction of its total trade:

$$b_i = \frac{\left| \sum_j (X_{ij} - M_{ij}) \right|}{\sum_j (X_{ij} + M_{ij})} \tag{1.10}$$

It follows from (1.10) that if all imbalances are one-sided then GL_i^B will always take the value of unity. This, and the fact that the correction is applied only at the highest level of aggregation, are considered undesirable features that have led others to propose alternative corrections. For example, Aquino (1978) replaces GL_i^B by $Q_i = 100 \left[1 - \left(\left| \sum_j (\hat{X}_{ij} - \hat{M}_{ij}) \right| \middle/ \left(\hat{X}_i + \hat{M}_i \right) \right) \right]$, where $\hat{X}_i$ and $\hat{M}_i$ are the hypothetical values of exports and imports under balanced trade, that is, $\hat{X}_i = X_i \left[\sum_j (X_{ij} + M_{ij}) \middle/ \sum_j 2X_{ij} \right]$ and similarly for $\hat{M}_i$. Other trade imbalance corrections have been proposed and used by Loertscher and Wolter (1980), Bergstrand (1983) and Balassa (1986). However, these alternative procedures introduce still other distortions.

Notes

1. However, economists can model the nature of demand differences as reflected, for example, by differences in income elasticities of demand or a bias toward home produced goods.
2. Here, economies of scale refer to economies of scale external to an industry. Economies of scale can also be internal to the firm and, if so, imply imperfectly competitive market structures.
3. One could also take the traditional supply side view and envision this trade to arise from differences in climate and soil between countries. Hence, French soil and climate are relative scarce (and hence expensive) in the US compared with US soil and climate. France therefore produces French wine relatively more cheaply that does the US. But if the soil and climate of France could be exactly duplicated in the US then trade in wine would not take place unless technology or the prices of other factor inputs also differed between these countries. The country that exported "French wine" would then be determined according to traditional comparative advantage considerations.
4. Note that the measurement concepts for world trade production (GDP) differ. The latter measures world value added whereas trade measures the value of shipments. Hence, the trade data "double count" the value of goods.
5. Technology transfer is facilitated by direct sales in foreign markets and, as discussed in Chapter 10, the spread of multinational corporations.
6. These growth rates are computed as $g = \ln(X_{2009}/X_{1979})/(2009-1979)$ where X is the trade share for a particular region.
7. The value 200 percent arises since with trade balance (exports = imports) the trade dependence ratio is effectively (exports + imports)/GDP = 2(exports)/GDP, and a country cannot in principle export more than it produces (that is, exports <= GDP). Note that a trade dependence ratio in excess of 200 percent could also reflect that trade values, unlike GDP, are not measured in terms of value added.

8. The commodity categories are defined according to the United Nations Standard International Trade Classification (SITC) Revision 3. The particular SITC level of detail shown in Table 1.6 is the 3-digit *group* level. See the Appendix to this book for further information on trade classification systems including the *Harmonized System* which has replaced the SITC.
9. Liesner (1958) first utilized an RCA index but Balassa (1966) refined and popularized its use. In fact, expression (1.1) is commonly referred to as the "Balassa index" of revealed comparative advantage.
10. Memedović (1994) critiques many of these *RCA* indices.
11. See Bowen (1983) and Hillman (1980).
12. The Appendix to this book discusses the measurement of such resources.
13. For example, if country i exports \$4 million of commodity j and imports \$6 million, then the amount of trade overlap is \$8 million (\$4 million of exports plus \$4 million of "matching" imports).
14. Grubel and Lloyd (1975). Other measures of trade overlap preceded that of Grubel and Lloyd. See Greenaway and Milner (1986) for a comparative review of these measures.
15. The Appendix to this book further discusses the SITC system as well as the more recently developed and used Harmonized System (HS) of classification.
16. Appendix 1.1 discusses alternative methods for aggregating values of GL_{ij}.
17. As the example suggests, measured trade overlap rises with the level of commodity aggregation. The literature on intra-industry trade has yet to reach agreement on what constitutes the appropriate level of aggregation for empirical purposes. In principle, the level of aggregation should reflect an "industry," that is, a collection of goods produced with the same or similar production function. In practice, studies often proceed from the 3-digit SITC level since corresponding data on industry characteristics, which are reported using a different system of classification, are only available at a similar level of disaggregation. See also the Appendix to this book.
18. More recent studies indicate that trade and labor flows (immigration) are likely to be complementary when one accounts for the presence of non-traded goods sectors (that is, services). For example, see Bowen and Wu (2011).
19. As with the intra-industry index (1.3) for trade flows, one can construct an intra-industry index of FDI flows. For example, see Norman and Dunning (1984).

References and additional reading

Globalization, trade and factor flows

Alfaro, L. and Charlton A. (2009), "Intra-industry Foreign Direct Investment," *American Economic Review*, 99 (5), 2096–2119.

Barro, R.J. and Lee, J.W. (2000), "International Data on Educational Attainment: Updates and Implications," Center for International Development Working Paper 42 (Cambridge, MA: Harvard University Press).

Bowen, H.P. and Wu, J-P. (2011), "Immigrant Specificity and the Relationship between Trade and Immigration: Theory and Evidence," Queens University of Charlotte McColl School of Business Discussion Paper 2011–01.

Bowen, H.P. and Sleuwaegen L. (2007), "European Integration: The Third Step," *Journal of International Economics and Policy*, 4 (3), 241–262.

Bowen, H.P. and Wiersema, M.F. (2005), "Foreign-based Competition and Corporate Diversification Strategy," *Strategic Management Journal*, 26 (12), 1153–1171.

De Benedictis, L. and Tajoli, L. (2011), "The World Trade Network," *The World Economy*, forthcoming.

Eaton, J. Kortum, S., Neimanx, B., and Romalis, J. (2010), "Trade and the Global Recession," University of Chicago, mimeo.

GATT (1990), *International Trade*, vols. 1 and 2 (Geneva: United Nations).

Heston, A. and Summers, R. (1991), "Penn World Table Version 5.6," Center for International Comparisons at the University of Pennsylvania.

Heston, A., Summers, and Aten, B. (2009), "Penn World Table Version 6.3," Center for International Comparisons of Production, Income and Prices at the University of Pennsylvania (August).

Leamer, E.E. (1984), *Sources of International Comparative Advantage: Theory and Evidence*, (Cambridge, MA: MIT Press).

Levchenko, A., Lewis, L., and Tesar, L. (2011), "The Collapse in Quality Hypothesis," *American Economic Review Papers and Proceedings*, 101 (3), 293–297.

Norman, G. and Dunning, J.M. (1984), "Intra-industry Foreign Direct Investment," *The Review of World Economics*, 120, 522–539.

Ricardo, D. (1817), *The Principles of Political Economy and Taxation*, reprinted in *Everyman's Library* (New York: Dutton), 1950.

Smith, A. (1776), *An Inquiry into the Wealth of Nations* (London: W. Straham and T. Cadwell).

Straubhaar, T. (1988), "International Labour Migration with A Common Market: Some Aspects of EC Experience," *Journal of Common Market Studies*, 27 (1), 45–62.

UNCTAD (2010), *World Investment Report 2010* (Geneva: United Nations).

US Department of Commerce (2010), *Survey of Current Business* (Washington, DC: US Government Printing Office), July, 20–35.

Wiersema, M.F. and Bowen, H.P. (2008), "Corporate International Diversification: The Impact of Foreign Competition, Industry Globalization and Firm Diversification," *Strategic Management Journal*, 2 (29), 115–132.

WTO (1995), *International Trade, Trends and Statistics* (Geneva: United Nations).

WTO (2010), *International Trade Statistics* (Geneva: United Nations).

Intra-industry and intra-firm trade

Aquino, A. (1978), "Intra-industry Trade and Inter-industry Specialization as Concurrent Sources of International Trade in Manufactures", *Journal of World Economics*, 114, 275–296.

Balassa, B. (1966), "Tariff Reductions and Trade in Manufactures Among the Industrial Countries,", *American Economic Review*, 56, 466–473.

Balassa, B. (1986), "Intra-industry Trade Among Exporters of Manufactured Goods," in D. Greenaway and P.K.M. Tharakan (Eds.), *Imperfect Competition and International Trade: Policy Aspects of Intra-industry Trade* (Brighton: Wheatsheaf).

Bergstrand, J.H. (1983), "Measurement and Determinants of Intra-industry International Trade," in P.K.M. Tharakan (Ed.), *Intra-industry Trade: Empirical and Methodological Aspects* (Amsterdam: North-Holland), 201–262.

Bernard, A., Jensen, J. and Schott, P. (2005), "Importers, Exporters and Multinationals: A Portrait of Firms in the US That Trade Goods," *NBER Working Paper 11404*.

Bowen, H.P. and Wiersema, M.F. (2009), "Firm Performance, International Diversification and Product Diversification: Their Interrelationships and Determinants," Queens University of Charlotte McColl School of Business Discussion Paper 2009–4.

Culem, C. and Lundberg, L. (1986), "The Product Pattern of Intra-industry Trade: Stability Among Countries and Over Time," *The Review of World Economics*, 122, 113–130.

Greenaway, D. (1983). Intra-industry and Inter-industry Trade in Switzerland, *Review of World Economics* (*Weltwirtschaftliches Archiv*), 119, 109–121.

Greenaway, D. and Milner, C. (1983), "On the Measurement of Intra-industry Trade," *The Economic Journal*, 93, 900–908.

Greenaway, D. and Milner, C. (1986), *The Economics of Intra-industry Trade* (Oxford: Basil Blackwell).

Greenaway, D. and Tharakan, P.K.M. (1986), *Imperfect Competition and International Trade: Policy Aspects of Intra-industry Trade* (Brighton: Wheatsheaf).

Grubel, H.G. and Lloyd, P.J. (1975), *Intra-industry Trade* (London: Macmillan).

Grubel, H.G. and Lee, H.-H. (2002), *Frontiers of Research on Intra-Industry Trade* (London: Palgrave).

Hummels, D., Ishii, J., and Yi, K. (2001), "The Nature and Growth of Vertical Specialization in World Trade," *Journal of International Economics*, 54 (1), 75–96.

Liesner, H.H. (1958), "The European Common Market and British industry," *Economic Journal*, 68, 302–16.

Loertscher, R. and Wolter, F. (1980), "Determinants of Intra-industry Trade: Among Countries and Across Industries," *The Review of World Economics*, 116, 280–93.

OECD (Organisation for Economic Co-operation and Development) (2002), *OECD Economic Outlook*, 2002 (1), 309–320.

OECD (Organisation for Economic Co-operation and Development) (2010), *OECD.stat*, http://www.oecd-ilibrary.org/economics/data/oecd-stat_data-00285-en.

Tharakan, P.K.M. (1983), *Intra-industry Trade: Empirical and Methodological Aspects* (Amsterdam: North-Holland).

Wiersema, M.F. and Bowen, H.P. (2011), "The Relationship Between International Diversification and Firm Performance: Why It Remains A Puzzle," *Global Strategy Journal*, 1 (1/2), 152–170.

Revealed comparative advantage

Balance, R.H., Forstner, H., and Murray, T. (1987), "Consistency Tests of Alternative Measures of Comparative Advantage," *The Review of Economics and Statistics*, 121, 346–350.

Bowen, H.P. (1983), "On the Theoretical Interpretation of Indices of Trade Intensity and Revealed Comparative Advantage," *The Review of World Economics*, 119 (3), 464–472.

Hillman, A. (1980), "Observations On The Relation Between 'Revealed Comparative Advantage' And Comparative Advantage As Indicated By Pre-Trade Relative Prices," *The Review of World Economics*, 116, 314–321.

Marchese, S. and De Simone, F.N. (1989), "Monotonicity of Indices of 'Revealed' Comparative Advantage: Empirical Evidence on Hillman's Condition," *The Review of World Economics*, 125, 158–167.

Memedović, O. (1994), *On the Theory and Measurement of Comparative Advantage, Book No. 65* (Rotterdam: Tinbergen Institute Research Series).

2

Trade policy instruments and environment

2.1   Instruments of trade policy

2.2   Administered protection and the WTO

2.3   Concluding remarks

A country's trade policy is defined as the set of taxes, subsidies, quantitative measures and other impediments or stimuli it undertakes with respect to transactions between its residents and the residents of foreign countries. The forms that these policies take are called the instruments of trade policy. Since one nation's trade policies will, by definition, affect the residents of other countries, trade laws and institutions have developed to offer a framework for mutually agreeable implementation of trade policies among countries and, when disputes arise, a mechanism for their resolution. These laws and institutions represent the environment of trade policy.

This chapter provides an overview of the main instruments of trade policy and discusses the rules that most countries have agreed will govern the use of these instruments.[1] These rules are, for the most part, contained in three agreements administered by the World Trade Organization (WTO): the General Agreement on Tariffs and Trade (GATT), the General Agreement on Trade in Services (GATS), and the Agreement on Trade-related Aspects of Intellectual Property Rights (TRIPs).[2] Members of the WTO are sovereign states or customs territories; as of December 2010 the WTO had 153 members and 31 observers.[3]

2.1   Instruments of trade policy

Tariffs

A tariff is a tax levied on imports of a good. Its effect is to raise the internal domestic price of the imported good above its external world price. This increase in the domestic price reduces the volume imported and thereby shields a country's domestic industries from foreign competition. A tariff rate can be either *ad valorem* or specific. An *ad valorem* rate is a percentage of the import value of the good while a specific rate is a fixed currency amount per unit of the good.

Ad valorem tariffs are the most widely used instrument for restricting trade. This is primarily due to the GATT, which recommends an *ad valorem* tariff as the preferred method for restricting trade. This recommendation is made for two reasons: first, an *ad valorem* tariff is transparent in the sense that its effect on price is readily observed and easily calculated; second, *ad valorem* rates are directly comparable across goods since they are stated in percentage terms. Such comparability is important when countries seek to negotiate reductions in trade barriers. Comparing specific rates across products is problematic since these depend on the units in which products are measured. One disadvantage of an *ad valorem* rate is that it is applied to the value of an imported good, and what constitutes the appropriate "value for duty" is then subject to interpretation and abuse.[4] The GATT therefore contains specific rules on "customs valuation" in order to limit the discretion of custom officials in setting a value for duty.

Bound versus applied rates

A country's *tariff schedule* lists the tariff rates applicable to imported goods. There are two types of tariff rates: the bound rate and the applied rate. The bound (or scheduled) rate is the rate a WTO member country has agreed will be the *maximum* rate that it will levy on a good imported from any other WTO member country. The applied rate is the actual rate a country applies on its imports (from any country). Table 2.1 shows, as of the conclusion of the Uruguay Round, the number of bound rates on industrial products as a percentage of the total number of tariffs rates (tariff lines) for major groupings of WTO members.

Tariff averages

As Table 2.1 suggests, a country's tariff schedule can contain thousands of commodity categories (tariff-line items). Applied analyses involving the use of tariff rate data will therefore require some method of aggregating individual rates.[5] The ideal would be a weighted average with weights equal to the amount of the product that a country would import under free trade. However, since free-trade import weights are not available, other approaches are taken. These include: 1) weighting by share of world imports, 2) weighting by share in categories corresponding to the end-use of goods (for example, final versus intermediate demand), 3) weighting by estimates of free-trade import levels where the estimates are derived from an econometric model or by adjusting import levels based on estimated import demand elasticities, 4) weighting by a product's share in a country's own imports and 5) foregoing weights and instead computing the unweighted average of individual rates.[6]

The use of world import share weights has the defect that it fails to recognize the production structure of any particular country. Weighting tariffs by end-use assumes that the ratio of imports to consumption would be more or less the same as under free trade which is, a priori, a reasonable assumption. However, this method requires comparable disaggregated import

Table 2.1 Bound tariffs on industrial products as of 1994

Country group	Number of tariff lines	Import value (billions of US $)	Percentage of tariff lines bound	Percentage of imports under bound rates
Developed economies	86,968	737.2	99	99
Developing economies	157,805	306.2	72	59
Transition economies	18,962	34.7	98	96

Source: GATT (1994).

data on end-use, which are not normally available. Using econometric methods to estimate the level of free trade imports requires a statement of the underlying determinants of trade flows and thus belief in the model's specification. But econometric estimates of tariff averages do have the distinct virtue of providing a measure of the uncertainty associated with the calculated averages. Weighting by a country's own import shares contains a systematic downward bias since goods subject to high tariffs have low weights while goods with low tariffs have relatively higher weights.[7] Despite the bias, many studies have used the last method since the data requirements are easily met, the direction of the bias is known, and the value of the weight given to each good approaches its theoretical value as tariffs are progressively lowered. Finally, an unweighted average of tariff rates gives inordinate weight to obscure products and there is a strong upward bias because the product breakdown is usually more detailed for highly protected, import sensitive, industries.

Table 2.2 shows three different average *ad valorem* tariff rates for different groupings of WTO member countries across selected product categories. These averages are simple averages rather than import share weighted averages. As might be expected, bound rates are higher than either the most favored nation (MFN) or effective applied rates, the latter being the rate actually applied. Across product groups, food and textiles show by far the highest rates. Among the lowest applied rates are those in the primary product categories ores and metals and fuels. Across WTO importer groups, less developed countries (LDCs) and developing countries, excluding the LDCs, generally apply higher tariff rates in most product categories than high-income WTO member countries.

The relative level of developing countries' tariffs shown in Table 2.2 partly reflects the important role of tariff revenue in supporting developing countries' policy objectives. Equally important is that many developing countries are relatively recent entrants into the WTO, and hence only recently subject to WTO disciplines regarding bound tariff rates. Similarly, the relatively low average tariff rates of high-income WTO members reflect decades of effort by these WTO members to reduce tariffs among themselves.

Table 2.3 provides further information on the structure of tariff protection by showing tariff averages for selected country groups with respect to their imports from developing market economies, least developed countries and Europe (as a representative of developed countries) in 1996 and 2008. Two tariff averages are shown: the MFN applied rate and a preferential rate that would be given, for example, due to a regional trade agreement. The values in Table 2.3 indicate a general decline in average tariffs between 1996 and 2008. As expected, preferential rates are lower than MFN rates. Most importers apply higher rates to imports from Europe than from developing countries.

Effective protection and tariff escalation

As detailed in Chapter 5, a tariff raises not only the internal domestic price of an imported good but also the price and production of the domestically produced goods with which it competes. This tariff-induced increase in the production of domestic "import competing" goods is sometimes called the "protective effect" of the tariff. However, the rise in domestic production is not an entirely satisfactory measure of protection since what one actually seeks to protect by limiting competition from imports is the income of the factors of production employed in import-competing industries. This income (value added) encompasses payments to primary factor inputs which can include pure economic profit. The amount by which a *nominal* tariff raises an industry's value added above its free trade level is called the effective rate of protection (*ERP*).

The relationship between the *ERP* afforded domestic producers of good j and the *nominal* tariff rate applied on good j is given by formula (2.1) below:

Table 2.2 Tariff averages by WTO importer group and major product categories, 2009[a]

Importer group (number of countries)	Duty rate[c]	Products[b]							
		All non-oil trade	Food	Ores & metals	Fuels	Chemicals	Machinery & transport equipment	Miscellaneous goods	Textiles
All WTO members (123)	Bound	29.75	50.99	22.60	25.9	24.18	25.15	22.17	28.26
	Effective	8.17	12.48	3.85	3.92	5.69	5.83	2.26	12.04
	MFN	9.34	15.39	4.65	4.77	5.61	6.64	5.36	13.00
High-income WTO members (21)	Bound	29.22	50.14	22.25	25.9	23.86	25.40	21.46	28.44
	Effective	7.86	13.43	3.96	3.91	5.52	5.95	2.54	11.52
	MFN	9.11	15.42	4.54	4.6	5.64	6.68	4.83	12.76
Developing WTO members (59) excl. LDCs	Bound	28.17	48.32	20.55	23.6	22.87	23.92	18.34	27.37
	Effective	8.31	11.94	3.76	3.67	5.70	5.62	2.12	12.26
	MFN	9.15	14.57	4.42	4.52	5.58	6.38	4.28	12.95
Low & middle income WTO members (102)	Bound	28.69	49.05	21.20	24.6	23.43	24.19	18.54	27.67
	Effective	8.44	11.86	3.75	3.92	5.85	5.71	1.95	12.33
	MFN	9.25	14.65	4.50	4.68	5.67	6.45	4.51	13.04
LDC WTO members (32)	Bound	30.60	46.46	22.95	36.6	35.50	25.70	12.85	26.67
	Effective	9.64	11.17	3.15	6.65	8.51	6.73	1.38	12.26
	MFN	11.91	13.57	4.26	7.02	9.60	8.21	3.21	15.36

[a] Averages are simple averages of tariff rates.
[b] Product categories are defined according to SITC groupings: Food (SITC 0 + 1 + 22 + 4); Ores & Metals (SITC 27 + 28 + 68); Fuels (SITC 3); Chemicals (SITC 5); Machinery & Transport Equipment (SITC 7); Miscellaneous Goods (SITC 9); Textiles (26 + 65 + 84 of SITC Rev.1).
[c] Bound is bound rate; effective is the effective applied rate; MFN is MFN applied rate.
Source: Authors, from data in World Integrated Trade Solution database (2010).

Table 2.3 Average MFN and preferential applied tariff rates, 1996 and 2008

Importer	Year	Exporter					
		Developing market economies		Least developed countries		Europe[a]	
		MFN	Preferential	MFN	Preferential	MFN	Preferential
Developed Market Economies	1996	9.9%	7.8%	8.1%	4.4%	9.2%	8.3%
	2008	7.9%	5.5%	6.8%	2.9%	7.2%	6.3%
Asia	1996	9.1%	5.4%	7.3%	3.2%	8.9%	7.7%
	2008	7.4%	5.7%	6.0%	1.2%	8.9%	8.6%
European Union (EU)	1996	10.5%	7.9%	7.7%	1.0%	9.8%	8.3%
	2008	8.6%	5.0%	6.8%	0.6%	7.0%	5.0%
North American Free Trade Agreement (NAFTA)	1996	8.7%	7.5%	8.3%	7.7%	7.9%	7.2%
	2008	6.8%	5.4%	6.9%	5.5%	6.3%	6.1%

[a]Europe is shown as a proxy for developed market economics.
Source: Authors, using data from United Nations (2010, Millennium Development Goals).

where t_j = nominal tariff rate on final product j;

t_z = nominal tariff rate on intermediate good z;

ϕ_{jz} = share of intermediate input z in the <u>value</u> of one unit (i.e., a dollar's worth) of good j when evaluated at free trade (external) prices.

$$ERP_j = \frac{t_j - \sum_z \phi_{jz} t_z}{1 - \sum_z \phi_{jz}} \qquad (2.1)$$

The term $(1 - \sum_z \phi_{jz})$ is the ratio of valued added to the value of total output computed on the basis of free trade (external or "world") prices. As (2.1) indicates, the emphasis of the *ERP* on factor incomes draws attention to the effect of tariffs on imported intermediate inputs. For example, a 10 percent tariff on rice imports and a 20 percent tariff on fertilizer imports used in rice production are unlikely to raise value added in domestic rice production.

For the purposes of illustration, Table 2.4 lists the *ERP* for selected commodities and countries in 1962. In most cases the *ERP* exceeds the nominal tariff rate but in some cases the *ERP* is negative. Although entirely possible, it is unlikely that an industry would allow its government to impose a tariff rate that reduced its valued added. One explanation for negative effective rates is that an industry receives direct or indirect subsidies which are not captured in the calculation of effective rates. Another explanation is that the measurement of the *ERP* is subject to bias since it assumes that input requirements are fixed.

From (2.1) it may be seen that the *ERP* will exceed the nominal rate of protection (t_j) if the nominal rate is above the weighted average of the nominal rates on intermediate goods. The *ERP* therefore rationalizes a stylized fact of tariff protection – tariff escalation – which refers to the tendency for tariff rates to rise with the stage of fabrication of goods. The phenomenon of tariff escalation was evident in Table 2.2 since the lowest tariff rates are those applied on primary products. Table 2.5 makes the relationship more explicit by showing the average tariff rate (across developed countries) applied in each of three product categories by stage of processing.

The *ERP* is an important concept for understanding the structure of a country's protection and its implications for internal resource allocation (since factors will tend to move to, or

Table 2.4 Nominal and effective rates of protection in selected countries and industries, 1962[a]

Product	United States		Japan		United Kingdom		EU	
	Nominal	ERP	Nominal	ERP	Nominal	ERP	Nominal	ERP
Thread and yarn	11.7	31.8	2.7	1.4	10.5	27.9	2.9	3.6
Textile fabrics	24.1	50.6	29.7	48.8	20.7	42.2	17.6	44.4
Clothing	25.1	35.9	25.2	42.4	25.5	40.5	18.5	25.1
Steel ingots/primary forms	20.6	106.7	13.0	58.9	11.1	98.9	6.4	28.9
Ships	5.5	2.1	13.1	12.1	2.9	−10.2	0.4	−13.2
Electrical machinery	12.2	18.1	18.1	25.3	19.7	30.0	14.5	21.5
Automobiles	6.8	5.1	35.9	75.7	23.1	41.4	19.5	36.8
Precision instruments	21.4	32.2	23.2	38.5	25.7	44.2	13.5	24.2

[a] All values in percent.
Source: Based on Balassa (1965).

Table 2.5 Example of tariff escalation in selected products[a]

Product Category	Stage of Processing		
	Raw Material	Semi-Finished	Finished
Textiles and Clothing	0.8	11.5	16.7
Leather, Footwear, Rubber and Travel Goods	0.0	4.4	10.2
Base Metals	0.0	3.2	5.9

[a] Sector trade-weighted tariff averages across developed countries.
Source: Based on Balassa and Balassa (1984).

remain in, sectors with rising value added). The calculation of effective rates is now less frequent owing to the increasing use of applied general equilibrium models (see Chapter 5) which permits one to directly compute the implications of a country's tariff structure for its resource allocation. Nonetheless, the principle underlying the *ERP* remains valid, as does its use for inferring the level of protection, particularly when high levels of commodity or sector detail are required.

Non-tariff barriers

Non-tariff barriers to trade (NTBs) encompass all actions except tariffs that impede transactions between foreign and domestic residents. These can include both trade-related restrictions as well government intervention in domestic markets via taxes or subsidies and also bureaucratic regulations. NTBs can thus affect trade both directly and indirectly. An example of a direct measure would be a longer delay in certifying that an import versus a domestically produced good meets a country's technical standards. An indirect measure might be an economy-wide wage subsidy.

The use of NTBs – and their importance in restricting trade – increased substantially in the 1970s and 1980s and created a major strain on the world trading system. One problem was that the GATT framework then in force lacked well-defined rules (disciplines) regarding many of the NTBs being adopted. While the growing use of NTBs reflected weaknesses in the existing GATT framework, their use also reflected one of the GATT's major strengths: cumulative and substantial reductions in bound tariff rates. Low bound rates meant that a WTO member wishing to increase protection of its domestic industries had relatively little latitude to achieve this protection by increasing tariffs.[8] Rather, they had to turn to other instruments of protection. As discussed in Section 2.2, recent changes in the GATT and the addition of new agreements have served to bring a number of NTBs, particularly quantitative restrictions such as quotas, within the discipline of the WTO framework. Specifically, the GATT now explicitly prohibits most NTBs. The following discusses some of the more important types of NTBs. A complete listing of the types of measure that constitute NTBs is given in Table 2.6.

Table 2.6 UNCTAD coding system for trade control measures (NTBs)

1000 Tariff measures	2400 decreed customs valuation
1100 statutory customs duties	2900 para-tariff measures n.e.s.
1200 MFN duties	
1300 GATT ceiling duties	**3000 Price control measures**
1400 tariff quota duties	3100 administrative pricing
1410 low duties	3110 minimum import prices
1420 high duties	3190 administrative pricing n.e.s.
1500 seasonal duties	3200 voluntary export price restraint
1510 low duties	3300 variable charges
1520 high duties	3310 variable levies
1600 temporary reduced duties	3320 variable components
1700 temporary increased duties	3330 compensatory elements
1710 retaliatory duties	3340 flexible import fees
1720 urgency and safeguard duties	3390 variable charges n.e.s
1900 preferential duties under trade agreements	3400 antidumping measures
1910 interregional agreements	3410 antidumping investigations
1920 regional and subregional agreements	3420 antidumping duties
1930 bilateral agreements	3430 price undertakings
	3500 countervailing measures
2000 Para-tariff measures	3510 countervailing investigations
2100 customs surcharges	3520 countervailing duties
2200 additional taxes and charges	3530 price undertakings
2210 tax on foreign exchange transactions	3900 price control measures n.e.s.
2220 stamp tax	
2230 import license fee	**4000 Finance measures**
2240 consular invoice fee	4100 advance payment requirements
2250 statistical tax	4110 advance import deposit
2260 tax on transport facilities	4120 cash margin requirement
2270 taxes and charges for sensitive product categories	4130 advance payment of customs duties
	4170 refundable deposits for sensitive product categories
2290 additional charges n.e.s.	4190 advance payment requirements n.e.s.
2300 internal taxes and charges levied on imports	4200 multiple exchange rates
2310 general sales taxes	4300 restrictive official foreign exchange allocation
2320 excise taxes	4310 prohibition of foreign exchange allocation
2370 taxes and charges for sensitive product categories	4320 bank authorization
2390 internal taxes and charges levied on imports n.e.s.	4390 restrictive official foreign exchange allocation n.e.s.

Table 2.6 (Continued)

4500 regulations concerning terms of payment for imports
4600 transfer delays, queuing
4900 finance measures n.e.s.

5000 Automatic licensing measures
5100 automatic license
5200 import monitoring
5210 retrospective surveillance
5220 prior surveillance
5270 prior surveillance for sensitive product categories
5700 surrender requirement
5900 automatic licensing measures n.e.s.

6000 Quantity control measures
6100 non-automatic licensing
6110 license with no specific *ex ante* criteria
6120 license for selected purchasers
6130 license for specified use
6131 linked with export trade
6132 for purposes other than exports
6140 license linked with local production
6141 purchase of local goods
6142 local content requirement
6143 barter or counter trade
6150 license linked with non-official foreign exchange
6151 external foreign exchange
6152 importers' own foreign exchange
6160 license combined with or replaced by special import authorization
6170 prior authorization for sensitive product categories
6180 license for political reasons
6190 non-automatic licensing n.e.s.
6200 quotas
6210 global quotas
6211 unallocated
6212 allocated to exporting countries
6220 bilateral quotas
6230 seasonal quotas
6240 quotas linked with export performance
6250 quotas linked with purchase of local goods
6270 quotas for sensitive product categories
6280 quotas for political reasons
6290 quotas n.e.s.
6300 prohibitions
6310 total prohibition
6320 suspension of issuance of licenses
6330 seasonal prohibition

6340 temporary prohibition
6350 import diversification
6370 prohibition for sensitive product categories
6380 prohibition for political reasons (embargo)
6390 prohibitions n.e.s.
6600 export restraint arrangements
6610 voluntary export restraint arrangements
6620 orderly marketing arrangements
6630 multifibre arrangement (MFA)
6631 quota agreement
6632 consultation agreement
6633 administrative co-operation agreement
6640 export restraint arrangements on textiles outside MFA
6641 quota agreement
6642 consultation agreement
6643 administrative co-operation agreement
6690 export restraint arrangements n.e.s.
6700 enterprise-specific restrictions
6710 selective approval of importers
6720 enterprise-specific quota
6790 enterprise-specific restrictions n.e.s.
6900 quantity control measures n.e.s.

7000 Monopolistic measures
7100 single channel for imports
7110 state trading administration
7120 sole importing agency
7170 single channel for sensitive product categories
7200 compulsory national services
7210 compulsory national insurance
7220 compulsory national transport
7900 monopolistic measures n.e.s.

8000 Technical measures
8100 technical regulations
8110 product characteristics requirements
8120 marking requirements
8130 labeling requirements
8140 packaging requirements
8150 testing, inspection and quarantine requirements
8160 information requirements
8170 requirement relative to transit
8180 requirement to pass through specified customs
8190 technical regulations n.e.s.
8200 pre-shipment inspection
8300 special customs formalities
8400 return obligation
8900 technical measures n.e.s.

Source: UNCTAD (2005).

Quantitative restrictions

A major category of NTB are quantitative restrictions, the most common being explicit import and export quotas. An import quota sets a limit on the amount of a good that can be imported over a specific period of time. To ensure compliance, the country imposing the quota will establish a system of import licensing. An import license permits the holder of the license to import a specified amount of the good. Similarly, an export quota sets a limit on the volume of a good that can be exported over a given period of time. Again, to ensure compliance, the country imposing the export quota will establish a system of (export) licensing.

Chapters 5 and 10 examine the economic effects of quantitative NTBs, including import and export quotas, in detail. A rough summary of these effects is that a quota raises the price of the good whose supply is being restricted and creates rents (pure profit) for the holder of the quota license[9] due to a difference between the demand and supply price of the restricted good. Who gets the rents generated by a quota is an important issue since these rents determine, in part, the quota's effect on the welfare of the importing and exporting countries.

Recognition that quantitative (and other) restrictions on trade can generate rents leads to the idea of *rent seeking activity*, that is, private agents who attempt to influence the nature of a country's trade policy in order to "capture" the rents these policies generate. Since the acquisition of these rents involves only a transfer of income between private agents, rent seeking activity is not productive. In fact, such activity imposes a cost on society since the activities involved in seeking to influence trade policies use up real resources (e.g., lobbying law makers or other government officials or hiring lawyers and other professionals in an effort to seek protection for one's industry). As discussed in Chapter 6, the possibility that rent-seeking activity may offer an explanation for the observed structure of protection within a country is part of a broader area of inquiry: the political economy of protection.

Voluntary export restraints

One class of NTB that has received close attention, particularly in the 1970s and 1980s, are voluntary export restraints (VERs). A VER is "voluntary" in the sense that an exporting country agrees to limit its exports in some way at the request of the importing country. A VER can involve an explicit export quota or, for example, a price agreement in which the exporting country agrees to not lower its export price (and, in fact, to raise its price to the importing country). Many VER agreements relate to trade in agricultural products which were not covered by GATT disciplines prior to 1994. As discussed in Section 2.2 below, the GATT now encompasses *all sectors* including agriculture and it prohibits the use of VERs.

Performance requirements

Performance requirements are another class of NTB that grew in importance during the 1970s and 1980s. These typically require foreign firms to meet objectives that may or may not apply to domestic firms. Examples include domestic content and export performance requirements. The former requires that some minimum fraction of a product's value added be derived from domestic factors of production. The stated intent of the policy is to maintain or raise domestic employment and income. A domestic content requirement may also be used to induce foreign firms to locate some or all of their production facilities in the importing country. Developing countries in particular have used such schemes in an effort to transfer the knowledge and skills possessed by a foreign firm to the local work force. Chapter 5 examines the economic implications of domestic content requirements.

An export performance requirement requires foreign firms producing in the "host" country, or host country firms wanting more favorable treatment, to export a certain percentage of their output. Several developing countries use export performance requirements to generate foreign exchange receipts. The GATT now prohibits most types of domestic content and export performance schemes, although developing countries often seek exemptions to retain many of these schemes as part of their "development" goals.

Government procurement

Government procurement and sourcing polices are another important class of NTB. Governments may prohibit foreign sourcing outright (for example, US civil servants must fly using US air carriers when traveling on official business) or simply make foreign sourcing more difficult. For example, foreign firms may be allowed to bid on government projects but only on special terms or conditions that end up favoring domestic bidders. Such restrictions can be of substantial importance. At present, the impact of such activities on trade is unknown. Due partly to this uncertainty over the impact on trade, only a subset of WTO member countries have agreed to rules governing government procurement.

Restrictiveness of NTBs

One factor that compounds the friction between countries regarding the use of NTBs is that the restrictiveness of NTBs is often difficult to quantify.[10] Without definite numbers there is considerable scope for countries to disagree about the importance of any given NTB. The difficulty in quantifying NTBs also creates a problem from the viewpoint of an applied analysis of NTBs. As discussed in Chapter 5, one approach to determining the restrictiveness of an NTB is to estimate its *ad valorem* equivalent (AVE), that is, the *ad valorem* tariff rate that would induce the same level of imports as the NTB in question. The restrictiveness of the NTB can then be determined by considering the effect of a change in this AVE rate on price and trade volume. However, as Chapter 5 discusses, estimating the effects of an NTB using AVE rates requires strong assumptions about the market for the good in question, including stable supply and demand curves during the period of estimation.

Another approach to gauging the restrictiveness of NTBs uses data on reported NTBs by country and sector to construct various indices intended to gauge the importance of NTBs.[11] One example is the frequency index (F_g) which measures, for a given country, the frequency of NTBs within a given commodity category g:

$$F_g = \frac{100}{N_g} \sum_{j \in g} D_j \tag{2.2}$$

where the binary variable D_j equals one when at least one NTB applies to good j and is zero otherwise and N_g is the number of commodities within commodity category g.[12] F_g equals zero when no NTBs are imposed on any of the N_g commodities comprising group g and equals 100 when each of the N commodities face at least one NTB.[13]

Table 2.7 shows values of the frequency index for different types of NTB in 1994 and 2004. Table 2.7 indicates that "non-core" NTB measures increased from 55.3 percent to 84.8 percent between 1994 and 2004 whereas the use of "core" NTBs (mostly quantity control, finance and price control measures) declined substantially. This decline in "core" measures reflects commitments by WTO member countries made during the Uruguay Round to reduce their use of such measures.

Table 2.8 breaks out the numbers in Table 2.7 by selected regions. When compared with the values for 1994, all regions show a switch from "core" to "non-core" measures. This happened most notably in Africa: over 50 percent of all measures applied in 1994 were core measures, but by 2004 this figure had fallen by 11.9 percent. Excluding non-core measures

Table 2.7 Frequency of NTB use by broad category

Trade control measure[a]	Description	1994 (%)	2004(%)
1	Tariff measures (tariff rate quota, etc)	5.8	0.3
3	Price control measures	7.1	1.8
4	Finance measures	2.0	1.5
417	Refundable deposit for sensitive products categories	0.0	0.6
5	Automatic licensing measures	2.8	1.7
6	Quantity control measures	49.2	34.8
617	Prior authorization for sensitive product categories	18.1	17.1
627	Quotas for sensitive product categories	0.2	0.2
637	Prohibition for sensitive product categories	2.5	6.8
7	Monopolistic measures	1.3	1.5
8	Technical measures	31.9	58.5
Non-core measures $(5 + 617 + 627 + 637 + 8)$		55.3	84.8
Core measures $(1 + 3 + 4 + 6 + 7 - (617 + 627 + 637))$		44.7	15.2
Number of countries		52	97
Total observations (Number of tariff lines)		97706	545078

[a]See Table 2.6 for definitions.
Source: UNCTAD (2005, Table 1).

such as technical measures and automatic licenses, the use in Africa of core NTBs fell from 68.5 percent in 1994 to 15 percent in 2004. With these changes, Africa's pattern of NTB use is now similar to that of countries in other regions.

Export promotion

Accompanying the rise in NTB restrictions on imports has been an increase in measures that instead promote exports. These measures include direct export subsidies and other types of export support programs. Like NTBs, the often opaque nature of export promotion measures results in their becoming a source of trade friction. Export promotion measures in particular raise tensions because they are seen by non-subsidized exporters as constituting "unfair" trade practices; they also result in visible output and employment reductions in non-subsidizing countries. Chapters 5 and 11 consider the pros and cons of export promotion measures in greater detail.

Since its inception, the GATT has explicitly prohibited the use of export subsidies, that is, subsidies contingent on export performance. However, the term "subsidy" was not actually defined in the GATT until 1994.[14] Pre-1994, the issue of what constituted an export subsidy, apart from overt and direct payments to exporters, was open to interpretation and hence dispute. If a subsidy for exports is deemed to exist, the GATT permits member countries to "countervail" (offset) the price reducing effect of the subsidy by assessing a countervailing duty on imports of the subsidized product. This *administered* (sanctioned) increase in protection, which comes in response to the trade policy of another country, is referred to as *contingent protection*.[15] Prior to 1994, countries routinely charged that other countries were subsidizing exports and, in response, the accusing countries countervailed these perceived

Table 2.8 Frequency of NTBs by region, 1994 and 2004[a]

Trade control measure[b]	Description	World (%)	Developed (%)	Developing (%)				C.E. Europe (%)
				Total	Africa	America	Asia	
1	Tariff measures (tariff rate quota, etc)	0.3 (5.8)	3.4 (16.3)	0 (0.3)	0 (0)	0 (0)	0.1 (0.7)	0.1 (0)
3	Price control measures	1.8 (7.1)	2.9 (9.4)	1.7 (6.1)	0.5 (15.3)	1.9 (2.7)	2.2 (6.9)	0 (0)
4	Finance measures	1.5 (2)	0.3 (0.1)	1.6 (3.1)	3.8 (0)	2 (0)	0 (7.7)	0 (0)
417	Refundable deposit for sensitive products categories	0.6 (0)	0.3 (0.1)	0.6 (0)	3.8 (0)	0 (0)	0 (0)	0 (0)
5	Automatic licensing measures	1.7 (2.8)	7.4 (5.3)	1.1 (1.5)	0.7 (0)	0.2 (0)	3 (3.7)	0.3 (0)
6	Quantity control measures	34.8 (49.2)	34.7 (45.8)	35.2 (53.1)	32 (62.5)	31.3 (48.1)	43.6 (55.6)	16.5 (9.9)
617	Prior authorization for sensitive product categories	17.1 (18.1)	16.7 (4.7)	17.2 (25.9)	10.5 (11.2)	21.3 (40.9)	14 (14.2)	13.5 (7.1)
627	Quotas for sensitive product categories	0.2 (0.2)	0.6 (0.5)	0.2 (0)	0.4 (0)	0 (0)	0.5 (0)	0 (0)
637	Prohibition for sensitive product categories	6.8 (2.5)	1 (1.5)	7.5 (3.1)	9.2 (0.6)	6.3 (2.7)	8.3 (4.4)	0 (0)
7	Monopolistic measures	1.5 (1.3)	0.7 (1.1)	1.6 (1.4)	2.6 (2.5)	0.6 (0.6)	2.6 (1.9)	0 (0)
8	Technical measures	58.5 (31.9)	50 (21.9)	58.6 (34.4)	60.4 (19.7)	63.9 (48.6)	48.4 (23.5)	83.1 (90.1)
Non-core measures (5 + 617 + 627 + 637 + 8)		15.2 (44.6)	23.5 (65.9)	14.7 (35)	15 (68.5)	8.1 (7.8)	25.8 (54.1)	3.1 (2.9)
Core measures (1 + 3 + 4 + 6 + 7 − (617 + 627 + 637))		84.8 (55.4)	76 (34.1)	85.3 (65)	85 (31.5)	91.8 (92.2)	74.2 (45.9)	96.9 (97.1)

[a]Numbers in parentheses are for 1994.
[b]See Table 2.6 for definitions.
Source: UNCTAD (2005, Tables 2a and 2b).

subsidies. However, lacking any definition of a subsidy, the method used to determine the appropriate magnitude of the countervailing duty was equally vague and hence also contentious. The GATT now contains specific rules and procedures for determining the subsidy rate and hence also the amount of the countervailing duty. It also delineates the kinds of subsidies that are actionable (see Section 2.2.).

Four commonly used export support programs are: subsidized export insurance, subsidized supplier credits, subsidized buyer credits and official development assistance (ODA).[16] The specifics of each program differ, but all share the goal of increasing the net revenue of exporting firms by either lowering the firm's costs or increasing the demand for its output.

Subsidized export insurance involves the home government underwriting all or part of the cost of insurance that an exporting firm buys. In so doing, it guarantees the exporter's receipts in domestic currency and hence eliminates a source of uncertainty at no cost to the exporting firm. Subsidized seller credits (also called "soft" loans) are loans a government grants the private sector at terms more favorable than those available in private capital markets. This effectively reduces the exporter's marginal cost. In contrast, subsidized buyer credits provide the foreign importer with more favorable financing than the exporter could provide. This effectively raises the demand facing exporters. Finally, when giving official development assistance (ODA), the donor country can stipulate that the recipient must purchase from the donor country's firm goods equal in value to the amount of the aid.[17]

Table 2.9 provides an illustration of the potential importance of such export promotion programs by showing the subsidy element (as a percentage of non-EU exports) associated with the export credit programs of Belgium, France and the UK during the period 1978–84. Although France's export promotion was the more substantial, such export credit subsidies generally rose in all three countries over the period.

Despite the continued use of export credit subsidies, export programs are in general a small fraction of the total subsidies granted to both industry and agriculture (see Table 2.10).[18]

Table 2.9   Export credit subsidies[a]

Year	Belgium	France	United Kingdom
1978	0.2	2.9	0.6
1979	0.3	2.8	0.9
1980	0.2	4.2	1.3
1981	0.3	5.1	1.7
1982	0.4	5.1	1.7
1983	0.4	3.8	1.0
1984	0.5	3.0	1.1

[a]Subsidies as a percentage of total exports to non-EU countries.
Source: Melitz and Messerlin (1987) and Abraham (1990).

Table 2.10   Sector distribution of subsidies of selected WTO members, yearly average 1999–2002 (percentages)

County/Group	Agriculture (%)	Industry (%)	Other (%)
Australia	30	51	19
European Community	42	8	50
EU (15)	1	19	80
Japan	78	22	0
United States	60	8	32

Source: WTO (2006, Table 9).

As noted, GATT prohibitions against overt export subsidies have been one factor limiting the size of export promotion schemes.

2.2 Administered protection and the WTO

Reference was made throughout Section 2.1 to the rules (disciplines) of the WTO and the GATT regarding the use of trade policy instruments by WTO member countries. It is important to note that these rules do not prohibit WTO member countries from imposing trade restrictions. Rather, they define the scope of such restrictions and a framework for consistent implementation – that is, for the administration of protection – hence the term *administered protection*. This section discusses the WTO and its key agreements in more detail.

The World Trade Organization

The WTO, established in January 1995, is one of the key outcomes of the 1986–94 Uruguay Round of multilateral trade negotiations. The primary responsibilities of the WTO are to provide a forum for multilateral trade negotiations and a framework for their implementation; 2) administer the trade policy review mechanism (TPRM); and 3) administer the dispute settlement procedures (DSPs).

Prior to the establishment of the WTO, the GATT was the only multilateral framework for administered protection. The latter now represents one of several agreements administered by the WTO (see Figure 2.1). In particular, the Uruguay Round gave rise to two new multilateral agreements: the General Agreement on Trade in Services (GATS) and the Agreement on Trade-related Aspects of Intellectual Property Rights (TRIPs). These agreements cover forms of trade and also issues previously outside the scope of the GATT. In addition, there are four plurilateral agreements covering government procurement, trade in civil aircraft, trade in bovine meat and trade in dairy products. A plurilateral agreement is binding only on countries that sign the agreement. In contrast, multilateral agreements such as the GATT are binding on all countries that agree to become WTO members.

The TPRM is both a function and a set of procedures whereby the WTO monitors the trade policies of member countries. To this end, each year WTO staff prepare a report on one or more member countries. Each report details the country's trade policies and provides an evaluation of these policies from an economic perspective. The stated intent of these reports is to

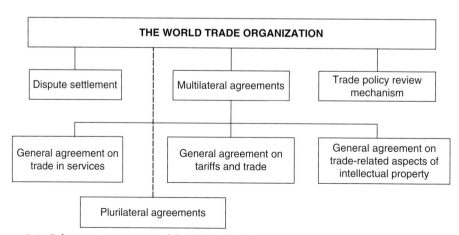

Figure 2.1 Schematic structure of the World Trade Organization

maintain transparency in the formulation and implementation of trade policies by providing a mechanism for multilateral surveillance of the trade practices of member countries.[19]

The dispute settlement function is a set of procedures that detail how a WTO member can initiate a complaint against the trade practices of another member and how this dispute is to be processed and ultimately resolved. Dispute settlement is discussed below as part of a more general discussion of the GATT.

General Agreement on Tariffs and Trade (GATT)

The GATT is the cornerstone agreement of the WTO. First signed in October 1947, the GATT was initially intended as an interim measure until a formal institutional body, the International Trade Organization (ITO), could be established. However, by the early 1950s, GATT members had failed to ratify an ITO charter and the GATT became the only formal statement of rules for administered protection. It is important to note that the GATT is only an agreement, not an institution. Prior to the establishment of the WTO, all monitoring and administration of the GATT was the responsibility of a small Secretariat based in Geneva. The WTO supplants this Secretariat and provides the formal institutional foundation for the GATT and other trade agreements. In recognition of this (and other) changes, the pre-WTO GATT is denoted GATT 1947 and the post-WTO GATT is denoted GATT 1994.

One function of the GATT (now WTO) is to provide a forum (i.e., a market) where countries can negotiate (i.e., exchange) reductions in their trade barriers; these forums are called multilateral trade negotiations and each such forum is called a "round." When GATT 1947 was first negotiated most of the significant trade barriers were tariffs. The GATT's Articles of Agreement therefore establish procedures for negotiating tariff reductions (*concessions*) among member countries and they delineate the rights and duties regarding these concessions. Once member countries agree on concessions these concessions become "bound." Binding a tariff rate means that no country can unilaterally increase that rate. As noted in Section 2.1, a bound tariff rate is a maximum rate that applies to all WTO members. However, the GATT does permit a country, under prescribed rules, to re-negotiate a previously bound rate. It also permits, under certain conditions (see safeguards below), a country to raise its tariff above the bound rate but, if it does, the country must then compensate the exporters harmed by its action.

Key principles

Two key principles underlying the GATT (and all multilateral agreements now forged by the WTO) are that of non-discrimination (Article I) and national treatment (Article III). The non-discrimination or "Most-Favored-Nation" (MFN) principle requires WTO member countries to treat products imported from different trading partners on the same basis.[20] The GATT does permit exceptions to MFN treatment. For example, customs unions are allowed as are certain historically recognized preferential trade relationships. In addition, developing countries may be granted tariff preferences under what is known as the generalized system of preferences (GSP).

National treatment requires that foreign goods, once inside the border of a country, be treated the same as domestically produced goods. One implication of national treatment is that trade barriers are only to be applied at the border; domestic policies should not therefore become barriers to trade. National treatment serves to limit the use of domestic policies to restrict trade and permits countries to identify more easily the trade barriers that they may need to overcome.

Tariff reductions and tariffication

An important function of the WTO is to facilitate reductions in trade barriers among its members. To this end, WTO members are required, when specified, to convert any non-tariff barrier to trade into its *ad valorem* equivalent, a process called *tariffication*. The purpose of tariffication is to make the level of protection afforded by NTBs transparent, and also comparable to tariff rates, for the ultimate purpose of negotiating their reduction.

As noted previously, negotiated reductions in trade barriers are conducted during "rounds" of multilateral trade negotiations. Since 1947 there have been eight completed rounds of multilateral tariff negotiations (see Table 2.11). A ninth round, called the Doha Round, was initiated in 2001 but has yet to be completed. The first five rounds, held between 1947 and 1962 were enormously successful in reducing tariffs. The sixth round (1964–67), known as the Kennedy Round, was important for two reasons. First, negotiators addressed both

Table 2.11 GATT/WTO trade rounds and tariff reductions, 1947–2007

Round or meeting	Period and number of parties	Subjects and modalities	Weighted tariff reduction[a]	Outcome
Geneva	1947 23 countries	Tariffs: item-by-item offer-request negotiations	−26%	Concessions on 15,000 tariff lines
Annecy	1949 33 countries	Tariffs: item-by-item offer-request negotiations	−3%	5,000 tariff concessions; 9 accessions
Torquay	1950 34 countries	Tariffs: item-by-item offer-request negotiations	−4%	8,700 tariff concessions; 4 accessions
Geneva	1956 22 countries	Tariffs: item-by-item offer-request negotiations	−3%	Modest reductions
Dillon Round	1960–1 45 countries	Tariffs: item-by-item offer-request negotiations, motivated in part by need to rebalance concessions following creation of the EEC.	−4%	4,400 concessions exchanged; EEC proposal for a 20 percent linear cut in manufactures tariffs rejected
Kennedy Round	1963–1967 48 countries	Tariffs: formula approach (linear cut) and item-by-item talks. Non-tariff measures: antidumping, customs valuation.	−38%	Average tariffs reduced by 35 percent; some 33,000 tariff lines bound; agreements on customs valuation and anti-dumping
Tokyo Round	1973–1979 99 countries	Tariffs: formula approach with exceptions. Non-tariff measures: anti-dumping customs valuation, subsidies and countervail, government procurement, import licensing, product standards, safeguards, special and differential treatment of developing countries.	−33%	Average tariffs reduced by one third to 6 percent for OECD manufactures imports; voluntary codes of conduct agreed for all non-tariff issues except safeguards.

| Uruguay Round | 1986–1994 103 countries in 1986, 117 as of end of 1993 | Tariffs: formula approach and item-by-item negotiations. Non-tariff measures: all Tokyo issues, plus services, intellectual property, pre-shipment inspection, rules of origin, trade-related investment measures, dispute settlement, transparency and surveillance of trade policies. | −38% | Average tariffs again reduced by one third on average. Agriculture and textiles and clothing subjected to rules; creation of WTO; new agreements on services and TRIPs; majority of Tokyo Round codes extended to all WTO members. |
| Doha Round | 2001 – 150 countries as of beginning 2007 | Tariffs: formula approach and item-by-item negotiations. Non-tariff measures: trade facilitation, rules, services, environment. | N/A | |

[a] MFN tariff reduction of industrial countries for industrial products (excluding petroleum); Tariff reductions for the first five rounds refer to the US only. The calculations of average rates of reductions are weighted by MFN import values.

Source: Adapted from WTO (2007, Tables 4 and 5).

tariff and non-tariff barriers and trade in agriculture goods. Second, bargaining was for across-the-board reductions on all product categories; previous rounds had instead involved only bilateral negotiations on a product by product basis. In the end, little agreement was reached in the areas of agriculture and non-tariff barriers (with the EU ultimately strengthening its Common Agricultural Policy), but tariffs on manufactured goods were cut by an average of one-third. These tariff cuts reduced the average tariff rate of most industrialized countries in manufactures to under 6 percent (see Table 2.12).

Table 2.12   Average applied tariff rates for selected countries, 2002

Region/Country	Manufactures	Textiles	Clothing
OECD countries	6.2	9.4	16.1
Australia	5.4	9.9	20.7
Canada	4.9	10.7	18.4
European Union	4.4	7.9	11.4
Japan	2.9	6.5	11
Korea	8	9.4	12.4
Mexico	17.3	20.5	34.4
New Zealand	3.1	2.4	13.7
Turkey	5.9	8.6	11.8
United States	4	9.1	11.4

60

Table 2.12 (Continued)

Region/Country	Manufactures	Textiles	Clothing
Developing countries	13.5	18.1	23
Asia			
China	9.6	9.7	16.1
Chinese Taipei	6.4	8.3	13.1
Hong Kong,	0	0	0
Indonesia	9	12.6	18.1
Malaysia	9.9	16.7	19.6
Philippines	7.4	10.7	19.2
Singapore	0	0	0
Thailand	16.1	18.7	39.7
South Asia			
Bangladesh	22.1	30.2	...
India	34.1	39	40
Sri Lanka	8	3.4	11
Latin America			
Argentina	16.1	20.1	22.9
Bolivia	9.6	10	10
Brazil	16.8	20	22.9
Chile	9	9	9
Colombia	12.1	18	19.9
Costa Rica	4.8	8.3	13.8
Dominican Republic	14.6	20.5	30.6
El Salvador	6.9	17	23.9
Jamaica	5.6	3.2	19.4
Paraguay	13.7	19.5	22.4
Peru	13.3	17	19.3
Uruguay	14.7	20.1	22.9
Venezuela	12.3	18	19.9
Africa			
Algeria	24.1	35.3	44.5
Egypt	22.3	42	39.7
Morocco	28.2	38.2	49.6
Tunisia	28.7	38	42.6
Sub-Saharan Africa	16.8	21.8	34.5

Notes: Simple average tariff rates for most recent year data available;
Manufactures: SITC 5–8 less 68; Textiles (65); Clothing (84).
Source: UNCTAD (2002, Table 8).

Failure during the Kennedy Round to mold agreement in the areas of agriculture and non-tariff barriers, and the emergence of certain developing countries as significant exporters of manufactured goods resulted in these issues being at the forefront of the subsequent Tokyo Round (1974–79). The Tokyo Round achieved an additional one-third cut in tariffs but failed to successfully address the issues of agricultural trade and the participation of developing countries in GATT disciplines. Non-tariff barriers received substantial attention; "codes of conduct" were adopted covering areas such as subsidies, countervailing and anti-dumping duties, health and safety regulations, import licensing procedures, government procurement, customs valuation and safeguards. However, these codes were plurilateral rather than multilateral, and hence binding only on members that signed the code (only about one-third of the members signed and most were developed countries).

The Uruguay Round, launched in 1986 and concluded on April 15 1994 dealt seriously with many of the issues addressed but left unfinished in the Tokyo Round. The Uruguay Round reached agreements in a number of areas, many of which have already been noted. These included: an additional one-third reduction in tariffs; the extension of GATT disciplines to cover trade in all goods, not just manufactured products – in particular, agricultural and textile products; the phase-out by 2006 of the Multi-Fiber Arrangement (MFA) governing trade in textiles;[21] improved rules on the use of temporary import restrictions (see safeguards below); restraint on the use of subsidies and clearer rules on countervailing duties (see below); tariffication of quantitative restrictions; extension of GATT rules to cover trade in services (the GATS); development of rules to remove adverse trade impacts of investment or "right-of-establishment" rules,[22] counterfeiting and intellectual property (TRIPs); and, finally, institutional reforms, most notably strengthening the GATT's dispute-settlement capabilities (see below) and replacement of the GATT Secretariat with the World Trade Organization (WTO). Many of the Uruguay Round agreements were more extensive versions of the Tokyo Round codes. Important, however, is that the Uruguay Round agreements derived from these codes apply to all WTO members – therefore raising them from plurilateral to multilateral status. The Uruguay Round agreements therefore signaled a commitment by WTO members to reverse the trend toward unilateralism and the unequal treatment of trading partners that occurred during the 1970s and 1980s.

The latest round – the Doha Round, started in 2001 – has so far failed to gain traction. Members failed to conclude negotiations by the original deadline of January 1 2005 and then also failed to meet a subsequent unofficial deadline of the end of 2006. Part of the explanation for the delay is that the Doha Round is the first round in which lower income countries have pushed for concessions they see as material to their development processes. Rapidly emerging countries such as India and Brazil have led a contingent of developing countries that insist on measures that recognize their developing status, and they have called on high income countries to grant various exemptions to different parts of the WTO agreements. For example, they have proposed new rules allowing developing countries to subsidize exports without facing countervailing measures if the subsidy program is deemed to have "legitimate development goals," and that least-developed countries should be exempt from the GATT's ban on export subsidies. A central area of contention is agriculture products. Developed countries (such as the US and the EU countries) support and protect their agricultural sectors with outright subsidies and trade distorting domestic measures (e.g., price supports) which they have been slow to phase out. The lower income countries have pushed for further liberalization of such measures but at the same time have sought protection (exemptions) for themselves (e.g., the right to restrict exports due to food security issues). Negotiations on these and many other issues are ongoing.

Dispute settlement

An important function of the GATT is the administration of a dispute settlement process. The dispute settlement process is important because it makes the commitments of member countries regarding tariffs or other agreements enforceable.

During the turbulent 1970s and 1980s, the dispute settlement process specified in GATT 1947 was found to be both time-consuming and weak. Disputes were first addressed by a panel of independent experts whose findings were then submitted to the GATT's governing council (i.e., all GATT members) and a consensus of members was required before the panel's recommendations could be implemented. If the offending country chose not to implement the findings of the panel, the country bringing the complaint could then ask the council for permission to retaliate. Such authorization again required a consensus of all GATT members. The entire process could therefore be blocked at two stages by either one of the parties involved in the dispute. In addition, the process was slow and its outcome highly uncertain. In practice, most disputes were settled before they got to the final stages.

Although cumbersome, the GATT 1947 dispute settlement process was generally successful until the 1970s. Thereafter, globalization and rapid changes in trade exposed a number of weaknesses in the process. One major failure was the inability of the system to deal with trade in politically sensitive sectors, such as agriculture, which were not covered by GATT 1947. The prolonged nature of the dispute process and the uncertainty of enforcement led to growing impatience with the entire system. While delays did permit issues to settle, many countries simply became unwilling to endure the process and often initiated retaliatory steps before receiving approval by the GATT council. The multilateral system of rules was in danger of collapse.

The Uruguay Round significantly overhauled and strengthened the GATT's dispute settlement process, thereby addressing many of the earlier frustrations. Under GATT 1994 it is now impossible for either party of a dispute to block an inquiry. In addition, the entire process was streamlined and is now subject to standard terms of reference (i.e., consistent and clear rules). An exact timetable for the completion of each procedural step is given. Assisting the repair of the dispute settlement process is that GATT 1994 disciplines cover trade in all goods. Hence, the process can now be used to resolve disputes arising over the trade in any good, not just manufactured goods.

Safeguards

Safeguards constitute a safety valve for the world trading system. As trade patterns change, a country may wish to temporarily alter its bound commitments in order to protect domestic sectors threatened by injurious import competition. To this end, the safeguards provision of the GATT allows a member to withdraw a bound concession under certain circumstances. For example, a country can impose temporary import restrictions to give an industry time to adjust when it is "seriously injured" by a rapid increase in imports. A country can also restrict all its imports to deal with a serious balance of payments deficit and it can restrict imports that threaten public safety, health, morals, the environment, the general public welfare or national security.

The stated intent of safeguards is to facilitate trade liberalization by allowing countries to impose temporary trade barriers, on a non-discriminatory basis, in order to protect producers seriously injured by trade liberalization. GATT 1994 prohibits the use of voluntary export restraints, orderly marketing arrangements or any other similar measure on the import or export side as a means of implementing protection under a safeguards provision. But despite this prohibition, GATT 1994 does permit an importing country seeking protection via a safeguards action to use a quantitative restriction, and this restriction can take the form of a quota imposed by exporters (i.e., an export quota) if mutually agreed between the importer and all affected exporters. The resolution of this seeming contradiction concerning the legal use of quotas is that, under GATT 1994, any quota must be global, that is, nondiscriminatory. Hence, while voluntary export restraints are prohibited under GATT 1994, VER-like actions are permitted if they are applied on a multilateral basis.[23]

Restrictions imposed under a safeguards provision can last for a maximum of eight years: four years initially but then extendible for another four years if injury persists and the domestic industry can demonstrate that it is adjusting. During the first three years the importing country is not required to compensate affected exports for its actions, but if the restriction is continued beyond three years affected exporters can demand compensation.

Anti-dumping and countervailing duties

The safeguard provisions also address so-called "unfair" trade practices, notably dumping and government subsidies. The protectionist measures taken under these provisions are conditional upon demonstrating that a particular circumstance has arisen. This explains why these measures often come under the heading *contingent protection*.

Dumping is defined as selling in an export market at a price below normal value. The latter is habitually defined as the price of the exported good in its country of origin. Under Article VI of GATT, normal value can also be construed as the comparable export price to a third country in the ordinary course of trade or – if the latter is unavailable or unreliable – the full cost of production, including all fixed and sunk costs, and a "normal" profit.[24]

The export price is compared with the normal value at the same or similar level of trade, normally the ex-factory level. The difference between price and normal value is called the margin of dumping and is often expressed as a percentage of the export price.

WTO rules allow, but do not mandate, anti-dumping measures when dumping has caused material injury to the home industry of like products, or when it threatens the emergence of a home industry that competes with the dumped imports.[25] The measures are intended to offset the injurious effects of dumping on the competing home industry. The extent of injury is assessed by a slew of indicators, for example the home industry's decline in sales, market share, profits, and capacity utilization. The only injury that is relevant to the question of whether a WTO member is allowed to adopt an anti-dumping measure is injury to the industry that produces similar products. Benefits or harm to other industries or consumers as a result of dumping are not germane to the question of whether the member may adopt anti-dumping measures.

The most commonly used anti-dumping measure is a duty (i.e., tax). WTO rules stipulate that the rate of duty may not exceed the margin of dumping.[26] The duty generally remains in effect for a number of years, but it is renewable upon expiry if the conditions that warranted its initial imposition persist.

Unlike a conventional tariff, the anti-dumping duty targets only the exports of like products that originate in the country whose firms are deemed to have dumped. It may apply to all exports of like products from the country whose exporters have dumped, or only to the exports of the firms whose dumping has been found to cause injury.

Anti-dumping procedures are initiated by the industry in the importing country that competes with the dumped imports. Upon a finding of dumping, the importing country typically levies a provisional anti-dumping duty on the subject imports. At this stage, a government agency or tribunal steps in to investigate whether the dumped imports have been a cause of injury. If it concludes in the affirmative then the duty is maintained.[27] If it does not, the case is withdrawn, and monies collected under the duty are refunded.

The alternative remedy to an anti-dumping duty is an "undertaking." An undertaking is a commitment by exporters to raise the export price by an agreed amount (a price undertaking), or to restrict the export volume (a quantity undertaking). Such commitments result in a termination of the legal proceedings.

Anti-dumping duties are on average much higher than the classical tariff. Prusa (2001) finds that the median anti-dumping duty levied by the US between 1980 and 1994 was 16 percent. In 20 percent of cases the rate of duty exceeded 50 percent. This contrasts with a 4 percent average classical tariff rate for the industries that sought anti-dumping protection during the same period.

Unlike anti-dumping duties, countervailing duties are aimed at the actions of foreign governments rather than foreign firms. A subsidy exists under WTO rules when a government or an entity entrusted by a government makes a financial contribution to an enterprise or industry, which confers an advantage to the recipient. The contribution may come in the form of a transfer of money, goods or services, or in the form of foregoing monies due to the government. Subsidies that target an enterprise or industry are called specific. Specific subsidies granted to an industry located in one country impinge on a second industry located elsewhere when: a) the second industry competes in its local market with the recipient of the subsidy; b) the subsidy impedes that industry's exports to the country granting the subsidy; c) the subsidy curbs the second industry's exports to third countries.

The subsidies that can be counteracted under WTO rules come under the following headings: prohibited and actionable. Prohibited subsidies are specific subsidies conditioned upon export performance or upon the use of local inputs in preference to imported ones. Other subsidies, provided they are specific (e.g., production subsidies to an industry), while not prohibited, may be counteracted.[28] Counteraction is either multilateral or unilateral. Under the multilateral process, the member country making the complaint requests the establishment of a panel to determine if the subsidy is WTO consistent. If the subsidy is found to belong to the prohibited class, it must be withdrawn. If it is not, the subsidizing country may face countermeasures proportionate to the subsidy granted.

The successful challenge of an actionable subsidy hinges on a finding that it: a) causes injury to the domestic industry of another member country; or b) nullifies or impairs the benefits that accrue to another WTO member; or c) causes serious prejudice to the interests of another member. If one of these conditions is established, and the subsidizing member refuses to withdraw the subsidy or remove its adverse effects, the injured member may be authorized to take countermeasures commensurate with the degree and nature of the subsidy's adverse effects.

If the counteraction is unilateral, the importing country is authorized to levy a countervailing duty on subsidized imports upon showing that these imports have caused injury to the domestic industry. The importing country is authorized to levy a countervailing duty on products that have benefitted from prohibited or actionable subsidies. The duty must be terminated within five years, unless renewed prior to this date on the basis of a review. Proceedings may be suspended or terminated without the imposition of countervailing duties upon acceptance of an undertaking by the subsidizing government to eliminate or limit the subsidy, or to take measures concerning its effects.[29]

These rules apply only to subsidies of non-agricultural goods. Farm subsidies are instead addressed in the Agreement on Agriculture. This requires countries to reduce domestic support of agriculture as measured by the aggregate measure of support (AMS), which includes domestic and border support.

Regional trade agreements

Regional trade agreements (RTAs), such as customs unions and free trade areas, are fundamentally at odds with the MFN principle underlying the GATT.[30] However, the GATT does allow such RTAs subject to certain conditions: 1) the trade restrictions against non-RTA members must not rise on average; 2) the agreement must eliminate all duties and other restrictions to trade between RTA members on "almost all" products that originate from RTA members; 3) the elimination of trade barriers between RTA members must occur with a reasonable length of time (presently less than ten years). If these and other requirements are met then WTO members can, by unanimous agreement, sanction the RTA. In practice, WTO enforcement of the GATT's RTA requirements has been relatively weak. One reason for this was the decision of GATT members during the late 1950s not to examine closely the agreements contained in the Treaty of Rome which established the EU. This precedent has resulted in subsequent RTAs being largely tolerated for political reasons.

Under GATT rules, if RTA members seek to increase bound rates in order to establish a common tariff boundary around RTA members then they must compensate RTA non-members. If agreement cannot be reached regarding compensation the GATT permits RTA non-member countries to retaliate against RTA members.

General Agreement on Trade in Services (GATS)

Since the mid-1980s, trade in services has continued to grow and is, by some measures, becoming a sizable fraction of all trade flows. The growing importance of trade in services led many services exporting countries to consider it in their interest to develop rules and procedures regarding such trade. To this end, the GATS sets forth a set of general principles and rules that apply to measures affecting trade in services. The GATS incorporates the MFN and national treatment principles, although, as under GATT, exceptions are permitted. The agreement prohibits, in principle, certain market access restrictions, namely limitations on: 1) the number of suppliers, 2) the value of transactions or assets, 3) the total quantity of service output, 4) the number of natural persons that may be employed, 5) the type of legal entity through which a service supplier is permitted to supply a service, 6) the share of equity ownership of a foreign investor or the absolute value of the foreign investment. In addition to these prohibitions, the GATS contains a number of sector-specific rules dealing with modes of market conduct and rights of establishment.

General Agreement on Trade-Related Intellectual Property Rights (TRIPs)

While tailored to recognize many of the unique characteristics of services, the GATS remains close to its GATT roots in terms of general principles and, in addition, there is no attempt to harmonize trade policies across countries. In contrast, the TRIPs agreement seeks uniformity by establishing minimum standards of intellectual property protection that must be achieved by all member countries. The TRIPs does not state how each government should enforce these minimum standards, but by specifying minimum standards the agreement does require countries to take positive action to protect intellectual property. This requirement for action is in sharp contrast to the GATT and GATS, since these do not require governments to undertake a specific policy but instead simply constrain governments regarding the types of policies they can pursue.

Like its sister agreements, the TRIPs adopts the MFN and national treatment principles but also permits exceptions. Regarding the protection of intellectual property, the obligations specify minimum periods of protection in areas of such as trademarks, industrial designs, copyright and patents, and that criminal procedures and penalties are to be applied to copyright abuses if these are on a commercial scale. The agreement also contains specific provisions dealing with the application of competition law to intellectual property protection, and it specifies in detail the procedures to be followed for enforcement and dispute settlement.

2.3   Concluding remarks

Countries use a variety of trade policy instruments to restrict or promote their trade. *Ad valorem* tariffs are the preferred and predominant instrument used to restrict trade. Other trade restricting instruments, called non-tariff barriers (NTBs), are also used and can take a variety of forms, the most common being quantitative restrictions in the form of export and import quotas. The promotion of exports is commonly effected through the use of subsidies. However, most countries have agreed to prohibit direct export subsidies and hence indirect subsidies are the most common form of export promotion.

Members of the World Trade Organization (WTO) agree to limit their choice of trade policy instruments and to follow prescribed rules (disciplines) in the application of these instruments. They further agree to reduce trade barriers among themselves. WTO rules are mainly contained in a set of multilateral agreements, the most important being the General Agreement on Tariffs and Trade (GATT). First signed in 1947, the GATT underwent a number of transformations during the Uruguay Round of multilateral trade negotiations that concluded in 1994. These changes were significant enough to distinguish the revised GATT from the original GATT. The latter is now called GATT 1947 and the new revised GATT is called GATT 1994.

By the late 1980s, the multilateral system of rules for the administration of protection was in jeopardy due to widespread and growing use of NTBs and a failure of GATT 1947 to address many of the disputes that arose between countries. In large measure, this failure resulted from the fact that GATT 1947 disciplines applied only to trade in manufactured goods. As an outcome of the Uruguay Round, GATT disciplines now cover trade in all goods. In addition, the system of NTBs, and the unilateral and bilateral protectionist measures built up during the 1970s and 1980s, is being dismantled. While hurdles remain in areas such as agriculture, WTO members have demonstrated a resolve to continue and strengthen the multilateral framework of administered protection.

Notes

1. Detailed treatment of the economic effects of trade policy instruments appears in Chapters 5 and 10.
2. These are the main multilateral agreements covering trade. See Section 2.2 for further discussion.
3. Observers must begin negotiations to enter ("ascend") into the WTO within five years.
4. Specific rates are therefore easier to administer since customs officials do not need to know the value of a good in order to determine the amount of duty. Also, there is little scope for customs officials to inflate the amount of duty by setting an arbitrary value on the product.
5. Until recently, the product classification system for tariffs was the Brussels Tariff Nomenclature (BTN) and the Customs Cooperation Council Nomenclature (CCCN). The current system is the Harmonized Commodity Description and Coding System (the "Harmonized System"), which provides greater product detail and the flexibility to incorporate new products easily. The design of a product classification is crucial to avoid misclassification and hence inaccurate application of duties by customs officials.

6. The computation of tariff averages is particularly important for the calculation of the welfare effects of tariffs. See Chapter 5 and also the articles by Leamer (1974), Anderson (1994) and Anderson and Neary (2005).

7. For example, a good subject to a prohibitive tariff – that is, one that eliminates all imports of the good – receives zero weight in the average.

8. As discussed in Section 2.2, a WTO member country can raise its bound rate but to do so it must justify the increase and it may also be required to compensate affected exporters.

9. This is not always the case since one must also account for how the license is obtained and at what cost. See Chapters 5 and 10.

10. This difficulty can be a virtue for the country adopting the NTB since it may permit the country to achieve a level of protection much higher than that suggested by its applied tariff rate.

11. Basic data for this purpose comes from The United Nations Council on Trade and Development (UNCTAD) which maintains an inventory of NTBs covering most of developed economies and about 80 developing countries at the tariff line level. These data consist of a brief description of the NTB and its coverage. See Table 2.6.

12. A category can be either a country's total imports or one of the product categories defined according to the trade classification system (e.g., SITC) in use (see Appendix).

13. Another index is the coverage ratio (C_g) which weights the incidence of NTBs by import value shares:

$$C_g = 100 \sum_{j \in g} \frac{D_j M_j}{\sum_{j \in g} M_j}$$

where M_j is the value of imports of good j and D_j is as defined for the frequency index. Like the frequency index, the coverage ratio takes values between 0 and 100.

14. A subsidy is deemed to exist when there is a financial contribution by a government and a benefit is thereby conferred.

15. Another form of contingent protection is an anti-dumping duty. An importing country can assess this duty against foreign firms deemed to have "dumped" their goods in the importing country's market. See Section 2.2.

16. Although export promotion measures receive widespread popular attention, they only affect a small number of industries which may, nonetheless, represent a sizable portion of a country's total import value.

17. Poor data has hampered empirical estimation of the effects of various export promotion schemes. Some progress in collecting consistent data has been made by the Commission of the European Communities and the European Free Trade Area (EFTA), but international comparisons remain difficult.

18. Export credit subsidies constitute the bulk of export assistance, whereas subsidies on export insurance are of minor importance – at most 1 percent of total exports. The importance of "tied" official development aid is more difficult to gauge, but available evidence suggests it is also of minor importance.

19. Aside from increasing the demand for the services of international economists, these TPRM reports represent an important source of data on trade barriers.

20. MFN arose partly for practical reasons related to the method by which negotiations to reduce tariffs were initially conducted. Specifically, bargaining over concessions on individual products was conducted on a bilateral basis between the importing country and its largest supplier. Concessions achieved between these two parties were then made available on an "unconditional MFN" basis to all other members.

21. The MFA involved a system of bilateral quotas between textile exporting and importing countries.

22. These are the so-called TRIMs – Trade Related Investment Measures.

23. However, the GATT does allow for selectivity in the application of a restriction if imports from some countries are shown to have increased "disproportionately." However, such discriminatory measures can be maintained for at most four years.

24. The below cost definition is used more often in some countries, in particular the US.

25. The discussion of WTO rules is based on Trebilcock and Howse (2005) and Mavroidis (2007).

26. In the EU, and to some extent in Australia, authorities also consider the injury margin when setting the anti-dumping duty. The margin is the amount by which the export price, net of transport cost, undercuts the domestically produced like product. The European Commission applies the lesser duty rule. Specifically, when the dumping margin exceeds the undercutting, the duty equals the latter.

27. The rate may be adjusted in response to pricing information that has become available after the provisional duty was set.

28. Non-actionable subsidies constitute a third heading under the Agreement on Subsidies and Countervailing Measures. The "safe harbor" for these subsidies no longer exists. See Mavroidis (2007).

29. A *de minimis* provision stipulates that investigations should terminate when the amount of subsidy is less than 1 percent *ad valorem*, or when the volume of subsidized imports is negligible.

30. Chapter 12 discusses the theoretical implications of regional trade agreements.

References and additional reading

The GATT and WTO

Baldwin, R.E. (1995), "An Economic Evaluation of the Uruguay Round Agreements," *Annual Trade Review*, Claremont-McKenna College.

Deardorff, A. and Stern, R.M. (Eds.). (1994), *Analytical and Negotiating Issues in the Global Trading System* (Ann Arbor: University of Michigan Press).

Hoekman, B. (1996), "Trade Laws and Institutions: Good Practices and the World Trade Organization," World Bank Discussion Paper 282 (Washington, D: The World Bank).

Jackson, J. (1989), *The World Trading System: Law and Policy of International Economic Relations* (Cambridge, MA: MIT Press).

Stern, R.M. (Ed.) (1993), *The Multilateral Trading System: Analysis and Options for Change* (Ann Arbor: University of Michigan Press).

GATT (1994), *The Results of the Uruguay Round of Multilateral Trade Negotiations* (Geneva: United Nations), (November).

Tariff and non-tariff protection

Anderson, J.E. (1994), "Tariff Index Theory," *Review of International Economics*, 32 (2), 156–173.

Anderson, J.E. and Neary, J.P. (2005), *Measuring the Restrictiveness of Trade Policy* (Cambridge, MA: MIT Press).

Balassa, B. and Balassa C. (1984), "Industrial Protection in the Developed Countries," *The World Economy*, 7, 179–196.

Balassa, B. (1965), "Tariff Protection in Industrial Countries: An Evaluation," *Journal of Political Economy*, 73 (6), 573–94.

Boltuck, R. and Litan, R.L. (1991), *Down in the Dumps: Administration of the Unfair Trade Laws* (Washington, DC: Brookings Institution).

Coughlin, C.C. (2010), "Measuring International Trade Policy: A Primer on Trade Restrictiveness Indices," *Federal Reserve Bank of St. Louis*, 92 (5), 381–394.

Deardorff, A.V. and Stern, R.M. (1998), *Measurement of Nontariff Barriers: Studies in International Economics* (Ann Arbor: University of Michigan Press).

Finger, J.M. and Olechowski, A. (1987), "Trade Barriers: Who Does What to Whom," in H. Giersch (Ed.), *Free Trade in the World Economy* (Tübingen: J.C.B. Mohr), 37–71.

GATT (various years), *Trade Policy Review Mechanism* (Geneva: United Nations).

Grossman, G. (1981), "The Theory of Domestic Content Protection and Content Preference," *Quarterly Journal of Economics*, 96 (4), 583–603.

Kee, H., Nicita, A., and Olarreaga, M. (2009), "Estimating Trade Restrictiveness Indices," *Economic Journal*, 119 (534), 172–199.

Laird, S. and Yeats, A. (1990), *Quantitative Methods for Trade Barrier Analysis* (Basingstoke: Macmillan).

Leamer, E.E. (1974), "Nominal Tariff Averages with Estimated Weights," *Southern Economic Journal*, 41, 34–46.

Mussa, M. (1984), "The Economics of Content Protection," NBER Working Paper No. 1457.

Nogués, J.J., Olechowski, A. and Winters, L.A. (1986), "The Extent of Non-Tariff Barriers to Industrial Countries' Imports," *The World Bank Economic Review*, 1, 181–199.

Schuknecht, L. (1992), *Trade Protection in the European Community* (Switzerland: Harwood Academic Publishers).

United Nations (2010), *Millennium Development Goals*, available at http://www.mdg-trade.org.

UNCTAD (2002), *Trade And Development Report 2002: Developing Countries in World Trade* (Geneva: United Nations).

UNCTAD (2005), *Methodologies, Classifications, Quantification and Development Impacts Of Non-Tariff Barriers: Note By The UNCTAD Secretariat*, Document TD/B/COM.1/EM.27/2, June 23.

World Integrated Trade Solution (2010), available at http://wits.worldbank.org/WITS/WITS/.

WTO (various years), *World Trade Report* (Geneva: United Nations).

Safeguards, export subsidies and dumping

Abraham, F. (1990), *The Effects On Intra-Community Competition Of Export Subsidies To Third Countries: The Case Of Export Credits, Export Insurance And Official Development Assistance*, Report prepared for the Commission of the European Communities.

Abraham, F., Couwenberg, I., and Dewit, G. (1991), "Towards an EU policy on export financing subsidies: Lessons from the 1980s and prospects for future reform," International Economics Research Papers Number 77, Centrum voor Economische Studiën, Katholieke Universiteit Leuven.

Finger, J.M. (1993), *Antidumping: How it Works and Who Gets Hurt* (Ann Arbor: University of Michigan Press).

Hindley, B. (1994), "Safeguards, VERs and Antidumping Action," in *The New World Trading System* (Paris: OECD), 91–103.

Mavroidis, P.C. (2007), *Trade in Goods: The GATT and the Other Agreements Regulating Trade in Goods* (Oxford: Oxford University Press).

Trebilcock, M.J. and Howse, R. (2005), *The Regulation of International Trade*, 3rd ed. (London: Routledge).

Competitive markets: trade and trade policy

3

The Ricardian framework

The edifice of international trade theory is constructed on the principle of comparative advantage. This basic principle, developed by David Ricardo, is the fundamental explanation of the benefits of specialization.

> Though an awareness of the benefits of specialization must go back to the dim mists of antiquity in all civilizations, it was not until Ricardo that this deepest and most beautiful result in all of economics was obtained. Though the logic applies equally to interpersonal, interfirm and interregional trade, it was in the context of international trade that the principle of comparative advantage was discovered and has been investigated ever since.
>
> (Findlay, 1988, 514)

Using this principle, Ricardo argued that trade between two countries of not too different size would be beneficial even if one had an absolute productive advantage (a lower price) in all goods. In the context of the economic and philosophical debates of the time, this principle not only refuted Adam Smith's principle of absolute efficiency as a determinant of trade but also provided an anti-mercantilist proof that trade can be beneficial for nations.

This chapter investigates the principle of comparative advantage in various forms and relates it to international trade. In Section 3.1, the concept is first illustrated in an elementary way, known as the Ricardian example. In Section 3.2 the concept is formalized as the Ricardian model. This model is then used to determine the international equilibrium and discuss the gains from trade. The remainder of the chapter discusses the implications of relaxing the main assumptions of the Ricardian model. Section 3.3 introduces the various concepts of scale economies and then looks at the pattern of trade and specialization when scale economies are external to the firm. Section 3.4 examines how comparative advantage operates when there is a continuum of goods and discusses the gains from trade in this context. In Section 3.5 this model is extended to encompass technological heterogeneity and a large number of countries. Finally, Section 3.6 summarizes the basic Ricardian propositions and the empirical tests to which they have been subjected.

3.1 The principle of comparative cost advantage

To illustrate the principle of comparative advantage, Ricardo used the example reproduced in panel A of Table 3.1. Each entry in panel A is the constant unit labor requirement for producing either wine or cloth in England and Portugal. In this example, Portugal has an absolute advantage in the production of both goods since it requires only 80 labor years per unit of wine and 90 labor years per unit of cloth compared with 120 and 100 labor years respectively in England.

Now consider the effect of international trade on the pattern of production. England could decide either to decrease its production of wine and thereby release labor resources to produce more units of cloth, or to increase its production of wine and reduce its production of cloth. Panel B of Table 3.1 outlines the outcome of the former, panel C the latter. If England decreases its production of wine by 5 units, it releases 600 labor years that can be used to produce 6 additional units of cloth. If Portugal then imports these 6 units of cloth, the clothing industry in Portugal can release 540 labor years. Of these, only 400 are needed to compensate for the loss of 5 units of wine in England. Hence, the remaining 140 labor years represent the efficiency gain in world production due to the re-arrangement of production made possible by trade. With 140 labor years Portuguese workers can produce 1.75 additional units of wine (as in panel B), 1.6 additional units of cloth or various combinations of both commodities (not shown). These gains could in turn be divided so that Portugal and England each benefit from trade between the two nations. This gain from trade can be exploited further until one of the following situations occurs: the whole labor force in England specializes in cloth production, or the whole labor force in Portugal specializes in wine production or both. Panel C shows the negative efficiency loss of specialization in the wrong commodities.

Table 3.1 The Ricardian example

A Labor requirements per unit of output

	Wine	Cloth
England	120	100
Portugal	80	90

B Trade and efficient labor reallocation (changes in production)

	Wine	Cloth
England	−5	+6
Portugal	6.75	−6
	1.75	0

C Trade and inefficient labor reallocation (changes in production)

	Wine	Cloth
England	+5	−6
Portugal	−5	4.44
	0	−1.56

The pattern of trade and specialization just described can also be determined by comparing autarky market prices. If labor markets are competitive, the autarky wage rate in each country is unique. If goods markets are competitive, the relative price of cloth (c) and wine (w) in each country is determined by the relative average cost of production. Using the data provided in panel A of Table 3.1 to compute the average costs of production we obtain the autarky prices: $(p_w/p_c)^P = 8/9$ and $(p_w/p_c)^E = 6/5$. Thus, in autarky, a unit of wine in Portugal exchanges for 8/9 of a unit of cloth, while in England a unit of wine exchanges for 6/5 of a unit of cloth. Since $6/5 > 8/9$, we say that England has a comparative advantage over Portugal in cloth relative to wine and, if trade takes place, England should export cloth and import wine. If we invert the inequality the converse holds as well. We can state that Portugal has a comparative advantage over England in wine versus cloth. Hence, comparative advantage explains how international trade can arise and provides a basis for predicting the direction of such trade.

Nothing has been said so far about absolute costs. To see why these do not affect the outcome, refer back to panel A of Table 3.1 and assume that the pre-trade nominal wage in each country equals unity. If the exchange rate is also fixed at unity, wine and cloth will be cheaper in Portugal as it has lower labor requirements for both goods. When trade opens, Portuguese firms will be confronted with increased demand for both commodities and will try to hire more workers, thereby bidding up wages and thus costs. In England, international competition will cause English wages to fall as English firms lay off workers. If this process of wage adjustment persists long enough for the Portuguese wage to exceed that in England by more than 100/90, the price of English cloth will become cheaper than in Portugal and England will start producing and exporting cloth. The wage adjustment process will stop when trade balance equilibrium is reached. The resulting equilibrium pattern of trade will be the same as that obtained under the comparative cost analysis.

In contrast to the comparative cost analysis using relative prices, the analysis of nominal cost differences explains the path (in value terms) of adjustment towards the pattern of international specialization. Since the above held the exchange rate fixed, the full weight of the adjustment fell on wages. In practice, both wages and exchange rates contribute to the adjustment toward trade balance.

3.2 The Ricardian model

This section formalizes the preceding discussion in an analytical framework known as the Ricardian model. In its barest essentials, the Ricardian model rests on several assumptions.

(1) Two countries: denoted "home" and "foreign" (marked *).

(2) Two final products: good 1 and good 2.

(3) Each good uses only one input (labor) in production. Labor is homogeneous in quality.

(4) Labor is inelastically supplied in each country.

(5) Labor is perfectly mobile within each country but internationally immobile.

(6) Constant labor requirement per unit of output. Let a_j and a_j^* be the quantity of home and foreign labor, respectively, required to produce one unit of good j ($j = 1, 2$). These requirements are invariant to the scale of production.

(7) Technologies differ between the two countries: $a_j \neq a_j^* (j = 1, 2)$.

(8) No cost of transportation, no trade barriers.

(9) Competition in factor and product markets.

The Ricardian model describes a static equilibrium and therefore assumes that the supply of resources in the economy is inelastic and that tastes and technology do not change.[1] Factors of production other than labor are ignored. The reason is that, since physical capital and raw materials are traded internationally much more than labor, the latter is likely to cause an uneven influence on comparative advantage.

Production equilibrium

Denote the price of the second commodity in terms of the first by $p = p_2/p_1$. According to the above assumptions, the production function of the jth industry is:

$$q_j = (1/a_j)L_j, \quad j = 1, 2 \tag{3.1}$$

where $(1/a_j)$ is the productivity of labor in industry j and L_j is the amount of labor employed in industry j. Since labor is assumed to be uniform in quality and costlessly mobile between sectors, the reward to labor is unique within the country. This, combined with the assumption of a competitive labor market, implies full employment of labor resources:

$$L_1 + L_2 = L \tag{3.2}$$

where L denotes the total labor supply. The substitution of (3.1) into (3.2) gives the economy's production possibility curve $T_1 T_2$ depicted in Figure 3.1:

$$q_1 = \frac{L}{a_1} - \frac{a_2}{a_1} q_2 \tag{3.3}$$

whose slope $(-a_2/a_1)$ is the negative of the ratio of labor requirements or, equivalently, the negative of the ratio of labor productivities $(-1/a_1/1/a_2)$.

Depending on the relative commodity price there are three possible output configurations:

$$p = a_2/a_1 \quad \text{incomplete specialization on segment } T_1 T_2$$
$$p > a_2/a_1 \quad \text{complete specialization in good 2 at } T_2 \tag{3.4}$$
$$p < a_2/a_1 \quad \text{complete specialization in good 1 at } T_1$$

If the two commodities are produced in positive amounts, competitive forces will equate each commodity price to its average cost, $p_j = a_j w$. As the wage rate is identical between sectors, the

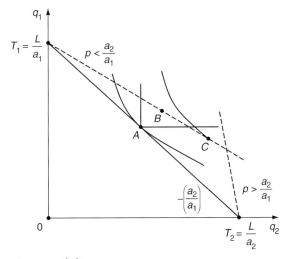

Figure 3.1 A production possibility curve

ratio of goods' prices $p = a_2/a_1$ is independent of the wage. Hence, if $p_2/p_1 > a_2 w / a_1 w$, then the relative value of one additional unit of good 2 is greater than the relative cost necessary to make it and firms would increase production of good 2 and reduce production of good 1. This process would continue until all labor is employed in sector 2. Similar reasoning applies if $p < a_2/a_1$.

Demand

Ricardo did not allow for consumer preferences to feature explicitly in the model. However, modern analysis incorporates traditional demand theory in the model in order to determine the world price and hence the trade equilibrium. Tastes of society are assumed to be represented by a set of social indifference curves, where each indifference curve depicts commodity combinations that yield a constant level of satisfaction for each member of society and for society as a whole. The objective of the community is to reach the highest possible indifference curve given the constraint imposed by national income, analogous to the utility maximization problem of a representative consumer. In general, social indifference curves do not have the usual properties of an individual indifference curve. In particular, changing income distributions usually result in intersecting community indifference curves. However, efforts have been made to salvage the concept by stating a set of assumptions that eliminate the problem of changing income distributions and thereby guarantee that a community indifference curve is just an aggregate version of an individual one.[2]

The problem of social preference maximization can be stated as:

$$\max_{d_1, d_2} U(d_1, d_2) \quad \text{s.t.} \quad d_1 + p d_2 \leq Y \tag{3.5}$$

where d_j is the quantity demanded of the jth commodity ($j = 1, 2$), U represents the social utility function and Y is national income available to consumers. Note that Y is national income expressed in terms of product 1. The first-order conditions for the above problem are $U_1(d_1, d_2) = \lambda$ and $U_2(d_1, d_2) = \lambda p$, where λ is the Lagrange multiplier and $U_j = \partial U / \partial d_j$ is the marginal utility of the jth commodity. These can be rearranged to give $U_2/U_1 = p$. Translated into well known geometry, this condition states the tangency condition between the slope of an indifference curve and the budget line. The general solution to this maximization problem is that demand functions depend on prices and income: $d_j = d_j(Y, p)$.

Excess demand functions

In the present framework we are able to calculate the wage rate and consequently national income for the given labor supply and commodity prices. This is made more explicit in (3.12) and (3.13) below. As long as the labor endowment remains unchanged, relative commodity prices comprise all the information needed to specify the demand functions and thus we are justified in writing:

$$d_j = d_j(p) \tag{3.6}$$

International equilibrium requires that world supply equals world demand for every commodity. In a two-country two-commodity world, this constraint is represented by the following two equations:

$$q_1(p) + q_1^*(p) = d_1(p) + d_1^*(p)$$
$$q_2(p) + q_2^*(p) = d_2(p) + d_2^*(p)$$

where starred variables indicate foreign country values. These equations can be rearranged to give:

$$[q_1(p) - d_1(p)] + [q_1^*(p) - d_1^*(p)] = 0 \qquad (3.7)$$

$$[q_2(p) - d_2(p)] + [q_2^*(p) - d_2^*(p)] = 0 \qquad (3.8)$$

The brackets in these equations enclose the positive or negative excess demands of the two countries for each of the two commodities. (3.7) and (3.8) contain only one argument, p. The system therefore appears to be over-determined. However, (3.7) and (3.8) are not independent. Consider the consumer budget constraints:

$$(q_1 - d_1) + p(q_2 - d_2) = 0 \qquad (3.9)$$

$$(q_1^* - d_1^*) + p(q_2^* - d_2^*) = 0 \qquad (3.10)$$

These equations state that, for each country, the value of production equals the value of consumption or, put differently, that trade must be balanced in each country. Adding (3.9) to (3.10) gives:

$$[(q_1 - d_1) + (q_1^* - d_1^*)] + p[(q_2 - d_2) + (q_2^* - d_2^*)] = 0 \qquad (3.11)$$

(3.11) is Walras's law with only two markets: when one of the markets is in equilibrium then by necessity the other market is also in equilibrium. Hence, it is sufficient to solve either (3.7) or (3.8) alone, since the solution to one equation necessarily implies that the other equation will also be satisfied.

Consider the market for the second commodity illustrated in Figure 3.2. By varying p we can generate the demand function $d_2 = d_2(p)$ and the supply function $q_2 = q_2(p)$ depicted in panel (a). The excess demand function for commodity 2 is derived as the horizontal difference between d_2 and q_2 for all values of p. The supply function of good 2, and hence the excess demand function, is not smooth everywhere and has two points of non-differentiability, T_1 and T_2. We know from earlier analysis that T_1 and T_2 correspond to the complete allocation of labor to sector 1 and sector 2, respectively. Autarky price is determined at point A and

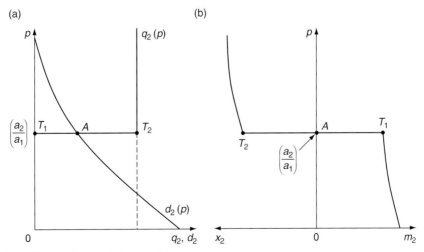

Figure 3.2 Excess demand for good 2

is therefore given by a_2/a_1. Below a_2/a_1 the home country imports commodity 2 in positive amounts $(m_2 = d_2 - q_2)$, while above a_2/a_1 it is a net supplier of good 2 $(d_2 - q_2 < 0)$ and will therefore export that good $(x_2 = q_2 - d_2)$. The foreign excess demand can be obtained in a similar way.

International equilibrium

Figure 3.3 describes how to obtain the international equilibrium price p_w. From (3.8) equilibrium implies $d_2 - q_2 = q_2^* - d_2^*$. The equilibrium price ratio is therefore determined by the intersection of the excess demand curves of the two countries. Hence, there exists an equilibrium price p_w such that the market for good 2 is cleared. At that price the domestic economy imports good 2 in exchange for its exports of good 1.

Implicitly, Figure 3.3 is constructed on the assumption that the home country has a comparative advantage in the first commodity. If one instead assumes that $a_2^*/a_1^* > a_2/a_1$ then the foreign excess demand curve is shifted upward such that the foreign autarky price lies above the domestic one. The international equilibrium is then found in the second quadrant where the second commodity is exported by the domestic economy. We have derived the following results relating to the pattern of trade.

Proposition 3.1 (Ricardo): A country exports the commodity in which it has a comparative labor-productivity advantage.

Proposition 3.2 (Mill): The international price ratio lies in the range spanned by the pre-trade price ratios of the two trading nations, that is $a_2/a_1 \geq p_w \geq a_2^*/a_1^*$ with strict inequality holding if relative country size is not great.

A corollary of the above theorems is that, with free trade, each country specializes completely in the good in which it has a comparative advantage. Mill's conclusion that the world price lies strictly between the pre-trade prices is not possible when the two trading nations are (1) identical in all respects, or (2) grossly unequal in size. The first case is trivial since it leaves no room for international trade. The equilibrium price would then be $a_2/a_1 = p_w = a_2^*/a_1^*$ and countries would be indifferent between domestic production and trade. The second case is illustrated in Figure 3.3. If the foreign country is comparatively small with an excess demand curve given by the broken curve then the international equilibrium price would be that of the domestic country. As a consequence, the foreign partner realizes the maximum gain in

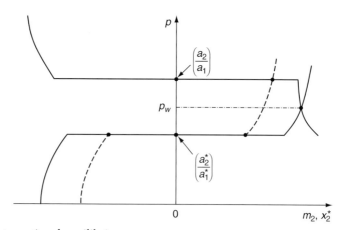

Figure 3.3 International equilibrium

its terms of trade (export price relative to import price). The domestic economy continues, however, to consume the same amount of both goods as before but its production mix changes to accommodate trade with the foreign country. Assuming that the world price lies between the autarky price ratios, trade leads each economy to completely specialize according to its comparative advantage: in the above example, the home country specializes in good 1 and the foreign country in good 2.

Gains from trade

Having determined the pattern of international trade, there remains another classic question of trade theory: is international trade beneficial to both countries? Put differently, is it possible to show that the reallocation of labor resources as a result of trade allows each country to consume beyond the boundaries of its autarkic production possibility frontier and thereby reach a higher community indifference curve?

The gains from trade are illustrated in Figure 3.1. An economy can potentially benefit from free trade if the relative world price differs from its autarkic level. In Figure 3.1, the equilibrium terms of trade are illustrated by the slope of the dashed line originating from T_1. Every possible autarkic consumption basket such as A is therefore dominated by a free trade consumption point such as B which allows consumption of more of both commodities. However, other free trade consumption patterns such as C could also take place, where more of good 2 and less of good 1 than at B is preferred while satisfying the same budget constraint.

The gains from trade can be conveniently broken down into gains from exchange and gains from specialization. This is illustrated in Figure 3.4. Point A represents the autarkic equilibrium and gives rise to the autarkic utility level u_a. Assume that, with free trade, the economy can trade at the international price p_w. Suppose for a moment that the economy cannot change its output. Production therefore remains at A but the decrease in the relative price of good 2 leads to the new consumption point B on a higher utility level u_b. The movement from A to B shows the gains from exchanging the autarky amounts produced. However, as the economy moves to the complete specialization point T_1 consumption takes place at C, showing a higher

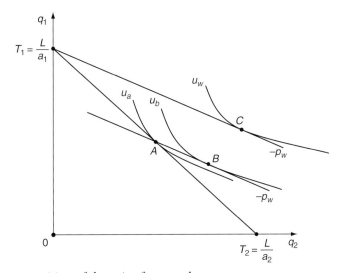

Figure 3.4 Decomposition of the gains from trade

utility level u_w. The movement from B to C indicates the gains from increased specialization in production.

Analytically the proof of the gains from trade is more complicated but offers an interesting application of the Ricardian model. A sufficient condition for the gains from trade is to see whether trade is beneficial to every individual in each country. One way to proceed is to look at domestic and foreign real wages – that is, the wage rates measured in terms of each good. If wages rise in terms of at least one commodity and do not decrease in terms of any other, then one can conclude that both countries are better off through trade.

Consider the autarkic equilibrium of the home country and assume that the country spends a constant share α of its income on the first commodity.[3] Referring to (3.5), this would be the case if $U(.)$ is of the Cobb-Douglas type in d_1 and d_2. On the production side, the domestic production functions are given by (3.1) and the labor resources by (3.2). It is easy to verify that the following is the unique autarky equilibrium if both goods are produced:

$$p_1^a = 1 \qquad p_2^a = \frac{a_2}{a_1} \qquad w^a = \frac{1}{a_1}$$

$$q_1^a = \frac{\alpha L}{a_1} \qquad q_2^a = \frac{(1-\alpha)L}{a_2} \qquad Y^a = \frac{L}{a_1} \qquad (3.12)$$

$$L_1^a = \alpha L \qquad L_2^a = (1-\alpha)L$$

Since the production structure is the same for the foreign country, a similar autarkic equilibrium is achieved with variables denoted by an asterisk. Assume that tastes are identical for the two countries, $\alpha = \alpha^*$ and consider a trading equilibrium in which the two countries have labor forces L and L^*. Assuming that:

$$\frac{a_2}{a_1} > \frac{a_2^*}{a_1^*}$$

we obtain the following solution for the trade equilibrium:

$$p_1 = 1 \qquad\qquad p_2 = \frac{a_2^*}{a_1} \frac{(1-\alpha)}{\alpha} \frac{L}{L^*} \qquad w = \frac{1}{a_1}$$

$$w^* = \frac{1}{a_1} \frac{(1-\alpha)}{\alpha} \frac{L}{L^*} \qquad q_1 = \frac{L}{a_1} \qquad\qquad q_2 = \frac{L^*}{a_2^*} \qquad (3.13)$$

When trade opens, the equilibrium terms of trade are given by p_2/p_1 and will lie strictly between the cost ratios of the two countries if:

$$\frac{a_2}{a_1} > \frac{a_2^*}{a_1} \frac{(1-\alpha)}{\alpha} \frac{L}{L^*} > \frac{a_2^*}{a_1^*} \qquad (3.14)$$

which simplifies to:

$$\frac{a_2}{a_2^*} > \frac{(1-\alpha)}{\alpha} \frac{L}{L^*} > \frac{a_1}{a_1^*} \qquad (3.15)$$

The inequality conditions (3.14) and (3.15) indicate the role of relative work forces (that is, relative country size) and of consumer preferences in establishing the international equilibrium price ratio. For example, an absolute size effect (a larger L) or a strong preference for good 2 (a lower α) narrows the difference between the domestic autarky price and world price but enlarges the gap between the foreign autarky price and the same world price, and vice versa. As long as (3.15) is satisfied, each economy completely specializes according to its comparative advantage.

To determine whether trade is beneficial we can compare the real wages in terms of both goods in autarky and in the trading equilibrium. Using (3.12) and (3.13), we can see that the home wage in terms of good 1 stays constant at $1/a_1$ while in terms of good 2 it is:

$$\frac{w^a}{p_2^a} = \frac{1}{a_2} \quad \frac{w}{p_2} = \frac{1}{a_2^*} \frac{\alpha}{(1-\alpha)} \frac{L^*}{L}$$

In contrast, the foreign real wage is constant in terms of good 2 (equals $1/a_2^*$) but varies in terms of good 1:

$$\frac{w^{*a}}{p_1^{*a}} = \frac{1}{a_1^*} \quad \frac{w^*}{p_1} = \frac{1}{a_1} \frac{(1-\alpha)}{\alpha} \frac{L}{L^*}$$

By comparing the real wages in terms of both goods in autarky and in the trading equilibrium, one sees that with trade real wages are not inferior in terms of both goods in the home and foreign country as long as:

$$\frac{1}{a_2^*} \frac{\alpha}{(1-\alpha)} \frac{L^*}{L} > \frac{1}{a_2} \quad \text{and} \quad \frac{1}{a_1} \frac{(1-\alpha)}{\alpha} \frac{L}{L^*} > \frac{1}{a_1^*}$$

which reduces to

$$\frac{a_2}{a_2^*} > \frac{(1-\alpha)}{\alpha} \frac{L}{L^*} > \frac{a_1}{a_1^*}$$

a condition equivalent to inequality (3.15) which determines the requirement for each country to improve its terms of trade. A difference in relative labor productivities between countries is therefore crucial to the conclusion that both countries gain from trade. Gains are likely to be greatest for trade between economies that are least similar in this regard. In addition, the closer the world price is to the foreign autarky price, the higher are the gains that accrue to the home country and vice versa. Hence, any improvement in the relative price of the home country's exports (its terms of trade) increases the home country's benefits from trade at the expense of the foreign benefits.

3.3 Economies of scale

Increasing returns to scale (IRS) are often presented as a basis for foreign trade even in the absence of other causes of trade. In this section we look at the consequences of introducing IRS into the Ricardian model. We start by defining the general concepts of internal and external scale economies, and national and international scale economies. We then illustrate the patterns of trade that arise when economies of scale are national and external to firms. Other ways of introducing IRS in trade models are discussed in Part III.

Concepts and definitions

Internal and external scale economies

Scale economies may be internal or external. These terms were first introduced by Marshall (1890) when analyzing industry production costs as a function of output:

> We may divide the economies arising from an increase in the scale of production of any kind of goods, into two classes—firstly, those dependent on the general development of the industry; and, secondly, those dependent on the resources of the individual houses of business engaged in it, on their organization and the efficiency of their management. We may call the former *external economies*, and the latter *internal economies*.
>
> (Marshall, 1972, 221)

In current terminology, scale economies are called internal to the firm if the firm's average costs depend upon, and decrease with, the firm's level of output. This type of scale economies is often attributed to individual firms that are characterized by high fixed costs combined with constant marginal costs. This implies that only a few large plants will satisfy total demand. In contrast, external economies of scale are effects that are external to the firm and only appear at the industry level. The firm's average costs then depend upon, and decrease with, the level of industry output. Some of the firm's activities that would otherwise be undertaken at the firm level are delegated at the industry level as the latter expands. Traditional examples include the construction of a dam for a hydroelectric power plant in a flood-prone rural area, and the Swiss watch industry, which created specific schooling and infrastructure facilities as the industry expanded. These examples suggest that in order to reap the benefits of external economies production needs to be geographically concentrated.[4]

With external economies, any expansion of a firm's output has no effect on the firm's costs as long as the size of the industry is unchanged. The assumptions of constant returns to scale (CRS) and price-taking behavior at the firm level can therefore be maintained. In contrast, internal economies have implications for the market structure. In particular, because of fixed costs, the number of firms cannot be too large since otherwise profit would be negative. Moreover, no firm can be in equilibrium at a level of output on the decreasing segment of its average cost curve since the firm will always want to increase production if firm entry is possible. Hence, perfectly competitive price-taking behavior cannot be assumed when scale economies are internal to the firm.[5]

National and international scale economies

Ethier (1979, 1982a) indicated that scale economies can work in other ways and introduced the concepts of national and international scale economies. Analogous with Adam Smith's division of labor in pin production, the idea is that industrial production becomes more efficient if it splits into separate stages. With each firm specialized in undertaking one of the individual steps in the process, a larger market will allow a greater division of production. Scale economies are therefore international if it is easy to ship products from place to place, as the various stages of production need not be located in the same country. These international scale economies will depend upon the size of the world market. However, sufficiently high trade barriers and transport costs will make these scale economies national since they force all stages of production to be located in the same country.[6]

External economies of scale

External economies are awkward to examine in a well structured and rigorous analysis since they stand for a mixture of static and dynamic factors.[7] Formally, economies or diseconomies of scale that are external to a firm j ($j = 1, \ldots, n$) are usually represented by a production function of the form $q_j = F_j(\mathbf{e}_j, q)$ where q_j is the output level of the jth firm, $\mathbf{e}_j$ is firm j's vector of factor inputs, and q is the size of either the national or the world industry. A property of this production function is that, for a given q, q_j is positively linear homogeneous in $\mathbf{e}_j$.

In the aggregate of all firms, the production structure can be given a useful representation. Consider the autarky equilibrium of the home economy whose resources are still given by (3.2) but replace the production functions (3.1):[8]

$$q_1 = \frac{1}{a_1} L_1 \tag{3.16}$$

$$q_2 = \frac{1}{a_2} L_2 q_2^{(\beta - 1)/\beta} \tag{3.17}$$

The substitution of production functions (3.16) and (3.17) into the labor supply constraint (3.2) gives the economy's production possibility curve:

$$q_1 = \frac{L}{a_1} - \frac{a_2}{a_1} q_2^{1/\beta} \tag{3.18}$$

where the marginal rate of transformation is:

$$\frac{\partial q_1}{\partial q_2} = -\frac{a_2}{a_1} \frac{1}{\beta} q_2^{(1-\beta)/\beta} < 0$$

The production function (3.17) conveniently summarizes the situations that could give rise to external and national scale economies. In particular, production of good 2 is homogeneous of degree β so that the value of β determines whether the set of feasible production points is convex or concave. With $\beta > 1$, (3.17) exhibits IRS. The marginal rate of transformation is then increasing in q_2 since each unit of labor transferred from q_1 to q_2 generates a larger increase in q_2 than the previous unit. This gives rise to the convex production frontier $T_1 T_2'$ depicted in Figure 3.5. With $\beta < 1$, (3.17) exhibits decreasing returns to scale and results in a concave production frontier (not shown) as the marginal rate of transformation is decreasing in q_2. With $\beta = 1, q_2$ is characterized by CRS and the marginal rate of transformation is a constant. This generates the linear production frontier $T_1 A T_2$ in Figure 3.5, similar to that of Figure 3.1.

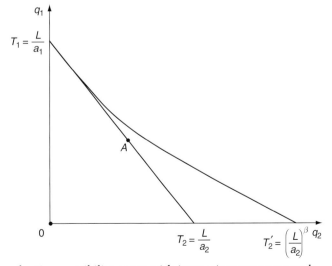

Figure 3.5 A production possibility curve with increasing returns to scale

Autarky with increasing returns to scale

Assume preferences are homothetic so that α is the expenditure share on the first commodity. Assuming $\beta = 2$ in (3.17), it is easy to obtain the autarkic equilibrium with IRS:

$$
\begin{aligned}
&p_1^a = 1 && p_2^a = a_2^2/a_1(1-\alpha)L && w^a = 1/a_1 \\
&q_1^a = \alpha L/a_1 && q_2^a = (1-\alpha)^2 L^2/a_2^2 && Y^a = L/a_1 \\
&L_1^a = \alpha L && L_2^a = (1-\alpha)L
\end{aligned}
\tag{3.19}
$$

A direct comparison with (3.12) points out a similar distribution of the labor force among sectors. Although the production of good 1 remains the same, the production of good 2 is now the square of that obtained under CRS. Also, the level of welfare under IRS is higher than that achieved in the absence of IRS since the new wage in terms of both goods is not inferior to that under CRS. An additional characteristic of the IRS autarkic equilibrium is that the pre-trade relative price, $(p_2^a/p_1^a) = a_2^2/a_1(1-\alpha)L$, depends upon consumer preferences and the country's labor endowment. Compared with the pre-trade price in (3.12), the present one falls short of the latter by the factor $a_2/(1-\alpha)L < 1$.

Free trade equilibrium with no trade

Now consider international trade. Suppose that the two countries have identical relative prices in autarky. By the above reasoning, this would be true if they were identical in all respects, with identical tastes and the same amount of labor. No trade is then a possible free trade equilibrium since trade would not take place in a comparative advantage sense. But this outcome would not be Pareto-optimal. Why? The pattern of production would be inefficient in the sense that scale economies have not been exploited. Thus scale economies provide a basis for trade independently of comparative advantage. To explore these issues further, assume the labor forces now differ between countries and assume that each country's labor is measured such that $a_1 = a_1^* = a_2 = a_2^* = 1$. There will be three types of equilibrium. For each type, there can be a mirror image equilibrium in which countries reverse roles, but this will not be illustrated here.

The Ricardian equilibrium (RE)

A possible equilibrium involves complete specialization in each country. A specialization pattern that is consistent with international equilibrium is:

$$
\begin{aligned}
&p_1 = 1 && p_2 = \frac{(1-\alpha)L}{\alpha L^{*2}} && w = 1 \\
&w^* = \frac{(1-\alpha)L}{\alpha L^*} && q_1 = L && q_2^* = L^{*2}
\end{aligned}
\tag{3.20}
$$

It is clear from (3.20) that the foreign wage in terms of both goods is higher than the autarky real wage. For the domestic country, a loss in welfare is not excluded, but it depends on the values of α and L/L^*. Hence, the present international equilibrium is undoubtedly preferable to the preceding one for the country that specializes in the IRS commodity. However, there is a mirror image to the equilibrium (3.20) in which the pattern of production and gains from trade are reversed. Hence, if the countries have governments conducting trade policy, each will try to ensure that it becomes the country specialized in producing the IRS commodity.

The wage equalization equilibrium (WE)

Another equilibrium involves one country that has completely specialized in one commodity and the other country that still produces both goods. It makes a great deal of difference which good is produced by both countries. If it is the CRS good 1, labor's value marginal product in good 1, and therefore wage, must be the same internationally which is in sharp contrast to (3.20). The equilibrium is:

$$p_1 = 1 \quad p_2 = \frac{1}{(1-\alpha)(L+L^*)} \quad w = w^* = 1$$

$$q_1 = \alpha L + (\alpha - 1)L^* \quad q_1^* = L^* \quad q_2 = (1-\alpha)^2(L+L^*)^2 \qquad (3.21)$$

$$L_1 = \alpha L + (\alpha - 1)L^* \quad L_2 = (1-\alpha)(L+L^*)$$

Consequently, both countries will achieve the same welfare level. While the free trade real wage in terms of good 1 equates to the autarky wage, the wage in terms of good 2 is higher. This is a case in which free trade is welfare-improving (when compared with autarky).

The Graham equilibrium

The last equilibrium is one in which one country specializes in producing the IRS good while the other country produces both the IRS and CRS goods. International wage equalization is unlikely to take place because the scale of production of the IRS good 2 in the incompletely specialized country is usually insufficient to obtain large gains in labor productivity. Since the price of good 2 is the same in both countries, the wage of the incompletely specialized country needs to be low to compensate for this low labor productivity. Hence, free trade may cause a welfare loss for this country.

Multiple Pareto-rankable equilibria

As illustrated above, IRS results in multiple trade equilibria. In some of these equilibria, free trade might lower the welfare of a country relative to autarky. The static model examined here cannot capture the dynamics of moving from autarky to one of these equilibria. However, the equilibria can be ranked as "bad" or "good" according to a welfare measure rule which, in the Ricardian model, is simply the wage rate in terms of both goods. For example, from the discussion in the preceding paragraphs, the following ranking applies to the domestic economy (for $L = L^*$ and $0 < \alpha < 1/2$): $RE <$ autarky $< WE$ where "$<$" stands for "is welfare inferior to." Hence, when there are multiple equilibria, if the economy is in a "bad" equilibrium (for example RE), there exists another equilibrium (for example WE), in which everyone would be better off. However, there is no way for this economy to move from this equilibrium to reach a better equilibrium due to what is called a coordination failure.[9] This refers to the inability of agents to coordinate their actions successfully in a many-person decentralized economy. The latter does not provide incentives such that firms could coordinate and jump to a "good" equilibrium. In contrast, an insightful planner could lead the economy to a Pareto equilibrium. Note that the above ranking of equilibria does not apply to the foreign country and, hence, can potentially lead to a conflict of interest between countries regarding the desired equilibrium.

3.4 A continuum of goods

Actual trade is characterized by the exchange of a large number of commodities. The Standard International Trade Classification (SITC) nomenclature (Revision 3) has 3,121 5-digit entries.

The number of goods actually traded is larger, however. Some commodities, such as textiles, are well represented (200 entries) but the trade classification does not fully account for the degree of product differentiation of many other items (such as bolts, automobiles and so on). This section extends the Ricardian model to the case of many goods using the continuum assumption originally developed by Dornbusch *et al.* (1977). Assuming a continuous rather than discrete number of goods simplifies the analysis and permits questions related to growth, demand shifts and exogenous technological change to be answered with ease.[10] In each case, the focus of the analysis is to determine (1) the dividing line between exported and imported goods, and (2) the position of the relative wage that guarantees trade balance.

The technology

The Ricardian model assumes that each good is produced with a constant unit labor requirement. For good z, let $a(z)$ and $a^*(z)$ be the unit labor requirement in the home and foreign countries respectively. As usual, an asterisk denotes the foreign country. The ratio $A(z) = a^*(z)/a(z)$ then represents the ratio of domestic to foreign labor productivity. If n commodities are produced, label them so that they are ranked in order of diminishing home comparative advantage:

$$A(1) > A(2) > \ldots > A(i) > \ldots > A(n) \tag{3.22}$$

Commodity 1, compared with any lower ranked commodity, is characterized by the highest relative domestic productivity and therefore confers the highest comparative advantage to that country. The above inequality could also be read in a different form: commodity n confers the highest comparative advantage to the foreign country.

In working with a continuum of goods, the above relative productivities can be represented by an index constructed on the interval [0, 1] in accordance with diminishing home comparative advantage. Although "holes" will exist (the number of traded goods is not infinite), these will be ignored by assuming that $A(z)$ is a smooth, continuous and decreasing function of z, $A'(z) < 0$. The function $A(z)$ is graphed in Figure 3.6 as the downward sloping schedule against z varying between 0 and 1.

Multiplying the productivity ratios by the relative foreign wage w^*/w gives an ordered set of relative foreign prices. The domestic country therefore produces the (first) subset of

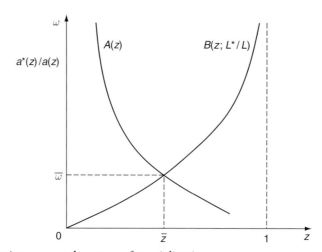

Figure 3.6 Relative wage and pattern of specialization

commodities that give a competitive margin with respect to foreign producers (price ratios exceeding one):

$$p(z) = a(z)w < a^*(z)w^* = p^*(z) \tag{3.23}$$

$$\omega = \frac{w}{w^*} < A(z) \tag{3.24}$$

The other country produces the remaining set of commodities whose price ratios are less than one. Given ω, there exists a borderline commodity $\tilde{z}$ whose production is equally efficient in both countries (price ratio equal to one):

$$\omega = A(\tilde{z}) \quad \text{and} \quad \tilde{z} = A^{-1}(\omega) \tag{3.25}$$

For each ω there is a different borderline commodity $\tilde{z}$. This can be written as $\tilde{z}(\omega)$ with $\tilde{z}'(\omega) < 0$. Given ω, the domestic country will produce efficiently the range of commodities:

$$0 \leq z \leq \tilde{z}(\omega)$$

while the foreign country will produce all commodities in the range:

$$\tilde{z}(\omega) \leq z \leq 1$$

Given ω and the state of technology, the above establishes the pattern of international specialization. The equilibrium borderline between these two sets of commodities depends, however, on demand conditions, but the ordering does not.

Demand and equilibrium

On the demand side, we again assume homothetic preferences and in particular that the demand functions derive from a Cobb-Douglas utility function. This specification of demand associates with each commodity a constant expenditure share $b(z)$:

$$b(z) = p(z)d(z)/S > 0$$

$$\int_0^1 b(z)dz = 1$$

where S denotes nominal expenditure, $d(z)$ the demand for, and $p(z)$ the price of commodity z. The fraction of expenditure spent on home goods is equal to:

$$v(\tilde{z}) = \int_0^{\tilde{z}} b(z)dz$$

with

$$v'(\tilde{z}) = b(\tilde{z}) > 0 \text{ and } 0 \leq v(\tilde{z}) \leq 1$$

The fraction spent on foreign goods is:

$$1 - v(\tilde{z}) = \int_{\tilde{z}}^1 b(z)dz$$

Identical tastes are assumed for the two countries. Consequently, everyone in the world spends a constant share of his or her income on each good z and this share $v(\tilde{z})$ is common to both countries.

Equilibrium in the market for home goods requires that the total value of spending on home goods equals domestic labor income. The world spending on home goods is $v(\tilde{z})$ times world income: the sum of the wages earned at home and abroad. The equilibrium relationship is:

$$wL = v(\tilde{z})(wL + w^*L^*) \tag{3.26}$$

An alternative interpretation of the equilibrium can be given by rewriting (3.26) as:

$$(1 - v(\tilde{z}))wL = v(\tilde{z})w^*L^* \tag{3.27}$$

This is the condition for trade balance: the value of domestic imports equals the value of exports. (3.26) and (3.27) imply a value of w/w^* corresponding to each $\tilde{z}$ such that market equilibrium obtains:

$$\omega = \frac{v(\tilde{z})}{1 - v(\tilde{z})} \frac{L^*}{L} = B(\tilde{z}; L^*/L) \tag{3.28}$$

This schedule is drawn in Figure 3.6. The relative wage ω starts at zero and approaches infinity as $\tilde{z}$ approaches unity. In this interval the curve slopes upward since the higher $\tilde{z}$ is the higher the numerator of $B(\cdot)$ and the lower the denominator of $B(\cdot)$. A characteristic of Figure 3.6 is that, while an economy always stays on its technological curve A $(\tilde{z})$, it can temporarily be off its B curve. To the right of the B curve, there is an excess demand for labor and a trade surplus; to the left, the economy has an excess supply of labor and a trade deficit. For example, holding ω fixed, an increase in the range of domestically produced goods could create an excess demand for labor, lower home imports and raise home exports, and thus create a trade surplus. A rise in the domestic relative wage would then be required to restore trade balance and labor market equilibrium.

By combining the demand side of the economy as represented by (3.28) with the condition for efficient specialization (3.25), one obtains the unique relative wage $\bar{\omega}$ and borderline good $\bar{z}$ at which the world is efficiently specialized, trade is balanced and national labor markets are in equilibrium:

$$\bar{\omega} = A(\bar{z}) = B(\bar{z}; L^*/L) \tag{3.29}$$

Graphically, the solution is given by the intersection of the two schedules. The commodities to the left of $\bar{z}$ are exported by the domestic country, while commodities to the right of $\bar{z}$ are exported by the foreign country. Commodity $\bar{z}$ is either non-traded or gives rise to intra- or inter-industry trade, depending on what is needed for trade balance.

Application: exogenous technical progress

Consider the effect of uniform technical progress in every industry abroad.[11] By the definition of $A(z)$, this implies a reduction in $a^*(z)$ and a proportional downward shift of the $A(z)$ schedule in Figure 3.7. At the initial equilibrium relative wage $\bar{\omega}_1$, this economy-wide productivity increase represents a loss of domestic industries at the margin in the range E_1E_1' and a trade deficit. A decrease in the home relative wage is therefore necessary to partially offset the decline in comparative advantage and to restore trade balance. Point E_2 is the new long-run

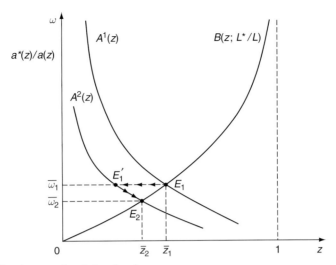

Figure 3.7 A foreign productivity shock

Table 3.2 Domestic welfare and foreign productivity shock

Interval	Price	Real wage	Welfare
$(0, \bar{z}_2)$	$p(z) = wa(z)$	$w/p(z) = 1/a(z)$	0
$(\bar{z}_2, \bar{z}_1)$	$p(z) < wa(z)$	$w/p(z) > 1/a(z)$	+
$(\bar{z}_1, 1)$	$p(z) = w^*a^*(z)$	$w/p(z) > (w/w^*)(1/a(z))$	+

equilibrium where the new range of home produced goods is $(0, \bar{z}_2)$ and the interval of foreign produced goods includes the previous range $(\bar{z}_1, 1)$ and the transitional goods $(\bar{z}_1, \bar{z}_2)$.

To remove any ambiguity about the domestic consequences of the foreign productivity improvement, consider the effect on domestic welfare. The latter can be examined by looking at the domestic real wage, that is, the wage in terms of each good in the continuum. If the domestic real wage either stays the same or rises, then the country is better off. The results are summarized in Table 3.2.

The domestic wage in terms of goods in the interval $(0, \bar{z}_2)$ remains constant because domestic labor productivity is unchanged. For any good z in the transitional interval $(\bar{z}_1, \bar{z}_2)$, the price is now lower than before the productivity shock and, hence, the domestic real wage rises in terms of these goods. In the interval $(\bar{z}_1, 1)$, the price of foreign goods is $p(z) = w^*a^*(z)$. Dividing w by this last expression gives the result in Table 3.2. Knowing that ω falls proportionally less than $a^*(z)$, the domestic real wage increases in this interval. Summing the effects for the three kinds of goods, domestic welfare unambiguously rises as a result of the increase in foreign labor productivity.

3.5 Technological heterogeneity

So far, the Ricardian theory may appear to be incomplete because it gives no explanation of differences in labor productivities across countries and hence it provides no guidance as to how labor productivity and comparative advantage can be expected to evolve. Recently, two rapidly expanding research fields have tackled this open question. A first strand of the literature deals with trade and institutions (and vice versa); the second deals with technological heterogeneity in international trade. The modeling standpoint of many of these studies is the continuum assumption of Dornbusch *et al.* (1977) (henceforth DFS) discussed in the preceding section.

Institutional differences can be a source of comparative advantage even when technology, as in the Ricardian model (or relative factor endowments as in the Heckscher-Ohlin-Samuelson model), is identical across countries. For example, Cuñat and Melitz (2011a, 2011b) focus on labor market regulations and show how labor market flexibility is a source of comparative advantage. Labor market regulations affect the extent to which firms can adjust to external shocks. In countries with more regulated labor markets, firms tend to produce more mature goods for which less severe shocks are expected. Levchenko (2004) studies the quality of institutions (for example the imperfect recognition of property rights and the quality of contract enforcement) and shows how this affects trade flows and the distribution of the gains between rich and poor countries. In Nunn (2007), Costinot (2009) and others, institutional differences across countries do have consequences not only for aggregate productivity but also for productivity differences across industries within a single country. Industries can differ in their institutional intensities because with bad courts leading to poor contract enforcement, or with imperfect recognition of property rights, firms will tend to under-invest in research and development and relation-specific investments for fear of *ex post* defection of the producer of the final good. Altogether institutional differences should generate scope for comparative advantage and hence international trade.

The realm of Ricardo's ideas has expanded with the introduction of technological heterogeneity into trade models. Recall that in the DFS world of two countries (home and foreign), goods z are ordered in descending order of the ratio $A(z) = a^*(z)/a(z)$ which represents the countries' relative efficiencies. Relative wages then determine the breakpoint in this chain of comparative advantage as in (3.25). However, with more than two countries, this analysis breaks down because a natural ordering of commodities no longer exists. This observation is the point of departure of Eaton and Kortum (2002) (henceforth EK), who construct a multi-country trading world assuming a probabilistic formulation of technological heterogeneity.

The technology

As in Table 3.1, countries have differential access to technology, so that efficiency varies across commodities and countries. We denote country i's efficiency in producing good $z, z \in [0, 1]$ as $Z_i(z)$. If labor were the only factor of production (as in previous sections) then $Z_i(z) \equiv 1/a_i(z)$ would denote the number of units of good z that can be produced with one unit of labor in country i. Input cost in country i is denoted as c_i. In Costinot *et al.* (2012) for example, input costs are simply wages. In EK, input costs are a composite variable that combines wages and the price of a bundle of intermediate inputs. With no fixed cost and CRS, the cost of producing a unit of good z in country i is $c_i/Z_i(z)$.

Country i's efficiency in producing good z is the realization of a random variable $Z_i(z)$. The randomness captures factors such as discoveries, weather, infrastructure, strikes and, more generally, institutions that are country-specific. It is drawn independently for each z from a country-specific probability distribution $F_i(\xi) = \Pr(Z_i(z) \leq \xi)$. Particularly, country i's efficiency is assumed to be drawn from a two-parameter Fréchet cumulative distribution function:

$$F_i(\xi) = e^{-T_i \xi^{-\theta}}$$

(3.30)

with $T_i > 0$ and $\theta > 1$. A random process modeled as in (3.30) is but one approach out of many, but it has the property of being parsimonious in terms of its number of parameters. Parameter θ, which is common to all countries, is a shape parameter that indexes (the inverse of) the dispersion of productivities: a larger θ implies a lesser variance. The country-specific parameter T_i is a scale parameter that positions the distribution of country i: a larger T_i implies that a high efficiency draw for any good z is more likely. There are three other useful properties: (1) By the law of large numbers $F_i(\xi)$ is also the fraction of goods for which country i's efficiency is below ξ; (2) if $Z_i(z)$ is distributed according to Fréchet, so too does $\lambda Z_i(z)$ for $\lambda > 0$; (3) for any two countries i and n, if $Z_i(z)$ and $Z_n(z)$ are distributed according to (3.30) then $\max\{Z_i(z), Z_n(z)\}$ has a Fréchet distribution.[12]

There are N trading nations which are separated by geographic barriers. Besides transport costs, these barriers include tariffs, non-tariff barriers and, more generally, costs of doing business. They are introduced using Samuelson's standard iceberg assumption that delivering one unit of a good to country n requires shipping $\tau_{in} \geq 1$ units from country i. Positive geographic barriers means $\tau_{in} > 1$ for $i \neq n$ and barriers within each country are assumed negligible, that is $\tau_{ii} = 1$ for all i. Cross-border arbitrage forces geographic barriers to obey a triangle inequality: for any three countries i, k and n, $\tau_{in} \leq \tau_{ik}\tau_{kn}$. Given this, delivering a unit of good z produced in country i to country n costs:

$$p_{in}(z) = \frac{c_i}{Z_i(z)}\tau_{in} \tag{3.31}$$

Perfect competition is assumed, so that $p_{in}(z)$ is also the prevailing price on this bilateral trade flow.[13] The price consumers in n actually pay for good z will be $p_n(z)$, the lowest across all sources i:

$$p_n(z) = \min\{p_{in}(z); i = 1, \ldots N\} \tag{3.32}$$

Demand and equilibrium

On the demand side, unlike the original DFS framework where demand functions derive from a Cobb-Douglas utility function, buyers purchase individual goods in amounts $d(z)$ to maximize a CES utility function:

$$U = \left[\int_0^1 d(z)^{(\sigma-1)/\sigma} dz\right]^{\sigma/(\sigma-1)} \tag{3.33}$$

where $\sigma > 1$ denotes the elasticity of substitution among differentiated goods. For any country n, this maximization is subject to prices given by (3.32) and a budget constraint denoted by S_n, country n's total expenditure.[14] Identical tastes are assumed for all countries. In a trade equilibrium where each country's trade with the rest of the world is balanced, some of these demands are met locally by the domestic economy (which may also export) and others by imports from foreign suppliers. In the model, comparative advantage creates potential gains from trade, the extent of which decreases with the resistance imposed by geographic barriers.

Counterfactual: benefits of foreign technology

Like most models in this chapter, the EK model is a general equilibrium model that solves for endogenous variables like wages, output and welfare. To make the model suitable for the computation of counterfactuals, numerical values for key parameters must be estimated. A realistic estimate of θ is found to be 8.28. Based on this estimate, EK derive country estimates of technology parameter T_i and geographic barriers τ_{in}. If the state of technology in the US is normalized to 1, then it is computed that $T_i = 0.89$ for Japan, $T_i = 0.81$ for Germany, $T_i = 0.07$ for Greece and so on. Regarding geographic barriers, it costs 25.7 percent less to export to the US compared with the sample average, 17.4 percent less in Japan, 11.4 percent less in Germany, but 33 percent more in Greece.

Given this, consider the general equilibrium response of technical progress in every industry in Germany, here represented by a 20 percent increase in the state of technology T_i for Germany. It is already known from Table 3.2 that trade does allow a country to benefit from a foreign technological progress. The contribution of the EK model is to quantify the magnitudes of these productivity gains and an important outcome is that any country n benefits more from a productivity improvement in country i, the smaller is τ_{in} and thus in general, the closer it is to the source. For example, the Netherlands would obtain 62 percent of the German productivity gains, compared with 9.7 percent in the US, 5.9 percent in Japan, and 38.9 percent in Greece. But for these large productivity gains to be obtained an important condition must be met, namely that labor is perfectly mobile across industries.

3.6 Tests of the Ricardian trade theory

Surprisingly, there is little empirical work on the Ricardian model, so it is easy to organize. Particularly, there are two main streams of formulated specifications. On the one hand, there are traditional empirical studies which run regressions that implicitly use the rationale of the two-country, multi-commodity framework of Section 3.4 and translate this into a multi-country regression. On the other hand, recent empirical studies test theoretically grounded hypotheses that derive directly from multi-sector multi-country models that assume firm heterogeneity as in Section 3.5. This section reviews the insights that are gained from both types of empirical analyses.

Tests of the two-country framework

Except for the borderline commodity, the sharp implication of the two-country multi-commodity Ricardian model concerns the extent of specialization. In practice, the actual commodity classification with which empirical researchers work does not allow goods to be identified unambiguously as either exports or imports. Even at sufficiently detailed levels of classification, intra-industry trade exists (see Chapter 1) and hence the Ricardian outcome of complete specialization is rejected in any data set. Looser versions of the Ricardian model are therefore empirically studied.

The assumptions about the wage structure will lead to as many different testing hypotheses about the trade model. The empirical literature makes three types of assumption about domestic and foreign wages. The first is that the wage rate in any industry is different both across industries and across countries. Hence, in a competitive economy, the pre-trade price of commodity z will equal its average cost: $p_z = a_z w_z$ where w_z is industry z's wage rate. Using the rationale of the previous section, but assuming a finite number J of traded commodities, this commodity z will be in the subset of domestically exported goods if it has a foreign pre-trade relative price ratio greater than one:

$$\frac{p_z^*}{p_z} = \frac{a_z^* w_z^*}{a_z w_z} > 1 \qquad z = 1, 2, \ldots, m$$

Similarly, the domestic country will import commodity j if:

$$\frac{p_j^*}{p_j} = \frac{a_j^* w_j^*}{a_j w_j} < 1 \qquad j = m+1, \dots J$$

Hence, combining the last two expressions:

$$\frac{a_z^* w_z^*}{a_z w_z} > \frac{a_j^* w_j^*}{a_j w_j} \qquad z = 1, 2, \dots, m; \; j = m+1 \dots, J$$

This is a statement of the Ricardian hypothesis in terms of comparative unit labor costs where the latter, and not labor productivity, is compared. This can be called a Type-I hypothesis.

If instead the inter-industrial pattern of wage rates is identical internationally, then $w_z^*/w_z = w_j^*/w_j$ equals a constant, and we can write:

$$\frac{a_z^*}{a_z} > \frac{a_j^*}{a_j} \qquad z = 1, 2, \dots, m; \; j = m+1 \dots, J$$

The Ricardian hypothesis is thus restated in its original form, that is, in terms of labor productivity. This can be called a Type-II hypothesis.

Finally, a Type-III hypothesis is obtained if, as in the previous section, the wage is assumed to be unique in each country but different across countries: $w = w_z = w_j, w^* = w_z^* = w_j^*$ where w^*/w is a constant. In this case, the above ranking of labor productivities is maintained but the relative wage now indicates the borderline that separates exported goods from imported goods:

$$\frac{a_z^*}{a_z} > \frac{w^*}{w} > \frac{a_j^*}{a_j} \qquad z = 1, 2, \dots, m; \; j = m+1 \dots, J \qquad (3.34)$$

This Type-III hypothesis fits closer to the DFS version of the Ricardian theory. MacDougall's (1951) pioneering study tested this Type-III hypothesis by examining the export performance of the US relative to the UK to third markets. His results are reported in Table 3.3. Using 1937 data, MacDougall notes that, at the going rate of exchange £1 = $4.769, wage rates in the US were approximately twice those in the UK. This is important to know since it is expected that the ratio of US exports to UK exports should exceed 1 whenever the US output per worker is more than twice that of the British and vice versa. On the whole, the data provided in Table 3.3 are supportive of the Type-III Ricardian hypothesis.

This study was followed by Stern (1962), Balassa (1963), MacDougall et al. (1962), McGilvray and Simpson (1973) and Golub and Hsieh (2000) who performed tests of all three hypotheses. Particularly, McGilvray and Simpson (1973) examine the Type-III hypothesis using the bilateral trade flows between the Republic of Ireland and the UK. As expected, Ireland and the UK are two actively trading nations, with the UK representing, in 1964, 70 percent and 50 percent of Irish merchandise exports and imports, respectively.

McGilvray and Simpson measure the bilateral trade flows between these two nations, not their relative shares in third country markets, and the scope of their analysis covers the whole of merchandise trade (34 merchandise sectors), not a few selected commodities. First, they rank sectors by their propensity to export (exports divided by gross domestic product (GDP)) and develop a parallel ranking of sectors by their propensity to import competing goods (imports divided by GDP *plus* imports). Second, they rank the sectorial ratios of Irish labor productivity (in value) relative to those of the UK in increasing value. Third, they compute

Table 3.3 UK relative to US unit labor requirements and exports, 1937

$a_{z(UK)}/a_{z(US)} > 2$	US exports/UK exports[a]
Wireless sets & valves	8
Pig iron	5
Motor cars	4
Glass containers	3 1/2
Tin cans	3
Machinery	1 1/2
Paper	1
$1.4 < a_{z(UK)}/a_{z(US)} < 2$	UK exports/US exports
Cigarettes	2
Linoleum, oilcloth, etc.	3
Hosiery	3
Leather footwear	3
Coke	5
Rayon weaving	5
Cotton goods	9
Rayon making	11
Beer	18
$a_{z(UK)}/a_{z(US)} < 1.4$	UK exports/US exports
Cement	11
Men's & boys' woolen outerclothing	23
Margarine	32
Woolen & worsted	250

Note: (*a*) Exceptions: US output per worker more than twice British output
per worker, but UK exports exceed US exports: electric lamps, rubber
tyres, soap, biscuits and matches (these represent about 3% of the value
of trade in the commodities listed).
Source: MacDougall (1951, Table 1, p. 698).

several Spearman rank correlation[15] analyses on these pairs of rankings as shown in Table 3.4. If the Type-III hypothesis is to be verified, one should expect to find a positive rank correlation between the labor productivity ranking and the ranking of sectors according to their propensity of export, and a negative rank correlation between the labor productivity ranking and the ranking of sectors according to their propensity to import. In Table 3.4, none of these computed correlation coefficients is significant and all but two are opposite in sign to what would be hypothesized if the Ricardian model were valid.

Following Bhagwati (1964), modern empirics of the Ricardian theory contend that the above regressions take the intuition of a two-country Ricardian model but translate this into a multi-country regression. Because these regressions did not follow directly from any general Ricardian model they could not be considered as a true test of the Ricardian model.

Table 3.4 Rank correlation coefficients for comparative labor productivities, and export and import propensities, Ireland, 1964 and United Kingdom, 1963

		Export propensity		Import propensity	
		(1)	(2)	(3)	(4)
	n	34	30	34	30
Comparative productivity of direct labor inputs	r_s	−0.10	−0.17	0.01	−0.15
	t	−0.54	−0.89	0.04	−0.80
Comparative productivity of direct labor *plus* indirect labor inputs from non-traded goods sectors	r_s	−0.15	−0.24	0.02	−0.14
	t	−0.88	−1.32	0.11	−0.77
Comparative productivity of direct *plus* all indirect labor inputs	r_s	−0.22	−0.31	0.21	0.09
	t	−1.30	−1.35	1.20	0.48

Notes: $n =$ number of observations ($n = 30$ with the 4 primary producing sectors excluded); $r_s =$ Spearman rank correlation coefficient; $t =$ Student $- t$.
Source: McGilvray and Simpson (1973, Table 1).

Multi-country regressions

Building on the EK model, Costinot *et al.* (2012) offer the first theoretically consistent Ricardian test. Compared with EK, they introduce one element of simplification in that labor is the only factor of production. On the other hand, there is one element of complication in that goods are supplied in different varieties. In particular: (1) there are $j = 1, \ldots, J$ goods; (2) each good j may come in an infinite number of varieties; (3) the productivity parameter is a random variable drawn independently from a Fréchet cumulative distribution function like (3.30) for each triplet comprising any country i, any good j and its corresponding varieties; (4) parameter θ, which is common to all countries and industries, measures intra-industry heterogeneity.

In this framework, Costinot *et al.* test a reduced-form specification that follows directly from the theoretical model. For any importer k, any pair of exporters i and i', and any pair of goods j and j', the following expression is estimated:

$$\ln\left(\frac{\tilde{x}_{ik}^{j}\tilde{x}_{i'k}^{j'}}{\tilde{x}_{ik}^{j'}\tilde{x}_{i'k}^{j}}\right) = \theta \ln\left(\frac{\tilde{z}_{i}^{j}\tilde{z}_{i'}^{j'}}{\tilde{z}_{i}^{j'}\tilde{z}_{i'}^{j}}\right) + \ln\left(\frac{\varepsilon_{ik}^{j}\varepsilon_{i'k}^{j'}}{\varepsilon_{ik}^{j'}\varepsilon_{i'k}^{j}}\right) \tag{3.35}$$

where variable $\tilde{x}_{ik}^{j}$ represents bilateral exports adjusted for the level of openness in country i and industry j; $\tilde{z}_{i}^{j}$ is observed productivity and ε_{ik}^{j} is an error term that combines the variation in trade costs and measurement errors in bilateral trade data. Parameter θ is thus a key coefficient of interest and the intuition suggests that $\theta > 0$. Using trade and productivity data for 21 Organisation for Economic Co-operation and Development (OECD) countries and 13 industries covering the manufacturing sector, estimation of (3.35) implies that, *ceteris paribus*, the elasticity of adjusted bilateral exports with respect to observed productivity is significantly positive and equal to 6.53. This outcome, which is consistent with the EK estimate of 8.28, (re-)confirms the important role of labor productivity in explaining bilateral trade as long as variables in the regressions are properly adjusted for multi-country variations.

3.7 Concluding remarks

The academic literature traditionally devotes a great deal of coverage to the Ricardian model. One reason is the simplicity of the argument, but there is also a widespread tendency to focus on labor productivity and to consider it as a good approximation of overall productivity (including capital).

It seems useful to summarize the main results of this chapter. First, comparative advantage arises from technological differences between countries. Trade allows for efficiency gains of specialization that can be shared among participating countries. Detailed information on the demand structure is, however, necessary to determine the actual world relative price and the actual pattern of production. Second, in the absence of technological differences, taste differences can give rise to comparative advantage as well. Third, if countries are similar in all respects, scale economies are a determinant of trade, as they allow countries to specialize in fewer tasks. Fourth, under IRS the trade pattern is characterized by the existence of multiple equilibria. These can be ranked according to a welfare measure rule into "bad" and "good" equilibria. If an economy is in a "bad" equilibrium, a decentralized economy may result in a coordination failure that prevents it from moving to a "good" equilibrium. Fifth, it is surprising to observe that, so far little empirical work has been done in testing Ricardian hypotheses derived from multi-sector multi-country models. Recent tests of theoretically-grounded hypotheses show, however, a significant impact of labor productivity on trade performance. Tests with scale economies await further research.

Overall, the Ricardian model seems to raise new questions about the sources of comparative advantage. Firm heterogeneity provides a useful though mechanistic guide as to how labor productivity and comparative advantage can be expected to evolve. However, it gives no explanation of whether one cumulative distribution function is a superior representation of differences in labor productivities across countries than another. In particular, the randomness of productivities will be questioned in the next chapter where we consider the Heckscher-Ohlin-Samuelson (H-O-S) model and the role of (deterministic) factor endowments.

Problems

3.1 Find the condition that guarantees that, at the uniquely determined world price ratio, world output of both commodities is greater with trade than its pre-trade level. Relate your answer to inequality (3.14).

3.2 Show that the consumption pattern can be a source of comparative advantage. A way to proceed is to assume $\alpha \neq \alpha^*$, and replace the technology of the Ricardian model described by (3.1) with fixed endowments of each commodity that are similar at home and abroad.

3.3 Consider the implications on the international equilibrium and country welfare of (1) increasing the foreign country's labor endowment and, (2) decreasing a_1^* and a_2^* in the same proportion (productivity growth). What are the benefits transferred to the other country?

3.4 Show that the convexity of the production possibility curve is reinforced in Figure 3.5 if both sectors have increasing returns.

3.5 Give the conditions under which a conflict of interest between the two countries arises, with one country gaining and the other losing from trade. This corresponds to Graham's (1923) argument for protection.

3.6 Instead of a uniform foreign productivity increase, show the implications for long-run equilibrium and domestic welfare of technical progress in a single foreign industry.

3.7 Analyze the full implications of a harmonization of technology across the world caused, for example, by a transfer of the least costly technology.

Notes

1. Dynamic effects of international trade are therefore not investigated. A series of recent contributions on endogenous growth have developed a set of formal techniques by which the relationship between international trade and long-run growth can be explored. See Chapter 14 for the growth and trade links.
2. Readers unfamiliar with the concept of community indifference curves can find a summary of the controversies in Chacholiades (1973, ch. 5). The few cases where the use of social indifference curves is justified are: (1) a Robinson Crusoe economy, (2) a totalitarian state, (3) a country inhabited by individuals with identical tastes and factor endowments, (4) individuals with identical and homothetic tastes and (5) if income is always reallocated among individuals in such a way as to maximize social welfare. In spite of the questionable validity of these assumptions, social indifference curves are used extensively in trade theory and we accordingly follow this tradition here.
3. This assumes homothetic preferences, a common assumption in trade models.
4. An analysis of the long-run trends in US regional specialization and localization over the period 1860–1987 does not, however, support explanations based on external economies (Kim, 1995). The empirical evidence seems more consistent with explanations based on internal scale economies and regional factor endowments (see Chapter 4).
5. See Chapter 8. Some forms of competitive interaction do imply competitive pricing, for example Bertrand competition as well as contestable markets.
6. Krugman and Venables (1995) examine how increased globalization affects the location of manufacturing as transportation costs are gradually reduced. International scale economies can spontaneously arise in the model and lead to uneven gains from trade between two regions with no inherent comparative advantage.
7. An exception is Okuno-Fujiwara (1988) who identifies the conditions that create Marshallian external economies, introducing interdependence of several industries and oligopolistic competition in at least one of them.
8. For more on the topic of this subsection, see Ethier (1982b, 1987). Ethier (1982b) assumes $a_1 = a_2 = 1$.
9. This literature has been initiated to characterize economies that exhibit underemployment equilibria, but where the results do not derive from the usual Keynesian assumptions of price rigidity (Diamond, 1982; Weitzman, 1982; Heller, 1988; Cooper and John, 1988). This concept is now used to characterize economies in a permanent state of underdevelopment, or certain forms of market structure (Okuno-Fujiwara, 1988).
10. Taylor (1993) extends the continuum Ricardian model of Dornbusch *et al.* (1977) to a dynamic framework. The model incorporates heterogeneity across industries in research and production technologies, and in the technological opportunity for innovation.
11. The material in the rest of this section depends upon Krugman and Obstfeld (1988, 36–38).

12. See the mathematical appendices to Bernard *et al.* (2003) for more properties of the Fréchet distribution.
13. Bernard *et al.* (2003) extend the analysis to allow for Bertrand competition to explain why exporting plants have higher productivity. With Bertrand competition, the lowest cost seller in any country n can set a price equal to the unit cost of the second most efficient supplier in that country. Though imperfect competition is introduced, it does not change the results as long as the distribution of markups is fixed. See Chapter 9 for more details.
14. The appendix to Chapter 8 is devoted to the solution of demands and relative prices when demands derive from a CES utility function.
15. The Spearman rank correlation coefficient is a non-parametric measure of association when ranks are used instead of actual observations. It measures in Table 3.4 the tendency of labor productivity and trade propensity to relate in a monotone way and, unlike the ordinary sample correlation coefficient, is not restricted to uncovering a linear relation between them. The Spearman coefficient is:

$$r_s = 1 - 6 \sum_{i=1}^{n} d_i^2 / n(n^2 - 1)$$

where n is the number of observations (either 30 or 34 in Table 3.4) and d_i the difference in the rank number between the two variables. Note that if several observations tie, their score is the sum of their ranks divided by the number of observed ties. Under the null hypothesis of no correlation, the sampling distribution of r_s has mean 0 and the standard deviation $\sigma(r_s) = 1/\sqrt{n-1}$. Since this sampling distribution can be approximated with a normal distribution, we base the test of the null hypothesis on the statistic $t = (r_s - 0)/(1/\sqrt{n-1})$ which has approximately the standard distribution.

References and additional reading

The Ricardian theory

Bhagwati, J.N. and Srinivasan, T.N. (1983), *Lectures on International Trade* (Cambridge, MA: MIT Press), chs 2–4.
Chacholiades, M. (1973), *The Pure Theory of International Trade* (London: Macmillan).
Findlay, R. (1988), "Comparative Advantage," in J. Eatwell, M. Milgate and P. Newman (Eds.), *The New Palgrave: A Dictionary of Economics* (London: Macmillan), 514–517.
Ricardo, D. (1821), *The Principles of Political Economy and Taxation* (London: J. Murray).

The Ricardian model with many goods

Bernard, A.B., Eaton, J., Jensen, J.B., and Kortum, S. (2003), "Plants and Productivity in International Trade," *American Economic Review* 93 (4), 1268–1290.
Chipman, J.S. (1965), "A Survey of International Trade: Part I – The Classical Theory," *Econometrica*, 33, 477–519.
Dornbusch, R., Fischer, S., and Samuelson, P.A. (1977), "Comparative Advantage, Trade, and Payments in a Ricardian Model with a Continuum of Goods," *American Economic Review*, 47 (5), 823–839.
Eaton, J. and Kortum, S. (2002), "Technology, Geography, and Trade," *Econometrica*, 70, 1741–1779.

Haberler, G. (1936), *The Theory of International Trade* (London: W. Hodge).

Krugman, P.R. and Obstfeld, M. (1988), *International Economics: Theory and Policy* (Glenview: Scott, Foresman), appendix to ch. 2, 36–41.

Taylor, M.S. (1993), "Quality Ladders and Ricardian Trade," *Journal of International Economics*, 34, 225–243.

Viner, J. (1937), *Studies in the Theory of International Trade* (New York: Harper).

Institutions and trade

Costinot, A. (2009), "On the Origins of Comparative Advantage," *Journal of International Economics*, 77 (2), 255–264.

Cuñat, A. and Melitz, M. (2011a), "Volatility, Labor Market Flexibility, and the Pattern of Comparative Advantage," *Journal of the European Economic Association*, forthcoming.

Cuñat, A. and Melitz, M. (2011b), "A Many-country, Many-good Model of Labor Market Rigidities as a Source of Comparative Advantage," *Journal of the European Economic Association, Papers and Proceedings*, forthcoming.

Levchenko, A.A. (2004), "Institutional Quality and International Trade," *Review of Economic Studies*, 74 (3), 791–819.

Nunn, N. (2007), "Relationship-Specificity, Incomplete Contracts, and the Pattern of Trade," *Quarterly Journal of Economics*, 122 (2), 569–600.

Economies of scale, decreasing costs, and the pattern of specialization

Ethier, W.J. (1979), "Internationally Decreasing Costs and World Trade," *Journal of International Economics*, 9, 1–24.

Ethier, W.J. (1982a), "National and International Returns to Scale in the Modern Theory of International Trade," *American Economic Review*, 72, 388–405.

Ethier, W.J. (1982b), "Decreasing Costs in International Trade and Frank Graham's Argument for Protection," *Econometrica*, 50 (5), 1243–1267.

Ethier, W.J. (1987), "The Theory of International Trade," in L.M. Officer (Ed.), *International Economics* (Boston: Kluwer Academic), 1–57.

Graham, F. (1923), "Some Aspects of Protection Further Considered," *Quarterly Journal of Economics*, 37, 199–227.

Kim, S. (1995), "Expansion of Markets and the Geographic Distribution of Economic Activities: The Trends in US Regional Manufacturing Structure, 1860-1987," *Quarterly Journal of Economics*, 110, 881–908.

Krugman, P.R. and Venables, A.J. (1995), "Globalization and the Inequality of Nations," *Quarterly Journal of Economics*, 110, 857–880.

Marshall, A. (1972), *Principles of Economics* (1890) (London: Macmillan; rev. edn 1972).

Okuno-Fujiwara, M. (1988), "Interdependence of Industries, Coordination Failure and Strategic Promotion of an Industry," *Journal of International Economics*, 25, 25–43.

Panagariya, A. (1981), "Variable Returns to Scale in Production and Patterns of Specialization," *American Economic Review*, 71, 221–230.

Coordination failure

Cooper, R. and John, A. (1988), "Coordinating Coordination Failures in Keynesian Models," *Quarterly Journal of Economics*, 103, 441–464.

Diamond P. (1982), "Aggregate Demand Management in Search Equilibrium," *Journal of Political Economy*, 90, 881–894.

Heller, W.P. (1988), "Coordination Failure with Complete Markets in a Simple Model of Effective Demand," in W.P. Heller,. R.M. Starr, and D.A. Starrett (Eds.), *Equilibrium Analysis: Essays in Honor of K.J. Arrow*, Vol. 2 (Cambridge: Cambridge University Press).

Weitzman, M. (1982), "Increasing Returns and the Foundations of Unemployment Theory," *Economic Journal*, 787–804.

Tests of the Ricardian model

Balassa, B. (1963), "An Empirical Demonstration of Classical Comparative Cost Theory," *Review of Economics and Statistics*, 45, 231–238.

Bhagwati, J. (1964), "The Pure Theory of International Trade: A Survey," *Economic Journal*, 74, 1–84.

Costinot, A., Donaldson, D., and Komunjer, I. (2012), "What Goods do Countries Trade? A Quantitative Exploration of Ricardo's Ideas," *Review of Economic Studies*, forthcoming.

Golub, S.S. and Hsieh, C.-T. (2000), "Classical Ricardian Theory of Comparative Advantage Revisited," *Review of International Economics*, 8 (2), 221–234.

Leamer, E.E. and Levinsohn, J. (1995), "International Trade Theory: The Evidence" in G. Grossman and K. Rogoff (Eds.), *Handbook of International Economics* (Amsterdam: North-Holland), Vol. 3, ch. 26, 1339–1394.

MacDougall, G.D.A. (1951), "British and American Exports: A Study Suggested by the Theory of Comparative Costs, Part I," *Economic Journal*, 61, 487–521.

MacDougall, G.D.A., Dowley, M., Fox, P. and Pugh, S. (1962), "British and American Productivity, Prices and Exports: An Addendum," *Oxford Economic Papers*, 14 (3), 297–304.

McGilvray, J. and Simpson, D. (1973), "The Commodity Structure of Anglo-Irish Trade," *Review of Economics and Statistics*, 55, 451–458.

Stern, R.M. (1962), "British and American Productivity and Comparative Costs in International Trade," *Oxford Economic Papers*, 14 (3), 275–296.

Time series techniques

Hamilton, J.D. (1994), *Time Series Analysis* (Princeton: Princeton University Press).

Mills, T.C. (1990), *Time Series Techniques for Economists* (Cambridge: Cambridge University Press).

4

The factor abundance model

The predominant explanation of the pattern of comparative advantage is the factor abundance theory. A twentieth-century development, this theory was first set out by Eli Heckscher in 1919 and further developed by Bertil Ohlin (1933). During the 1950s Paul Samuelson set out a general equilibrium formalization of the insights of Heckscher and Ohlin (H-O) and subsequently derived a set of important theorems. In recognition of Samuelson's contribution, the H-O theory came to be known as the Heckscher-Ohlin-Samuelson (H-O-S) theory. More recently, this theory has been labeled simply the "factor abundance" theory, in reference to its central tenet: comparative advantage, and hence trade, is the result of differences in the relative supplies of factors between countries.

The analytical foundation of the factor abundance theory is a general equilibrium model of an economy producing J goods using H primary factors of production under conditions of perfect competition in both product and factor markets. The H-O-S model augments this essentially closed economy model by introducing another country and by making additional assumptions about the interaction between countries. These additional assumptions include the international identity of production functions and the international immobility of factors. These additional assumptions serve to eliminate all causes of difference in autarky relative prices between countries except that of differing relative factor supplies.

This chapter presents the H-O-S model, that is, the analytical model underlying the factor abundance theory. Two methods of presentation are used: a traditional approach which uses production and direct utility functions and a modern approach which uses duality theory to express supply and demand in terms of revenue and expenditure functions. We first consider the supply side of the model and establish two key relationships: that between relative factor prices and an industry's use of factors, and that between relative factor prices and relative output prices. We then demonstrate three important comparative statics results: the Rybczynski theorem, the Stolper-Samuelson theorem and the reciprocity relations. Next, we present the demand side of the model, and combine this with the supply elements to determine the trade equilibrium. Following this we consider the effect of trade on the domestic allocation of resources and the distribution of income. Finally, we demonstrate the two main predictions of the factor abundance theory: the H-O theorem concerning the pattern of trade, and the Factor Price Equalization theorem concerning the effect of trade on the pattern of factor prices between countries.

4.1   Production equilibrium

In this section we present the production relationships that describe the supply side of an economy and develop the conditions for the maximization of the economy's income. The following assumptions are maintained throughout this chapter:

Assumption 1: There is perfect competition in both product and factor markets.

Assumption 2: Factors of production are homogeneous in quality and costlessly mobile between industries.

Assumption 3: The total supply of each factor is independent of its reward – that is, the national supply of each factor is perfectly inelastic.

Additional assumptions needed to derive the basic propositions of the factor abundance theory will be introduced when appropriate.

Traditional analysis

The traditional presentation of the H-O-S model reduces the dimensionality of the underlying general equilibrium model from J goods and H factors to that of a "simple" two-sector model with two goods and two factors of production: capital and labor. The presentation below adopts this convention. A general version of the model is presented in Chapter 5 when discussing applied modeling in general equilibrium.

The production function

We assume an economy produces two commodities, q_1 and q_2, using two primary factors, capital K and labor L. The production function for industry j is:

$$q_j = F_j(K_j, L_j) \quad j = 1, 2 \tag{4.1}$$

where K_j and L_j are the levels of capital and labor employed in industry j, respectively. The production function is assumed to satisfy the following properties:

(1) Some of each factor is required for production:

$$F_j(0, L_j) = F_j(K_j, 0) = 0, \quad j = 1, 2$$

(2) Linear homogeneity (homogeneity of degree one): for $\gamma > 0$,

$$F_j(\gamma K_j, \gamma L_j) = \gamma F_j(K_j, L_j) = \gamma q_j, \quad j = 1, 2$$

(3) Factor marginal products are positive but diminishing:

$$\frac{\partial F_j(K_j, L_j)}{\partial K_j} > 0 \qquad \frac{\partial F_j(K_j, L_j)}{\partial L_j} > 0 \quad j = 1, 2$$

$$\frac{\partial^2 F_j(K_j, L_j)}{\partial K_j^2} < 0 \qquad \frac{\partial^2 F_j(K_j, L_j)}{\partial L_j^2} < 0 \qquad j = 1, 2$$

A production function satisfying properties (1) to (3) is called a neoclassical production function.[1] Since linear homogeneity is crucial to establishing the main factor abundance theorems, the remainder of this section discusses some implications of linear homogeneity for the production function.

By linear homogeneity, a proportional change in all inputs will change output in the same proportion – that is, production exhibits constant returns to scale (CRS).[2] Given this, (4.1) can be expressed in several equivalent forms. For example, applying property (2) with $\gamma = 1/q_j$ gives (4.1) as:

$$1 = F_j(a_{jK}, a_{jL}) \tag{4.2}$$

where $a_{jK} = K_j/q_j$ and $a_{jL} = L_j/q_j$ are the *unit factor input requirements*, that is, the amount of each factor required to produce one unit of output. (4.2) implicitly defines the unit isoquant: the combinations of capital and labor required to produce one unit of output.[3]

Another form of the production function is obtained by setting $\gamma = 1/L_j$:

$$q_j = L_j f_j(k_j) \tag{4.3}$$

where $k_j = K_j/L_j$ is industry j's capital–labor ratio. This form illustrates another implication of linear homogeneity: factor average and marginal products only depend on the industry capital–labor ratio.[4] This is directly evident for labor's average product by simply rearranging (4.3):

$$\frac{q_j}{L_j} = f_j(k_j) \tag{4.4}$$

where

$$\frac{\partial(q_j/L_j)}{\partial k_j} > 0$$

Capital's average product is similarly expressed by setting $\gamma = 1/K_j$ to obtain $q_j/K_j = f_j(1/k_j)$ where

$$\frac{\partial(q_j/K_j)}{\partial k_j} < 0$$

The dependence of factor marginal products on the industry capital–labor ratio is demonstrated by differentiating (4.3) with respect to each factor:

$$\frac{\partial q_j}{\partial K_j} = \frac{\partial(L_j f_j(k_j))}{\partial k_j} \frac{\partial k_j}{\partial K_j} = f_j'(k_j) > 0$$

$$\frac{\partial q_j}{\partial L_j} = \frac{\partial(L_j f_j(k_j))}{\partial k_j} \frac{\partial k_j}{\partial L_j} = f_j(k_j) - k_j f_j'(k_j) > 0$$

where "'" indicates differentiation of the function with respect to its argument. Using these expressions, property (3) can be written compactly as $f_j'(k_j) > 0$ and $f_j''(k_j) < 0$ for all $k_j > 0$, $(j = 1, 2)$.[5]

Figure 4.1 illustrates the per worker production function (4.4). As implied by properties (1) to (3), this function is an increasing, monotonic and strictly concave function of k_j whose slope decreases from infinity at $k_j = 0$ to zero at $k_j = \infty$.

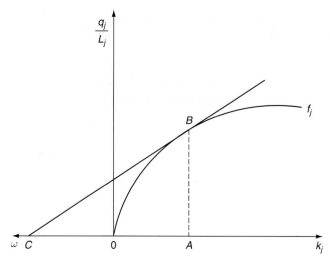

Figure 4.1 A neoclassical per worker production function

A final implication of linear homogeneity is the "adding-up" condition, also known as Euler's law:

$$q_j = L_j(f_j - k_j f_j') + K_j f_j' = f_j \quad j = 1, 2$$

which states that output equals the sum of the contributions made by each factor.

Optimal resource allocation

We now establish the conditions for optimal resource allocation which, for given output prices, imply the maximization of national income. Industry j's profit maximization problem is:[6]

$$\Pi_j(p_j, w_j, r_j) = \max_{L_j, K_j} (p_j q_j - w_j L_j - r_j K_j) \text{ subject to } q_j = L_j f_j(k_j) \qquad (4.5)$$

where $\Pi_j(p_j, w_j, r_j)$ denotes industry j's maximum profit for the given wage rate (w_j), rental rate (r_j) and output price (p_j), each measured in some arbitrary unit of account. Assuming both commodities are produced in equilibrium, the solution to (4.5) yields the condition that, in each industry, each factor will be paid its value marginal product:

$$w_j = p_j(f_j - k_j f_j') \quad j = 1, 2 \qquad (4.6)$$
$$r_j = p_j f_j'$$

Since factors are homogeneous and costlessly mobile between industries, the values of w_j and r_j are common across industries ($w_j = w$ and $r_j = r, \forall j$). Given this, (4.6) implies the following condition for optimal factor allocation between industries:

$$p_1(f_1 - k_1 f_1') = w = p_2(f_2 - k_2 f_2') \qquad (4.7)$$
$$p_1 f_1' = r = p_2 f_2'$$

Hence, for given output prices, national income is maximized when factors are allocated so as to equate their value marginal product across industries.

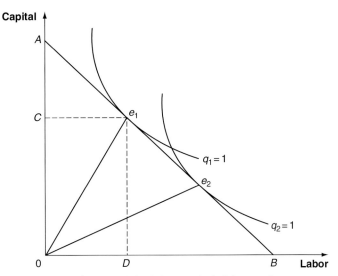

Figure 4.2 Unit isoquants and cost-minimizing capital–labor ratios

Figure 4.2 illustrates the above allocation rule by showing each industry's unit isoquant (4.2) together with an iso-cost line (*AB*) whose slope equals (minus) the economy's wage–rental ratio.[7] The point of tangency between the iso-cost line and each unit isoquant (points e_1 and e_2) determines an allocation of capital and labor satisfying (4.7) in that the ratios of factor marginal products in each industry are equated via the common wage–rental ratio. Note that for given factor prices, points e_1 and e_2 determine a unique cost-minimizing capital–labor ratio in each industry as measured by the slope of rays Oe_1 and Oe_2.[8]

Whereas the above defines optimal factor allocations between industries, we must also take into account that the economy as a whole is limited by its supply of capital and labor. Since factor markets are perfectly competitive, this factor supply constraint is embodied in the equilibrium condition that resources be fully employed. If K and L denote the economy's total supply of capital and labor, respectively, then the conditions for full employment are:

$$K = K_1 + K_2 \tag{4.8}$$

$$L = L_1 + L_2 \tag{4.9}$$

These constraints can be combined by dividing (4.8) by (4.9) to express the economy's overall capital–labor ratio as a weighted average of industry capital–labor ratios:

$$k = \lambda_1 k_1 + \lambda_2 k_2 \tag{4.10}$$

where $\lambda_j = L_j/L$ is the proportion of the labor force allocated to sector *j*. Since $\lambda_1 + \lambda_2 = 1$, and assuming $k_1 \neq k_2$, (4.10) can be solved to give the following alternative expressions for λ_1 and λ_2:

$$\lambda_1 = \frac{k - k_2}{k_1 - k_2} \quad \text{and} \quad \lambda_2 = \frac{k_1 - k}{k_1 - k_2} \tag{4.11}$$

Inserting expressions (4.11) into (4.3), the per capita output of each industry can be expressed as a function of both industry and national capital–labor ratios:[9]

$$\frac{q_1}{L} = \lambda_1 f_1(k_1) = \frac{k - k_2}{k_1 - k_2} f_1(k_1) \tag{4.12}$$

$$\frac{q_2}{L} = \lambda_2 f_2(k_2) = \frac{k_1 - k}{k_1 - k_2} f_2(k_2)$$

We now discuss two key relationships in the H-O-S model: the relationship between factor prices and factor inputs, and the relationship between factor prices and output prices.

Factor prices and factor use

Dividing w by r in (4.6) gives the economy's wage–rental ratio (ω) as a function of an industry's capital–labor ratio:

$$\omega(k_j) = \frac{f_j(k_j)}{f_j'(k_j)} - k_j \quad j = 1, 2 \tag{4.13}$$

Since $\dfrac{d\omega}{dk_j} = -\dfrac{f_j f_j''}{(f_j')^2} > 0$, (4.13) can be inverted to express each k_j uniquely in terms of the economy's wage–rental ratio, that is, $k_j = k_j(\omega)$ with:

$$\frac{dk_j}{d\omega} = -\frac{(f_j')^2}{f_j f_j''} > 0, \quad j = 1, 2 \tag{4.14}$$

The positive relationship between k_j and ω obtained in (4.14) derives from the fact that a rise in the wage–rental ratio leads producers in each industry to substitute capital for labor, thus raising the capital–labor ratio.

Figure 4.3 illustrates the function $k_j(\omega)$ for each industry. Consistent with (4.14), each curve is drawn positively sloped. The relative placement of the two curves assumes industry 1 is

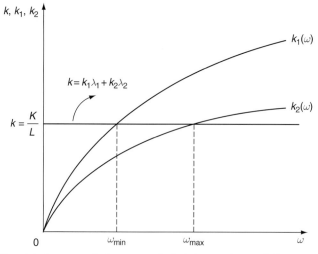

Figure 4.3 Relationship between industry capital–labor ratios and the wage–rental ratio

capital-intensive (equivalently, industry 2 is labor-intensive).[10] Whereas the function $k_j(\omega)$ is defined for all values of ω, the full employment constraint (4.10) restricts the range of ω. For example, if the economy's overall capital–labor ratio is $K/L = k$, Figure 4.3 indicates that ω is restricted to the interval $[\omega_{\min}, \omega_{\max}]$. To see why, note that when $\omega = \omega_{\min}$ the economy is completely specialized in the production of good 1 since $k_1 = k$ and thus $\lambda_1 = 1$. Inserting these values into (4.13) gives the value of $\omega_{\min}$ as:

$$\omega_{\min} = \frac{f_1(k)}{f_1'(k)} - k$$

Conversely, when $\omega = \omega_{\max}$ the economy is completely specialized in the production of good 2 since $k_2 = k$ and thus $\lambda_2 = 1$. From (4.13) the value of $\omega_{\max}$ is:

$$\omega_{\max} = \frac{f_2(k)}{f_2'(k)} - k$$

Since $\omega_{\min}$ and $\omega_{\max}$ correspond to complete specialization in one good or the other, we must have $\omega_{\min} < \omega < \omega_{\max}$ if both goods are to be produced in equilibrium.

Factor prices and commodity prices

If both goods are produced in equilibrium, conditions (4.7) imply that we can write:

$$p(\omega) = \frac{f_1'(k_1(\omega))}{f_2'(k_2(\omega))} \tag{4.15}$$

which gives the relative price of good 2 ($p = p_2/p_1$) as a function of ω alone. Totally differentiating (4.15), and making use of (4.13) and (4.14), we obtain:

$$\frac{1}{p}\frac{dp}{d\omega} = \frac{k_1(\omega) - k_2(\omega)}{(\omega + k_2(\omega))(\omega + k_1(\omega))} \gtreqless 0 \quad \text{as } (k_1(\omega) - k_2(\omega)) \gtreqless 0 \tag{4.16}$$

which indicates that the slope of the relationship between relative output prices and relative factor prices depends upon which industry is capital-intensive. Figure 4.4 illustrates (4.15) assuming, as in Figure 4.3, that industry 1 is capital-intensive at all values of ω (that is, $(k_1 - k_2) > 0, \forall \omega > 0$).[11] Note that this "strong factor intensity" assumption ensures a one-to-one relationship between $p(\omega)$ and ω. Since this assumption is important for establishing several key results in the H-O-S model we state it explicitly:

> **Assumption 4 (no factor intensity reversals):** The ordering of industry capital–labor ratios is invariant to changes in ω.

Finally, in Figure 4.4, the function $p(\omega)$ is drawn continuous outside the interval $[p_{\min}, p_{\max}]$ since nothing restricts the sale of a good at an increasingly favorable price.

Changes in factor supplies and output prices

The equations (4.6), (4.11), (4.12), (4.13) and (4.15) comprise a model with ten endogenous variables $\{q_j, k_j, \lambda_j, p_j, w, r\}$. Taking p_j as known, this system can be solved for the remaining eight variables in terms of the economy's factor supplies and commodity prices. Note that this model only covers the supply side of the economy. To derive equilibrium commodity prices we must add demand. This is discussed in Sections 4.2 and 4.3.

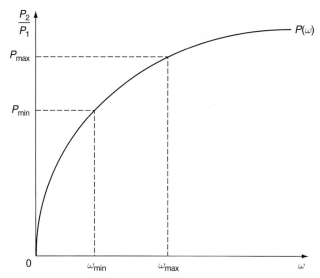

Figure 4.4 Relationship between relative commodity and factor prices

Since commodity prices and national factor supplies are given, we can consider how a change in one of these exogenous variables would affect the values of the model's endogenous variables. Two important cases are considered below: the effect of an output price change on factor prices and the effect of a factor supply change on outputs.

With both commodities produced, (4.16) states that a rise in the price of good j will raise (lower) the relative return (ω) to labor if the industry producing good j is labor-intensive (capital-intensive). Given this, we need consider here only the effect of a price change on individual factor rewards.

Consider an increase in p_1, an increase in p_2 being analyzed by analogy. Totally differentiating (4.6) with respect to p_1 yields:

$$\frac{dw}{dp_1} = \frac{k_2 f_1}{k_2 - f_1} \gtreqless 0 \quad \text{as } (k_2 - k_1) \gtreqless 0 \tag{4.17}$$

$$\frac{dr}{dp_1} = \frac{-f_2}{k_2 - k_1} \gtreqless 0 \quad \text{as } (k_2 - k_1) \gtreqless 0 \tag{4.18}$$

As indicated, an increase in the price of good 1 will raise the nominal return to the factor used intensively in the production of good 1.

The effect on real factor rewards can be established by comparing the proportional change in nominal factor prices to the proportional change in output price. Writing (4.17) and (4.18) in elasticity form, and making use of (4.13), we can, after some manipulation, write:

$$\frac{dw}{dp_1} \frac{p_1}{w} = -\frac{k_2(\omega + k_1)}{\omega(k_1 - k_2)} \tag{4.19}$$

$$\frac{dr}{dp_1} \frac{p_1}{r} = \frac{\omega + k_1}{k_1 - k_2} \tag{4.20}$$

If industry 1 is capital-intensive ($k_1 > k_2$) then:

$$\frac{dr}{dp_1} \frac{p_1}{r} > 1 \text{ and } \frac{dw}{dp_1} \frac{p_1}{w} < 1^{12}$$

Hence, if industry 1 is capital-intensive, a rise in the price of good 1 will raise the real return to capital and lower the real return to labor (both returns measured in units of good 1). Since p_2 is held fixed, these changes also apply to the real returns measured in units of good 2.

The preceding effects on factor rewards in response to a change in output price are summarized by the Stolper-Samuelson theorem:

Proposition 4.1 (Stolper-Samuelson): An increase in the price of any good raises the nominal, relative and real return to the factor intensive in the production of that good and lowers the nominal, relative and real return to the other factor.

The effect on production of an exogenous change in national factor supplies is contained in the Rybczynski theorem:

Proposition 4.2 (Rybczynski): If capital–labor ratios differ between industries then, at constant commodity prices, an increase in the supply of one factor alone will cause an expansion of the good intensive in the use of that factor and an absolute decline in the output of the other good.[13]

It will suffice to consider an increase in capital since an increase in labor can be analyzed by analogy. With reference to Figures 4.1 and 4.3 (or (4.10) and (4.13)), fixing output prices implies that the values of ω, the k_j, and thus the $f_j(k_j)$, are also fixed. Hence, any change in outputs $q_j = L_j f_j(k_j)$ must come from a change in L_j (equivalently, λ_j, since L is given).[14] Differentiating expressions (4.11) with respect to K gives:

$$\frac{dL_1}{dK} = \frac{1}{k_1 - k_2} \tag{4.21}$$

$$\frac{dL_2}{dK} = -\frac{1}{k_1 - k_2} \tag{4.22}$$

Using these, the effect on production is:

$$\frac{dq_1}{dK} = \frac{f_1}{k_1 - k_2} \gtreqless 0 \quad \text{as } (k_1 - k_2) \gtreqless 0 \tag{4.23}$$

$$\frac{dq_2}{dK} = \frac{-f_2}{k_1 - k_2} \gtreqless 0 \quad \text{as } (k_1 - k_2) \gtreqless 0 \tag{4.24}$$

which establishes the proposition.

Finally, we note three additional results related to this topic. First, the total effect on national income ($Y = p_1 L_1 f_1 + p_2 L_2 f_2$) of an increase in capital is:

$$\frac{dY}{dK} = p_1 f_1 \frac{dL_1}{dK} + p_2 f_2 \frac{dL_2}{dK} = r > 0 \tag{4.25}$$

Hence, at constant output prices, each unit of accumulated capital unambiguously raises national income by an amount equal to its rental price. Second, by manipulating (4.23) and (4.24) we can obtain the following inequality:

$$\hat{q}_1 > \hat{K} > \hat{L} = 0 > \hat{q}_2$$

where the "∧" denotes the relative change in a variable (e.g., $\hat{q} = dq/q$). This states that the relative change in capital (labor) must lie between the relative change in outputs. This result is known as a "magnification effect."

Finally, by dividing (4.24) by (4.23) we obtain an expression for the relative change in outputs due to the change in capital:

$$\left. \frac{dq_1}{dq_2} \right]_{\hat{L}=0} = -\frac{f_1}{f_2} < 0 \qquad\qquad (4.26)$$

where $\hat{L} = 0$ denotes that labor is held constant. This equation implicitly defines a line in (q_1, q_2) space (with slope given by (4.26)) called a Rybczynski line (R-line). Geometrically, an R-line connects the production point on the initial production frontier to the production point on the new production frontier resulting from the change in factor supply, with commodity prices held fixed.

Whereas (4.26) relates to an increase in capital, similar reasoning with respect to a change in labor alone leads to the R-line for labor:

$$\left. \frac{dq_1}{dq_2} \right]_{\hat{K}=0} = -\frac{f_1 k_2}{f_2 k_1}$$

In general, an R-line is negatively sloped, with the magnitude of the slope depending on the initial values of $k_1(\omega)$ and $k_2(\omega)$ or, equivalently, the initial output prices since the capital–labor ratios are functions of ω which is in turn a function of relative output prices. The effect on outputs of a combined change in both capital and labor can also be derived by totally differentiating (4.11).

Simulation analysis

The effect of factor supply changes on outputs and factor employment can be illustrated using the computer model of Problem 4.5. Table 4.1 lists these effects under three scenarios: a 10 percent increase in K alone, a 10 percent increase in L alone and a combined 10 percent increase in both factors. The numbers shown are the percentage change in each variable relative to its initial solution value obtained from Problem 4.5 and reproduced in column (1).

As expected, an increase in either factor alone leads to an absolute increase in the output of the industry intensive in the growing factor and an absolute decline in the output of the

Table 4.1 Effects of an exogenous increase in factor supplies

Variable	Base solution	% change in variable due to a 10% increase in:		
		Capital	Labor	Both
	(1)	(2)	(3)	(4)
Capital-intensive industry 1				
Output (q_1)	0.956	17.5	−7.5	10
Capital employed (K_1)	0.686	17.5	−7.5	10
Labor employed (L_1)	1.333	17.5	−7.5	10
Labor-intensive industry 2				
Output (q_2)	0.429	−35	45	10
Capital employed (K_2)	0.114	−35	45	10
Labor employed (L_2)	0.667	−35	45	10

other industry. The combined 10 percent increase in labor and capital provides an intermediate outcome: the output of both industries increases by 10 percent by the linear homogeneity of production functions. Note that when the supply of both factors is increased the "magnification effect" on outputs is not obtained. Since goods prices are fixed by assumption, relative price effects are excluded and industries' capital–labor ratios are constant. This, together with expressions (4.21), explains why industry j's uses of factors must change at the same rate as industry j's output.

Duality

The preceding section studied the problem of national income maximization and optimal resource allocation in terms of factor inputs and commodity outputs. In this section, these issues are approached from the dual perspective of cost minimization defined by factor prices and output prices.[15] Since the adjustment within the neoclassical model is based on relative price changes, one can argue that it is preferable to deal with cost functions, as these deal directly with prices, rather than production functions, which relate to quantities and are only indirectly affected by prices. A strong advantage of this approach is that we can observe cost functions directly, which is not the case for production functions. Duality allows for a general treatment using the vector method. In what follows we will assume H factor inputs (capital, skilled and unskilled labor, resources and so on) and J commodities. But, for some practical applications, the vector dimension will be reduced to two.

The minimum cost function

Consider an economy consisting of J competitive industries. Each industry employs H factor inputs $\mathbf{e}_j = (e_{j1}, \ldots, e_{jH})$ to produce an amount q_j of a single good using the production function $q_j = F_j(\mathbf{e}_j)$. By the duality between production and cost functions, there exists a minimum cost function:

$$C_j(\mathbf{w}, q_j) = \min_{\mathbf{e}_j} \left\{ \mathbf{w}.\mathbf{e} = \sum_{h=1}^{H} w_h e_{jh} : F_j(\mathbf{e}_j) \geq q_j \right\} \tag{4.27}$$

which serves as a sufficient description of the technology.[16] The set of input requirements comprises all those that can produce at least the output level q_j according to the production function $F_j(\mathbf{e}_j)$. Given an input price vector $\mathbf{w} = (w_1, \ldots, w_H)$, a firm chooses its optimal factor requirements to minimize its total cost (factor payments). Under certain regularity conditions,[17] the minimum cost function $C_j(\mathbf{w}, q_j)$ and the production function $F_j(\mathbf{e}_j)$ completely determine each other and are thus equivalent representations of the same underlying technology.

Input demands

If $F_j(\mathbf{e}_j)$ is linearly homogeneous then the cost function can be written as $C_j(\mathbf{w}, q_j) = q_j c_j(\mathbf{w})$, where $c_j(\mathbf{w})$ is the unit cost function that represents both average and marginal production cost. An important property of the unit cost function is Shephard's lemma:[18] if $c_j(\mathbf{w})$ is differentiable with respect to $\mathbf{w}$ at the factor price vector $\mathbf{w}'$ then the demand for factor h per unit of output is given by the partial derivative of the unit cost function with respect to its price:

$$\frac{\partial c_j(\mathbf{w}')}{\partial w_h} = a_{jh} \tag{4.28}$$

where a_{jh} is the demand for factor h per unit of output j – that is, the optimal unit factor input requirement. Given (4.28), industry j's total demand for factor h is obtained as $e_{jh} = a_{jh}q_j$.

Production equilibrium

We now express the conditions for a competitive equilibrium in the economy in terms of the above unit cost function. The profit maximization problem for industry j is:

$$\Pi_j(p_j, \mathbf{w}) = \max_{q_j} \{q_j[p_j - c_j(\mathbf{w})], q_j \geq 0\} \quad j = 1, \ldots, J$$

where $\Pi_j(p_j, \mathbf{w})$ denotes industry j's maximum profit for given factor prices $\mathbf{w}$ and output price p_j. The solution to this problem requires that output be chosen so as to equate price and marginal cost. Combining this condition with the long-run equilibrium requirement of zero profits in each industry, a competitive equilibrium requires the following conditions to be satisfied:

$$q_j[p_j - c_j(\mathbf{w})] = 0 \quad j = 1, \ldots, J \tag{4.29}$$

$$c_j(\mathbf{w}) - p_j \geq 0 \quad j = 1, \ldots, J \tag{4.30}$$

Together, (4.29) and (4.30) state that any good produced in a long-run equilibrium ($q_j > 0$) must yield zero profit, whereas any good with negative profit will not be produced ($q_j = 0$).[19] To (4.29) and (4.30) we add the factor market equilibrium (full employment) conditions:

$$\sum_{j=1}^{J} a_{jh} q_j \leq e_h \quad h = 1, \ldots, H \tag{4.31}$$

where e_h is the national supply of factor h and the a_{jh} are as defined in (4.28). If the price of input h is positive ($w_h > 0$) then (4.31) holds with equality – that is, factor h is fully employed. If $w_h = 0$ then factor h is in excess supply (underemployed).

Finally, multiply (4.29) by q_j and sum over j to state the equality between national income and gross domestic product (GDP) at market prices:

$$\sum_{j=1}^{J} q_j c_j(\mathbf{w}) = \sum_{j=1}^{J} p_j q_j = \mathbf{pq} \tag{4.32}$$

An equivalent statement in terms of factor payments is obtained by multiplying (4.31) by w_h and summing over h:

$$\sum_{j=1}^{J} q_j \sum_{h=1}^{H} a_{jh} w_h = \sum_{j=1}^{J} q_j c_j(\mathbf{w}) = \sum_{h=1}^{H} w_h e_h = \mathbf{we} \tag{4.33}$$

Hence, in equilibrium, GDP at market prices equals the payments to factors (i.e. $\mathbf{pq} = \mathbf{we}$), the latter being GDP at factor cost.

Expressions (4.28), (4.29), (4.30) and (4.31) comprise a J-sector model which can be solved for the input requirements (a_{jh}), input prices (w_h) and outputs (q_j) in terms of the given national factor supplies (e_h) and commodity prices (p_j). When $H = 2$ and $J = 2$, the production equilibrium described above is identical to that of the traditional analysis of this section.

The revenue function

Expression (4.32) gives the revenue an economy receives for a particular configuration of output prices (**p**) and factor supplies (**e**). Another choice of **p** and **e** would generate another value for the economy's revenue. Hence, there exists a revenue function $G(\mathbf{p}, \mathbf{e})$ that records the highest attainable revenue for a given set of output prices and factor supplies:

$$G(\mathbf{p}, \mathbf{e}) = \mathbf{p} \cdot \mathbf{q}(\mathbf{p}, \mathbf{e}) \tag{4.34}$$

where $\mathbf{q}(\mathbf{p}, \mathbf{e})$ denotes the vector of profit maximizing output choices for given output prices and factor supplies.[20] An important property of the revenue function is Hotelling's lemma: if $G(\mathbf{p}, \mathbf{e})$ is differentiable with respect to **p** at the commodity price vector $\mathbf{p}^0$ then the output supply function of good j is given by the partial derivative of the revenue function with respect to the price of commodity j:

$$\frac{\partial G(\mathbf{p}, \mathbf{e})}{\partial p_j} = q_j \quad j = 1, \ldots, J \tag{4.35}$$

From (4.33) we can also write this as:

$$\frac{\partial G(\mathbf{p}, \mathbf{e})}{\partial e_h} = w_h \quad h = 1, \ldots, H \tag{4.36}$$

that is, the equilibrium price of factor h is given as the partial derivative of the revenue function with respect to the supply of factor h.[21]

As an example, consider the maximization of income for an economy producing two goods q_1 and q_2. For given prices p_1 and p_2, national income is then $GDP = p_1 q_1 + p_2 q_2$. Fixing the value of GDP as some level, say $\overline{GDP}$, this equation can be solved to express the combinations q_1 and q_2 that would yield, at the given prices, the income level $\overline{GDP} : q_1 = \overline{GDP}/p_1 - (p_2/p_1)q_2$. As shown in Figure 4.5, this equation defines an "iso-income" line whose intercepts measure real income in units of the good recorded on the particular axis (that is, $\overline{GDP}/p_j, j = 1, 2$) and whose slope is (minus) the relative price of good ($p = p_2/p_1$ in the example).

Given the economy's transformation curve[22] $O_1 A O_2$, the economy's maximal income is obtained by producing the combination of outputs given by point A, where an iso-income line is tangent to the transformation curve. Any other combination of outputs (e.g., point B or C)

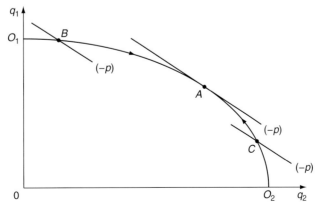

Figure 4.5 National income maximization

would lie on a lower iso-income line of the same slope. Finally, we can verify Hotelling's lemma for good 2:

$$\frac{\partial G(\mathbf{p}, \mathbf{e})}{\partial p_2} = q_2 + p_1(\partial q_1/\partial p_2) + p_2(\partial q_2/\partial p_2) = q_2$$

since $\partial q_1/\partial q_2 = -p_1/p_2$ at point A.

The reciprocity condition

An important implication of the duality between production and cost functions as expressed in (4.35) and (4.36) is the reciprocity condition:

$$\frac{\partial q_j}{\partial e_h} = \frac{\partial w_h}{\partial p_j} \quad j = 1, \ldots, J; \quad h = 1, \ldots, H \tag{4.37}$$

This is established by differentiating (4.35) with respect to p_j and differentiating (4.36) with respect to e_h and noting that:

$$\frac{\partial^2 G}{\partial e_h \partial p_j} = \frac{\partial^2 G}{\partial p_j \partial e_h}$$

In words, (4.37) says that the effect of a change in the supply of factor h on the production of good j is equal in magnitude to the effect of a change in the price of good j on the price of factor h (w_h). The left-hand side of (4.37) derives from the Rybczynski theorem, whereas the right-hand side derives from the Stolper-Samuelson theorem. The reciprocity condition has important empirical significance since it means that we do not need to estimate the effect of factor supply changes and price changes separately: we can instead infer one from the other.

The factor price frontier

Assume two goods and two factors (capital and labor) and let the price of good 1 be the numeraire. The zero profit conditions in this case are:

$$p = a_{2L}w + a_{2K}r \tag{4.38}$$
$$1 = a_{1L}w + a_{1K}r \tag{4.39}$$

where a_{jh} is the equilibrium requirement of factor h per unit of output j and factor prices w and r are measured in units of good 1.[23] Solving (4.38) and (4.39) individually for w, and noting that $a_{jK}/a_{jL} = k_j(\omega)$, we obtain:

$$w = \frac{1}{a_{2L}}p - k_2(\omega)r \tag{4.40}$$

$$w = \frac{1}{a_{1L}} - k_1(\omega)r \tag{4.41}$$

Figure 4.6 depicts (4.40) and (4.41) as the iso-price curves p and 1, respectively. The absolute value of the slope of each curve at a particular combination of w and r equals the industry's capital–labor ratio. By (4.14), each curve is convex to the origin since the capital–labor ratio is an increasing function of the wage–rental ratio. The intersection of the two curves (point A) determines the economy's equilibrium wage ($\bar{w}$) and rental rate ($\bar{r}$) consistent with zero profits

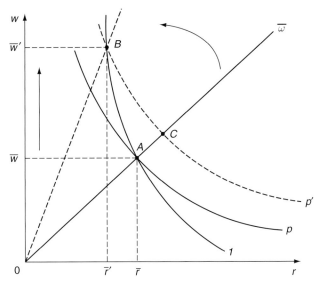

Figure 4.6 Factor price frontiers

in both industries. That the iso-price curves intersect only once is due to the assumption of no factor intensity reversals.

The Stolper-Samuelson theorem again

Using (4.40) and (4.41), it is a simple matter to determine the effect of a change in commodity prices on factor prices. Consider Figure 4.6 and assume the relative price of good 2 increases from p to p'. This price increase shifts the iso-price curve from p to p' and establishes a new zero profit equilibrium at point B. Hence, $\overline{w}$ rises to $\overline{w}'$ and $\overline{r}$ falls to $\overline{r}'$. The resulting rise in the wage–rental ratio induces both industries to substitute capital for labor as reflected by the steeper slope of each curve at point B relative to point A.

Since good 1 is the numeraire and p has risen, capital's real return has fallen in terms of both goods whereas labor's real return has risen in terms of good 1. To determine labor's return in terms of good 2, note that any point along the line $O\overline{\omega}$ corresponds to the increase in factor rewards proportional to an increase in p. For example, point C is consistent with a constant ratio of w (or r) to p'. Since point B lies above the ray $O\overline{\omega}$, the wage has thus also increased relative to the price of good 2. Finally, Figure 4.6 indicates that there is a "magnification effect" associated with the relative change in output price and the relative change in factor prices, namely:

$$\hat{w} > \hat{p} > 0 > \hat{r}$$

This relationship can be derived analytically using (4.38) and (4.39) with p replaced by p'.

Simulation analysis

As with factor supply changes, the effect of an output price change can be illustrated using the computer model of Problem 4.5. In this regard, the first column of Table 4.2 reproduces the base solution of the model already discussed in Table 4.1. The second column shows the disturbed solution of factor prices, factor employment and outputs due to a 10 percent increase in the price of good 2. As expected, a rise in the price of good 2 shifts production from the

Table 4.2 General equilibrium of a 10 percent increase in the price of good 2

Variable	Base solution	10% increase in p
Outputs		
Industry 1 (q_1)	0.956	0.515
Industry 2 (q_2)	0.429	0.995
Factor prices		
Rental rate	0.697	0.576
Wage rate	0.359	0.434
Ratio (w/r)	0.515	0.753
Factor inputs		
Capital–labor ratio		
Industry 1 (k_1)	0.515	0.753
Industry 2 (k_2)	0.171	0.251
Labor employed in		
Industry 1 (L_1)	1.333	0.594
Industry 2 (L_2)	0.667	1.406
Capital employed in		
Industry 1 (K_1)	0.686	0.447
Industry 2 (K_2)	0.114	0.353

capital-intensive industry 1 to the labor-intensive industry 2. Consistent with the Stolper-Samuelson theorem, this price increase raises the wage rate and lowers the rental rate, and the resulting rise in the relative wage leads each industry to increase its use of capital relative to labor.

4.2 Specification of demand

Traditional analysis

With identical preferences, utility maximization by consumers results in demand functions that depend on prices and national income: $d_j = d_j(Y, \mathbf{p})$, where national income Y is measured in units of good 1. If these optimal demands are substituted back into the utility function we obtain the indirect utility function, $V(Y, \mathbf{p}) = U(d_1(Y, \mathbf{p}), d_2(Y, \mathbf{p}))$. The indirect utility function records the maximum utility attainable for a particular configuration of prices $\mathbf{p}$ and national income Y. A useful property of the indirect utility function is Roy's identity:

$$d_j(Y, \mathbf{p}) = -\frac{\partial V(Y, \mathbf{p})/\partial p_j}{\partial V(Y, \mathbf{p})/\partial Y} \quad j = 1, \dots, J \tag{4.42}$$

which establishes that the ordinary demand function for good j can be derived from the indirect utility function as the ratio of partial derivatives with respect to the price of good j and income, respectively.

Duality

Just as duality between output maximization and cost minimization in production gives rise to the GDP or revenue function, duality between utility maximization and expenditure minimization gives rise to the spending (expenditure) function:

$$S(\mathbf{p}, \bar{u}) = \min_{\mathbf{d}} \left\{ \mathbf{p} \cdot \mathbf{d} = \sum_{j=1}^{J} p_j d_j : u(\mathbf{d}) \geq \bar{u}, \mathbf{d} \geq 0 \right\} \tag{4.43}$$

where $\bar{u}$ denotes a given level of utility and $\mathbf{d}$ is the vector of quantities demanded. The expenditure function records, for given prices $\mathbf{p}$, the minimum expenditure (cost) necessary to obtain utility level $\bar{u}$. By analogy to Shephard's lemma, differentiation of (4.43) with respect to the price of good j yields the compensated (Hicksian) demand functions:

$$\frac{\partial S(\mathbf{p}, \bar{u})}{\partial p_j} = h_j(\mathbf{p}, \bar{u}) \quad j = 1, \ldots, J \tag{4.44}$$

To relate these compensated demand functions to the ordinary demand functions $(d_j(\mathbf{p}, Y))$ we assume that consumers spend all of their money income in achieving maximum utility so that $Y = S(\mathbf{p}, \bar{u})$. Given this, replace Y in $d_j(\mathbf{p}, Y)$ to express d_j as a function of prices and the utility level $\bar{u}$:

$$h_j(\mathbf{p}, \bar{u}) = d_j(\mathbf{p}, S(\mathbf{p}, \bar{u})) \tag{4.45}$$

Alternatively, solve $Y = S(\mathbf{p}, \bar{u})$ for the level of utility $\bar{u}$ in terms of prices and income, that is, $\bar{u} = V(Y, \mathbf{p})$ where V is the indirect utility function, and then substitute this into $h_j(\cdot)$ to express it as a function of prices and income:

$$h_j(\mathbf{p}, V(\mathbf{p}, Y)) = d_j(\mathbf{p}, Y) \tag{4.46}$$

The effect of a price change on demand can be examined by differentiating (4.45) with respect to p_i:

$$\frac{\partial d_j}{\partial p_i} = \frac{\partial h_j}{\partial p_i} - \frac{\partial d_j}{\partial S} \frac{\partial S}{\partial p_i} \tag{4.47}$$

This states the known result that the effect of a price change on demand is composed of a substitution effect $\partial h_j/\partial p_i$ and a real income effect $(-\partial d_j/\partial S)(\partial S/\partial p_i)$.

Homothetic preferences

If the utility function is assumed to be homothetic or, more specifically, linear homogeneous[24] the spending function has the simple form $S(\mathbf{p}, \bar{u}) = \bar{u} \, s(\mathbf{p})$ where $s(\mathbf{p}) = S(\mathbf{p}, 1)$ is the "unit utility" spending function. Since $\bar{u} = V(\mathbf{p}, Y)$, the indirect utility function takes the special form:

$$V(Y, \mathbf{p}) = S(\mathbf{p}, \bar{u})/s(\mathbf{p}) = Y/s(\mathbf{p}) \tag{4.48}$$

In addition, the compensated demand functions take the form:

$$\frac{\partial S(\mathbf{p}, \bar{u})}{\partial p_j} = \bar{u} \frac{\partial s(\mathbf{p})}{\partial p_j} \tag{4.49}$$

whereas the ordinary demand functions, by Roy's identity, become:

$$d_j(\mathbf{p}, Y) = Y\frac{\partial s(\mathbf{p})/\partial p_j}{s(\mathbf{p})} = Y\zeta(\mathbf{p}) \tag{4.50}$$

where $\zeta(p)$ is some function of relative output prices. A primary implication of homothetic preferences is that the ratio of demands $d_j(\mathbf{p}, Y)/d_i(\mathbf{p}, Y)$ is independent of the level of income or utility. Equivalently, the share of total expenditure spent on any good $(d_j(\mathbf{p}, Y)/Y = \zeta(\mathbf{p}))$ only depends on relative prices.

4.3 Autarky and international equilibria

The preceding sections have presented the supply and demand elements of the competitive general equilibrium model underlying the H-O-S model. This section combines these elements to demonstrate first the determination of a country's autarky prices and then the determination of the post-trade (world) equilibrium prices. We then discuss the stability of the world equilibrium.

Autarky price determination

Figures 4.7 and 4.8 portray the general equilibrium of an economy in autarky, a situation where all commodities are produced and consumed in equilibrium. Figure 4.7 considers the question using the traditional approach, Figure 4.8 using duality.

Figure 4.7 superimposes a social indifference map on the transformation curve O_1AO_2. Autarkic equilibrium is located where the economy attains the highest possible indifference curve given its production possibilities – that is, point A. At this point, the economy produces and consumes q_1^a units of good 1 and q_2^a units of good 2, the equilibrium being achieved at price p_a. Tangency of O_1AO_2 to the indifference curve u_a implies the equality between the autarkic relative price, the rate of transformation in production and the rate of substitution in consumption.

Figure 4.8 depicts the autarkic equilibrium employing the revenue function (4.34) and the expenditure function (4.43). National revenue and expenditure are measured along the vertical axis. Price p_j is measured along the horizontal axis. Given the equilibrium values for all other prices, the expenditure function $S(p_1, \ldots, p_j, \ldots, p_J : u_a)$ gives for each value of

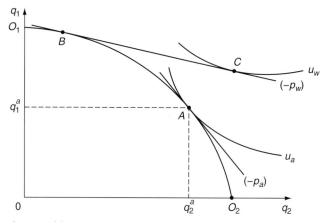

Figure 4.7 Autarkic equilibrium and community indifference curve

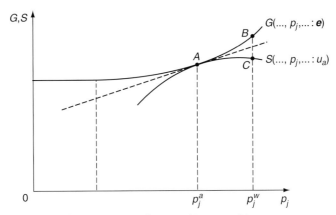

Figure 4.8 Autarkic equilibrium, national expenditure and income

p_j the expenditure necessary to obtain the same autarkic utility u_a. The revenue function $G(p_1, \ldots, p_j, \ldots, p_J : \mathbf{e})$ records the increase in national income as the price of good j rises (see Note 21). The slopes of $G(\,.\,)$ and $S(\,.\,)$ are q_j and h_j respectively, by (4.35) and (4.44). At point A, $h_j = q_j$, so that the autarkic equilibrium price is p_j^a.

After having determined the equilibrium of an isolated economy, the next step is to consider international trade. The opening of international trade implies the introduction of foreign consumers and producers, and therefore a world price ratio that, in general, will be different from the one that prevails under autarky. The next section considers the international equilibrium and extends the concepts first introduced in Section 3.2.

World price determination

Assuming there are only two goods, Figure 4.9 illustrates both the demand and supply functions for good 2 and the associated excess demand function for good 2. The excess demand function is the difference between the demand and supply of good 2 at alternative values of $p = p_2/p_1$.[25] By definition, excess demand is zero at the autarky price p_a. Below p_a, excess demand is positive and corresponds to the country's import demand: $m_2 = d_2(p) - q_2(p)$. Above p_a, there is an excess supply (negative excess demand) of good 2; this corresponds to

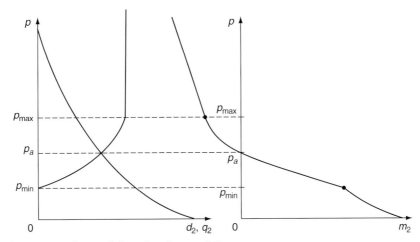

Figure 4.9 Excess demand function for good 2

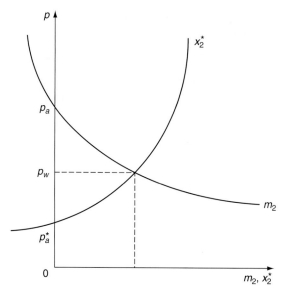

Figure 4.10 World price determination

the country's export supply $(-m_2 \equiv x_2(p) = q_2(p) - d_2(p))$. Since limited factor supplies constrain the supply of good 2, the excess demand function is not smooth everywhere and there are two points of non-differentiability: p_{min} and p_{max}. Assuming good 2 is capital-intensive, the economy produces only good 1 for $p \leq p_{min}$ and produces only good 2 for $p \geq p_{max}$.

In similar fashion, the foreign country's autarky price p_a^* and excess demand function can be derived from its underlying demand and supply functions. Assuming $p_a > p_a^*$, Figure 4.10 combines the excess demand functions of each country in one graph. Given these, trade will result in the equilibrium world price p_w as determined by the point of intersection between the home country's import demand and the foreign country's export supply. Note that p_w equates, by definition, the world demand and world supply of good 2 since the equality of excess demands at p_w can also be written as $d_2(p_w) + d_2^*(p_w) = q_2(p_w) + q_2^*(p_w)$. By Walras's Law, the price $1/p_w$ also clears the world market for good 1.[26]

The decline in the relative price of good 2 from p_a to p_w is illustrated in Figure 4.7 as a movement of the domestic production point from A to B and of the domestic consumption point from A to C. Point C is better than point A as it lies on a higher indifference curve. This shows the gains from trade. Likewise, gains from trade arise in Figure 4.8 but stem from the curvature of $G(\,.\,)$ and $S(\,.\,)$. A world price of p_j^w, for example, would provide, *ceteris paribus*, a gain from trade equivalent to the distance BC. This is obtained since $G(\,.\,) > S(\,.\,)$ for any price greater than p_j^a.

Import demand and market stability

A key point to be learned from Figure 4.10 is that the price elasticities of the import demand and export supply functions derive from the properties of the underlying domestic demands and supplies. Since these demand and supply functions have been derived in a general equilibrium setting, the elasticities associated with these functions are also general equilibrium, not partial equilibrium.[27] Below we break the import and export price elasticities down into their fundamental components and show that the values of these elasticities are crucial for determining the stability of the international equilibrium.

Totally differentiating the expression for the import demand for good 2, that is, $m_2 = d_2(p, Y) - q_2(p)$ and nothing that $S = Y$ gives:

$$dm_2 = \frac{\partial d_2}{\partial p}dp + \frac{\partial d_2}{\partial S}\frac{\partial Y}{\partial p}dp - \frac{\partial q_2}{\partial p}dp \qquad (4.51)$$

Using (4.47) we can replace $\partial d_2/\partial p$ in (4.51) to get:

$$dm_2 = \left[\frac{\partial h_2}{\partial p} - \frac{\partial q_2}{\partial p}\right]dp - \frac{\partial d_2}{\partial S}\left[\frac{\partial S}{\partial p} - \frac{\partial Y}{\partial p}\right]dp \qquad (4.52)$$

Dividing (4.52) by m_2 and noting that

$$\left(\frac{\partial S}{\partial p} - \frac{\partial Y}{\partial p}\right) = (d_2 - q_2) = m_2$$

(4.52) can be written:

$$\hat{m}_2 = \left[\frac{p}{m_2}\frac{\partial h_2}{\partial p} - \frac{p}{m_2}\frac{\partial q_2}{\partial p} - p\frac{\partial d_2}{\partial S}\right]\hat{p} \qquad (4.53)$$

where "^" denotes the relative change in a variable (e.g., $\hat{p} = dp/p$). Finally, divide both sides of (4.53) by $\hat{p}$ to obtain the expression for the price elasticity of import demand ($e = -\hat{m}_2/\hat{p}$):

$$e = e_1 + e_2 + e_3 \qquad (4.54)$$

where $e_1 = -(p/m_2)(\partial h_2/\partial p)$ is the compensated price elasticity, $e_2 = (p/m_2)(\partial q_2/\partial p)$ is the supply elasticity and $e_3 = p(\partial d_2/\partial S)$ is the marginal propensity to consume good 2 (that is, the fraction of an increase in expenditure that is spent on importables). Note that $0 < e_3 < 1$ for normal goods, $e_3 > 1$ if good 1 is inferior and $e_3 < 0$ if good 2 is inferior. All elasticities are defined as positive.[28]

Market stability

Stability of the international equilibrium refers to the ability of the system to return to its original equilibrium after a disturbance. For example, suppose p were to fall below its equilibrium value. The market for good 2 is then stable if this price decline causes home imports of good 2 to rise relative to foreign exports of good 2, thereby creating a world excess demand for good 2, that is, $(\hat{x}_2^* - \hat{m}_2)/\hat{p} > 0$. From the definition of the trade elasticities (see also Problem 4.10), the world excess demand for good 2 will rise as p falls if $e - (-f^*) = e + f^* > 0$. Since $f^* = e^* - 1$ the condition for a fall (rise) in p to generate a world excess demand (supply) for good 2 becomes:

$$e + e^* > 1 \qquad (4.55)$$

This condition, known as the Marshall-Lerner condition, states that the trade equilibrium will be stable if the sum of the price elasticities of domestic and foreign import demand exceeds unity.

Given the importance of market stability, an important empirical question is whether the values of actual price elasticities of import demand satisfy the Marshall-Lerner condition. Table 4.3 reports home and foreign import price elasticity estimates for a number of countries.

Table 4.3 Estimated price elasticities of import demand and the Marshall-Lerner condition[a]

Country	Home (e) (1)	Foreign (e*) (2)	Sum[c] (e+e*) (3)
Belgium	–	1.57[b]	–
Canada	1.02	0.83	1.85 (0.20)
France	–	1.33[b]	–
Germany	0.60	0.66	1.26 (0.20)
Italy	–	3.29[b]	–
Japan	0.93	0.93	1.86 (0.33)
Netherlands	–	2.73[b]	–
UK	0.47	0.44	0.91 (0.21)
USA	0.92	0.99	1.91 (0.42)
Other industrial	0.49	0.83	1.32 (0.18)
Developing countries	0.81	0.63	1.44 (0.32)
OPEC	1.14	0.57	1.71 (0.28)

[a] Taken from Marquez (1990), except where indicated.
[b] Taken from Goldstein and Khan (1978).
[c] Standard error in parentheses.

The import price elasticities (e and e^*) are correctly signed and range between 0.44 and 2.73. Where computable (column (3)), the hypothesis that the Marshall-Lerner condition fails to hold can be rejected for all countries except the United Kingdom (UK) on the basis of point estimates. It is important to note that estimates of Table 4.3 are obtained using standard single-equation and simultaneous equation techniques. However, recent developments in econometrics reveal that most data used in this type of estimation are non-stationary, in which case inferences might not be valid. Bahmani-Oskooee and Niroomand (1998) use cointegration techniques to yield non-spurious results. In a sample of 30 countries, they show that the Marshall-Lerner condition is satisfied for most of them and that, as in previous studies, the condition is not satisfied for the UK.

4.4 The factor abundance theorems

We now demonstrate the two central theorems of the factor abundance theory: the H-O theorem for the pattern of trade and the factor price equalization (FPE) theorem for the effect of trade on factor prices. These theorems are demonstrated in terms of the "simple" two-factor, two-good H-O-S model. The extension of these theorems to arbitrary numbers of goods and factors is discussed in Chapter 7. The following summarizes the assumptions used to establish these theorems:

(1) Perfect competition prevails in both commodity and factor markets.
(2) Factors of production are homogeneous in quality and costlessly mobile between industries within a country.

(3) The production function for each good is of the neoclassical type and is, in particular, homogeneous of degree one.

(4) Production functions differ between industries.

(5) Consumers have identical and homothetic preferences.

(6) There are no taxes, costs of transport, or other impediments to the *domestic* movement of goods.

(7) There are two countries, two goods and two factors of production.

(8) There are no factor intensity reversals.

(9) Factors of production are immobile between countries and inelastically supplied within each country.

(10) The production function for each good is identical across countries.

(11) There are no taxes, costs of transport or other impediments to the *international* movement of goods.

(12) Consumer preferences are identical across countries.

In listing these assumptions we have tried to group them into those representing the competitive general equilibrium model (assumptions (1) to (6)) and those representing the H-O-S extensions of the model (assumptions (7) to (12)) applied to an international context.

Comparative advantage and trade

The factor abundance theorem concerning the basis of comparative advantage and hence the pattern of trade between two countries is the Heckscher-Ohlin (H-O) theorem:

Proposition 4.3 (Heckscher-Ohlin): Given assumptions (1) to (12), a country will have a comparative advantage in, and therefore export, the good that uses its relatively abundant factor intensively in production.

To demonstrate this theorem we must define the concept of factor abundance, the concept of factor intensity having been previously defined. Given two factors – capital and labor – the home economy is defined to be abundant in capital compared with labor if either

$$k \equiv \frac{K}{L} > \frac{K^*}{L^*} \equiv k^*$$

or

$$\omega_a > \omega_a^*$$

where an asterisk denotes foreign (rest of world) variables. The first definition is the *physical* definition of abundance since it compares the relative quantities of factors between countries. The second is the *price* definition of abundance since it compares the *autarky* relative factor prices between countries. Like the definition of factor intensity, these definitions of factor abundance involve a relative comparison: that is, what matters is the relative size of K/L and K^*/L^*, of ω_a and ω_a^*, not the numerical value of each ratio.

To illustrate the H-O theorem we use an augmented Harrod-Johnson diagram (Viaene, 1993) as shown in Figure 4.11. This diagram combines Figures 4.3, 4.4 and 4.10, with the latter figure shown in the third quadrant. The first quadrant of Figure 4.11 is drawn assuming industry 1 is capital-intensive and that the home country is capital-abundant on both definitions – that is, $k > k^*$ and $\omega_a > \omega_a^*$.

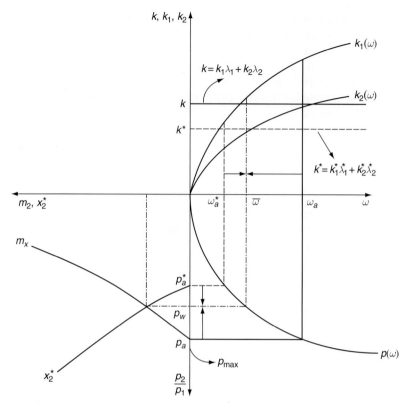

Figure 4.11 The augmented Harrod-Johnson diagram

Closer inspection of Figure 4.11 raises the following question: if $k > k^*$ how can we verify that indeed $\omega_a > \omega_a^*$? Or in Ohlin's words (Ohlin, 1933, 13) "in what way [do] differences in equipment come to be expressed in differences in money costs and prices?" For example, if consumers in the home country have a strong bias for the capital-intensive good 1 then ω_a may be less than ω_a^*, despite the fact that the home country is physically capital-abundant. The assumption that preferences are identical and homothetic across countries (assumptions (5) and (12)) prevents such demand biases and hence ensures a one-to-one correspondence between the physical and price definitions of factor abundance.

Since industry technologies are identical across countries (assumption (10)), the relationships shown in both the first and fourth quadrants of Figure 4.11 apply to both countries. Moreover, since consumers everywhere have the same tastes, the home country's relative capital abundance will be reflected in a higher autarky wage–rental ratio: $\omega_a > \omega_a^*$. The one-to-one correspondence between factor prices and output prices in turn implies that the home country's autarky price ratio exceeds that of the foreign country (that is, $p_a > p_a^*$). Hence, the capital-abundant country has the comparative advantage in the capital-intensive good and, with trade, the home country will export good 1.

Empirical link: The Leontief paradox

The first empirical test of the H-O theorem was conducted by Leontief (1954). Leontief conjectured that if the United States (US) is capital-abundant and the H-O theory is true, then capital per worker embodied in US exports should exceed the capital per worker embodied in US imports.[29] Before discussing Leontief's analysis in detail, we must first consider the meaning of "embodied factor services."

The "embodied services" of a factor refer to the amount of a factor's services used up in producing a given amount of some good. For example, the total amount of labor embodied in the production of an economy's entire set of outputs is, with full employment, equal to the economy's total labor supply. Similarly, the services of factor h embodied in, for example, a country's exports is computed by multiplying the *total* requirement of factor h needed to produce a unit of good j (z_{hj}) times the amount of good j that is exported (x_j) and then summing the results over all exported goods:

$$\sum_{j=1}^{J} x_j z_{hj} = \text{services of factor } h \text{ embodied in exports}$$

The *total* unit factor input requirements z_{hj} differ from the *direct* unit factor input requirements a_{hj} (defined previously) in that they take into account the fact that an industry uses both primary factors and intermediate goods to produce a unit of output. That is, the total input requirement z_{hj} measures the amount of factor h required both directly (in industry j) and indirectly (via the production of intermediate goods purchased by industry j) to produce a unit of good j.

Total factor input requirements are calculated from the direct unit factor input requirements and an input–output (I-O) matrix which characterizes the interdependence between industries in an economy. The (i, j) entry in an I-O matrix records the amount of sector i's output purchased by sector j for the purpose of producing sector j's output. These purchases by sector j from sector i are expressed per unit of sector j's gross output. Hence, each entry in the I-O matrix is a "unit intermediate goods requirement." If b_{ij} denotes these unit intermediate goods requirements then the equilibrium value added (final demand) in industry j (d_j) can be written as:

$$d_j = q_j - \sum_{i=1}^{J} q_i b_{ij} \quad j = 1, \dots, J \tag{4.56}$$

Stacking expressions (4.56) into one vector yields the vector of final demands as:

$$\mathbf{d} = \mathbf{q} - \mathbf{Bq} \equiv (\mathbf{I} - \mathbf{B})\mathbf{q} \tag{4.57}$$

where $\mathbf{d}$ is the $J \times 1$ vector of final demands, $\mathbf{q}$ is the $J \times 1$ vector of gross outputs, $\mathbf{B}$ is the $J \times J$ input–output matrix of unit intermediate good requirements and $\mathbf{I}$ is the $J \times J$ identity matrix. Since the matrix $(\mathbf{I} - \mathbf{B})$ is square, it can be inverted to solve (4.57) for the levels of gross outputs required to produce the vector of equilibrium final demands:

$$\mathbf{q} = (\mathbf{I} - \mathbf{B})^{-1} \mathbf{d} \tag{4.58}$$

To calculate the amount of each primary factor absorbed in producing the equilibrium final demands $\mathbf{d}$, let $\mathbf{A}$ denote the $H \times J$ matrix of equilibrium (direct) unit factor input requirements (a_{hj}). Pre-multiplying both sides of (4.58) by $\mathbf{A}$ gives:

$$\mathbf{Aq} = \mathbf{Zd} \tag{4.59}$$

where $\mathbf{Z} = \mathbf{A}(\mathbf{I} - \mathbf{B})^{-1}$ is the $H \times J$ matrix of total (direct *plus* indirect) primary input requirements. With full employment, $\mathbf{Aq} = \mathbf{e}$, where $\mathbf{e}$ is the $H \times 1$ vector of national factor supplies. Hence (4.59) can also be written:

$$\mathbf{e} = \mathbf{Zd} \tag{4.60}$$

which demonstrates that the elements of the matrix $\mathbf{Z}$ are indeed the *total* factor input requirements per unit of final demand.

Assuming the total input requirements to be fixed by the conditions of technology, Leontief imagined a scenario in which US exports and imports were reduced by $1 million, with the reduction distributed across industries in proportion to their initial share in total US exports or total US imports.[30] As a consequence of these reductions, domestic production would rise in order to replace the lost imports and it would fall due to the export reduction. By computing the changes in factor employment associated with these changes in domestic production one could then infer the net change in factor employment. Leontief conjectured that, if the US is capital-abundant and the H-O theory is true, the ratio of capital to labor released due to the export decline will exceed the ratio of capital to labor absorbed in replacing the lost imports with domestic production.

If $\mathbf{S}_x$ and $\mathbf{S}_m$ denote the vectors of commodity export and import shares respectively, Leontief's calculation of the changes in labor and capital employment due to a $1 million change in exports and imports can be expressed as:

$$\Delta L_x = -\mathbf{z}_L \mathbf{S}_x \Delta x, \, \Delta L_m = -\mathbf{z}_L \mathbf{S}_m \Delta m \tag{4.61}$$

$$\Delta K_x = -\mathbf{z}_K \mathbf{S}_x \Delta x, \, \Delta K_m = -\mathbf{z}_K \mathbf{S}_m \Delta m \tag{4.62}$$

where $\mathbf{z}_L$ and $\mathbf{z}_K$ are the $1 \times J$ vectors of total labor and total capital requirements per unit of final demand and the scalars Δx and Δm are, by assumption, equal to (minus) $1 million. Given (4.61) and (4.62), Leontief's hypothesis was that the following ratio should exceed one:[31]

$$\gamma = \frac{\Delta K_x / \Delta L_x}{\Delta K_m / \Delta L_m} \tag{4.63}$$

Table 4.4 reports Leontief's calculations, which used 1947 data on US trade and the US input–output matrix.

These numbers indicate, for example, that the expansion of US production required to replace $1 million of US imports would require an additional $3.09 million in capital services (investment) and an additional 170,004 man-years of labor. Since total input requirements are assumed to be fixed, this implies that, on average, the capital–labor ratio across US import-competing industries is about 18.2. In contrast, the average capital–labor ratio in US export industries is around 14. Computing (4.63) the average capital–labor ratio in US import-competing industries is about 30 percent higher than the average capital–labor ratio in US export industries, a finding contrary to the H-O theorem.

Leontief's "paradoxical" result generated considerable debate as to its causes, and it is fair to say that for some 25 years after Leontief's findings most empirical work directly or indirectly attempted to explain his result. However, one question never addressed by the literature

Table 4.4 Capital and labor services embodied in 1947 US exports and imports replacements

Variable	Exports	Imports
Capital ($, 1947 prices)	2 550 780	3 091 339
Labor (man-years)	182 313	170 004
Capital–labor ratio	13.99	18.18

was whether γ accurately reveals a country's abundant factor. That is, if a country is capital-abundant, does the H-O theory imply that γ must exceed unity? Chapter 7 addresses this question in detail and provides a negative answer.

Trade and factor prices

The second factor abundance theorem concerns the effect of trade on factor price differences between countries:

Proposition 4.4 (factor price equalization): Given assumptions (1) to (12), trade in goods will cause the absolute and relative prices of factors between countries to move toward equality. Complete equalization will be achieved if both countries continue to produce both goods in the trading equilibrium.

Consider first the case of relative factor prices. As Figure 4.11 shows, trade results in the single world price p_w. In moving from autarky to the trade equilibrium, the change in relative output prices causes each country's export industry to expand and its import-competing industry to contract. These shifts in production imply corresponding changes in factor demands and factor prices within each country.

Consider the home country. With the opening of trade, production of good 1 expands, production of good 2 contracts, and capital and labor are released from industry 2 to be re-employed in industry 1. However, since industry 2 is labor-intensive, the amount of labor per unit of capital released from industry 2 exceeds that which the capital-intensive industry 1 can absorb at the autarky wage and rental rate. Hence, the initial effect of trade on the home country's factor markets is to induce an excess supply of labor or, equivalently, an excess demand for capital, at the home country's autarky factor prices. Restoration of factor market equilibrium therefore requires the wage–rental ratio (ω) to fall. Of course, the same effects are occurring in the foreign country, but in the opposite direction. In particular, an excess supply of capital (excess demand for labor) arises as industry 2 expands and industry 1 contracts. Hence, ω^* must rise in order to restore factor market equilibrium in the foreign country.

The restoration of factor market equilibrium in each country therefore implies that, relative to their autarky values, ω^* will rise and ω will fall until equality is reached at $\bar{\omega}$ (which corresponds to p_w). Note that complete equality can occur only if neither country is completely specialized in production at the equilibrium world price p_w. One rule of thumb for the likelihood of equality is that the difference in the countries' relative factor supplies should not be too great.

The equalization of absolute factor prices is easily demonstrated using duality relationships. Under free trade both countries face the same prices and hence, given identical production functions, the iso-price curves (denoted $p = p_w$ and 1) in Figure 4.6 are the same for each country. As such, the factor prices given at the point of intersection ($\bar{w}$ and $\bar{r}$) of these iso-price curves are also identical between countries.

Data link

The proposition that trade in goods can equalize the prices of internationally immobile factors is an extremely powerful prediction. Most would agree that, in reality, absolute factor prices are not equalized between countries. However, such an interpretation of the data is a great misrepresentation of the power of the FPE proposition. A more useful interpretation is that increased trade can be expected to lower the reward to factors intensive in sectors that compete with imports and to raise the reward to factors intensive in export sectors. That is, the FPE is a statement about a convergence of factor rewards over time. Complete convergence is not expected since the assumptions under which equality is expected are absent in the real

Table 4.5 Convergence of nominal levels of compensation per hour across the
euro area

Sector	1993	2004
Total economy	0.38	0.31
Agriculture	0.46	0.45
Industry (excl. construction)	0.42	0.35
Construction	0.39	0.35
Trade and transport	0.41	0.32
Financial intermediation	0.40	0.31
Other services	0.35	0.30

Notes: (a) For each year hourly compensations in any country and/or sector
are relative to that of the euro area average (set to 100). Euro area in
calculations includes the initial 12: Austria, Belgium, Finland, France,
Germany, Greece, Ireland, Italy, Luxembourg, Netherlands, Portugal,
Spain; (b) Entries are coefficients of variation (standard deviation over the
sample mean).
Source: Andersson *et al.* (2008). This table is available from the European Central
Bank website, www.ecb-europa.eu.

world. The prevalent use of trade restrictions and, as will be made clearer in later chapters,
institutional constraints also hamper the functioning of the market mechanism. Given the
facts of the world, the idea of testing the hypothesis of complete factor price equalization
is absurd; this strong form of the FPE theorem can simply be rejected without consulting
the data.

Consider, then, what evidence there is in favor of the weaker hypothesis that trade tends
to move factor prices toward equality. Table 4.5 compares nominal levels of hourly wages
across the euro area (composed of the initial 12 countries) for each economy as a whole as
well as their major sectors in 1993 and 2004 (Andersson *et al.*, 2008). For each year an average
nominal hourly compensation has been computed for all 12 countries and set to 100. Raw
wage data in each country are therefore relative to those of the euro area. In 2004 for example, the maximum observation is 135 for Belgium and Luxembourg, implying that the hourly
compensation in these two countries is 35 percent higher than the average in the euro area.
In contrast, the lowest observation is 44 for Portugal, implying a substantially lower wage
level. Using these raw data, Table 4.5 reports the coefficient of variation computed over the
set of 12 countries, for each economy as a whole and for six sectors. A standard deviation relative to mean earnings moving closer to zero reflects a movement toward wage equalization
across countries. Complete equalization would imply a mean of 100, a zero standard deviation
and a zero coefficient of variation.

Table 4.5 indicates some tendency towards an equalization of labor's earnings in that, over
time, the standard deviations move closer to zero. The sectoral breakdown reveals that standard deviations decline more in service sectors such as financial intermediation but less so
in sectors such as agriculture and construction. Although both statistics (means and standard deviation) have fluctuated over time, this provides evidence of a movement toward wage
equalization in the course of economic integration and increased trade within the European
Monetary Union.

To conclude this section we note that hourly wage dispersion in the euro area is still
around 30–40 percent higher than that observed across US states. At the same time, Faber

and Stokman (2009) found that over the last 40 to 50 years there has been strong evidence of price level convergence in Europe towards levels that have been observed in the US for a long time. As the cost of capital is almost equal across countries of the euro area, these observations reveal remaining cross-country differences in labor productivity and differences in institutional frameworks.

4.5 Concluding remarks

This chapter has presented the elements of the competitive general equilibrium model underlying the factor abundance theory. Denoted as the H-O-S model, it is used to study the determinants of comparative advantage and the effect of trade upon factor rewards and the distribution of income. This chapter has emphasized relative factor supplies and their role in determining factor prices, production costs and autarky prices. The following summarizes key conclusions[32] about the real-world phenomena the H-O-S model helps us to understand.

(1) Countries should export those goods whose production makes relatively intensive use of their relatively abundant factors.

(2) Trade (and gains from trade) should be greatest between countries with the greatest differences in economic structure. If the ratios of resources were the same in all countries then there would be no trade.

(3) Trade should cause countries to specialize in production. The production characteristics of the goods a country exports should be distinctly different from those of the goods it imports.

(4) Factor prices between countries should become more equal as trade increases between those countries and also the more similar are the country's relative factor supplies.

(5) Domestic interest groups lobbying for changes in the terms of trade should be defined on the basis of their function in the production process (e.g., laborers, capitalists and land-owners) rather than on the basis of the identity of the industries where they are employed.

Chapters 5–7 will judge the H-O-S model's prediction on the basis of its empirical relevance. As the above implications derive from a set of assumptions of a very close texture, several assumptions will be first relaxed and looked at both theoretically and empirically.

Problems

4.1 Show that at point e_1 in Figure 4.2 the marginal product of capital and labor are *1/OA* and *1/OB*, respectively. Extend this analysis to show that at point e_1 the marginal rate of substitution of labor for capital (dK_j/dL_j) equals the ratio of labor's marginal product to capital's marginal product.

4.2 Given Equation (4.13), use Figure 4.1 to show that if $k_1 = OA$ then $\omega = CO$. Also, verify graphically that a rise in w/r raises the cost-minimizing capital–labor ratio of each industry.

4.3 Show that Equation (4.14) is related to the elasticity of substitution of capital for labor and verify that the relationship is positive.

4.4 Verify that if $\omega < \omega_{min}$ or $\omega > \omega_{max}$ some resource must be unemployed.

4.5 Let production in each sector be described by the following Cobb-Douglas functions: $q_1 = K_1^\alpha L_1^{1-\alpha}$ and $q_2 = K_2^\beta L_2^{1-\beta}$. (a) Derive relationship (4.15) and its inverse – that is, the relationship between the industry capital–labor ratio and relative factor prices. Does the possibility for factor intensity reversals exist? (b) Assume the following values for the parameters and exogenous variables of the model: $\alpha = 0.5, \beta = 0.25, p = 0.743, K = 0.8$ and $L = 2$. Using the production model described so far, construct a computer program to solve for the level of all endogenous variables $\{q_j, k_j, \lambda_j, w, r\}$.

4.6 The transformation curve in Figure 4.5 is drawn strictly concave with respect to the origin. Show that this is due to the assumption of constant returns to scale, to the difference in industry factor intensities and to the assumption of competitive markets.

4.7 Demonstrate that if an economy produces at a point like B or C in Figure 4.5, market clearing via price adjustment would bring the economy back to equilibrium at point A. How important is the concavity assumption of the transformation curve for this result?

4.8 Assume that the utility function is of the Cobb-Douglas type $U = d_1^\gamma d_2^{1-\gamma}$ with $\gamma = 0.5$. Solve the computable model of Problem 4.5 for the variables of demand, import and export. Add to this the level of social welfare as measured by the value of U.

4.9 Using the parameter and exogenous values of Problems 4.5 and 4.8: (a) solve the general equilibrium model for the autarkic level of all endogenous variables of the model (including social welfare U); (b) discuss the sensitivity of your results in (a) with respect to changes in the parameters α, β and γ; (c) solve for the international price as a result of trade between two countries similar in all respects except for a higher foreign endowment of labor, namely $L^* = 2.2$. Check that countries are not worse off with the opening of international trade.

4.10 Define the price elasticity of home export supply as $f = -\hat{x}_1/\hat{p}$. Show that $f = e - 1$. Define $f^* = \hat{x}_2^*/\hat{p}$ and $e^* = \hat{m}_1^*/\hat{p}$ and show that similar relations hold for the foreign country.

4.11 Using Figure 4.6, demonstrate that even with large differences in countries' relative factor supplies, factor prices can still be equalized if capital and labor are highly substitutable within industries and the difference in industries' capital–labor ratios is not too great.

Appendix

The transformation curve

The transformation or production possibility curve characterizes an economy's technology and factor supplies. Geometrically, the transformation curve can be derived from the Edgeworth-Bowley box diagram (Figure 4.12), where the dimensions of the box are the total supplies of capital and labor.

   Within this box are reproduced the unit isoquants of Figure 4.2. The outputs are measured by reference to the origins, O_1 for good 1 and O_2 for good 2. For example, point A gives one allocation of capital and labor between the two industries which would produce one unit of each good. Point A is not an efficient allocation of the factors between industries since it is possible, as at point C', to produce more of good 2 and no less of good 1. Likewise, at S', it is possible to produce more of good 1 with no less of good 2. Points C' and S' are Pareto-efficient allocations of capital and labor between industries because, at each point, any reallocation of inputs would result in a decrease in the output of at least one commodity (as at D).

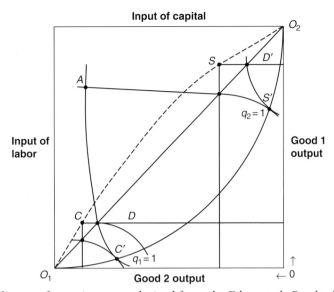

Figure 4.12 The transformation curve derived from the Edgeworth-Bowley box diagram

The locus of Pareto-efficient factor allocations (curve $O_1C'S'O_2$) is the contract curve. Here, the contract curve lies below the diagonal because we assume that industry 1 is capital-intensive. Given this, the transformation curve can be derived simply by recording the isoquant numbers at each point along the contract curve.

An alternative method of deriving the transformation curve is Savosnick's (1958) graphical technique. To demonstrate this technique, we first rescale the axes such that, with respect to the origin labeled O, the output of good 2 is measured along the bottom horizontal axis and the output of good 1 is measured along the right-hand vertical axis. Then we project vertical and horizontal lines to these axes from the point of intersection between each isoquant and the main diagonal O_1O_2. These projections are then reflected back from the vertical and horizontal axes to determine their point of intersection in the interior of the Edgeworth-Bowley box (e.g., point S or C). Repeating this process for all points of intersection with the main diagonal, the transformation curve is traced out as the locus of all such meeting points. In Figure 4.12 this process results in the curve O_1CSO_2.

Savosnick's technique exploits the "replication" property of homogeneous functions – that is, the entire isoquant map can be found once one isoquant is specified. This is illustrated in Figure 4.12 for the case of good 1. The unit isoquant q_1 cuts the main diagonal O_1O_2 at point D. The diagonal also cuts an unknown isoquant for good 1 at the point D'. To determine the number of units of good 1 produced on the unknown isoquant, it suffices to measure the ratio of distances $\frac{O_1D'}{O_1D} = \lambda$ that is, the point D' lies on the isoquant corresponding to the output level $\lambda q_1 = \lambda$. Note that since changes in output of good 1 can be measured along the ray O_1O_2, the properties of triangles imply that the same changes in output (ratio of distances) apply along the vertical axis.

Notes

1. See Note 5 for limit conditions on the production function and factor marginal products.
2. Alternatively, CRS means that the level of output (scale) is unimportant for determining the characteristics of the production process. For this reason the H-O-S model focuses on the ratio of variables and not their level.

3. A related concept is the unit *value* isoquant, which indicates the combinations of capital and labor that can produce one dollar (or other unit of account) of output. This is obtained from (4.1) by setting $\lambda = 1/p_j q_j$, where p_j is the price of good j.

4. It will be seen in Section 4.4 that property plays a central role in establishing the factor price equalization theorem as well as many of the theory's predictions about the effect of trade on the distribution of income among factor owners.

5. Written in this form, the following limit conditions are appended to property (3):

$$\lim_{k_j \to 0} f_j(k_j) = 0, \lim_{k_j \to \infty} f_j(k_j) = \infty, \lim_{k_j \to \infty} f_j'(k_j) = 0, \lim_{k_j \to 0} f_j'(k_j) = \infty$$

6. Since national income is the sum of income generated by each industry, national income is maximized when each industry achieves its maximum profit.

7. The iso-cost line is $K_j = \overline{C}_j/r - (w/r)L_j$ where $\overline{C}_j$ is a fixed level of expenditure on inputs K_j and L_j at the given prices r and w, respectively.

8. By linear homogeneity, these cost-minimizing capital–labor ratios are invariant to the level of output in each industry.

9. The economy's transformation function ($q_1 = T(q_2)$) can be found by simultaneously solving expressions (4.12) for q_1 as a function of q_2.

10. By definition, industry i is capital-intensive relative to industry m if $k_i(\overline{\omega}) > k_m(\overline{\omega})$ for some $\overline{\omega} > 0$. Note that the concept of factor intensity is unrelated to the specific value of an industry's capital–labor ratio. For example, industry i can still be capital-intensive even if both k_i and k_m are less than unity.

11. Graphically, this means that the curves in Figure 4.3 never intersect.

12. This is established by subtracting 1 from both sides of (4.19) and (4.20) and verifying the sign of the resulting expressions.

13. This proposition can be interpreted in two ways: either as a comparison of production equilibria within a country after a change in a factor supply or as a cross-country comparison of production equilibria between countries, similar in all respects, except for a difference in K or L.

14. The Rybczynski theorem assumes factor supply changes as purely exogenous and not the result of a change in factor rewards. See Kemp (1969) and Martin (1976) for an analysis of the case of variable factor supplies.

15. The duality between cost and production functions was first established by Shephard (1953) and is surveyed in Diewert (1982). Dixit and Norman (1980) and Woodland (1982) present several applications of duality to international trade. The present treatment follows Woodland (1977) and Mussa (1979).

16. Brackets {} such as those in (4.27) denote a set while the colon means "such that." Vectors are printed in **bold face**. No distinction is made between row and column vectors unless warranted.

17. The cost function $C(\mathbf{w}, q)$ must be a non-negative and continuous function defined over $\mathbf{w} > 0$ and $q \geq 0$. Moreover, it is homogeneous of degree one in $\mathbf{w}$, non-decreasing in $\mathbf{w}$, concave in $\mathbf{w}$ and non-decreasing in q. Any minimum cost function with these properties will serve as a suitable description of technology.

18. See Woodland (1982) or Cornes (1992) for proofs of Shephard's and Hotelling's lemmas.

19. The solution $q_j = +\infty$ is also possible but is incompatible with competitive equilibrium since factor prices could no longer be assumed constant if output were to expand without bound.

20. $G(\mathbf{p}, \mathbf{e})$ is a non-negative, non-decreasing, linearly homogeneous function of $\mathbf{p} > 0$ and $\mathbf{e} > 0$ and is concave in $\mathbf{e}$ and convex in $\mathbf{p}$.

21. By (4.35) an increase in the price of good j cannot decrease GDP, and will increase GDP if good j is produced in equilibrium. Similarly, by (4.36), more of any factor cannot reduce GDP, and will increase GDP if that factor is productive at the margin (a positive shadow price).

22. The appendix discusses the derivation of the transformation function and shows its dependence on the economy's technology and resources supplies.

23. These equations are dual to the unit isoquants (4.2).

24. Since utility functions are unique only up to a monotonic transformation, assuming linear homogeneity makes no sacrifice of generality.

25. In the present framework, we are able to calculate factor prices and consequently the level and distribution of national income as a function of national endowments and commodity prices. As long as endowments remain unchanged, commodity prices comprise all the information needed to specify the demand functions that can be written as $d_j = d_j(p)$.

26. For further details see equations (3.7) to (3.11) in Chapter 3.

27. See Jones (1969) and Ethier (1983) for further details on partial versus general equilibrium elasticities.

28. Similarly, the price elasticity of foreign imports is $e^* = e_1^* + e_2^* + e_3^*$.

29. McGilvray and Simpson's (1973) analysis of Anglo-Irish trade is an application of Leontief's original test.

30. The levels of non-competitive imports (imported goods not produced domestically) were assumed to remain unchanged.

31. Leontief was specifically interested in capital and labor but γ can be calculated with respect to any two factors.

32. See Ethier (1987).

References and additional reading

The neoclassical model

Bhagwati, J.N. and Srinivasan, T.N. (1983), *Lectures on International Trade* (Cambridge, MA: MIT Press), chs 5 and 6, 50–81; appendix B, 384–396.

Chacholiades, M. (1973), *The Pure Theory of International Trade* (London: Macmillan), chs 4–6, 81–169.

Dinwiddy, C.L., and Tal, F.J. (1988), *The Two-Sector Equilibrium Model: A New Approach* (Oxford: Philip Allan).

Ethier, W.J. (1983), *Modern International Economics* (New York: Norton), appendix I, 511–556.

Ethier, W.J. (1987), "The Theory of International Trade," in L.M. Officer (Ed.), *International Economics* (Boston: Kluwer Academic), 1–57.

Hazari, B.R. (1978), *The Pure Theory of International Trade and Distortions* (London: Croom Helm), ch. 1, 7–29.

Jones, R.W. (1965), "The Structure of Simple General Equilibrium Models," *Journal of Political Economy*, 73, 557–572.

Jones, R.W. (1969), "Tariffs and Trade in General Equilibrium: Comment," *American Economic Review*, 59, 418–424.

Kemp, M.C. (1969), *The Pure Theory of International Trade and Investment* (Englewood Cliffs: Prentice-Hall), chs 1–4, 5–118.

Metzler, L.A. (1949), "Tariffs, the Terms of Trade, and the Distribution of National Income," *Journal of Political Economy*, 57, 1–29.

Ohlin, B. (1933), *Interregional and International Trade* (Cambridge, MA: Harvard University Press).

Samuelson, P.A. (1953), "Prices of Factor and Goods in General Equilibrium," *Review of Economic Studies*, 21, 1–20.

Viaene, J.-M. (1993), "The Harrod-Johnson Diagram and the International Equilibrium," *International Economic Journal*, 7 (1), 83–93.

Duality theory

Cornes, R. (1992), *Duality and Modern Economics* (Cambridge: Cambridge University Press).

Diewert, W.E. (1982), "Duality Approaches to Microeconomic Theory," in K.J. Arrow and M.D. Intrilligator (Eds.), *Handbook of Mathematical Economics* (Amsterdam: North-Holland), 535–599.

Dixit, A. and Norman, V. (1980), *Theory of International Trade* (Cambridge: Cambridge University Press).

Kohli, U. (1991), *Technology, Duality, and Foreign Trade: The GNP Function Approach to Modeling Imports and Exports* (Ann Arbor and London: University of Michigan Press and Harvester Wheatsheaf).

Mussa, M. (1979), "The Two-Sector Model in Terms of Dual: A Geometric Exposition," *Journal of International Economics*, 9, 513–526.

Shephard, R.W. (1953), *Cost and Production Functions* (Princeton, NJ: Princeton University Press).

Woodland, A.D. (1977), "A Dual Approach to Equilibrium in the Production Sector in International Trade Theory," *Canadian Journal of Economics*, 10 (1), 50–68.

Woodland, A.D. (1982), *International Trade and Resource Allocation* (Amsterdam: North-Holland).

Production possibility curve

Krauss, M.B., Johnson, H.G., and Skouras, T. (1973), "On the Shape and Location of the Production Possibility Curve," *Economica*, 40 (159), 305–310.

Melvin, J.R. (1971), "On the Derivation of the Production Possibility Curve," *Economica*, 38 (151), 281–294.

Savosnick, K.M. (1958), "The Box Diagram and the Production Possibility Curve," *Ekonomisk Tidsskrift*, 60 (3), 183–197.

The Leontief paradox and the input–output accounting system

Klein, L.R. (1983), *Lectures in Econometrics* (Amsterdam: North-Holland), 21–36.

Leontief, W. (1954), "Domestic Production and Foreign Trade: the American Position Re-examined," *Economica Internazionale*, 7, 3–32.

McGilvray, J. and Simpson, D. (1973), "The Commodity Structure of Anglo-Irish Trade," *Review of Economics and Statistics*, 55, 451–458.

Variable factor supply

Kemp, M.C. (1969), *The Pure Theory of International Trade and Investment* (Englewood Cliffs: Prentice-Hall), ch. 5, 119–133.

Martin, J.P. (1976), "Variable Factor Supplies and the HOS Model," *Economic Journal*, 820–831.

Price elasticities

Bahmani-Oskooee, M. and Niroomand, F. (1998), "Long-run Price Elasticities and the Marshall-Lerner Condition Revisited," *Economics Letters*, 61, 101–109.

Goldstein, M. and Khan, M.S. (1978), "The Supply and Demand for Exports: A Simultaneous Approach," *Review of Economics and Statistics*, 60, 275–286.

Goldstein, M. and Khan, M.S. (1985), "Income and Price Effects in Foreign Trade," in R.W. Jones and P.B. Kenen (Eds.), *Handbook of International Economics*, Vol. 2 (Amsterdam: North-Holland), ch. 20, 1041–1105.

Leamer, E.E. (1981), "Is it a Demand Curve or is it a Supply Curve? Partial Identification through Inequality Constraints," *Review of Economics and Statistics*, 63, 319–327.

Marquez, J. (1990), "Bilateral Trade Elasticities," *Review of Economics and Statistics*, 72, 75–86.

Convergence

Andersson, M., Gieseck, A., Pierluigi, B., and Vidalis, N. (2008), "Wage Growth Dispersion across the Euro Area Countries: Some Stylised Facts," Occasional Paper Series No. 90, European Central Bank (Frankfurt: European Central Bank).

Faber, R.P. and Stokman, A.C.J. (2009), "A Short History of Price Level Convergence in Europe," *Journal of Money, Credit and Banking*, 41 (2–3), 461–477.

5

Trade policy

A nation's trade policy encompasses the instruments it uses to restrict or promote trade. In this chapter, we examine the effects on welfare and resource allocation of alternative trade policy instruments in competitive markets. We first examine the theoretical implications of trade policy instruments that target prices, such as a tariff or export subsidy. We then consider trade policy instruments that do not directly target prices by examining three specific forms of quantitative restrictions: an import quota, an export quota and a domestic content requirement. Following the theoretical presentation, we discuss methods for estimating the welfare effects that arise from various trade policy instruments, including computable general equilibrium (CGE) models which are now commonly used to estimate the effects of various trade policies. This chapter is an important foundation for Chapter 10, which considers the use of trade policy instruments in a world of imperfect competition.

5.1 Tariffs

A tariff is a tax levied on imports. The tariff rate or duty can be stated as either an *ad valorem* or specific rate. An *ad valorem* tariff rate states the tax as a percentage of import value; a specific tariff rate states the tax as a fixed currency amount per unit of the good imported. These two forms of tariff are not equivalent, but it is common when analyzing the effects of a tariff to assume it is *ad valorem*.

To examine the effects of a tariff we adopt the two-good model developed in Chapter 4 and assume that the home country imposes the *ad valorem* tariff τ on its imports of good 2 (good 1 is exported). This tariff "drives a wedge" between the world relative price of good 2 (p_w) and the domestic or internal relative price of good 2 (p_d):[1]

$$p_d = (1 + \tau)p_w.\,^2$$

(5.1)

A tariff will alter the pattern of consumption, production and trade since it changes the domestic, and possibly the international, price of the imported good. Moreover, since a tariff creates a price distortion it also alters national and world welfare. We now turn to a detailed examination of these economic effects.

Small country

Figure 5.1 illustrates a trading equilibrium for a small country that is unable to affect the prices of its imports or exports on world markets. Under free trade, the country achieves welfare level u_2 by producing at point A and consuming at point B, and hence exporting aA units of good 1 in exchange for aB units of good 2. Since the world price p_w is fixed, imposing the tariff on good 2 raises the domestic relative price of imports according to (5.1). Producers respond to this increase in the domestic relative price by shifting production to point A'. The tariff therefore raises domestic production of good 2 and lowers domestic production of good 1. This shift in production reduces the economy's gross domestic product (GDP) valued at world prices by the amount ef when measured in terms of numeraire good 1 (EF measured in terms of good 2). Since international equilibrium requires the value of a country's exports to equal the value of its imports at international prices, the economy's new consumption point must lie on the international budget line eE. Since this budget line lies everywhere below the pre-tariff international budget line fF, the country must be worse off as the result of the tariff.

The exact welfare level achieved under the tariff is determined by locating the country's new consumption point after imposition of the tariff. To do so, note first that the tariff generates revenue for the government and one must consider how this revenue is spent. A common assumption is that the government redistributes this revenue back to consumers via a lump-sum transfer. Consumers will therefore spend the country's entire income according to their preferences. Given this, the new consumption point is found as follows. First, as noted above, trade balance requires consumption to take place along the international budget line eE. Second, consumers will equate their marginal rate of substitution between goods 1 and 2 to the tariff-inclusive domestic price p_d. These two requirements imply that consumption must occur at point B', which is the only point on budget line eE where a social indifference curve

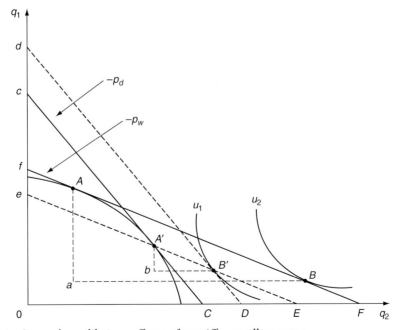

Figure 5.1 General equilibrium effects of a tariff – small country

exhibits a slope equal to the tariff inclusive domestic price p_d. The tariff revenue, expressed in terms of good 1, equals cd. The tariff therefore reduces national welfare from u_2 to u_1, and in the new equilibrium the country imports bB' units of good 2 in exchange for $A'b$ exports of good 1. Hence, the tariff also reduces the volume of trade.

Distributional effects

The economy-wide welfare reduction illustrated in Figure 5.1 masks changes in the welfare of different agents within the economy (e.g., consumers, producers and the government). Understanding how, and in what direction, tariff protection alters the welfare of different domestic agents is important for understanding the motives for different groups to favor or oppose a tariff and other forms of protection. To examine the distributional effects of a tariff we take a partial equilibrium approach[3] that focuses on the domestic market for the imported good. Panel (a) of Figure 5.2 illustrates this market.

In Figure 5.2, the foreign export supply (x_2^*) is drawn infinitely elastic at the world price p_w reflecting the assumption of a small country. The free trade equilibrium occurs at the intersection of the domestic demand (d_2) and the market supply curve Q_2 (which equals the horizontal summation of the domestic and foreign supply curves), the latter derived as the sum of the domestic (q_2) and foreign export supply curves. Under free trade, the domestic price of good 2 will therefore equal the world price p_w. At this price, consumers demand d_f units of good 2, of which q_f are supplied by domestic producers and hence $(d_f - q_f)$ units are imported.

Imposing a tariff raises the market supply curve to Q_2' and raises the domestic equilibrium price from p_w to p_d. This price increase lowers domestic consumption from d_f to d_t, raises domestic production from q_f to q_t, and lowers imports to $(d_t - q_t)$ units.

The increased domestic price of good 2 clearly harms consumers. A measure of their loss is the decrease in consumer surplus given by the trapezoidal area $p_d a b p_w$. This loss to consumers can be broken down into income transfer and efficiency cost components. The income transfer component has two sub-components: a transfer from consumers to producers measured by area C and a transfer from consumers to their government measured by area I (which equals tariff revenue). The tariff therefore benefits domestic producers and the government at the expense of domestic consumers of good 2.

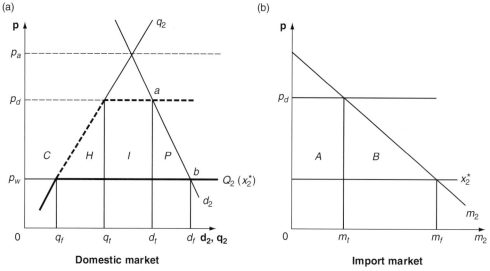

Figure 5.2 Partial equilibrium analysis of a tariff – small country

The efficiency cost of the tariff also has two sub-components: a production cost measured by area H and a consumption cost measured by area P. The production cost is the additional cost to the importing country of obtaining $(q_t - q_f)$ units of good 2 from domestic producers rather than on world markets at the lower cost $p_w(q_t - q_f)$.[4] The consumption cost measures the loss that arises as consumers substitute away from good 2 and into good 1 (more generally, into other goods) as the price of good 2 rises above its true resource cost. Since the income transfer components are a redistribution of income among domestic agents, the net change in welfare for the country as a whole is the sum of the production and consumption efficiency costs.

Panel (b) of Figure 5.2 gives an equivalent illustration of the effects of the tariff but now in terms of the market for imports alone. The import demand curve (m_2) is derived as the horizontal difference between the domestic demand (d_2) and domestic supply (q_2) in panel (a) for each price below the autarky price p_a. This construction assumes that good 2 is homogeneous across countries and hence that the domestic and imported goods are perfect substitutes. The initial free trade equilibrium occurs at the intersection of the home country's import demand and the foreign export supply (x_2^*). A tariff raises the foreign export supply and hence the equilibrium domestic price of imports which results in a fall in the volume of imports. Consumers of the import good experience a welfare loss equal to the loss in consumer surplus as measured by areas A and B in panel (b). By construction, area A equals area I in panel (a) and area B equals the sum of areas H and P in panel (a). Area B therefore measures the country's net welfare loss from the tariff, and hence the change in consumer surplus in panel (b) excludes the income transfer from consumers to domestic producers (i.e., area T in panel (a)).

Large country

We now assume the country is large and hence able to influence the prices of goods on world markets. This assumption is illustrated in Figure 5.3 by the positively sloped foreign export supply function (x_2^*). As drawn, foreign export supply is assumed elastic at the initial free trade equilibrium denoted as point a. Since a tariff raises the domestic price of the imported good, domestic residents will import less of good 2 at any given world price. As shown in Figure 5.3,

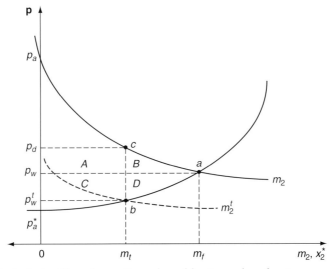

Figure 5.3 Effect of a tariff on domestic and world prices when foreign export supply is elastic

the tariff displaces the import demand curve downward from m_2 to m_2^t so that the new "tariff-ridden" international equilibrium occurs at point b. The tariff inclusive domestic price is then p_d with cb/bm_t being the *ad valorem* tariff rate τ. Since export supply is upward sloping, the new equilibrium involves a lower world price and lower imports, and hence a lower value of imports at world prices relative to the free trade equilibrium. The magnitude of the change in world price and volume of imports depends importantly on the elasticity of the foreign export supply; the less elastic is foreign export supply, the larger will be the fall in world price and the smaller the fall in the quantity of imports.

Welfare

In Figure 5.3, the net welfare change due to the tariff is given as area C minus area B. This is demonstrated as follows. Relative to free trade, the tariff reduces the welfare of domestic consumers by the loss in consumer surplus which equals areas A and B in Figure 5.3. Tariff revenue to the government equals areas A and C. Areas C and D equal the loss in the surplus of foreign exporters due to a deterioration in their country's terms of trade. Note that area C, which accrues to the importing country as tariff revenue, measures the gain to the importing country arising from an improvement in its terms of trade. The net change in the importing country's welfare is therefore area C minus area B which, for some values of τ, could be positive. Since areas A and C are, respectively, income transfers within and between countries, areas B and D measure the reduction in world welfare arising from the tariff. Finally, since the importing country's terms of trade gain is a terms of trade loss for the foreign country, the latter may retaliate by imposing a restriction on its imports from the home country. Such retaliation would eliminate some or all of the importing country's terms of trade gain. Moreover, since retaliation will further reduce the volume of trade it would also increase the efficiency costs, and hence the welfare loss, at the world level.

A formal statement of the general equilibrium welfare changes suggested by Figure 5.3 can be made by assuming that welfare is measured by the following indirect utility function:

$$V(p, S) \equiv U(d_1(p, S), d_2(p, S)), \qquad (5.2)$$

where $d_j(p, S)$ is the demand for commodity j ($j = 1, 2$) and S is expenditure (spending) at domestic prices as given by the economy's budget constraint:

$$S(p_d, u_1) \equiv q_1 + p_d q_2 + (p_d - p_w)m_2 = Y + \tau p_w m_2, \qquad (5.3)$$

where u_1 is the post-tariff level of utility. Expression (5.3) states the equality, at domestic prices, between total expenditure and income from all sources (i.e., production plus tariff revenue). Totally differentiating (5.2) and applying Roy's identity (i.e., $d_2(p, S) = -(\partial V/\partial p)/(\partial V/\partial S)$), the welfare change due to the tariff can be expressed as a function of the change in domestic prices:

$$dW = dS - d_2 dp_d \qquad (5.4)$$

where $dW = (\partial V/\partial S)^{-1} dV$ (with $\partial V/\partial S > 0$) measures the change in real income (in units of the numeraire) that is equivalent to the change in utility (dV).[5] The welfare change in (5.4) can also be expressed as a function of the world price and volume of imports. To do this, we first obtain expressions for dp_d and dS by totally differentiating equations (5.1) and (5.3) and then substituting these expressions into (5.4) to obtain:

$$dW = -m_2 dp_w + \tau p_w dm_2. \qquad (5.5)$$

Expression (5.5) indicates that the net change in the welfare of the tariff-imposing country is the sum of two components.[6] The first relates to the change in the country's terms of trade (dp_w) while the second relates to the change in import volume (dm_2). Since $\tau p_w = p_d - p_w$, the second component measures the efficiency cost of the tariff arising from the distortion between the domestic and world price of imports. As shown in Figure 5.3, the tariff reduces both the world price and the volume of imports, that is, $dp_w < 0$ and $dm_2 < 0$.[7] By (5.5), the terms of trade improvement raises welfare while the fall in import volume reduces welfare. Since these two effects have opposite signs the change in welfare could be positive – that is, a tariff could raise the welfare of a large country. By definition, the terms of trade effect is zero for a small country and hence (5.5) reconfirms that a tariff must reduce the welfare of a small country.

Metzler's paradox

Figure 5.3 assumes that foreign export supply is elastic at the free trade equilibrium. In contrast, Figure 5.4 illustrates the extreme case in which the foreign export supply curve is backward bending at the free trade equilibrium point a. In this case, the tariff reduces not only the world price but also the domestic price of good 2 and hence the quantity imported increases. Figure 5.4 therefore suggests that a tariff could raise, lower or leave unchanged the domestic price of the imported good. These possibilities then raise a question concerning the expected effect of a tariff on domestic resource allocation. In particular, if a tariff lowers the domestic price of imports then domestic production of good 2 will fall, not rise. This decline in domestic production may be contrary to what policymakers had intended by imposing the tariff. The possibility that a tariff could lower the domestic price of the imported good was first pointed out by Metzler (1949) and is hence known as Metzler's paradox. The conditions under which this paradoxical outcome does not occur are stated below.

Metzler condition: The imposition of a tariff increases the domestic price of the imported good if and only if the price elasticity of foreign import demand exceeds the domestic marginal propensity to spend on the export good.

To derive the Metzler condition, write (5.1) in relative change form:

$$\hat{p}_d = \hat{p}_w + \frac{d\tau}{(1+\tau)}. \tag{5.6}$$

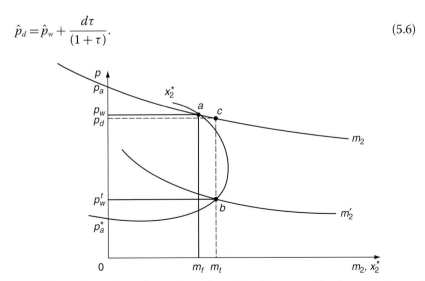

Figure 5.4 Effect of a tariff on domestic and world prices when foreign export supply is backward-bending

International equilibrium requires that home and foreign trade balances be zero. In turn, this implies that the value of imports in each country be equal: $m_2 p_w = m_1$. Writing this relationship in relative change form gives:

$$\hat{p}_w = \hat{m}_1 - \hat{m}_2. \tag{5.7}$$

Expressions (5.6) and (5.7) indicate that we need to find expressions for $\hat{m}_1$ and $\hat{m}_2$ in terms of the world price and tariff rate. Consider first $\hat{m}_2$ and assume that the tariff revenue is returned to domestic consumers via a lump sum transfer.[8] Since import demand is $m_2 = d_2(p_d, S(p_d, u_1)) - q_2(p_d)$, where expenditure (S) is given by (5.3), we can repeat the steps taken to derive (4.53) to obtain:

$$\hat{m}_2 = -e\hat{p}_w - (e_1 + e_2)d\tau. \tag{5.8}$$

Recall from Chapter 4 that e and e_1 are, respectively, the uncompensated and compensated price elasticities of import demand, while e_2 is the elasticity of domestic supply of good 2. Derivation of (5.8) assumes the country was initially in free trade – that is, $\tau = 0$ and $p_d = p_w$. For a given level of imports $(\hat{m}_2 = 0)$, the term $(e_1 + e_2)d\tau$ in (5.8) indicates the size of the downward displacement of the import demand curve illustrated in Figure 5.3 or Figure 5.4.

Turning now to $\hat{m}_1$, foreign import demand will react normally to the change in world price so the expression for $\hat{m}_1$ takes the simpler form:

$$\hat{m}_1 = \hat{p}_w e^*, \tag{5.9}$$

where e^* is the price elasticity of foreign import demand. Substitution of (5.8) and (5.9) into (5.7) gives:

$$\hat{p}_w = -\frac{e_1 + e_2}{e^* + e - 1}d\tau. \tag{5.10}$$

Expression (5.10) is negative since $e_1 > 0, e_2 > 0$, and trade balance stability requires $(e^* + e - 1) > 0$.[9] The tariff will therefore improve the home country's terms of trade unless the country is small (i.e., $e^* = \infty$). The effect of this terms of trade improvement on the domestic price of the imported good is found by substituting (5.10) into (5.6) to obtain (with $\tau = 0$):

$$\hat{p}_d = \frac{e^* - (1 - e_3)}{e^* + e - 1}d\tau \begin{array}{c} > \\ = \\ < \end{array} 0 \text{ as } e^* \begin{array}{c} > \\ = \\ < \end{array} (1 - e_3) \tag{5.11}$$

where use has been made of (4.54). Expression (5.11) states the Metzler condition: a tariff will raise the domestic price of the imported good if the foreign import price elasticity e^* exceeds the domestic marginal propensity to spend on the export good $(1 - e_3)$. A tariff that lowers the domestic price of the imported good relative to its free trade level will lower domestic production of the import-competing good and hence make the domestic industry worse off compared with free trade. A fall in the domestic price also implies a fall in the relative and real return to the factor used intensively in the import-competing industry. This change in factor rewards is opposite to that predicted by the Stolper-Samuelson theorem (which assumes a small country). While theoretically possible, no case of Metzler's paradox has been demonstrated empirically.[10]

The optimum tariff

Expression (5.5) indicates that a tariff can raise the welfare of a large country through an improvement in its terms of trade. However, (5.5) also indicates that the welfare gain from an improved terms of trade is set against a loss arising from the distortion between domestic and world prices introduced by the tariff. These offsetting effects on welfare suggest that there exists a tariff rate that would just balance these gains and losses at the margin, and hence maximize the welfare of the tariff-imposing country. This welfare-maximizing tariff rate is called the optimum tariff. Its value is found by setting dW to zero in (5.5) and solving for τ:

$$\tau^* = \frac{1}{\hat{m}_2/\hat{p}_w} = \frac{1}{f^*}. \qquad (5.12)$$

The second equality in (5.12) follows from (5.7) and (5.9) and the equality $f^* = e^* - 1$. As (5.12) indicates, the size of the optimum tariff is inversely related to the elasticity of foreign export supply. Note that expression (5.12) further confirms that a small country maximizes its welfare under free trade since $\tau^* = 0$ when $f^* = \infty$.

Tariffs versus export subsidies

In the home market, a tariff gives domestic producers of the good that competes with the imported good (i.e., domestic import-competing producers) an advantage over foreign producers. In contrast, an export subsidy gives domestic exporters an advantage over foreign producers in foreign markets. Since a subsidy is a negative tax, the preceding analyses of a tariff are easily adapted to examine the welfare and resource allocation implications of an export subsidy. Specifically, the welfare implications of an export subsidy can be inferred from (5.5) by assuming that good 2 is instead exported so that $-m_2 = x_2$ and p_w is now the country's terms of trade. Then, by (5.5), an export subsidy unambiguously decreases the welfare of the subsidizing country. The subsidy causes the country's terms of trade to deteriorate ($dp_w < 0$), and the trade volume effect, which in this case measures the increase in domestically financed subsidy payments consequent to the increase in exports, adds to this welfare loss.[11]

Taking an export subsidy as representative of policies that stimulate trade and a tariff as representative of polices that restrict trade, the above analyses imply the following proposition regarding a country's optimal choice of trade policy instrument:

Trade policy prescription: *When markets are perfectly competitive, trade policy should take the form of restrictions rather than stimulants to trade.*

Symmetry of import and export taxes

A tariff changes the pattern of domestic production and consumption because it changes the domestic *relative* price of imports. We now show that the *relative* price change induced by a tariff, and hence the effects of the tariff, can be duplicated if the country instead imposes a tax on its exports. Consider first the case of a tariff. The domestic nominal price of imports is $p_{2d} = (1 + \tau)p_{2w}$ while the domestic nominal price of the export good equals the world price ($p_{1d} = p_{1w}$). The domestic relative price of imports is therefore $p_{2d}/p_{1d} = (1 + \tau)p_{2w}/p_{1w}$. Now let the country instead impose an *ad valorem* tax τ on its exports of good 1. By assumption, the domestic price of imports now equals the world price ($p_{2d} = p_{2w}$) but the domestic nominal price of exports (net of the tax) is now below the world price since $p_{1d}(1 + \tau) = p_{1w}$ or $p_{1d} = p_{1w}/(1 + \tau)$. The domestic relative price of imports is therefore $p_{2d}/p_{1d} = (1 + \tau)p_{2w}/p_{1w}$ which is the same as the case of a tariff. Hence, a tax on imports and a tax on exports result in the same change in domestic relative prices and in this sense they are equivalent. This result is known as the Lerner Symmetry Theorem:

Lerner Symmetry Theorem: *A tax on exports has the same effect on domestic relative prices as an equal tariff on imports.*

Since a uniform tariff on all imports has exactly the same effect as a uniform tax on all exports, all the preceding conclusions about the resource allocation effects of a tariff apply without change to the case of an export tax. In particular, this symmetry implies the existence of an optimum export tax equivalent to the optimum tariff.

5.2 Quantitative restrictions

Tariffs and other "price" measures distort relative prices from their free market value and reduce trade volumes. Under perfect competition, the same results in terms of prices and trade volumes can be attained by policies that target quantities rather than prices. Quantitative restrictions can be explicit, for example when they take the form of export and import quotas, or implicit, as when they take the form of a domestic content requirement (DCR). Below we examine the effects of such restrictions in a partial equilibrium framework. Although the price and volume effect of a quantitative restriction can often be duplicated by an appropriate tariff, these policies generally differ in their welfare effects. In particular, tariffs generate revenue for the home government, while quantitative restrictions generate pure economic profit (rent) for those who hold the right to import or export the restricted good. If the holders of these "quota rights" are not domestic agents then the quota rent is a transfer of domestic income to foreigners which is then added to the efficiency costs that a country experiences from restricting its trade.

Import quotas

Figure 5.5 illustrates the case of a large country. The initial free trade equilibrium is at point a where the domestic price of the imported good equals the world price p_w and the volume of imports is m. An import quota that limits imports to $\overline{m}$ units implies that the import demand becomes vertical (downward) at point c and a new international equilibrium is established at point b. The import quota therefore lowers the world price from p_w to p'_w. However, the price that clears the domestic market for imports is p_d. Since the same world and domestic prices, and therefore quantity imported, would result if a tariff $\tau = (p_d - p'_w)/p'_w$ had instead

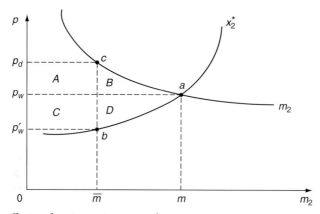

Figure 5.5 The effects of an import quota – large country

been imposed,[12] the quota imposes the same welfare cost to consumers, namely the decrease in consumer surplus equal to areas A and B. However, under the quota, areas A and C are not tariff revenue but rather pure economic profit (rent). Assuming this rent accrues to domestic importers, the *net* change in the quota imposing on the country's welfare is the same as under a tariff, namely area C minus area B, while the loss to the foreign country again equals areas C and D. However, this is not the only possible outcome. Any part of the quota rents that fails to accrue to domestic agents would entail an uncompensated loss of income for the importing country. In the extreme, all rents could go to foreign agents; a possibility discussed in the next section. But regardless of who captures the quota rents, world welfare falls by an amount equal to areas B and D.

Who earns the rents generated by a quota depends on how, and by whom, the quota is administered. Import quotas are always administered by the importing country, which sets a limit on the volume of imports that can be admitted over a given period of time. A global import quota limits imports from all suppliers, while a country-specific quota limits imports from only certain countries, normally just the largest suppliers.

The administration of an import quota usually takes one of two forms: imports enter on a first-come, first-served basis until the total volume of imports reaches the prescribed limit or the importing country issues licenses which identify the importer and the volume of imports covered by the license. Under the first scheme, importers who are first to import goods up to the limit set by the quota get the quota rents. Under the second scheme, the government can either issue licenses on a first-come, first-served basis, or allocate licenses to importers based on predetermined criteria[13] or by selling the licenses at an auction. If licenses are simply issued (essentially for free) then importers who receive licenses get the quota rents.[14] If licenses are sold at auction, the revenue earned by the government equals, in theory, the quota rents.[15] If so, then an "auctioned import quota" is equivalent in both its revenue and welfare effect to that of a tariff.[16]

Export quotas

Export quotas are always administered by the exporting country, which sets a limit on the volume of exports that can be shipped over a specified period of time. The methods for administering an export quota are the same as those for an import quota: the country can allow exports to be shipped on a first-come, first-served basis or export licenses can be issued or sold at auction. Whoever acquires the right to export will capture the rents generated by the quota (except if the licenses are auctioned by the government). Before considering the economic effects of an export quota we note that, just as there is always a tariff that can duplicate the price and volume effects of an import quota, there is also always an export tax that can duplicate the price and volume effects of an export quota. Given this, the Lerner Symmetry Theorem between export and import taxes implies a similar symmetry between export and import quotas – that is, there exists an export quota that has the same price and volume effects as an import quota.

Voluntary export restraint

Countries sometimes use export quotas to limit sales of "strategic" goods such as natural resources or "sensitive" technology. More prevalent, however, are export quotas that arise from a voluntary restraint agreement (VRA). A VRA is negotiated between an importing country and one or more of its supplier countries with the intent of limiting its imports. Since the importing country "requests" exporters to limit their supply, this type of export quota is called a voluntary export restraint (VER).[17]

The effect of a VER on the importing country can be illustrated using Figure 5.5. Starting from the free trade equilibrium (point a), a quota that limits exports to $\overline{m}$ units implies that the foreign export supply becomes vertical at point b and hence the new international equilibrium is established at point c. The world price of exports therefore rises from p_w to p_d which is also the new domestic price in the importing country. The rise in the world price under the VER contrasts with the fall in world price (from p_w to p'_w) that arises in the case of an import quota that limits imports to $\overline{m}$ units. That is, a VER causes the importing country's terms of trade to deteriorate, while an import quota improves its terms of trade. The terms of trade deterioration implies a loss in consumer surplus equal to areas A and B. Since foreign exporters receive the price p_d but supply $\overline{m}$ units at a marginal cost of p'_w they receive a rent of $(p_d - p'_w)$ per unit exported. Total rents are therefore equal to areas A and C in Figure 5.5. The importing country's net welfare loss is then areas A and B.[18] Since this loss exceeds that arising under an equal import quota where the rents accrue to domestic importers we can conclude that, for the importing country, a VER is welfare inferior to an import quota as a policy for reducing its imports.[19]

In the exporting country, the export quota reduces producer surplus by areas C and D but generates rent equal to areas A and C. The net benefit to the exporting country is therefore area A minus area D. If the foreign government auctioned export licenses it could capture the quota rents (areas A and C) which, by assumption, would be redistributed to (foreign) consumers. In this case, the distributional effects of the quota within the foreign country would be identical to an *ad valorem* export tax $t = (p_d - p'_w)/p'_w$ (assuming the tax proceeds are redistributed to consumers). Finally, like an import quota, the VER leads to a net decline in world welfare equal to areas B and D.

Domestic content requirements

A domestic content requirement (DCR) requires firms that sell in the domestic market to purchase a specified minimum proportion of their intermediate inputs from domestic suppliers.[20] If firms comply with the requirement, import duties are waived on imported intermediate goods or some other benefit is granted. If firms fail to meet the requirement then a penalty can be imposed or the firm may be prohibited from selling its final product in the domestic market.[21] A DCR is therefore a quantitative restriction that involves a minimum purchase requirement.

A DCR can be specified in physical terms or in terms of value-added. The physical base is usually applied when the imported and domestic inputs are homogeneous while the value-added base is applied if the inputs are heterogeneous. When defined as a required share of value-added, several refinements are possible. For example, capital costs may be excluded from the definition of value-added.

The essential aspects of a DCR can be understood using a partial equilibrium model in which a final good is produced using one intermediate "component" good.[22] It is assumed that production of one unit of the final good requires one unit of the component and that domestic and imported components are perfectly substitutable in producing the final good. The importing country is assumed to be small so the supply of imported components (x^*) is infinitely elastic at the fixed world price p_w. The supply of domestic components (q) is given by the (inverse) supply function $p_d = p_d(q)$ where p_d is the price of domestic components and $\partial p_d/\partial q > 0$. The assumption of a fixed input–output relation between the component and final good implies that total domestic demand for components (D) is just the amount produced of the final good (z):

$$D = q + x^* = z \tag{5.13}$$

where x^* is the quantity of the imported component. Now assume that the government imposes a DCR that specifies that the fraction $\lambda(0 \leq \lambda \leq 1)$ of all components purchased must be purchased from domestic suppliers. This restriction implies that the demand for domestically produced components (d) is:

$$d = \lambda(q + x^*) = \lambda z. \tag{5.14}$$

The minimum purchase requirement also implies that final good producers now pay an average price ($\bar{p}$) for components equal to:

$$\bar{p} = \lambda p_d + (1 - \lambda)p_w. \tag{5.15}$$

Figure 5.6 illustrates the domestic market for components. Under free trade, equilibrium occurs at point e with the domestic price of components equaling the world price p_w. At this price, final good producers purchase D_0 components, of which q_0 units are purchased from domestic suppliers while $D_0 - q_0$ units are imported. The imposition of the DCR implies that final good producers face a "composite" supply function ($\bar{q}$) for components which, assuming $\lambda \neq 1$ or 0, lies between the domestic and import supply functions.[23] Therefore, under the DCR, final good producers demand a total of $\bar{D}$ components at the average price $\bar{p}$ given by (5.15). Of this total, $q_1 = \lambda \bar{D}$ components must be purchased from domestic suppliers. To supply these q_1 units domestic component producers must receive the price p_d. In summary, the price of domestic components rises from p_w to p_d, domestic production of components rises from q_0 to q_1 units and imports of components fall to $\bar{D} - q_1$ units.

Comparing the welfare effects of the DCR to a tariff ($\tau = (p_d - p_w)/p_w$) that would also raise the production of domestic components to q_1 we note that, from Figure 5.6, the tariff brings about the same deadweight loss (area A) as the DCR on the production side. However, the consumption deadweight loss (area B) is smaller under the DCR than under the tariff (areas B, C and E) since, under the tariff, final good producers will demand a total of D_t components. Intuitively, a DCR involves a lower welfare cost than a tariff since the former allows imported components to be purchased at the world price whereas the tariff raises the price of both domestic and imported components. A DCR is therefore superior to a tariff if the intent is to raise production of domestic components.

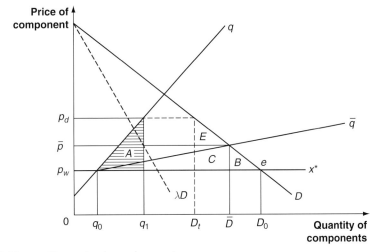

Figure 5.6 Domestic content requirement

5.3 Estimating welfare effects

This section presents partial and general equilibrium methods used to estimate the distributional and net welfare effects of trade policies. The calculation of these effects is an important area of applied work in international trade. Quantifying the welfare costs and benefits of trade policies provides important input into the policy-making process – the decision by government officials to grant or remove protection is often influenced by the magnitude of the calculated effects. The calculated welfare effects can also serve as data for empirical investigations of the motives for protection and other areas of research.

The calculation of welfare effects arising from trade policy changes has traditionally been made using formulae derived from a partial equilibrium analysis. The first half of this section presents and discusses this approach. Although partial equilibrium methods have been used to measure welfare changes arising from large-scale changes in trade policy, such as multilateral tariff reductions, their use is now overshadowed by the widespread use of CGE models. CGE models simplify the measurement of net welfare changes since they assume an explicit form for the utility function. The second half of this section discusses the basic structure of CGE models and the methods used to compute welfare changes. Although widely used, the data and computational requirements of a CGE model are orders of magnitude greater than that of a partial equilibrium analysis. Traditional partial equilibrium methods therefore remain preferred when only a few products are to be examined, and such methods are often the only feasible way to proceed when welfare effects are to be computed at a detailed commodity level.

Partial equilibrium methods

Partial equilibrium methods for calculating the welfare effects of trade policies ignore the price and quantity changes for all but a few commodities. Moreover, these methods use demand functions that treat income as exogenous and therefore ignore the income effects that arise from a trade policy change. Our analysis of partial equilibrium methods assumes two goods: one imported and the other domestically produced. We begin with the case of a small country and consider estimating the welfare effects that arise from complete removal of an existing tariff. Since this analysis makes the simplifying assumption that the relevant demand and supply functions are linear, we illustrate extension to the case of nonlinear demand and supply functions by considering the case of a large country that implements a partial tariff reduction. The section concludes by considering estimation of the welfare effects associated with a change in non-tariff barriers, as illustrated by the cases of a partial reduction in an import quota and an export quota.

Tariffs

Small country

To illustrate as simply as possible the methods used to estimate the welfare effects of trade policies consider first the case of a small country that has in place an *ad valorem* tariff τ on its imports of a homogeneous good. This case is depicted by panels (a) and (b) of Figure 5.2. Looking first at panel (a), elimination of the tariff implies four effects to be estimated: the two transfer effects (areas C and I) and the two efficiency cost effects (areas H and P). If the demand and supply functions are linear then these effects are easily calculated for given values of the tariff and the elasticities of demand and supply. Since we are interested in the effects of complete tariff elimination, the effect on tariff revenue (area I) does not require estimation since the government will lose the existing tariff revenue, and the value of the latter is directly observable. Given this, let $\Delta p = (p_w - p_d) < 0$, $\Delta d = (d_f - d_t) > 0$ and $\Delta q = (q_f - q_t) < 0$ denote, respectively, the changes in domestic price, domestic demand and domestic production that will arise from tariff elimination. Noting that $\Delta p / p_d = -\tau/(1+\tau)$, the reader can verify the following expressions for computing the value of each of the three remaining areas shown in panel (a) of Figure 5.2:

$$\text{Area } C: \quad -\Delta p(q_t + \Delta q/2) = \frac{\tau V_q}{2(1+\tau)}\left(2 - \frac{\tau \varepsilon_d}{(1+\tau)}\right) \tag{5.16}$$

$$\text{Area } H: \quad \Delta p \Delta q/2 = \left(\frac{\varepsilon_d V_q}{2}\right)\left(\frac{\tau^2}{(1+\tau)^2}\right) \tag{5.17}$$

$$\text{Area } P: \quad -\Delta p \Delta d/2 = \left(\frac{\eta_d V_d}{2}\right)\left(\frac{\tau^2}{(1+\tau)^2}\right) \tag{5.18}$$

In these expressions, $\eta_d > 0$ and $\varepsilon_d > 0$ are, respectively, the price elasticities of domestic demand and domestic supply, and $V_q = p_d q_t$ and $V_d = p_d d_t$ are, respectively, the values of domestic production and domestic consumption at the tariff inclusive domestic price. Except for the elasticity values, these expressions involve variables readily available from national statistics on trade and production.

The sum of (5.16) – (5.18) plus the tariff revenue (i.e., $-\Delta p(d_t - q_t)$) equals the change in the surplus of domestic consumer (ΔCS):

$$\Delta CS = \frac{\tau V_d}{2(1+\tau)}\left(2 + \frac{\eta_d \tau}{(1+\tau)}\right). \tag{5.19}$$

The economy-wide net change in welfare (ΔW) is the sum of (5.17) and (5.18):

$$\Delta W = \left(\frac{\varepsilon_d V_q + \eta_d V_d}{2}\right)\left(\frac{\tau^2}{(1+\tau)^2}\right). \tag{5.20}$$

Multiplying (5.20) by V_m / V_m, where $V_m = p_d m_t$ is the initial (tariff inclusive) value of imports, and using $\eta_m = \frac{V_q}{V_m}\varepsilon_d + \frac{V_d}{V_m}\eta_d$, where $\eta_m > 0$ is the elasticity of import demand, (5.20) can also be written:

$$\Delta W = \frac{V_m \eta_m \tau^2}{2(1+\tau)^2}. \tag{5.21}$$

As expected, expression (5.21) is the value of area B in panel (b) of Figure 5.2.

The above formulae are widely used to calculate the distributional and net welfare effects of tariff elimination. By reversing the logic, the estimated effects can be interpreted as the transfer and efficiency costs incurred by maintaining the existing tariff. Hence, these formulae collectively provide for the measurement of the various aspects of the "cost of protection."

A major attraction of these formulae is their simplicity in terms of data requirements. Tariff rates and import values are readily obtained from published statistics. More difficult is obtaining the values of the demand and supply elasticities. Values of these elasticities are either estimated by the analyst or culled from the literature. Often several estimates are available, and these may refer to "commodities" at higher or lower levels of aggregation than the "commodity" being examined. When several estimates are available, a "best guess" value (usually the average of available estimates) is used. Regardless of the source, the elasticity values are only an estimate of the "true" elasticity. To some, the uncertainty about the "true" value of elasticity represents a weakness of these formulae since it implies that the "true" size of the effects cannot be known. However, this view is too strong. Rather, although rarely done, such uncertainty can be incorporated by using the upper and lower values of, for example, a 95 percent confidence interval for the relevant elasticity estimate.[24] The estimated transfer and welfare effects would then be presented as interval estimates with an associated level of confidence. Finally, because of the difficulties in obtaining elasticity values, the net change in welfare effect is usually calculated using (5.21) rather than (5.20) since the latter formula only requires one elasticity value to be available.

Large country

We now consider the case of a large country. To analyze this, we will extend the preceding small country analysis in two ways. First, we will assume that the initial tariff τ_1 is to be reduced to a new level $\tau_2 \neq 0$; this represents a partial reduction rather than full elimination of the tariff. Second, we will dispense with the assumption of linear import demand and export supply functions. As we will see, the analysis of a partial tariff reduction for a small country with nonlinear import demand and export supply can be handled as a special case of the large country example presented below.

Figure 5.7 illustrates the case of a large country as implied by the positively sloped import supply (x^*) curve. In the initial tariff-ridden equilibrium, consumers import m_1 units at the tariff inclusive domestic price p_1. Given the world price p_w^1 the tariff revenue equals areas A, C and E. A partial reduction in the tariff from τ_1 to τ_2 shifts the tariff inclusive import supply from x_1^* to x_2^* and lowers the domestic price of imports to p_2. Since import supply is positively sloped, the world price rises to p_2^w (a terms of trade deterioration for the importing country).

The tariff reduction benefits consumers of the imported good by the change in consumer surplus (areas A and B), which can be measured as:

$$\Delta CS = \int_{p_2}^{p_1} m(p_m)\, dp_m. \tag{5.22}$$

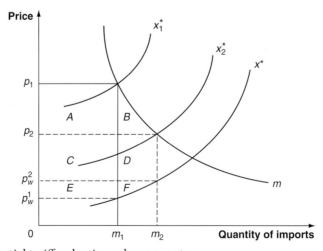

Figure 5.7 A partial tariff reduction – large country

where $m(p_m)$ is the inverse import demand function. The change in tariff revenue $\Delta R = (p_2 - p_w^2)dm - (dp_w - dp)m_1$ equals area D minus areas A and E in Figure 5.7. This change can also be measured as areas B, D and F minus areas A, B, E and F:

$$\Delta R = \int_{m_1}^{m_2} (p_m(m) - p_w(m))\, dm \quad (\text{areas } B + D + F)$$

$$- \int_{p_2}^{p_1} m(p_m)\, dp_m \quad (\text{areas } A + B)$$

$$- \int_{p_w^1}^{p_w^2} x^*(p_w)\, dp_w \quad (\text{areas } E + F) \tag{5.23}$$

where $p_w = p_w(m)$ and $m = x^*(p_w)$ are, respectively, the inverse and direct import supply functions. Adding expressions (5.22) and (5.23), the net change in welfare is:

$$\Delta W = \int_{m_1}^{m_2} (p_m(m) - p_w(m))\, dm - \int_{p_w^1}^{p_w^2} x^*(p_w)\, dp_w \tag{5.24}$$

which equals areas B and D minus area E in Figure 5.7. Given functional forms for import demand and export supply one can directly compute the integrals in (5.24) to compute the change in welfare.[25] Absent specific functional forms, the value of (5.24) can instead be approximated using the trapezoid rule which applied to (5.24) yields:[26]

$$\Delta W \cong \frac{1}{2}\left(\Delta m(p_1(1 + p_2/p_1) - p_{w1}(1 + /p_w^1)) - \Delta p_w x_1^*(1 + x_2^*/x_1^*)\right). \tag{5.25}$$

where $\Delta p_w = (p_{w2} - p_{w1}) > 0$. We now want to express the price and quantity changes in (5.25) in terms of the underlying elasticities of import demand and supply. To do so, first define the "pass-through" coefficients:

$$\rho_m = \hat{p}_m = (p_2/p_1) - 1$$
$$\rho_w = \hat{p}_w = (p_w^2/p_w^1) - 1 \tag{5.26}$$

which measure, respectively, the percentage change in the domestic and world price of the import good. Using (5.26), and setting $x_2^*/x_1^* = \hat{x}^* + 1$, (5.25) can be written:

$$\Delta W \cong \frac{1}{2}(\Delta m((\rho_m + 2)p_1 - p_w^1(\rho_w + 2)) - \Delta p_w x_1^*(\hat{x}^* + 2))$$

Multiplying the first expression in parentheses by m_1/m_1 and using $m_1 = x_1^*$ as well as $p_w^1 = p_1/\gamma_1$, where $\gamma_1 = (1 + \tau_1)$ gives:

$$\Delta W \cong \frac{V_1}{2\gamma_1}\left(\hat{m}(\gamma_1(\rho_m + 2) - (\rho_w + 2)) - \rho_w(\hat{x}^* + 2)\right) \tag{5.27}$$

Using $\hat{m} = -\eta_m \rho_m$ and $\hat{x}^* = \varepsilon_m \rho_w$, where ε_m denotes the elasticity of import supply, the preceding expression can be written:

$$\Delta W \cong \frac{V_1}{2\gamma_1} \left(-\eta_m \rho_m \left(\gamma_1 (\rho_m + 2) - (\rho_w + 2) \right) - \rho_w (\varepsilon_m \rho_w + 2) \right) \qquad (5.28)$$

Values for the pass-through coefficients are obtained by solving the equilibrium condition $-\eta_m \rho_m = \varepsilon_m \rho_w$ (i.e., $\hat{m} = \hat{x}^*$) with the equation for the change in the domestic price of imports: $\rho_m = \hat{\gamma} + \rho_w$, where $\hat{\gamma} = d\gamma/\gamma = d(1+\tau)/(1+\tau)$:

$$\rho_m = \frac{\hat{\gamma}}{(\varepsilon_m + \eta_m)}$$

$$\rho_w = \frac{-\eta_m \hat{\gamma}}{(\varepsilon_m + \eta_m)} \qquad (5.29)$$

Inserting these values into (5.28), one can after considerable manipulation write (5.28) as:

$$\Delta W \cong \frac{-V_1 \eta_m}{2\gamma_1} \left(\mu \left(\left(\frac{\hat{\gamma} \varepsilon_m}{(\varepsilon_m + \eta_m)} + 1 \right)^2 - 1 \right) + 2\hat{\gamma} \eta_m \right) \qquad (5.30)$$

where $\mu = (1 + \eta_m + \gamma_1 \varepsilon_m)$.

The formula for the welfare change of a small country that implements a partial tariff reduction can be found by repeating the above steps using $\Delta W = \int_{m_1}^{m_2} (p_m(m) - p_w) \, dm$ instead of expression (5.24) (see Problem 5.7). Doing this will result in the following expression (trapezoid approximation):

$$\Delta W \cong V_1 \eta_m \frac{(\tau_1)^2 - (\tau_2)^2}{2(1 + \tau_1)^2} \qquad (5.31)$$

Comparing this formula with (5.30) indicates that the only complication introduced by assuming a large country is that an estimate of the import supply elasticity is needed. However, the literature contains relatively few estimates of import supply elasticities for individual commodities. For this reason, welfare estimates using (5.30) are often presented for a range of assumed values for the supply elasticity (e.g., $\varepsilon_m = 1$ and $\varepsilon_m = 10$).

Table 5.1 shows calculated income transfer and efficiency costs associated with removing tariffs on selected US commodities.[27] One feature to note is the size of the net welfare effect relative to the size of the income transfers (tariff revenue plus producer surplus), with the latter typically much larger than the former.[28] The last column of Table 5.1 lists the ratio of the change in consumer surplus to the change in industry employment estimated to result from tariff removal. This ratio is an estimate of the cost to domestic consumers of maintaining employment in the industry via the tariff. For example, the first row shows that US consumers paid the equivalent of $145,400 per year (1998 dollars) to maintain the average job in the US footwear industry. Since this amount is substantially in excess of the annual wage of a worker in the footwear industry, consumers would be better off if the tariff were removed and consumers simply paid each subsequently unemployed footwear worker his or her wage.

This section has shown that obtaining an estimate of the welfare gain or loss arising from a tariff change is relatively simple. However, a number of practical and theoretical considerations arise when implementing these formulae. First, each layer of complexity added to

Table 5.1 Partial equilibrium estimates of welfare changes from removing selected US tariffs[a]
(values in millions of 1988 US dollars unless noted)

Product	Consumer surplus (gain)	Tariff revenue (loss)	Producer surplus (loss)	Net welfare[b] (gain)	Cost per job protected[c]
Footwear	290.8	−190.1	−72.1	28.5	145.4
Ceramic tile	96.5	−77.6	−16.7	2.3	24.1
Luggage	205.5	−139.8	−59.6	6.1	137.0
Leather gloves	33.8	−15.0	−17.5	1.3	67.6
Women's handbags	145.5	−103.4	−39.6	2.5	132.3
Glassware	238.6	−99.0	−132.5	7.2	91.8
Electronic capacitors	94.1	−42.3	−49.3	2.5	62.7
Bicycles	42.1	−26.4	−15.0	0.8	105.2
Optical instruments	18.6	−11.2	−7.0	0.4	46.5
Canned tuna	88.8	−21.4	−62.2	5.2	126.9

[a] Estimates are for 1988 and assume that the elasticity of domestic supply is unity.
[b] Sum of reduction in production and consumption efficiency costs.
[c] Total change in consumer surplus divided by change in industry employment estimated to arise from tariff removal, in thousands of US dollars.
Source: Adapted from United States International Trade Commission (1989).

the underlying model increases the number of elasticities whose values need to be known. Unfortunately, estimates of the elasticities needed to implement a full supply and demand model are rarely available. One way around this problem is to assume that certain elasticities take a range of values and to then present the corresponding range of welfare estimates. Alternatively, one can make assumptions that reduce the number of required elasticity values. A common assumption in this regard is that import supply is infinitely elastic (small country).

Second, when a welfare formula involves only one elasticity the uncertainty associated with the estimated value of this elasticity can be incorporated by presenting the welfare calculation as an interval estimate. However, when a formula involves several elasticities there is no simple way to summarize the joint uncertainty associated with the elasticity estimates. One way around this problem is to forego formulae stated in terms of underlying supply and elasticities and instead directly estimate the change in imports arising from a tariff change. This alternative approach requires the estimation of an econometric model that links import volumes to prices and tariffs.[29] Having estimated such a model, the import change arising from a tariff change can then be forecast and used to calculate the welfare change. Since the standard error of the forecast will incorporate the joint uncertainty of the estimate parameters a confidence interval can easily be constructed for the estimated welfare change. One caution in using this approach is that tariff rates may be endogenous since protection may have been obtained at the request of industries undergoing significant import competition. Hence, high tariffs may be associated with industries with high imports. This relationship between tariff rates and import volumes creates a "simultaneity bias" that would be expected to lead to estimates of the effects of tariffs (or other trade barriers) on imports volumes that are smaller than the true size of the effects. If so, any calculated welfare change would also be smaller than the true change in welfare.[30]

Multiple tariff changes

Estimation of the total change in welfare arising from a change in several tariff rates can be made by summing the individual partial equilibrium estimate for each good. However, each estimate ignores the income effect associated with a tariff change so that the summation of these estimates only compounds the error of omitting income effects. Since the accuracy of the estimated total welfare change is likely to fall as the scope of the tariff changes increases, welfare changes arising from large-scale tariff changes (e.g., multilateral tariff reductions) are now estimated using CGE models. However, when the analysis covers commodities at a detailed level of disaggregation a CGE model may be impractical due to data requirements. In such cases, the summation of the individual partial equilibrium estimates may be the only practical method for presenting the "total" effect of multiple tariff changes.

Non-tariff barriers

We now examine methods for estimating the welfare effects of non-tariff restrictions to trade by considering quantitative restrictions in the form of import and export quotas. Since the price and quantity effects of quotas can, under perfect competition, be duplicated by a tax on trade, the results of the preceding section are directly applicable to estimating the welfare effects of quotas. All that is required in most cases is to estimate the change in the domestic price of the traded good implied by the quantitative restriction and to then plug this change into the appropriate formula. The methods used to estimate the welfare effects of quotas apply equally well to other forms of non-tariff barriers as long as the price (or quantity) effects of the restriction can be determined. However, since quotas and other non-tariff restrictions often create economic rents, a careful assessment of the distribution of these rents is needed when determining the correct formula for calculating welfare changes.

Import quota

Figure 5.8 illustrates the case of a partial reduction in an import quota. The supply of imports is assumed to be infinitely elastic at the world price p_w (small country) and we ignore any

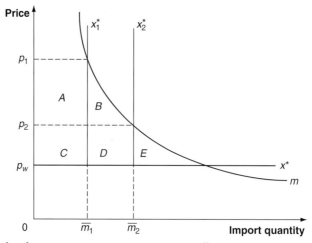

Figure 5.8 Partial reduction in an import quota – small country

cross-price effects between the imported and domestic good. Assuming an initial import quota of $\overline{m}_1$ units, import supply is given by x_1^* and the domestic price of imports is therefore p_1. An expansion of the quota to $\overline{m}_2$ units raises import supply to x_2^* and domestic price falls from p_1 to p_2.

Areas A and B in Figure 5.8 measure the gain to consumers of the imported good that arises from expansion of the quota. Since this change in consumer surplus is the same as that arising from a tariff reduction this change in consumer surplus can be measured using the trapezoid approximation:

$$\Delta CS \cong -\Delta p (\overline{m}_2 + \overline{m}_1)/2.$$

where $\Delta p = (p_2 - p_1) < 0$. Since the change in import quantity is known[31] we must now infer the price change Δp. The simplest method is to use the elasticity formula: $\Delta p = -p_1 \hat{m}/\eta_m$. Substituting this into the above expression, the formula for the change in consumer surplus is:

$$\Delta CS \cong \frac{V_1}{2\eta_m} \hat{m} (\hat{m} + 2)$$

In this expression $V_1 = p_1 \overline{m}_1$ is the initial value of imports. Now consider the change in quota rents which equals area D minus area A in Figure 5.8. Assuming these rents accrue to domestic agents, the change in quota rent is then equivalent to a change in tariff revenue. This implies that the expression for the net welfare change from partial relaxation of the quota is then given as:

$$\Delta W = \int_{\overline{m}_1}^{\overline{m}_2} \left\{ p_m(m) - p_w \right\} dm.$$

This expression equals areas B and D in Figure 5.8. Approximating this expression by the trapezoid rule yields:

$$\Delta W \cong \eta_m \{ (p_2 - p_w) + (p_1 - p_w) \}/2 \tag{5.32}$$

Expression (5.32) can be calculated by substituting estimates for the price changes in (5.32) or, equivalently, one can use expression (5.31) with the tariff rates replaced by *ad valorem* equivalent (AVE) tariff rates defined as $\tau_1^* = (p_1/p_w - 1)$ and $\tau_2^* = (p_2/p_w - 1)$.[32] The resulting expression (trapezoid approximation) can be written:

$$\Delta W \cong V_1 \eta_m \frac{(\tau_1^*)^2 - (\tau_2^*)^2}{2(1 + \tau_1^*)^2} \tag{5.33}$$

Since $p_1 = V_1/\overline{m}_1$ and $p_w = V_w/\overline{m}_1$ are observable, where V_w is the value of imports at world prices, only an estimate of p_2, and hence τ_2^*, is required.[33] By definition, $p_2 = (1 - \eta_m \hat{m})p_1$. Hence, using the preceding definitions of p_1 and p_w, the value of p_2/p_w can be estimated as

$$p_2/p_w = (1 - \eta_m \hat{m}) \frac{V_1}{V_w}.$$

Given this, the AVE tariff rates corresponding to quota levels $\overline{m}_1$ and $\overline{m}_2$ are computed as, respectively,

$$\tau_1^* = \frac{V_1}{V_w} - 1 \tag{5.34}$$

and

$$\tau_2^* = \frac{(1 - \eta\hat{m})V_1 - V_w}{V_w}. \qquad (5.35)$$

The above discussion implies that calculation of the welfare effects in the case of a large country only requires an estimate of the applicable AVE tariff rates. These rates can then be inserted into the appropriate formula derived for a tariff change. Since the initial AVE tariff rate is always that given by (5.34), only an expression for $\tau_2^* = (p_2/p_w - 1)$ is needed. For a large country, it is easily verified that an estimate of the AVE tariff rate is:[34]

$$\tau_2^* = \left(p_2/p_w^2 - 1\right) = \frac{\varepsilon_m V_1(\eta_m - \hat{m})}{\eta_m V_w(\varepsilon_m + \hat{m})} - 1$$

Hence, if quota rents accrue to domestic agents and the import quota is binding at $\bar{m}_2$ units then the calculation of welfare effects requires only minor modification to the formulae derived for a tariff change.

Export quotas

The methods for calculating the welfare effects of an export quota are the same as those for an import quota. In particular, AVE tariff rates can be calculated and inserted into the appropriate welfare formula. One practical difficulty is that computation of the AVE tariff rates requires data on producer prices in the exporting country which are often difficult to obtain. In addition, the accuracy of the AVE tariff rates is likely to be less than in the case of an import quota since differences between domestic and world prices may arise for any number of reasons, including costs of transport within a country.[35]

Our analysis of an export quota considers a partial reduction in a VER. In this case, interest normally focuses on the welfare changes in the importing country rather than the exporting country. Figure 5.9 illustrates this case for a large country. Given an initial voluntary export quota of $\bar{x}_1$ units and a world price equal to p_w^1 exporters receive rent of $p_w^1 - p_1$ on each unit exported. Expansion of the quota from $\bar{x}_1$ to $\bar{x}_2$ reduces the world price from p_w^1 to p_w^2 and raises the producer price from p_1 to p_2. Per unit rent therefore falls to $p_w^2 - p_2$.

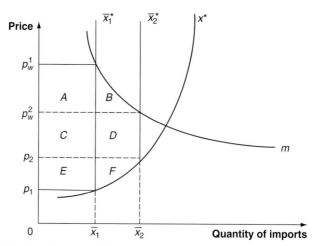

Figure 5.9 Partial reduction in a voluntary export restraint – large country

Table 5.2 Partial equilibrium estimates of welfare changes arising from removal of VERs on selected products imported by the US

(All values in millions of US dollars unless noted)

Product	Change in				
	Consumer surplus	Tariff revenue[a]	Foreign quota rents	Domestic producer surplus	Net welfare[b]
Carbon and specialty steel	895.5	−486.0	−22.6	−343.0	66.6
Machine tools	56.0	−29.0	−5.5	−19.1	7.9

[a] Estimates also include the effects of removing pre-quota tariffs. Estimates are for 1988 and assume that the elasticity of domestic supply is 1.38.
[b] Sum of reduction in production and consumption deadweight losses plus repatriation of quota rents earned by foreign entities.
Source: Adapted from United States International Trade Commission (1989).

The benefit of the quota expansion to the importing home country is the gain in consumer surplus given by areas *A* and *B* in Figure 5.9. The exporting country loses quota rents equal to areas *A* and *E* but gains rent equal to area *D*. In addition, exporter surplus rises by areas *E* and *F*. The net change in foreign welfare is therefore areas *F* and *D* minus area *A*. We leave to the reader the task of writing down the expressions for these welfare changes in terms of the AVE tariff rates and the underlying supply and demand elasticities.

Table 5.2 lists estimated welfare gains and losses from removing VERs on selected products imported into the US. Since foreigners receive the quota rents generated by these VERs, the net welfare gain to the US from removing these restrictions is substantially larger than in the case of tariffs.

Quota removal

The methods discussed above have assumed a partial expansion of a quota rather than complete removal. A partial change in a quota simplifies estimation of the price change (or the AVE tariff rate) arising from the quota expansion since the amount traded after the quota change is simply the new level set by the quota. However, if the quota were instead being eliminated or the new quota level could not be assumed to be binding then the new volume of trade and hence the change in trade must be estimated. Estimation of the hypothetical quantity change is often done using an econometric model of the market being examined.[36] The estimated quantity change is then used to calculate the hypothetical price change or AVE tariff rate which is then used to calculate welfare changes using the formulae developed in this section.

Price changes and unit values

Estimates of the welfare effects arising from a quota require data on the domestic and world price of the restricted good. However, these price data are rarely available. Instead, prices are calculated by dividing the value of exports or imports of a good by its quantity. This would be valid if the good were homogeneous. However, in practice a "good" is often an aggregate category consisting of several varieties (e.g., footwear). Since price varies across varieties, dividing a value by a quantity gives an average price. This average price is called a unit value. The value of a unit value depends on both the prices of the individual items and the composition of items within the aggregate category. Hence, actual changes in unit values will reflect changes in both components. However, when unit values are used to estimate price changes, and hence AVE tariff rates, the composition of items is implicitly held fixed. The failure to account for changes in the composition of items leads to an underestimation of the actual price change that will result when the quota is changed. For example, tightening a quota raises the prices of all items covered by the quota but the proportionate increase in the price of low price items will exceed the proportionate increase in the price of high price items. Consumers respond to these relative price changes by increasing their demand for high price relative to low price items. Similarly, expanding a quota lowers the prices of all items but the proportionate fall in the prices of low price items will exceed the proportionate fall in the prices of high price items. Consumers respond by increasing their demand for low price relative to high price items. Since the estimated price change does not take account of these changes in consumer spending it understates the size of the actual price change. Hence, calculated welfare gains and losses will also be understated.[37]

General equilibrium methods

This section first presents a theoretical derivation of the net welfare change arising from a change in trade policies in general equilibrium. This analysis extends the welfare decomposition analysis presented in Section 5.1 to the case of many goods and when imported and domestically produced goods are imperfect substitutes. Following this, we discuss CGE modeling as an approach to obtaining estimates of the net welfare change that arises in general equilibrium.

Welfare changes

Assume there are J goods, and each good is produced domestically and also imported.[38] Denote the vector of world prices of imported goods as $\mathbf{p}_w = (p_{w1},\ldots,p_{wJ})$ and the vectors of domestic prices of domestic and imported goods as $\mathbf{p}_d = (p_{d1},\ldots,p_{dJ})$ and $\mathbf{p}_m = (p_{m1},\ldots,p_{mJ})$, respectively. The utility level (u_0) a country achieves under its current set of trade policy instruments (e.g., tariffs or quotas) can be found by equating its expenditure (S) with its current income from all sources:

$$S\left(\mathbf{p}_d, \mathbf{p}_m, \mathbf{p}_w, u_0\right) = G\left(\mathbf{p}_d\right) + \sum_{j=1}^{NJ} (p_{mj} - p_{wj})m_j \tag{5.36}$$

Expression (5.36) is the J-good analogue of (5.3). The right-hand side of (5.36) states that income derives from two sources: production, as given by the economy's GDP function $G(\mathbf{p}_d)$, and tariff revenue or quota rents, as reflected by the difference between the domestic and world prices of imports.[39] By definition of the expenditure function, this income level (just) allows the economy to achieve utility level u_0.

We now need a measure of the welfare change a country would experience if it adopted a different set of trade policies. Let u_1 denote the utility level that would obtain under the new set of trade policies. A widely used measure of welfare changes is the equivalent variation (EV).[40] In the present context, the EV measures the amount of income that consumers would need to receive (give up), at the prices existing under the initial trade policies, to obtain the utility level u_1. The expression for this amount of income is:

$$EV = S(\mathbf{p}_d, \mathbf{p}_m, \mathbf{p}_w, u_1) - S(\mathbf{p}_d, \mathbf{p}_m, \mathbf{p}_w, u_0) \tag{5.37}$$

If the income change given by (5.37) is positive (negative) then the new set of trade policies would represent a welfare gain (loss) compared with the existing trade policies. If the form of the expenditure function (S) is known, (5.37) can be used to calculate the welfare gain (loss) due to any change in trade policies. CGE models perform exactly this calculation since they normally assume an explicit form of the utility function and can therefore derive its associated expenditure function.

If the form of expenditure function is unknown then one can calculate a local approximation to the welfare change given in (5.37). To see how, substitute (5.36) into (5.37) to get:[41]

$$EV = \left(G(\mathbf{p}_d) + \sum_{J=1}^{NJ} (p_{mj} - p_{wj})m_j \right) - S(\mathbf{p}_d, \mathbf{p}_m, \mathbf{p}_w, u_0) = 0. \qquad (5.38)$$

Holding utility constant at the level u_0, total differentiation of (5.38) gives:

$$dEV = \sum_{j=1}^{NJ} \left[\frac{\partial G}{\partial p_{dj}} dp_{dj} + \left((dp_{mj} - dp_{wj})m_j + (p_{mj} - p_{wj})dm_j \right) \right.$$
$$\left. - \left(\frac{\partial S}{\partial p_{dj}} dp_{dj} + \frac{\partial S}{\partial p_{mj}} dp_{mj} \right) \right] \qquad (5.39)$$

By the properties of the income and expenditure functions we have $\partial y/\partial p_{dj} = q_j$, $\partial S/\partial p_{dj} = d_j$ and $\partial S/\partial p_{mj} = m_j$, where q_j and d_j are the production and consumption of domestic good j. Substituting these expressions in (5.39) gives:

$$dEV = \sum_j \left[\left((q_j - d_j)dp_{dj} - m_j dp_{wj} \right) + (p_{mj} - p_{wj})dm_j \right] \qquad (5.40)$$

This expression is the J-good analogue of (5.5) and holds for a small change in trade policies. As in (5.5), the net change in welfare derives from two sources. First there is the change in the terms of trade, which now encompasses both exports $(q_j - d_j)$ and imports. Second is the price distortion or trade volume effect which measures the change in tariff revenue or quota rents as the volume of imports changes. The value of (5.40) can be computed if the price and quantity changes are known. However, the price and quantity changes in (5.40) are general equilibrium changes that take into account all interactions between markets. The computation of these changes therefore requires a fully specified general equilibrium model. In the absence of such a model, the price and quantity changes in (5.40), and hence the net welfare change, can be approximated using partial equilibrium analysis.

General equilibrium modeling

In the early 1970s analysts began to develop and use CGE models to evaluate the welfare and resource allocation effects of trade and domestic tax policies. CGE models are also called applied general equilibrium (AGE) models. These models are "computable" because they posit explicit forms for demand and supply functions[42] which make it possible to explicitly solve for the equilibrium values of prices and quantities once the model is fitted to a set of data. CGE models capture the interactions that take place between markets and provide the policy-maker with considerable detail on production and consumption effects, as well as the welfare changes, arising from trade policy changes.

The focus of all CGE models is the computation of changes in the equilibrium values of a model's endogenous variables arising from changes in exogenously given policy variables (e.g., tariffs). These changes in endogenous variables are obtained using one of two methods. The first derives the global changes in the model's endogenous variables while the second method derives the local, comparative static, changes. Calculation of welfare effects arising from policy changes is made using the expenditure function implied by the assumed form of the utility function or by summing the welfare change in each market as in (5.40).

Implementing a CGE model can involve considerable time and effort in terms of data collection and model specification. Since the details of each model vary with the interests of the modeler and the set of policy questions to be examined, no one account of a "CGE model" is possible. Therefore, in this section we provide an outline of the main elements of CGE modeling and leave the specific details of the many alternative models to the references listed at the end of this chapter.

Theoretical foundation

The theoretical foundation for all CGE models is the competitive general equilibrium model. Hence, it is appropriate to begin our discussion of CGE modeling with a review of this model in the case of many goods and many factors.[43] Most CGE models introduce modifications to the assumptions of this standard model. In particular, unlike here, goods are assumed to be imperfectly substitutable and the production sector uses intermediate goods as well as primary factor inputs. To these extensions are often added assumptions concerning factor mobility, unemployment, imperfectly competitive pricing or economies of scale. However, regardless of the assumptions, the model ultimately reduces to a system of demand and supply equations and a set of income-expenditure identities.[44]

Consider first the supply side of the economy, which determines factor prices and therefore national income. Assume there are J competitive industries. Each industry is assumed to employ H factor inputs to produce an amount q_j of a single homogeneous good using the production function $q_j = F_j(\mathbf{e}_j)$, where $\mathbf{e}_j = (e_{j1}, \ldots, e_{jH})$ is the vector of factor inputs employed in industry j. Since the production function for industry j ($j = 1, \ldots, J$) is assumed to be linear homogeneous it can also be expressed as

$$1 = F_j(a_{j1}, \ldots, a_{jH}) \tag{5.41}$$

where $a_{jh} = e_{jh}/q_j$ is the demand for factor h per unit of output j. Since factors of production are assumed homogeneous and perfectly mobile between industries, equilibrium requires that a factor's value marginal product equals its market price. Denote the vector of factor prices as $\mathbf{w} = (w_1, \ldots, w_h)$ and the vector of commodity prices as $\mathbf{p} = (p_1, \ldots, p_j)$. Then the conditions for equilibrium are:

$$p_j(\partial F_j/\partial e_h) \leq w_h \quad j = 1, \ldots, J; \ h = 1, \ldots, H. \tag{5.42}$$

These equations hold with equality of every factor actually used in production.

Let $\mathbf{e} = (e_1, \ldots, e_H)$ denote the vector of total factor supplies. The supply of each factor is assumed to be perfectly inelastic so that $\mathbf{e}$ can be regarded as a vector of constants. Full employment of factors requires:

$$e_h = \sum_j e_{jh} = a_{1h}q_1 + \cdots + a_{Jh}q_J \quad h = 1, \ldots, H. \tag{5.43}$$

Equations (5.41) to (5.43) are sufficient to determine the supply side of the model. Together, there are $J + JH + H$ independent equations to determine JH optimal unit factor requirements, H factor prices and J output supplies. It is therefore possible to solve for an equilibrium in terms of the given values of the factor supplies and commodity prices.

Now consider demand. As long as factor supplies are fixed, relative commodity prices contain all the information needed to specify the demand functions:

$$d_j = d_j(p_1, \ldots, p_j, \ldots, p_J) \quad j = 1, \ldots J. \tag{5.44}$$

These functions are homogeneous of degree zero in prices. We now consider the market clearing and income-expenditure identities that must hold in general equilibrium.

Consider first an isolated economy for which the supply always equals the demand for each good:

$$q_j = d_j \quad j = 1, \ldots J. \tag{5.45}$$

These market clearing identities are not independent by virtue of the income-expenditure identity:

$$\sum_{j=1}^{J} p_j q_j \equiv \sum_{h=1}^{H} w_h e_h = \sum_{j=1}^{J} p_j d_j \tag{5.46}$$

Thus, we can drop any one equation in (5.45). If we now count the number of equations we find $J + JH + H + J - 1$ independent relations to determine the J outputs, JH factor demands, H factor prices and J commodity prices. Hence, the number of endogenous variables exceeds by one the number of independent relations. To resolve this, prices are expressed in terms of any one good (i.e., the numeraire) whose price is then set equal to unity. Given this, the autarky equilibrium is determinate – that is, the model can be solved for the outputs, factor demands, factor prices and $J - 1$ relative prices in terms of the given factor supplies.

Now assume there are N separate trading countries where each is described by the above technology and tastes. A superscript is used to denote each country $n = 1, \ldots, N$. With trade, it is no longer true that production and consumption of each good be equal within a country. Instead, production must equal consumption for the world as a whole:

$$\sum_{n=1}^{N} d_j^n = \sum_{n=1}^{N} q_j^n \quad j = 1, \ldots, J. \tag{5.47}$$

Assuming balanced trade in each country implies that the total value of production equals the total value of consumption for each country, that is:

$$0 = p_1^n(q_1^n - d_1^n) + \cdots + p_j^n(q_j^n - d_j^n) + \cdots + p_J^n(q_J^n - d_J^n) \quad n = 1, \ldots, N. \tag{5.48}$$

Summing (5.48) over countries, and noting that free trade equates commodity prices across countries, we obtain:

$$0 = p_1 \sum_{n=1}^{N}(q_1^n - d_1^n) + \cdots + p_j \sum_{n=1}^{N}(q_j^n - d_j^n) + \cdots + p_J \sum_{n=1}^{N}(q_J^n - d_J^n). \tag{5.49}$$

This is Walras's Law with J markets: when $(J-1)$ markets are in equilibrium then by necessity the remaining market is also in equilibrium. Hence, it is sufficient to solve $(J-1)$ of the equations in (5.47) for the $(J-1)$ world relative prices.

Given the world prices, the J equations in (5.41), the JH equations in (5.42), the H equations in (5.43) and the J equations in (5.44) in each of the N countries solve for the $(JH + 2J + H)$ country unknowns, namely, the a_{ij}, q_j, d_j and w_h. The equilibrium is therefore determinant for a given distribution of world factor endowments among countries.

Implementation

Implementing a CGE model typically involves five steps:

1) Model selection;
2) Specification;
3) Data collection;
4) Calibration and verification;
5) Counterfactual policy simulations.

The following summarizes each of these steps.

Model selection

CGE models can be country-specific or multilateral. The majority of CGE models are single country models. Such models are common because the data are available to provide greater detail on industry and consumer behavior and the analyst can concentrate on incorporating specific institutional details such as wage rigidities or specific domestic policies. The next level of generality is achieved by multi-country models which incorporate interactions between countries as reflected in the world markets for their goods. Multi-country models can be global or regional. A regional model typically specifies sector detail for a subset of countries while treating the remaining countries as a "rest of world" residual. An example of a regional model is that developed to examine the effects of the creation of the North American Free Trade Agreement (NAFTA) between Canada, the US and Mexico (see Chapter 12). Global models typically sacrifice industry detail (due to data limitations) but model the interactions among all countries. To give orders of magnitude, a typical single country model might specify supplies and demands for some 60 sectors while a regional model might reduce this to 20 or 30 sectors. A global model might reduce this to 10 or 12 sectors. The principal limitations are data on the input–output technologies of different countries and difficulties in reconciling national systems of data classification.

Specification

Specification of a CGE model involves choosing both the underlying behavioral structure of the model and explicit functional forms for the supply and demand equations. CGE models typically use a combination of Cobb-Douglas and CES (Constant Elasticity of Substitution) functions to represent either utility and production functions or, equivalently, supply and demand functions. Table 5.3 lists some of the common functional forms used in CGE models. Which functional form is chosen depends on the interests of the modeler and the availability of data on the elasticity parameters that characterize these functions. Since elasticity values are crucial to CGE models (they cannot be solved without them) modelers maintain inventories of elasticity estimates culled from the literature or estimate elasticities as needed.

CGE models commonly assume that the pattern of demand is determined by a multistage budgeting process. In the first stage, expenditure is allocated among goods. Preferences

Table 5.3 Common functional forms used in CGE modeling

	Cobb-Douglas	Constant elasticity of substitution (CES)	Linear expenditure system (Cobb-Douglas Variety)
Utility or production function	$\prod_i x_i^{\alpha_i}$	$\left(\sum_i \alpha_i^{1/\sigma} x_i^{(\sigma-1)/\sigma}\right)^{\sigma/(\sigma-1)}$	$\prod_i (x_i - c_i)^{\alpha_i}$
Demand equation	$x_i = \alpha_i Z / p_i$	$x_i = \alpha_i Z / \left(p_i^{\sigma} \sum_{j \neq i} \alpha_j p_j^{(1-\sigma)}\right)$	$x_i = c_i + \left(\frac{\alpha_i}{p_i}\right)\left(I - \sum_j p_j c_j\right)$
Expenditure or cost function	$\prod_i (p_i/\alpha_i)^{\alpha_i}$	$\left(\sum_i \alpha_i p_i^{(1-\sigma)}\right)^{(1-\sigma)}$	$\prod_i (p_i/\alpha_i)^{\alpha_i}$
Side conditions	$\sum_i \alpha_i = 1$	$\sum_i \alpha_i^{1/\sigma} = 1$	$\sum_i \alpha_i = 1;$

Notes: x_i is the quantity of good or factor i; p_i is the price of x_i; σ is the elasticity of substitution between any pair x_i and x_j; Z is either income (commodity equation) or output (input demand); α_i is an expenditure (or cost) share depending on the definition of x_i. In the LES specification, c_i is the minimum demand requirement of good i.

at this stage are modeled either as Cobb-Douglas or as a Linear Expenditure System (see Table 5.3). In the second stage, expenditure on each good is then allocated between imports and a domestically produced variety. The specification of second stage preferences varies across models although most adopt some form of the Armington (1969) specification that goods are differentiated by their country of production (see below). Some models forego the assumption of a constant elasticity of substitution and instead utilize a "flexible" functional form that permits the elasticity of substitution to vary over pairs of goods. Finally, some models forego the assumption of product differentiation entirely and instead assume that imports and domestic goods are perfect substitutes. These different assumptions are not without importance. In particular, output responses will be larger when perfect substitutes are assumed.

Armington assumption

Most CGE trade models adopt the Armington (1969) assumption of national product differentiation when modeling the demand for goods. Under this assumption imports are differentiated by country of origin and thus, symmetrically, each country is the sole producer of its export good. Consumers within a country then use a two-stage budgeting procedure to determine their demand for imports. In the first stage, they choose the total amount to be spent on imports without regard to country of origin. In the second stage they determine the allocation of their aggregate spending on imports across supplier countries. This process leads to conditional import demand functions[45] which are implemented by modeling them as CES functions of domestic and imported varieties of goods.

A central attraction of the Armington specification is that it serves to model, without explaining, the phenomena of intra-industry trade observed in the trade data. It thus allows goods to be modeled as imperfect substitutes (and hence differentiated). However, while convenient, the Armington specification is restrictive since it assumes that while all varieties of a domestically produced good are perfect substitutes, these varieties are imperfect substitutes for the varieties produced by other countries.[46] In addition, the specification implies that a country, no matter how small, enjoys market power with respect to its export good. Another troubling aspect of the Armington specification is the implied cross-price effects that arise between imported goods and their domestically produced, and exported, substitutes. These cross-price effects imply export market price changes whose effect on welfare is the opposite to that arising in the domestic markets for imported goods. Sufficiently strong cross-price effects can therefore result in net welfare changes that are opposite to those expected when import restrictions are reduced. In fact, these cross-price induced welfare changes have generally been found to dominate the import market efficiency gains associated with import liberalization with the result that the calculated net welfare change from tariff reductions is often found to be negative.[47]

The Armington specification is one example of a specification that gives rise to the nesting of functions that is common in CGE models. Figure 5.10 gives a schematic of the type of nesting that might be used to model the output of a given sector. In this figure, gross output of the sector is modeled as a Leontief function of both value-added and an intermediate input. This would be represented as $q_j = \min(V_j/a_{Vj}, H_j/a_{Hj})$ where V_j is sector j's value-added, H_j is the composite intermediate input, and a_{vj} and a_{Hj} are the unit input requirements of, respectively, value-added and the composite intermediate. The value-added (net output) function is then modeled as a CES function of capital (K_j) and labor input (L_j), which can be written as: $V_j = \gamma_j \left(\alpha_{jL} L_j^{(\sigma_j-1)/\sigma_j} + \alpha_{jK} K_j^{(\sigma_j-1)/\sigma_j} \right)^{\sigma_j/(\sigma_j-1)}$. In this function, γ_j is a scale parameter whose value is determined during the calibration stage (see below). The composite intermediate H_j is then modeled as a Leontief function of M composite intermediates (i.e., $H_j = \min (Z_{ji}/a_{ji}; i = 1, \ldots, M)$. Each of these M composite intermediates is itself a CES function of a domestically produced and imported variety. If the imported intermediate were further disaggregated by country of export then the CES composite function would be an implementation of the Armington assumption. The structure shown in Figure 5.10 allows substitution between domestic and imported varieties of each primary intermediate, but no substitution occurs between the composites of these intermediates, nor between the intermediate and value-added.

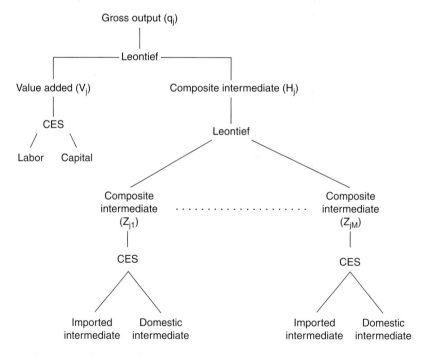

Figure 5.10 Example of a nested production structure

Data

The data used to implement a CGE model are the flows of income and expenditure between agents within an economy and with the rest of the world. Modelers often represent these flows in the form of a Social Accounting Matrix (SAM). The rows and columns of the SAM denote groupings of economic agents while the entries in the matrix are the expenditure-income flows among agents.

Table 5.4 shows a simplified SAM for an economy consisting of five agents or institutional groupings: suppliers, households, government, rest of world and a capital account reflecting savings and investment. The entries in each column record the transaction flow from group *j* to group *i* while the entries in a given row record the income received by group *i* from group *j*. The sum of the elements in column *j* is the total expenditure by group *j* while the sum of the elements in row *i* is the total income received by group *i*. If the income-expenditure identities are satisfied then the sum of the elements in any row *i* equals the sum of the elements in any column *j*.

The primary purpose of constructing a SAM is to check the consistency of the data and thus ensure that the accounting identities are satisfied. This consistency check is crucial since the data are often collected from several different sources. In addition, one usually needs to reconcile differences in the units in which income and expenditure are measured (e.g., the value of sales measured at producer prices versus household expenditure measured at market prices). A SAM is also the format in which many of the computer programs[48] developed to solve CGE models expect the data to be provided.

The level of disaggregation within a SAM will reflect the degree of detail desired by the modeler. Generally, the supplier group is divided into "activities" and "commodities." Activities are the basic production units of the economy in that they purchase intermediate inputs and hire factor services to produce commodities. The "commodities" combine domestic supply with imports and distribute these goods for intermediate use and final demand. The activities and commodities can then be further disaggregated into individual product categories to provide sector detail. Additional disaggregation of agents would identify "factors" (which receive value added) and "enterprises" (which receive profits).

Table 5.4 A simplified social accounting matrix (SAM)

Receipts by	Expenditures by					Total
	(1) Suppliers	**(2)** Households	**(3)** Government	**(4)** Rest of world	**(5)** Capital account	
(1) Suppliers		Purchases	Purchases	Exports	Investment	**Aggregate Demand**
(2) Households	Income					**Income**
(3) Government		Taxes				**Taxes**
(4) Rest of world	Imports					**Imports**
(5) Capital account		Savings	Savings	Savings		**Aggregate Savings**
Total	**Aggregate Supply**	**Expenditure**	**Expenditure**	**Foreign Exchange**	**Investment**	

Calibration

Calibration involves "fitting" a CGE model to a given set of data. There are two aspects to calibration. The first involves the selection of elasticity values and the use of observed data to compute values of function parameters such as factor shares, consumption expenditure shares, and so on – all of which are parameters that appear in the demand and supply equations. The second aspect of calibration involves calculating the value of parameters that represent the units of measurement of the variables. This second type of calibration is required only if a global solution to the model is sought. If the effects of policy changes will instead be calculated using local, comparative, static, approximations then the process of calibration ends with the selection of elasticity values and the computation of the various function parameters.

If a global solution for the model is to be computed, the model must be adjusted to account for differences in the units of measurement of the variables. This adjustment involves estimating the value of scale parameters, one of each equation, so that the model fits the observed data in levels. This process can be envisioned by thinking of a single linear equation $y = a + bx$ in which the value of the slope coefficient "b" is known. Given data on y and x, calibration to the level of y then amounts to finding the value of the intercept parameter "a" (i.e. $a = y - bx$).

In practice, the scale parameters are estimated by arbitrarily setting all prices in the model to unity. Since prices and the values of all other endogenous variables are then known, the equations can be solved to determine the unknown scale parameters. The solution values of the scale parameters are then appended to the corresponding equations as known parameters and the full model is then solved, this time for the vector of equilibrium prices. By construction, the solution values of the prices should be unity. However, computational accuracy often results in prices that are slightly different from unity (e.g., 0.999998). These prices, and the solution values of the model's other endogenous variables, then become the *benchmark* or initial solution data set against which all subsequent counterfactual solutions are compared.

The process of solving for the equilibrium prices and the benchmark data set is referred to as model verification. Once the model is solved, not only does it fit the adjusted data (and vice versa), but if the prices are found to differ greatly from unity then the modeler knows that either incorrect values of the scale parameter have been entered or there is some other data inconsistency. Hence, model verification serves to check for data entry errors either in parameter values or equations as well as generating the benchmark equilibrium data set.

Counterfactuals

Two methods are used to obtain the effects of counterfactual changes in policy variables: the global solution method and the Johansen method.[49] The global solution method involves resolving the model for each alternative choice for the policy variable(s) and then comparing each new set of equilibrium values to those of the benchmark equilibrium.

The Johansen method uses the comparative static derivatives implied by the model to compute the change in endogenous variables that arise from changes in the exogenous policy variables. The main difference between the global solution and Johansen methods is that the effects of policy changes computed using the latter are local approximations to the global changes obtained using the global solution method. The comparative static derivatives are found by first totally differentiating the (log-linear) system of supply and demand equations and then expressing these derivatives as relative changes in the variables.[50] The result of this differentiation is then a system of linear equations which, by construction, has as many unknowns (the relative changes in the endogenous variables) as equations. Since the equation system is linear, solutions for the unknown comparative static derivatives can be found by matrix inversion. Once the solution matrix of comparative static changes is found, post-multiplying this matrix by a vector of relative changes in the policy variables then gives the corresponding changes in the endogenous variables of the model. The Johansen method is often used to compute the effects of policy changes[51] despite the fact that algorithms for computing a global solution are now widely available and relatively simple to implement.

To indicate the type of results obtained from a CGE model, Table 5.5 and Table 5.6 show the results of a global solution simulation conducted at the conclusion of the Uruguay Round of General Agreement on Tariffs and Trade (GATT) negotiations. The model used contained 19 sectors and 13 countries/regions. The model also used two alternative specifications for production and market conduct: constant returns to scale and perfect competition (CRS/PC) and increasing returns to scale and imperfect (monopolistic) competition (IRS/IP).

Table 5.5 shows projected changes in the real wage and relative price of labor expected to occur once the trade liberalizations agreed to in the Uruguay Round were implemented. Table 5.6 shows the projected welfare changes for each country/region as a percentage of its GDP in 1992 (the benchmark equilibrium year). For each country/region, the welfare change is broken down into four product groups to indicate the sources of the income change. The measure of welfare change is the equivalent variation (see (5.37)). Hence, the welfare changes measure the increase in national income that would be necessary at base year (1992) prices to achieve the welfare gain (or loss) projected to arise from the Uruguay Round liberalizations.

The results in Table 5.5 indicate that the agreed liberalizations were expected to raise the real wage in all countries/regions while the wage-rental ratio was generally expected to fall in industrial countries. These across-the-board real wage increases can occur because the model assumes that labor also derives income from the ownership of capital. The real wage gains appear to be largest in China, East Asia and South Asia. Increasing returns to scale and

Table 5.5 Estimates of percentage change in real and relative wages due to trade barrier reductions under Uruguay Round agreements
(Percentage change relative to 1992 base values)

Country/Region	Real wage (percent change)		Wage-rental ratio (percent change)	
	CRS/PC[a]	IRS/IP	CRS/PC	IRS/IP
Australia/New Zealand	0.71	0.04	−0.12	−0.35
Japan	0.13	0.13	−0.01	−0.19
Canada	0.67	0.61	−0.04	0.03
United States	0.30	0.32	−0.04	−0.17
European Union	0.29	0.33	−0.00	−0.01
EFTA	0.33	0.29	0.05	0.12
Africa	0.41	0.71	0.21	0.36
China	1.89	1.69	0.46	1.67
East Asia	1.93	1.49	0.39	1.35
South Asia	2.13	2.84	0.59	4.15
Latin America	0.65	0.63	−0.12	−0.20
Transition Economies	0.17	0.25	−0.03	−0.05
Rest of World[b]	3.10	3.39	0.13	0.27

[a]CRS = constant returns to scale; PC = perfect competition; IP = imperfect competition.
[b]Mostly Turkey and South Africa.
Source: Adapted from Tables 15 and 16, Francois, McDonald and Nordström (1995).

Table 5.6 Estimates of welfare changes due to trade barrier reductions under Uruguay Round agreements[a]
(Percentage of 1992 GDP)

Country/Region	Total[a]		Industrial products		Agricultural products		Non-agricultural primary products	
	CRS/PC	IRS/IP	CRS/PC	IRS/IP	CRS/PC	IRS/IP	CRS/PC	IRS/IP
Australia & New Zealand	0.09	0.03	−0.11	−0.17	0.18	0.18	0.02	0.01
Japan	0.04	0.16	0.05	0.17	0.01	−0.01	−0.00	−0.00
Canada	0.13	0.12	−0.01	0.03	0.13	0.07	0.01	0.02
United States	0.17	0.28	0.16	0.29	0.00	−0.01	0.00	0.00
European Union	0.22	0.26	0.14	0.25	0.07	0.01	0.01	0.01
EFTA	0.03	0.04	0.10	0.03	−0.07	0.00	−0.00	−0.00
Africa	0.24	0.81	0.23	0.51	−0.05	0.16	0.07	0.13
China	0.84	2.79	0.79	2.69	0.03	0.06	0.01	0.03
East Asia	0.35	2.00	0.38	1.95	0.00	0.04	−0.01	0.00
South Asia	0.37	2.77	0.43	2.89	−0.07	−0.06	−0.00	−0.06
Latin America	0.01	0.33	−0.01	0.25	0.02	0.09	0.00	−0.00
Transition Economies	−0.04	0.21	0.05	0.17	−0.09	0.03	0.01	0.01
Rest of World[c]	0.98	2.28	0.51	2.40	.20	0.03	−0.10	−0.14
Total	0.17	0.44	0.07	0.42	0.02	0.02	0.00	0.01

[a]Equivalent variation measured as a percentage of 1992 base GDP.
[b]CRS = constant returns to scale; PC = perfect competition; IP = imperfect competition.
[c]Mostly Turkey and South Africa.
Source: Adapted from Tables 17 and 19, Francois, McDonald and Nordström (1995).

imperfect competition tend to give more or less the same real wage changes, while changes in the wage-rental ratio are larger under the IRS/IP specification than under the CRS/PC specification.

As shown in Table 5.6, the projected welfare gains arise mostly from liberalization of industrial products and other primary products, which indicates the importance of the agreed liberalization of tariffs and non-tariff barriers to trade (NTBs) in these sectors. With the exception of Latin America, the gains from liberalization favor developing regions. The relatively large gains for China, East Asia and South Asia reflect the then impending liberalization of trade in textiles and apparel. This trade had previously been covered by a system of export quotas known as the Multi-Fiber Arrangement (MFA). In the Uruguay Round, WTO member countries agreed to end the MFA and to extend coverage of the GATT agreements to such trade.

Caveats

CGE models make it possible to calculate sectoral output and employment consequences of alternative trade policies as well as net welfare effects. While many praise the efforts of CGE modelers to quantify the detailed workings of a trading world, CGE modeling has its critics.

One substantive criticism is that the values calculated from such models have no statistical foundation since the estimates derived have no associated standard error. Hence, there is no way to assess the reliability of the estimates. In principle, the remedy would be to estimate the parameters of the model's equations using times series observations on all relevant variables. However, the data to do this are simply not available at the level of detail required.

A second criticism is that CGE models lack transparency – that is, the detailed inter-relationships and nesting of functions make it extremely difficult to determine what drives the results of any particular model. In response, CGE modelers often conduct sensitivity analyses by varying the values of one or more elasticity parameters and reporting the difference this makes for key results. Although helpful, this type of sensitivity analysis does not fully reveal the dependence of the results on particular linkages within the model or on the functional forms chosen to represent the equations of it.

5.4 Concluding remarks

This chapter has examined the impact of trade restricting and trade promoting measures under the assumption that firms operate in perfectly competitive markets. Generally, when firms operate in perfectly competitive markets, a country imposing a restriction on trade suffers a loss of welfare due to a misallocation of resources that creates economic inefficiencies in both production and consumption. An exception is the case of a large country that can use its market power to set a price for its exports that extracts "monopoly rents" from foreign buyers, with the transfer of income offsetting the costs the country incurs from misallocating resources. A similar idea – that an income transfer from foreigners can offset the deadweight loss from resource misallocation – arises in Chapter 10 when, for example, an export subsidy is analyzed in the context of imperfectly competitive markets. While the "optimum tariff" is a theoretical possibility, it is important to remember that such a tariff may engender retaliation that can make all countries worse off than under free trade.

Finally, we examined both partial and general equilibrium methods for estimating the welfare effects of tariff and non-tariff barriers. While partial equilibrium methods are often used, particularly when detailed commodities are examined, the use of CGE modeling has become routine for assessing large-scale changes in trade policy in a multi-country, multi-commodity setting.

Problems

5.1 Demonstrate that the distance cd in Figure 5.1 equals the tariff revenue $\tau p_w m_t$ where m_t is the post-tariff level of imports (i.e., the distance bB′ in Figure 5.1).

5.2 Use the computer program of the small open economy developed in Chapter 4 to incorporate the effects of a tariff on imports, production and consumption as presented in Figure 5.1. Assume that $\tau = 0.1$ and compare your results with the free trade solution from Chapter 4.

5.3 Demonstrate that a subsidy to domestic producers that raises their production from q_f to q_t in panel (a) of Figure 5.2 would involve a lower net welfare cost to the country than if the same increase in production were obtained via a tariff. List some reasons why a country might use a tariff rather than a direct production subsidy if the intent was to increase domestic production.

5.4 Preferential government procurement is a policy that favors domestic firms in the granting of government contracts. Show that this policy is equivalent to a production subsidy. Does the relative size of government contracts with respect to industry matter? Explain.

5.5 Using the analysis that leads to equation (5.5), examine the consequences for a large country that introduces an export subsidy. What are the domestic and global welfare consequences of this policy?

5.6 When discussing the effects of an import quota it was stated that the price and quantity effects of a quota can be duplicated by a tariff. Examine whether the Metzler paradox is also possible under an import quota – that is, is it possible for an import quota to lower the domestic price of the import good relative its initial free trade level?

5.7 Derive expression (5.31). That is, derive the expression for the change in welfare that will arise when a small country implements a partial reduction in a tariff from τ_1 to τ_2.

Appendix

Measures of welfare change

This appendix reviews three commonly used measures of welfare change: the Hicksian compensating and equivalent variation and the Marshallian consumer surplus.[52]

Compensating and equivalent variation

Hicks (1939) proposed the compensating variation (CV) and equivalent variation (EV) as concepts for empirically measuring the change in welfare that arises from price changes. Each concept measures a change in real income (measured in units of the numeraire) that is equivalent to a change in utility. The concepts differ only with respect to the reference set of prices used to evaluate the consumer's consumption decision. In this regard, the CV uses the new set of prices while the EV uses the initial set of prices. Assume there are J goods and let $\mathbf{p}_0 = (p_2^0,\ldots,p_J^0)$ and $\mathbf{p}_1 = (p_2^1,\ldots,p_J^1)$ denote two alternative vectors of relative goods prices (good 1 is the numeraire). Using the expenditure function, the compensating and equivalent variations can be defined as:

$$CV = S(\mathbf{p}_1, u_1) - S(\mathbf{p}_1, u_0) \tag{5.50}$$

$$EV = S(\mathbf{p}_0, u_1) - S(\mathbf{p}_0, u_0) \tag{5.51}$$

where u_0 and u_1 are, respectively, the utility levels achieved at prices $\mathbf{p}_0$ and $\mathbf{p}_1$. By definition, the CV is the amount of income (in units of the numeraire) that at prices $\mathbf{p}_1$ would just restore the consumer's utility to the level u_0 (i.e., $S(\mathbf{p}_1, u_0) = S(\mathbf{p}_1, u_1) - CV$). Hence, if the CV is negative it implies a loss to the consumer since he or she would need to be given (compensated) the CV amount of income to be as well off after the price change as before the price change. Alternatively, if the CV is positive then the price change from $\mathbf{p}_0$ to $\mathbf{p}_1$ represents a gain to the consumer since he or she could give up income equal to the CV and be just as well off after the price change as before it.

The EV measures the income change that, at the initial price $\mathbf{p}_0$, would allow the consumer to achieve the welfare level u_1 in the absence of the price change. In this sense, the EV is the income change that is "equivalent" to the welfare change arising from the price change from $\mathbf{p}_0$ to $\mathbf{p}_1$. Again, a positive (negative) EV represents a gain (loss) due to the price change.

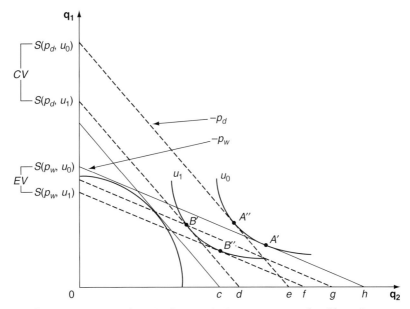

Figure 5.11 Compensating and equivalent variation measures of welfare change

Figure 5.11 illustrates the measurement of the *CV* and *EV* concepts for the case of two goods. In this figure, the price change is assumed to result from a tariff imposed on imports of good 2 (in this sense Figure 5.11 is comparable to Figure 5.1). Under free trade consumers face prices $\mathbf{p}_0 = p_w$ and achieve utility level u_0 by consuming at point A′. Under the tariff consumers face domestic prices $\mathbf{p}_1 = p_d$ and achieve utility level u_1 by consuming at point B′. By definition, $CV = S(p_d, u_1) - S(p_d, u_0)$ and $EV = S(p_w, u_1) - S(p_w, u_0)$. Since the *CV* and *EV* are negative the price change (i.e., the tariff) results in a welfare loss. We note that if measured in units of good 2, the *CV* equals (the negative of) distance *de* while *EV* equals (the negative of) distance *fh* in Figure 5.11. Note also that the *EV* can be decomposed into two parts: a consumption loss (*fg*) and a production cost (*gh*), where the latter measures the welfare change at prices p_w associated with the increase in the production of good 2 (and decline in the production of good 1) arising from the tariff.

Calculation of the compensating or equivalent variation is possible if the form of the expenditure function is known.[53] As discussed in Section 5.3, CGE models typically assume a specific form for the utility function and can therefore derive the form of the associated expenditure function.

Consumer surplus

Closely related to the above Hicksian measures is the Marshallian concept of consumer surplus.[54] Under this concept, the effect of a price change on a consumer's welfare is measured by the area to the left of the demand curve and between the new and old price. This measure is shown in Figure 5.12 as the area $p_d B' A' p_w$ associated with the ordinary (money income constant) demand curve $d_2(p, Y)$.

Figure 5.12 also shows the Hicksian (compensated) demand functions $h_2(p, u_0)$ and $h_2(p, u_1)$ for good 2. These give the change in demand resulting from a price change while maintaining utility constant at either u_0 or u_1, respectively. For comparison, the price-quantity points in Figure 5.12 correspond to the similarly labeled points in Figure 5.11. At the price p_w, $d_2(p, Y)$

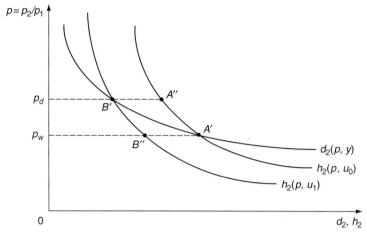

Figure 5.12 Hicksian and Marshallian measures of welfare change

and $h_2(p, u_0)$ yield the same quantity demanded. This is a direct application of equations (4.45) and (4.46) which state the equality of these demands when income Y equates to the minimum expenditure (i.e., $S(p, u_0)$) necessary to attain utility level u_0. The compensated demand functions $h_2(p, u_0)$ is steeper than $d_2(p, Y)$ at A' if good 2 is normal, and flatter than $d_2(p, Y)$ if good 2 is inferior (see (4.47)). The two curves coincide if demands are unresponsive to income.

It can be shown that the CV measured in units of good 2, the distance de in Figure 5.11, equals area $p_d B' B'' p_w$ in Figure 5.12 and that EV, the distance fh in Figure 5.11, corresponds to the area $p_d A'' A' p_w$ in Figure 5.12.[55] As suggested by Figure 5.12, the Marshallian consumer surplus measure lies between the EV and the CV measures unless demands are unresponsive to income.

Notes

1. In practical applications, the world price p_w is taken to be the cost, insurance, freight (*cif*) price of imports – that is, the price at the boundary of the importing country. The domestic internal price is then the *cif* price plus the tariff. The price received by exporters is measured by the free on board (*fob*) price. The difference between the *cif* and *fob* prices of a good is often used to measure the cost of transport. For simplicity, the analysis of this chapter ignores transport and related costs.
2. For a specific tariff τ^* the relationship *is* $p_d = p_w + \tau^*$. For a constant world price, a specific tariff of $\tau^* = \tau p_w$ has the same effect on p_d as an *ad valorem* tariff of τ. The equivalence breaks down if p_w changes. For example, a fall in p_w reduces p_d proportionately less under a specific tariff but in equal proportion under an *ad valorem* tariff.
3. The demand functions therefore treat income and the prices of all other goods as exogenous, unlike the general equilibrium demand functions in Chapter 4.
4. Recall that the height of the domestic supply curve measures the opportunity cost (in terms of foregone output of good 1) of producing an additional unit of good 2.
5. This income measure of the change in utility is the Hicksian equivalent variation. See the Appendix to this chapter.

6. The decomposition of the welfare change due to a small change in trade policy appears in a variety of contexts. Examples include Lloyd's (1982) analysis of a customs union and Viaene's (1987) analysis of land reclamation. Application to the case of imperfectly competitive markets includes Rodrik (1988), Helpman and Krugman (1989) and Feenstra (1995). The Section "General equilibrium methods" in this Chapter extends this welfare decomposition to the case of many goods and when imported and domestic goods are imperfect substitutes.

7. See, however, the following section on Metzler's paradox.

8. Metzler (1949) also considers the extreme cases in which the government spends the tariff revenue either entirely on the export good or entirely on the import good.

9. This is the Marshall-Lerner condition. See equation (4.55) in Chapter 4.

10. However, the second column of Table 4.3 shows that some estimated values of e^* are less than one. Hence Metzler's paradox is empirically possible.

11. Note that a foreign export subsidy only affects the welfare of the home country via a terms of trade effect. Hence, while a foreign export subsidy creates a distortion between the world and domestic price of exports in the foreign country, no such distortion exists in the importing country. The latter therefore benefits from the lower import price and its welfare increases. As such, countering the foreign export subsidy with, say, a countervailing tariff, would only serve to offset the importing country's welfare gain and may even turn it into a net loss.

12. This tariff rate is known as an "implicit" or "*ad valorem* equivalent" tariff rate. Implicit tariff rates are often used to estimate the welfare effects of non-tariff barriers to trade. See Section 5.3.

13. For example, licenses might be "proportionally distributed," that is, distributed to importers in proportion to their share of pre-quota imports or some other measure of pre-quota market presence.

14. Note that an "importer" can be either a domestic or foreign entity. Hence, the allocation of quota rights by the importing country does not guarantee that the quota rents accrue only to domestic entities. If the domestic importer is a foreign-owned entity then quota rents may be transferred abroad either by the direct repatriation of profits or indirectly by setting higher transfer prices between the parent "exporter" and its subsidiary "importer." Taxation of repatriated profits by the importing country could recapture some of these quota rents. Note that the issue of domestic versus foreign "importers" is moot if the government instead auctions the quota licenses.

15. Since the (maximum) price each importer is willing to pay to import one unit of the good equals the difference between the post-quota domestic price (p_d) and the world price (p_w).

16. This may not be the case when markets are imperfectly competitive. See Chapter 10.

17. One widely studied VER is that between the US and Japan in which Japan agreed to limit its exports of certain motor vehicles to the US. Another important example is the MFA (Multi-Fiber Arrangement) which specified a system of quotas on textile exports vis-à-vis industrial country importers (as noted in Chapter 2, the MFA was abolished in 2006 after a ten-year phase-out following the Uruguay Round Agreements). These are but some of the many VRAs that have been negotiated.

18. To see this, consider the equivalent case of an import tariff where the tariff-imposing country transfers all tariff revenue to the foreign country. In this case, home consumers lose areas A and B since the home government collects revenue equal to areas A and C and then transfers this revenue to the foreign government.

19. This raises the question of why an importing country would negotiate a VER rather than impose an import quota. One reason is that GATT rules prohibit countries from undertaking unilateral import restrictions unless "justified." Even if deemed justified, GATT rules require the importing country to compensate affected exporters by reducing trade barriers on other products it imports from the affected countries. During the 1980s, many importing countries found these rules cumbersome and the GATT's process of obtaining approval for "justified" import restrictions too slow. Negotiating with an "offending" exporter to limit exports was much faster, and also provided compensation to the exporter in the form of a potential welfare gain equal to area A minus area D. Moreover, prior to the GATT's Uruguay Round negotiations which concluded in 1994, bilateral agreements that limited exports were not covered under GATT rules and hence explicit compensation was not required. Exporting countries often agreed to VERs for fear that not doing so would bring even greater limits on their trade should the importing country instead adopt import restrictions. Agreements reached under the Uruguay round phased out the use of bilateral VER agreements.

20. Johnson (1971) and Corden (1971) contain some of the earliest work on this subject.

21. In some cases firms can offset a portion of a DCR by exporting rather than using domestically produced components. For example, in order to satisfy a Mexican DCR, US auto firms in Mexico exported Mexican-produced components to the US even though these components were cheaper to produce in the US.

22. This model follows the analysis of Vousden (1987).

23. The composite inverse supply function (5.15) can be written: $\bar{p}(z, p_w, \lambda) = \lambda p_d(\lambda z) + (1 - \lambda)p_w$ since under the DCR $q = \lambda z$. With λ and p_w fixed, $d\bar{p}/dz = \lambda^2(dp_d/dz)$ so that, for example, if $\lambda = .5$ then the slope of the composite inverse supply curve ($\bar{q}$) in Figure 5.6 is one-quarter that of the domestic inverse supply curve (q).

24. Computable general equilibrium models also ignore the uncertainty associated with elasticity values (and other model parameters) when making welfare calculations.

25. A common approach is to assume import demand has the constant elasticity form $m = kp_m^{-\eta m}$ (or $p_m = (m/k)^{-1/\eta m}$), where k is a constant representing all other variables in the demand equation, and to then use this functional form when computing price and quantity changes. One can similarly assume that the import supply function takes the constant elasticity form $x^* = k_1 p_w^{\varepsilon m}$.

26. The trapezoid rule states that an integral of the form $\int_a^b f(x)dx$ can be approximated as $(b - a)((f(a) + f(b))/2$ and that the error associated with this approximation is no greater than $(b - a)^3(Z/12)$. The number Z is chosen so as to satisfy $\left| \partial^2 f(x)/\partial x^2 \right| \leq Z$ for $a \leq x \leq b$. The approximation error is therefore zero when $f(x)$ is affine (i.e., linear).

27. These estimates assume the imported and domestically produced goods are imperfect substitutes.

28. Finding that the net welfare change is small relative to income transfers is common in studies of the costs of protection.

29. For example, see Grossman (1986).

30. Trefler (1993) found that treating tariff rates as endogenous resulted in an estimate of the restrictiveness of US tariffs to be ten times larger than when tariffs were taken to be exogenous.

31. This assumed the import quota is binding at the new level $\bar{m}_2$, that is, $\bar{m}_2$ is the below the level of imports that would obtain under free trade.

32. These are also called "implicit tariffs." The ratio of the domestic to world price is sometimes called a "nominal protection coefficient."

33. Of course, p_1 and p_w are themselves estimates in the sense that they computed by dividing a total value by a measure of quantity. See the discussion of unit values later in this section.

34. This is derived using $p_w = V_w/m_1, p_1 = V_1/m_1, p_2 = p_1\left(1 - \hat{m}/\eta_m\right)$ and $p_w^2 = p_w^1\left(1 - \hat{m}/\varepsilon_m\right)$.

35. See Baldwin (1989) for a critique of AVEs and other methods for measuring the price impact of NTBs.

36. See Pelzman (1986) for examples of this approach.

37. The shift toward high priced varieties when a quota is tightened is referred to as "quality upgrading." While this terminology suggests a gain to consumers, "upgrading" is actually a loss since consumer choice is restricted to buying higher price items. Expanding an import quota (or VER) implies "quality downgrading" and more choice, and hence a welfare gain. Boorstein and Feenstra (1997) find that the welfare gain associated with quality downgrading is equal in size to the traditional welfare gain calculated from price changes alone. Hence, by ignoring compositional changes, the traditional welfare calculation may understate by as much as one-half the actual welfare gain from reducing a trade restriction.

38. It may be helpful to think of there being N classes of goods, where each class consists of a domestic and imported variety.

39. This assumes that all quota rents accrue to domestic agents.

40. The Appendix reviews this and other measures of welfare change.

41. Alternatively, (5.38) is just the difference between the left- and right-hand sides of (5.36).

42. If you worked out problems 4.5, 4.8 and 4.9 in Chapter 4 you have already developed a CGE model without calibration.

43. The classic treatment of this model is Samuelson (1953).

44. This is not strictly true since under imperfect competition supply functions do not exist. Instead, equations that specify pricing rules assume this role.

45. Conditional on total expenditure allocated to imports. See any advanced text on microeconomics (e.g., Varian 1992) for a discussion of conditional demand functions.

46. For example, all varieties of German automobiles are perfect substitutes as are all varieties of Japanese automobiles, but German and Japanese automobiles are imperfect substitutes.

47. Such results have led many AGE modelers to question the Armington specification as a method for modeling product differentiation. In particular, Brown (1987) shows that the substitution possibilities implied by the Armington specification imply excessive terms of trade changes. Hence AGE models that use this specification are biased toward finding negative welfare changes from trade liberalization. Brown's findings have led some to suggest that product differentiation should be modeled at the level of the firm rather than the level of country.

48. For example, see Brooke, Kendrick and Meeraus (1988).

49. Named for Johansen (1960), who is usually credited with conducting the first CGE analysis.

50. This is the approach used by Jones (1965) in presenting his analysis of the two-sector general equilibrium model.

51. Examples include Deardorff and Stern (1986) and Dixon et al. (1982).

52. Other measures include the equivalent and compensating surpluses (Hicks 1939) and the money metric approach. These concepts are, however, methodologically related to the equivalent and compensating variations. See Deaton and Muelbauer (1980) and Boadway and Bruce (1984) for reviews of alternative measures.

53. More generally, computation of the *CV* or *EV* requires that u_0 and u_1 be known. Willig (1976), Seade (1978), Vartia (1983) and others have developed techniques that overcome this estimation problem and also allow a direct comparison with the Marshallian measure discussed below.
54. This concept is originally due to Dupuit, but Marshall (1890) popularized the concept as an important tool in applied welfare economics.
55. An algebraic demonstration of this is given in Burns (1973).

References and additional reading

Impediments to trade

Helpman, E. and Krugman, P.R. (1989), *Trade Policy and Market Structure* (Cambridge, MA: MIT Press).
Lerner, A. (1936), "The Symmetry between Import and Export Taxes," *Economica*, 3, 306–313.
Metzler, L.A. (1949), "Tariffs, the Terms of Trade, and the Distribution of National Income," *Journal of Political Economy*, 57, 1–29.
Schuknecht, L. (1992), *Trade Protection in the European Community* (Chur, Switzerland: Harwood Academic Press).
Vousden, N. (1990), *The Economics of Trade Protection* (Cambridge: Cambridge University Press).

Decomposition of welfare changes

Helpman, E. and Krugman, P.R. (1989), *Trade Policy and Market Structure* (Cambridge, MA: MIT Press), section 2.7, 22–25.
Lloyd, P.J. (1982), "3 x 3 Theory of Customs Unions," *Journal of International Economics*, 12, 41–63.
Rodrik, D. (1988), "Imperfect Competition, Scale Economies, and Trade Policy in Developing Countries," in Robert E. Baldwin (Ed.), *Trade Policy Issues and Empirical Analysis* (Chicago: University of Chicago Press).
Varian, Hal R. (1992), *Microeconomic Analysis*, 3rd ed. (W.W. Norton: New York).
Viaene, J.-M. (1987), "Factor Accumulation in a Minimum-Wage Economy," *European Economic Review*, 31, 1313–1328.

Welfare measures

Boadway, R.W. and Bruce, N. (1984), *The Pure Theory of Welfare Economics* (Oxford: Basil Blackwell).
Burns, M.E. (1973), "A Note on the Concept and Measure of Consumer's Surplus," *American Economic Review*, 63, 335–344.
Deaton, A. and Muellbauer, J. (1980), *Economics and Consumer Behavior* (Cambridge: Cambridge University Press).
Hicks, J. (1939), "Foundations of Welfare Economics," *Economic Journal*, 49, 696–712.
Marshall, A. (1890), *Principles of Economics* (London: Macmillan).
Seade, J. (1978), "Consumer's Surplus and Linearity of Engel Curves", *Economic Journal*, 88, 511–523.
Vartia, Y. (1983), "Efficient Methods of Measuring Welfare Change and Compensated Income in Terms of Ordinary Demand Functions," *Econometrica*, 51, 79–98.

Willig, R.D. (1976), "Consumer's Surplus without Apology," *American Economic Review*, 66, 589–597.

Domestic content protection

Beghin, J.C. and Knox Lovell, C.A. (1993), "Trade and Efficiency Effects of Domestic Content Protection: The Australian Tobacco and Cigarette Industries," *Review of Economics and Statistics*, 75, 623–669.

Corden, W.M. (1971), *The Theory of Protection* (London: Allen and Unwin).

Grossman, G.M. (1981), "The Theory of Domestic Content Protection and Content Preference," *Quarterly Journal of Economics*, 9, 583–603.

Hollander, A. (1987), "Content Protection and Transnational Monopoly," *Journal of International Economics*, 23, 283–297.

Johnson, H.G. (1971), *Aspects of the Theory of Tariffs* (London: Allen and Unwin).

Krishna, K. and Itoh, M. (1988), "Content Protection and Oligopolistic Interactions," *Review of Economic Studies*, 55, 107–125.

Krishna, K. and Krueger, A.O. (1994), "Implementing Free Trade Areas: Rules of Origin and Hidden Protection," in A. Deardorff, J. Levinhson and R. Stern (Eds.), *New Directions in Trade Theory* (Ann Arbor: University of Michigan Press).

Richardson, M. (1991), "The Effects of a Content Requirement on a Foreign Duopsonist," *Journal of International Economics*, 31, 143–155.

Vousden, N. (1987), "Content Protection and Tariffs under Monopoly and Competition," *Journal of International Economics*, 23, 263–282.

Trade policy modeling

Armington, Paul A. (1969), "A Theory of Demand for Products Distinguished by Place of Production," *International Monetary Fund Staff Papers*, 16, 159–176.

Baldwin, R.E. (Ed.) (1988), *Trade Policy Issues and Empirical Analysis* (Chicago: University of Chicago Press and National Bureau of Economic Research).

Baldwin, R.E. (1989), "Measuring Nontariff Trade Policies," NBER Working Paper 2978 (May).

Ballard, F., Shoven, J. and Whalley, J. (1985), *A General Equilibrium Model for Tax Policy Evaluation* (Chicago: University of Chicago Press).

Boorstein, R. and Feenstra, R.C. (1987). "Quality Upgrading and its Welfare Cost in US Steel Imports, 1969–74," National Bureau of Economic Research Working Paper 2452 (Cambridge, MA: National Bureau of Economic Research).

Brooke, A., Kendrick, D., and Meeraus A. (1988), *GAMS, A User's Guide* (California: The Scientific Press).

Brown, D.K. (1987), "Tariff, the Terms of Trade, and National Product Differentiation," *Journal of Policy Modeling*, 9 (4), 503–526.

de Melo, J. and Tarr, D. (1992), *A General Equilibrium Analysis of U.S. Foreign Trade Policy* (Cambridge, MA: MIT Press).

Dixon, P., Parmenter, B., Sutton, J., and Vincent, D. (1982), *ORANI: A Multi-Sector Model of the Australian Economy* (Amsterdam: North-Holland).

Deardorff, A. and Stern, R.M. (1986), *The Michigan Model of World Production and Trade* (Cambridge, MA: MIT Press).

Deardorff, A. and Stern, R.M. (1990), *Computation Analysis of Global Trading Arrangements* (Ann Arbor: The University of Michigan Press).

Feenstra, R. (Ed.) (1988), *Empirical Methods for International Trade* (Cambridge, MA: MIT Press).

Feenstra, R. (Ed.) (1989), *Trade Policies for International Competitiveness* (Chicago: University of Chicago Press and National Bureau of Economic Research).

Feenstra, R. (1995), "Estimating the Effects of Trade Policy," ch. 30 in G. Grossma- and K. Rogoff (Eds.), *Handbook of International Economics*, Vol. 3 (Amsterdam: North-Holland).

Francois, J.F. and Reinert, K.A. (Eds.) (1997), *Applied Methods for Trade Policy Analysis: A Handbook* (Cambridge: Cambridge University Press).

Francois, J.F., McDonald, B.J. and Nordström, H. (1995), "Assessing the Uruguay Round," in W. Martin and L.A. Winters (Eds.), *The Uruguay Round and the Developing Economies*, discussion paper #307 (Washington, DC: World Bank).

Ginsburgh, V. and Keyzer, M. (1997), *The Structure of Applied General Equilibrium Models* (Cambridge, MA: MIT Press).

Grossman, G. (1986), "Imports as a Cause of Injury: The Case of the US Steel Industry," *Journal of International Economics*, 20, 201–223.

Hufbauer, G., Berliner, D. and Elliott, K.A. (1986), *Trade Protection in the United States: 31 Case Studies* (Washington, DC: Institute for International Economics).

Johansen, L. (1960), *A Multi-Sectoral Study of Economic Growth* (Amsterdam: North-Holland).

Jones, R.W. (1965), "The Structure of Simple General Equilibrium Models". *The Journal of Political Economy*, 73 (6):557-572.

Laird, S. and Yeats, A. (1990), *Quantitative Methods for Trade-Barrier Analysis* (New York: New York University Press).

Leamer, E.E. (1988), "Measures of Openness," in R.E. Baldwin (Ed.) *Trade Policy Issues and Empirical Analysis* (Chicago: University of Chicago Press and National Bureau of Economic Research).

Pelzman, J. (1986), "The Tariff Equivalents of the Existing Quotas under the Multifiber Arrangement". Paper presented at the Southern Economic Association meetings, November 23–25.

Roussland, D. and Soumela, J. (1985), "Calculating the Consumer and Net Welfare Costs of Import Relief", *United States International Trade Commission Staff Research Study #15*.

Samuelson, P.A. (1953), "The Prices of Goods and Factors in General Equilibrium," *The Review of Economics and Statistics*, 21 (54), 83–93.

Saxonhouse, G.R. (1989), "Differentiated Products, Economies of Scale and Access to the Japanese Market," in R.C. Feenstra (Ed.), *Trade Policies for International Competitiveness* (Chicago: University of Chicago Press and National Bureau of Economic Research).

Shoven, J. and Whalley, J. (1984), "Applied General-Equilibrium Models of Taxation and International Trade: An Introduction and Survey," *Journal of Economic Literature*, 22 (3), 1007–1051.

Shoven, J. and Whalley, J. (1992), *Applying General Equilibrium* (New York: Cambridge University Press).

Trefler, D. (1993), "Trade Liberalization and the Theory of Endogenous Protection: An Econometric Study of US Import Policy," *Journal of Political Economy*, 101, 138–160.

US International Trade Commission (USITC) (1989), "The Economic Effects of Significant US Import Restraints," USITC Publication 2222 (Washington, DC : US International Trade Commission), October.

6

Factor mobility and trade

Faced with weak empirical support for traditional theories,[1] many analysts have looked for alternative theories that can explain trade between countries. This chapter examines one such alternative approach: the gravity equation, which is the predominant functional form to describe variations in the bilateral volume of trade. The gravity equation says that trade flows between any pair of countries should be positively related to both countries' market size and negatively to the distance between them. The focus is on bilateral trade rather than on the commodity pattern of trade, and in that sense it should not be viewed as an alternative to the models of Chapters 3 and 4.[2] It is a popular framework, mainly because of the strength of its explanatory power in empirical analyses. Its success depends also on its ability to infer trade effects of trade costs but also changes in institutions such as regional trading agreements and exchange rate regimes. Although this model has been traditionally applied to bilateral trade, recent theoretical developments validate its use in explaining international factor movements as well (see, e.g., Martin and Rey, 2004; Bergstrand and Egger, 2007; Anderson, 2010).

The assumptions of the two-factor H-O-S model are also modified one by one to see which phenomena might be explained. This chapter considers three such modifications and examines their influence both theoretically and empirically: (1) international mobility of factors to see whether trade and factor flows are substitutes or complements; (2) international labor mobility and a minimum wage floor, thereby introducing the possibility of illegal immigration; and (3) the specific factors model, which weakens the assumption of domestic factor mobility and contributes to the political economy of trade policy.

6.1   The gravity equation

Given the empirical success of the gravity equation, there have been numerous attempts to develop its theoretical foundation. A key result of the last decade is that the gravity specification can be derived from any of our general trade models but that current empirical tests have not yet found ways to discriminate among them. The gravity equation has been obtained in the literature assuming product differentiation and imperfect competition (see Anderson,

1979; Helpman and Krugman, 1985; Bergstrand, 1989; Anderson and van Wincoop, 2003) but also in the literature building on perfect competition and technological differences (see Eaton and Kortum, 2002) and on perfect competition and complete specialization (see Deardorff, 1998). We use the latter framework to derive a first version of the gravity specification, after which we outline estimation procedures and estimation results.

The basic gravity equation

Consider a particular trading equilibrium where N separate countries produce N different goods. Each country produces an amount q_j of its single good at the price p_j. Preferences are assumed to be similar across countries and are Cobb-Douglas. Consumers in all countries therefore spend a fixed proportion β_j of their incomes on good j. With free trade and with perfect competition, sellers of good j should receive the same price p_j in all markets. Given this, country j's income is $Y_j = p_j q_j$. For each commodity j, there is market clearing such that country supply is equal to world demand:

$$Y_j = p_j q_j = \sum_{n=1}^{N} \beta_j Y_n = \beta_j Y_w \qquad (6.1)$$

which implies $\beta_j = Y_j / Y_w$ with $Y_w = \sum_{n=1}^{N} Y_n$ being world income. If we define m_{jn} as bilateral imports of any country n from country j then:

$$m_{jn} = \beta_j Y_n = \frac{Y_j Y_n}{Y_w} \qquad (6.2)$$

This equation measures consumption expenditure in country n on goods made in country j. (6.2) shares the idea of the gravity equation except that it is unrelated to distance. The reason is that imports are valued on a cost, insurance, freight (*cif*) quotation that is inclusive of transport costs. But gravity models usually focus on exports and these are usually valued on a free on board (*fob*) basis that is exclusive of transport costs. To highlight the difference let x_{jn} denote bilateral exports of country j to country n. Transport costs are of Samuelson's iceberg type – namely the cost of moving goods involves the loss of some proportion of the product in transit: only a fraction of the good shipped abroad actually arrives. Let the transport factor between j and n be τ_{jn}. This is one plus the transport cost, the difference $(\tau_{jn} - 1)$ representing the cost of transport from j to n. Ultimately consumers abroad have one unit of the good at their disposal but the buyers' price for goods coming from country j is $\tau_{jn} p_j$ and thus varies according to their location. Given this:

$$x_{jn} = \frac{m_{jn}}{\tau_{jn}} = \frac{1}{\tau_{jn}} \frac{Y_j Y_n}{Y_w} \qquad (6.3)$$

If transport costs are related to distance, then (6.3) gives the basic gravity equation. Given this specification, the rest of this section outlines the various functional forms to be estimated and discusses empirical results.

Functional forms

Different models have been used in the empirical literature to formally assess the effects of variables like gross domestic product (GDP) and distance on trade (Baltagi, 2005). The first model is the so-called one-way error component model where a dependent variable x_{jnt} is explained by a vector of K explanatory variables $\mathbf{x_{jnt}}$ and time-invariant unobserved country fixed effects α_j and α_n. Formally, the model is written as:

$$\ln x_{jnt} = \alpha_j + \alpha_n + \boldsymbol{\beta} \mathbf{x_{jnt}} + \varepsilon_{jnt}, \qquad j, n = 1, \ldots N; \; j \neq n; \; t = 1, \ldots T, \quad (6.4)$$

where $\boldsymbol{\beta}$ is the vector of parameters, N is the number of countries and T the number of observations. ε_{jnt} is the remainder stochastic disturbance with $\varepsilon_{jnt} \sim \text{IID}(0, \sigma^2)$. In estimation, $\ln x_{jnt}$ stands for the natural logarithm of exports of country j to country n and $\mathbf{x_{jnt}}$ includes explanatory variables such as in (6.3) but now expressed in natural logarithm. Application of model (6.4) leads to the estimation of $2N$ country parameters. The fixed effects of exporter country j and importer country n are included to control for time-invariant country-specific heterogeneity. This model is used in cross-section regressions of the gravity model derived by Anderson and van Wincoop (2003) that includes "multilateral resistance" terms capturing country j's and country n's resistance to trade with all regions of the sample. Since multilateral resistance terms are not observables, Feenstra (2002) shows that consistent estimates of the model can be obtained by using exporter and importer fixed effects.

An alternative specification of the one-way error component model is the bilateral fixed effects model where α_j and α_n in (6.4) are replaced by time-invariant unobserved country pair effects α_{jn}:

$$\ln x_{jnt} = \alpha_{jn} + \boldsymbol{\beta} \mathbf{x_{jnt}} + \varepsilon_{jnt}, \qquad j, n = 1, \ldots N; \; j \neq n; \; t = 1, \ldots T, \quad (6.5)$$

The estimation of (6.5) involves estimating $N(N-1)$ country pair parameters α_{jn}. Bilateral fixed effects between countries j and n are included to control for influences on the trade of a country pair. Border transactions, seasonal trade, bilateral treaties and so on are controlled for with these time-invariant specific effects.

The second model is the two-way error component model that accounts for any time-specific effect that is not included in the regression:

$$\ln x_{jnt} = \alpha_j + \alpha_n + \lambda_t + \boldsymbol{\beta} \mathbf{x_{jnt}} + \varepsilon_{jnt}, \qquad j, n = 1, \ldots N; \; j \neq n; \; t = 1, \ldots T, \quad (6.6)$$

where λ_t denotes the unobservable time effect. There is T such time effects. This model controls for omitted variables that vary over time (e.g., business cycles) but remain constant across countries. Likewise, the counterpart of (6.5) with unobservable time effects is:

$$\ln x_{jnt} = \alpha_{jn} + \lambda_t + \boldsymbol{\beta} \mathbf{x_{jnt}} + \varepsilon_{jnt}, \qquad i, j = 1, \ldots N; \; i \neq j; \; t = 1, \ldots, .T. \quad (6.7)$$

However, in panel data regressions, an alternative specification of (6.4) is also used:

$$\ln x_{jnt} = \alpha_{jt} + \alpha_{nt} + \boldsymbol{\beta} \mathbf{x_{jnt}} + \varepsilon_{jnt}, \qquad i, j = 1, \ldots N; \; i \neq j; \; t = 1, \ldots T, \quad (6.8)$$

where the country fixed effects are now made time-dependent. (6.8) includes $2NT$ dummies in the regression. It is unusual to estimate time-dependent country pair effects in (6.7) since the specification includes $N(N-1)T$ dummies and its estimation suffers from too large a loss of degrees of freedom.

Some estimates

Table 6.1 reproduces some panel data estimates of equations (6.4) to (6.7) obtained by Brouwer *et al.* (2008). Though the objective of the study is to quantify the trade effects of

Table 6.1 Estimates of the gravity equation[a,b]

Explanatory variables	Bilateral exports: ln x_{jn}			
	Eq. (6.4)	Eq. (6.5)	Eq. (6.6)	Eq. (6.7)
ln GDP$_j$	0.353 (0.00)[c]	0.480 (0.00)	0.426 (0.00)	0.522 (0.00)
ln GDP$_n$	0.415 (0.00)	0.568 (0.00)	0.461 (0.00)	0.590 (0.00)
—	—	—	—	—
ln distance	−0.714 (0.00)		−0.714 (0.00)	
Contiguity	0.396 (0.00)		0.398 (0.00)	
Language	0.218 (0.00)		0.218 (0.00)	
$\overline{R}^2$ adjusted	0.934	0.991	0.935	0.992

Notes: (a) This table reports panel least squares estimates.
(b) No. of observations = 4152.
(c) p-values in parentheses.
Source: Brouwer *et al.* (2008).

institutional arrangements like the European Union (EU) and Economic and Monetary Union (EMU), it is useful to illustrate the main features of the gravity model. They use a sample of 29 countries ($N = 29$) that includes all 25 countries that were EU members in 2004 and a group of non-EU countries consisting of Switzerland, Japan, Canada and the United States (US). This gives 28 bilateral relationships per country over a period ranging from 1990 until 2004 and, in principle, a balanced dataset of 12,180 observations. However, because of missing observations this dataset is unbalanced. All nominal variables are expressed in US dollars.

Estimates in Table 6.1 include also standard gravity variables like distance, contiguity and language. Distance measures the number of kilometers between capital cities of country j and n; contiguity is a binary variable that takes the value 1 when countries j and n share a common border, 0 otherwise. Language is also a binary variable that is 1 when countries j and n share a common official language, 0 otherwise. These variables are not included in specifications with country pair fixed effects as they are time-invariant characterizations of bilateral transactions among source and destination countries.

Across the four model specifications, we have a number of robust and significant parameter estimates. For example, it is clear that GDPs have a positive effect on trade, the elasticity ranging between 0.353 and 0.590, the effect being larger when country pair fixed effects are used. The sign of distance is negative for trade with the elasticity being −0.714, indicating a 10 percent increase in distance, lowering bilateral trade by about 7 percent. Contiguity and common languages matter as well. Taking estimates of the first column, the marginal effect of contiguity on bilateral exports can be approximated as the difference between the anti-logarithm of the contiguity parameter when a value 1 is reported ($e^{0.396}$) and when a value 0 is given (e^0) : $(e^{0.396} − 1) * 100 \approx 48.6$. This indicates that contiguous countries trade on average 48.6 percent more that non-contiguous countries. Likewise the marginal export effect of common language is $(e^{0.218} − 1) * 100 \approx 24.4$ and shows that countries with at least one common official language trade on average 24.4 percent more than otherwise.

Distance

The above estimates of distance are puzzling in an age of unlimited access to information and of almost free communication. That distance matters is confirmed in the meta-analysis of

Disdier and Head (2008) comprising 1,467 estimates spanning a long period – from 1870 to 2001. One of their findings is that the estimated impact of distance on trade slightly decreased until 1950 but rose after that to remain high. The mean elasticity is −0.9 and is even higher (in absolute value) than that of Table 6.1. A reason for the difference might be that contiguity and language are directly controlled for in Table 6.1 and that the sample contains mostly European countries where distance is less of an issue.

Transport costs

Though distance also captures institutional and cultural differences on trade, it co-varies mostly with transport costs. A reason why transport costs are not introduced directly into regression analyses is that they are difficult to come by and when available they are approximate measures of true costs. A straightforward measure used in the literature on trade and growth is the "matched partner technique" that computes the ratio $[cif/fob − 1] * 100$ to approximate *ad valorem* transport costs. Applying this formula for the period 1965–1990 Radelet and Sachs (1998) estimate that transport costs are on average 10.3 percent for Australia, 4.9 percent for the US, 3.0 percent for Germany and so on. Though Hummels and Lugovskyy (2006) show the limits of the "matched partner technique" by providing the extent of measurement errors, Hummels (2007) confirms the finding that transport costs seem larger and exhibit greater variability across exporters and across time than do tariffs. In particular, although costs of air shipping have declined sharply in the last decades, this is not the case for the costs of ocean shipping.

6.2 Goods and factors: substitutes or complements?

In this section we relax the H-O-S assumption of international factor immobility and examine the coexistence of international trade in goods and factors. One issue in this context is whether goods flows and factor flows are substitutes or complements. Markusen's (1983) analysis offers explanations as to why they may be complements. In contrast, the Mundell theorem establishes a substitution between commodity and factor movements. If empirically valid, the theorem has an important policy implication: as international labor movements are sensitive to wage differentials countries can, by liberalizing their trade, reduce the wage differentials and thereby moderate the flux of foreign immigrants. Recent examples of such trade liberalization are the 1991 reunification of East and West Germany and the 1993 Free Trade Agreement between Mexico and the US.

Case for substitution

Mundell (1957) is credited with the first formal analysis of the interaction between the international flow of goods and factors. Adopting the H-O-S model, but relaxing the assumption of international factor immobility, Mundell derived the following result:

Proposition 6.1 (Mundell): An increase in trade impediments stimulates factor movements and an increase in restrictions to factor movements stimulates trade.

In extreme form, this result implies that if factors are internationally mobile then trade in goods will cease. More generally, the result states that goods trade and factor flows are substitutes. Below we examine the analysis that establishes the first part of this proposition.[3]

Consider a trading equilibrium for a *small* economy such as that depicted in Figure 6.1. Production occurs at point Q, consumption is at point D, and good 2 is imported at the free trade price p_w. The country's post-trade level of income, measured in terms of numeraire

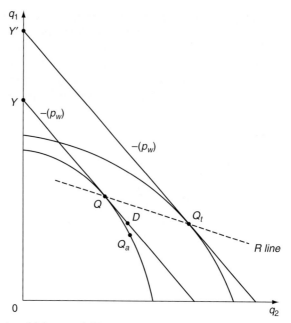

Figure 6.1 International labor mobility

good 1, is OY. This equilibrium assumes trade has equalized factor prices between countries and that factors are internationally immobile. If factors were now allowed to move
internationally, no flows would in fact take place since factor prices have already equalized
between countries. Therefore, to generate an international flow of factors we must introduce
a difference in factor returns.

Assume the country depicted in Figure 6.1 now imposes a prohibitive tariff on the labor-
intensive good 2. By definition, this will cause trade to cease as production moves to the
autarky point Q_a. Since good 2 is labor-intensive, the resulting increase in the production of
good 2 will, by the Stolper-Samuelson theorem, raise labor's marginal product and lower capital's marginal product. If labor is now allowed to be internationally mobile (capital remaining
internationally immobile), the rise in labor's marginal product will induce an inflow of labor
from the rest of the world. By assumption, output prices and factor marginal products are
constant in the rest of the world. Consequently, the inflow of labor will continue until factor
rewards in the tariff-imposing country return to their pre-tariff level. Hence, with marginal
products unchanged, so also is the real income accruing to domestic factors. This means that
the post-tariff consumption point must lie along the pre-tariff income line YQ in Figure 6.1 –
that is, consumption will remain at D.

Whereas the income of domestic factors is unchanged, some production now takes place
using foreign labor and thus a part of the economy's income must be paid to these foreign
workers. This implies that the new production equilibrium must generate income greater
than OY so that, once wage payments are remitted abroad, the country will retain its original,
pre-tariff, income level OY. The production equilibrium satisfying this requirement is Q_t in
Figure 6.1. Production at Q_t is feasible since the inflow of labor expands the country's transformation curve. That Q_t is the new equilibrium production point is confirmed by noting that at
any production point to the left of Q_t, and along the Rybczynski line, the country would need
to import good 2 (since consumption must take place at D). However, imports are not possible
due to the prohibitive tariff. At Q_t, income from production (GDP) is OY'. Of this income, OY
(GNP) is retained by domestic factors, YY' is remitted abroad as payment to the "imported"

labor and is financed by an equal amount of exports of good 2. In this new equilibrium, the inflow of foreign workers has replaced the exports of good 1 and, in this sense, trade and factor flows are substitutes.

Given this new equilibrium, the tariff could be completely removed without affecting production, consumption, or trade. That is, by prohibiting trade in goods but allowing international factor mobility, the resulting equalization of factor rewards has resulted in the equalization of goods prices. This is just the factor price equalization theorem "turned on its head" to become a commodity price equalization theorem.

As Mundell shows, the above result does not depend on the tariff rate – any positive tariff will eliminate the trade in goods. The assumption that the country is small (and therefore faces constant terms of trade) is also unimportant. Rather, the important assumptions are those that ensure factor price equalization, including incomplete specialization. It is also important that only one country imposes the restriction on trade. If both countries impose restrictions then trade need not vanish since both factor prices and commodity prices need not be equalized.

Case for complementarity

Correlations between the international flow of goods and factors offer mixed evidence on the above proposition of substitutability. Analysis of international labor flows to the EU corroborates substitutability but casual observation suggests complementarity between long-term capital flows and goods trade. This has led some to search for an explanation of such complementarity within the context of received trade models.

Markusen's (1983) analysis offers one such attempt. The model assumes a world of two identical countries (including identical factor endowments) and all H-O-S assumptions satisfied. As such, the initial equilibrium is one of no trade. Given this, it is then asked which assumption, when relaxed, would lead to: (1) trade; (2) an inequality in factor rewards across countries; (3) a relatively higher price for the factor used intensively in the production of a country's export good. The latter condition ensures that once factor mobility is allowed, there will be an inflow of the country's abundant factor. The motives for trade examined by Markusen include a foreign production tax, monopoly, returns to scale, factor taxes and differences in production technology. We only take up the case of a foreign production tax.

Assume two identical countries and let point A in Figure 6.2 denote each country's autarky equilibrium along its production possibility curve $T_1 T_2$. Now suppose the foreign country imposes an *ad valorem* tax rate τ^* on the production of labor-intensive good 2. A reason for this tax might be excess pollution associated with the production of good 2. Since the tax lowers the price received by foreign producers and raises the price to foreign consumers, the foreign country's autarky equilibrium will move to a point such as B. Since autarky prices are now different across countries, allowing trade gives rise to the home country exporting good 2. Why? Assuming internationally immobile factors, trade will cause the relative price facing consumers in each country to converge to the world price p_w. At this price, the home economy produces at point H and consumes at point C whereas the foreign country produces at point F and consumes at point D. Balanced trade is implied by the equality of the distances CH and DF.

Whereas home producers receive the world price p_w, foreign producers receive the net price $p_d^* = p_w/(1 + \tau^*)$. This gap in producer prices implies a cross-country difference in factor rewards. Since $p_d^* < p_w$, it must be that labor earns more, and capital earns less, at home than abroad. Hence, if factors are allowed to flow across borders, the home economy will attract foreign labor and generate an outflow of capital. As such, the home (foreign) country's supply of capital relative to labor falls (rises). As established below, these factor movements imply that the volume of trade between the two countries will increase. Hence, we have the result

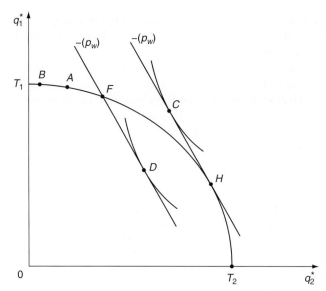

Figure 6.2 Production tax as a determinant of trade

that factor movements lead to an increased willingness of countries to trade and, in this sense, factor movements and trade in goods are complementary.[4]

We now establish that trade will increase as each country receives more (less) of the factor used intensively in the production of its export (import) good. Consider the foreign country that experiences an increase in its capital stock and a decrease in its labor force. As shown in panel (a) of Figure 6.3, the increase in capital shifts the production point from F to F' along the Rybczynski line (R line). Moreover, the inflow of capital raises aggregate income and, since preferences are assumed homothetic, consumption moves from D to D'. Consequently, the new trade vector becomes $F'D'$, which exceeds the initial trade vector FD.

Panel (b) of Figure 6.3 shows the separate effect of the shrinking of the labor endowment. In this case, the labor outflow shrinks production from F to F' along the Rybczynski line while consumption moves from D to D'. Again, the new trade vector $F'D'$ exceeds the initial trade vector FD. Repeating this analysis for all possible terms of trade confirms the proposition that

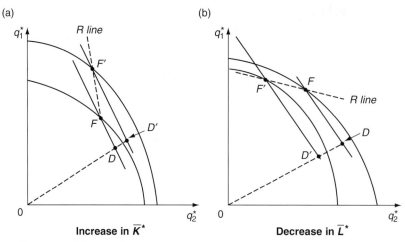

Figure 6.3 Factor mobility and trade

trade will rise if factor movements raise the relative supply of the factor used intensively in the export industry.

A final point concerns the equalization of factor rewards across countries. Because the production tax creates a wedge between the world price and the price received by foreign producers, the equilibria explained thus far do not involve an equality of factor rewards between countries. Hence, factors will continue to flow between countries which will push them toward complete specialization in production. Only when one country reaches specialization can factor rewards be equalized.

Empirical analysis

Having presented alternative theoretical models that predict opposite results concerning the relationship between the international trade in goods and in factors, it is a matter of empirical research to characterize this relationship. The main reference of this section is Wong (1988), who estimated the effects of the movements of capital and labor on the volume of trade and factor prices of the US over the period 1948–83.

Consider the problem of a competitive economy that produces and exports two goods, durables (d) and non-durables and services (n), and imports non-domestically produced goods and services (m). There are three primary factors, land (a), labor (l) and capital (k), available in the fixed quantity $\mathbf{e} = (e_a, e_l, e_k)$. This economy trades freely with the rest of the world at the vector of fixed prices $\mathbf{p} = (p_d, p_n, p_m)$ and gives a transfer of b abroad.

The production technology is represented by the revenue function $G(\mathbf{p,e})$.[5] The preferences of the consumers are represented by the indirect trade utility (ITU) function $T(\mathbf{p}, \mathbf{e}, b)$. This function, first introduced by Woodland (1980), gives the maximum level of utility $V(\mathbf{p}, G(\mathbf{p,e})-b)$ that this economy achieves at the fixed prices $\mathbf{p}$ and the national expenditure $G(\mathbf{p,e})-b$. The usefulness of using the ITU function follows from the following derivatives:

$$\frac{\partial T(\mathbf{p}, \mathbf{e}, b)}{\partial \mathbf{p}} = \lambda(\mathbf{q} - \mathbf{d}) \equiv \lambda\, \mathbf{x}(\mathbf{p}, \mathbf{e}, b) \tag{6.9}$$

$$\frac{\partial T(\mathbf{p}, \mathbf{e}, b)}{\partial \mathbf{e}} = \lambda\, \mathbf{w}(\mathbf{p}, \mathbf{e}, b) \tag{6.10}$$

$$\frac{\partial T(\mathbf{p}, \mathbf{e}, b)}{\partial b} = -\lambda \tag{6.11}$$

where λ is the marginal utility of income, $\mathbf{w}$ is the vector of factor prices, and $\mathbf{q}$, $\mathbf{d}$ and $\mathbf{x}$ are the vectors of commodity supply, commodity demand and net exports respectively.

The functional form that has been chosen for T and G for the purpose of econometric estimation is the transcendental logarithmic (translog). A first advantage of a translog function is that it takes explicit account of the constraints imposed by homogeneity and symmetry. A second advantage of the function is that, by making use of (6.9) – (6.11) combined with (4.35) and (4.36), the shares of net exports in domestic expenditure, $p_j x_j/(G - b)$, and the shares of factor payments in the domestic product, $w_h e_h/G$, are dependent upon all domestic endowments, all commodity prices and the transfer b ($j = d, n, m; h = a, l, k$). Our particular interest lies in the estimated response of the vector of net exports with respect to the vector of endowments.

Table 6.2 shows the elasticities ε_{jh} ($j = d, n, m; h = l, k$) of exports and imports with respect to labor and capital endowments. There are two main conclusions that can be drawn from this table. First, all elasticities in the table are significantly different from zero. Second, and more importantly, all elasticities are positive except in one year for ε_{nk} suggesting, for the US, a strong complementarity result between factor supplies and international trade. This implies

Table 6.2 Elasticities of exports and imports with respect to factor supply[a]

Year	ε_{dk}	ε_{dl}	ε_{nk}	ε_{nl}	ε_{mk}	ε_{ml}
1948	0.4041	0.2044	−0.0492	0.8158	0.2237	0.8494
1953	0.6678	0.7846	0.0325	1.7120	0.3038	1.2146
1958	0.6277	0.7005	0.0137	1.4305	0.2880	1.1170
1963	0.6539	0.7932	0.0489	1.4579	0.3448	1.2884
1968	0.6513	1.0108	0.1229	1.7957	0.3517	1.3466
1973	0.6211	1.3890	0.1681	1.7248	0.3679	1.5378
1978	0.6661	1.5688	0.3589	2.0711	0.4282	1.5624
1983	0.7028	1.4878	0.4249	2.1900	0.4496	1.5295
Standard error[b]	0.1283	0.1794	0.1173	0.1659	0.0041	0.0170

[a] ε_{jh} = Elasticity of exports ($j = d, n$) and of imports ($j = m$) with respect to factor endowments ($h = l, k$).
[b] Standard errors are calculated using the values of variables for 1972.
    Source: Wong (1988).

that any increase in US factor endowments causes an increase in the volume of US trade (exports and imports) with the rest of the world.

6.3 International labor migration

In this section we relax the assumption of international labor immobility and examine the economy-wide effects of immigration. International labor migration deserves a separate treatment because its impact on host economies is a hotly debated issue. Also there is a fundamental asymmetry between labor movements and physical capital flows. With physical capital the owner of physical capital is separate from the capital service its equipment supplies. With labor, ownership and labor services cannot be separated. While capital services may move across borders, ownership need not be mobile. In contrast, labor services and ownership move together. This distinction matters because it affects the allocation of benefits across countries.

International labor migration: labor only

Consider the basic Ricardian framework of Chapter 3 and suppose that a free trade equilibrium is attained at an international price lying strictly between the cost ratios of the two countries and that the home country completely specializes in good 1. Then the equilibrium wage is such that:

$$p_1 = a_1 w$$

while, in the foreign country,

$$p_2 = a_2^* w^*$$

Dividing these two equations gives:

$$\frac{w^*}{w} = \frac{(1/a_2^*)}{(1/a_1)} \frac{p_2}{p_1}$$

The ratio of foreign to home wage rates now depends on the ratio of foreign to home labor productivities and on the world relative price. The ratio w^*/w must rise if either p_2/p_1 or the ratio of labor productivities increases. Taking the ratio of w^* and w from the trading equilibrium in (3.13) directly provides an alternative expression:

$$\frac{w^*}{w} = \frac{(1-\alpha)}{\alpha}\frac{L}{L^*} \tag{6.12}$$

(6.12) expresses w^*/w in terms of consumer preferences and the relative size of the domestic to foreign labor force: the ratio must rise as either α or L^* decrease as both changes lead to a rise in the world price of p_2. This indicates clearly that the international trade equilibrium achieved in the Ricardian model is not characterized by wage equalization, unless by a fluke. Since this wage difference would be expected to give rise to international labor migration, it explains why Ricardo assumed international labor immobility from the start.

Integrated equilibrium

Consider now the so-called integrated equilibrium of the world economy. This equilibrium is defined by Dixit and Norman (1980) as the resource allocation that the world would have if goods and factors were perfectly mobile. Applying this concept to our framework of two countries the following question arises: if international labor mobility is allowed, how much labor will flow across borders? Denoting labor migration into the domestic country by ΔL, the latter will be such that w^*/w in (6.12) equates to unity:

$$1 = \frac{(1-\alpha)}{\alpha}\frac{(L+\Delta L)}{(L^*-\Delta L)}$$

A simple manipulation of this last expression gives:

$$\frac{\Delta L}{L^*} = (1-\alpha)\frac{L}{L^*}\frac{(w-w^*)}{w^*} \tag{6.13}$$

where the wage rates w^* and w are the pre-mobility equilibrium wage rates. By (6.13), migration as a proportion of the foreign labor force is a product of three terms: the wage gap, relative labor forces L/L^* and $(1-\alpha)$. With $w > w^*$ initially, the ensuing labor movement to the domestic economy ($\Delta L > 0$) causes production of good 1 to increase and that of good 2 to decrease, and an increase in the equilibrium price p_2/p_1 (but good 1 being the numeraire, $p_1 = 1$). According to (3.14) and (6.12), the home wage decreases in terms of good 2 but stays constant in terms of good 1; vice versa the foreign wage is constant in terms of good 2 but increases in terms of good 1. The inflow of foreign workers therefore causes a loss in national welfare but a gain in foreign welfare when compared with the pre-mobility equilibrium. The Ricardian model thus establishes a conflict of interest between host country labor and source country labor.

Empirical results

In the empirical literature (6.13) is an often used framework to quantify the response of migration flows to key explanatory variables. For example, in an attempt to explain migration from the United Kingdom (UK) between 1870 and 1913, Hatton (1995) obtained the following results:

$$M_t = -3.49 + 9.85 \, \Delta \ln(w^*/w)_t + 6.97 \, \ln(w^*/w)_{t-1}$$
$$(0.79) \quad (1.91) \qquad\qquad (1.92)$$
$$+ 38.09 \, \Delta \ln L_t^* + 7.35 \, \Delta \ln L_t + 34.40 \, \ln L_{t-1}^*$$
$$(2.54) \qquad\qquad (1.00) \qquad\qquad (3.03)$$
$$- 18.28 \, \ln L_{t-1} + 16.77 \, MST_t + 0.03 \, Time + 0.44 \, M_{t-1} \qquad\qquad (6.14)$$
$$(3.20) \qquad\qquad (0.63) \qquad\quad (0.78) \qquad\quad (3.11)$$
$$\overline{R}^2 = 0.81 \quad RSS = 22.36 \quad LM(1) = 1.01 \quad RESET = 6.02 \quad HETERO = 0.34$$

where

M_t = net migration rate per 1,000 of population (net emigration from the UK divided through by the UK population)

w, w^* = wage in the UK; weighted average of wages in the US (weight of 1/2), Australia (weight of 1/4) and Canada (weight of 1/4)

L, L^* = UK employment rate; foreign employment rate (constructed as w^*)

MST = immigrant stock of UK born abroad (thousands)

$Time$ = time trend

It is clear from (6.14) that studies of migration patterns use variables other than wages, mainly to characterize the employment conditions in the country of origin and destination. The main reason for the inclusion of these variables lies in the recognition that, unlike in the Ricardian model, labor markets are imperfect because of, for example, built-in downward nominal wage rigidities. In this spirit, (6.14) includes the employment rates (a proxy for cyclical conditions), the stock of previous emigrants (one aspect of attractiveness of emigration), a time trend (a proxy for the fall in emigration costs) and a lagged dependent variable (the "friends and relatives" effect).

(6.14) explains more than four-fifths of the variation in net emigration. It gives the expected signs on all variables except for the change in the UK employment rate, which turns out positive. However, the lagged level term has the correct sign and is particularly strong. Setting the Δ's to zero and $M_t = M_{t-1}$ we obtain the steady state solution for M. From this, one can read the estimated long-run semi-elasticities for the right-hand side variables on the migration rate: 12.45 ($= 6.97/(1 - 0.44)$) for the relative wage, 61.43 for the foreign employment rate, -32.64 for the UK employment rate and 29.95 for the migrant stock. Thus, a permanent 10 percent increase in the overseas wage relative to the home wage would increase the net emigration rate by about 1.25 per thousand. A permanent 10 percent increase in the overseas employment rate has a more powerful impact, raising the net emigration rate by 6.14 per thousand. The impact of the home employment rate is half this size. Finally, each increase of 1,000 existing migrants draws about 30 new migrants overseas.

Extensions

The above analysis raises two points. The first is related to the following question: why do some people migrate while others do not? This is not explained by (6.14), but there are attempts to construct a more general theory which encompasses more aspects of migration, the wage variable being a necessary but not sufficient condition for international labor mobility (Stark, 1992). Many studies have also emphasized a self-selection effect – namely that migrants are not randomly selected but generally represent the upper tail of the skills distribution of the working population of source countries (see Borjas and Bratsberg, 1996;

Chiswick, 1999). The second point is related to the fundamental conflict between national and foreign welfare. Empirical studies other than (6.14) address the conflict indirectly by using opinion surveys. For example, Facchini and Mayda (2008) empirically confirm that voters are on average very opposed to migration in the majority of host countries and that their negative opinion is largely based on economic factors.

International labor migration: labor and capital

Since policymakers take public opinion on migration issues seriously we would expect migration policies based on the preceding analysis to be much more restrictive than we observe. As this is not the case, there must be other important determinants of migration policies. The empirical analysis of Facchini and Mayda (2008) concludes that pro-migration lobbies are powerful players in shaping the migration policy in the US.

To illustrate the emergence of a pro-migration lobby let us introduce a second factor of production – physical capital – in a framework of two countries called home (H) and partner (P). Each country produces a single good by means of two primary factors: capital K and labor L. The production functions $F(K_h, L_h)$ and $F(K_p, L_p)$, respectively, are neoclassical and have similar functional forms (see Section 4.1). The national capital–labor ratios are assumed to be different, with H being relatively more capital-abundant than P – that is, $(K_h/L_h) > (K_p/L_p)$. Normalizing the goods price at unity, nominal wage rates are equal to the respective value marginal product: $w_h = F_L(K_h, L_h)$ at home and $w_p = F_L(K_p, L_p)$ abroad, where $F_L(.)$ is the marginal product of labor.[6]

Figure 6.4 depicts the optimal allocation of labor, holding fixed the allocation of capital. The left and right vertical axes measure labor's real wage in H and P, respectively. The total labor of both countries is measured by the distance OO^* along the horizontal axis. Before international migration, the initial allocation of labor between H and P is assumed to be such that OL_0 and L_0O^* workers are in H and P, respectively. Curves hh and pp, drawn with reference to origins O and O^* respectively, are labor's physical marginal product in each country. The law of diminishing returns implies that the marginal product of labor is higher in the labor-scarce economy ($w_h^0 > w_p^0$).

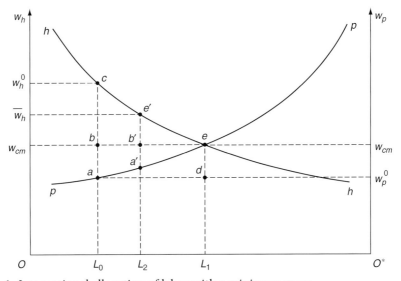

Figure 6.4 International allocation of labor with a minimum wage

Total home output produced with labor OL_0 is equal to the area under the curve hh up to L_0. To see this, consider:

$$\int_0^{L_0} F_L(K_h, L_h)\, dL_h = F(K_h, L_0) - F(K_h, 0) = F(K_h, L_0)$$

where $F(K_h, 0) = 0$ since it is a property of neoclassical production functions that a single factor does not produce any output in the absence of the other. Under our assumptions, the part of output that goes to domestic labor equals the wage rate times the labor force, $(w_h^0 . OL_0)$. The part of output that goes to capital is the remaining area under each curve. The partner country's output and income distribution are obtained by analogy.

If labor mobility is allowed, immigration will occur only to the labor-poor country, and will continue until point e where capital–labor ratios, real wages and capital returns are equalized. At point e, H absorbs the quantity L_0L_1 of P labor and the new equilibrium real wage is w_{cm}. Given this, H production increases by:

$$\Delta Y_h = \int_{L_0}^{L_1} F_L(K_h, L_h) dL_h = \text{area } ecL_0L_1 \tag{6.15}$$

but, against this increase, there is a less than offsetting wage bill paid to migrants given by the area ebL_0L_1, thus yielding a home gain of ecb. This gain accrues exclusively to home capitalists who also absorb the real wage loss of home labor, the area $cbw_{cm}w_h^0$. Clearly, the inflow of foreign workers causes a gain in national welfare but the gains are all reaped by capital owners. As in the Ricardian framework, domestic labor loses.

Asymmetry

As the real wage in P has increased from w_p^0 to w_{cm}, partner labor (whether migrants or non-migrants) gains at the expense of partner capitalists. Whether this translates in an overall gain in P depends on whether the labor units L_0L_1 productive in H are border workers or migrants who reside in H. The distinction is important because it affects the composition of national incomes and determines under which jurisdiction – that is, tax system – these labor units fall. In the former case, national income in P increases by eba, that is, the difference between the repatriated wage bill ebL_0L_1 and the loss in P output eaL_0L_1. In the latter case, area ebL_0L_1 is part of the domestic product of H that then appropriates all the allocation gains. Those who are left behind in P face an uncompensated aggregate loss corresponding to the area eda. Partner country, essentially partner capital, is a net loser from this type of labor mobility.

Wage floor and illegal immigration

Most economies in Northern America and Western Europe subject their entire labor market to a minimum wage floor. Specifics of the minimum wage regulation, though, vary across countries. For example, 20 of the 27 EU member states set a statutory national minimum wage. In the other seven countries collective agreements are the main mechanism used to regulate low wages.[7] In the US, there is a federal minimum wage and a state one, the latter being usually but not always higher. In states like Alabama, Louisiana and so on, where there is no defined minimum wage, the federal wage becomes the default.[8]

Suppose instead that H subjects its entire labor market to a minimum wage floor. Define this minimum wage by $\overline{w}_h$ in Figure 6.4. If labor mobility is free, home firms will hire partner labor until the marginal product of labor equals $\overline{w}_h$. The direct effect of the wage floor is to restrict the number of immigrants to L_0L_2 compared with L_0L_1 before. A differential in marginal products will therefore remain, indicating that though gains are realized they are not exhausted. Compared with the free mobility equilibrium e, workers lose less as they regain the area $b'e'\overline{w}_h w_{cm}$ while capital owners lose $ee'\overline{w}_h w_{cm}$, the net loss to the domestic economy being $eb'e'$.

Though further potential gains can be realized by lowering $\overline{w}_h$, these gains do not accrue to all groups in the society. Home labor sees its marginal product decline with immigration and will therefore object to a lower $\overline{w}_h$. In contrast, the marginal product of home capital increases with immigration and owners of capital will therefore favor a lowering of $\overline{w}_h$. If this is not possible, capital owners have incentives to hire illegal immigrants by offering foreign-born workers a wage slightly above the marginal product they earn in P. This practice enables domestic capital owners to capture the area $ee'a'$ since they hire $L_1 L_2$ clandestine migrants to produce goods with higher domestic marginal products.

Extensions

In Figure 6.4 the introduction of a minimum wage has the indirect effect of restricting the number of migrants. In reality, immigration quotas constitute the major policy tool aimed at directly limiting migration into high-income countries. However, there is an equivalence result between the two policy instruments: a minimum wage $\overline{w}_h$ and a quota of $L_0 L_2$ foreign-born workers are equivalent in terms of illegal migration, domestic output and incentives.

It is also the case that illegal migrants cannot fully exploit their human capital as their illegal status prevents access to health facilities and to the job market for their skills. Hence, illegality causes a *brain waste* for skilled individuals (see, e.g., Mattoo *et al.*, 2008) and increases the likelihood of skilled illegal migrants returning home, since the opportunity cost of returning is low for the most educated migrants (see, e.g., Coniglio *et al.*, 2009).[9]

6.4 The specific factors model

Since it characterizes the long-run equilibrium of an economy, the H-O-S theory assumes that factors of production are costlessly mobile within a country. However, recent empirical evidence on the dispersion of wages and capital returns across industries questions this assumption. For example, even after correcting for differences in worker ability, persistent wage differences across industries and over time have been found for both the US and Germany (Krueger and Summers, 1988; Katz and Summers, 1989; Fels and Gundlach, 1990). Recent empirical evidence also shows that the human capital of workers is largely occupation- or industry-specific (Kambourov and Manovskii, 2008, 2009). Evidence for the returns to capital also suggests persistent, long-run, differences across industries (Grossman and Levinsohn, 1989). These findings suggest that both capital and labor may be relatively immobile between industries, even in the long run.

The specific factors (SF) model modifies the H-O-S assumption of long-run factor mobility by allowing some or all factors to be immobile between industries. In particular, the SF model characterizes the extent of domestic factor immobility in terms of three periods: the short run, the medium run and the long run. In the short run all factors are completely immobile between industries. In the long run, there is complete factor mobility as in the H-O-S model. Between these extremes is the medium run, in which some factors are mobile while others are immobile. A key feature of the SF model is that the extent of factor mobility influences how factor prices, and hence factor incomes, respond to shocks such as an exogenous change in output prices.

In the next section we describe the production equilibrium, and hence optimal factor allocations, in the SF model (Neary, 1978). We then trace the effect of an output price change on production, factor employment and income distribution in moving from the short run to the long run. Interpreting the output price change to be the result of a tariff, it is then shown how the changes in factor incomes imply transitional coalitions of factor owners that either favor or oppose the tariff. This analysis of interest groups serves as an introduction to the political economy of protection: that part of trade theory that deals with the endogenous determination of trade policy (Ethier, 2011).

Optimal factor allocation

The implications of the SF model can be brought out with the aid of panels (a) and (b) in Figure 6.5. Each panel presents an alternative view of the allocation of an economy's labor and capital between two industries. Panel (a) depicts the optimal allocation of labor, holding fixed the allocation of capital. Panel (b) shows an Edgeworth-Bowley production box, which depicts the allocation of both factors simultaneously.[10] Together, panels (a) and (b) trace the transition of factor allocation, production and factor incomes from the short run to the long run.

In panel (a), the economy's total labor force is measured by the distance $O^1 O^2$ along the horizontal axis. The right and left vertical axes measure labor's nominal wage in industry 1 and industry 2, respectively. Since the length of the horizontal axis measures the economy's total labor force, any point on the axis denotes an allocation of labor between the two industries. Curves V_1^a and V_2^a, drawn with reference to origins O^1 and O^2, respectively, are labor's value marginal product in each industry. Each curve is a decreasing function of

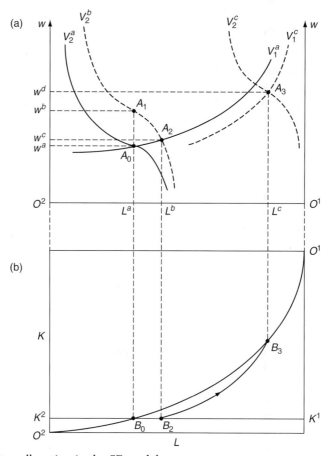

Figure 6.5 Factor allocation in the SF model

industry employment owing to diminishing marginal returns. By definition, the curve for each sector is drawn holding fixed the price of its output and the amount of capital employed. In panel (b), the horizontal axes measure the economy's total labor force and the vertical axes measure the economy's total supply of capital. The optimal long-run allocations of capital and labor between industries occur along the contract curve $O_1 O_2$.

Given these figures, the optimal allocation of factors is determined as follows. In the absence of complete specialization, competition and perfect factor mobility imply equality between value marginal products and nominal factor rewards:

$$p_1 F_1^L(K_1, L_1) = w = p_2 F_2^L(K_2, L_2) \tag{6.16}$$

$$p_1 F_1^K(K_1, L_1) = r = p_2 F_2^K(K_2, L_2) \tag{6.17}$$

where superscripts denote marginal products, w is the nominal wage, r is nominal rental on capital and p_j is the nominal price of good j ($j = 1, 2$). These conditions imply, in panel (a), the equilibrium wage and labor allocation given at the intersection point A_0. At the wage w^a, the quantity of labor employed in sector 1 is $L^a O^1$ and the quantity of labor in sector 2 is $O^2 L^a$. At any other wage, the implied allocation of labor between industries would leave some of the economy's labor unemployed (holding fixed the levels of capital employed). In panel (b), the optimal allocation of capital and labor between sectors is at point B_0. The levels of capital employed in each industry are given by the distances $O_1 K_1$ and $O_2 K_2$. These levels of capital are implicit in the positions of curves V_1^a and V_2^a in panel (a).

Adjustment to changes in output price

We now suppose there is an exogenous increase in the price of good 2 alone. In panel (a), this price increase leaves V_1^a unaffected but shifts V_2^a upward (to V_2^b) in proportion to the price increase. Assuming both factors are immobile, a new short-run equilibrium occurs at A_1 in panel (a) and at B_0 in panel (b). With neither factor mobile, re-establishing the equality between value marginal products and factor rewards in each sector now requires factor rewards to differ between sectors. In particular, nominal wages and rentals in sector 2 must rise in proportion to the price increase while wages and rentals in sector 1 remain unchanged. These changes in nominal factor rewards imply that, if one excludes the extreme case that each individual spends exclusively on his own produced commodity, the real income of the owners of the factors employed in sector 2 increases while the real income of the owners of the factors employed in sector 1 falls. The following inequality summarizes these short-term changes in nominal factor returns:

$$\hat{w}_2 = \hat{r}_2 = \hat{p}_2 > \hat{w}_1 = \hat{r}_1 = \hat{p}_1 = 0 \tag{6.18}$$

where a "hat" (ˆ) over a variable denotes its percentage change with respect to the initial long-run equilibrium.

Moving to the medium run, we assume labor becomes mobile while capital remains immobile. Given the short-run wage differential, labor will now flow from sector 1 to sector 2 until nominal wages are again equalized. This implies a new equilibrium at point A_2 in panel (a) and B_2 in panel (b). Since capital employment remains fixed, this reallocation of labor raises the output of good 2 and reduces the output of good 1.

We now inquire further into the changes in factor returns. Note that we can measure these changes relative to either the initial long-run values or the short-run values determined above. Measured relative to the initial long-run values, labor's nominal wage has risen (from w^a to w^c in panel (a)). Since the proportional rise in the nominal wage is less than the proportional increase in $p_2 (= w^b / w^a)$, labor's real return has fallen in terms of good 2 ($\hat{w} < \hat{p}_2$) and risen in terms of good 1 ($\hat{w} > \hat{p}_1$). These conflicting movements in real returns mean that the change in labor's welfare is ambiguous – that is, it depends on labor's preferences for good 2 versus good 1.[11] Finally, when measured relative to their preceding short-run values, labor's nominal and real return fell in sector 2 but increased in sector 1.

Turning to the return to capital, the flow of labor from sector 1 to sector 2 raises capital's marginal product in sector 2 but lowers it in sector 1.[12] Since p_2 increased but p_1 did not change, these changes in capital's marginal product imply that its nominal return fell in sector 1 but rose in sector 2. These changes in nominal returns, coupled with the change in p_2, imply that the real income of the owners of capital employed in sector 1 declined in terms of either good (both r_1/p_1 and r_1/p_2 fell) while the real income of the owners of capital employed in sector 2 increased (both r_2/p_1 and r_2/p_2 rose). These same changes in capital's nominal and real return occur if the changes are measured relative to their short-run values. The following summarizes the medium-run changes in factor rewards when measured relative to the initial equilibrium A_0:

$$\hat{r}_2 > \hat{p}_2 > \hat{w} > \hat{p}_1 = 0 > \hat{r}_1 \tag{6.19}$$

Moving to the long run, we assume that both capital and labor are mobile. In view of the medium-run differential in capital's return across sectors, capital will now move from sector 1 to sector 2 until its return is equalized. The final equilibrium is shown at A_3 in panel (a) and at B_3 in panel (b). The curve $B_2 B_3$ in panel (b) depicts a possible path for this real-location of capital. In panel (a), the reallocation of capital shifts V_1 and V_2 to the right since an increase (decrease) in the quantity of capital employed raises (decreases) labor's marginal product at all levels of employment. To determine the changes in returns relative to their initial long-run values, we can employ the Stolper-Samuelson theorem to conclude that, if sector 2 is labor-intensive, nominal and real wages must rise whereas nominal and real rentals must fall:

$$\hat{w} > \hat{p}_2 > \hat{p}_1 = 0 > \hat{r} \tag{6.20}$$

Note that the medium-run ambiguity over the change in labor's real income is resolved in the long run (compare (6.20) with (6.19)).[13]

Winners and losers from protection

The above changes in factor incomes imply "winners" and "losers" from protection. To see this, we need only interpret the increase in the price of good 2 to be the result of a tariff imposed on imports of good 2. Given this, Figure 6.6 summarizes the evolution of nominal factor returns from which real returns can be derived by comparison with the relative price movements (Ethier, 1987). Initially, the nominal prices of goods and factors are assumed to be normalized to unity by an appropriate choice of units. Therefore, imposition of a tariff at time SR raises both the domestic relative price of good 2 ($p_d = p_2/p_1$), and the nominal return to each factor in sector 2, from unity to $(1 + \hat{p}_d)$.[14] Looking now at the return to capital, the transition from SR to MR involves a further rise in the nominal and real return to capital in sector 2 and a fall in the returns to capital in the unprotected sector. Proceeding from MR to LR, the return to capital in sector 2 declines until, at time LR, the nominal and real returns to capital are below their pre-tariff value of unity. The path of returns to labor shows that labor in the protected sector gains in the short run while labor (overall) gains even more in the long run. Note that, in moving from SR to MR, nominal and real wages rise in sector 1 but fall in sector 2; this corresponds to the above noted ambiguity over the change in labor's welfare at this stage.

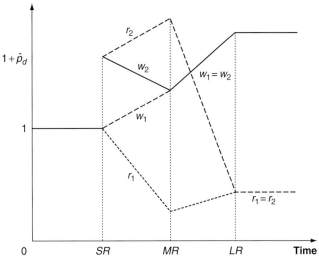

SR = short run; MR = medium run; LR = long run.

Figure 6.6 Protection of good 2 and nominal factor rewards

The political economy of tariffs

The political economy of protection deals with the endogenous determination of commercial policy. It asks, among other questions, why different countries have different structures of protection and what gives rise to any particular structure. A conventional assumption is that self-interest governs the behavior of economic agents, who then join interest groups according to whether they are potential gainers or losers from a policy. Individual interest groups or coalitions of several groups then attempt to achieve their preferred policy through the political system by lobbying lawmakers or supporting political candidates (Grossman and Helpman, 2002).

Coalition formation

For example, what coalitions of domestic factor owners might we expect to form if a country's residents were offered the choice of free trade or protection? Assuming capital is immobile except in the long run, Table 6.3 indicates the coalitions that would be predicted to form in different "runs." If factor owners consider only their long-run interests, the Stolper-Samuelson theorem would predict that capital owners and labor owners would form separate and opposing coalitions. However, if both short- and medium-run interests are considered, the SF model is applicable. Note that the short-run and long-run interests of some factor owners can differ (e.g., labor in sector 1 (L_1) and capital in sector 2 (K_2)). Note also that, in contrast to the Stolper-Samuelson case, workers and capital owners within the same industry might, at some stage, jointly demand either free trade or protection.

Table 6.3 Factor owner coalitions (capital immobile except in the long run)

Periods	Favor free trade	Favor protection	Ambiguous
SR	K_1, L_1	K_2, L_2	–
MR	K_1	K_2	L_1, L_2
LR	K_1, K_2	L_1, L_2	–

Empirical analysis

As discussed above, the SF and H-O-S models offer alternative predictions about the way a society's lobbying activities might be organized. With imperfect factor mobility, the SF model predicts coalitions based largely on industry affiliation whereas the H-O-S model, in assuming perfect factor mobility, predicts coalitions based solely on factor ownership (that is, the Stolper-Samuelson case).

Magee (1980) examined the empirical merits of these predictions about lobbying activity by considering three hypotheses, each of which corresponds to the prediction of the Stolper-Samuelson theorem:

▲ *Marxian hypothesis*: capitalists and workers will oppose each other on the issue of free trade or protection in an industry, with capital favoring free trade and labor favoring protection if the country is capital-abundant and labor scarce (underlying assumptions of Table 6.3).

▲ *Unanimity hypothesis*: each factor will favor either free trade (capital) or protection (labor) but not both (see third row of Table 6.3).

▲ *Independence hypothesis*: a factor's position does not depend on whether it works in the export sector or in the import-competing sector.

To test each proposition, Magee used data on the position taken by labor unions and industry trade associations on the issue of either increasing or reducing protection during US Congressional hearings on the US Trade Reform Act of 1973. With respect to the first proposition, Table 6.4 shows the pairing of interests in 21 of the 33 US industries where both labor and capital (the industry association) expressed an unambiguous preference. These results are contrary to the H-O-S model, since the two interest groups adopted a common position on trade policy in all but two industries (tobacco and petroleum).

If the country in question were capital-abundant, the unanimity hypothesis would imply that, in all industries, capital would favor free trade while labor would favor protection. Table 6.4 reveals no such unanimity for the (capital-abundant) US. This finding is corroborated in an even larger sample of industries than that reported here.[15] Again, these findings are consistent with the theoretical predictions of the SF model (see the first and second row of Table 6.3) and do not support Stolper-Samuelson's factor mobility assumption.

Table 6.4 Lobbying on the 1973 Trade Reform Act: industry agreement (disagreement) of labor and capital

		Position of the industry's labor	
		Protection	*Freer trade*
Position of the industry's capital owners	*Protection*	Distilling, shoes, chemicals, textiles, stone products, apparel, iron & steel, cutlery, plastics, hardware, rubber shoes, bearings, leather, watches	Tobacco
	Freer trade	Petroleum	Paper, machinery, trucks, aviation, tractors

Source: Magee (1980).

Table 6.5 Free trade or protection: labor's and capital's position by industry

	Industry	Protection	Free trade	Odds ratio
Capital (obs. = 24)	Import-competing	10 ($p_{11}=0.42$)	3 ($p_{12}=0.12$)	4.0
	Export	5 ($p_{21}=0.21$)	6 ($p_{22}=0.25$)	
Labor (obs. = 21)	Import-competing	11 ($p_{11}=0.52$)	1 ($p_{12}=0.05$)	8.8
	Export	5 ($p_{21}=0.24$)	4 ($p_{22}=0.19$)	

Source: Magee (1980).

The third hypothesis states that a factor's preferred policy is independent of the industry in which it works. Table 6.5 shows, for each factor, its policy preference versus its industry affiliation. Each cell measures responses as both an absolute count and as a proportion of the total number of observations. For example, 10 of the 24 capitalists (42 percent) associated with the import-competing sector preferred protection.

The odds ratio shown in Table 6.5 is defined as $(p_{11}/p_{12})/(p_{21}/p_{22})$, where p_{ij} is the proportion of responses in cell (i,j) relative to the number of observations. The numerator of this ratio measures the preference for protection versus free trade for a factor working in the import-competing sector; the denominator measures this relative preference for a factor working in an export sector. A value of unity therefore implies independence between industry affiliation and a factor's preferences whereas values above unity favor the SF model since this implies low values for p_{12} and p_{21}.

Table 6.5 indicates that the odds of capital in the import-competing sector favoring protection are four times those of capital in the export sector; for labor the odds ratio is 8.8. Statistically, the hypothesis of independence can be rejected at the 5 percent level of significance for capital and at the 10 percent level of significance for labor.[16]

6.5 Concluding remarks

The seeming lack of empirical support for the predictions of the factor endowments theory led to a systematic search for alternative trade models. This chapter examined one such alternative theory – the gravity model, where market size, distance and transport costs matter. Also, some assumptions of the one-factor Ricardian and two-factor H-O-S models were modified one by one to see which phenomena might be explained. This chapter considered three such attempts and examined their influence both theoretically and empirically. The international mobility of factors was considered first. In this case, trade in goods and international factor movements are substitutes in the standard H-O-S model. However, if trade in commodities is not based on the difference in factor endowments, then trade and factor flows can be complementary. More specifically, trade in factors causes trade in commodities. International labor migration was then considered to examine the benefits of immigration to both host and source countries and to identify pro-migration lobbies. Also it was shown how a minimum wage floor and migration quotas give rise to illegal immigration. Lastly, the specific factors model was introduced. It assumes some factors are domestically immobile.

In this model, a price shock leads to transitional changes in the real income of factor owners which differ from the income changes predicted by the H-O-S model. Also, the specific factors model explains the phenomenon that coalitions for or against trade policy issues form on the basis of industry affiliation rather than factor ownership (laborers, capitalists, landowners and so on), as predicted by the H-O-S model.

Problems

6.1 Show graphically the second part of the Mundell proposition – that is, an increase in restrictions to factor movements stimulates trade.

6.2 A comparison of the columns of Table 6.2 suggests that $\varepsilon_{dk} > \varepsilon_{mk} > \varepsilon_{nk}$ and that, except for some years, $\varepsilon_{nl} > \varepsilon_{ml} > \varepsilon_{dl}$. Given this, which of the goods are capital-intensive and which are labor-intensive? What are the assumptions about demand that allows such characterization? Explain.

6.3 Show that world production with factor mobility (that is, factors moving from low to high productivity countries) is more efficient than the trading equilibrium when one of the two countries has an absolute advantage.

6.4 Consider the production function of the domestic economy (subscript h) and of the foreign economy (subscript p): $Q_h = K_h^{\alpha_h} L_h^{1-\alpha_h}$, $Q_p = K_p^{\alpha_p} L_p^{1-\alpha_p}$. Before labor market integration between H and P, national capital–labor ratios are assumed as follows: $K_h/L_h = 2 > K_p/L_p = 1$. Take $L_h = L_p = 1$ and $\alpha_h = \alpha_p = 0.3$. Given this information: (1) Derive the marginal products of labor in the two countries under autarky. Quantify these with the parameter values given above; (2) Introduce a domestic minimum-wage $\overline{w}_h$ such that it is equal to the marginal product of labor under autarky. Given this, if one allows for international labor mobility (physical capital remaining immobile), how much labor will flow from one country to the other? Make a distinction between documented and illegal labor migration; (3) Repeat the steps of (2) for different values of $\overline{w}_h$; (4) Quantify remittances from abroad, assuming that labor income is returned to the source country. Compute the percentage difference between gross national income (GNI) (with migration) and GDP (in autarky) in both countries.

6.5 Suppose instead that labor is the immobile factor except in the long run. Capital is therefore mobile except in the short run where both factors are immobile. Fill in the cells of Table 6.3 corresponding to that particular case. Make statements over the consequences of a tariff on good 2 for the reward of the immobile factor in general.

Notes

1. See the Leontief paradox and the measurement of intra-industry trade.
2. As a matter of fact, the converse is true. For example, equation (10) in the multi-country Ricardian model of Eaton and Kortum (2002) bears a resemblance to the standard gravity equation.
3. We consider only the first part of the proposition since the second part proceeds by reversing the steps of the analysis.
4. It is important to note that in the H-O-S model the difference in factor endowment is the cause of trade in commodities. In Markusen's model, trade in commodities is the result of other determinants of comparative advantage and of differences in factor endowments that emerge endogenously in response to these determinants of comparative advantage.

5. The properties of the revenue function are given by (4.35) and (4.36) and further explored in that section.
6. This is our adaptation of MacDougall (1960) to the case of international labor mobility. MacDougall's original idea is described in Chapter 12, where the integration of markets for physical capital is analyzed.
7. Since 1999, Eurostat has published a cross-country comparison of the level of minimum wages in the EU. In the report of January 2009, the gross monthly minimum wage ranged between 123 euros in Bulgaria and 1,642 euros in Luxembourg (see the Eurostat website: http://epp.eurostat.ec.europa.eu). The seven countries where low wages are regulated by collective agreements are: Austria, Cyprus, Denmark, Finland, Germany, Italy, and Sweden.
8. In cases where an employee is subject to both state and federal minimum wage laws, he or she is entitled to the higher of the two minimum wages (see the US Department of Labor website: www.dol.gov). For an overview of the minimum wage regulations and their implications, see Card and Krueger (1995).
9. Other applications of the minimum wage model include Brecher (1980) and Viaene (1987), among others. Brecher examines factor accumulation and finds that for a small country (fixed terms of trade), foreign investment might worsen, rather than improve, employment and welfare. In a similar vein, Viaene found that the existence of a minimum wage reduced the possibility of favorable welfare and employment effects from land reclamation.
10. See appendix of Chapter 4.
11. Real income in terms of good 1 (w/p_1) and good 2 (w/p_2) corresponds to the intercepts of a worker's budget constraint. If w/p_1 and w/p_2 change in opposite directions then knowledge of a worker's preferences is needed to determine his/her change in real income (level of utility). Ruffin and Jones (1977) call this the "neo-classical ambiguity."
12. These changes in capital's marginal product as labor alone is changed derive from the technological complementarity between capital and labor inherent in a two-factor neoclassical production function.
13. The comparison of (6.19) and (6.20) suggests two other remarks. First, equalization of commodity prices through free trade will, in general, not lead to the equalization of factor rewards in the short and medium run. Second, one appealing element of the SF model is that (6.19) holds regardless of the assumption on the relative factor supply, while the Stolper-Samuelson result (6.20) depends crucially on it.
14. In sector 2, w rises to $w_2 = (1 + \hat{p}_d)w_0$ and r rises to $r_2 = (1 + \hat{p}_d)r_0$, where $r_0 = w_0 = 1$.
15. In the overall sample, Magee found that 37 percent of the capital owners, and 24 percent of the labor unions supported freer trade.
16. See Magee (1980) for more details on these significance tests.

References and additional reading

Gravity models

Anderson, J.E. (1979), "A Theoretical Foundation for the Gravity Equation," *American Economic Review*, 69, 106–116.
Anderson, J.E. (2010), "The Gravity Model," NBER Working Paper Series, 16576 (Cambridge, MA: NBER).

Anderson, J.E. and van Wincoop, E. (2003), "Gravity with Gravitas: A Solution to the Border Puzzle," *American Economic Review*, 93, 170–192.

Baltagi, B.H., Egger, P., and Pfaffermayr, M. (2003), "A Generalized Design for Bilateral Trade Flow Models," *Economics Letters*, 80 (3), 391–397.

Bergstrand, J.H. (1989), "The Generalized Gravity Equation, Monopolistic Competition, and the Factor-Proportions Theory in International Trade," *Review of Economics and Statistics*, 71 (1), 143–153.

Bergstrand, J.H. and Egger, P. (2007), "A Knowledge- and Physical-capital Model of International Trade Flows, Foreign Direct Investment and Multinational Enterprises," *Journal of International Economics*, 73, 278–308.

Bergstrand, J.H. and Egger, P. (2011), "Gravity Equations and Trade Frictions," in D. Bernhofen, R. Falvey, D. Greenaway and U. Kreickemeier (Eds.), *Palgrave Handbook of International Trade* (Basingstoke: Palgrave Macmillan), ch. 17.

Brouwer, J., Paap, R., and Viaene, J.-M. (2008), "Trade and FDI Effects of EMU Enlargement," *Journal of International Money and Finance*, 27 (2), 188–208.

Deardorff, A.V. (1998), "Determinants of Bilateral Trade: Does Gravity Work in a Neoclassical World?" in J.A. Frankel (Ed.), *The Regionalism of the World Economy* (Chicago: University of Chicago Press), 7–28.

Eaton, J. and Kortum, S. (2002), "Technology, Geography, and Trade," *Econometrica*, 70, 1741–1779.

Feenstra, R.C. (2002), "Border Effects and the Gravity Equation: Consistent Methods for Estimation," *Scottish Journal of Political Economy*, 49, 491–506.

Helpman, E. and Krugman, P. (1985), *Market Structure and Foreign Trade, Increasing Returns, Imperfect Competition, and the International Economy* (Cambridge, MA and London: MIT Press).

Martin, P. and Rey, H. (2004), "Financial Super-markets: Size Matters for Asset Trade," *Journal of International Economics*, 64, 335–361.

Distance and transport costs

Davis, D.R. (1998), "The Home Market, Trade, and Industrial Structure," *American Economic Review*, 88, 1264–1277.

Disdier, A.-C. and Head, K. (2008), "The Puzzling Persistence of the Distance Effect on Bilateral Trade," *Review of Economics and Statistics*, 90 (1), 37–48.

Hummels, D. (2007), "Transportation Costs and International Trade in the Second Era of Globalization," *Journal of Economic Perspectives*, 21 (3), 131–154.

Hummels, D. and Lugosvskyy, V. (2006), "Are Matched Partner Trade Statistics a Usable Measure of Transportation Costs?" *Review of International Economics*, 14 (1), 69–86.

Radelet, S. and Sachs, J. (1998), "Shipping Costs, Manufactured Exports, and Economic Growth," mimeo, AEA Meetings, Harvard University.

International factor mobility

Burgess, D.F. (1978), "On the Distributional Effects of Direct Foreign Investment," *International Economic Review*, 19, 647–664.

Dixit, A. and Norman, V. (1980), *Theory of International Trade: A Dual, General Equilibrium Approach* (Cambridge: Cambridge University Press).

Jones, R.W., Neary, J.P., and Ruane, F.P. (1983), "Two-Way Capital Flows," *Journal of International Economics*, 14, 357–366.

Markusen, J.R. (1983), "Factor Movements and Commodity Trade as Complements," *Journal of International Economics*, 14, 341–356.

Melvin, J.R. (1970), "Commodity Taxation as a Determinant of Trade," *Canadian Journal of Economics*, 3, 62–78.

Mundell, R. (1957), "International Trade and Factor Mobility," *American Economic Review*, 47, 321–335.

Wong, K.-Y. (1988), "International Factor Mobility and the Volume of Trade: An Empirical Study," in R.C. Feenstra (Ed.), *Empirical Methods for International Trade*, (Cambridge, MA: MIT Press), 231–250.

Wong, K.-Y. (1995), *International Trade in Goods and Factor Mobility* (Cambridge MA: MIT Press).

Woodland, A.D. (1980), "Direct and Indirect Trade Utility Functions," *Review of Economic Studies*, 47, 907–926.

International labor migration

Borjas, G.J. and Bratsberg, B. (1996), "Who leaves? The Emigration of the Foreign-born," *Review of Economics and Statistics*, 78 (1), 165–167.

Chiswick, B.R. (1999), "Are Immigrants Favorably Self-Selected?" *American Economic Review*, 89 (2), 181–185.

Coniglio, N.D., De Arcangelis, G. and Serlenga, L. (2009), "Clandestine Migrants: Do the High-Skilled Return Home First?" mimeo, Sapienza University, Rome.

Facchini, G. and Mayda, A.M. (2008), "From Individual Attitudes towards Migrants to Migration Policy Outcomes: Theory and Evidence," *Economic Policy*, 56, 653–713.

Facchini, G. and Mayda, A.M. (2009), "Does the Welfare State Affect Individual Attitudes towards Immigrants? Evidence across Countries," *Review of Economics and Statistics*, 91 (2), 295–314.

Hatton, T. (1995), "A Model of UK Emigration, 1870–1913," *Review of Economics and Statistics*, 77 (3), 407–415.

MacDougall, G.D.A. (1960), "The Benefits and Costs of Private Investment from Abroad: A Theoretical Approach," *Economic Record*, 36, 13–35.

Mattoo, A., Neagu, I.C., and Ozden, C. (2008), "Brain Waste? Educated Immigrants in the US Labor Market," *Journal of Development Economics*, 87, 255–269.

Michael, S.M. (2003), "International Migration, Income Taxes and Transfers: A Welfare Analysis," *Journal of Development Economics*, 72, 401–411.

Stark, O. (1992), *The Migration of Labor* (Oxford: Blackwell).

Minimum wage

Brecher, R.A. (1974), "Minimum Wage Rates and the Pure Theory of International Trade," *Quarterly Journal of Economics*, 88 (1), 98–116.

Brecher, R.A. (1980), "Increased Unemployment from Capital Accumulation in a Minimum-Wage Model of an Open Economy," *Canadian Journal of Economics*, 13, 152–158.

Card, D. and Krueger, A.B. (1995), *Myth and Measurement: The New Economics of the Minimum Wage* (Princeton: Princeton University Press).

Viaene, J.-M. (1987), "Factor Accumulation in a Minimum-Wage Economy," *European Economic Review*, 31, 1313–1328.

Specific factors model

Ethier, W.J. (1987), "The Theory of International Trade," in L.M. Officer (Ed.), *International Economics* (Boston: Kluwer Academic), 1–57.

Ethier, W.J. (2011), "Political Economy of Protection," in D. Bernhofen, R. Falvey, D. Greenaway, and U. Kreickemeier (Eds.), *Palgrave Handbook of International Trade* (Basingstoke: Palgrave Macmillan), ch. 10.

Fels, J. and Gundlach, E. (1990), "More Evidence on the Puzzle of Interindustry Wage Differentials: The Case of West Germany," *Weltwirtschaftliches Archiv*, 3, 544–560.

Grossman, G.M. and Levinsohn, J.A. (1989), "Import Competition and the Stock Market Return Capital," *American Economic Review*, 79 (5), 1065–1087.

Grossman, G.M. and Helpman, E. (2002), *Interest Groups and Trade Policy* (Princeton: Princeton University Press).

Kambourov, G.T. and Manovskii, I. (2008), "Rising Occupational and Industry Mobility in the United States: 1968–1997," *International Economic Review*, 49 (1), 41–79.

Kambourov, G.T. and Manovskii, I. (2009), "Occupational Specificity of Human Capital," *International Economic Review*, 50 (1), 63–115.

Katz, L.F. and Summers, L.H. (1989), "Industry Rents: Evidence and Implications," in M.N. Baily, and C. Winston (Eds), *Brookings Papers on Economic Activity: Microeconomics* (Washington, DC: Brookings Institution), 208–275.

Kohli, U. (1993), "US Technology and the Specific-Factors Model," *Journal of International Economics*, 34, 115–136.

Krueger, A.B. and Summers, L.H. (1988), "Efficiency Wages and the Inter-industry Wage Structure," *Econometrica*, 56, 259–293.

Magee, S.P. (1980), "Three Simple Tests of the Stolper-Samuelson Theorem," in P. Oppenheimer (Ed.), *Issues in International Economics* (London: Oriel Press), 138–153.

Neary, J.P. (1978), "Short-Run Capital Specificity and the Pure Theory of International Trade," *Economic Journal*, 88, 488–510.

Ruffin, R. and Jones, R. (1977), "Protection and Real Wages: The Neo-Classical Ambiguity," *Journal of Economic Theory*, 14, 337–348.

Panel data estimation

Baltagi, B.H. (2005), *Econometric Analysis of Panel Data*, 3rd ed. (Chichester: John Wiley and Sons).

7

The factor abundance theory in higher dimensions

This chapter extends the theoretical propositions of the Heckscher-Ohlin-Samuelson (H-O-S) model to arbitrary numbers of goods and factors and discusses empirical methods and evidence for testing these propositions. Following a review of the equilibrium conditions for a closed economy with *J* goods and *H* factors, we consider a generalization of the concept of comparative advantage. We then consider the Heckscher-Ohlin theorem and methods of testing its predictions for the pattern of trade.[1] Following this, we consider an extension of the Stolper-Samuelson and Rybczynski propositions and review efforts to empirically evaluate them. Finally, we consider the factor price equalization (FPE) theorem. Theoretical extension of the Heckscher-Ohlin theorem will normally involve a comparison of pre-trade and post-trade equilibrium conditions expressed in terms of an economy's domestic income and expenditure functions under the assumption that firms minimize cost and consumers maximize utility. The properties of the income and expenditure functions are then used to derive inequalities that are interpreted as *average* relationships that must hold between prices, outputs and inputs. For empirical purposes, these average relationships are interpreted as *correlations* that should exist between prices, outputs and inputs.

7.1   Autarky equilibrium with *J* goods and *H* factors

Let $\mathbf{p} = (p_1, p_2, \ldots, p_J)$ be a vector of *J* product prices, $\mathbf{e} = (e_1, e_2, \ldots, e_H)$ a vector of *H* national factor supplies and $\mathbf{q} = (q_1, q_2, \ldots, q_J)$ a vector of national outputs.[2] As discussed in Chapter 4, a country's gross domestic product (GDP) function $G(\mathbf{p}, \mathbf{e})$ gives the maximum income that the country can achieve when facing prices $\mathbf{p}$ and endowed with resource supplies $\mathbf{e}$. The GDP function is derived from the maximization of national income with respect to outputs for a given set of prices and subject to the constraint imposed by the economy's transformation function. Thus, G($\mathbf{p}$, $\mathbf{e}$) depends upon technology as well as factor supplies. By definition,

$$G(\mathbf{p}, \mathbf{e}) = \mathbf{pq} \tag{7.1}$$

where the outputs are those that maximize national income at prices $\mathbf{p}$ and are feasible – that is, can be produced from the given factor supplies and technology. By Hotelling's Lemma, differentiation of (7.1) with respect to the price of good j yields the output supply function of good j:

$$\frac{\partial G(\mathbf{p}, \mathbf{e})}{\partial p_j} = q_j(\mathbf{p}) \tag{7.2}$$

In Chapter 4, it was also shown that total income from production must equal the total payments to the factors of production:

$$G(\mathbf{p}, \mathbf{e}) = \mathbf{pq} = \mathbf{we} \tag{7.3}$$

where $\mathbf{w} = (w_1, w_2, \ldots, w_H)$ is the vector of equilibrium factor prices. This income identity implies a dual interpretation of G($\mathbf{p}$, $\mathbf{e}$): it is the minimum amount that can be paid to an economy's factors with the average cost of production no less than price in each industry (that is, industry profits are at most zero).[3] Thus, in (7.3), $\mathbf{w}$ is the vector of factor prices that minimize expenditure on factors subject to the constraint that profits in each industry must be non-positive.

While the GDP function summarizes the supply side of an economy, the domestic expenditure or spending function S($\mathbf{p}$, u) summarizes the demand side. The expenditure function gives the minimum expenditure at prices $\mathbf{p}$ that would enable a country to purchase a mix of commodities that provide a level of welfare no less than u.[4] By definition:

$$S(\mathbf{p}, u_0) = \mathbf{ph}. \tag{7.4}$$

The commodity demands $\mathbf{h}$ are chosen to minimize expenditure subject to the constraint that the utility level is u_0. By Shephard's Lemma, differentiation of (7.4) with respect to the price of good j gives the (compensated) demand function for good j:

$$\frac{\partial S(\mathbf{p}, u_0)}{\partial p_j} = h_j(\mathbf{p}, u_0). \tag{7.5}$$

The GDP and expenditure functions permit us to determine an economy's equilibrium price vector and equilibrium level of utility. In particular, the equilibrium conditions are:

$$\frac{\partial G(\mathbf{p}, \mathbf{e})}{\partial p_j} = \frac{\partial S(\mathbf{p}, u)}{\partial p_j} \quad j = 1, \ldots, J. \tag{7.6}$$

$$G(\mathbf{p}, \mathbf{e}) = S(\mathbf{p}, u). \tag{7.7}$$

Expression (7.6) states the equality of demand and supply for each good while (7.7) is the economy's overall budget constraint. However, (7.7) is redundant since it can be derived by multiplying both sides of (7.6) by p_j and summing over j. Thus, of the $(J + 1)$ equations in (7.6) and (7.7), only J are independent. These J equations allow determination of $(J - 1)$ relative prices and u, the level of utility achieved in equilibrium. Since the economy does not, by assumption, engage in trade, the equilibrium price vector $\mathbf{p}$ is the economy's autarky price vector and the equilibrium level of utility is the level of utility obtained under autarky.

7.2 Generalized law of comparative advantage

The law of comparative advantage states that trade results from, and can thus be predicted by, differences in autarky relative product prices between countries. In Chapter 3, the law of comparative advantage was generalized to many goods and a single (or single composite) factor in the form of the Ricardian chain proposition. In this section, the law of comparative advantage is extended to an arbitrary number of goods and factors.

We first state some very general relationships between price changes and quantity changes which derive from properties of the income and expenditure functions in competitive equilibrium. These relationships are then used to demonstrate that differences in autarky prices between countries will be correlated with the pattern of a country's net exports. The relationships derived are very general in that they hold irrespective of the exact form of a country's technology and preferences. The only restrictions are the convexity requirements needed to insure solutions to the underlying producer (profit maximization) and consumer (utility) optimizations implicit in the definitions of the GDP and expenditure functions.

Let $\mathbf{q}_0$ be the output vector produced at equilibrium prices $\mathbf{p}_0$ and let $\mathbf{q}_1$ be the output vector produced at equilibrium prices $\mathbf{p}_1$. From the definition of the GDP function, the optimum output bundles at their respective prices yield maximum income. As such, we can write the following inequalities:

$$\mathbf{p}_0\mathbf{q}_0 \geq \mathbf{p}_0\mathbf{q}_1 \Rightarrow \mathbf{p}_0(\mathbf{q}_0 - \mathbf{q}_1) \geq 0 \tag{7.8}$$

$$\mathbf{p}_1\mathbf{q}_1 \geq \mathbf{p}_1\mathbf{q}_0 \Rightarrow -\mathbf{p}_1(\mathbf{q}_0 - \mathbf{q}_1) \geq 0. \tag{7.9}$$

Adding these inequalities gives:

$$(\mathbf{p}_0 - \mathbf{p}_1)(\mathbf{q}_0 - \mathbf{q}_1) \geq 0. \tag{7.10}$$

This states that price changes and output changes are, on average, positively correlated and, in this sense, price changes can be said to predict output changes.

A similar set of inequalities derives from the expenditure function. Specifically, if $\mathbf{h}_0$ and $\mathbf{h}_1$ are the demands at prices $\mathbf{p}_0$ and $\mathbf{p}_1$ when utility is held constant then we can write:

$$\mathbf{p}_0\mathbf{h}_0 \leq \mathbf{p}_0\mathbf{h}_1 \Rightarrow \mathbf{p}_0(\mathbf{h}_0 - \mathbf{h}_1) \leq 0 \tag{7.11}$$

$$\mathbf{p}_1\mathbf{h}_1 \leq \mathbf{p}_1\mathbf{h}_0 \Rightarrow -\mathbf{p}_1(\mathbf{h}_0 - \mathbf{h}_1) \leq 0. \tag{7.12}$$

Combining these inequalities gives:

$$(\mathbf{p}_0 - \mathbf{p}_1)(\mathbf{h}_0 - \mathbf{h}_1) \leq 0. \tag{7.13}$$

This states that price changes and demand changes are, on average, negatively correlated and, in this sense, price changes predict demand changes.

Combining inequalities (7.11) and (7.13) permits us to derive a statement about the change in prices when moving from autarky to trade and the accompanying changes in outputs and demands. It may be guessed that since domestic outputs respond, on average, positively to price changes while domestic demands respond, on average, negatively to price changes, the difference between supply and demand (net exports) should respond, on average, positively to price changes. That is, when moving from autarky to trade, goods whose prices were lower in autarky will on average be associated with rising domestic supply and falling domestic demand – that is, positive net exports. Conversely, goods whose prices were higher in autarky will on average be associated with falling domestic supply and rising domestic demand, that is, negative net exports (= net imports).

Let $\mathbf{p}_T$ denote the vector of prices under free trade and let $\mathbf{p}_A$ denote a country's autarky price vector. Using (7.10), the relationship between autarky and free trade incomes can be written:

$$(\mathbf{p}_A - \mathbf{p}_T)(\mathbf{q}_A - \mathbf{q}_T) \geq 0. \tag{7.14}$$

It is assumed that the production mix with trade ($\mathbf{q}_T$) is feasible – that is, producible from the country's resources and technology. Likewise, (7.13) can be expressed in terms of autarky and free trade expenditure:

$$(\mathbf{p}_A - \mathbf{p}_T)(\mathbf{h}_A - \mathbf{h}_T) \leq 0. \tag{7.15}$$

Combining inequalities (7.14) and (7.15) yields:

$$(\mathbf{p}_A - \mathbf{p}_T)(\mathbf{h}_A - \mathbf{h}_T) \leq (\mathbf{p}_A - \mathbf{p}_T)(\mathbf{q}_A - \mathbf{q}_T) \tag{7.16}$$

$$(\mathbf{p}_A - \mathbf{p}_T)(\mathbf{h}_A - \mathbf{q}_A) - (\mathbf{p}_A - \mathbf{p}_T)(\mathbf{h}_T - \mathbf{q}_T) \leq 0 \tag{7.17}$$

$$-(\mathbf{p}_A - \mathbf{p}_T)(\mathbf{h}_T - \mathbf{q}_T) \leq 0 \tag{7.18}$$

since $(\mathbf{h}_A - \mathbf{q}_A) = 0$ by definition of autarky. Finally, if $\mathbf{t} = -(\mathbf{h}_T - \mathbf{q}_T) = (\mathbf{q}_T - \mathbf{h}_T)$ denotes the vector of commodity net exports (excess supplies) then (7.18) becomes

$$(\mathbf{p}_A - \mathbf{p}_T)\mathbf{t} \leq 0. \tag{7.19}$$

Proposition 7.1: *In moving from autarky to free trade, the difference between a country's autarky prices and the prices existing under free trade will, on average, be negatively correlated with changes in the country's excess supplies of goods. Goods with higher prices in autarky relative to free trade will, on average, have negative excess supplies (be imported) whereas goods with lower prices in autarky will have positive excess supplies (be exported).*

Note that Proposition 7.1 does not say that each good that has a lower price in autarky will be exported – that is, we are unable to predict the *commodity composition* of trade.

An immediate implication of (7.19) is that, if it holds, then the value of a country's net trade (net exports) at autarky prices must be strictly negative:

$$\mathbf{p}_A \mathbf{t} < 0 \tag{7.20}$$

This follows immediately by imposing the trade balance condition $\mathbf{p}_T \mathbf{t} = 0$ in (7.19) and assuming that the elements of the trade vector $\mathbf{t}$ are not all zero.

Repeating the above analysis for the foreign country (rest of the world) yields:

$$(\mathbf{p}_A^* - \mathbf{p}_T)\mathbf{t}^* \leq 0. \tag{7.21}$$

where an asterisk denotes foreign country variables. We can now state a relationship between the difference in autarky prices between countries and the pattern of trade. With balanced world trade (that is, $\mathbf{p}_T\mathbf{t}^* = -\mathbf{p}_T\mathbf{t}$) and noting that $\mathbf{t}^* = -\mathbf{t}$, conditions (7.19) and (7.21) imply:

$$(\mathbf{p}_A - \mathbf{p}_A^*)\mathbf{t} \leq 0. \tag{7.22}$$

Proposition 7.2 (generalized law of comparative advantage): *Assuming that in each country firms minimize costs and consumers maximize utility, the difference in countries' autarky prices will be negatively correlated with the pattern of net exports that exists under free trade.*

Proposition 7.2 is completely general; it does not rely on any specific assumption about the nature of technology or preferences. However, this generality comes at a price: we are unable to predict the exact commodity composition of trade between countries.

Empirically testing proposition 7.2 (equivalently proposition 7.1) would not appear feasible, since it requires data on autarky prices. Yet Bernhofen and Brown (2004) overcame this limitation by using the opening up of Japan to international trade in the nineteenth century after 200 years of isolation as a natural experiment to test the generalized law of comparative advantage prediction. Since (7.20) must hold if (7.19) is true, they used data on Japan's trade vector during its "free trade" period from 1868 to 1875 and prices on those goods from Japan's "autarky" period 1851–53. They found that (7.20) was satisfied in every year between 1868 and 1875.

7.3 Factor abundance and trade

The above generalized law of comparative advantage is now recast in terms of factor input requirements and factor abundance in order to generalize the Heckscher-Ohlin factor abundance model. As usual, we will want to consider factor abundance measured either by autarky factor prices (the price version) or autarky factor supplies (the quantity version).

We begin by stating the set of equations that must be satisfied by an economy in a competitive general equilibrium:

$$(\mathbf{p} - \mathbf{w}\mathbf{A}(\mathbf{w}))\mathbf{q} = 0 \tag{7.23}$$

$$\mathbf{p} \leq \mathbf{w}\mathbf{A}(\mathbf{w}) \tag{7.24}$$

$$\mathbf{A}(\mathbf{w})\mathbf{q} = \mathbf{e} \tag{7.25}$$

In these equations, $\mathbf{A}(\mathbf{w})$ denotes the $H \times N$ matrix of equilibrium input requirements per unit of output which are a function of factor prices so that $\mathbf{w}\mathbf{A}(\mathbf{w})$ is then the vector of unit cost functions. Equation (7.23) states the condition for zero profits in each industry whereas (7.24) states the requirement that for any good, average cost must equal or exceed its price. Together, equations (7.23) and (7.24) insure that positive production of any good ($q_j > 0$) must yield zero profits. Finally, (7.25) states the requirement for factor market equilibrium (that is, full employment).

Now consider a change in goods prices under the assumption that the set of goods produced is the same both before and after the price change. Given this assumption, the change in goods prices can be characterized by the total differential of the zero profit condition (7.24) (with strict equality):

$$d\mathbf{p} = d\mathbf{w}\mathbf{A}(\mathbf{w}) + \mathbf{w}d\mathbf{A}(\mathbf{w}). \tag{7.26}$$

Since $\mathbf{w}d\mathbf{A}(\mathbf{w}) = 0$ when costs are minimized, the above reduces to:

$$d\mathbf{p} = d\mathbf{w}\mathbf{A}(\mathbf{w}) \tag{7.27}$$

Post-multiplying both sides of (7.27) by the vector of price changes yields:

$$d\mathbf{p}d\mathbf{p} = d\mathbf{w}\mathbf{A}(\mathbf{w})d\mathbf{p} > 0. \tag{7.28}$$

This expression is strictly positive since the left-hand-side of (7.28) is the sum of squared price changes. Given this, (7.28) states that small changes in goods prices ($d\mathbf{p}$) are positively correlated with $d\mathbf{w}\mathbf{A}(\mathbf{w})$ or, equivalently, that small changes in factor prices ($d\mathbf{w}$) are positively correlated with changes in $\mathbf{A}(\mathbf{w})d\mathbf{p}$. In either case, (7.28) suggests the following:

Proposition 7.3: *Small changes in goods prices will on average be associated with increases in the prices of those factors employed most intensively in producing those goods whose prices have risen the most, and associated with decreases in the prices of factors employed less intensively in producing those goods whose prices have fallen.*

Note that this proposition follows from the assumption of cost minimization in competitive markets and does not depend on special characteristics of technology or even the number of goods and factors. Again, however, the price for this generality is that we cannot say anything about the relationship between the price of a specific factor and the price of a specific good; we can only speak of an average relationship between changes in factor prices and changes in goods prices.

Factor prices and trade

We now link Proposition 7.3 to the factor abundance model and trade. Post-multiplying (7.27) by the vector of commodity excess supplies ($\mathbf{t}$) gives:

$$d\mathbf{p}\mathbf{t} = d\mathbf{w}\mathbf{A}(\mathbf{w})\mathbf{t}. \tag{7.29}$$

Since $d\mathbf{p}\mathbf{t} \leq 0$ (see (7.19)), we can write:

$$d\mathbf{w}\mathbf{A}(\mathbf{w})\mathbf{t} \leq 0. \tag{7.30}$$

Equation (7.30) provides one statement of the link between factor abundance, factor inputs, and trade. First, we can interpret the vector of factor price changes ($d\mathbf{w}$) as the difference between home and foreign autarky factor prices. Thus, negative elements of $d\mathbf{w}$ indicate factors whose autarky prices are lower in the home country than in the foreign country and, in this sense, are abundant in the home country. Given that each element of the matrix $\mathbf{A}(\mathbf{w})$ is positive, (7.30) then implies the following:

Proposition 7.4: *A country will tend, on average, to be a net exporter of goods whose production is intensive in those factors that are relatively inexpensive (abundant) in autarky and a net importer of goods whose production is intensive in those factors that are relatively expensive (scarce) in autarky.*

Since Proposition 7.4 only specifies the average relationship between factor prices, factor use, and goods trade it need not hold with respect to any particular factor and good. In this sense, Proposition 7.4 is a *weak* form of the Heckscher-Ohlin theorem.

Expression (7.30) can also be interpreted as a statement about the relationship between factor abundance and a country's trade in factor services:

$$d\mathbf{w}\mathbf{f} \leq 0. \tag{7.31}$$

where $\mathbf{f} = \mathbf{A}(\mathbf{w})\mathbf{t}$ is the factor content of (net) trade.[5] Hence, Proposition 7.4 can be stated in the following equivalent form:

Proposition 7.5: *A country will tend, on average, to be a net exporter of the services of its less expensive (abundant) factors and a net importer of the services of its expensive (scarce) factors.*

A caveat concerning both (7.30) and (7.31) is that they hold strictly only for small price changes since $\mathbf{A}(\mathbf{w})$ is the home country's autarky factor requirements, that is, the factor requirements associated with the home country's (initial) autarky factor prices. Since a move from autarky to free trade is expected to change factor prices and thus factor input requirements we need to restate (7.28) in a way that holds for arbitrary (large) price changes.

Consider two alternative equilibria characterized by output price vectors $\mathbf{p}_0$ and $\mathbf{p}_1$ and associated factor price vectors $\mathbf{w}_0$ and $\mathbf{w}_1$ (which we can interpret as the autarky prices in the home and foreign country, respectively). We continue to assume that in each equilibrium the same goods are produced. Given this, define the scalar valued function $z(\mathbf{w}) = \mathbf{w}\mathbf{A}(\mathbf{w})(\mathbf{p}_1 - \mathbf{p}_0)$ and consider the change in this function between the two equilibria. Using the mean-value theorem[6] this change can be expressed as

$$z(\mathbf{w}_1) - z(\mathbf{w}_0) = (\mathbf{w}_1 - \mathbf{w}_0)dz(\overline{\mathbf{w}}), \tag{7.32}$$

where $\overline{\mathbf{w}}$ is some factor price vector that lies "between" $\mathbf{w}_0$ and $\mathbf{w}_1$. The differential $dz(\overline{\mathbf{w}})$ equals $[\mathbf{A}(\overline{\mathbf{w}}) + \overline{\mathbf{w}}d\mathbf{A}(\overline{\mathbf{w}})](\mathbf{p}_1 - \mathbf{p}_0)$ which can be simplified by noting (as in deriving (7.27)) that the term $\overline{\mathbf{w}}d\mathbf{A}(\overline{\mathbf{w}})$ vanishes by virtue of cost minimization. Hence,(7.32) can be written

$$z(\mathbf{w}_1) - z(\mathbf{w}_0) = (\mathbf{w}_1 - \mathbf{w}_0)\mathbf{A}(\overline{\mathbf{w}})(\mathbf{p}_1 - \mathbf{p}_0) \tag{7.33}$$

or, since $z(\mathbf{w}_1) - z(\mathbf{w}_0) = (\mathbf{p}_1 - \mathbf{p}_0)(\mathbf{p}_1 - \mathbf{p}_0)$,[7]

$$(\mathbf{p}_1 - \mathbf{p}_0)(\mathbf{p}_1 - \mathbf{p}_0) = (\mathbf{w}_1 - \mathbf{w}_0)\mathbf{A}(\overline{\mathbf{w}})(\mathbf{p}_1 - \mathbf{p}_0). \tag{7.34}$$

Since the left-hand-side of (7.34) is strictly positive we can write:

$$(\mathbf{w}_1 - \mathbf{w}_0)\mathbf{A}(\overline{\mathbf{w}})(\mathbf{p}_1 - \mathbf{p}_0) > 0. \tag{7.35}$$

This result is similar to (7.29) but differs in that there is some freedom in the choice of a factor price vector and thus a factor input requirements matrix.[8]

As with (7.30), (7.34) can be used to link autarky factor prices and trade flows. Specifically, eliminate the term $(\mathbf{p}_1 - \mathbf{p}_0)$ from both sides of (7.34) and then post-multiply both sides of the resulting equation by $\mathbf{t}$ to obtain:

$$(\mathbf{p}_1 - \mathbf{p}_0)\mathbf{t} = (\mathbf{w}_1 - \mathbf{w}_0)\mathbf{A}(\overline{\mathbf{w}})\mathbf{t}. \tag{7.36}$$

Since $(\mathbf{p}_1 - \mathbf{p}_0)\mathbf{t} \geq 0$ (see (7.19)), we can write:

$$(\mathbf{w}_1 - \mathbf{w}_0)\mathbf{A}(\overline{\mathbf{w}})\mathbf{t} \geq 0. \tag{7.37}$$

Alternatively, we can express (7.37) in terms of a country's trade in factor services:

$$(\mathbf{w}_1 - \mathbf{w}_0)\bar{\mathbf{f}} \geq 0, \tag{7.38}$$

where $\bar{\mathbf{f}} = \mathbf{A}(\bar{\mathbf{w}})\mathbf{t}$ is the vector of factor contents. Expressions (7.37) and (7.38) have the same interpretation as (7.30) and (7.31), respectively, with respect to the average relationship between abundant factors (in the price sense) and net trade or net factor service flows. The primary difference is that (7.37) and (7.38) relate to large price changes and in this sense are more general.

Factor intensity reversals

Whereas (7.37) and (7.38) are more general than (7.30) and (7.31), this additional generality is not without difficulty since (7.37) and (7.38) assume that countries use the same factor input requirements (that is, $\mathbf{A}(\bar{\mathbf{w}})$), as would be the case if trade equalized factor prices between countries. The generality of (7.37) and (7.38) is thus limited since factor prices may not be equalized by trade, and also that higher dimensional analogs to factor intensity reversals might exist.[9] To resolve this issue we need to find a factor input matrix such that (7.37) or (7.38) hold even if factor prices are not equalized or high order "factor intensity reversals" are present.

To understand the difficulty, consider the 2x2 example of a factor intensity reversal in which the trading equilibrium is such that countries' post-trade factor prices lie on either side of this reversal. Given this, suppose that the home country exports good x and imports good y and that good x is capital-intensive in the home country. The foreign country exports good y but, due to the factor intensity reversal, y is capital-intensive in the foreign country. If we were to calculate, for each country, the factor content of its trade using its domestic techniques of production we would observe that both the home country and the foreign country are net exporters of capital services. However, based on autarky factor price differences, only one country can be capital abundant. Thus, it is impossible for each country to be a net exporter of the services of its <u>abundant</u> factor.

A solution to this problem can be seen by considering the calculation of factor contents in the above 2x2 case. Let the home country's unit capital and labor requirements be a_{Kx}, a_{Lx} in industry x and a_{Ky} and a_{Ly} in industry y and let $t_x > 0$ denote the net exports of good x and let $t_y < 0$ denote the home country's net imports of good y. By choice of units, the goods prices can be normalized to unity so that the condition for balanced trade can be written $-t_x = t_y$. Given this, the factor content of the home country's trade vector can be written:

$$\begin{pmatrix} a_{Kx} & a_{Ky} \\ a_{Lx} & a_{Ly} \end{pmatrix} \begin{pmatrix} t_x \\ t_y \end{pmatrix} = \begin{pmatrix} a_{Kx} & a_{Ky} \\ a_{Lx} & a_{Ly} \end{pmatrix} \begin{pmatrix} t_x \\ -t_x \end{pmatrix} = \begin{pmatrix} (a_{Kx} - a_{Ky})\,t_x \\ (a_{Lx} - a_{Ly})\,t_x \end{pmatrix} \tag{7.39}$$

Since $t_x > 0$ by assumption and industry x is capital-intensive ($(a_{Kx} - a_{Ky}) > 0$), the country exports the services of capital ($(a_{Kx} - a_{Ky})t_x > 0$) and imports the services of labor ($(a_{Lx} - a_{Ly})t_x < 0$) via its imports of the labor-intensive good y. Letting an asterisk denote foreign input requirements, and remembering that industry y is capital-intensive in the foreign country (i.e., $(a_{Ky}^* - a_{Kx}^*) > 0$) and that $-t_i^* = t_i (i = x, y)$, the factor content of the foreign country's trade vector can be written:

$$\begin{pmatrix} a_{Kx}^* & a_{Ky}^* \\ a_{Lx}^* & a_{Ly}^* \end{pmatrix} \begin{pmatrix} t_x^* \\ -t_x^* \end{pmatrix} = \begin{pmatrix} a_{Kx}^* & a_{Ky}^* \\ a_{Lx}^* & a_{Ly}^* \end{pmatrix} \begin{pmatrix} -t_x \\ t_x \end{pmatrix} = \begin{pmatrix} (a_{Ky}^* - a_{Kx}^*)\,t_x \\ (a_{Lx}^* - a_{Ly}^*)\,t_x \end{pmatrix}. \tag{7.40}$$

As expected, the foreign country exports the services of capital ($(a_{Ky}^* - a_{Kx}^*)t_x > 0$) and imports the services of labor ($(a_{Lx}^* - a_{Ly}^*)t_x < 0$).

One solution to this problem is to note that, if the home country is capital abundant (capital is cheaper relative to labor in the home country compared to the foreign country), it must be the case that each industry in the home country employs more capital per unit of labor than does the corresponding industry in the foreign country. This follows from the property that, within any industry, the higher is the price of labor compared with the price of capital, the higher will be the amount of capital employed per unit of labor. This property implies the following inequalities:

$$(a_{Kx} - a_{Kx}^*) > 0 \text{ and } (a_{Ky} - a_{Ky}^*) > 0 \tag{7.41}$$

$$(a_{Lx} - a_{Lx}^*) < 0 \text{ and } (a_{Ly} - a_{Ly}^*) < 0. \tag{7.42}$$

Since $a_{Kx}^* > a_{Ky}^*$ and $a_{Lx}^* < a_{Ly}^*$, inequalities (7.41) and (7.42) imply, respectively, the following:

$$(a_{Kx} - a_{Ky}^*) > 0 \text{ and } (a_{Lx} - a_{Ly}^*) < 0. \tag{7.43}$$

The monotonic relationship between factor input requirements and relative factor prices in an industry suggests we should calculate the factor content of a country's trade using the factor requirements of the country of origin of a good (the exporting country). That is, we should use the home country's factor requirements for good x and the foreign country's factor requirements for good y. Adopting this procedure, the factor content of home's trade becomes:

$$\begin{pmatrix} a_{Kx} & a_{Ky}^* \\ a_{Lx} & a_{Ly}^* \end{pmatrix} \begin{pmatrix} t_x \\ -t_x \end{pmatrix} = \begin{pmatrix} (a_{Kx} - a_{Ky}^*)\, t_x \\ (a_{Lx} - a_{Ly}^*)\, t_x \end{pmatrix}. \tag{7.44}$$

Given (7.43) we have $(a_{Kx} - a_{ky}^*)t_x > 0$ and $(a_{Lx} - a_{Ly}^*)t_x < 0$, that is, the home country exports the services of capital and imports the services of labor. Applying this procedure to the foreign country's trade vector gives:

$$\begin{pmatrix} a_{Kx} & a_{Ky}^* \\ a_{Lx} & a_{Ly}^* \end{pmatrix} \begin{pmatrix} t_x^* \\ -t_x^* \end{pmatrix} = \begin{pmatrix} (a_{Kx} - a_{Ky}^*)\, t_x^* \\ (a_{Lx} - a_{Ly}^*)\, t_x^* \end{pmatrix}. \tag{7.45}$$

Since $t_x^* < 0$, (7.43) implies $(a_{Kx} - a_{ky}^*)t_x^* < 0$ and $(a_{Lx} - a_{Ly}^*)t_x^* > 0$, that is, foreign imports the services of capital and exports the services of labor.

We now extend this procedure to an arbitrary number of goods and factors. Let $\bar{\mathbf{A}}$ be the factor input requirements matrix whose j^{th} column represents the input requirements of the country exporting good i. If $\mathbf{t}$ denotes a country's net export vector, the factor content of its trade is then $\bar{\mathbf{f}} = \bar{\mathbf{A}}\mathbf{t}$.

Now consider a trading equilibrium between two countries, and let $\mathbf{h}_T$ denote a country's free trade consumption vector. Since countries share the same technologies (production functions), it would be possible for a country to produce for itself the vector $\mathbf{h}_T$ by using factors $\mathbf{e} + \bar{\mathbf{f}}$. One way to imagine this is that the factors $\bar{\mathbf{f}}$ are made available to the country not through goods trade but rather by the direct movement of the factors. Alternatively, the country could simply cease producing exports and instead produce its bundle of imports using the same techniques used in the exporting country. In any event, this alternate production plan is unlikely to be profitable when valued at the country's autarky prices $\mathbf{w}_A$ and $\mathbf{p}_A$:

$$\mathbf{w}_A(\mathbf{e} + \bar{\mathbf{f}}) \geq \mathbf{p}_A \mathbf{h}_T \tag{7.46}$$

In this expression, $\mathbf{w}_A(\mathbf{e} + \bar{\mathbf{f}})$ is the total cost of employing factors $(\mathbf{e} + \bar{\mathbf{f}})$ at their prices $\mathbf{w}_A$ and $\mathbf{p}_A\mathbf{h}_T$ is the expenditure that would be required to purchase the post-trade consumption bundle valued at autarky prices. Since the country chose the consumption bundle $\mathbf{h}_T$, it must be the case that this bundle costs at least as much as bundle $\mathbf{h}_A$ at prices $\mathbf{p}_A$, since otherwise the country would have chosen $\mathbf{h}_T$ since it involves higher utility – that is, $\mathbf{p}_A\mathbf{h}_T \geq \mathbf{p}_A\mathbf{h}_A$. Combining this inequality with that in (7.46) gives:

$$\mathbf{w}_A(\mathbf{e} + \bar{\mathbf{f}}) \geq \mathbf{p}_A\mathbf{h}_A. \tag{7.47}$$

Rearranging this expression gives:

$$\mathbf{w}_A\bar{\mathbf{f}} \geq (\mathbf{p}_A\mathbf{h}_A - \mathbf{w}_A\mathbf{e}) = 0. \tag{7.48}$$

A similar expression can be derived for the rest of the world, namely $\mathbf{w}_A^*\bar{\mathbf{f}}^* \geq 0$. Since $\bar{\mathbf{f}} = -\bar{\mathbf{f}}^*$, these inequalities can be combined to yield:

$$(\mathbf{w}_A - \mathbf{w}_A^*)\bar{\mathbf{f}} \geq 0. \tag{7.49}$$

Proposition 7.6: *Using as the factor input requirements for good i the factor input requirements of the country exporting good i, a country will on average be a net exporter of the services of its abundant factors and a net importer of the services of its scarce factors, where abundance is defined in terms of autarky factor prices.*

Lastly, substitute $\bar{\mathbf{f}} = \bar{\mathbf{A}}\mathbf{t}$ into (7.49) to relate factor price differences to factor use and commodity trade:

$$(\mathbf{w}_A - \mathbf{w}_A^*)\bar{\mathbf{A}}\mathbf{t} \geq 0. \tag{7.50}$$

The interpretation of this inequality is now familiar: countries will on average export goods which make relatively intensive use of their abundant (relatively inexpensive) factors.

This section has related differences in autarky factor prices to a country's use of factors and its trade in goods, and also to its trade in factor services. Despite the validity of each set of relationships, it can be argued that the relationship between factor prices, factor use and trade in goods are perhaps less "precise" than that between factor prices and factor services trade since the former depends on a somewhat ad hoc definition of factor intensity (that is, the elements of the factor input requirements).

Factor supplies and trade

We now consider the relationship between trade flows and factor abundance where the latter are measured by factor supplies rather than autarky factor prices. The first step is to place restrictions on demand so as to rule out "demand biases" that could reverse the normally expected negative relationship between relative factor supplies and relative factor prices. As in the 2x2 model, demand reversals are precluded by assuming countries have identical and homothetic preferences. Given this, we now establish the multifactor, multi-commodity relationship between physical factor abundance and factor prices between countries.

As shown in Chapter 4 (Section 4.2), the assumption of homothetic preferences permits us to write the expenditure function in the separable form:[10]

$$S(\mathbf{p}_A; u_A) = u_A s(\mathbf{p}_A) \tag{7.51}$$

where u_A is the utility level reached under autarky at prices $\mathbf{p}_A$. Using this, equilibrium condition (7.7) becomes

$$u_A s(\mathbf{p}_A) = G(\mathbf{p}_A; \mathbf{e}) = \mathbf{we}. \tag{7.52}$$

where $\mathbf{w}$ is the vector of factor prices that minimize expenditure on factors subject to the constraint of non-positive profits in all industries.

Suppose an autarky equilibrium is characterized by output prices $\mathbf{p}_A$ and factor prices $\mathbf{w}_A$. Then by (7.52) we can write $G(\mathbf{p}_A; \mathbf{e}) = \mathbf{w}_A \mathbf{e}$. By definition, any other price vectors $\mathbf{p}$ and $\mathbf{w}$ would yield either lower income or greater expenditure on factors. Thus, given the equilibrium $G(\mathbf{p}_A; \mathbf{e}) = \mathbf{w}_A \mathbf{e}$, it must be true that $\mathbf{w}_A^* \mathbf{e} \geq \mathbf{w}_A \mathbf{e}$ and $G(\mathbf{p}_A; \mathbf{e}) \geq G(\mathbf{p}_A^*; \mathbf{e})$ where the asterisk denotes foreign country prices. These inequalities imply:

$$\mathbf{w}_A^* \mathbf{e} \geq G(\mathbf{p}_A^*; \mathbf{e}). \tag{7.53}$$

Now, if u_0 is the utility level achievable at foreign prices (that is, $G(\mathbf{p}_A^*; \mathbf{e}) = u_0 s(\mathbf{p}_A^*)$) then it must be that $u_0 \geq u_A$ since the possibility to exchange at prices other than one's autarky prices ($\mathbf{p}_A$) must involve higher utility. Given this, and (7.53), we can write

$$\mathbf{w}_A^* \mathbf{e} \geq G(\mathbf{p}_A^*; \mathbf{e}) = u_0 s(\mathbf{p}_A^*) = u_0 \frac{u_0 s(\mathbf{p}_A^*)}{u_0 s(\mathbf{p}_A)} s(\mathbf{p}_A) = \lambda G(\mathbf{p}_A; \mathbf{e}) = \lambda \mathbf{w}_A \mathbf{e} \tag{7.54}$$

or

$$(\mathbf{w}_A^* - \lambda \mathbf{w}_A)\mathbf{e} \geq 0 \text{ where } \lambda = \frac{s(\mathbf{p}_A^*)}{s(\mathbf{p}_A)}. \tag{7.55}$$

Letting u_1 be the level of utility obtainable by the foreign country when facing home country autarky prices $\mathbf{p}_A$, the above logic when applied to the foreign country implies:

$$\mathbf{w}_A \mathbf{e}^* \geq G(\mathbf{p}_A; \mathbf{e}^*) = u_1 \bar{s}(\mathbf{p}_A) = u_1 \frac{u_1 s(\mathbf{p}_A)}{u_1 s(\mathbf{p}_A^*)} \bar{s}(\mathbf{p}_A^*) = \lambda^* G(\mathbf{p}_A^*; \mathbf{e}^*) = \lambda^* \mathbf{w}_A^* \mathbf{e}^* \tag{7.56}$$

or

$$(\mathbf{w}_A - \lambda^* \mathbf{w}_A^*)\mathbf{e}^* \geq 0 \tag{7.57}$$

where $\lambda^* = \dfrac{s(\mathbf{p}_A)}{s(\mathbf{p}_A^*)}$. Since $\lambda = 1/\lambda^*$, this can be written

$$(\lambda \mathbf{w}_A - \mathbf{w}_A^*)\mathbf{e}^* \geq 0. \tag{7.58}$$

The scalar λ is a measure of foreign relative to domestic price levels. By choice of numeraire, we can normalize the price levels in each country so that $\lambda = 1$. Given this, subtract (7.58) from (7.55) to obtain:

$$(\mathbf{w}_A - \mathbf{w}_A^*)(\mathbf{e} - \mathbf{e}^*) \leq 0, \tag{7.59}$$

where we have used $(\mathbf{w}_A^* - \lambda \mathbf{w}_A) = -(\lambda \mathbf{w}_A - \mathbf{w}_A^*)$ to reverse the inequality. Since positive (negative) elements of the vector $(\mathbf{e} - \mathbf{e}^*)$ indicate factors in greater (lesser) supply in the home compared with the foreign country, while negative (positive) elements of $(\lambda \mathbf{w}_A - \mathbf{w}_A^*)$ indicate factors that are cheaper (more expensive) in the home country compared with the foreign country, (7.59) states that countries will tend, on average, to have lower prices of those factors that are in relatively greater supply.

We now relate factor supply differences to differences in autarky goods prices. A direct way of doing this would be to replace the autarky factor price differences in (7.59) by the relationship between factor prices and output prices. The link between output prices and input prices is given by the zero profit conditions in each country:

$$\mathbf{p}_A = \mathbf{c}(\mathbf{w}_A)$$
$$\mathbf{p}_A^* = \mathbf{c}(\mathbf{w}_A^*). \tag{7.60}$$

The elements of $\mathbf{c}(\bullet)$ are industry unit cost functions. If we could solve these zero profit equations for factor prices in terms of output prices, we could place these solutions into (7.59) to arrive at a relationship between autarky output prices and factor supplies. That is, if the functions $\mathbf{c}(\mathbf{w}_A)$ and $\mathbf{c}(\mathbf{w}_A^*)$ are invertible, then we could write $\mathbf{w}_A = \mathbf{w}(\mathbf{p}_A)$ and $\mathbf{w}_A^* = \mathbf{w}(\mathbf{p}_A^*)$ and write (7.59) as:

$$\left(\mathbf{w}\left(\mathbf{p}_A\right) - \mathbf{w}\left(\mathbf{p}_A^*\right)\right)(\mathbf{e} - \mathbf{e}^*) \leq 0 \tag{7.61}$$

The problem, of course, is the conditions under which the unit cost functions are invertible. This issue, known as the univalence problem, is related to the 2x2 problem of factor intensity reversals. Essentially, what is required is that the mapping from factor prices to output prices be one-to-one. Suffice to say that invertibility requires severe restrictions on the cost functions.[11]

To complete our discussion, we will assume the cost functions are invertible. Solving the zero profit equations $\mathbf{p} = \mathbf{w}\mathbf{A}(\mathbf{w})$ for $\mathbf{w}$ gives $\mathbf{w} = \mathbf{p}\mathbf{A}(\mathbf{w})^{-1}$, where $\mathbf{A}(\mathbf{w})^{-1}$ is the inverse of the factor requirements matrix. Since $\mathbf{A}(\mathbf{w})^{-1}$ is square, we are assuming that the number of goods equals (or exceeds) the number of factors.

We now apply the same logic used to derive (7.37). First, expand (7.61) to get:

$$w(\mathbf{p}_A)(\mathbf{e} - \mathbf{e}^*) - w(\mathbf{p}_A^*)(\mathbf{e} - \mathbf{e}^*) \leq 0 \tag{7.62}$$

Now replace $\mathbf{w}(\mathbf{p})$ by $\mathbf{p}\mathbf{A}(\mathbf{w})^{-1}$ to get

$$[\mathbf{p}_A \mathbf{A}(\mathbf{w}_A)^{-1}(\mathbf{e} - \mathbf{e}^*)] - [\mathbf{p}_A^* \mathbf{A}(\mathbf{w}_A^*)^{-1}(\mathbf{e} - \mathbf{e}^*)] \leq 0 \tag{7.63}$$

This difference can be characterized as the difference between a scalar valued function $z(\mathbf{p}, \mathbf{e}) = \mathbf{p}\mathbf{A}(\overline{\mathbf{w}})^{-1}(\mathbf{e} - \mathbf{e}^*)$ evaluated at the two points $\mathbf{p}_A$ and $\mathbf{p}_A^*$, that is,

$$z(\mathbf{p}_A, \mathbf{e}) - z(\mathbf{p}_A^*, \mathbf{e}^*) \leq 0. \tag{7.64}$$

As done for (7.32), this difference can be specified using the mean-value theorem applied to the function $z(\mathbf{p}, \mathbf{e})$. Thus, for some vector of prices $\overline{\mathbf{p}}$ between $\mathbf{p}_A$ and $\mathbf{p}_A^*$[12] (7.64) can be expressed as:

$$z(\mathbf{p}_A) - z(\mathbf{p}_A^*) = (\mathbf{p}_A - \mathbf{p}_A^*)\frac{\partial z(\overline{\mathbf{p}})}{\partial \mathbf{p}} \tag{7.65}$$

By definition, the matrix of partial derivatives[13] $\dfrac{\partial z(\overline{\mathbf{p}})}{\partial \mathbf{p}}$ equals $\mathbf{A}(\overline{\mathbf{w}})^{-1}(\mathbf{e} - \mathbf{e}^*)$ so we can write:

$$z(\mathbf{p}_A) - z(\mathbf{p}_A^*) = (\mathbf{p}_A - \mathbf{p}_A^*)\mathbf{A}(\overline{\mathbf{w}})^{-1}(\mathbf{e} - \mathbf{e}^*) \tag{7.66}$$

Finally, by (7.63), we can write

$$(\mathbf{p}_A - \mathbf{p}_A^*)\mathbf{A}(\overline{\mathbf{w}})^{-1}(\mathbf{e} - \mathbf{e}^*) \leq 0. \tag{7.67}$$

If the elements of $\mathbf{A}(\overline{\mathbf{w}})^{-1}$ are taken to be measures of factor intensity then (7.67) implies the following proposition:

Proposition 7.7: *Countries will tend, on average, to have lower autarky prices (that is, a comparative advantage) of those goods that make intensive use of factors that are relatively abundant in the physical sense.*

Finally, since trade flows are inversely related to the difference in autarky prices (see (7.22), the following proposition may be inferred from (7.67):

Proposition 7.8: *Countries will, on average, export those goods that make intensive use of the factors that are relatively abundant in the physical sense.*

In contrast to the price version (i.e., (7.37)), the above quantity version involves the inverse of the factor requirements matrix. Since inversion of the factor input matrix is only possible if the number of goods is as least as large as the number of commodities, it can be concluded that the above quantity version will not hold when there are more factors than goods.

Finally, greater structure is obtained if it is not only assumed that goods at least outnumber factors but also that free trade results in factor price equalization. In this case, the inverted factor requirements matrix $\mathbf{A}(\overline{\mathbf{w}})^{-1}$ is the same for every country and it is observable since $\overline{\mathbf{w}}$ is now the vector of observable factor prices in the trading equilibrium. Denoting these factor prices as $\mathbf{w}$, a country's trade in factor services can be written as:

$$\mathbf{A}(\mathbf{w})\mathbf{t} = \mathbf{A}(\mathbf{w})\mathbf{q} - \mathbf{A}(\mathbf{w})\mathbf{h} \tag{7.68}$$

Given full employment ($\mathbf{A}(\mathbf{w})\mathbf{q} = \mathbf{e}$), the above can be written:

$$\mathbf{A}(\mathbf{w})\mathbf{t} = \mathbf{e} - \mathbf{A}(\mathbf{w})\mathbf{h}. \tag{7.69}$$

If preferences are assumed identical and homothetic, the factor content of consumption $\mathbf{A}(\mathbf{w})\mathbf{h}$ can be written $\alpha \mathbf{A}(\mathbf{w})(\mathbf{h} + \mathbf{h}^*)$ where α is the country's share of world GDP. In addition, since world consumption equals world production $(\mathbf{h} + \mathbf{h}^*) = (\mathbf{q} + \mathbf{q}^*)$, we can write $\alpha \mathbf{A}(\mathbf{w})(\mathbf{h} + \mathbf{h}^*) = \alpha \mathbf{A}(\mathbf{w})(\mathbf{q} + \mathbf{q}^*) = \alpha(\mathbf{e} + \mathbf{e}^*)$, where $(\mathbf{e} + \mathbf{e}^*)$ is the vector of world factor supplies. Given this, we can then write (7.69)) as

$$\mathbf{A}(\mathbf{w})\mathbf{t} = \mathbf{e} - \alpha(\mathbf{e} + \mathbf{e}^*). \tag{7.70}$$

Pre-multiplying both sides of (7.70) by the vector $(\mathbf{e}^* - \alpha(\mathbf{e} + \mathbf{e}^*))$ gives:

$$(\mathbf{e} - \alpha(\mathbf{e} + \mathbf{e}^*))\mathbf{A}(\mathbf{w})\mathbf{t} = (\mathbf{e} - \alpha(\mathbf{e} + \mathbf{e}^*))(\mathbf{e}^* - \alpha(\mathbf{e} + \mathbf{e}^*)). \tag{7.71}$$

Since the right-hand-side is a non-negative scalar we may write:

$$(\mathbf{e} - \alpha(\mathbf{e} + \mathbf{e}^*))\mathbf{A}(\mathbf{w})\mathbf{t} \geq 0 \tag{7.72}$$

This expression can also be written in terms of the trade in factor services as

$$(\mathbf{e} - \alpha(\mathbf{e} + \mathbf{e}^*))\mathbf{f} \geq 0. \tag{7.73}$$

If a country is defined to be abundant in factor k if $(e_k - \alpha(e_k + e_k^*)) > 0$, and likewise scarce in factor k if $(e_k - \alpha(e_k + e_k^*)) < 0$, then (7.72) implies:

Proposition 7.9: *If free trade equalizes factor prices between countries and countries have identical and homothetic preferences then each country will, on average, be a net exporter of those goods that make relatively intensive use of the country's physically abundant factors.*

Similarly, (7.73) implies:

Proposition 7.10: *If free trade equalizes factor prices between countries and countries have identical and homothetic preferences then each country will, on average, be a net exporter of the services of its physically abundant factors and a net importer of its physically scarce factors.*

Expression (7.73), and hence Proposition 7.10, is the foundation for the Heckscher- Ohlin-Vanek (H-O-V) rank and sign propositions, which relate physical factor abundance to trade in factor services when factor prices are equalized. The next section details these and other propositions of the H-O-V model, which has become the standard framework for empirically testing the factor abundance theory in the N good, H factor setting.

7.4 Testing the factor abundance model

The predictions of the H-O-S model derive from a complex interaction between three sets of variables (trade, factor use and factor supplies) and any empirical investigation of the model should therefore employ measures of all three sets of variables. Only in the mid-1980s did empirical tests of the H-O-S model begin to meet this requirement. Since earlier tests of the H-O-S model beginning with Leontief (1953)[14] were incomplete either in terms of data or model specification, the results of much of this work were considered inconclusive with respect to the validity of the H-O-S model. However, significant advances have occurred over the past 25 years on how the H-O-S model can and should be empirically evaluated. These advances have led to acceptance of the H-O-V model as the de facto framework for translating the predictions of the H-O-S model into testable hypotheses when there are many goods, factors and countries. This section develops the H-O-V model and discusses its use for empirically testing the factor abundance model.

The H-O-V model

Assume there are J commodities, H productive factors and N countries. Let $\mathbf{q}_i$ and $\mathbf{c}_i$ denote, respectively, the $J \times 1$ vectors of net outputs and final demand of country i.[15] The $J \times 1$ vector of net trades for country i is then $\mathbf{t}_i \equiv \mathbf{q}_i - \mathbf{c}_i$. Let $\mathbf{A}_i$ be the $H \times J$ matrix of equilibrium total factor input requirements.[16] An element a_{hj} of $\mathbf{A}_i$ is the amount of factor h used to produce one unit of net output of good j given the equilibrium factor prices and state of technology.[17] Pre-multiplying the vector of net trades ($\mathbf{t}_i$) by $\mathbf{A}_i$ yields country i's net trade in factor services ($\mathbf{f}_i$)

$$\mathbf{f}_i \equiv \mathbf{A}_i \mathbf{t}_i = \mathbf{A}_i \mathbf{q}_i - \mathbf{A}_i \mathbf{c}_i. \tag{7.74}$$

This expression is the most general statement of the H-O-V model since it places no restriction on the characteristics of demand or supply; in fact, (7.74) is an accounting identity. Adding structure to the model requires assumptions regarding factor markets, technology, and preferences.

Let $\mathbf{e}_i$ denote the $H \times 1$ vector of country i's factor supplies. Assuming full employment of all resources means $\mathbf{e}_i = \mathbf{A}_i \mathbf{q}_i$. If preferences are identical and homothetic across countries then the final demand vector of country i is proportional to the world final demand vector

$(\mathbf{c}_w)$: $\mathbf{c}_i = \mu_i \mathbf{c}_w$ where μ_i is country i's share of world expenditure. Since, for each good, world final demand equals world net output[18] we can also write $\mathbf{c}_i = \mu_i \mathbf{q}_w$ where $\mathbf{q}_w$ is the $J \times 1$ vector of world net outputs. Substituting these full employment and final demand relationships in (7.74) gives:

$$\mathbf{f}_i \equiv \mathbf{A}_i \mathbf{t}_i = \mathbf{e}_j - \mu_i \mathbf{A}_i \mathbf{q}_w \qquad (7.75)$$

If we further assume that free trade in goods equalizes factor prices across countries then all countries will use the same factor input requirements, that is, $\mathbf{A}_i = \mathbf{A} \; \forall i$. Given this, $\mathbf{A}\mathbf{q}_w$ in (7.75) equals the vector of world factor supplies $\mathbf{e}_w$ since $\mathbf{A}\mathbf{q}_w = \mathbf{A} \sum_{z=1}^{N} \mathbf{q}_z = \sum_{z=1}^{N} \mathbf{A}\mathbf{q}_z = \sum_{z=1}^{N} \mathbf{e}_z = \mathbf{e}_w$.

Finally, the expenditure share can be written $\mu_i = \alpha_i - \lambda_i$ where $\alpha_i = Y_i / Y_w$ is the ratio of country i's income (GDP) to world income (expenditure) and $\lambda_i = B_i / Y_w$, is the ratio of country i's trade imbalance to world income.[19] Substituting the expressions for $\mathbf{A}_i \mathbf{q}_w$ and μ_i in (7.75) gives:

$$\mathbf{f}_i = \mathbf{e}_i - (\alpha_i - \lambda_i)\mathbf{e}_w \qquad i = 1, \ldots, N \qquad (7.76)$$

The expressions in (7.76) are referred to as the H-O-V equations. Except for the explicit inclusion of the trade balance term λ_i, (7.76) is the extension of (7.70) to N countries. Each equation links country i's net trade in the services of a factor to the country's excess supply (supply minus demand) of that factor.

Definitions of factor abundance

The derivation of H-O-S-type propositions in the H-O-V model requires a definition of factor abundance. Two commonly used definitions are given below.

Relative factor abundance: Factor h is abundant relative to factor z in country i if country i's world share of factor h exceeds its world share of factor z, that is, if $e_{ih}/e_{wh} > e_{iz}/e_{wz}$, where $e_{i\bullet}$ and $e_{w\bullet}$ are the factor supplies in country i and the world, respectively.

The definition of relative abundance implies that a ranking of all H factor shares for one country defines that country's "structure of factor abundance."

Absolute factor abundance: Factor h is absolutely abundant in country i if country i's share of the world supply of factor h exceeds the country i's share of world income, that is, if $e_{ih}/e_{wh} > Y_i/Y_w = \alpha_i$.[20]

Note that an *absolutely* abundant factor can be *relatively* scarce compared with some other factor. In addition, all absolutely abundant factors are also *relatively* abundant compared with all *absolutely* scarce factors.

Given these factor abundance definitions, the H-O-V model (7.76) implies two propositions about the relationship between factor services trade and factor abundance.

Proposition S (sign proposition): If trade is balanced, a country exports (net) the services of its absolutely abundant factors and imports (net) the services of its absolutely scarce factors.

Proposition R (rank proposition): If country i is abundant in factor h *relative* to factor z, then country i's *proportionate* net trade in the services of factor h exceed its *proportionate* net trade in the services of factor z.

The *proportionate* net trade is the net trade in the services of a factor divided by either the country's total supply of that factor or the world supply of that factor. A third proposition, which is similar to proposition R, is:

Proposition L (Leontief proposition): If country i is abundant in factor h *relative* to factor z, then the ratio of its exports of factor h to its exports of factor z exceeds the ratio of its imports of factor h to its imports of factor z.

Propositions R and L differ in their concept of net trade, the latter measuring it as the ratio of exports to imports. Proposition L was initially investigated by Leontief (1953).

Propositions S, R and L may hold even if equations (7.76) are not exact (that is, hold as equalities) and are therefore considered "weakened" forms the exact H-O-V hypothesis of strict equality between the net trade in factor services and the excess supply of factors. A test of the exact H-O-V hypothesis would involve measuring the trade vector $\mathbf{t}_i$, the factor input matrix $\mathbf{A}$, and the vector of excess factor supplies $(\mathbf{e}_i - (\alpha_i - \lambda_i)\mathbf{e}_w)$ and then computing the extent to which these data violate the equalities in (7.76). In contrast, tests of propositions S, R, and L only require conformity between the right and left-hand-sides of (7.76) in terms of sign or rank.

In addition to being weaker forms of the exact H-O-V hypothesis, propositions S, R and L share the idea that the trade in factor services "reveals" factor abundance (that is, the left-hand side of (7.76) "reveals" the right-hand side of (7.76). Because of these similarities, and the fact that proposition L was the first to be subjected to empirical verification (by Leontief), these propositions, and their corresponding tests, are referred to as "Leontief-type."

Leontief-type tests

The Leontief proposition

For almost 30 years after Leontief's classic paper (Leontief, 1953), proposition L was at the core of any test of the H-O-S theory. Testing proposition L is no longer desirable since it can be shown that it may not hold even when the H-O-V model is true (see Problem 7.7). That proposition L may fail to hold is convincingly demonstrated by Leamer's (1980) examination of Leontief's original data for the United States (US). Using proposition R, Leamer ranked the US's *proportionate* net trade in capital and labor services (see Table 7.1). This ranking revealed capital to be abundant relative to labor, contrary to Leontief's finding.

Sign proposition

Unlike proposition L, propositions S and R are direct implications of the H-O-V model. However, testing these propositions requires careful formulation and, in particular, attention to the influence of any trade imbalance.

Consider first proposition S. The H-O-V equation for factor h is:

$$f_{ih} = e_{ih} - \alpha_i e_{wh} + \lambda_i e_{wh}. \tag{7.77}$$

Table 7.1 Factor content of 1947 US trade and production

Factor Services Embodied in:	Capital ($ millions)	Labor (million man years)
Net Trade	23,450	1.99
Production	328,519	47.273
Ratio of Net Trade to Production	0.0714	0.0424

Source: Leamer (1980).

The possibility of a trade imbalance can be taken into account by defining the *adjusted* net trade in factor h (f_{ih}^A):

$$f_{ih}^A \equiv f_{ih} - \lambda_i e_{wh} = e_{ih} - \alpha_i e_{wh}. \tag{7.78}$$

The adjusted factor content f_{ih}^A is the net trade in factor h that would be observed if trade were balanced.[21] From (7.78), $sign(f_{ih}^A) = sign(e_{ih} - \alpha_i e_{wh})$ and proposition S follows immediately from the definition of absolute factor abundance.[22]

Given data on the adjusted net trade in a factor and the excess supply of that factor, proposition S can be tested by examining whether the sign of the former matches the sign of the latter. One shortcoming of using proposition S to test the H-O-V model is that the alternative hypothesis associated with rejecting proposition S is unclear about the alternative model against which the H-O-V model is being tested.

Rank proposition

Proposition R states that the ranking of country i's *proportionate* net trade (adjusted for any trade imbalance) in the services of each of H factors duplicates its structure of factor abundance, that is, the ranking

$$\frac{f_{i1}^A}{z_i} > \cdots > \frac{f_{ih}^A}{z_h} > \cdots > \frac{f_{iH}^A}{z_H} \tag{7.79}$$

duplicates the ranking of world resource shares

$$\frac{e_{i1}}{e_{w1}} > \cdots > \frac{e_{ih}}{e_{wh}} > \cdots > \frac{e_{iH}}{e_{wH}}$$

The variable z_h in (7.79) can be either the supply of factor h in the world or in country i.

Given data on the *proportionate* adjusted factor contents and world resource shares, proposition R can be tested by comparing the ranking of the former to the ranking of the latter. Methods for gauging the conformity of these rankings have included computing the coefficient of rank correlation and the number of correct pairwise rankings among factors (or countries)[23] out of all possible pairwise rankings.

Like tests of proposition S, tests of proposition R face the problem that the alternative hypothesis is unclear regarding the alternative model. As discussed in Kohler (1991), tests of proposition R face an additional problem. Since in practice the H-O-V equations are not equalities, the form in which the factor contents and factor supplies are expressed can lead to alternative results. For example, the following are equivalent ways of expressing proposition R.

R1 : $rank(f_{ih}^A) = rank(e_{ih} - \alpha_i e_{wh})$.

R2 : $rank(f_{ih}^A / e_{wh}) = rank(e_{ih} / e_{wh} - \alpha_i)$.

R3 : $rank(f_{ih}^A / e_{ih}) = rank(1 - \alpha_i e_{wh} / e_{ih})$.

R4 : $rank(f_{ih}^A / \alpha_i e_{wh}), = rank(e_{ih} / \alpha_i e_{wh} - 1)$.

R5 : $rank(f_{ih}^A / \alpha_i) = rank(e_{ih} / \alpha_i - e_{wh})$.

These alternative expressions for proposition R can be thought to be generated by a linear transformation of the factor contents and excess factor supplies.[24] Kohler (1991) shows that these alternative formulations of proposition R can produce different rankings. Hence, all forms should be computed and analyzed when testing proposition R.

Table 7.2 Tests of H-O-V sign proposition (country by country)

Country	Proportion of sign matches (%)
Argentina	33
Australia	33
Austria	67
Belgium-Luxembourg	50
Brazil	17
Canada	75
Denmark	42
Finland	67
France	25
Germany	67
Greece	92
Hong Kong	100
Ireland	92
Italy	58
Japan	67
Korea	75
Mexico	92
Netherlands	58
Norway	25
Philippines	50
Portugal	67
Spain	67
Sweden	42
Switzerland	67
United Kingdom	92
United States	58
Yugoslavia	83

Source: Bowen, Leamer and Sveikauskas (1987).

Table 7.2 to Table 7.5 indicate of the type of results obtained when propositions S and R are tested. Table 7.2 and Table 7.3 report the proportion of correct matches when comparing the sign of the adjusted net trade in the services of a factor to the sign of the excess supply of that factor according to (7.78). Overall, proposition S holds for 61 percent of these pairwise comparisons. When comparisons are made country by country (Table 7.2), proposition S holds more convincingly for some countries than others (for example, Hong Kong versus Argentina). When the comparisons are made factor by factor (Table 7.3), proposition S holds less frequently.

While the results in Table 7.2 and Table 7.3 indicate that proposition S fails to hold in a number of instances, do such results permit one to reject proposition S and by implication the H-O-V model? This question raises the issue of choosing a level of significance. For example,

Table 7.3 Tests of H-O-V sign proposition (factor by factor)

Factor	Proportion of sign matches (%)
Capital	52
Labor (Total)	67
Professional/Technical	78
Managerial	22
Clerical	59
Sales	67
Service	67
Agricultural	63
Production	70
Land	
Arable	70
Pasture	52
Forest	70

Source: Bowen, Leamer and Sveikauskas (1987).

whereas a lower bound of 50 percent on the proportion of correct sign matches seems reasonable, the choice of a higher (critical) value for the proportion is problematic unless it equals 100 percent At best, such results only indicate that the H-O-V equations are not exact, but do not indicate the source of inexactness. As discussed below, recent work has gone a long way toward addressing the issue of why the H-O-V equations are not exact.

Table 7.4 and Table 7.5 show the corresponding tests of proposition R (form R4). Each table presents two sets of results. First is the rank correlation between the factor contents and factor abundances. Second is the proportion of correct rankings when the ordering of factor contents and factor abundances are compared two at time. Both the correlations and the proportion of correct pairwise rankings suggest that proposition R holds more often than proposition S. Yet, the rankings are not exact, and since the choice of a critical value for the proportion of correct rankings is largely subjective, the extent to which proposition R is considered validated is also subjective.

In summary, tests of proposition S or R do permit a test of the H-O-V model in that they indicate the extent of conformity between the left and right-hand sides of (7.76). Alternatively, if the H-O-V model (7.76) is assumed valid, then appeal to these propositions allows one to use the factor content of trade to "reveal" the structure of a country's factor abundance. In general, the alternative hypotheses associated with testing propositions S and R (as presently formulated) are unclear regarding the model against which the H-O-V model is being tested. Consequently, the reasons for rejecting the H-O-V model, if it is rejected, are also unclear. These difficulties lead one to consider alternative methods for testing the H-O-V model.

Regression approach to the H-O-V model

The H-O-V equations (7.76) specify an exact relationship between the factor content of trade and excess factor supplies. A test of this relationship is therefore to compute the extent to which the factor content vector deviates from the vector of excess factor supplies. But such an analysis requires some sensible way of measuring the distance between the two vectors,[25]

Table 7.4 Tests of the H-O-V rank proposition (country by country)

Country	Rank correlation	Proportion of correct pairwise rankings (%)
Argentina	0.164	58
Australia	−0.127	44
Austria	0.091	56
Belgium-Luxembourg	0.273	64
Brazil	0.673	86
Canada	0.236	64
Denmark	−0.418	29
Finland	0.164	60
France	0.418	71
Germany	0.527	76
Greece	0.564	80
Hong Kong	0.745	89
Ireland	0.491	76
Italy	0.345	69
Japan	0.382	71
Korea	0.345	69
Mexico	0.673	86
Netherlands	−0.236	38
Norway	−0.236	38
Philippines	0.527	78
Portugal	0.091	56
Spain	0.200	62
Sweden	0.200	62
Switzerland	0.381	69
United Kingdom	0.527	78
United States	0.309	67
Yugoslavia	−0.055	49

Source: Bowen, Leamer and Sveikauskas (1987).

that is, measuring the extent to which the equations are not exact. Leontief-type tests provide one indication of the inexactness of the H-O-V equations but are inadequate since the alternative hypotheses associated with these tests are unclear. One alternative is to study the H-O-V equations using regression analysis. This approach, properly formulated, permits one to test the hypotheses embodied in (7.76) against unambiguous alternative hypotheses. Another alternative, discussed in the section 'Measurement approach to the H-O-V model', is to assess how the use of country-specific factor input requirements and departures from the assumption of proportional consumption can make the H-O-V equations hold exactly.

Table 7.5 Tests of the H-O-V rank proposition (factor by factor)

Factor	Rank correlation	Proportion of correct pairwise rankings (%)
Capital	0.140	45
Labor (Total)	0.185	46
Professional/Technical	0.123	33
Managerial	−0.254	34
Clerical	0.134	48
Sales	0.225	47
Service	0.282	44
Agricultural	0.202	47
Production	0.345	48
Land		
Arable	0.561	73
Pasture	0.197	61
Forest	0.356	65

Source: Bowen, Leamer and Sveikauskas (1987).

Regression analysis of the H-O-V equations requires one to first specify the relationship between factor contents and factor supplies, and thus a set of parameters to estimate, under one set of assumptions. Changing one or more of these initial assumptions then implies an alternative specification and a corresponding set of parameters. In some cases, changing an assumption may simply correspond to restricting the value of certain parameters in the original specification. If so, conventional procedures for testing the significance of parameter restrictions can be employed. Such analysis permits one to identify those assumptions that may account for any failure of the H-O-V equations to be exact.

Relaxing the assumptions underlying the H-O-V model is likely to impose costs in terms of increasing the complexity of the relationship between factor contents and factor supplies. For example, incorporating economies of scale may lead to nonlinearities which can complicate, or even preclude, estimation. In practice, some compromise will need to be made between the generality of the specification and the tractability of estimation.

The procedure outlined above for testing the H-O-V model normally involves testing one or more of the *assumptions* of this model rather than an alternative theory, per se. This reflects that models which attempt to explain the composition of trade are built upon the principle of comparative costs. Thus, testing one model against another is really an attempt to discover which of the many potential determinants of relative costs is the more important. For example, if relaxing the assumption of identical technologies improves our ability to predict the pattern of trade, then both technological differences and factor supply differences must be considered as important determinants of the difference in relative costs. Determining which influence is the relatively more important may prove difficult, but should nonetheless represent one goal of the analysis.

To illustrate the methods for testing the H-O-V model in a regression framework, consider testing the H-O-V assumption of identical technologies against the alternative assumption that technologies differ across countries. Maintaining all other assumptions of the H-O-V model, including that of identical and homothetic preferences across countries, the vector of country i's net trades in factor services is given by (7.75). To model technological differences we assume that these differences are neutral across countries. This assumption implies that input matrices are proportional between countries and therefore that the input matrix of country i can be expressed in terms of the input matrix of some "reference" country, that is, $\delta_i \mathbf{A}_i = \mathbf{A}_R$ where subscript "R" denotes the reference country and δ_i is a positive scalar. By definition, $\delta_R = 1$ so that values of δ_i below (above) unity imply that country i is less (more) productive than the reference country. Multiplying (7.75) through by δ_i and using $\delta_i \mathbf{A}_i = \mathbf{A}_R$ gives:

$$\mathbf{f}_i^R = \delta_i \mathbf{e}_i - \mu_i \sum_{z=1}^{N} \delta_z \mathbf{e}_z, \tag{7.80}$$

where we have also used $\mathbf{q}_w = \sum_{z=1}^{N} \mathbf{A}_z^{-1} \mathbf{e}_z = \mathbf{A}_R^{-1} \sum_{z=1}^{N} \delta_z \mathbf{e}_z$. In (7.80), $\mathbf{f}_i^R$ denotes that country i's trade in the factor services is computed using the input requirements matrix of the reference country. With this parameterization, imposing the H-O-V assumption of identical technologies corresponds to restricting $\delta_i = 1$ for all i.[26] Finally, note that the assumption of neutral differences in technology preserves the linearity of the model, an important consideration for estimation purposes.

The specification in (7.80) can be used to test if the pattern of trade in factor services is better explained when neutral differences in technology are allowed. In particular, given data across countries on the factor contents ($\mathbf{f}_i^R$), factor supplies ($\mathbf{e}_i$) and the expenditure shares (μ_i) in a particular year, estimation of (7.80) will yield parameter estimates $\hat{\delta}_i$. Re-estimating (7.80) with the values of the δ_i restricted to the theoretical value of unity then allows one to test the null hypothesis of identical technologies against the alternative of neutral technological differences. The significance of the parameter restrictions is determined using a standard F-test.

Using specifications more general than (7.80), the pioneering work by Bowen et al. (1987) investigated a number of alternatives to the assumptions underlying the H-O-V model including neutral technological differences and non-proportional consumption.[27] Using 1966 data and defining the US as the reference country, Bowen et al. found they could reject the H-O-V assumption of identical technologies in favor of neutral technological differences but could not reject the H-O-V assumption of proportional consumption (that is, identical and homothetic preferences) across countries. Trefler (1995) extends their analysis of technological differences and alternative preference assumptions and also examines data for 1983. Like Bowen et al., Trefler (1995) found that the data favored the assumption of neutral technological differences[28] and the H-O-V assumption of homothetic preferences. However, Trefler also found support for the assumption that consumption is biased toward home goods.[29]

Table 7.6 lists the estimates of the neutral technological differences parameters (the δ_i in (7.80)) obtained by Trefler for 1966 and 1983. Also shown is the value of each country's real GDP per capita relative that of the US (see columns i and iv). Since a country whose productivity is half that of the US is expected to also have a per capita income half that of the US, these relative GDP per capita numbers should be highly correlated with the estimates of relative productivity (the δ_i). In fact, the correlation is 0.89 for 1983 and 0.71 for 1966.

Regression analysis of the H-O-V equations is an extremely useful method for testing the assumptions of the H-O-V model against a number of sensible alternative assumptions (models). As noted, the evidence from such studies is that the H-O-V assumption of identical technologies is not supported by the data and, while the hypothesis of proportional consumption (homothetic preferences) is not rejected, there is some evidence of a bias toward home

Table 7.6 H-O-V regression estimates of technological differences

Country	1983			1966[b]		
	(i)	(ii)	(iii)	(iv)	(v)	(vi)
	GDP per capita[a]	Productivity	t-statistic	GDP per capita	Productivity	t-statistic
Argentina	na	na	na	0.32	0.34	13.01
Australia	na	na	na	0.73	0.13	29.72
Austria	0.65	0.65	2.73	0.49	0.48	4.49
Bangladesh	0.04	0.03	47.71	na	na	na
Belgium	0.67	0.72	2.66	0.58	0.65	3.07
Brazil	na	na	na	0.17	0.22	19.68
Canada	0.95	0.48	2.11	0.77	0.59	7.44
Colombia	0.21	0.28	3.24	na	na	na
Denmark	0.72	0.57	4.09	0.70	0.68	2.16
Finland	0.70	0.65	2.17	0.52	0.55	3.51
France	0.73	0.69	1.80	0.61	0.61	8.33
Greece	0.35	0.42	9.40	0.24	0.41	4.58
Hong Kong	0.61	0.45	4.63	0.28	0.17	5.02
Indonesia	0.11	0.10	39.51	na	na	na
Ireland	0.39	0.58	8.04	0.35	0.54	1.92
Israel	0.60	0.60	3.03	na	na	na
Italy	0.66	0.47	1.25	0.48	0.67	5.56
Japan	0.66	0.74	4.84	0.41	0.41	17.95
Korea	na	na	na	0.10	0.07	15.11
Mexico	na	na	na	0.30	0.33	11.95
Netherlands	0.69	0.78	3.80	0.61	0.54	4.93
New Zealand	0.62	0.40	4.12	na	na	na
Norway	0.82	0.73	1.92	0.59	0.48	3.48
Pakistan	0.08	0.09	32.10	na	na	na
Panama	0.23	0.29	11.35	na	na	na
Philippines	na	na	na	0.11	0.11	17.70
Portugal	0.30	0.16	18.41	0.19	0.22	5.75
Singapore	0.66	0.38	7.89	na	na	na
Spain	0.41	0.55	2.91	0.40	0.43	8.14
Sri Lanka	0.12	0.17	23.80	na	na	na
Sweden	0.75	0.60	7.16	0.72	0.65	3.65
Switzerland	0.91	0.55	9.82	0.93	0.52	4.41
Thailand	0.16	0.14	9.63	na	na	na
Trinidad	0.69	0.49	2.91	na	na	na

Table 7.6 (Continued)

Country	1983			1966[b]		
	(i)	(ii)	(iii)	(iv)	(v)	(vi)
	GDP per capita[a]	Productivity	t-statistic	GDP per capita	Productivity	t-statistic
United Kingdom	0.66	0.70	7.15	0.59	0.57	8.67
United States	1.00	1.00	–	1.00	1.00	–
Uruguay	0.31	0.09	14.85	na	na	na
West Germany	0.73	0.79	1.41	0.63	0.57	10.95
Yugoslavia	0.30	0.11	19.46	0.20	0.21	12.04

na = not available.
[a] GDP per capita and productivity are measured relative to that of the US; t-statistic is the asymptotic t-statistic for testing the null hypothesis that a country's relative productivity parameter equals unity (i.e., $\delta_i = 1$).
[b] Uses 1967 trade data and 1966 factor supply data.
Source: Trefler (1995) Tables 2 (columns *i*, ii and iii) and Table 4 (columns i, ii and iii).

produced goods. As discussed in the next section, these findings led researchers to explore alternative methods to better understand the sources of the apparent empirical failure of the H-O-V model.

Measurement approach to the H-O-V model

The regression approach of the previous section assesses statistically the importance of departures from various assumptions that give rise to the H-O-V equations (7.76). An alternative approach, which we will call the measurement approach, seeks to find values of the factor input requirement matrix $\mathbf{A}_i$ and of consumption that make the H-O-V equations (7.74) for each country hold with equality. That is, if one correctly measures the total factor input requirements matrix $\mathbf{A}_i$, and if consumption is proportional to world consumption, then the left and right-hand sides of (7.76) must by definition be equal. This follows simply from the fact that the starting point for deriving (7.76) is the accounting identity that states that trade equals the difference between production and consumption. Conversely, if the two sides of (7.76) are not equal, then the task is to uncover what prevents the measured factor contents from equaling the measured excess factor supplies. This is the focus of the measurement approach, and one of its main virtues is that it forces one to directly confront reasons why the total factor input requirements matrix $\mathbf{A}_i$ may not be correctly measured. This emphasis has led researchers to examine the role of imported intermediate goods and how these can be incorporated to correctly measure the total factor input requirements matrix $\mathbf{A}_i$. The measurement approach is similar to the regression approach since it embeds alternative hypotheses regarding differences in technology and consumption, but it differs from the regression approach by focusing on the computational question of finding the correct measures of the factor input requirements and the factor content of consumption that will make (7.76) hold with exact equality.

The measurement approach is theoretically simple but difficult to implement empirically due largely to the difficulty of obtaining comparable factor input requirement matrices across countries and the problem how to account for imported intermediate goods. As previously stated, the theoretical foundation for the measurement approach is simply the accounting identity (7.74). This means that if a country's factor input requirements and net outputs are correctly measured then its measured use of factors $\mathbf{A}_i\mathbf{q}_i$ __must__ equal its available supply of these factors $\mathbf{e}_i$. Hence, if $\mathbf{A}_i$ and $\mathbf{q}_i$ are correctly measured, failure of the H-O-V equations to hold exactly must be due to incorrect measurement of factor consumption ($\mathbf{A}_i\mathbf{c}_i$ in (7.74)). This means that if the factor input requirements matrix $\mathbf{A}_i$ is measured correctly then failure of (7.76) to hold exactly must reflect violation of the assumption that a country's consumption is proportional to world consumption, that is, $\mathbf{c}_i = \mu_i\mathbf{c}_w$. Given this, researchers using the measurement approach have searched for ways to measure more correctly the total factor input requirements matrix $\mathbf{A}_i$.

An exceedingly ambitious effort toward this goal is Davis and Weinstein (2001), who investigate alternative specifications of how factor input requirements might differ among countries, including that factor prices are not equalized across all countries but are instead equalized only within subsets of countries. This specification implies that countries produce in different cones of diversification, with factor prices equalized between countries within a given cone. Davis and Weinstein (2001) also examine alternative assumptions regarding the consumption side of the model using gravity equation specifications (see Chapter 6).

The assumption that countries produce in different cones of diversification implies that input requirements vary with relative factor endowments. For example, capital (relative to labor) abundant countries will use production techniques that use more capital per unit of output and less labor per unit of output compared with the production techniques used in capital scarce countries. Equivalently, all industries in capital abundant countries will use more capital per worker than that used in capital scarce countries. Davis and Weinstein (2001) capture this relationship between input requirements and country factor supplies by estimating an equation of the form:[30]

$$\ln(a_{ijh}) = \alpha_i + \beta_{jh} + \delta_h\left(\frac{K_i}{L_i}\right) + \varepsilon_{ijh} \tag{7.81}$$

In this expression, a_{ijh} is the input requirement coefficient, that is, the amount of factor h used to produce one unit of good j in country i. The ratio K_i/L_i is country i's capital–labor endowment ratio and ε_{ijh} is a random error term. The equation expresses that each input requirement coefficient depends on three components. The first (α_i) is specific to each country but the same across all industries. This component therefore captures a neutral difference in technology between countries identical to that modeled by Bowen *et al.* (1987) and Trefler (1993, 1995). The second component β_{jh} is specific to factor h and industry j but common across countries, and can therefore be interpreted to be a measure of the average use (across countries) of factor h per unit of output in industry j. The final component δ_h captures the assumption that countries operate in different cones of diversification and hence that the input requirement of factor h will vary systematically with capital–labor endowments across countries.

Using (7.81), Davis and Weinstein (2001) estimate input requirement coefficients that vary by factor, industry and country and then use these estimates to construct a unique factor input requirements matrix $\mathbf{A}_i$ for each country. As noted in Section 7.3 when discussing factor intensity reversals, a statement of the H-O-V theorem in the absence of factor price equalization requires that one compute the factor content of each nation's trade using the factor input requirements of the exporting country. Davis and Weinstein follow exactly this procedure to construct the factor contents for each of 20 Organisation for Economic Co-operation and Development (OECD) countries plus a "rest of world" residual. They also use this procedure to attempt to correct for the presence of imported intermediate inputs.

Having estimated (7.81), Davis and Weinstein investigate the implications of different assumptions of how factor input requirements might differ across countries by computing a country's net trade in factor services using alternative estimates of factor input requirements. They then test proposition S by comparing the conformity between the signs of the factor contents and excess factor supplies under each assumption.

For example, they construct an input requirements matrix using only the estimates of the β_{jh} in (7.81) and then compute the net factor content of each country's trade and compare this to the excess factor supplies across countries. Sign test results using these average factor input requirements indicated a sign match in 45 percent of the cases. They then augmented the average input requirement estimates with the country-specific neutral technological differences (α_i) and recomputed the net factor contents for each country. For this case, the sign test indicated a sign match in 50 percent of the cases. While an improvement, this proportion of sign matches is little better than would be achieved by a coin toss. However, when the third component of (7.81) was included to estimate the factor input requirements, the proportion of sign matches rose to 86 percent, suggesting that an absence of factor price equalization, or equivalently non-neutral differences in factor input requirements, is important for explaining the weak sign test results of earlier studies.

Perhaps the definitive work using the measurement approach is Trefler and Zhu (2010). Importantly, they derive the correct expression for the total factor input requirements matrix $\mathbf{A}_i$ when there are traded intermediate goods among all countries. They note that prior efforts, such as Davis and Weinstein (2001), to account for traded intermediate goods by using the total factor requirements of the exporting country fail to account for the entire global network of traded intermediate goods. Specifically, using the total factor requirements of the exporting country ignores that the exporting country itself imports intermediate goods and hence factor services from other countries. For example, the US auto industry imports steel from Germany, but Germany imports iron ore from Brazil to make the steel. Using only the German total input requirements to compute the factor content of US steel imports fails to account for the factor inputs used in Brazil to produce the iron ore. Taking the global network of intermediate goods trade into account leads them to compute a matrix of total factor input requirements that measures a nation's total absorption of factors regardless of the country where these factors are employed. For each factor, measuring the correct amount of factor services absorbed through intermediate goods imports means that, when netted against the amount absorbed in producing a nation's exports, one correctly measures only the net flow of the services of factors that reside within a nation.[31]

As indicated previously, if one constructs the correct total factor input requirements matrix $\mathbf{A}_i$, then any failure of (7.76) to hold exactly must be due to the failure of the assumption that a nation's consumption vector is proportional to the world's consumption vector (i.e., $\mathbf{c}_i = \mu_i \mathbf{c}_w$). Trefler and Zhu (2010) demonstrate this convincingly. For each of 41 countries, they compute the labor content of trade using each country's own total factor input requirements matrix $\mathbf{A}_i$ (correctly measured to take account of imported intermediate inputs) and compare this to the computed labor content of each country's trade using only the US factor input requirements matrix ($\mathbf{A}_{US}$). Using a sign test, the proportion of correct sign matches is 34 percent when only $\mathbf{A}_{US}$ is used, but is 95 percent when each country's own factor requirements matrix ($\mathbf{A}_i$) is used. The implication of this result is that the major reason why (7.76) fails to hold exactly is a difference in technology across countries. Investigating the source of the remaining lack of conformity between the factor contents and excess supplies they find four sectors that uniformly fail to satisfy the assumption of proportional consumption: Construction, Government, Agriculture and Food. They note that Construction and Government mainly produce non-traded goods and services while the Agriculture and Food sectors are the most distorted by subsides and trade barriers. When consumption in each of these four sectors is computed using the proportional consumption assumption the sign test indicates that the proportion of correct sign matches rises to 98 percent.

The findings of Trefler and Zhu (2010) demonstrate that technological differences are by far the most important reason for the failure of (7.76) to hold with equality. As they note (p. 204), their use of factor requirements matrices that correctly account for multilateral trade in intermediate goods adds little toward accounting for the failure of the H-O-V equations (7.76) to hold with equality. Similarly, deviations from the assumption of proportional consumption play only a minor role, and arise mainly in sectors producing non-traded goods or goods that are heavily protected. These broad conclusions are in line with the earlier findings from the regression approach which indicated that the data favored a model with proportional consumption but technological differences.

Trade in goods

Prior to the use in the 1980s of the H-O-V model as a rigorous framework for testing the predictions of the factor abundance model, empirical evaluations focused on the trade in goods, and used mainly either an inter-industry or a cross-country regression framework. These two approaches are easily understood by representing the pattern of world trade at a point in time by a matrix of trade flows (see Figure 7.1) where rows index countries and columns index commodities (industries).

An inter-industry analysis/regression focuses on one country (a row of the matrix) and seeks to explain variation in the pattern of that country's trade across commodities (the columns of the matrix). This approach makes it necessary to select industry characteristics (for example, factor input requirements) as the explanatory variables. Since only trade and industry characteristics are observed, the estimation can be interpreted as inferring unobserved characteristics (e.g., factor supplies) of the selected country.

A cross-country analysis/regression instead focuses on one commodity/industry (a column) and seeks to explain variation in the pattern of trade in that commodity across countries (rows). This approach forces one to select country characteristics (such as factor supplies) as the explanatory variables. Since only trade and country characteristics are observed, the estimation can be interpreted as inferring unobserved characteristics (such as factor requirements) of the selected industry.

Neither of these two regression approaches is a legitimate method for testing the H-O-S model since they use only two of the three variables (trade, factor supplies and factor inputs) needed for a proper test of the H-O-S model. Moreover, as Leamer and Bowen (1981) demonstrate, the sign of a coefficient estimated from an inter-industry regression of trade on factor

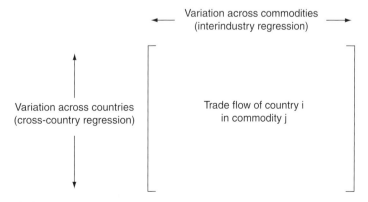

Figure 7.1 Trade flow matrix

input requirements does not reveal the sign of a country's factor content vector $(\mathbf{A}_i \mathbf{t}_i)$ and hence will not, assuming the H-O-V model is true, reveal the sign of a country's excess factor supplies unless, as later proved by Aw (1983), the regression design matrix $(\mathbf{A}_i \mathbf{A}_i)^{-1}$ is diagonal with strictly positive elements (see Problem 7.2). Since Aw's "no factor complementarities" condition is unlikely to hold in actual data, Bowen and Sveikauskas (1992) investigate this issue by comparing the signs of the estimated coefficients from inter-industry regression with those of the factor content vector $\mathbf{A}_i \mathbf{t}_i$ for each of 27 countries. For factor inputs measured as broad aggregates such as capital, skilled and unskilled labor and land, they found that the sign of a regression coefficient (when significant) matched the sign of the corresponding factor content in over 90 percent of the comparisons. Thus, for aggregate definitions of factor inputs, coefficient signs did appear to be reliable indicators of the net trade in factor services. But even if coefficient signs are more reliable than theory would suggest, directly computing the factor contents, rather than inferring their signs from regression coefficients, is a much simpler and more direct way to infer factor abundances.

Although these regression approaches are deficient as methods for testing the H-O-S theory, they can nonetheless be useful for extracting other information from the pattern of trade. For example, the inter-industry approach can, for example, be used to infer differences in relative factor prices between countries.[32] Similarly, as discussed in the next Section, the cross-country approach can be used to estimate Rybczynski effects which, by the reciprocity conditions, are also the Stolper-Samuelson effects. Since the inter-industry and cross-country methods discussed in this section are not strictly appropriate for testing the H-O-S model they will not be considered further. However, each approach played a very important role in the history of empirically evaluating the H-O-S theory prior to the adoption of the H-O-V model, so the reader is strongly encouraged to read the survey articles and related papers on each approach referenced at the end of this chapter. Baldwin (2008) in particular is an excellent recent treatise on these two methods and their shortcomings.

7.5   The Stolper-Samuelson and Rybczynski theorems

In this section, we extend the Stolper-Samuelson and Rybczynski theorems to higher dimensions. After discussing each theorem, the section concludes with discussion of empirical evidence regarding their validity.

The Stolper-Samuelson theorem

To extend the Stolper-Samuelson theorem beyond the 2x2 case we consider the effect of output price changes on nominal and real factor returns. The effect on nominal factor rewards is already contained in (7.35) which is reproduced below:

$$(\mathbf{w}_1 - \mathbf{w}_0)\mathbf{A}(\overline{\mathbf{w}})(\mathbf{p}_1 - \mathbf{p}_0) > 0. \tag{7.82}$$

This states that, on average, factor rewards will tend to increase the most for those factors that are used most intensively in the production of goods whose relative prices increased the most and, conversely, factor rewards will tend to decrease the most for those factors used least intensively in industries whose relative prices have fallen the most.[33]

To deduce the effect of price changes on real rewards we first consider a rise in the price of only one good, for example good z. Assuming this good was produced in the initial equilibrium then its price initially equaled its average cost of production:

$$p_z = \sum_{h=1}^{H} w_h a_{zh}. \tag{7.83}$$

Subsequent to a rise in p_z, competition will serve to constrain any rise in the cost of production of good z to be greater than or equal to the rise in price. Hence, we can write

$$\hat{p}_i = \hat{p}_z = \sum_{h=1}^{H} \hat{w}_h \theta_{zh} \qquad (7.84)$$

where $\theta_{zh} > 0$ is the share of factor k in the total cost of producing good z and $\sum_h \theta_{zh} = 1$. Since the prices of all other goods are held constant ($\hat{p}_j = 0, \forall\, j \neq z$), (7.84)) implies that for some factor, for example the first, the following relationship must hold:

$$\hat{w}_1 \geq \hat{p}_z > \hat{p}_j = 0, \forall\, j \neq z. \qquad (7.85)$$

This states that the return to some factor, here factor 1, will rise in terms of all goods and fall in terms of no good.

We now establish that the real return to some other factor must fall as a result of the rise in the price of good z. By assumption, the price of good m (m $\neq z$) did not change ($\hat{p}_m = 0$). Hence, if good m is produced in the new equilibrium, then it must be the case that the proportional rise in its price exceeded the rise in its average costs, that is,

$$0 = \hat{p}_m \geq \sum_h \hat{w}_h \theta_{mh}. \qquad (7.86)$$

By assumption, factor 1 is employed in producing good m so that $\theta_{m1} > 0$. In addition, it was established above that $\hat{w}_1 > 0$. Hence, since $\sum_h \theta_{mh} = 1$, it must be the case that for some factor, say factor 2, $\hat{w}_2 < 0$ and thus

$$\hat{w}_2 < \hat{p}_m = 0 < \hat{p}_z, \forall\, m \neq z. \qquad (7.87)$$

This states that the return to factor 2 rose in terms of no good and fell strictly in terms of good z. These results can be summarized by saying that every good is a "friend" to some factor and is an "enemy" to some other factor.[34]

Proposition 7.11: *A rise in the price of one good alone will raise the real reward of some factor in terms of all other goods and lower it in terms of no good, and it will lower the real return to some other factor in terms of all goods.*[35]

Proposition 7.11 is a generalization of the 2x2 model's *magnification effect* of an output price change on factor prices (see Chapter 4, Section 4.1). Note that this proposition is very general as no restrictions have been imposed on the number of goods relative to the number of factors. Finally, note that Proposition 7.11 applies to arbitrary changes in the relative price of goods.[36]

The Rybczynski theorem

The effect of factor supply changes on outputs is extended by considering initial and terminal equilibria characterized by endowment vectors $\mathbf{e}_1$ and $\mathbf{e}_2$, respectively. Assuming factor prices are initially equalized across countries, full employment in each equilibrium means that $\mathbf{e}_1 = \mathbf{A}(\mathbf{w})\mathbf{q}_1$ and $\mathbf{e}_2 = \mathbf{A}(\mathbf{w})\mathbf{q}_2$. Note that factor prices, and hence factor input requirements, are the same in each equilibrium. This follows from the fact that, with factor prices initially equalized, a sufficiently small change in factor supplies will leave factor prices unchanged (that is, only outputs need change). Given this, we can write:

$$\mathbf{e}_2 - \mathbf{e}_1 = \mathbf{A}(\mathbf{w})(\mathbf{q}_2 - \mathbf{q}_1). \qquad (7.88)$$

Pre-multiplying both sides by $(e_2 - e_1)$ gives:

$$(e_2 - e_1)A(w)(q_2 - q_1) > 0 \qquad (7.89)$$

This is analogous to the Stolper-Samuelson correlation given by (7.82).

Proposition 7.12: *Factor supply changes will raise, on average, the output of goods that make relatively intensive use of those factors whose supply has increased the most, and will reduce, on average, the output of goods that make relatively little use of those factors whose supply has increased the most.*

Since Proposition 7.12 requires factor price equalization, it applies only when the number of goods equals or exceeds the number of factors.

To obtain a more general statement of the effect of factor supply changes we mimic the preceding analysis for the Stolper-Samuelson theorem. Specifically, suppose the supply of one factor alone increases, for example the first (i.e., $\hat{e}_1 > 0, \hat{e}_h = 0, \forall\, h \neq 1$). With factor prices unchanged, the subsequent rise in the demand for the growing factor must, if factor prices are unchanged, equal or exceed the growth in the supply of that factor:

$$\hat{e}_1 \le \sum_j \lambda_{j1}\hat{q}_j, \qquad (7.90)$$

where $\lambda_{j1} > 0$ is the fraction of factor 1 employed in sector j and $\sum_j \lambda_{j1} = 1$. Given this, (7.90)) implies that there must be one good, say good j, for which $\hat{q}_j \ge \hat{e}_1 > 0 = \hat{e}_h, \forall\, h \neq 1$. Moreover, if good j also uses another factor, for example factor 2, which is initially fully employed then

$$0 = \hat{e}_2 \ge \sum_j \lambda_{j2}\hat{q}_j, \qquad (7.91)$$

where $\lambda_{j2} > 0$ is the fraction of factor 2 employed in sector j and $\sum_j \lambda_{j2} = 1$. Since $\hat{q}_j > 0$ and by assumption $\lambda_{j2} > 0$, (7.91) requires for some good, for example good m, that $\hat{q}_m < 0$. Hence, we have $\hat{q}_j \ge \hat{e}_1 > 0 > \hat{q}_m$.

Proposition 7.13 : *A rise in the supply of any one factor will, at unchanged factor prices, raise the output of at least one good and lower the output of some other good, provided that the growing factor is subsequently fully employed and that every industry which uses the factor also uses another factor that is fully employed.*

Whereas Proposition 7.13 is very general, it does require factor prices to remain fixed as factor supplies change. Whether this condition is satisfied depends on the relative numbers of goods and factors. When the number of goods equals or exceeds the number of factors, Proposition 7.13 holds.[37] However, if factors outnumber goods then Proposition 7.13 fails since then factor prices also depend on factor supplies and hence cannot remain constant when the latter change. This dimensionality issue was not important for the Stolper-Samuelson Proposition 7.11.

Empirical evidence

Empirical assessment of the Stolper-Samuelson theorem has centered on detecting whether changes in factor prices are explained by changes in goods prices, or alternatively by the changes in the pattern of trade that arises from changes in goods prices. The impetus for most studies has not been to empirically verify the Stolper-Samuelson theorem per se, but rather to discover if the rising skill premium – the rise in the ratio of the wages of skilled to unskilled workers – observed for the US particularly over the period from 1979 to 1995 is explained by the changes in the US trade pattern that has accompanied the growing globalization of world markets. Similarly, studies that estimate Rybczynski effects are not testing the predictions of the theorem per se, they instead examine the sign of an estimated effect to assess if a particular factor is a "friend" or an "enemy" either with respect to production of a particular good (or the price of the factor in the case of the Stolper-Samuelson theorem).

Different approaches have been taken to estimating Rybczynski effects. The first, based on the H-O-V model, was pioneered in Leamer (1984). Given the assumptions of the H-O-V model and assuming equal numbers of goods and factors, Leamer showed that the trade in good j in country i can be written as a linear function of country i's excess factor supplies:[38]

$$t_{ij} = (\mathbf{a}_{ij})^{-1}(\mathbf{e}_i - (\alpha_i - \lambda_i)\mathbf{e}_w),$$ (7.92)

where $(\mathbf{a}_{ij})^{-1}$ is a $1 \times J(=H)$ vector whose elements a_{ijh}^{-1} are the elements (row) of the inverse of the factor requirements matrix corresponding to industry j. Assuming balanced trade ($\lambda_i = 0$) and full employment ($\mathbf{A}_i\mathbf{q}_i = \mathbf{e}_i$), the expenditure share $\alpha_i = Y_i/Y_w$ can be written:

$$\alpha_i = \frac{\mathbf{p}\mathbf{q}_i}{Y_w} = \frac{\mathbf{p}(\mathbf{A}_i^{-1}\mathbf{e}_i)}{Y_w} = \frac{\mathbf{w}\mathbf{e}_i}{Y_w}$$ (7.93)

where $\mathbf{p}$ is the $J \times 1$ vector of world output prices and $\mathbf{w}$ is the $H \times 1$ vector of world factor prices. The term $\mathbf{w}\mathbf{e}_i$ is national expenditure at *factor cost*, and follows directly from the zero profit conditions $\mathbf{w} = \mathbf{p}\mathbf{A}_i^{-1}$. Inserting (7.93) into (7.92) and using the condition for world full employment $((\mathbf{A}'_{ij})^{-1}\mathbf{e}_w = q_{wj}$, where q_{wj} is the world output of commodity j), we can express (7.92) as

$$t_{ij} = \left[(\mathbf{a}_{ij})^{-1} - \frac{q_{wj}\mathbf{w}}{Y_w}\right]\mathbf{e}_i = \mathbf{r}_{ij}\mathbf{e}_i$$ (7.94)

where $\mathbf{r}_{ij}$ is a $1 \times H(=J)$ vector with elements $r_{ijh} = (a_{ijh}^{-1} - q_{wj}w_h/Y_w)$. These elements are the net effect (production minus consumption) of a change in the supply of resource h on country i's net trade in good j. The term a_{ijh}^{-1} is the Rybczynski effect, that is, the amount by which the production of good j will change when the supply of factor h changes by one unit (i.e., $a_{ijh}^{-1} = \partial q_{ij}/\partial e_{ih}$). Unlike (7.92), (7.94) expresses trade as a function only of country i's factor supplies. Hence, this specification does not require one to measure world factor supplies or world expenditure in order to perform estimation of the relationship between net trade and factor supplies.

Although specifications (7.92) and (7.94) are direct implications of the H-O-V model, they require the assumption of equal numbers of goods and factors. If the number of goods exceeds the number of factors then there are multiple solutions to the H-O-V equations (7.76) (i.e., multiple values of the $(\mathbf{a}_{ij})^{-1}$). If the number of factors instead exceeds the number of goods, then the solution to the H-O-V equations (7.76) is nonlinear, making the choice of model specification problematic.

Using 1958 and 1975 data on the net trade in ten commodity aggregates and 11 factor endowments for 58 countries, Leamer (1984) estimated several variants of (7.92) for each of the ten commodity aggregates. For each industry, he found that the variation in the net trade across countries is significantly related to variation in factor supplies, and that each industry generally evidences at least one friend and one enemy factor.

The second approach, undertaken by Harrigan (1995), estimated the relationship between the output in a given industry and factor supplies rather than between net trade and factor supplies. This approach removes the consumption effect embedded in (7.94) so the estimates obtained are directly the Rybczynski effects a_{ijh}^{-1}. Harrigan (1995) estimated Rybczynski effects for capital, skilled labor, unskilled labor and land using a panel data set on the gross output in each of ten industries across 20 OECD countries for the years 1970 to 1985. The results were mixed, with the overall power of the variation in factor endowments to explain variation in industry output across countries relatively low. However, he found that each industry had at least one statistically significant friendly factor and one statistically significant enemy factor in nine of the ten industries investigated.

Harrigan (1997) extended Harrigan (1995) by allowing, among other modifications, for technological differences among industries and countries. In addition, his estimates were derived by estimating GDP share equations derived from a translog specification of a nation's GDP (revenue) function along the lines pioneered by Kohli (1990). Using a 20 year panel dataset on ten OECD countries, seven manufacturing industries, and capital, land and labor divided into three groups based on their level of educational attainment, he found that differences in technology among countries and industries are important for explaining variation in industry output. He also obtained stronger results with respect to the estimated Rybczynski effects.

Overall, the findings of Leamer (1984) and Harrigan (1995, 1997) indicate that factor supplies are significant for explaining cross-country variation in trade and outputs. However, as indicated in Harrigan (1997), technological differences are also important, a finding consistent with the findings of the studies (Section 7.4) that have tested for the validity of the H-O-V model.

Turning to the Stolper-Samuelson prediction, it was noted above that empirical studies have centered on whether this prediction – that a rise in price of a good will raise the relative return to the factor used intensively in producing that good – explains the rising skill premium in the US observed from 1979 to 1995. Among the first such studies is Lawrence and Slaughter (1993). Examining changes during the 1980s in export, import and domestic goods prices and changes in the ratio of employment of nonproduction ("skilled labor") relative to that of production workers ("unskilled labor"), they concluded that the observed changes in goods prices were inconsistent with the Stolper-Samuelson prediction. In particular, they observed that the prices of goods intensive in skilled labor actually fell over the 1980s while the ratio of skilled to unskilled labor employed rose, suggesting that the skill premium should have been falling instead of rising. They concluded that some other effect – possibly technological progress – was raising the demand for skilled workers, and that this was behind the rising skill premium.

Leamer (1998) reformulates the zero profit conditions (7.26) to express changes in goods prices by industry in terms of changes in the prices of factors employed and changes in total factor productivity. Controlling for the influence of productivity changes on prices, he finds evidence that, particularly during the 1970s, changes in factor prices are significantly related to changes in goods prices unrelated to technology, and in the direction predicted by the Stolper-Samuelson theorem.

Baldwin and Cain (2000) also use the zero profit conditions to explain changes in goods prices but augment their relationship to use total (direct plus indirect) factor cost shares and industry capital usage. They conclude from their results that rising import competition in sectors employing less-educated labor and technical change biased toward saving less-educated labor appear to account for much of the relative wage changes over the period 1979 to 1987.

Harrigan and Balaban (1999) estimate Stolper-Samuelson elasticities based on a translog specification of the US GDP function. Overall, their results suggested that relative price changes did account for increasing wage inequality. However, many of their elasticity estimates for traded goods sectors were not statistically significant.

Fenestra and Hanson (2003) brings a new perspective to this literature by arguing that observed wage changes have a substantial within-industry component. From this, they argue that global "production sharing" (trade in intermediate products) is an omitted consideration that affects the relative demand for skilled workers, and may account for the observed increase in the relative use of skilled labor (as does skilled-biased technological change) as well as the rising skill premium. Estimating a model that incorporates production sharing they conclude that foreign outsourcing accounts for 50 percent or more of the increase in skilled labor usage, and that, for the US, outsourcing is an important factor in contributing to changes in industry productivity and product prices that would in turn increase the relative price of skilled labor.

The preceding discussion indicates that refinements to the basic mechanisms through which changes in trade may change factor prices have improved our understanding of the basic prediction of the Stolper-Samuelson theorem. Overall, the empirical evidence indicates that goods prices, factor supplies and the globalizing nature of trade flows are important for explaining changes in factor prices. Whether these forces or skills-biased technological change is the major explanation for the changing price of skilled relative to unskilled labor remains fertile ground for research.

7.6 Factor price equalization

Whether free trade in goods equalizes factor prices between countries has been the subject of considerable study since the mid-1950s. From an empirical perspective, factor price equalization (FPE) is perhaps less interesting than weaker hypotheses concerning the effects of trade on factor prices (e.g., that goods trade tends to reduce factor price differences between countries, with no presumption that they will become equal). However, for completeness, this section considers the theoretical issues concerning the likelihood of factor price equalization in the context of many goods and factors. A key concept to emerge from this analysis is that of an integrated equilibrium.

Initial inquiry into factor price equalization focused on the question of the global univalence of the mapping between goods prices and factor prices. Assuming equal numbers of goods and factors, and that all countries produce the same set of goods, the question of global univalence centers on the issue of finding technological restrictions such that the zero profit conditions

$$\mathbf{p} = \mathbf{w}\mathbf{A}(\mathbf{w}). \tag{7.95}$$

yield a one-to-one mapping between $\mathbf{w}$ and $\mathbf{p}$. In two dimensions the requirement is that of no factor intensity reversals. In higher dimensions, the non-singularity of $\mathbf{A}$ guarantees local univalence between $\mathbf{p}$ and $\mathbf{w}$ but not global univalence. A sufficient condition for the latter was provided by Gale and Nikaido (1965) who established that (7.95) is globally univalent if the principle minors of $\mathbf{A}$ are all positive (in which case $\mathbf{A}$ is called a P-matrix). Unfortunately, the conditions for the global univalence of (7.95) embody little economic intuition; and while these conditions are of theoretical importance, their relevance for empirical applications has yet to become evident.

A more intuitive approach to the likelihood of factor price equalization involves the concept of an integrated equilibrium. The essential idea is as follows. Consider a world economy without "countries" and assume that all factors and goods are mobile. An equilibrium in this world economy would then entail one set of goods prices and one set of factor prices. Now partition this world into arbitrary "countries" by assigning to each country some amount of the world's supply of each factor. This division of world resources then implies a pattern of production and consumption across countries. We then ask whether this partition of factor supplies supports a pattern of production such that each country can fully employ its share of factors using the integrated economy's production techniques. If the answer is yes, then there exists a trade equilibrium in which all countries have the same factor prices as in the integrated equilibrium (i.e., factor prices are equalized). If the answer is no, then the post-partition equilibrium will involve a different set of factor and goods prices, with the former differing across countries. The discussion below formalizes this idea.

Integrated equilibrium[39]

Let there be J goods, H factors and, for simplicity, two countries. Countries are assumed to share the same CRS production function for each good and product and factor markets are assumed perfectly competitive. Letting an asterisk denote foreign variables and functions when they differ from those of the home country, the following are the equilibrium conditions for each country:

$$\mathbf{w}A(\mathbf{w}) \geq \mathbf{p}\,\mathbf{q} \geq 0 \tag{7.96}$$

$$\mathbf{w}^*A(\mathbf{w}^*) \geq \mathbf{p}\,\mathbf{q}^* \geq 0 \tag{7.97}$$

$$A(\mathbf{w})\mathbf{q} = \mathbf{e} \tag{7.98}$$

$$A(\mathbf{w}^*)\mathbf{q}^* = \mathbf{e}^* \tag{7.99}$$

$$\mathbf{q} + \mathbf{q}^* = \mathbf{d}(\mathbf{p}, \mathbf{w}, \mathbf{e}) + \mathbf{d}^*(\mathbf{p}, \mathbf{w}^*, \mathbf{e}^*).^{[40]} \tag{7.100}$$

In these expressions, $A(\mathbf{w})$ is the $H \times J$ matrix of factor input requirements and $\mathbf{w}A(\mathbf{w})$ are the unit cost functions. Equations (7.96) and (7.97) are the conditions for production equilibrium, (7.98) and (7.99) are the conditions for factor market equilibrium, and (7.100) are the conditions for world output market equilibrium.

Equations (7.96) to (7.100) comprise a system of $2J + 3H$ equations in as many unknowns (the elements of $\mathbf{p}, \mathbf{w}, \mathbf{e}, \mathbf{q}, \mathbf{w}^*, \mathbf{e}^*, \mathbf{q}^*$). Deducting one unknown by the choice of normalization for prices, and one equation by Walras' law, this system is determinate and we assume it has a unique solution.

We now seek the conditions under which the solution to the above system will have the property that $\mathbf{w} = \mathbf{w}^*$. Suppose such a common solution $\overline{\mathbf{w}}(= \mathbf{w} = \mathbf{w}^*)$ exists. Then, with all goods produced somewhere, appropriate selection from among equations (7.96) implies that equilibrium goods prices will be given as $\overline{\mathbf{p}} = \overline{\mathbf{w}}A(\overline{\mathbf{w}})$. Substituting this into the demand functions permits world demand to be expressed as a function of the common factor prices, for example $\mathbf{d}(\overline{\mathbf{w}})$.[41] If $\overline{\mathbf{q}}$ represents the world output vector then the above system can be written:

$$\overline{\mathbf{w}}A(\overline{\mathbf{w}}) = \overline{\mathbf{p}} \tag{7.101}$$

$$A(\overline{\mathbf{w}})\overline{\mathbf{q}} = \overline{\mathbf{e}} \tag{7.102}$$

$$\overline{\mathbf{q}} = \mathbf{d}(\overline{\mathbf{w}}) \tag{7.103}$$

where $\overline{\mathbf{q}} = \mathbf{q} + \mathbf{q}^*$ and $\overline{\mathbf{e}} = \mathbf{e} + \mathbf{e}^*$. Comparing this equation system to that in (7.96)–(7.100), it may be seen that equations (7.101) to (7.103) describe an equilibrium in an integrated world economy in which both factors and goods are mobile. Equation (7.102) is just the addition of (7.98) and (7.99) when $\mathbf{w} = \mathbf{w}^* = \overline{\mathbf{w}}$. Hence, system (7.101) to (7.103) demonstrates that any trade equilibrium in which factor prices are equal but factors are immobile must also be an equilibrium in which goods and factors are mobile. Given this, the likelihood of factor prices being equalized by trade can be judged by considering the conditions under which a division of world production (via a division of world factor supplies) between countries will replicate the integrated equilibrium. Hence, we seek the conditions under which a partition of world output $\overline{\mathbf{q}} = \mathbf{q} + \mathbf{q}^*$ into non-negative components is also a solution to (7.96) to (7.100).

Given a solution $(\overline{\mathbf{q}}, \overline{\mathbf{w}}, \overline{\mathbf{p}})$, any division of $\overline{\mathbf{q}}$ between countries will satisfy conditions (7.96), (7.97) and (7.100). Hence, the issue reduces to whether a given partition of $\overline{\mathbf{q}}$ will also satisfy the factor market conditions (7.98) and (7.99). This will be possible if and only if the equations

$$\mathbf{A}(\overline{\mathbf{w}})\mathbf{q} = \mathbf{e} \qquad (7.104)$$

have a solution in $\mathbf{q}$ such that $0 \le \mathbf{q} \le \overline{\mathbf{q}}$. If so, then foreign production $\mathbf{q}^*$ is easily determined as $\mathbf{q}^* = \overline{\mathbf{q}} - \mathbf{q}$. Hence, the possibility of factor price equalization reduces to the condition that equations (7.104) have a non-negative solution in $\mathbf{q} \le \overline{\mathbf{q}}$.

These ideas are best understood in terms of a geometric representation of the set of all factor supply allocations that would replicate the integrated equilibrium. Consider first the set of all two-country worlds defined by different allocations of the world resources. This set can be represented as an H-dimensional rectilinear box with the lengths of its sides given by amounts of world resources. Any point in this box then denotes a division of world resources such that amounts $\mathbf{e}$ are located in the home country and amounts $\mathbf{e}^* = \overline{\mathbf{e}} - \mathbf{e}$ are located in the foreign country. Given this, suppose there exists an integrated world equilibrium with solution values $\overline{\mathbf{q}}$, $\overline{\mathbf{w}}$, and $\overline{\mathbf{p}}$. Then the set of factor allocations that will replicate the integrated equilibrium can be defined as:

$$\Omega = \{\mathbf{e} | \mathbf{A}(\overline{\mathbf{w}})\mathbf{q} = \mathbf{e}, 0 \le \mathbf{q} \le \overline{\mathbf{q}}\} \qquad (7.105)$$

For all values of $\mathbf{e}$ (that is, partitions of $\overline{\mathbf{e}}$ between $\mathbf{e}$ and $\mathbf{e}^*$) that lie within this set there will be an equilibrium with the same factor prices even when only goods are mobile. Partitions of $\overline{\mathbf{e}}$ that lie outside this set will entail different factor prices across countries.

What are the properties of this set of factor allocations? First, note that since $\mathbf{A}(\overline{\mathbf{w}})\mathbf{q} = \overline{\mathbf{e}}$ in the integrated equilibrium, the factor allocations given by $\mathbf{A}(\overline{\mathbf{w}})(\lambda \mathbf{q}) = \lambda \mathbf{A}(\overline{\mathbf{w}})\mathbf{q} = \lambda \overline{\mathbf{e}}$ (where $0 \le \lambda \le 1$), is also an element of Ω. This means that as λ is varied between zero and one we trace out the diagonal of the box of factor allocations. Hence, if countries have the same factor proportions there will be factor price equalization. Further details of the set Ω can be deduced by denoting $\mathbf{a}_j(\overline{\mathbf{w}})$ as the jth column of $\mathbf{A}(\overline{\mathbf{w}})$. This H-dimensional vector gives the unit factor requirements for good j in the integrated equilibrium. Using this, we can write

$$\mathbf{e} = \mathbf{A}(\overline{\mathbf{w}})\mathbf{q} = \sum_j \begin{bmatrix} a_{1j} \\ \vdots \\ a_{Hj} \end{bmatrix} q_j = \sum_j \mathbf{a}_j(\overline{\mathbf{w}})q_j. \qquad (7.106)$$

Using (7.106), the set Ω can be expressed in an alternative form that facilitates geometric interpretation. Specifically, let $\lambda_j = q_j/\overline{q}_j$ be the home country's share of the integrated equilibrium's production of good j. Given this, substitute $q_j = \lambda_j\overline{q}_j$ on the right-hand-side of (7.106) to get

$$\mathbf{e} = \sum_j \mathbf{a}(\overline{\mathbf{w}})q_j = \sum_j \lambda_j\mathbf{a}_j(\overline{\mathbf{w}})\overline{q}_j. \qquad (7.107)$$

This expresses the factor allocation $\mathbf{e}$ as a convex combination of the integrated equilibrium sectoral employment vectors $\mathbf{a}_j(\overline{\mathbf{w}})\overline{q}_j$. Given this, the set Ω can be written in the equivalent form

$$\Omega = \left\{ \mathbf{e} \mid \exists\, \lambda_j, 0 \le \lambda_j \le 1 \;\forall\, j \text{ s.t. } \mathbf{e} = \sum_j \lambda_j \mathbf{a}_j(\overline{\mathbf{w}})\overline{q}_j \right\}.^{42} \tag{7.108}$$

As the λ_j are varied between zero and unity, the vector sum $\sum_j \lambda_j \mathbf{a}_j(\overline{\mathbf{w}})\overline{q}_j$ yields convex combinations of the industry employment vectors $\mathbf{a}_j(\overline{\mathbf{w}})\overline{q}_j$. Hence, if the number of goods equals or exceeds the number of factors ($J \ge H$) these linear combinations will span at most a subset of H-dimensional real space. However, if factors outnumber goods ($H > J$) then it will in general not be possible to construct the set Ω since we have only J factor employment vectors. Hence, when $H > J$, factor price equalization is unlikely.

Consider, for simplicity, the even case ($J = H$) of two goods and two factors. Figure 7.2 shows the box of world factor allocations between two countries. The length of the box is the world supply of labor and the height is the world supply of capital. A point in the box divides these resources between the two countries. Assuming goods and factors are mobile, we can derive a unique integrated equilibrium solution $\overline{\mathbf{q}}$, $\overline{\mathbf{w}}$ and $\overline{\mathbf{p}}$ which then defines the equilibrium factor input requirements vectors $[\mathbf{a}_1(\overline{\mathbf{w}}), \mathbf{a}_2(\overline{\mathbf{w}})] \equiv \mathbf{A}(\overline{\mathbf{w}})$. These vectors correspond to rays OR_1 and OR_2 in Figure 7.2. The lengths $C_1 = \mathbf{a}_1(\overline{\mathbf{w}})\overline{q}_1$ and $C_2 = \mathbf{a}_2(\overline{\mathbf{w}})\overline{q}_2$ along rays OR_1 and OR_2, respectively, are the sectoral factor employment levels in the integrated equilibrium. That is, full employment in the integrated equilibrium requires the allocation C_1 of capital and labor to the production of good 1 and the allocation C_2 of capital and labor to the production of good 2. The vector sum of OC_1 and OC_2 is thus the world supply vector ($\overline{\mathbf{e}}$) which defines the parallelogram $OC_1\overline{e}C_2$.

Now suppose the home country receives the allocation $\mathbf{e}_1$ (foreign receives $\mathbf{e}_2 = \overline{\mathbf{e}} - \mathbf{e}_1$) of world capital and labor. This allocation can be decomposed into components parallel to OC_1 and OC_2 to yield points D_1 and D_2 which are the allocations of capital and labor across sectors that yield full employment in the home country. Hence, $\lambda_1 = OD_1/OC_1$ and $\lambda_2 = OD_2/OC_2$. As shown, a similar decomposition can be performed for the foreign country's allocation $\mathbf{e}_2$.

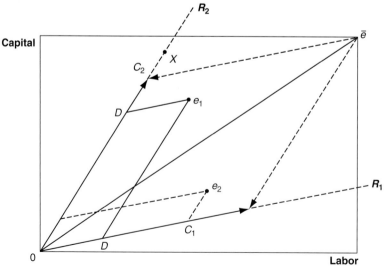

Figure 7.2 Integrated equilibrium and factor price equalization

As shown, the allocation $\mathbf{e}_1$ permits each country to produce less than the total amount of each good produced in the integrated equilibrium – that is, allocation $\mathbf{e}_1$ permits positive levels of production with full employment in each country. Hence, this division of world factor supplies (production) between countries replicates the integrated equilibrium and hence is also a trade equilibrium with equal factor prices.

It can be verified that any allocation of world factor supplies outside the parallelogram $OC_1\bar{e}C_2$ would require negative production of some good, or equivalently unemployed resources, in order to replicate production in the integrated equilibrium. For example, suppose the home country receives the allocation denoted X in Figure 7.2. In this case, full employment would require it to employ all its capital and labor in sector 2 and thus it would specialize in producing good 2. However, the home country's employment levels in sector 2 exceed those at C_2 (i.e., $X/C_2 > 1$) which means its production of good 2 exceeds that in the integrated equilibrium ($\lambda_2 > 1$). Hence, to achieve the integrated equilibrium production levels, the foreign country must produce a negative amount of good 2. Since it is not possible, using the integrated equilibrium factor input requirements, to replicate the integrated equilibrium with outputs that are weakly positive, factor allocation X cannot be a trade equilibrium with equal factor prices.

Figure 7.2 suggests that the "likelihood" of FPE can be measured by the size of Ω (the parallelogram) relative to the size of the box. If so, then FPE is unlikely when factors (H) outnumber goods (J) since, as noted earlier, the J factor input vectors can span, at most, an J-dimensional factor space. If goods outnumber factors then there are more factor input vectors than needed to span H-dimensional factor space. This implies that while a trade equilibrium with FPE is possible when $J > H$, production and trade patterns will be indeterminate since, with equal factor prices, there are many production patterns that can fully employ a given set of factors in each country.

Figure 7.3 illustrates the case of three goods and two factors. In Figure 7.3, we have added a third factor input requirement vector OR_3 corresponding to sector 3. To construct the set Ω,

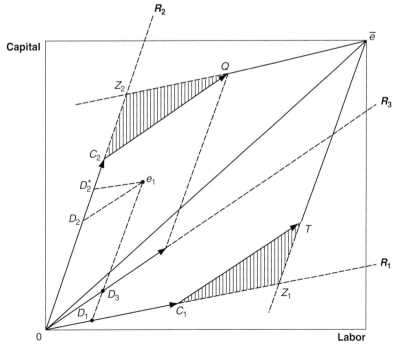

Figure 7.3 Factor price equalization with three goods and two factors

we determine the integrated equilibrium which determines rays OR_j and lengths $OC_j = a_j(\overline{w})\overline{q}_j$ along these rays. The vector sum of the OC_js equals the world supplies of capital and labor ($\overline{e}$) reflecting factor market clearing (full employment) in the integrated equilibrium. Given this, the set of factor allocations compatible with FPE (the set Ω) is given by the parallel-sided hexagon $OC_2Q\overline{e}TC_1$. Comparing this region to the case of two goods and two factors (the parallelogram $OZ_1\overline{e}Z_2$ in Figure 7.3), the addition of good 3 reduces the size of Ω by an amount equal to the two shaded regions.

Now consider the factor allocation e_1. The home country could fully employ these factors by employing OD_2 in sector 2, OD_3 in sector 3 and none in sector 1. Alternatively, it could employ OD_2^* in sector 2 and OD_1 in sector 1 and thus not produce good 3. Several other full employment production patterns are possible.[43] Hence, whereas the integrated equilibrium solution may be unique when goods outnumber factors, the country patterns of production and trade when factor prices are equalized is indeterminate.

Finally, while the pattern of trade in goods is indeterminate when goods outnumber factors, the factor content of trade is determinant. This is shown in Figure 7.4, which adds to Figure 7.3 the iso-income line GG passing through e_1. The slope of GG equals (minus) the wage-rental ratio in the integrated equilibrium.[44] With identical homothetic preferences across countries (as assumed here), the intersection of line GG with the diagonal of the box (point z) gives the factor content of the home country's consumption vector – that is, the capital and labor service it consumes (denoted K_c and L_c).[45] Subtracting the home country's factor supply (e_1) from its desired consumption of factors (z) defines its trade in factor services, that is, its factor content of net trade. In the present case, the home country exports the services of capital ($K_1 - K_c > 0$) and imports the services of labor ($L_1 - L_c < 0$).

In summary, if countries' factor supply vectors lie within the "cone" defined by the integrated equilibrium factor input requirement vectors then a trade equilibrium with immobile factors will replicate the integrated equilibrium and hence factor prices will be equalized.

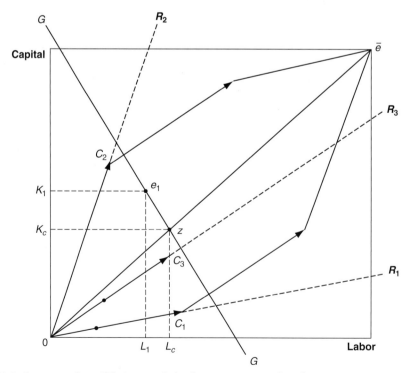

Figure 7.4 Integrated equilibrium and the factor content of trade

In general, this requires the number of goods to equal or exceed the number of factors and the factor supply vectors of countries not to differ "too greatly."

Empirical evidence

As indicated in Section 7.4, formal tests of the H-O-V model indicate that differences across countries in the relative productivity of factors are an important explanation of the failure of the H-O-V equations to hold with equality. These findings alone imply that differences in relative factor prices across countries are likely and hence that FPE does not obtain. However, the question arises as to whether these differences exist only between subsets of countries, for example between industrial and non-industrial countries. This would arise if one group of countries lies in one cone of diversification while another group of countries lies in a different cone of diversification, with relative factor prices equalized between countries in the same cone of diversification.

Schott (2003) examines this question by investigating for the nature of the cross-country relationship between output per worker in a given industry and country capital–labor endowment ratios (following on the analysis of Davis and Weinstein (2001)). Under FPE, this relationship would be linear, but if countries lie in different cones then the relationship is instead a spline function for which the slope of the relationship changes as one moves from one cone to another. His findings, using data for 1990 on 45 countries and 28 industries, indicate that OECD countries generally lie in one cone of diversification while non-OECD countries lie in a different cone of diversification. In addition to indicating the absence of relative factor price equalization between these two groups of countries, the findings also suggest countries will tend to specialize in producing only a subset of the complete range of all goods produced in the world.

Debaere and Demiroglu (2003) investigate for the likelihood of FPE based on the integrated equilibrium approach of the previous section. Specifically, they construct the region or "lens" defined by the integrated equilibrium techniques of production and investigate whether country endowments lie with this region. Using data on the capital–labor ratios in 28 manufacturing industries and the capital–labor endowments of 28 countries they find the conditions for FPE to be violated. However, they find that the endowments of OECD countries do lie within the region implied by integrated equilibrium, supporting Schott's (2003) finding that developed and developing countries lie in different cones of diversification.

7.7 Concluding remarks

The concept of comparative advantage, the price and quantity versions of the Heckscher-Ohlin (H-O) theorem, the Stolper-Samuelson and Rybczynski propositions and the factor price equalization theorem remain largely intact when considered in the context of a general J good, H factor perfectly competitive model. Where dimensionality is important, the critical requirement is that the number of goods exceeds the number of factors.[46] This requirement on the relative numbers of goods and factors applies most stringently to strong forms of the Rybczynski proposition, the quantity version of the H-O theorem and the likelihood of factor price equalization. However, assuming only that firms minimize costs and that consumers maximize utility, without regard to the exact form of technology or preferences, or the relative numbers of goods and factors, these propositions (except factor price equalization) do hold in the weaker form of correlations between (variously) factor prices, goods prices, factor use and trade.

While general results in the form of correlations can be derived, nothing can be said about individual components. For example, one is unable to predict the commodity composition of trade in goods in the case of the weakened H-O theorem. In these cases, the concept of a country's trade in factor services proves particularly useful as a parallel generalization of the H-O theorems. The factor services formulation also permits one to resolve cases in which the pattern of production, and hence trade in goods, is indeterminate (that is, when $J > H$).

When there are many goods and factors, the empirically testable statement of the factor abundance theory is the Heckscher-Ohlin-Vanek (H-O-V) model and its equations which link a country's net trade in factor services to its relative abundance of factors. Theoretically valid tests of the factor abundance model must involve a direct analysis of the H-O-V equations which relate the net trade in factor services to excess factor supplies. Importantly, this analysis must also make use of data on three independent sets of variables: factor supplies, commodity trade and factor inputs.

The first complete tests of the factor abundance theory using the H-O-V model indicated rejection of the theory. However, unlike earlier tests, these initial analyses tested the H-O-V model against clear alternative hypotheses (i.e., different assumptions about the nature of technology or consumption). The findings indicated that differences in technology across countries were significant for explaining the rejection of the "pure" H-O-V model which assumes identical, constant returns to scale, for production functions across countries. The most recent work has focused on uncovering both the nature of technological differences and the importance of these differences relative to consumption bias in accounting for the failure of the H-O-V equations to hold with equality. These efforts convincingly indicate that non-uniform differences in technology across countries are important, and that countries produce in different cones of diversification – a result that can arise when factor price equalization does not obtain. At the most general level, the findings indicate that differences in technology account for most of the failure of the H-O-V equations to hold with equality. Consumption bias in the form of deviations from the assumption of proportional consumption appears a far less important reason for the failure of the H-O-V equations to be exact.

Empirical evidence as to the validity of the Stolper-Samuelson and Rybczynski theorems generally supports their predications. But refinements in modeling the channels through which these effects operate needs to better confront the reality of international trade flows, and in particular the role of traded intermediate goods.

Lastly, the proposition that free trade in goods will equalize factor prices between countries led to consideration of an integrated world equilibrium in which goods and factors are mobile. If country factor supplies do now differ too greatly, then it is possible for factor prices to be equalized when the number of goods equals or exceeds the number of factors. Like the results from the formal tests of the H-O-V model, the empirical evidence indicates that groups of countries lie in different cones of diversification, suggesting that countries will tend to specialize in producing only a subset of the goods produced worldwide.

Problems

7.1   Use the following data for a three factor, three good model to calculate the factor supply vectors $\mathbf{e}_i$ and $\mathbf{e}_w$, the expenditure share $(\alpha_i + \lambda_i)$, the excess factor supply vector and the factor content of trade. Does the pattern of factor contents conform to absolute factor abundance? To relative factor abundance?

$$\mathbf{A} = \begin{bmatrix} 3 & 2 & 3 \\ 4 & 1 & 4 \\ 2 & 1 & 1 \end{bmatrix}, \mathbf{q}_i = \begin{bmatrix} 1 \\ 2 \\ 6 \end{bmatrix}, \mathbf{q}_w = \begin{bmatrix} 12 \\ 4 \\ 12 \end{bmatrix}, \mathbf{p} = \begin{bmatrix} 2 \\ 1 \\ 1 \end{bmatrix}, \mathbf{t}_i = \begin{bmatrix} -2 \\ 1 \\ 3 \end{bmatrix}$$

7.2 (Inter-industry regression) Suppose an inter-industry regression analysis estimates, for country i, the following relationship: $\mathbf{t}_i = \mathbf{A}_i \boldsymbol{\beta}_i + \boldsymbol{\varepsilon}_i$, where $\mathbf{t}_i$ is a $J \times 1$ vector of net trades, $\boldsymbol{\beta}_i$ is the $H \times 1$ vector of "slope" coefficients and $\boldsymbol{\varepsilon}_i$ is a $J \times 1$ vector of random errors. The equation has no constant term. Common practice interprets the sign of each estimated slope coefficient $\hat{\beta}_{ij}$ to indicate that factor j is either abundant (positive) or scarce (negative) in country i.

a) State the matrix formula for computing the estimates $\hat{\boldsymbol{\beta}}_i$.
b) Assume trade balance and use (7.76) to write the formula obtained in (a) to express it as a function of the excess factor supplies of country i. Would you expect the signs of the estimated coefficients to equal the signs of the country's excess factor supply? Why or why not?
c) What condition would ensure that the signs of the regression estimates equaled the signs of the corresponding excess factor supplies? What might such a condition imply about the use of factor inputs across industries?

7.3 (Inter-industry regression) Use your analysis of Problem 7.2 and the data in Problem 7.1 to compute the value of the regression coefficients $\hat{\beta}_i$. Do the signs of these coefficients equal the signs of the country's net trade in factors? Do the sign and rank of these coefficients conform to the country's absolute and relative factor abundance?

7.4 The assumption of neutral technological differences introduced in 'Regression approach to the H-O-V model' in Section 0 can be extended by assuming that subsets of industries exhibit neutral technological differences, where these neutral differences are different for different industry subsets. How would this assumption be stated in terms of differences in the factor requirements matrices between countries? Derive a specification for the H-O-V equations assuming such neutral differences with respect to two industry groups (such as manufacturing and agriculture). How would one attempt to estimate such an equation?

7.5 The H-O-V model (7.76) is stated in terms of the quantities of goods and factors. Using the fact that $diag(\mathbf{p}_i)^{-1}\mathbf{A}_i diag(\mathbf{w}_i) = \mathbf{w}_i\ \mathbf{e}_i$, where $\mathbf{p}_i$ is the J element vector of goods prices in country i and $\mathbf{w}_i$ is the $H \times 1$ vector of factor prices in country i, reformulate the H-O-V equations (7.76) in terms of the values of trade and factor supplies. Then formulate definitions of factor abundance such that propositions similar to S and R can be stated.

7.6 (Cross-country regression): Show that the signs of the estimated regression coefficients from estimating a cross-country regression of the form $\mathbf{t}_i = \mathbf{A}_i^{-1}\beta$ (which derives from the H-O-V equations as $\mathbf{t}_i = \mathbf{A}_i^{-1}(\mathbf{e}_i - (\alpha_i - \lambda_i)\mathbf{e}_w)$) will always match the signs of the country's factor content vector, and hence also the signs of the excess factor supplies if the H-O-V equations (7.76) are true.

7.7 (Proposition L) Write the H-O-V equations (7.76) for capital and labor. Denote the net factor trade in capital as $K_T = K_x - K_m$ and the net factor trade in labor as $L_T = L_x - L_m$.

(a) Use these expressions to form expressions for the ratios K_x/L_x and K_m/L_m.
(b) Now subtract the expression for K_m/L_m from that for K_x/L_x.
(c) Use the expression derived in (b) to establish that if trade in not balanced, the difference $(K_x/L_x - K_m/L_m)$ can be positive (i.e., $(K_x/L_x)/(K_m/L_m) - 1 > 0$) even if the country is abundant in labor.
(d) What conclusion do you reach for part c if trade is instead balanced?

Notes

1. Sections 7.4 to 7.6 can be read independently from Sections 7.1 to 7.3.
2. In this chapter, bold lower case letters denote vectors; bold upper case letters denote matrices. In addition, for notational simplicity, the transpose symbol "'" is omitted and vectors and matrices are instead assumed to be conformable for the indicated multiplication.
3. Formally $G(\mathbf{p}, \mathbf{e}) = \min_w \{\mathbf{we} \mid c_j(\mathbf{w}) \geq p_j, \forall j\}$ where $c_j(\mathbf{w})$ is industry j's unit cost function (see Chapter 4).
4. As in other chapters, this chapter maintains the assumption that there exists a collective utility function that depends upon the aggregate consumption of each good.
5. The factor content of net trade measures a country's net exchange of factor services that is implicit in its exchange of goods through trade.
6. If the function $y = f(x)$ is continuous and differentiable on the interval $[x_1, x_0]$ then the mean value theorem states that there exists some $\bar{x}$ between points x_1 and x_0 such that
$$y(x_1) - y(x_0) = \frac{\partial f(\bar{x})}{\partial x}(x_1 - x_0).$$
7. By definition, $z(\mathbf{w}_0) = \mathbf{w}_0 \mathbf{A}(\mathbf{w}_0)(\mathbf{p}_1 - \mathbf{p}_0)$ and $z(\mathbf{w}_1) = \mathbf{w}_1 \mathbf{A}(\mathbf{w}_1)(\mathbf{p}_1 - \mathbf{p}_0)$. Hence $z(\mathbf{w}_1) - z(\mathbf{w}_0) = \mathbf{w}_1 \mathbf{A}(\mathbf{w}_1)(\mathbf{p}_1 - \mathbf{p}_0) - \mathbf{w}_0 \mathbf{A}(\mathbf{w}_0)(\mathbf{p}_1 - \mathbf{p}_0)$. Using the zero profit condition $\mathbf{p} = \mathbf{w} \mathbf{A}(\mathbf{w})$, $z(\mathbf{w}_1) - z(\mathbf{w}_0) = \mathbf{p}_1(\mathbf{p}_1 - \mathbf{p}_0) - \mathbf{p}_0(\mathbf{p}_1 - \mathbf{p}_0) = (\mathbf{p}_1 - \mathbf{p}_0)(\mathbf{p}_1 - \mathbf{p}_0)$.
8. Note that (7.36) can be considered a generalized form of the Stolper–Samuelson proposition. Section 7.5 contains further details.
9. In addition, the factor price vector $\bar{\mathbf{w}}$ may not correspond to the factor price vector that exists under free trade. That is, the mean value theorem states only that (7.33) holds for *some* $\bar{\mathbf{w}}$ between $\mathbf{w}_0$ and $\mathbf{w}_1$. But no guidance is given as to how $\bar{\mathbf{w}}$ should be selected.
10. See also Dixit and Norman (1980), pp. 325–326.
11. See Section 7.5.
12. Alternatively, a vector of factor prices $\bar{\mathbf{w}}$ between $\mathbf{w}_A$ and $\mathbf{w}_A^*$ since output prices uniquely determine input prices when factor supplies $\mathbf{e}$ are given.
13. Note that factor supplies $\mathbf{e}$ and $\mathbf{e}^*$ are being held fixed.
14. See Section "The factor abundance theorems" in Chapter 4.
15. By definition, the vector of net outputs is $\mathbf{q}_i = (\mathbf{I} - \mathbf{B})\mathbf{g}_i$ where $\mathbf{I}$ is a $J \times J$ identity matrix, $\mathbf{B}$ is the $J \times J$ matrix of domestic intermediate goods requirements and $\mathbf{g}_i$ is the $J \times 1$ vector of gross outputs.
16. The model assumes intermediate goods are not traded between countries. The importance of this assumption is discussed in 'Measurement approach to the H-O-V model' in Section 7.4.
17. Let $\mathbf{D}_i$ denote the $H \times J$ matrix of equilibrium direct factor input requirements. Then, with reference to footnote 15, the matrix of total (direct plus indirect) factor input requirements is $\mathbf{A}_i = \mathbf{D}_i(\mathbf{I} - \mathbf{B})^{-1}$. This formulation assumes no imported intermediate goods (see 'Measurement approach to the H-O-V model' in Section 7.4).
18. That is, $c_w = \sum_{z=1}^{N} c_z = \sum_{z=1}^{N} q_z = q_w$.
19. Let $\mathbf{p}$ be the $J \times 1$ vector of world prices of goods. Pre-multiply the net trade identity $\mathbf{t}_i = \mathbf{q}_i - \mu_i \mathbf{c}_w$ by this price vector and solve for the expenditure share to get $\mu_i = (\mathbf{pq}_i - \mathbf{pt}_i)/\mathbf{pc}_w = (Y_i - B_i)/Y_w$.
20. An equivalent statement of absolute factor abundance is: factor h is absolutely abundant in country i if income per unit of factor h in the world exceeds the income per unit of factor h in country i, that is, if $(Y_w/e_{wh}) > (Y_i/e_{ih})$.

21. The form of the adjustment will depend on what is assumed about preferences. Here the adjustment assumes preferences are identical and homothetic across countries.

22. Proposition S led Brecher and Choudhri (1983) (B&C) to declare that Leamer's resolution of the Leontief paradox raised another paradox. Specifically, in Leamer's data the US exported labor services. By proposition S, B&C argued that the US should then also have an excess supply of labor. However, B&C then noted that the difference between US per capita GDP and world per capita GDP implied an *absolute* scarcity of labor in the US. B&C's paradox is then that proposition S did not hold. Casas and Choi (1985) (C&C) later argued that B&C did not account for trade imbalance. With balanced trade, they showed that the US *imported* labor (that is, $f_{iL}^A < 0$). Thus, proposition S does hold and there is no paradox. Note that this debate mixes the definitions of *absolute* and *relative* factor abundance. For example, Leamer infers *relative* abundance while B&C and C&C infer *absolute* abundance. Leamer's inference of US abundance in capital relative to labor would therefore remain valid even if C&C had not validated proposition S.

23. The traditional statements of propositions S and R refer to a given country so the comparison of signs or ranks is made across factors. The reader should verify that similar statements of these propositions can also be made for a given factor and that in this case the comparison of signs or ranks would be made across countries.

24. For example, R2 can be obtained by multiplying both sides of R1 by $1/e_{wh}$ whereas R3 is obtained by multiplying R1 by $1/e_{ih}$.

25. More generally, between two matrices, one with columns equal to the factor contents of trade for each country, and the other the matrix with columns equal to the excess factor supplies for each country.

26. The terms $\delta_i \mathbf{e}_i$ in (7.80) indicate that assuming neutral differences in technology is equivalent to assuming neutral differences in the efficiency ("quality") of factors across countries.

27. Specifically, that consumption depends upon per capita income.

28. Importantly, Trefler also found evidence of non-neutral differences in productivity across factors so that, for example, capital rich countries use relatively capital-intensive techniques while labor rich countries use relatively labor intensive techniques. As discussed in 'Measurement approach to the H-O-V model' in section 7.4, this implies capital rich and capital poor countries lie in different cones of diversification, and hence relative factor prices are equalized only within each group of countries.

29. This can be modeled by modifying the H-O-V consumption equation $\mathbf{c}_i = \mu_i \mathbf{q}_w$ to be $\mathbf{c}_i = \mu_i(\lambda_i \mathbf{q}_i + (1 - \lambda_i)(\mathbf{q}_w - \mathbf{q}_i))$ where $\mathbf{q}_i$ is home goods, $\mathbf{q}_w - \mathbf{q}_i$ is foreign goods and $0 < \lambda_i \leq 1$ measures consumption bias toward home goods.

30. Davis and Weinstein estimate several variants of (7.81).

31. That is, just as one needs to measure the indirect use of factor services though purchases of domestically produced intermediate goods, one also needs to measure the indirect use of factors though purchases of foreign produced intermediate goods. As shown in Trefler and Zhu (2010), this effectively requires construction of a regional input–output model in which regions are countries and all bilateral flows of intermediate goods are taken into account.

32. See Baldwin and Hilton (1983).

33. Recall from Section 7.4.1 that $\mathbf{A}(\overline{\mathbf{w}})$ defines factor input requirements at some intermediate wage $\overline{\mathbf{w}}$ between the $\mathbf{w}_0$ and $\mathbf{w}_1$. Hence, there is the possibility, due to "factor intensity reversals," that the change in $\mathbf{w}$ may change factor requirements to such an extent that (7.82) may no longer be valid.

34. See Jones and Scheinkman (1977).

35. As Ethier (1984) notes, this requires $\theta_{jh} > 0$ for all j in both the initial and new equilibria. This means every factor employed by the industry whose price has risen must be re-employed somewhere else in the economy in the new equilibrium.
36. See Ethier (1984).
37. In fact, even more general statements are possible in this case. See Ethier (1984).
38. This follows from pre-multiplying (7.76) by $\mathbf{A}_i^{-1}$.
39. This section based on Dixit and Norman (1981).
40. This assumes identical tastes among consumers in each country.
41. This also assumes that the distribution of factor ownership across countries is fixed so that demands are independent of where factor incomes are generated. See Dixit and Norman (1981, pp. 107) for further discussion.
42. With N countries, the set of factor allocations that will replicate the integrated equilibrium is:

$$\Theta = \left\{ \mathbf{e}_1, \dots, \mathbf{e}_N \,|\, \exists\ \lambda_{ij}, 0 \le \lambda_{ij} \le 1\ \forall\, j\ \text{s.t.}\ \mathbf{e}_i = \sum_j \lambda_{ij} \mathbf{a}_i\, (\overline{\mathbf{w}})\, \overline{q}_j \right\}$$

where j indexes goods, i indexes countries and each $\mathbf{e}_i$ is an H-element vector of factor supplies allocated to country i. The trade equilibrium output of good j in country i when all resources are fully employed is $q_{ij} = \lambda_{ij} \overline{q}_j$.
43. In general, if $J > H$ then equations $\overline{\mathbf{e}} = \mathbf{A}(\overline{\mathbf{w}})\mathbf{q}$ have potentially many solutions since at most H of the J columns of $\mathbf{A}$ can be linearly independent. This means that (at most) $J - H$ outputs can be expressed in terms of the remaining H outputs.
44. For country i, this line is derived from $GDP_i = \overline{r}K_i + \overline{w}L_i$.
45. With identical homothetic preferences, country i will consume the fraction $\alpha_i = GDP_i / \sum_i GDP_i$ of every good, $0 < \alpha_i \le 1$. It then follows that country i's consumption vector ($\mathbf{d}_i$) is proportional to the integrated world's output (= consumption) vector ($\overline{\mathbf{q}}$): $\mathbf{d}_i = \alpha_i \overline{\mathbf{q}}$. To see this, pre-multiply the latter equation by the factor requirements matrix to derive country i's implicit consumption of factors as $\mathbf{A}(\overline{\mathbf{w}})\mathbf{d}_i = \alpha_i \mathbf{A}(\overline{\mathbf{w}})\overline{\mathbf{q}}$. Since $\mathbf{A}(\overline{\mathbf{w}})\overline{\mathbf{q}} = \overline{\mathbf{e}}$ we have $\mathbf{A}(\overline{\mathbf{w}})\mathbf{d}_i = \alpha_i \overline{\mathbf{e}}$.
46. Ethier (1984) suggests that the relevant requirement is that the number of international markets should exceed the number of factors. This derives from the fact that the dimensionality issue concerns the number of linearly independent columns (rows) in the $H \times J$ factor input matrix $\mathbf{A}(\mathbf{w})$. For example, in the case of FPE let H_T factors be traded internationally and H_N factors be immobile. In this case the prices of the traded factors will be determined in international markets so that the dimensionality requirement in terms of $\mathbf{A}(\mathbf{w})$ becomes $J \ge H_N$. Since $H_T + H_N = H$, the latter can also be written as $J + H_T \ge H$ which states that the number of international markets (in goods and factors) should exceed the number of factors.

References and additional reading

Generalizing the H-O-S Model

Bernhofen, D.M. and Brown, J.C. (2004), "A Direct Test of the Theory of Comparative Advantage: The Case of Japan," *Journal of Political Economy*, 112 (1), 48–67.
Deardorff, A.V. (1979), "Weak Links in the Chain of Comparative Advantage," *Journal of International Economics*, 9 (2), 197–209.

Deardorff, A,V. (1980), "The General Validity of the Law of Comparative Advantage," *Journal of Political Economy*, 88 (5), 941–957.

Deardorff, A.V. (1982), "The General Validity of the Heckscher-Ohlin Theorem," *American Economic Review*, 72, 683–694.

Dixit, A. and Norman, V. (1980), *Theory of International Trade* (London: Cambridge University Press).

Ethier, W. (1984), "Higher Dimensional Issues in Trade Theory," ch. 3 in R. Jones and P. Kenen (Eds.), *Handbook of International Economics*, Vol. 1 (Amsterdam: North-Holland), 131–184.

Gale, D. and Nikaido H. (1965), "The Jacobian Matrix and the Global Univalence of Mappings," *Mathematische Annalen*, 159, 81–93.

Jones, R. and Scheinkman, J. (1977), "The Relevance of the Two-Sector Production Model in Trade Theory," *Journal of Political Economy*, 85, 909–935.

Woodland, A. (1982), *International Trade and Resource Allocation* (New York: North-Holland).

General Surveys: Testing the H-O-S Model

Baldwin, R.E. (2008), *The Development and Testing of Heckscher-Ohlin Trade Models: A Review* (Cambridge, MA: MIT Press).

Bernhofen, D.M. (2010), "The Empirics of General Equilibrium Trade Theory: What Have We Learned?" Münchener Gesellschaft zur Förderung der Wirtschaftswissenschaft (CESifo)   Working Paper No. 3242 (Munich: Münchener Gesellschaft zur Förderung der Wirtschaftswissenschaft, CESifo GmbH).

Leamer, E.E. and Levinsohn, J. (1995), "International Trade Theory: The Evidence," ch. 26 in G. Grossman and K. Rogoff (Eds.) *Handbook of International Economics*, Vol. 3 (Amsterdam: North-Holland).

The H-O-V Model

Bowen, H.P., Leamer, E.E., and Sveikauskas, L. (1987), "Multicountry, Multifactor Tests of the Factor Abundance Theory," *American Economic Review*, 77 (5), 791–809.

Brecher, R. and Choudhri, E. (1982), "The Leontief Paradox, Continued," *Journal of Political Economy*, 90, 820–823.

Brecher, R. and Choudhri, E. (1988), "The Factor Content of Consumption in Canada and the United States: A Two Country Test of the Heckscher-Ohlin-Vanek Model," in Robert C. Feenstra (Ed.) *Empirical Methods for International Trade* (Cambridge, MA: MIT Press), 5–17.

Casas, F. and Choi, E. (1985), "The Leontief Paradox, Continued or Resolved?" *Journal of Political Economy*, 93, 610–615.

Davis, D. and Weinstein, D. (2001), "An Account of Global Factor Trade," *American Economic Review*, 91 (5), 1423–1453.

Davis, D. and Weinstein, D. (2003), "The Factor Content of Trade," in E.K. Choi and J. Harrigan (Eds.), *Handbook of International Trade* (Malden, MA: Blackwell).

Debaere, P. (2003), "Relative Factor Abundance and Trade," *Journal of Political Economy* 111 (3), 589–610.

Hamilton, C. and Svensson, L.E.O. (1983), "Should Direct or Total Factor Intensities Be Used in Tests of the Factor Proportions Hypothesis?" *Weltwirtschaftliches Archiv*, 119 (3), 453–463.

Hakura, D. (2001), "Why Does HOV Fail? The Role of Technological Differences within the EC," *Journal of International Economics*, 54 (2), 361–382.

Kohler, W. (1991), "How Robust Are Sign and Rank Order Tests of the Heckscher-Ohlin-Vanek Theorem," *Oxford Economic Papers*, 43 (1), 158–171.

Leontief, W. (1953), "Domestic Production and Foreign Trade: The American Capital Position Re-Examined," *Proceeding of the American Philosophical Society*, 97, 332–349.

Leamer, E.E. (1980), "The Leontief Paradox Reconsidered," *Journal of Political Economy*, 88 (3), 495–503.

Reimer, J. (2006), "Global Production Sharing and Trade in the Services of Factors," *Journal of International Economics*, 68 (2): 384–408.

Staiger, R.W. (1986), "Measurement of the Factor Content of Foreign Trade with Traded Intermediate Goods," *Journal of International Economics*, 21 (3/4), 361–368.

Trefler, D. (1993), "International Factor Price Differences: Leontief was Right!" *Journal of Political Economy*, 101(6), 961–987.

Trefler, D. (1995), "The Case of the Missing Trade and Other Mysteries," *American Economic Review*, 85 (5): 1029–1046.

Trefler, D. and Zhu, S. (2010), "The Structure of Factor Content Predictions," *Journal of International Economics*, 82, 195–207.

Inter-industry regression

Aw, B-Y. (1983), "The Interpretation of Cross-section Regression Tests of the Heckscher-Ohlin Theorem with Many Goods and Factors," *Journal of International Economics*, 14 (1/2), 163–167.

Baldwin, R.E. (1971), "Determinants of the Commodity Structure of US Trade," *American Economic Review*, 61, 126–146.

Baldwin, R.E. and Hilton, S. (1983), "A Technique for Indicating Comparative Costs and Predicting Changes in Trade Ratios," *Review of Economics and Statistics*, 105–110.

Bowen, H.P. and Sveikauskas, L. (1992), "Judging Factor Abundance," *Quarterly Journal of Economics*, 107 (2), 599–620.

Kohler, W. (1988), "Modeling Heckscher-Ohlin Comparative Advantage in Regression Equations: A Critical Survey," *Empirica*, 15 (2), 263–293.

Leamer, E.E. and Bowen, H.P. (1981), "Cross-Section Tests of the Heckscher-Ohlin Theorem: Comment," *American Economic Review*, 71 (4), 1040–1043.

Stern, R.M. and Maskus, K.V. (1981), "Determinants of US Foreign Trade, 1958-76," *Journal of International Economics*, 11 (2), 207–224.

Cross-Country Regression

Bowen, H.P. (1983), "Changes in the International Distribution of Resources and their Impact on US Comparative Advantage," *Review of Economics and Statistics*, 65, 402–417.

Hunter, L. and Markusen, J. (1988), "Per-Capita Income as a Determinant of Trade," in R.C. Feenstra (Ed.) *Empirical Methods for International Trade* (Cambridge, MA: MIT Press).

Leamer, E.E. (1984), *Sources of International Comparative Advantage: Theory and Evidence* (Cambridge, MA: MIT Press).

Stolper-Samuelson, Rybczynski and Factor Price Equalization

Baldwin, R.E. and Cain, G. (2000), "Shifts in Relative US Wages: The Role of Trade, Technology, and Factor Endowments," *Review of Economics and Statistics*, 82, 580–595.

Debaere, P. and Demiroglu, U. (2003), "On the Similarity of Country Endowments," *Journal of International Economics*, 59, 101–136.

Feenstra, R.C. and Hanson, G.H. (2003), "Global Production Sharing and Rising Inequality: A Survey of Trade and Wages," in E.K. Choi and J. Harrigan (Eds.), *Handbook of International Trade* (Oxford: Blackwell).

Harrigan, J. and Balaban, R. (1999), "US Wage Effects in General equilibrium: The Effects of Prices, Technology and Factor Supplies, 1963–1991," National Bureau of Economic Research Working Paper no. 6981 (Cambridge, MA: NBER).

Harrigan, J. (1997), "Technology, Factor Supplies and International Specialization: Estimating the Neoclassical Model," *American Economic Review*, 87, 475–494.

Harrigan, J. (1995), "Factor Endowments and the International Location of Production: Econometric evidence for the OECD, 1970–1985," *Journal of International Economics*, 39, 123–141.

Lawrence, R.Z. and Slaughter, M. (1993), "International Trade and American wages in the 1980s: Giant Sucking Sound or Small Hiccup?" Brookings Papers on Economic Activity: Microeconomics, 2, 161–226.

Leamer, E.E. (1988), "In Search of Stolper-Samuelson Linkages between International Trade and Lower Wages," in S.M. Collins (Ed.), *Imports, Exports, and the American Worker* (Washington, DC: Brookings Institution Press).

Leamer, E.E. (1984), *Sources of International Comparative Advantage: Theory and Evidence* (Cambridge, MA: MIT Press).

Kohli, U. (1990), "Price and Quantity Elasticities in International Trade," *Economic Letters*, 33, 277–281.

Schott, P. (2003), "One Size Fits All? Heckscher-Ohlin Specialization in Global Production," *American Economic Review*, 93 (3), 686–708.

Imperfectly competitive markets: trade and trade policy

8

Imperfect competition

The models presented in earlier chapters explain the direction and composition of trade on the basis of differences in countries' technologies and factor endowments. However, they do not account for two striking features of the data presented in Chapter 1. First is the disproportionately large volume of trade that flows between industrialized countries. Assuming that these countries have similar endowments and technologies, the Ricardo and Heckscher-Ohlin theories would suggest that trade between them as a proportion of their individual GDP would be rather smaller than between countries dissimilar in terms of technology and factor endowments. Second, the models do not account for the existence and extent of intra-industry trade and have little to say about its consequences.

This chapter reconciles theory with these observed features of international trade. It relaxes the assumptions of the conventional theory regarding market structure and the conditions of production by focusing on monopoly power, scale economies and product differentiation. The recognition that these factors can serve as independent explanations of trade is not recent, but it is only since the early 1980s that they have been integrated into general equilibrium models.

Imperfect competition modifies some fundamental relationships encountered in earlier chapters. The partial equilibrium analysis of oligopolistic markets conducted in section 8.1 clarifies in what ways it does. It shows in particular that when the number of competitors is small, the consequences of trade depend crucially on the form of oligopolistic interaction, and on whether the number of producers is given or adjusts in response to profit opportunities. Interestingly, it also shows that when firms hold market power an opening of borders to trade can generate a welfare gain even when it does not give rise to actual trade.

The sections that form the bulk of this chapter look at markets in which firms engage in monopolistic competition. In such markets, each firm produces a variety of a product that is distinct from the varieties produced by rival firms. Trade produces welfare gains by expanding the assortment of varieties of many goods accessible to each country's consumers. Section 8.2 shows that when firms operate in monopolistically competitive environments the emergence of trade does not depend on the existence of difference endowments of technologies. But, when gaps in endowments do exist, they retain their predictive power for the direction of trade. This is shown in section 8.3, which establishes how endowments and country sizes jointly determine the volume of total trade among countries and the portion of that trade that is intra-industry. A technical appendix derives the conditions that characterize equilibrium under monopolistic competition when consumer preferences are of the Dixit-Stiglitz type, as this chapter and the next one assume.

8.1   Market power and the gains from trade

We examine first how the interaction of country size and market structure determines the direction of trade. We consider an industry with n identical home firms and n^* identical foreign firms. Each home firm produces q units of output at a cost $F + cq$. It sells q_l units in its local market and exports q_x units. The home industry's total output is $Q = nq$. Total industry output divides into output sold locally (Q_l) and output exported (Q_x). Starred variables denote the same for the foreign country. The inverse demands for the home and foreign country are given as:

$$p = p(Q) \text{ and } p^* = p^*(Q^*) \text{ where } Q = Q_l + Q_x^* \text{ and } Q^* = Q_x + Q_l^*$$

We use the superscripts "a" and "f" to emphasize, where necessary, that a particular condition applies to an autarky or a trading equilibrium.

Cournot rivalry[1]

Recall that under Cournot rivalry all firms choose quantity simultaneously on the basis of their beliefs about their rivals' choices. Now assume that foreign consumers demand λ times as many units as home consumers at any price, that is: $p^*(x) = p(x/\lambda)$ for all $x > 0$. Demand elasticities are then equal in both countries when prices are the same.

Autarky equilibrium when the number of firms is given

When all home firms have the same cost function $C(q) = cq + F$ they earn a profit $\pi = p(\overline{Q} + q)q - cq - F$, where $\overline{Q} = Q - q$ denotes the combined output of the firm's $(n - 1)$ rival producers. Maximization of the profit function with respect to q yields the first order condition:

$$\frac{\partial \pi}{\partial q} = p(\overline{Q} + q) + q \frac{dp(\overline{Q} + q)}{d(\overline{Q} + q)} \frac{\partial (\overline{Q} + q)}{\partial q} - c = p(Q) + q \frac{dp(Q)}{dQ} - c = 0 \quad (8.1)$$

where $\partial \overline{Q}/\partial q = 0$ follows from the assumption that all firms choose their quantity simultaneously. Condition (8.1) gives the firm's profit maximizing quantity as a function of the combined production of its rival producers and is therefore called a *best response function*. Because $Q = nq$, (8.1) can be expressed as:[2]

$$mr(Q_a) \equiv p(Q_a) + \frac{Q_a}{n} \frac{dp(Q_a)}{dQ_a} = c \quad (8.2)$$

Note that $mr(Q)$ is marginal revenue as perceived by the individual firm. It is larger than industry marginal revenue, denoted as $MR(Q) \equiv p(Q) + Q \dfrac{dp(Q)}{dQ}$ for all $Q > 0$. The reason is that the industry produces n times as many units as the individual firm. Hence, an increase in quantity lowers the industry's revenue from the sale of infra-marginal units

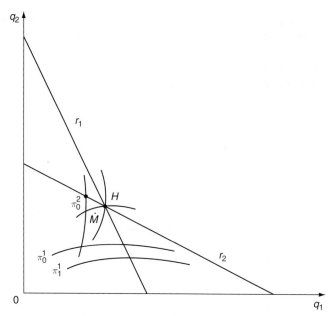

Figure 8.1 Best responses under Cournot rivalry

by n times as much as it lowers the revenue from the sale of infra-marginal units by the individual firm.

Figure 8.1 displays two loci of quantity combinations (q_1, q_2) under which the duopoly profits earned by firm 1 are π_0^1 and π_1^1. These loci are upward sloping when q_1 is small; they are downward sloping when q_1 is large. The reason is that for small q_1 the left-hand side of (8.1) is larger than c. If so, the profits earned by firm 1 increase when q_1 increases. It therefore takes an increase in q_2 to maintain the profits at their initial level. By contrast, when q_1 is large the firm's perceived marginal revenue exceeds its marginal cost. The firm's profits now fall when q_1 increases further. Hence, a decrease in q_2 is needed to maintain the profits at their initial level.

Since for *any* q_1 the profits earned by firm 1 decrease when q_2 increases, it must be true that $\pi_0^1 < \pi_1^1$. More generally, quantity combinations produce a higher profit for firm 1 when they lie on an iso-profit curve closer to the horizontal axis. Similarly, combinations of q_1 and q_2 yield a higher profit for firm 2 when they lie on a locus like π_0^2 which is closer to the vertical axis.

The best response function of firm 1 – denoted r_1 – intersects the maxima of firm 1's iso-profit curves. Similarly, r_2 – the best response of firm 2 – joins the right-most point of the iso-profit curves of firm 2. The best response functions are straight lines when demand is linear and marginal costs are constant. They intersect at point H, whose coordinates represent the Cournot equilibrium. Note that joint profits are not maximized at point H. They are highest at point M where the iso-profit curves of the two firms are tangent to each other.

One can show that r_1 has a slope less than -1 when perceived marginal demand is steeper than demand – that is, when $2p'(Q) + qp''(Q) < p'(Q)$. The same condition entails that the slope of r_2 is bounded by 0 and -1.[3] The implication is that each firm's optimal response to an increase in the output of the rival producer is to decrease its own output, but by a lesser amount. By differentiating (8.2) we obtain $dQ/dn > 0$ and $dq/dn < 0$. The latter, and the condition $p'(Q) < 0$, jointly imply that profit earned by the individual firms falls when n increases.

Denoting the elasticity of market demand by $\eta(p) \equiv [dp(Q)/dQ][Q/p(Q)]$, we can express the autarkic first order conditions in the home and foreign countries as:

$$p(Q_a)\left[1 + \frac{1}{n\eta(p_a)}\right] = c \quad \text{and} \quad p(Q_a^*/\lambda)\left[1 + \frac{1}{n\eta^*(p_a^*)}\right] = c^* \qquad (8.3)$$

We now show that allowing trade perturbs the autarky equilibrium even when autarky prices are the same in both countries.

Free trade equilibrium for a given number of firms

We begin by considering the case $c = c^*$ and $n = n^*$ which ensures that autarky prices are the same in both countries, even when country sizes are different. Opening borders to trade creates a single market with inverse demand given by $p = p\left[(Q + Q^*)/(1 + \lambda)\right]$. At every price, the elasticity of this demand equals the elasticity of the home and the foreign demand. The implication is that if all firms maintained their autarkic production levels, the price $\tilde{p}$ in the integrated market would be the same as the autarky prices p_a and p_a^*. That is, $\tilde{p}(Q_a + Q_a^*) = p\left((Q_a + Q_a^*)/(1 + \lambda)\right) = p_a(Q_a) = p_a^*(Q_a^*)$. However, since $\tilde{\eta}(p_a) = \eta(p_a) = \eta^*(p_a)$, it follows from (8.3) that $\tilde{p}(Q_a + Q_a^*)\left[1 + \frac{1}{(n + n^*)\tilde{\eta}(\tilde{p})}\right] > c$. Because marginal revenue is downward sloping, the latter inequality implies that each firm produces a larger quantity under free trade than under autarky. The intuition behind this result is that, when borders open, each firm gains access to the other country's market, but it must share its own market with a larger number of competitors. Competition intensifies and brings price closer to marginal cost.

Consider now the direction of trade, assuming $\lambda > 1$. Because all home and foreign firms produce the same quantity under free trade, and because the foreign market absorbs a quantity λ times larger than the home country, it must be true that the home industry exports in the trading equilibrium. The transition from autarky to free trade unambiguously increases total welfare in the smaller country. To see why, note first that total welfare in the home country would have increased had the quantity produced by the home industry expanded by an amount equal to the increase in quantity demanded by local consumers. As price would have fallen, consumers' gains would have surpassed producers' losses. But in response to the move to free trade, the home country's output expands by an amount that exceeds the increase in quantity demanded by local consumers. The extra production is exported. The export profits earned by firms based in the smaller country make a further contribution to that country's welfare.

The same cannot be said about the foreign country. If the output of the foreign industry expands at all, it does so by less than the quantity demanded by local consumers. The ensuing fall in profits earned by foreign firms may well surpass the gain from increased competition which accrues to foreign consumers.

In the particular case where the two industries and countries are mirror images of each other, that is, when $\lambda = 1$, $n = n^*$ and $c = c^*$, the transition to free trade does not set off a cross-border flow of products. Even so, consumer welfare and total welfare increase. The reason is that price falls as competition intensifies.

The analysis is more complicated when $n \neq n^*$. When $c = c^*$, the autarky price is lower in the country that has the larger number of firms. Because the free trade price is lower than the lowest of the autarky prices, consumer welfare in both countries is higher. In the trading equilibrium, the home industry's share of world output is $n/n + n^*$. Since trade equalizes prices between countries, home consumers demand a portion $1/(1+\lambda)$ of world output. Hence, the home country exports (imports) if λ is larger (smaller) than n^*/n.

Freedom of entry and exit

We now extend the analysis by examining the case where firms are free to enter and exit the industry in response to profit opportunities. The assumption that the number of active firms adjusts in response to profits is clearly out of place if only one firm possesses the necessary technology, or if entry, or perhaps exit, is prohibited by regulation. Generally, this assumption is less applicable in the short run than in the long run. When examining the effects of a transition from autarky to free trade, one takes the long-term perspective. When investigating how a change in trade policy influences the variables of interest, it is appropriate also to consider short-run effects.

A firm that contemplates joining an industry must think about the type of competition it will face following entry. It will enter if and only if it expects to earn a profit post-entry. A market served by n symmetric firms is said to be in a Cournot free-entry equilibrium if and only if n is the largest integer that satisfies the first order condition (8.4) below and the free entry conditions (8.5):

$$p(Q) + qp'(Q) - c = 0 \tag{8.4}$$

$$p(Q)\frac{Q}{n} - c\frac{Q}{n} - F \geq 0 \quad \text{and} \quad p(Q)\frac{Q}{m} - c\frac{Q}{m} - F < 0 \text{ where } m > n \tag{8.5}$$

We can clarify the role of the fixed cost F, or more generally of scale economies, by going through the following thought experiment: start from a situation where firms earn positive profits and let F increase slightly. At first, the profits of all firms fall, and output per firm remains constant. If F increases further it eventually reaches a threshold at which condition (8.5) ceases to hold. As this point, a first firm exits and the output of each remaining firm increases. If F increases further, output per firm remains constant at the new higher level until a second threshold is crossed. At that point, a second firm exits and output of the remaining firms again jumps upward. This process continues as F increases further until fixed cost attains a value where even a monopoly producer can no longer earn a profit.

Because condition (8.5) does not lend itself to comparative statics analysis, it is customary to replace the weak inequality sign by an equality sign, and to treat the number of firms as a continuous variable. Differentiation of (8.4) and the modified condition (8.5), which now reads $p(Q)\frac{Q}{n} - c\frac{Q}{n} - F = 0$, yields $dn/dF < 0$. Because in reality n is an integer, this negative sign is interpreted to mean that a small increase in F will either leave n unchanged or lower it.

The question of how a transition from autarky to free trade affects the number of active firms is easily addressed in a framework in which the home and foreign firms share the same cost function and have identical demands. For an insight into this we consider the following thought experiment. We freeze the number of firms in each country at the free-entry autarky equilibrium. We then open the borders to trade. The ensuing intensification of competition due to the increase of the number of competitors lowers profits below the autarky level. Because profits were initially zero they now become negative. We now unfreeze the number of firms. Since producers are free to exit, some cease production. A new Cournot equilibrium emerges in which the number of firms is smaller than under autarky. Because the mark-up is smaller than under autarky the firms that remain active must produce a larger quantity in order to cover their fixed costs. Consumers gain as price is lower; total surplus, which equals consumer surplus since profits are zero, also increases.

Transport costs

Although transport costs have come down significantly in the past few decades they still account for a significant portion of the delivered cost for many goods. Hummels (2007) estimates that in 2004 the average freight cost on US imports accounted for about 6 percent of import value in the case of ocean shipping and about 5 to 10 percent in the case of air shipping. He also determines that the median individual shipment of US imports incurred 9 dollars in transportation costs in 2004 for every dollar in duty paid.

When firms bear transportation costs, the mere opening of borders to trade does not necessarily equalize prices across countries. It does, however, bring about a convergence of prices when the gap in autarky prices exceeds the marginal transportation cost. Specifically, when the transportation cost is τ *per unit*, the gap between the home and foreign price under free trade satisfies one of the conditions in (8.6) below:

$$|p - p^*| < \tau \text{ or } |p - p^*| = \tau \tag{8.6}$$

A greater price disparity brings about entry by traders who purchase the good in the country where price is lower and resell it in the country where price is higher. This arbitrage operation reduces the gap until it equals τ.[4]

We will say that markets are *segmented* when the first condition in (8.6) holds; when the second condition holds we will say that markets are *connected by arbitrage*, or simply *connected*.

Segmented markets[5]

When home and foreign firms sell in their local market and also export, their respective profits are given by:

$$\pi = p(Q_l + Q_x^*)q_l + p^*(Q_x + Q_l^*)q_x - c(q_l + q_x) - F \tag{8.7}$$

$$\pi^* = p(Q_l + Q_x^*)q_x^* + p^*(Q_x + Q_l^*)q_l^* - c^*(q_l^* + q_x^*) - \tau\, q_x^* - F \tag{8.8}$$

where $Q_l = nq_l$, $Q_x = nq_x$, $Q_l^* = n^*q_l$ and $Q_x^* = n^*q_x$. The quantities q_l and q_x that home and foreign firms sell in the home country satisfy the first order conditions:[6]

$$p(Q_l + Q_x^*) + q_l p'(Q_l + Q_x^*) = c \tag{8.9}$$

$$p(Q_l + Q_x^*) + q_x^* p'(Q_l + Q_x^*) = c^* + \tau \tag{8.10}$$

Conditions (8.9) and (8.10) clearly indicate that the equilibrium values of q_l and q_x^* do not depend on the characteristics of demand in the foreign country. The reason is that marginal costs are constant. In fact, (8.9) and (8.10) are identical to the first order conditions one would obtain under autarky if the n^* foreign firms were also located in the home market and produced at a marginal cost $c^* + \tau$.

Condition (8.10) and the corresponding condition for the foreign country yield positive q_x^* and q_x for sufficiently small c, c^* and τ. Thus, in equilibrium there is cross-hauling of an identical commodity across borders.

To understand what drives such two-way trade, we revert to the case where the two countries have the same consumer demand, the same number of firms and the same production costs. Clearly, autarky prices are then equal in both countries. As soon as borders are opened to trade, each firm sees the opportunity to increase its profit by allocating a first unit of output to the foreign country, where its contribution to profits equals the foreign country's autarky price less delivered cost.[7] Cross-hauling takes place as long as the delivered marginal cost of exports remains smaller than the marginal revenue from exports.

Brander and Krugman (1983) show that such *cross-hauling* gives rise to reciprocal dumping. Specifically, it produces an equilibrium in which the price net of transportation cost at which each firm sells in its export market is lower than the price at which it sells in its local market.

A fall in τ stimulates competition. It produces a greater inter-penetration of markets and reduces price in both countries. However, the effect on world welfare is ambiguous. To see why, assume that demand in each country originates from a utility function $u = U(Q) + M$, where M is consumption of a competitively supplied "numeraire" good.[8] The industry's contribution to world welfare $\left(W^{world}\right)$ can then be expressed as:

$$W^{world} = \left[U(Q_l + Q_x^*) - cQ_l - (c + \tau)Q_x - nF\right]$$
$$+ \left[U^*(Q_x + Q_l^*) - c^*Q_l^* - (c^* + \tau)Q_x^* - n^*F\right]$$

where the first and second terms denote the welfare in the home and foreign country, respectively. Differentiating this expression and using $p = U'(Q)$ yields:

$$\frac{dW^{world}}{d\tau} = -\frac{d\tau(Q_x + Q_x^*)}{d\tau} + \left[(p - c)\frac{d(Q_l + Q_x^*)}{d\tau} + (p^* - c^*)\frac{d(Q_l^* + Q_x)}{d\tau}\right]$$
$$- (c^* - c)\frac{d(Q_x^* - Q_x)}{d\tau} \tag{8.11}$$

The first term on the right is the change in total transport cost. The third term captures the welfare effect from the savings in production cost that arise from the replacement of imports by local production, or vice versa. The middle term captures the effect on welfare resulting from the change in the intensity of competition. Because price exceeds marginal cost, its effect on welfare moves in the same direction as total quantity.

We now show that $dW^{world}/d\tau$ may be positive or negative. To do so, it is sufficient to establish that the sign of the derivative is ambiguous for the special case $n = n^*$ and $c = c^*$. We note first that:

$$\frac{d\tau(Q_x + Q_x^*)}{d\tau} = \begin{cases} Q_x + Q_x^* > 0 & \text{for } \tau = 0 \\ \\ \tau_{\max}\dfrac{d\left(Q_x + Q_x^*\right)}{d\tau} < 0 & \text{for } \tau = \tau_{\max} \end{cases} \tag{8.12}$$

where $\tau_{\max}$ is the threshold transportation cost at which all exports cease.

We also note that the middle term of (8.11) is negative. Indeed, differentiation of (8.9) and (8.10) yields $dQ_x^*/d\tau < 0$ while $p' + qp'' < 0$ implies $-1 < dQ_l/dQ_x^* < 0$. Thus, total output sold in the home country declines as τ increases. It then follows from (8.12) that $dW^{world}/d\tau < 0$.

We now observe that $p^* = c + \tau_{\max} = p = c^* + \tau_{\max}$ when $\tau = \tau_{\max}$. Given this, the middle term of (8.11) equals $\tau_{\max}\left[d\left(Q_x + Q_x^*\right)/d\tau + d\left(Q_l + Q_l^*\right)/d\tau\right]$ which implies $dW^{world}/d\tau < 0$. On the basis of continuity, we infer that the transportation cost affects word welfare as shown in Figure 8.2. An increase in τ when τ is small lowers output, and the latter contributes to a welfare loss in proportion to the gap between price and marginal cost. This gap is larger for larger τ. The ambiguous welfare effect of τ derives from transportation cost. When τ is small an increase in τ produces an increase in total transportation cost because the quantity

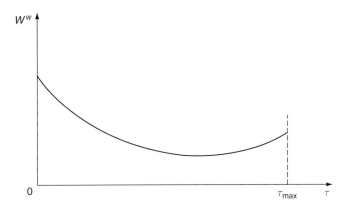

Figure 8.2 World welfare and transport cost

transported is large. The combined effect of lower sales in each country and of increased total transportation cost reduces welfare. By contrast, when τ is large, a further increase reduces total transportation cost. Welfare increases in τ when the fall in total transportation cost surpasses the loss attributable to the decline in quantity sold in each country.

Jointly, conditions (8.9) and (8.10) show that the bilateral exchange of an industry's products is balanced when demand and cost are the same in both countries, and when each country's industry has the same number of firms. Bernhofen (1999) shows that when one of these conditions does not hold *and the others do*, the Grubel-Lloyd (GL) index of intra-industry trade relates inversely to the gap in the variable for which the two countries are asymmetric. He calculates the GL index for bilateral US–German trade flows of 38 undifferentiated bulk chemicals produced by both countries. Then he estimates an equation that has the GL index as the dependent variable and cross-country differences in cost, country size and in the number of producers as explanatory variables. Estimation results reveal a negative and highly significant association between each of these differences and the GL index.[9]

Markets connected by arbitrage

When the transportation cost τ is smaller than the gap in prices that satisfy the conditions (8.9) and (8.10) one of the following conditions (8.13) must hold true:

$$p = p^* + \tau \quad \text{or} \quad p^* = p + \tau \tag{8.13}$$

Producers optimally choose quantities with the understanding that an extra unit sold in either lowers prices in both countries. To be precise, a portion $p^{*'}/(p^{*'} + p')$ of every additional unit produced in either country is ultimately consumed in the home country, and the share $p'/(p^{*'} + p')$ in the foreign country. Firms do not see distinct marginal revenues for each country as in the case of market segmentation. They see a single marginal revenue function that depends on their total sales.

When $p = p^* + \tau$, a foreign firm is indifferent between the following: (a) selling a quantity q at the price p^* in the foreign market and letting parallel traders export a portion of that quantity to the home market; (b) selling the very same portion into the home market at the price p, and bearing a transport cost τ per unit exported. The same cannot be said about home firms. Home firms can sell locally at p, but only obtain the net price $p^* - \tau = p - 2\tau$ per unit exported. Thus, when $p = p^* + \tau$ output produced in the foreign country is the only output exported. Similarly, only the home country exports when $p^* = p + \tau$. Cross-hauling of the same good does not take place.

Whether markets are in fact segmented or connected depends not only on the transportation cost. The number of firms in each market and the gap in costs across countries also matter.

Bertrand rivalry

Firms that sell a homogeneous good engage in Bertrand competition when they set a price and commit to sell any quantity demanded from them at that price. Consumers buy only from the seller who sets the lowest price. A firm captures the entire market when it undercuts, however slightly, the prices set by other producers. Firms that set the same price share equally in consumer demand if their common price is lower than the prices set by rival producers.

When the cost of the second-lowest-cost producer is higher than the price the lowest cost firm would set as a monopoly, the equilibrium price equals the price the lowest-cost firm sets as a monopoly. When the monopoly price exceeds the unit cost of the second-lowest-cost firm, the lowest-cost firm optimally sets a price marginally lower than the unit cost of the second-lowest-cost producer, and the second-lowest-cost firm sets a price equal or higher than its cost.[10]

Consider now an n-firm home industry and an n^*-firm foreign industry. Assume that $c < c^*$, and that transportation costs are zero. Also assume that the foreign firm's unit cost is lower than the price a home firm would set as a monopoly, formally, $p_m(c) \geq c^*$. When $n = n^* = 1$, autarky prices are $p_m(c)$ and $p_m^*(c^*)$. In the trading equilibrium the price is c^* in both countries (or, more precisely, $c^* - \varepsilon$) and the home country firms serves consumers in both countries. Consumer welfare is higher in both countries than under autarky because price is lower. World welfare is higher than under autarky because the average cost of world output is lower and because prices are closer to marginal (and average) cost. The foreign firm loses from the move toward free trade because its profits drop to zero. The home firm may gain or lose depending on the relative size of the two markets, and on its cost advantage over the foreign firm.

When $n = n^* \geq 2$, autarky prices are equal to the unit cost of local producers and the free trade price is c. Moving from autarky to free trade increases welfare in the foreign country because foreign consumers gain and the profits of foreign firms remain at zero. The home country's welfare is unaffected since consumer and producer surplus in that country are unchanged. The home firms sell a larger quantity under free trade but their profit margin remains zero.

Positive transport costs increase the number of possible outcomes. In particular, they may allow firms to set prices independently in each country. We consider two cases: 1) $c < c + \tau < c^*$ and 2) $c < c^* < c + \tau$. When $n = n^* = 1$ and monopoly prices satisfy the conditions $p_m(c) > c^* + \tau$ and $p_m^*(c^*) > c + \tau$, a transition from autarky to free trade lowers the home price to $c^* + \tau$ regardless of whether $c^* - c$ is larger or smaller than τ. In the trading equilibrium, the home firm sells into both countries when the gap is larger than τ; it sells only into the home country when it is smaller. The move from autarky to free trade raises the surplus of home and foreign consumers and world welfare in both cases.

When the gap in costs is smaller than τ, welfare increases because the move to free trade lowers price below a country's autarky price; the foreign firm earns lower profits in the trading equilibrium. When the gap in costs is larger than τ world welfare increases because the transition to free trade reduces average production costs. However, trade eliminates the profits of the foreign firm. When $n \geq 2$ and $n^* \geq 2$, autarky prices equal average production costs in both countries. Hence, moving from autarky to free trade increases a country's welfare only if it lowers the cost of producing the output consumed in that country. We already know this will happen when $c < c + \tau < c^*$.

Bertrand versus Cournot competition

The intuitively appealing feature of Bertrand competition is that firms actually set their price. When they instead set quantity (as in Cournot) it is unclear how prices are determined in the absence of an auctioneer. In contrast, the appealing feature of Cournot competition is that the equilibrium price converges gradually towards marginal cost as the number of firms becomes larger; under Bertrand competition the competitive price emerges as soon as two firms produce at the same cost. When firms produce distinct varieties of a good – an assumption that will be made in subsequent sections – the difference between quantity and price competition is not as stark. Also, the existence of equilibria in which firms compete in price is no longer contingent on average variable cost being constant.

Openness to trade and market power: Trade liberalization in Turkey

The finding that trade brings price closer to marginal cost lends itself to empirical verification. Such verification typically relies on the estimation a relationship derived from the first order conditions (8.14):

$$p(Q) + q_i \frac{dp(Q)}{dQ} \psi_i = \frac{dC(q_i)}{dq_i} \quad i = \{1 \ldots . n\} \tag{8.14}$$

where $\sum_{i=1}^{n} q_i = Q$; $\psi_i = \partial Q/\partial q_i$. The term ψ_i is called the conjectural variation. When $\psi_i = 1$ for all i, the n equations that form the system (8.14) determine a Cournot equilibrium. When $\psi_i = 0$ they characterize a competitive equilibrium regardless of the number of firms. When $\psi_i = n$, (8.14) yields the equilibrium one would obtain if firms maximized joint profits.

This relationship between ψ_i and marginal cost is apparent when rewriting (8.14) as:

$$\beta_i \equiv \frac{p}{dC(q_i)/dq_i} = \left[1 - \frac{q_i}{Q} \frac{\psi_i}{\eta}\right]^{-1} \text{ where } \eta = -\frac{dQ}{dp} \frac{p}{Q}. \tag{8.15}$$

An older interpretation of the conjectural variation parameter is that it represents the effect of a firm's quantity choice on rivals' quantity choices. Such an interpretation is nonsensical in a static model since firms cannot observe their rivals' actions when they are choosing their own quantities. Since they cannot observe them they cannot be influenced by them. Nevertheless, models based on specifications such as (8.15) are common in empirical studies. These studies take the view that a decrease in β_i reflects an intensification of competition in some unobserved dynamic game.

At the end of 1983, Turkey's government announced a number of significant import liberalization measures that were implemented almost immediately. Levinsohn (1993) examines how these liberalization measures affected the market power enjoyed by Turkish firms. He assumes that the production function of firm i at period t has the form $q_{it} = \phi_{it} f(\underline{e}_{jt})$, where $\underline{e}_{jt}$ is an H-dimensional vector of input quantities, and ϕ_{jt} is a productivity shock. A linear approximation of the production function around q_{jt} gives $\Delta q_{it} = \phi_{it} \left[\sum_{i=1}^{H} \frac{\Delta f_{it}}{\Delta e_{ijt}} \Delta e_{ijt}\right] + f_{it} \Delta \phi_{it}$ where $\Delta x_t = x_t - x_{t-1}$. Since $\phi_{it} \frac{\Delta f_{it}}{\Delta e_{ijt}} = w_{ijt} \frac{dC(q_{it})}{dq_{it}}$ where w_{ijt} denotes the price paid by firm i for factor j at time t, the production function can be expressed as $\Delta q_{it} = \beta_{it} \left[\sum_{i=1}^{H} \frac{w_{ijt}}{p_t} \Delta e_{ijt}\right] + f_{it} \Delta \phi_{it}$.

Levinsohn assumes that firms are subject to a yearly industry-wide productivity shock and a firm-specific shock.[11] His estimating equation is:

$$\Delta q_{jt} = \beta_1 \left[\sum_{i=1}^{H} \frac{w_{ijt}}{p_t} \Delta e_{ijt} \right] D_1 + \beta_2 \left[\sum_{i=1}^{H} \frac{w_{ijt}}{p_t} \Delta e_{ijt} \right] D_2 + f_{jt}(\gamma_t + \upsilon_{jt})$$

where β_1 and β_2 capture pre- and post- liberalization price-cost margins and:

$$D_1 = \begin{cases} 1\,for\,t = 1984 \\ 0\,for\,t = 1985 - 86 \end{cases} \quad and \quad D_2 = \begin{cases} 0\,for\,t = 1984 \\ 1\,for\,t = 1985 - 86 \end{cases}$$

The estimation results indicate that three out of the ten industries in the sample had a mark-up significantly larger than 1 during the pre-liberalization period whereas only one industry had a coefficient $\beta > 1$ (at the 95 percent level of confidence) after liberalization. Levinsohn then partitions the industries into three groups: (1) industries with a pre-liberalization high mark-up, in which protection decreased; (2) industries in which protection increased; and (3) industries with zero or negative price-cost margins that experienced trade liberalization. He finds that, in accordance with theory, the price-cost margin fell in all three industries belonging to the first group. The declines are significant at the 90 percent level for two industries. Levinsohn also finds as theory predicts, an increase in the mark-up for industries in the second group. Theory does not yield any prediction about the effects of liberalization for the third group and no clear pattern of change in the price-cost margin emerges from the data.

8.2 Product differentiation and intra-industry trade

Products can be differentiated horizontally or vertically. Two varieties of a good are vertically differentiated if all consumers prefer to purchase the same variety when the two varieties are equally priced. Differentiation is horizontal when under the same circumstances some consumers prefer the first variety and other consumers prefer the second variety.

There are two modeling approaches to horizontal differentiation. The first posits that consumers are identical and have a taste for variety. That is, consumers' utility is higher when their total consumption of any given product is spread over a larger assortment of varieties of that product. Under this approach, international trade proceeds from consumers' desire for a wider assortment of varieties than is produced by the local industry. The alternative approach postulates that consumers differ from one another, have no taste for variety and that they purchase only the variety that gives them the highest utility per dollar spent.[12] In this case, the individual consumer purchases either a locally produced variety or an imported one. Intra-industry trade takes place when each country is home to some consumers who derive the largest surplus from a variety produced in another country. The following sections consider only the first "love of variety" approach.[13]

Trade, real wages and the number of varieties

We first consider the Krugman (1979) model, which assumes a representative consumer who is identical in the home and foreign country and has preferences represented by the utility $V(v_1, v_2 \ldots \ldots) = \sum_{i=1}^{n} u(v_i)$ [$u' > 0$ and $u'' < 0$], where v_i denotes the consumption of variety i. Because the sub-utilities $u(.)$ enter the utility function symmetrically, consumers optimally purchase the same quantity of each variety when all varieties are equally priced.

On the production side, labor is the sole input, and firms use l_i units of labor to produce q_i units of a single variety i: the demand for labor is given as $l_i = a + cq_i$. The home country is endowed with L workers (consumers) who earn a wage w. The total production cost of q_i units of variety i is then $C(q_i) = wl_i = w(a + cLv_i)$. When all firms share the same cost function and all varieties enter the utility function symmetrically, all firms produce the same quantity and set the same price. This price satisfies the first order condition:

$$p\left(1 - \frac{1}{\eta}\right) = wc \quad \text{or} \quad \frac{p}{w}\left(1 - \frac{1}{\eta}\right) = c \tag{8.16}$$

where $\eta = -(\partial q / \partial p)p/q$ denotes the elasticity of demand faced by the individual firm. Freedom of entry ensures equality between price and average cost:[14]

$$p = w\left[\frac{a}{q} + c\right] \tag{8.17}$$

Since firms are symmetric the zero profit condition under autarky can be expressed as:

$$\left.\frac{p}{w}\right|_a = \left[\frac{a}{Lv_a} + c\right] \tag{8.18}$$

where the subscript "a" again indicates that (8.18) is an autarky condition. Figure 8.3 displays this zero profit condition as the downward sloping curve labeled ZP.

When $d\eta(v)/dv < 0$, condition (8.16) can be represented by the upward sloping curve labeled FO in Figure 8.3. In equilibrium, individual consumption of each variety and the real price (p/w) are then given by the coordinates of A. The number of producers and consumers follows from:

$$L = n(a + cq) = n(a + cLv) \tag{8.19}$$

Condition (8.18) shows that when country size increases, the ZP curve shifts downward. The new equilibrium has lower individual consumption per variety, and a lower real price p/w.

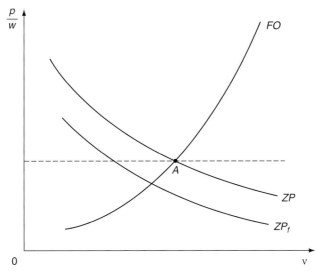

Figure 8.3 Free-entry equilibrium when goods are differentiated

In addition, because v is smaller, it follows from (8.19) that the larger economy produces a larger number of varieties. The implication is that welfare under autarky is higher in a larger country because: 1) the prevailing wage allows consumers to purchase a larger quantity; 2) that quantity is spread over a wider assortment of varieties.

We now assume that the home country trades at zero cost with a foreign country. The foreign country uses the same technology and is endowed with L^* workers (consumers). The opening to trade creates a single market of size $L + L^*$. Consumers now maximize the utility $U(v_1, v_2 \ldots \ldots) = \sum_{i=1}^{n} u(v_i) + \sum_{i=n+1}^{N} u(v_i)$, where $N = n + n^*$ is the total number of available varieties and n^* is the number of varieties produced in the foreign country.

In the trade equilibrium free entry into the integrated market ensures:

$$\frac{p}{w}\bigg|_f = \left[\frac{a}{(L+L^*)v_f} + c\right] \qquad (8.20)$$

Figure 8.3 displays condition (8.20) as the curve ZP_f. Because (8.16) is the same as under autarky, if follows that p/w and consumption per variety are lower in the trading equilibrium than under autarky.

Output per firm in the trading equilibrium is $q_f = (L+L^*)v_f$. Because p/w is lower in the trading equilibrium, it must be true [see (8.17)] that $q_f > q_a$. It is the lower mark-up in the trading equilibrium which requires that firms produce a larger quantity in order to cover their fixed cost. Since $q_f > q_a$ implies $l_f > l_a$ and since labor endowments are fixed, it must be true as well that in the trading equilibrium each country has fewer firms than under autarky.

The equilibrium number of consumed varieties in the trading equilibrium follows from the full employment condition $L + L^* = N[a + cq_f] = N[a + c(L+L^*)v_f]$. Clearly, $N > \max(n_a, n_a^*)$ as $L + L^* > \max(L, L^*)$ and $v_f < v_a$. This means that workers (consumers) in both countries gain from the move from autarky to free trade because: 1) they consume more units per hour worked; and 2) they can spread their consumption over a larger number of varieties.

Because home and foreign firms produce the same quantity in the open economy, each country's share of firms is equal to its share of the world's labor endowment. Moreover, since preferences, prices and wages are the same in both countries, the value of each country's imports (M and M^*) is equal to the country's income (wL for the home country) multiplied by the proportion of varieties produced by the other country. Specifically,

$$M = wL\frac{L^*}{L+L^*} = wL^*\frac{L}{L+L^*} = M^* \qquad (8.21)$$

Thus, trade in the differentiated good is balanced. The large country imports fewer varieties but spends more on each imported variety. Condition (8.21) also shows that for given $L + L^*$ the volume of trade is highest when $L = L^*$.

The constant elasticity of substitution (CES) utility

Consider now the CES utility function $V = \left[\sum_{i=1}^{n} v_i^\rho\right]^{\frac{1}{\rho}}$, where $\rho = (\sigma - 1)/\sigma$ and σ denotes the elasticity of substitution among varieties. This utility function generates demands for individual varieties that have constant price elasticity. Since this type of demand is easy to work with it has been used extensively in the trade literature. The appendix to this chapter characterizes the equilibrium that emerges from monopolistic competition when demands derive from CES utility.

The appendix shows that when the cost function is $C(q) = (F + cq)w$, where w and q denote respectively the wage and the quantity of output, all firms produce the quantity $q = \frac{a}{b}(\sigma - 1)$ in equilibrium and set a real price $\frac{p}{w} = c\frac{\sigma}{\sigma - 1}$. Neither the equilibrium price nor the quantity produced by individual firms depends on country size.

A first implication is that, in the absence of trade costs, a transition from autarky to free trade does not change output per firm. Because the transition has no effect on labor endowments, it also follows that the number of varieties produced in each country remains the same.[15] Even so, the price index P falls when countries open their borders to trade. The reason is that the number of varieties accessible to their consumers becomes larger.

The first order condition (8.16) can be represented by the dotted horizontal line shown in Figure 8.3. A move from autarky to trade shifts the ZP curve downward and therefore the new intersection involves lower consumption per variety, but unchanged p/w.

Based on the Krugman model, Feenstra (1994) proposes an index that captures how the introduction of new varieties affects a country's CES-based price index. The index treats a country's entire production of a product as a single variety and assumes that no two countries produce an identical variety. Broda and Weinstein (2006) generalize the Feenstra index to the case of several CES aggregate goods. They calculate that the expansion of the range of varieties accessible to US buyers from 1972 to 2001 contributed to an annual fall of 1.2 percent in the "true" import price index. They also determine that US consumers would have been willing to forgo 2.6 percent of their income to extend the range of varieties they obtained through imports. In contrast, Arkolakis *et al.* (2008) find that the new varieties imported into Costa Rica following its liberalization contributed little to the country's welfare. They argue that the gains from trade hardly depend on what happens to total variety.

The home market effect

We now examine how transport costs affect the cross-country allocation of production. We assume an economy that has a perfectly competitive industry producing a homogeneous product by means of constant returns to scale technology, and a monopolistic competitive industry producing a differentiated product. The homogeneous product serves as the numeraire. The representative consumer is the same in both countries, and has preferences represented by the utility $U = H^{1-\alpha}V^{\alpha}$, where H denotes consumption of the homogeneous good and $V(v_1, v_2, \ldots)$ is the CES function discussed above. Exporters of the homogenous good incur no transportation costs. Under this assumption, each country will have the same wage w when trade is free, and each country will produce the homogeneous good. Exporters of the differentiated good bear an iceberg type transportation cost – that is, they must ship $\tau > 1$ units to ensure that 1 unit arrives at the intended destination. Firms set their prices independently in each market.

The existence of a transportation cost τ for the differentiated good implies that foreign consumers pay τp for a variety that the home firm sells locally at the price p. Likewise, home consumers pay τp^* for an imported variety that sells for p^* in the foreign country. Because all varieties enter utility symmetrically, and because the wage and the technology are the same in both countries, it must be true that $p = p^*$. The home and foreign price indices are therefore given by $P = [np^{1-\sigma} + n^*(\tau p)^{1-\sigma}]^{1/1-\sigma}$ and $P^* = [n(\tau p)^{1-\sigma} + n^* p^{1-\sigma}]^{1/1-\sigma}$.[16] This in turn implies that the home and foreign demand for individual varieties produced in the home country are $(p^{-\sigma}/P^{1-\sigma})\alpha wL$ and $[(\tau p)^{-\sigma}/(P^*)^{1-\sigma}]\alpha wL^*$, where wL and wL^* stand for home and foreign national income. Likewise, the demands by home and foreign consumers for each variety produced in the foreign country are $[(\tau p)^{-\sigma}/P^{1-\sigma}]\alpha wL$ and $[p^{-\sigma}/(P^*)^{1-\sigma}]\alpha wL^*$.

Because firms must ship $\tau > 1$ units to have 1 unit delivered in a foreign market, the sum of outputs produced by all home-based firms satisfies condition (8.22), and correspondingly the total output produced by foreign firms satisfies condition (8.23):

$$nq = n(p^{-\sigma}/P^{1-\sigma})\alpha wL + n[(\tau p)^{-\sigma}/(P^*)^{1-\sigma}]\alpha wL^*\tau \qquad (8.22)$$

$$n^*q = n^*[(\tau p^{-\sigma})/P^{1-\sigma}]\alpha wL\tau + n^*[p^{-\sigma}/(P^*)^{1-\sigma}]\alpha wL^* \qquad (8.23)$$

By choosing units such that $w = p = 1$, and setting $\varsigma \equiv \tau^{1-\sigma} < 1$, conditions (8.22) and (8.23) can be expressed as:

$$\frac{q}{\alpha} = \frac{1}{n+n^*\varsigma}L + \frac{\varsigma}{n\varsigma+n^*}L^* = \frac{\varsigma}{n+n^*\varsigma}L + \frac{1}{n\varsigma+n^*}L^*. \qquad (8.24)$$

From this it follows that:

$$\frac{n}{n+n^*} = \frac{1}{1-\varsigma}\left[(1+\varsigma)\frac{L}{L+L^*} - \varsigma\right] \text{ for } \frac{\varsigma}{1+\varsigma} < \frac{L}{L+L^*} < \frac{1}{1+\varsigma} \qquad (8.25)$$

Because $0 < \varsigma < 1$, (8.25) implies the following: 1) the larger country's share of firms exceeds its share of workers/consumers; 2) increasing the relative size of the larger country produces a proportionately larger increase in the share of firms based in that country; 3) the larger country's share of firms relates positively to transportation costs.

Because all home and foreign firms produce the same quantity, and since $n/n + n^* > L/L + L^*$ whenever $L > L^*$, it also follows that the larger country is a net exporter of the differentiated good. Condition (8.25) also shows that a country does not produce the differentiated good when its share of population is smaller than $\varsigma/1 + \varsigma$ and that it is the only producer of the differentiated good when its share of the population is larger than $1/1 + \varsigma$.

Krugman (1980) refers to the predisposition of production to concentrate in larger markets in the presence of scale economies and transportation costs as the "home market effect." The intuition behind this effect is a simple one: being located in the larger country allows firms to avoid the transportation cost on the greater part of their sales.[17]

Davis (1998) shows that the home market effect vanishes when the cost of transporting the homogenous good is not substantially lower than the cost of transporting the good produced by the increasing returns to scale industry. He stresses that there exists no convincing empirical evidence to support a claim that transportation costs or trade barriers are on average higher in industries that produce differentiated products, and they are certainly not of an order of magnitude that would give rise to a home market effect. However, in subsequent work Krugman and Venables (1999) show that the home country effect can materialize in a multiple good world where some homogeneous goods have low transportation costs and where some industries that produce differentiated goods do not bear a fixed cost.

Hanson and Xiang's (2004) model assumes a continuum of differentiated industries and that countries differ in size but are identical in terms of consumer preferences and technology. By locating in the larger country where the wage is higher, firms trade off more costly production against lower transportation costs. The model predicts a positive relationship between country size and the propensity to produce more highly differentiated goods which are costly to transport.

Hanson and Xiang (2004) also provide a test. First, they classify a sample of industries into two groups: group m, which contains industries that produce mostly differentiated goods that also have high transportation costs; and group o, which consists of industries that produce the least differentiated goods and have low transportation costs. To isolate the effect of size, they select pairs of exporting countries that face common trade policy barriers in their destination markets. This pairing eliminates biases that would arise from differences in the trade barriers erected by importing countries. Then they estimate the equation:

$$\ln \frac{S_{mlk}/S_{msk}}{S_{olk}/S_{osk}} = \alpha + \beta f \left[\frac{Y_l}{Y_s} \right] + \Phi \left(X_l - X_s \right) + \theta \ln \left[\frac{d_{lk}}{d_{sk}} \right] + \varepsilon_{molks}$$

where S_{rik} is sales of product $r(=m,o)$ by country $i = \{$large (l) or small $(s)\}$ to country k, Y_i is market size of country i as measured by its *GDP* and f is an increasing function, X_i is a vector of controls that capture the relative production cost in country i of industries m and o, d_{ik} is the distance between the exporting country i and importing country k, and ε_{mojks} is the error term.

The numerator of the dependent variable is the ratio of exports of a large country relative to exports of a small country for goods produced by an industry belonging to group m. The denominator is the same ratio for an industry belonging to group o. By using a ratio of ratios as the dependent variable, Hanson and Xiang scale out the size of the importing country. To test for the the home market effect is to test that $\beta > 0$, that is, larger countries export more highly differentiated, high transport cost goods relative to smaller countries.

The estimation results lend support to the theoretical model. The dependent variable is found to increase in relative exporter *GDP*. The estimated β is 0.42 and is highly significant. It shows that an exporting country that is 10 percent larger than another exporting country has on average exports of goods from industries belonging to group m that are 4.2 percent larger than the exports of such goods by a smaller country, where the m group exports are normalized by the two countries' relative exports of goods produced by industries belonging to group o.

8.3 Factor endowments and monopolistic competition

We now consider the role that differences in factor endowments play in determining the direction and composition of trade when goods are differentiated. Following Helpman (1981) and Helpman and Krugman (1985), we embed monopolistic competition in a two-sector Heckscher-Ohlin framework. One industry produces a homogeneous good by means of a constant returns to scale technology; this good serves as the numeraire. The second industry uses an increasing returns to scale technology to produce a differentiated good. Firms in the differentiated good sector engage in monopolistic competition whereas firms in the homogeneous sector are perfect competitors. Both industries use labor and capital as inputs. Production technologies are identical in both countries, but the differentiated industry is more capital-intensive. The home country is capital abundant, that is, $K/L > K^*/L^*$.

Consumer preferences are represented by a two-level homothetic utility function $U = U[H, V(v_1, v_2, \ldots.)]$, where H denotes consumption of the homogeneous good and $V = \left[\sum_{i=1}^{n} v_i^{\rho} \right]^{\frac{1}{\rho}}$ is a sub-utility of the form encountered in section 8.2. Utility maximization involves a two-step process. First, consumers allocate their total income between the homogeneous and the differentiated good. Second, they allocate their total expenditure on the differentiated good to the individual varieties. When the upper tier utility function $U[\cdot]$ is the Cobb-Douglas function $H^{1-\alpha}V^{\alpha}$, the share of aggregate spending on the differentiated good is α. An equal quantity of each variety is consumed when all are equally priced. The price index of the differentiated good is given as $P = n^{1/1-\sigma}p$, where n is the number of varieties and p is the common price of all varieties.[18] For given prices and total spending, consumer welfare increases when the number of varieties increases.

Inter-industry and intra-industry trade

Figure 8.4 displays the factor allocation in the integrated economy endowed with $L + L^*$ units of labor and $K + K^*$ units of capital. In this integrated economy, all goods and factors are perfectly mobile across borders and industries. The labor and capital used in production of the homogeneous good are given by the coordinates of point Q_H^W when measured with respect to origin O. By proper choice of units, the quantity of the homogeneous good is represented by the length of the vector $\overline{OQ_H^W}$. Similarly, the quantity of the differentiated good is represented by the length of the vector $\overline{OQ_D^W}$. The quantities of labor and capital used in production of the differentiated goods industry are given by the coordinates of point Q_D^W when measured with respect to origin O. The slopes of the vectors $\overline{OQ_H^W}$ and $\overline{OQ_D^W}$ are the factor intensities in the production of each good.

We now consider the question of how output is allocated across countries when labor and capital cannot cross national borders. Let the coordinates of point E (measured with respect to origin O) be the labor and capital endowments of the home country; the coordinates of point E with respect to O^* then denote the labor and capital endowments of the foreign country.

It is apparent from Figure 8.4 that the home country can fully employ its factors of production by producing quantities $\overline{OQ_H}$ and $\overline{OQ_D}$ of the homogeneous and differentiated good, using capital and labor in the same proportion as the integrated economy. The foreign country can also fully employ its labor and capital using the factor intensities of the integrated economy. The foreign country produces the quantity $\overline{O^*Q_H^*} = \overline{Q_H Q_H^W}$ of the homogeneous good and quantity $\overline{O^*Q_D^*} = \overline{Q_D Q_D^W}$ of the differentiated good. Thus, given their endowments, the two countries can jointly produce the same quantities of goods produced in the integrated economy with the world amounts of labor and capital fully employed. As discussed in Chapter 7, this implies factor price equalization, that is, factor prices will be the same across countries, and free trade will ensure the equality of goods prices.

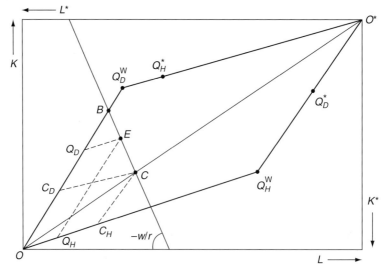

Figure 8.4 Endowments, inter-industry and intra-industry trade

We now establish the pattern of consumption. Since the total value of consumption equals total factor income, the line through E with its slope equal to the negative of the wage-rental ratio $(-w/r)$ is appropriately interpreted as a budget constraint. Since both countries consume goods in the same proportion, it must be true that the factor content of consumption is identical in the two countries. This implies that the factor content of consumption is given by the coordinates of C, the point where the budget line intersects the main diagonal OO^*. Because factor income equals the value of consumption, the ratio $OC/OO^* = z$ represents the home share of world consumption and income.

To determine home consumption, we pass through point C lines that are parallel to $\overline{OQ_H^W}$ and $\overline{OQ_D^W}$. The length of the vector $\overline{OC_H}$ then measures home consumption of the homogeneous good and the length of vector $\overline{OC_D}$ measures home consumption of the differentiated good. Foreign consumption of each good is similarly obtained by constructing a parallelogram through E and O^*. Given this, Figure 8.4 shows that the home country is a net exporter of the differentiated good. The length of the vector $\overline{C_D Q_D}$ measures its net exports, that is, the difference between the volume of home varieties exported and the volume of foreign varieties imported. The length of the vector $\overline{Q_H C_H}$ measures the home country's imports of the homogeneous good.

Dividing the outputs of the differentiated good (shown as $\overline{OQ_D}$ and $\overline{O^*Q_D^*}$ in Figure 8.4) by the equilibrium output per firm q yields the number of home and foreign varieties, denoted n and n^*. Note that output per firm is the same in both countries since prices and technologies are the same. Given this, world output of the differentiated good is $nq + n^*q$. Home consumption of the differentiated good is $z(nq + n^*q)$ and foreign consumption is $z^*(nq + n^*q)$, where $z^* = 1 - z$. Thus, $nq - z(nq + n^*q) = (z^*n - zn^*)q$ represents the home country's net exports of the differentiated good.

We observe that the capital abundant country is the net exporter of the capital-intensive good, and of the services of capital. In this regard, the vector $\overline{EC}$ shows the factor content of the home country's trade. We remark that, in contrast to the prediction of the classical Heckscher-Ohlin model, trade does not vanish when the endowment point lies on the diagonal OO^*. Instead, the inter-industry component of trade disappears, the net factor content of trade becomes zero. All trade is therefore intra-industry.

Finally, if both industries produce differentiated goods then all trade is intra-industry. The country abundant in capital is a net exporter of the capital-intensive differentiated good and a net importer of the labor-intensive differentiated good.

The volume of trade

We now examine how the value of total world trade (VTT) relates to factor endowments. Denoting by p the free trade price of the differentiated good, the value of total world trade can be written:

$$VTT = z^* p Q_D + \left\{ z p Q_D^* + \left[z(Q_H + Q_H^*) - Q_H \right] \right\}$$

where the first term denotes the value of home exports (equal to the value of foreign imports of the differentiated good) and the term in curly brackets denotes the value of home imports. The latter is the sum of home imports of differentiated goods and the difference between home consumption and home production of the homogeneous good. Because trade is balanced, the second term equals the first term, implying:

$$VTT = 2z^* p Q_D \tag{8.26}$$

In Figure 8.4, consider a shift of the endowment point E inside the parallelogram $OQ_D^W O^* Q_H^W$. Because this shift does not influence factor or goods prices, its effect on total trade can be decomposed as:

$$\frac{dVTT}{VTT} = \frac{dz^*}{z^*} + \frac{dQ_D}{Q_D} \tag{8.27}$$

This expression states that the volume of total world trade increases with an increase in the relative size of the foreign country (the net importer of the differentiated good) and also with an increase the production of the differentiated good in the home country.

We now consider a movement in the endowment point E in Figure 8.4 that leaves the home country's capital to labor ratio unchanged. This change will bring about an equi-proportionate change in the home country's production of both goods. Since price will remain the same, the home country's GDP will change in the same proportion as the increase in its endowments, that is $dz/z = dQ_D/Q_D = dGDP/GDP$. Since $z^* = 1 - z$ implies that $dz/z = -(dz^*/z^*)(z^*/z)$, (8.27) can be expressed as:

$$\frac{dVTT}{VTT} = \left[1 - \frac{z}{z^*}\right]\frac{dz}{z} \tag{8.28}$$

This expression states that the value of total world trade increases in the size of the home country as long as the home country's share of world income is smaller than the foreign country's share. The value of total world trade decreases if the home country's share of world income exceeds the foreign country's share. Thus the value of total world trade is highest when the two countries are equally sized. Condition (8.28) also implies, in contrast to the Heckscher-Ohlin model, that movements of the endowment point E along the main diagonal influence the volume of trade.

When the endowment point moves along the line that passes through E and C, country sizes remain constant – that is, dz/z. In this case, condition (8.27) reduces to:

$$\frac{dVTT}{VTT} = \frac{dQ_D}{Q_D} \tag{8.29}$$

It follows from (8.29) that a reallocation of factors that raises the capital per worker endowment in the capital abundant country increases the volume of total world trade. This is also predicted by the traditional Heckscher-Ohlin framework.

When both goods are differentiated, each country imports a fixed share of the production of every variety of every good produced by its trading partner. Letting $p_1 = 1$ and p_2 denote respectively the price of the first and the second differentiated good, we can express the total volume of world trade as:

$$VTT = z\left[Q_1^* + p_2 Q_2^*\right] + z^* \left[Q_1 + p_2 Q_2\right] = zGDP^* + z^* GDP$$

In this expression, the first term on the right is the value of the home country's imports; the second term on right hand side is the value of its exports. When trade is balanced, the expression reduces to:

$$VTT = 2zGDP^* = 2zz^* GDP^{world} \text{ where } GDP^{world} = GDP + GDP^* \tag{8.30}$$

Since world GDP is unaffected by movements of the endowment point inside the factor price equalization set, the volume of world trade is determined only by the product zz^*. Since, $z = 1 - z^*$ it follows that VTT is largest when $z = z^*$.

Figure 8.5 displays the loci of constant VTTs as downward sloping lines. The volume of trade is largest along the line that passes through M, the midpoint of the diagonal. The volume of trade declines as the endowment point moves towards iso-volume lines farther from M.

Expression (8.30) generalizes to a multi-sector, multi-country, multi-factor world, and it also applies to a subgroup of countries whose trade is not balanced. Specifically, for any subgroup A of countries one can show (see Problem 8.6):

$$\frac{VTT^A}{GDP^A} = z^A \left[1 - t^A + \sum_{j \in A} z_j^A t_j^A - \sum_{j \in A} \left(z_j^A \right)^2 \right] \tag{8.31}$$

where $z^A = GDP^A / GDP^{world}$ is the share of world GDP accounted for by countries belonging to group A; $z_j^A = GDP_j / GDP^A$ is the share of country j's GDP in the group A's GDP; t_j^A is the excess of exports over imports of country j as a proportion of GDP^A; and $t^A = \sum_{j \in A} t_j^A$. Note that when $t_j = 0$ for all j's, the bracketed term in (8.31) becomes $\left[1 - \sum_{j \in A} \left(z_j^A \right)^2 \right]$. The expression $\left[1 - \sum_{j=1}^{n} (z_j)^2 \right]$ is called the similarity index because it increases as countries become more equal in size.[19]

Empirical evidence

Helpman (1987) provides the first empirical evidence regarding relationship (8.32). He calculates the annual value of intra-group trade for a set of 14 Organisation for Economic Co-operation and Development (OECD) countries relative to their joint GDP for the years 1956 to 1981. Choosing OECD countries is sensible since the bulk of the trade among such developed countries is intra-industry. He then graphs the yearly value of the world trade ratio against the contemporaneous values of the term $\left[1 - t^A + \sum_{j \in A} z_j^A t_j^A - \sum_{j \in A} \left(z_j^A \right)^2 \right]$. The graph reveals a clear positive relationship, but the small sample size precludes an assessment of the statistical significance of the positive relationship.

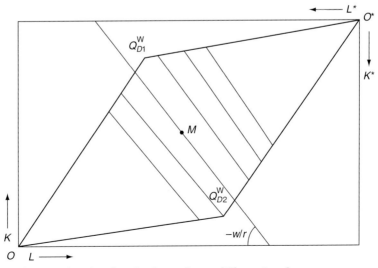

Figure 8.5 Volumes of trade when both goods are differentiated

Hummels and Levinsohn (1995) take a different approach. The country groups they form are country-pairs. This is appropriate since (8.31) holds for groups of any size. By grouping countries in pairs they generate 91 observations for each year between 1962 and 1983. This sample size is large enough to allow statistical testing of the relationship. The estimating equation is:

$$\ln\left(VTT_t^{i+j}\right) = \alpha \ln\left[GDP_t^{i+j} \times \left(1 - (z_t^{i,ij})^2 - (z_t^{j,ij})^2\right)\right] + v^{ij} + \varepsilon_t^{ij} \qquad (8.32)$$

where GDP_t^{i+j} is the joint GDP of countries i and j in year t; $z_t^{i,ij}$ denotes country i's share of the joint GDP of countries i and j at time t; $v^{ij} = \mu^{ij} + \ln(z^{ij})$ is a country fixed effect that is assumed constant over time, and ε_t^{ij} is an idiosyncratic disturbance term.[20] Non-random factors such as trade barriers, distance, a common border and language, which systematically affect bilateral trade flows, are captured by country-pair fixed effects.

Column 1 of Table 8.1 shows the baseline estimation result obtained by Hummels and Levinsohn (1995) for OECD countries. The estimated coefficients are consistent with the hypothesis that country size dispersion positively influences trade volumes. Interestingly, the authors also find a positive and significant relationship when they estimate equation (8.32) in a random sample of non-OECD countries. This finding is surprising since the assumptions that demands are similar and competition is monopolistic are generally thought to be inappropriate for such countries.

Hummels and Levinsohn note that in the data sample of non-OECD country pairs the dependent variable is zero for 142 of the 1456 observations. Since this may bias results, they also estimate the equation below which is expressed in levels rather than logs:

$$VTT_t^{i+j} = \alpha\left[GDP_t^{i+j} \times \left(1 - (z_t^{i,ij})^2 - (z_t^{j,ij})^2\right)\right] + v^{ij} + \varepsilon_t^{ij} \qquad (8.33)$$

Column 2 of Table 8.1 reports the findings from fixed effects estimation. The results clearly show a significant positive sign for country similarity.[21]

Debaere (2005) claims that the positive coefficient in Hummels and Levinsohn (2005) derives from a positive correlation between countries' size and their trade volume rather than

Table 8.1 Estimated effects for total trade and country size

	Hummels & Levinsohn OECD (1)	Hummels & Levinsohn Non-OECD (2)	Debaere OECD Log (3)	Debaere Non-OECD Log (4)	Debaere OECD Tobit (5)	Debaere Non-OECD Tobit (6)
α_0	1.405	1.57E-3				
	(110.8)	(24.4)				
α_1			1.57	−0.96	−0.06	4E-05
			(14.3)	(0.99)	(6.00)	(1.33)
α_2			0.47	1.98	0.013	0.046
			(9.4)	(2.1)	(3.3)	(9.2)
R^2	.865/.981	.304/6.71	0.61	0.02	0.28	−.08
# of obs	2002	1456	1820	1320	1820	1320

t-statistic in brackets.
Source: Hummels and Levinsohn (1995) and Debaere (2005).

from the similarity of country pairs' *GDP*s. He argues that the larger trade volumes of larger counties could explain a positive estimate for α, even if similarity of size has no effect on total trade. Debaere also argues that Hummels and Levinson's test is weak because their model does not account for changes over time in country pairs' share of world output. Accordingly, he estimates equation (8.34) which accounts for the term z^A in (8.31):

$$\ln VTT_t^{ij} - \ln GDP_t^{ij} = \gamma^{ij} + \alpha_1 \ln z_t^{ij} + \alpha_2 \ln \left(1 - (z_t^{i,ij})^2 - (z_t^{ji,ij})^2\right) + \varepsilon_t^{ij} \quad (8.34)$$

This specification allows a separate measurement of the impact of joint country size in relation to world *GDP*, as well as the similarity of country sizes. It does not impose equality of the coefficients of country size and size similarity as does (8.31). Also, the equation captures bilateral trade frictions using a multiplicative fixed effect.

Column 3 of Table 8.1 shows the Debaere's estimates from fixed effect regression with time-specific effects for the group of OECD countries. The coefficients show that country similarity and the share of country pair in the world economy each contribute positively to the volume of bilateral trade. The coefficients are statistically different from zero and different from each other.

For the sample of non-OECD country pairs, Debaere's (2005) encounters the same problem as Hummels and Levinsohn (2005) in that a substantial proportion (about 7 percent) of the observations show zero bilateral trade. He proposes two solutions to this problem. The first is to act as if the reported zeroes in fact represent small numbers. He can then use the logarithm of a small number whenever a zero trade value is reported. The second solution is to specify the equation in levels (as in (8.33)) and use the Tobit technique for estimation. Columns 4 and 6 of Table 8.1 display the estimation results for each method.

The estimated coefficient for similarity reported in column 4 contrasts with the coefficient for similarity shown in column 3. Not only is the similarity coefficient not significant for the non-OECD group, its sign suggests an effect opposite to that predicted by Helpman (1987). Column 6 on the other hand reveals a positive, but not significant, effect of similarity.

Debaere (2005) concludes that his overall findings corroborate the positive effect of similarity for OECD countries but not for non-OECD countries. He stresses that only the logarithmic specification allows for the inclusion of transportation costs that have the theoretically preferred multiplicative form. He also notes that the R^2's are much higher for the OECD sample than for the non-OECD sample.

Recent work by Kamata (2010) stresses that the equations estimated by Hummels and Levinsohn (1995) and by Debaere (2005) fail to account for the fact that countries, including those belonging to the OECD, also trade homogeneous goods. Taking this fact into account, he finds that country-pair volumes of bilateral trade in differentiated products, as a proportion of their joint production of differentiated products, is a function of the similarity of the countries' *GDP*s and the share of their *GDP*s derived from the production of differentiated goods.

The intra-industry share of trade

The value of intra-industry trade is measured as the value of the matching two-way trade in goods within the same industry. Equivalently, intra-industry trade is the component of total trade whose elimination would not alter the value of net trade in an industry. When net trade (exports minus imports) is zero, the value of intra-industry trade equals twice the difference between total trade and inter-industry trade. In the two-country, two-sector world we have studied in this chapter, the value of intra-industry trade is $2pzQ_D^*$. It then follows from (8.26) that the share of intra-industry trade in total trade (*IITS*) will be given as:

$$IITS = \frac{zQ_D^*}{z^*Q_D} = \frac{zn^*}{z^*n}$$

As indicated when discussing Figure 8.5, changes in endowments that keep the endowment point E inside the factor price equalization set do not change p. Therefore, such changes will affect *IITS* only though their effect on the quantity of the differentiated good that each country produces. Hence, endowment changes that increase the capital–labor endowment ratio in the capital-abundant home country increase Q_D at the expense of Q_D^*. As a result, the intra-industry share of total trade falls.

In a multi-country setting with M industries, the share of intra-industry trade between countries i and j is measured by the Grubel-Lloyd index (see Chapter 2):

$$IITS^{ij} = \frac{2 \sum_{m \in M} p_m \min\left[z^i Q_m^i, z^j Q_m^i\right]}{\sum_{m \in M} p_m \min\left[z^i Q_m^j + z^j Q_m^i\right]} \tag{8.35}$$

Unfortunately, the analysis of the effects of factor endowment changes on the Grubel–Lloyd index does not carry over in a straightforward manner in the multidimensional setting. Helpman and Krugman (1985) provide insights by using the Lerner diagram displayed as Figure 8.6. Figure 8.6 depicts the iso-value curves, also called unit value isoquants, for four goods. Each curve is the locus of the amounts of labor and capital required to produce one dollar's worth of output. Good "a" is the most capital-intensive and good "d" is the least capital-intensive. Country i's endowment of capital relative to labor is given by the slope of the ray labeled $k_i = K_i/L_i$. The country's unit cost line is shown as the line with slope $-w_i/r_i$.

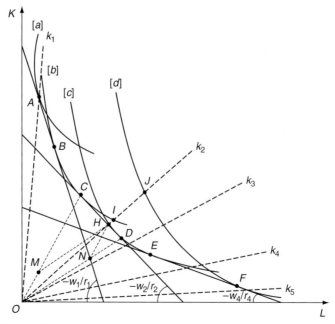

Figure 8.6 A Lerner diagram

Each country produces either a single good or two goods. To see why, consider country 2. To generate one dollar of value from the production of good "d" the country would utilize the amounts of labor and capital given by the coordinates of point J. Clearly, it would be more efficient to produce the same dollar value via good "b", as this would require inputs given by the coordinates of point I. But it would be even more efficient to produce only good "c". This implies that country 2 will use its factors most efficiently (and fully employ its factors) when it produces both good "b" and good "c". The amount of labor and capital used to produce each good is given by the coordinates of points M and N. These points are found by drawing through H (the point where the ray k_2 intersects the line with slope $-w_2/r_2$) lines parallel to the rays that go from the origin to points D and C. These are the points at which the iso-cost line with slope $-w_2/r_2$ is tangent to the iso-value curves "b" and "c".[22]

More generally, a country whose endowment ray k_i intersects a unit cost line connecting the tangency points of two iso-value curves will produce a combination of the corresponding two goods. For example, country 1 with a capital per worker endowment shown by the slope of k_1 will produce goods "a" and "b", country 4 will produce goods "c" and "d", and country 3 will produce only good "c".

Figure 8.6 shows that a pattern of trade emerges when industries are ranked by their factor intensity. When goods are differentiated, there is intra-industry trade and inter-industry trade between the countries whose relative factor supplies are not too far apart. For example, trade arises between countries 1 and 2, between countries 2 and 3 and between countries 2 and 4. Because countries with very similar endowments either produce the same good, or the same two goods, their bilateral trade is only intra-industry. At the other end of the spectrum one finds countries whose endowments are far apart, such as countries 1 and 4 and countries 2 and 5. Their bilateral trade is exclusively inter-industry trade.

These observations suggest the following hypotheses: 1) the share of intra-industry bilateral flows is larger for countries with similar endowments and 2) the share of intra-industry trade within a group of countries is larger the smaller the disparity of incomes within the group.

Helpman (1987) tests the first hypothesis by calculating the intra-industry trade share in total trade between all pairs of of OECD countries. He then estimates the following equation for every year between 1970 and 1981:

$$IITS^{ij} = \alpha_0 + \alpha_1 \ln \left| \frac{GDP^i}{N^i} - \frac{GDP^j}{N^j} \right| + \alpha_2 \min \left[\ln GDP^i, \ln GDP^j \right]$$
$$+ \alpha_3 \max \left[\ln GDP^i, \ln GDP^j \right] + \varepsilon^{ij} \qquad (8.36)$$

In this equation, N^i and N^j denote the populations of countries i and j. The absolute difference in per capita $GDPs$ is a proxy for the gap in endowments; the "min" and "max" variables control for country size effects.

Helpman (1987) finds that, in accordance with theory, estimation of (8.36) yields a negative value of α_1, although evidence for this negative relationship becomes weaker toward the end of his sample period. In addition, he finds that the size of the smaller country correlates positively and the size of the larger country correlates negatively with the intra industry share in total trade (IITS), although the latter coefficient is not statistically significant.

Hummels and Levinsohn (1995) call attention to two possible weaknesses of Helpman's (1987) analysis. They stress that per capita income is a weak proxy for differences in endowments when more than two factors enter production. They also point to a long-standing debate on the question of whether similarity in per capita income proxies for similarity in endowments, or similarity in consumer tastes. This question dates back to Linder's hypothesis that a country manufactures a good for the home market before it exports it. The implication is that countries with similar levels of per capita income have similar tastes, and for that reason develop similar goods for local use. They will at a later date export similar products. If the latter is true, a positive estimate of α_1 might reflect the impact of similarity of demands rather than similarity in endowments.

Hummels and Levinsohn (1995) explore this hypothesis by estimating an equation in which the dependent variable is the logistic transformation of *IITS*, and where $\ln \left| GDP^i/N^i - GDP^j/N^j \right|$ is replaced by two variables:[23] $\ln \left| K^i/L^i - K^j/L^j \right|$ and $\ln \left| T^i/L^i - T^j/L^j \right|$, where K^i, T^i and L^i denote the capital stock, the land endowment and the working population of country *i*. The sample consists of annual data for the period 1962 to 1983. Hummels and Levinsohn find a negative and significant effect for the difference in land endowments, which they attribute to the lack of intra-industry trade in agricultural products. Their regression reveals that the gap in capital per worker has a negative and significant effect on the *IITS* in early years of their sample, but that this negative effect loses significance by the middle years of their sample period and in fact turns positive in the last two years of their data. The estimated sign of the "min" term is positive for all years and significant for the years 1962–76. The sign of the "max" term is negative for all sample years, but is never significant.

Finally, Hummels and Levinsohn (1995) take advantage of the panel nature of their data and pool their 22 years of observations. Pooling allows them to assess the effect of changes in endowments over time. This allows a more natural test because the theory only predicts how *ITTS* evolves as endowments change for a given country pair, holding all other things constant: a condition that cannot be captured by the use of cross-sectional data alone.

Hummels and Levinsohn use a fixed effects method to estimate the following equation:

$$IITS_t^{ij} = \alpha_1 \ln \left| \frac{K_t^i}{L_t^i} - \frac{K_t^j}{L_t^j} \right| + \alpha_2 \min \left[\ln GDP_t^i, \ln GDP_t^j \right]$$

$$+ \alpha_3 \max \left[\ln GDP_t^i, \ln GDP_t^j \right] + v^{ij} + \varepsilon_t^{ij}$$

where v^{ij} is a country-pair specific variable that sweeps out the country-pair specific effects. Estimation yields a positive and significant coefficient for the gap in capital per worker.[24] The sign of the coefficient of the "min" variable is again positive and highly significant. The hypothesis that idiosyncratic differences explain much of the observed intra-industry trade is borne out by the fact that a very large proportion of the variation in *ITTS* is explained by the country-pair dummies. This suggests that factors not accounted for in the model – possibly distance and tax policy toward multinationals – play an important role.

8.4 Concluding remarks

This chapter has explored the causes and consequences of trade under oligopoly and monopolistic competition. When markets are oligopolistic, countries may trade with partners with whom they share the same technologies and factor costs. The direction and welfare effects of such trade depend in a complex way on the relative size of the trading partners and the structure of national industries. Interestingly, the opening to trade may produce welfare gains even when no actual trade takes place. The gains arise from a reduction of monopoly power in national markets that brings prices closer to marginal costs. Empirically, the effect of trade on market power can be assessed, and in this regard the effects predicted by the theory are generally supported by the data.

Transportation costs introduce an extra element. When such costs are substantial, the transition from autarky to free trade can set off a wasteful cross-hauling of identical commodities. The existence of such two-way trade is contingent on Cournot rivalry and on the segmentation of national markets.

The assumption that consumers value variety provides a different motive for intra-industry trade. Under monopolistic competition, the gains from trade then include that consumers gain access to a wider assortment of product varieties. When trade reduces the margin between price and marginal cost, firms that do not exit the industry increase their rate of output to ensure that their fixed costs are covered. The increased exploitation of scale economies constitutes an additional gain from trade. The monopolistic competition model also explains the "home market effect," that is, why industries that produce highly differentiated goods that incur high transportation costs tend to locate in the largest markets.

When embedded in a general equilibrium framework that assumes countries differ from each other in endowments only, the monopolistic competition model yields predictions consistent with the Heckscher-Ohlin theory. Specifically, the monopolistic competition model predicts that the capital abundant country will export more varieties and will export a larger total quantity of the more capital-intensive differentiated good than it imports. Unlike the prediction of the standard Heckscher-Ohlin model, the monopolistic competition model does not predict that trade vanishes when countries are equally endowed in terms of capital per worker; instead, the inter-industry component of trade disappears leaving only intra-industry trade.

The general equilibrium framework also generates predictions regarding the volume of bilateral trade between groups of countries. In this regard, the model predicts that the volume of such trade depends on the combined income of the group and on the disparity in national incomes within the group. These predictions find a measure of empirical support with regard to trade among OECD countries, whose bilateral trade is primarily intra-industry, and whose consumers can be reasonably assumed to share the same tastes. No such support for the model's predictions has yet been found for the trade among poorer countries.

Although the general equilibrium framework discussed in this chapter generates a gravity equation specification (see Chapter 6), one should not infer that the superior performance of such a specification represents support for the monopolistic competition model. Alternative models that have complete specialization may generate similar specifications for total trade. As stressed by Feenstra (2004), in order to test whether monopolistic competition explains trade flows one should look for hypotheses that arise only in this model. One such hypothesis is the home market effect.

Problems

8.1 Let the home and foreign demands be $Q = a - p$ and $Q^* = (a - p^*)\lambda$ where $\lambda > 1$. Assume $n = n^* = 2$ and $c = c^* = 0$. Also assume that all firms are Cournot competitors and that transportation costs are zero. Determine the range of λ for which welfare increases in both countries in response to a move from autarky to free trade. Define welfare as the sum of consumer surplus and industry profits.

8.2 Let the home and foreign demands be $Q = 12 - pQ$ and $Q^* = 12 - p^*$. Let $c = 4$ and let $n^* = \mu n$. Transportations cost are zero and firms are Cournot competitors. Find the combinations (c^*, μ) for which the home country exports.

8.3 The inverse demands in the home and foreign country are $p = a - y$ and $p^* = a - y^*$ where y and y^* are the per capita quantities consumed. There are L consumers in the home country and L^* consumers in the foreign country. Firms are Cournot competitors. Marginal production cost and transportation cost are zero. Fixed cost is F in both countries. Explore how moving from autarky to free trade affects the total number of active firms and how it affects welfare.

8.4 Assume that the home and foreign countries' inverse demands are respectively $p = 1 - Q$ and $p^* = 1 - Q^*/\lambda$ where $\lambda \geq 1$. There are n Cournot firms in the home country and $n^* = \mu n$ foreign firms. Home and foreign firms produce at a unit cost $c < 1$. The cost of transporting a unit of output from one country to another is τ. Determine the values of λ, μ and τ for which both countries consume locally produced and imported output.

8.5 Assume that inverse demands in the home and foreign country are $p = 1 - Q$ and $p^* = \theta - Q^*$ [$\theta > 1$]. Also assume $n = n^* = 1$ and $1 > c = c^*$. Indicate the range of parameter values for which markets are segmented, and determine the equilibrium prices when markets are connected by arbitrage. Also determine prices when markets are connected. Assume that the unit transportation cost is τ and that firms are Cournot rivals.

8.6 Derive expression (8.31).

Appendix

Monopolistic competition with Dixit-Stiglitz preferences

Consumers

Assume that the representative consumer's preferences can be represented by the Cobb-Douglas utility function $U = H^{1-\alpha} V^\alpha$ [$0 < \alpha < 1$], where H is consumption of a homogeneous good. The sub-utility is $V \equiv \left[\sum_{i=1}^{n} v_i^\rho\right]^{\frac{1}{\rho}}$ [$0 < \rho < 1$], where n denotes the number of varieties of the differentiated good.[25] All consumers spend a portion α of their income on the differentiated good and a portion $1 - \alpha$ on the homogeneous good.

Let p_i and I denote respectively the price of variety i and the representative consumer's income. Maximization of V^ρ subject to the consumer's budget constraint $\sum_{i=1}^{n} p_i v_i = \alpha I$ yields the first order conditions $\rho v_i^{\rho-1} = \lambda p_i$, [$i = 1, \ldots n$]. The latter imply $v_i/v_j = (p_i/p_j)^{1/(\rho-1)}$. It then follows that $v_i = v_j \left(p_i/p_j\right)^{1/(\rho-1)}$ and $\alpha I = \sum_{i=1}^{n} p_i v_i = \left[v_j/p_j^{1/(\rho-1)}\right] \sum_{i=1}^{n} p_i^{1+1/(\rho-1)}$. Thus,

$$v_j = \frac{\alpha I}{\sum_{i=1}^{n} p_i^{1+1/(\rho-1)}} p_j^{1/(\rho-1)} = \frac{\alpha I}{\sum_{i=1}^{n} p_i^{1-\sigma}} p_j^{-\sigma} = \frac{\alpha I}{P}\left(\frac{p_j}{P}\right)^{-\sigma} \tag{A8.1}$$

where $\sigma \equiv 1/(1 - \rho)$ is the elasticity of substitution between individual varieties and $P \equiv \left[\sum_{i=1}^{n} p_i^{1-\sigma} \right]^{1/(1-\sigma)}$ is a "true" price index. To see the latter note that:

$$U = \left[\sum_i v_i^{(\sigma-1)/\sigma} \right]^{\frac{\sigma}{\sigma-1}} = \left[\sum_{i=1}^{n} \left(\frac{\alpha I}{P} \right)^{\frac{\sigma-1}{\sigma}} \left(\frac{p_i}{P} \right)^{1-\sigma} \right]^{\frac{\sigma}{\sigma-1}}$$

$$= \frac{\alpha I}{P^{1-\sigma}} \left[\sum_{i=1}^{n} p_j^{1-\sigma} \right]^{\frac{\sigma}{\sigma-1}} = \frac{\alpha I P^\sigma}{P^{1-\sigma}} = \frac{\alpha I}{P}$$

When $p_i = p$ for all I we have $P = n^{1/1-\sigma} p$. Note that an increase in n that does not change individual prices lowers P by an amount inversely related to the elasticity of substitution between varieties.

When the economy has L consumers, aggregate expenditure on the differentiated good equals $E=LI$, and the market demand for variety j is:

$$q_j = \frac{\alpha E}{\sum_{i=1}^{n} p_i^{1-\sigma}} p_j^{-\sigma} = \frac{\alpha E}{P} \left(\frac{p_j}{P} \right)^{-\sigma} \tag{A8.2}$$

Defining the quantity index $Q \equiv \left[\sum_{j=1}^{n} q_j^\rho \right]^{\frac{1}{\rho}}$ and using (A8.2) yields:

$$Q = \left[\sum_{j=1}^{n} p_j^{-\sigma\rho} \right]^{\frac{1}{\rho}} \frac{\alpha E}{P^{1-\sigma}} = \left[\sum_{j=1}^{n} p_j^{1-\sigma} \right] \left[\sum_{j=1}^{n} p_j^{1-\sigma} \right]^{\frac{1}{\rho}-1} \frac{\alpha E}{P^{1-\sigma}}$$

$$= \left[\sum_{j=1}^{n} p_j^{1-\sigma} \right]^{-\frac{1}{1-\sigma}} \alpha E = \frac{\alpha E}{P} \tag{A8.3}$$

Jointly, (A8.2) and (A8.3) imply:

$$q_j = Q \left(\frac{p_j}{P} \right)^{-\sigma} \tag{A8.4}$$

Producers

The differentiated sector uses labor as the sole input. The production technology is:

$$q_i = \begin{cases} 0 & \text{when } l_i \leq F \\ (-F + \varphi_i l_i) & \text{when } l_i \geq F \end{cases}$$

where l_i denotes the units of labor used by firm i, F is a fixed labor usage, and φ_i denotes the marginal productivity of labor in firm i. The firm's total cost is then $C_i(q_i) = (F + c_i q_i)w$ for $q_i > 0$, where w denotes the wage, and $c_i \equiv 1/\varphi_i$ denotes the additional units of labor required per additional unit of output.

To characterize the equilibrium one must answer the following questions: 1) How many varieties will a firm produce in order to maximize profits? 2) Will a specific variety be produced by more than one firm? 3) Will firms choose price or quantity?

Starting with the last question, we assume that each firm produces a single variety and that no variety is produced by more than one firm. The profit function $\pi_i = (p_i - c_iw)q_i - Fw_i$ is maximized when $p_i[1 - 1/\eta_i] = c_iw$, where η_i is firm i's perceived elasticity of demand. This elasticity generally depends on whether the firm sets price or quantity. When it sets price, taking the prices of rival producers as given, the elasticity is:

$$\eta_i^p = -\frac{\partial q_i}{\partial p_i}\frac{p_i}{q_i} = -\frac{\alpha E}{\sum_i p_i^{1-\sigma}}\left[-\sigma p_i^{-\sigma-1} - \frac{(1-\sigma)p_i^{-\sigma}}{\sum_i p_i^{1-\sigma}}\right] \frac{p_i}{\alpha E p_i^{-\sigma}\bigg/\sum_i p_i^{1-\sigma}}$$

$$= \sigma - (\sigma-1)\frac{p_i^{1-\sigma}}{\sum_i p_i^{1-\sigma}} = \sigma - (\sigma-1)\left(\frac{p_i}{P}\right)^{1-\sigma} = \sigma - (\sigma-1)z_i$$

where $z_i = (q_i/Q)^{(\sigma-1)/\sigma} = (p_i/P)^{1-\sigma}$ follows from (A8.4). When the firm instead sets quantity (taking the quantities of rival producers as given), the inverse of its perceived elasticity of demand for variety i is $\dfrac{1}{\eta_i^q} = \dfrac{1}{\sigma} + \dfrac{\sigma-1}{\sigma}z_i$.[26] Note η_i^p and η_i^q are larger when z_i is smaller. Also, $\eta_i^p \to \sigma$ and $\eta_i^q \to \sigma$ when $z_i \to 0$. The latter certainly applies when there is a continuum of varieties, and the international trade literature assumes that it also applies for the discrete version of the model. Implicit in this approach is the belief that the number of firms is sufficiently large to ensure that the conditions hold approximately, and this in turn implies that the equilibrium is the same whether the firm sets price or quantity.

The price-cost mark-up is given by:

$$\frac{p_i}{wc_i} = \frac{\sigma}{\sigma-1} \tag{A8.5}$$

Note that this mark-up does not depend on the number of active firms. We now consider the question of why two firms would never produce the same variety of a good. Suppose they did, and that they choose price as the decision variable. In this case, the ensuing Bertrand competition would yield a zero mark-up; producing a different variety ensures a positive mark-up. If firms instead set quantity, their profits from all producing the same variety would be lower than if they all produced a different variety. Jointly, (A8.4) and (A8.5) imply:

$$q_i/q_j = (p_i/p_j)^{-\sigma} = (r_i/r_j)^{\sigma/(\sigma-1)} = (c_i/c_j)^{-\sigma} = (\varphi_j/\varphi_i)^{-\sigma} \tag{A8.6}$$

where $r_i \equiv p_iq_i$. It then follows from (A8.5) that:

$$\pi_i = r_i - w[F + c_iq_i] = r_i - wF - p_i\frac{\sigma-1}{\sigma}q_i = r_i\left(1 - \frac{\sigma-1}{\sigma}\right) - wF$$

$$= \frac{r_i}{\sigma} - wF \tag{A8.7}$$

Upon using (A8.3), (A8.4) and (A8.5), condition (A8.7) implies that firm i' variable profit is:

$$\tilde{\pi}_i = \frac{r_i}{\sigma} = \frac{\alpha E}{\sigma}\left[\frac{\sigma}{\sigma-1}\frac{wc_i}{P}\right]^{1-\sigma} \tag{A8.8}$$

When $c_i = c$ for all i, all firms produce the quantity $q = (\sigma - 1)F/c$. When entry is free their revenue is $r = wc(\sigma/\sigma - 1)q = w\sigma F$. Note that the quantity produced depends only on the technology and factor cost; it does not depend on the amount spent by consumers on the differentiated good. From (A8.3) and the definition of P, it can be seen that the number of active firms will be larger the larger is the amount of spending (E). Note that a change in E does not affect the price each firm sets nor the quantity it produces, because P falls when n increases, and as a result welfare increases.

Consider now the question of whether a firm will ever produce more than one variety. Because the varieties are substitutes, a firm that produces two varieties sets higher prices for these varieties than the prices that would be set if these varieties were produced by two separate firms. Given this, freedom of entry implies that a firm that produces two varieties could be undercut by a firm that uses the same technology and produces just one of the varieties. Thus, a firm that produces two or more varieties cannot exist in equilibrium.

Notes

1. The main sources of this section are Brander and Krugman (1983) and Helpman and Krugman (1985).
2. Equation 8.2 is spelled out with the superscript "a" to emphasize that is applies in autarky only.
3. In applied economies this condition, which ensures the stability of the equilibrium, is generally assumed. Seade (1980) shows that the condition does not hold in a neighborhood where demand is sufficiently convex.
4. The activities of these agents – referred to as parallel traders – limit firms' ability to price discriminate across national markets.
5. This section draws on Brander (1981).
6. Because the conditions applicable to the foreign market mirror those of the home market, we only show the latter.
7. Delivered cost = production cost + transportation cost.
8. Because the marginal utility of the numeraire is constant, welfare changes are exactly measured by the standard surplus method.
9. The author recognizes that, strictly speaking, this approach does produce a proper test as the theory predicts a negative sign only when two of the variables are symmetric.
10. To see that this is indeed an equilibrium note first that since the cost of the second-lowest-cost producer is below the monopoly price, the profits earned by the lowest-cost producer fall when it sets a price below the cost of the second-lowest-cost producer. Setting a price equal to that of the second-lowest-cost producer halves his profits. Similarly, the second-lowest-cost producer does not deviate as a higher price maintains profits at zero and a lower price makes them negative.
11. In particular, $\Delta\phi_{jt} = \gamma_t + \upsilon_{jt}$ with $E(\gamma_t) = E(\upsilon_{jt}) = 0$, $E(\gamma_t\gamma_s) = \sigma_\gamma^2$ and $E(\upsilon_{it}\upsilon_{is}) = \sigma_\upsilon^2$ for $t = s$.
12. The latter approach has been pioneered by Lancaster (1979).
13. Helpman and Krugman (1985) show that the two approaches yield very similar predictions at the aggregate level.
14. Because the first order conditions and the free entry conditions are the same for all firms, the subscript i is dropped in the remainder of this section.
15. The following sections show that this outcome is contingent on the absence of transportation costs.
16. See Helpman and Krugman (1985).

17. Head *et al.* (2002) determine that a home market effect also emerges when the utility function has the Ottaviano-Tabushi-Thisse form (as in problem 8.5). It also arises in a Brander (1981) framework in which firms produce a homogeneous good. Surprisingly, Head *et al.* (2002) find a reverse home market effect when products are sufficiently differentiated across countries but not within countries.

18. The appendix to this chapter derives the price index.

19. The sum of squares of market shares is called the Hirschman-Herfindahl concentration index. Using $\sum_{j=1}^{n}(z_j)=1$ one easily shows that $\sum_{j=1}^{n}(z_j)^2=1/n+nVar(z)$.

20. The term μ^{ij} captures the many influences, such a as trade resistance, that affect bilateral trade flows.

21. Neither column 1 nor column 2 are significantly affected by the use of a random effect estimator, by removing the trend in the data, and by using factor endowments as instruments to account for possible endogeneity of *GDP*. Note that equation (8.33) also holds in the absence of intra-industry trade when all of the following conditions hold: 1) each good is produced in a single country; 2) tastes are identical across countries and homothetic; 3) prices are uniform across countries.

22. Note that Figure 8.6 assumes that factor prices are not equal across countries, which contrasts with our previous analysis of monopolistic competition in which factor price equalization was assumed.

23. They transform the variable because the dependent variable is bounded between 0 and 1 which makes the use of OLS estimators questionable. The transformed variable *ln[ITTS/1–ITTS]* can theoretically take any value in the interval $(-\infty,+\infty)$.

24. The land endowments gap variable does not appear in the equation as it is highly collinear with the country-pair dummies.

25. This is the discrete version of the sub-utility. The continuous version reads $V\equiv\left[\int_0^n(v(i)^\rho di)\right]^{1/\rho}$ and yields identical demands and pricing conditions as the discrete version examined in this appendix.

26. (A8.3) and (A.8.4) jointly entail $q_i=Q^{1-\sigma}p_i^{-\sigma}E^{-\sigma}$. Thus, $dq_i=(\alpha E)^{-\sigma}[(1-\sigma)Q^{-\sigma}p_i^{-\sigma}dQ-\sigma p^{-\sigma-1}Q^{1-\sigma}dp_i]$. But $dQ=(q_i/Q)^{\rho-1}dq_i=z_idq_i$ $1=dQ/dq_i=z_i^{\rho-1}$. Substitution for dQ yields $1/\eta_i^q$.

References and additional reading

Oligopoly

Bernhofen, D.M. (1999), "Intra-Industry Trade and Strategic Interaction: Theory and Evidence," *Journal of International Economics*, 47, 225–244.

Brander, J.A. (1981), "Intra-Industry Trade in Identical Commodities," *Journal of International Economics*, 1, 1–14.

Brander, J. A. and Krugman, P. (1983), "A 'Reciprocal Dumping' Model of International Trade," *Journal of International Economics*, 15 (3/4), 313–321.

Bresnahan, T.F. (1989), "Empirical Studies of Industries with Market Power," Chapter 8 in R. Schmalensee and R.D. Willig (Eds.), *Handbook of Industrial Organization*, Vol. 2 (Amsterdam: North-Holland).

Caves, R.E. (1985), "International Trade and Industrial Organization: Problems, Solved and Unsolved," *European Economic Review*, 28, 377–395.

Kreps, D.A. and Scheinkman, J.A. (1983), "Quantity Precommitment and Bertrand Competition Yield Cournot Outcomes," *Bell Journal of Economics*, 4, 326–337.

Levinsohn, J. (1993), "Testing Imports as Market Discipline Hypothesis, *Journal of International Economics*," 35 (1/2), 1–22.

Roberts, M.J. and Tybout, J. (1997), "The Decision to Export in Colombia: An Empirical Model of Entry with Sunk Cost," *American Economic Review*, 87 (4), 545–564.

Seade, J. (1980), "On the Effects of Entry," *Econometrica*, 48, 479–489.

Trefler, D. (2004), "The Long and Short of the Canada-US Free Trade Agreement," *American Economic Review*, 94 (4), 870–895.

Weinstein, D. (1989), "Competition, Unilateral Dumping and Firm Profitability," University of Michigan Research Seminar in International Economics Seminar Discussion Paper 249.

Monopolistic competition

Anderson, S. P., de Palma, A., and Thisse, J.F. (1990), "Demand for Differentiated Products, Discrete Choice Models, and the Characteristics Approach," *Review of Economic Studies*, 56, 21–35.

Arkolakis, C., Demidova, S., Klenow, P. J., and Rodríguez-Clare, A. (2008), "Endogenous Variety and the Gains from Trade," *American Economic Review*, 98 (2), Papers and Proceedings of the One Hundred Twentieth Annual Meeting of the American Economic Association, 444–450.

Balassa, B. and Bauwens, L. (1987), "Intra-Industry Specialization in a Multi-Industry Framework," *Economic Journal*, 97, 923–939.

Bergstrand, J.H. (1989), "The Generalized Gravity Equation, Monopolistic Competition, and the Factor-Proportions Theory in International Trade," *Review of Economics and Statistics*, 71 (1), 143–153.

Bergstrand, J.H. (1990), "The Heckscher-Ohlin-Samuelson Model, the Linder Hypothesis, and the Determinants of Bilateral Intra-Industry Trade," *Economic Journal*, 100, 1216–1229.

Broda, C. and Weinstein, D.E. (2006), "Globalization and the Gains from Variety," *Quarterly Journal of Economics*, 121, 541–585.

Caves, R.E. (1985), "International Trade and Industrial Organization: Problems, Solved and Unsolved," *European Economic Review*, 28, 377–395.

Chen, N., Imbs, J., and Scott, A. (2009), "The Dynamics of Trade and Competition," *Journal of International Economics*, 77, 50–62.

Davis, D.R., (1998), "The Home Market, Trade, and Industrial Structure," *American Economic Review*, 88 (5), 1264–1276.

Debaere, P. (2005), "Monopolistic Competition and Trade Revisited: Testing the Model without Testing for Gravity," *Journal of International Economics*, 66, 249–266.

Dixit, A. and Stiglitz, J. (1977), "Monopolistic Competition and Optimum Product Diversity," *American Economic Review*, 67, 297–303.

Dixit, A.K. and Norman, V. (1980), *Theory of International Trade* (Cambridge: Cambridge University Press).

Feenstra, R.C. (1994), "New Product Varieties and the Measurement of International Prices," *American Economic Review*, 84 (1), 157–177.

Feenstra, R.C., Romalis, J., and Schott, P.K. (2002), "US Imports, Exports, and Tariff Data, 1989-2001," *NBER Working Paper 9387*.

Fujita, M., Krugman, P., and Venables, A.J. (1999), *The Spatial Economy: Cities, Regions, and International Trade* (Cambridge, MA: MIT Press).

Greenaway, D., Hine, R., and Milner, C. (1995), "Vertical and Horizontal Intra-Industry Trade: A Cross Industry Analysis for the United Kingdom," *Economic Journal,* 105, 1505–1518.

Hanson, H.H. and Xiang, C. (2004), "The Home-Market Effect and Bilateral Trade Patterns," *American Economic Review*, 94 (4), 1108–1129.

Head, K., Mayer, T., and Ries, J. (2002), "On the Pervasiveness of Home Market Effects," *Economica*, 69, 371–390.

Helpman, E. (1981), "International Trade in the Presence of Product Differentiation, Economies of Scale, and Monopolistic Competition: A Chamberlin-Heckscher-Ohlin Approach," *Journal of International Economics,* 11, 305–340.

Helpman, E. (1987), "Imperfect Competition and International Trade: Evidence from Fourteen Industrial Countries," *Journal of the Japanese and International Economies*, 1, 62–81.

Helpman, E. and Krugman, P. (1985), *Market Structure and Foreign Trade* (Cambridge, MA: MIT Press).

Hummels, D. (2007), "Transportation Costs and International Trade in the Second Era of Globalization," *Journal of Economic Perspectives*, 21 (3), 131–154.

Hummels, D.L. and Levinsohn, J. (1995), "Monopolistic Competition and International Trade: Reconsidering the Evidence," *Quarterly Journal of Economics,* 110, 799–835.

Kamata, I. (2010), "Revisiting the Revisited: An alternative Test of the Monopolistic Competition Model of International Trade," La Follette School of Public Affairs, Working paper 2010-007, available at http://papers.ssrn.com/sol3/papers.cfm?abstract_id=1649129.

Krugman, P.R. (1979), "Increasing returns, Monopolistic Competition and International Trade," *Journal of International Economics*, 9 (4), 469–479.

Krugman, P.R. (1980), "Scale Economies, Product Differentiation and the Pattern of Trade," *American Economic Review*, 70 (5), 950–959.

Krugman, P.R. and Venables, A.J. (1999), "How Robust Is the Home Market Effect?" Mimeo, MIT and LSE.

Lancaster, K., (1966), "A New Approach to Consumer Theory," *Journal of Political Economy*, 31, 1–26.

Lancaster, K. (1979), *Variety, Equity and Efficiency* (New York: Columbia University Press).

Levinsohn, J. (1993), "Testing Imports as Market Discipline Hypothesis," *Journal of International Economics*, 25, 1–2.

Linder, S. (1961), *An Essay on Trade and Transformation* (New York: Wiley).

Roberts, M.J. and Tybout, J. (1997), "The Decision to Export in Columbia: An Empirical Model of Entry with Sunk Cost," *American Economic Review*, 87 (4), 545–564.

Seade, J. (1980), "On the Effects of Entry," *Econometrica*, 48, 479–89.

Trefler, D. (2004), "The Long and Short of the Canada-US Free Trade Agreement," *American Economic Review*, 94 (4), 870–895.

Venables, A.J., Rice, P.G., and Stewart, M. (2003), "The Geography of Intra-industry Trade: Empirics," *Topics in Economic Analysis & Policy*, 3 (1), article 11.

Weinstein, D. (1989), "Competition, Unilateral Dumping and Firm Profitability," University of Michigan Discussion Paper 249.

Yang, X. and Heijdra, B.J. (1993), "Monopolistic Competition and Optimum Product Diversity: Comment," *American Economic Review*, 83, 295–301.

9

Heterogeneous firms

9.1   The Melitz (2003) model and extensions

9.2   Endogenous mark-ups

9.3   Endogenous comparative advantage

9.4   The diversity of export destinations

9.5   Measuring the impact of trade costs

9.6   Concluding remarks

The models studied in Chapter 8 assumed that all firms in an industry are equally productive and that all varieties of the good produced by the industry are equally appreciated by consumers. Because of these symmetry assumptions, the models of Chapter 8 cannot explain why the propensity to export varies so much across firms within industries.

In this regard, the data show that even in comparative advantage industries only a minority of firms export. For example, the 2002 United States (US) Census of Manufactures reveals that, while exporting firms in the US are mostly found in skill-intensive industries, these firms are a minority of the firms within those industries – even in the most skill-intensive industries, less than 40 percent of firms export.[1] Eaton *et al.* (2004) report a similar exporting pattern within French industries.

Sections 9.1 and 9.2 explain why the propensity to export varies across firms within industries. The models studied in these sections show how the transition from autarky to free trade produces an intra-industry reallocation of output that increases the output shares of the most productive firms. This yields a welfare gain from trade not encountered in earlier chapters.

Section 9.3, embeds a heterogeneous monopolistically competitive industry in a Heckscher-Ohlin framework. The embedded model shows that a transition from autarky to free trade creates a Ricardian productivity gap at the industry level that magnifies the endowment-based source of comparative advantage. Trade improves productivity in all industries, but the improvement is greatest in the industry that has the comparative advantage.

The models of sections 9.1 to 9.3 still assume that all varieties of a good enter consumers' utility symmetrically. However, they are not equally priced because they are produced by firms that are not equally productive. The less productive firms survive competition because consumers value variety – that is, consumers are better off when they spend part of their budget on higher priced varieties produced by less productive firms than if they instead spend their entire budget on only the narrow range of lower priced varieties offered by the most productive firms.

Section 9.4 introduces a model that focuses on the interaction between the number of countries served by exporters and transportation costs. The model explains the observed positive correlation between a firm's efficiency and the number of export markets it serves.

Section 9.5 summarizes the findings of a study that tests several of the predictions of the models discussed in this chapter. Among other findings, the study shows how changes in US tariff rates and transportation costs have impacted on the productivity of US industries.

9.1 The Melitz (2003) model and extensions

Melitz (2003) considers an industry into which there is a continuum of potential entrants. Payment of a fee F_E buys a potential entrant the right to draw a productivity φ from a distribution $G(\varphi)$ of productivity values defined on the interval $(0, \infty)$. The fee can be considered the cost of developing or adopting a new technology. A key assumption is that this fee becomes a sunk cost as soon as it is incurred. Upon drawing a productivity the firm becomes an active producer if it is able to earn an operating profit at least as large as its fixed production cost F.

Each active firm produces a single variety of a differentiated product, using labor as the sole input. Specifically, a firm that draws productivity φ – henceforth called firm φ – uses $l = F + q/\varphi$ units of labor to produce q units of output. The fixed cost of production F is the same for all firms. Given a wage w, the firm's marginal cost is $c(\varphi) = w/\varphi$ and its fixed cost is wF.

The representative consumer's utility, which is the same in all countries, is represented by the function:

$$U = \left[\int_\Omega v(\varphi)^\rho \, d\varphi \right]^{1/\rho}$$

where $v(\varphi)$ denotes the individual's consumption of the variety produced by firm φ and Ω is the set of all consumed varieties. This utility function is the continuous version of the constant elasticity of substitution (CES) function studied in Chapter 8, and it generates demand functions that have the same properties. Specifically, profit maximization entails (see (A8.5) in Chapter 8):

$$p(\varphi)(1 - 1/\sigma) = c(\varphi) = w/\varphi \tag{9.1}$$

This expression indicates that all active firms will have the same mark-up $p(\varphi)/c(\varphi)$ if they pay the same wage w.

Firm φ produces the quantity $q(\varphi) = Lv(\varphi)$, where L denotes the number of consumers/workers in the economy. Then, denoting the firm's revenue by $r(\varphi) \equiv p(\varphi) q(\varphi)$, we can write:[2]

$$v(\varphi_1)/v(\varphi_2) = q(\varphi_1)/q(\varphi_2) = (\varphi_1/\varphi_2)^\sigma = \left[p(\varphi_1)_i/p(\varphi_2) \right]^{-\sigma}$$
$$= [r(\varphi_1)/r(\varphi_2)]^{\sigma/\sigma - 1} \tag{9.2}$$

Condition (9.2) implies that the profits of firm φ can be expressed as:

$$\pi(\varphi) = r(\varphi) - wl = r(\varphi) - w[F + q(\varphi)/\varphi] = r(\varphi) - r(\varphi)[1 - 1/\sigma] - wF$$
$$= r(\varphi)/\sigma - wF \tag{9.3}$$

Melitz (2003) assumes that entry into a foreign market requires an investment in "export development." This includes factors such as developing a marketing channel, adapting a product and possibly learning about foreign bureaucratic procedures.[3] An active firm enters foreign markets if its productivity is sufficient to generate an operating profit from exports that surpasses the fixed cost of export development.

Exporters set prices independently in each market, and they incur an iceberg-type transportation cost $\tau > 1$. Given this, we can express the relationship between delivered marginal costs in the local and foreign market as:

$$c_x(\varphi) = \tau \, c_l(\varphi) = \tau w/\varphi \tag{9.4}$$

where the subscripts "l" and "x" indicate that a variable pertains to the local or foreign market. It follows from (9.1), (9.2) and (9.4) that the following condition holds for all firms that export:

$$c_l(\varphi)/c_x(\varphi) = p_l(\varphi)/p_x(\varphi) = q_l(\varphi)/q_x(\varphi)\tau^\sigma \quad \text{and} \quad r_l(\varphi) = r_x(\varphi)\tau^{\sigma-1} \tag{9.5}$$

The autarky equilibrium

Let φ_D denote the minimal cut-off productivity needed to become an active producer and let φ_X denote the minimal productivity required to enter an export market. These threshold productivities play a central role in the Melitz (2003) model. Indeed, for any distribution of productivities G, they determine the price, quantity and profit of the average firm in the industry. All industry-level variables can be expressed in terms of the price and quantity set by the average firm.

Normalizing the wage to 1, we define the survival productivity φ_D as:

$$\pi(\varphi_D) - F = r(\varphi_D)/\sigma - F = 0 \tag{9.6}$$

where the first equality follows from (9.3). The distribution of active firms can now be expressed as:

$$\mu(\varphi) = \begin{cases} g(\varphi)/(1 - G(\varphi_D)) & \text{for} \quad \varphi \geq \varphi_D \\ 0 & \text{for} \quad \varphi < \varphi_D \end{cases} \tag{9.7}$$

where $\int_{\varphi_D}^{\infty} g(\varphi)d\varphi = 1 - G(\varphi_D)$.

Condition 9.8 below defines $\tilde{\varphi}$, which expresses the weighted mean of the productivities of the active producers as a function of the survival threshold φ_D:

$$\tilde{\varphi} = \left[\int_0^{\infty} \varphi^{\sigma-1} \mu(\varphi)d\varphi \right]^{\frac{1}{\sigma-1}} = \left[\frac{1}{1 - G(\varphi_D)} \int_{\varphi_D}^{\infty} \varphi^{\sigma-1} g(\varphi)d\varphi \right]^{\frac{1}{\sigma-1}} \tag{9.8}$$

The latter, together with (9.2), implies $r[\tilde{\varphi}(\varphi_D)]/r(\varphi_D) = [\tilde{\varphi}(\varphi_D)/\varphi_D]^{\sigma-1}$. This and condition (9.3) then allow us to write:

$$\pi(\tilde{\varphi}^a) = [\tilde{\varphi}^a(\varphi_D^a)/\varphi_D^a]^{\sigma-1} [r(\varphi_D^a)/\sigma] - F = Fk(\varphi_D^a) \text{ where } k(\varphi_D)$$
$$= [\tilde{\varphi}(\varphi_D)/\varphi_D]^{\sigma-1} - 1 \tag{9.9}$$

Since $k' < 0$, it follows from (9.9) that $\pi(\tilde{\varphi}^a)$ and φ_D^a are negatively related.[4] Melitz (2003) refers to this relationship between the profit of the average active firm and the cut-off productivity φ_D as the "zero cut-off profit" (ZCP) condition.

To determine the autarky values $\pi(\tilde{\varphi}^a)$ and φ_D^a, it is necessary to have a second relationship, which Melitz (2003) derives from his assumptions regarding entry and exit. He assumes that firms retain the same productivity as long as they remain active, which may not be forever. A firm exits an industry if it is hit by a "fatal shock," which is assumed to occur with probability δ during each period that the firm is active. Because in a stationary equilibrium active firms earn the same profit during each period, the post-entry value of a firm's φ is given by:

$$V(\varphi) = \sum_{t=0}^{\infty} (1-\delta)^t \pi(\varphi) = \pi(\varphi)/\delta. \tag{9.10}$$

Since there is a continuum of potential entrants, the *expected* profit from investing in the entry fee F_E is driven to zero. Specifically, since $1 - G(\varphi_D^a)$ denotes the probability of becoming an active firm, we can write:[5]

$$[1 - G(\varphi_D^a)]\pi(\tilde{\varphi}^a)/\delta - F_E = 0 \tag{9.11}$$

Condition (9.11) is called the free entry condition *(FE)*, and it indicates a positive relationship between $\pi(\tilde{\varphi}^a)$ and φ_D^a. Jointly, the ZCP^a and the *FE* conditions determine the autarky cut-off productivity φ_D^a and the profit of the average active firm $\pi(\tilde{\varphi}^a)$. Figure 9.1 displays the equilibrium as point A.[6]

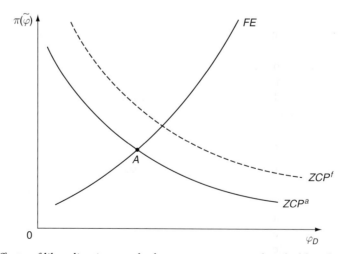

Figure 9.1 Effects of liberalization on the home country cost threshold and number of supplies

Having determined φ_D^a and $\pi(\tilde{\varphi}^a)$, we can use (9.7) and (9.8) to derive $\tilde{\varphi}$. Given the latter, we can then use (9.1), (9.2) and (9.3) to derive the price set by the firm with average productivity and hence its revenue and profit. None of these firm-level equilibrium values depend on country size.

The *FE* curve shown in Figure 9.1 shifts upward when the entry fee increases. This produces a new equilibrium in which both the post-entry profit of the average active firm and the probability of becoming active increase. The *ZCP*^{a} curve shifts upward when the fixed production cost F increases. This brings about an increase in the average firm's profit and lowers the probability than a productivity draw will result in entry.

Denoting by M the number or perhaps more accurately the mass of active firms, and letting $p(\tilde{\varphi})$ denote the price of the firm with average productivity, we can express the industry price index P in autarky as:

$$P^a = \left[\int_0^\infty p(\varphi)^{1-\sigma} M^a \mu(\varphi) \, d\varphi \right]^{\frac{1}{1-\sigma}} = M^{a\frac{1}{1-\sigma}} p(\tilde{\varphi}^a) = M^{a\frac{1}{1-\sigma}} \frac{\sigma}{\sigma-1} \frac{1}{\tilde{\varphi}^a} \quad (9.12)$$

This price index decreases in M because consumers appreciate variety. Other industry-level variables can similarly be expressed as a function of the productivity of the average firm. Specifically, the aggregate quantity index is $Q = M^{\frac{\sigma}{\sigma-1}} q(\tilde{\varphi})$, total industry revenue is $R \equiv PQ = Mr(\tilde{\varphi})$, and total industry profit is $\Pi = M\pi(\tilde{\varphi})$.

In the stationary equilibrium in which all aggregate variables are constant, the number of firms entering the industry equals the number of firms exiting. We can express this as: $\delta M = [1 - G(\varphi_D)] M_E$, where M_E stands for the number of firms that pay the entry fee in each period. Denoting the number of workers engaged in the production of entry services by L_E, the total cost of entry is given as $wL_E = L_E$. Freedom of entry implies: $L_E = M_E F_E = \delta M F_E / [1 - G(\varphi_D)] = M\pi(\tilde{\varphi})$, where the last equality follows from (9.11). Given this, we can write industry revenue as $R = L_p + n\pi(\tilde{\varphi})$, where L_p represents aggregate payments to production workers. Together, these expressions allow us to write:

$$R = L_P + L_E = L \text{ and } M^a = \frac{R^a}{r(\tilde{\varphi}^a)} = \frac{L}{\sigma[\pi(\tilde{\varphi}^a) + F]} \quad (9.13)$$

Condition (9.13) indicates that when the distribution of productivities, fixed production costs and the elasticity of substitution between varieties in an industry are the same in two countries, the larger country will produce a larger number of varieties and therefore enjoy a higher level of welfare in autarky. In addition, the larger country's real wage $w/P = 1/P$ will be higher in autarky since the average price is the same in each country but the price index P is smaller (see (9.12)) in the larger country.

The trading equilibrium

When trading costs are zero, a move towards free trade is formally equivalent to an enlargement of country size. Because demands originate from a CES utility, the number of active firms in the integrated market will be the sum of the number of active firms in autarky in each country. Prices are the same as in autarky. Welfare increases in all trading countries since consumers gain access to a larger number of varieties.

We now consider the more realistic hypothesis that penetration of foreign markets requires investment in export development. Melitz (2003) assumes that each export market has a development cost $\hat{F}_X$. Upon learning its productivity, each firm determines whether or not it will make the investment in export development. Exporters are assumed to bear a transportation cost per unit exported. Because all export markets are identical, firms that choose to export will do so to all N foreign countries. Given this, we can express the post-entry per period profit of firm φ as:

$$\pi(\varphi) = \begin{cases} \pi_l(\varphi) + N\pi_x(\varphi) = [r_l(\varphi)/\sigma - F] \\ \quad\quad +N[r_x(\varphi)/\sigma - F_x] & \text{if it exports} \\ \pi_l(\varphi) = r_l(\varphi)/\sigma - F & \text{if it does not export} \end{cases} \tag{9.14}$$

where $\pi_j(\varphi)$ and $r_j(\varphi)$ respectively denote profits and revenue derived from market $j = \{l = local, x = foreign\}$. The per period cost of export development F_X is equivalent to the one-off payment $\hat{F}_X$ where $\hat{F}_X = \sum_{t=0}^{\infty}(1-\delta)^t F_X = F_X/\delta$. Given this, it follows from (9.4) and 9.5 that the export cut-off φ_X will satisfy the condition:

$$r_x(\varphi_X)/\sigma - F_X = \tau^{1-\sigma}r_l(\varphi_X)/\sigma - F_X = 0 \tag{9.15}$$

Expression (9.15) implies that all firms export when $\varphi_D = \varphi_X$, and that only firms with productivities φ in the interval (φ_D, φ_X) export when $\varphi_D < \varphi_X$. Since $\pi_l(\varphi_D) = \pi_x(\varphi_X) = 0$, it follows from (9.5), (9.6) and (9.15) that:

$$\frac{F_x}{F} = \frac{r_x(\varphi_X)}{r_l(\varphi_D)} = \left[\frac{1}{\tau}\frac{\varphi_X}{\varphi_D}\right]^{\sigma-1} \tag{9.16}$$

Condition (9.16) expresses φ_X as a function of φ_D and fixed costs. Melitz (2003) proceeds under the assumption that $\tau^{\sigma-1}F_X > F$. This inequality ensures that $\varphi_D < \varphi_X$ and is therefore consistent with the empirical observation that industries typically include exporting and non-exporting firms. The *ex ante* probability that a successful entrant will export is given by: $p_X = 1 - G(\varphi_X)/1 - G(\varphi_D)$.

To determine the productivity thresholds in an open economy, we proceed along lines similar to those followed for the analysis of autarky. First, the per period profit of the average active firm is:

$$\bar{\pi}^f = \pi_l^f\left(\tilde{\varphi}^f\right) + p_X N\pi_x^f\left(\tilde{\varphi}_X^f\right) = Fk\left(\varphi_D^f\right) + p_X NF_X k\left(\varphi_X^f\right) \tag{9.17}$$

where $k(\varphi)$ is defined as in (9.9) and $\tilde{\varphi}_X^f$ denotes exporters' average productivity. By virtue of (9.16) the export threshold φ_X, and consequently $\tilde{\varphi}_X^f$, is determined by φ_D^f as a function of the two fixed costs.

Condition (9.17) represents one relationship between φ_D^f and average profit in the open economy. A second relationship follows from the conditions of entry and exit which require:

$$\left[1 - G\left(\varphi_D^f\right)\right]\bar{\pi}^f/\delta = F_E \quad \text{or} \quad \bar{\pi}^f = \frac{\delta}{1 - G\left(\varphi_D^f\right)}F_E \tag{9.18}$$

Condition (9.17) is indicated as ZCP^f in Figure 9.1, while condition (9.18) is shown as *FE*. Jointly, these relationships determine the free trade average profit $\bar{\pi}^f$ and the survival cut-off productivity φ_D^f which, in turn, determines φ_X^f, $\tilde{\varphi}^f$, *and* $\tilde{\varphi}_X^f$ as well as the price and quantity produced by the average firm.

Under free trade, the revenue of the average firm is: $\bar{r}^f = r_l(\tilde{\varphi}^f) + p_x N r_x(\tilde{\varphi}_X^f) = \sigma\left[\bar{\pi}^f + F + p_X NF_x\right]$, where the second equality follows from (9.3). Since $R = L$ also holds in the open economy, the number of active firms in each country is given by:

$$M^f = \frac{R^f}{\bar{r}^f} = \frac{L}{\sigma\left[\bar{\pi}^f + F + p_X NF_x\right]} \tag{9.19}$$

The number of varieties to which each country's consumers have access is the sum of the number of locally produced and imported varieties. Because the probability of becoming an exporter is the same in each country, the total number of available varieties accessible to consumers everywhere is $M_{tot}^f = (1 + Np_x)M^f$. Note that no country consumes all varieties produced in the world and some firms do not export.

The open versus closed economy

The free entry condition has the same form in the open economy as in the closed economy. Condition (9.17) – shown as the dotted line in Figure 9.1 – associates to every φ_D a higher average profit than condition (9.4), that is, $\bar{\pi}^f > \bar{\pi}^a$ and $\varphi_D^f > \varphi_D^a$. It then follows from (9.13), and (9.19) that $M^f < M^a$. Although the number of locally produced varieties is smaller in the trading equilibrium, the number of varieties available to consumers (M_{tot}^f) may be larger or smaller than in autarky. Interestingly, welfare is higher in the trading equilibrium even when $M_{tot}^f < M_{tot}^a$. To see why, note that the real wage under autarky and free trade is: $(1/P)^j$ $[j = \{a, f\}]$. Since $\varphi_D^f > \varphi_D^a$, and $P^j = (M^j)^{\frac{1}{\sigma-1}} p(\tilde{\varphi}^j) = \frac{(M^j)^{\frac{1}{\sigma-1}}}{\rho \tilde{\varphi}^j} = \frac{(M^j)^{\frac{1}{\sigma-1}}}{\rho \varphi_D^j}\left[\frac{r(\tilde{\varphi}^j)}{r(\varphi_D^j)}\right]^{\frac{1}{\sigma-1}} = \frac{(M^j)^{\frac{1}{\sigma-1}}}{\rho \varphi_D^j}\left[\frac{L/M^j}{r(\varphi_D^j)}\right]^{\frac{1}{\sigma-1}} = \frac{1}{\rho \varphi_D^j}\left[\frac{L}{\sigma F}\right]^{\frac{1}{\sigma-1}}$ it follows that consumers are better off in the trading equilibrium. Moreover, since $r_l^j(\varphi) = \left[\varphi/\varphi_D^j\right]^{\sigma-1} \sigma F$, it also follows that firms' revenue from local sales are lower in the trading equilibrium than in autarky.

All firms that export in the open economy do not gain from a transition from autarky to free trade. The transition changes exporter's profits by an amount equal to: $\pi^f(\varphi) - \pi^a(\varphi) = \left[r_l^f(\varphi) + Nr_X^f(\varphi) - r^a(\varphi)\right]/\sigma - NF_X$. As indicated, the term in square brackets is positive for finite τ, but it is larger than NF_X only for firms with the highest φ. Thus, exporters are partitioned into a class with high φ that benefit from free trade, and a class with lower φ that are better off under autarky. Firms in the second group – which includes the firms whose $\varphi = \varphi_X$ – are worse off because the loss they suffer from having to share the local market with foreign producers exceeds the profit they earn from exporting.

The transition from autarky to free trade exposes all active firms to foreign competition in their home market, but only the more productive among them compete in export markets. As a result, production shares among surviving firms shifts from the less productive to the more productive firms. Prospective entrants pay the entry fee F_E in the hope of drawing a technology that will allow them to export. The demand for labor by these prospective entrants, and also by incumbents who enter foreign markets, pushes up the wage. The higher wage drives the least productive firms out of the industry as their variable profit can no longer cover their fixed production costs.

Finally, $k' < 0$ (see (9.9)) implies an upward shift of the ZCP^f curve shown in Figure 9.1 in response to a fall in τ. This implies that a fall in the variable trade cost has qualitatively the same effect as a transition from autarky to free trade.

Asymmetrical countries

Baldwin and Forslid (2004), Falvey *et al.* (2006) and Demidova (2008) extend the analysis to the case where firms draw their productivity from country-specific distributions. They formalize the idea of a cross-country gap in technology by letting entrants in one country draw their productivity from a distribution that dominates the distribution from which entrants in other countries draw their productivity.[7] Survival and export thresholds are then country-specific and satisfy the condition:[8]

$$\frac{\varphi_X^*}{\varphi_D} = \frac{\varphi_X}{\varphi_D^*} = \tau \left[\frac{F_x}{F} \right]^{1/\sigma - 1} \tag{9.20}$$

This relationship between the home and foreign thresholds becomes transparent when we consider a hypothetical sequence of events. As in Melitz (2003), we begin by assuming identical technology distributions in each of two countries. In this symmetric case, the two countries export different varieties, but their trade in the differentiated good is balanced. Now let the distribution in the home country "improve" slightly. This means more home firms will be prepared to pay the entry fee since they now have a better chance of drawing a higher productivity and becoming exporters. As additional firms pay the entry fee, competition intensifies in the home market and, as a result, the home survival productivity φ_D increases. It then follows from (9.20) that the foreign export cut-off φ_X^* also increases. The reason is that foreign firms are now compelled to compete in a tougher home market and must own better technology to earn a positive profit from exporting. But, if the latter is true, then it must also be true that the foreign survival productivity cut-off φ_D^* is lower since, if it were not, the foreign entrant's expected profits could not remain equal to the cost of entry. Given this, the home export threshold φ_X must also be lower by virtue of (9.20) since home-based exporters now compete in a foreign market where local producers are on average less productive.

This hypothetical sequence of adjustments implies that when the home country has a small technological advantage the relationship between thresholds is given as $\varphi_D^* < \varphi_D^{Melitz} < \varphi_D < \varphi_X < \varphi_X^{Melitz} < \varphi_X^*$, where the "Melitz" superscript identifies the cut-offs when productivity distributions are identical. This ranking of thresholds suggests that when two countries are equal in size, the technologically leading country has a trade surplus in the differentiated good.[9]

A technological improvement in the home country lowers the average price locally as additional home entrants are drawn into the industry. Also, the home survival and average productivities increase and foreign firms exit. Although fewer foreign firms export, home consumers have access to more varieties due to the surge in entry into the home market. Demidova (2008) shows that in this case welfare in the foreign country falls since the increased imports of home varieties cannot make up for the fall in foreign productivity and the ensuing decline in the number of varieties produced in the foreign country. This finding contrasts sharply with the welfare effect of a technological improvement in the standard Ricardian model, which predicts that a country benefits from an improvement in its trading partner's productivity. However, the adverse effect on foreign welfare arises only when both countries produce the differentiated good. When the productivity gap crosses a critical value, the foreign country specializes in the homogeneous good. From that point onward, further upgrading of the home productivity distribution increases foreign welfare. It does so by improving the foreign country's terms of trade – as in the Ricardian framework – and by providing additional varieties to foreign consumers.

In Melitz (2003), the export opportunities of all countries change uniformly when trade costs fall. Falling trade costs intensify competition, raise productivity thresholds and increase welfare in all countries. In contrast, Demidova (2008) shows that the export opportunities generated by falling trade costs disproportionately benefit firms in the technologically leading country. While all home and foreign firms lose local sales to imports, these losses are relatively larger in the case of firms based in the technologically lagging country. Also, in the lagging country, the disappearance of locally produced varieties may not be fully compensated by the increase in the number of imported varieties. The conclusion is that while a fall in trade costs increases welfare in the technologically more advanced country, it has an ambiguous effect on welfare in the technologically lagging country. It is more likely to lower welfare in the technologically lagging country when the cross-country technology gap is wider.

9.2 Endogenous mark-ups

Melitz and Ottaviano (2008) revisit the issues addressed in Melitz (2003) by allowing mark-ups to respond to changes in the intensity of competition. They assume an economy producing two goods: a homogeneous good and a differentiated good. Both goods use labor as the sole input and are produced by means of a constant returns technology. There are L consumer/workers and each consumes $v(i)$ units of variety i of the differentiated good.

Firm i in the differentiated goods sector faces the linear demand $q(i) = Lv(i) = L\left[\dfrac{\alpha}{\kappa n + \gamma} - \dfrac{1}{\gamma}p(i) + \dfrac{\kappa n}{\kappa n + \gamma}\dfrac{\bar{p}}{\gamma}\right]$, where $p(i)$ is the price of variety i, n is the measure (number) of consumed varieties in the set Ω^*, γ is the degree of differentiation between varieties and $\bar{p} = (1/n)\int_{i\in\Omega^*} p(i)di$ is the average price of consumed varieties. Ω^* is the largest subset of varieties that satisfies the condition:

$$p(i) \leq \left[\gamma\alpha + \eta n\bar{p}\right]/\left[\eta n + \gamma\right]) \equiv p_{max} \tag{9.21}$$

where the right-hand side represents the price at which demand for a variety is driven to zero. For given $\bar{p}$, the elasticity of the demands for each variety increases as n increases.

Potential entrants into the differentiated goods industry draw a marginal cost c from a Pareto distribution $G(c) = [c/c_M]^k$ where $c \in [0, c_M]$ and $k \geq 1$[10] and, in contrast to Melitz (2003), firms do not bear a fixed production cost.

A firm with unit cost c – called firm c – sets the price $p(c)$. Similar notation is used for firm output, profit and revenue. The survival and export cost thresholds are c_D and c_X. Given this, the cost for the average firm is $\bar{c} = [\int_0^{c_D} cdG(c)]/G(c_D) = (k/k+1)c_D$.

The closed economy

Because the survival threshold c_D is the common intercept of linear demands for all varieties, equilibrium firm-level values of the endogenous variables are:

$$p(c) = \frac{1}{2}[c_D + c] \quad q(c) = \frac{L}{2\gamma}[c_D - c] \quad p(c)q(c) = \frac{L}{4\gamma}\left[(c_D)^2 - c^2\right]$$

$$\pi(c) = \frac{L}{4\gamma}[c_D - c]^2 \tag{9.22}$$

Clearly, firms with higher c will have lower price cost gaps $p(c) - c$, lower revenue and lower profits. Also, $p(c) - c$ and $q(c)$ converge to zero as c approaches c_D. The latter explain why the draw of a marginal cost $c > c_D$ on entry triggers exit, even though there is no fixed cost of production.

Using (9.22), we can express firm-level variables of the average firm as:

$$\bar{p} = \frac{2k+1}{2(k+1)} c_D \quad \bar{\pi} = F_E \left(\frac{c_M}{c_D} \right)^k \quad \bar{r} = \frac{L}{2\gamma} \left(\frac{1}{k+2} \right) (c_D)^2$$

$$\bar{p} - \bar{c} = \frac{1}{2(k+1)} c_D \quad \frac{\bar{p}}{\bar{c}} = 1 + \frac{1}{2k} \tag{9.23}$$

Free entry entails $\int_0^{c_D} \frac{L}{4\gamma} [c_D - c]^2 \, d \, (c/c_M)^k = F_E$. This condition pins down the autarkic survival threshold as:

$$c_D^a = \left[\frac{\gamma \phi}{L} \right]^{1/(k+2)} \quad \text{where } \phi \equiv 2(k+1)(k+2)(c_M)^k F_E \tag{9.24}$$

Note that, in contrast to Melitz (2003), survival now requires the threshold cost to be lower or, equivalently, the threshold productivity to be higher in the larger country. To see why, note first that if expected profits net of the fixed entry cost are zero in a smaller country that has n_s firms, then expected profits must be positive in a larger country that also has n_s firms. But this can only mean that entry into the larger market comes to a halt when the number of active firms is larger than n_s. Since prices relate negatively to the number of producers, it then follows that the average price is lower in the larger country. Consequently, survival in the larger country requires a lower cost (c_D). The latter, and the fact that the larger country produces more varieties, implies that under autarky welfare is higher in the larger country.

The equilibrium number of firms in autarky is obtained by setting $p_{\max} = c_D$ and using conditions (9.21) and (9.23) to yield:

$$n^a = \frac{2(k+1)\gamma}{\kappa} \frac{\alpha - c_D^a}{c_D^a} \tag{9.25}$$

Condition (9.25) shows that n^a and c_D^a are negatively related. It also shows that for given c_D, the equilibrium number of firms is positively related to γ.

The open economy

We assume that countries are identical, with the possible exception of size. When transportation costs are zero, the transition from autarky to free trade creates a single integrated market and every active firm sells into both countries. The transition to an open economy affects average costs, mark-ups and welfare in the same way as an increase in country size.

When the transportation cost to the home country (τ) and to the foreign country (τ^*) are both positive, each country's differentiated goods industry will have exporters and non-exporters. As in Melitz (2003), the productivity of exporters will be higher than that of firms that only sell locally.

We now let c_D and c_D^* denote respectively the home and foreign country survival cost cut-offs. Similarly, we let c_X and c_X^* represent the home and foreign country export cost thresholds. Since markets are segmented, equilibrium requires that each country's survival threshold be equal to the threshold cost of the other country's exporters. Formally:

$$\tau^* c_X = c_D^* \quad \text{and} \quad \tau c_X^* = c_D \tag{9.26}$$

The simplicity of (9.26) compared to (9.16) follows from the assumption that firms do not incur a fixed export development cost. Such fixed export cost is not required to partition the industry into exporters and non-exporters when demands are linear. The reason is that the mark-up on exports sales goes to zero when $c \to c_X$.

In the open economy, freedom of entry in the home country entails:

$$\int_0^{c_D} \pi_D(c)dG(c) + \int_0^{c_X} \pi_X(c)dG(c) = \int_0^{c_D} (L/4\gamma)(c_D - c)^2 d(c/c_M)^k$$

$$+ \int_0^{c_X} (L^*/4\gamma)(\tau^*)^2(c_X - c)^2 d(c/c_M)^k = F_E$$

This condition can be restated as $L(c_D)^{k+2} + L^*(\tau^*)^{-k}(c_D^*)^{k+2} = \gamma\phi$ upon substitution from (9.26) with ϕ defined by (9.24). Similarly, free entry in the foreign country entails: $L^*(c_D^*)^{k+2} + L(\tau)^{-k}(c_D)^{k+2} = \gamma\phi$. Jointly, these two free entry conditions yield the free trade survival cut-offs

$$c_D^f = \left[\frac{\gamma\phi}{L}\frac{1-(\tau^*)^{-k}}{1-(\tau\tau^*)^{-k}}\right]^{1/k+2} \quad \text{and} \quad c_D^{*f} = \left[\frac{\gamma\phi}{L^*}\frac{1-\tau^{-k}}{1-(\tau\tau^*)^{-k}}\right]^{1/k+2} \tag{9.27}$$

Conditions (9.27) show that when transportation costs are positive, a country's survival cut-off is negatively related to its own size but not the trading partner's size. Melitz and Ottaviano (2008) explain that this is a consequence of a mutual cancelling effect; trade with a larger market provides greater opportunities on the export side but it also intensifies competition in the local market.

The conditions (9.27) also reveal that a country's survival threshold relates negatively to the transportation costs of its imports and positively to the transportation costs of its exports. Because τ and τ^*, are larger than 1, (9.27) and (9.24) also establish that each country's survival threshold is lower in the open economy than in autarky.[11] The latter result, in combination with (9.21) and $p_{max} = c_D$, implies that the number of firms that serve each country is larger in the open economy than under autarky.

The lower survival cut-off under free trade entails a lower average cost and a lower average price.[12] The price set by the home firm with marginal cost $c \in [0, c_D^f]$ in its local market is $p_l(c) = (c_D^f + c)/2$; the price set in the home market by a foreign producer with marginal cost $c \in [0, c_D^f/\tau]$ is $p_x^*(c) = (c_D^f + \tau c)/2$. The price distribution of locally produced and imported varieties is the same because the distributions of local production costs and delivered costs of imported varieties are identical. Thus, in both countries, the free trade average price is lower than the autarky price. As the average price-cost margin is also lower, average output per firm must be higher under free trade to ensure zero expected profits.

We conclude that a transition from autarky to free trade increases welfare in all trading countries via: 1) increased product variety, 2) lower prices and 3) lower production costs. When transport costs are the same ($\tau = \tau^*$) the larger country will have the lower survival cost threshold (see (9.27)), and welfare in the larger country, already higher than in the small country under autarky, will stay higher under free trade. The reason for this is that in the open economy, as in autarky, consumers in the larger country enjoy access to a larger number of varieties and can purchase them at a lower average price.

Trade liberalization

Since changes in tariffs and transportation costs affect prices, quantities and profits in the same way, we can examine the impact of liberalization by considering how a change in τ and τ^* perturbs the trading equilibrium. We will consider both short run and long run effects, where the short run is a period of time sufficiently brief to ensure that the number of firms in each country remains constant so that only rates of production will change. In the long run, trade liberalization will also determine the number of firms in each market via entry and exit.[13]

The long run

The home and foreign entrants draw a technology from the Pareto distributions $G(c) = (c/c_M)^k$ and $G^*(c^*) = (c^*/c_M^*)^k$. As in previous sections, the home market is served by home firms with average cost $c < c_D$ and by foreign firms with average cost $c^* < c_D/\tau$. Similarly, the foreign market is served by foreign-based firms having average cost $c^* < c_D^*$ and by home-based firms with average cost $c < c_D^*/\tau^*$.

The zero profit condition pins down the number of firms in each country. Using (9.26) and the zero profit conditions we then obtain:

$$c_D = \left[\frac{\gamma\phi}{L} \frac{1 - (\tau^* c_M/c_M^*)^{-k}}{1 - (\tau\tau^*)^{-k}} \right]^{1/k+2} \quad \text{and} \quad c_D^* = \left[\frac{\gamma\phi}{L^*} \frac{1 - (\tau^{-k} c_M^*/c_M)}{1 - (\tau\tau^*)^{-k}} \right]^{1/k+2} \tag{9.28}$$

Conditions (9.28) indicate that a country's survival threshold depends on its size, its fixed costs (via ϕ as shown by (9.24)), trading costs and the parameters of the marginal cost distributions.

The equilibrium number of suppliers of the home and foreign market – denoted N and N^* – is:

$$N = \frac{2(k+1)\gamma}{\kappa} \frac{\alpha - c_D}{c_D} \quad \text{and} \quad N^* = \frac{2(k+1)\gamma}{\kappa} \frac{\alpha - c_D^*}{c_D^*} \tag{9.29}$$

Note that (9.29) has the same form as (9.25). However, unlike (9.25), the N suppliers to the home market include both home and foreign producers. The same applies to the N^* suppliers to the foreign market. Given this, the number of firms located in each country – denoted n and n^* – are determined by the equalities $N = n(c_D/c_M)^k + n^*(c_D/\tau\, c_M^*)^k$ and $N^* = n^*(c_D^*/c_M^*)^k + n\left(c_D^*/\tau^*\, c_M\right)^k$.

Figure 9.2 displays the first condition (9.29) as the downward sloping curve *RR*. The equilibrium value of N is at the intersection of *RR* and the line *TT*, whose distance from the horizontal axis is determined by (9.28).

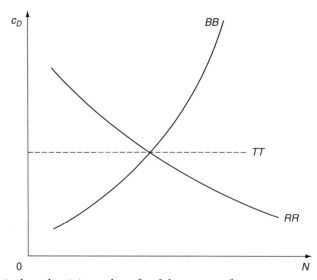

Figure 9.2 Survival productivity and profit of the average firm

A fall in τ (leaving τ^* unchanged) shifts the TT line upward, bringing about a new equilibrium in which the number of suppliers to the home market is lower and the home survival threshold is higher. Thus, the average price in the home country increases. In the foreign country, the survival threshold c_D^* falls as a result of exit from the home market and entry into the foreign market. This reshuffling of firms takes place because the lower τ makes it less costly to serve the home market from the foreign base.

Condition (9.28) also indicates that when trade costs are equal in both directions, the survival threshold decreases proportionately in both countries when trade costs fall in tandem. The effect on firm and industry level variables is qualitatively the same as for a transition from autarky to free trade.

The short run

Let the number of home and foreign based firms be $\bar{n}$ and $\bar{n}^*$. With these numbers fixed, a change in trade costs affects the equilibrium only via the survival thresholds c_D and c_D^*. Since the proportion of home and foreign firms serving the home country are $(c_D/c_M)^k$ and $(c_D/\tau\, c_M^*)^k$ respectively, the total number of varieties sold in the home and foreign countries by local and non-local firms will satisfy the following conditions:

$$ N = \bar{n}\,(c_D/c_M)^k + \bar{n}^*\big(c_D/\tau\, c_M^*\big)^k \text{ and } N^* = \bar{n}^*\big(c_D^*/c_M^*\big)^k + \bar{n}\,\big(c_D^*/\tau^*\, c_M\big)^k \quad (9.30)$$

Conditions (9.30) indicate that the number of varieties obtainable in each country relates positively to the country's survival threshold. Figure 9.2 displays this relationship as the curve BB. A fall in τ shifts BB to the right, with the resulting new intersection with RR involving a higher N and lower c_D. Higher cost home firms cease production. The average cost of home-based firms and the average home price fall.

The mark-up of the average firm $(\bar{p}/\bar{c})$ is pushed down by increased competition, but it is also pulled up by the exit of the highest cost firms (with the lowest mark-ups). These two effects cancel each other out, as is apparent from (9.23) which indicates that $\bar{p}/\bar{c}$ does not depend on c_D.

9.3 Endogenous comparative advantage

In order to determine how endowments affect trade when firms are heterogeneous Bernard *et al.* (2007) embed the Melitz (2003) model in a Helpman and Krugman (1985) framework. Their model assumes that firms use skilled labor (S) and unskilled labor (L) to produce two differentiated goods, labeled *1* and *2*. Both factors of production are internationally immobile but perfectly mobile across industries within each country. Good *1* is skill intensive and the home country is assumed to be abundant in skilled labor, that is: $\bar{S}/\bar{L} > \bar{S}^*/\bar{L}^*$.

On the production side, firms bear a variable cost and a fixed cost. The factor intensity of the processes that generate the fixed cost is the same as the intensity of the processes that generate the variable cost. The home skilled and unskilled wages are w_S and , w_L, respectively. The total cost of a home firm belonging to industry i with productivity φ can therefore be expressed as $C(\varphi)_i = \big[F_i + q_i/\varphi\big]\,W$, where q_i is the quantity of output and $W \equiv (w_S)^{\beta_i}(w_L)^{1-\beta_i}$, $[1 > \beta_1 > \beta_2 > 0]$.

Entrants draw their productivity φ from the distribution $G(\varphi)$ which is identical across industries and countries. As in Melitz (2003), firms that draw a productivity lower than the threshold φ_D exit immediately. Among active firms, those with $\varphi > \varphi_X$ sell locally and export; the active firms with lower productivity only sell locally. The cost of entry into the industry becomes sunk as soon as it is incurred. The entry process utilizes the two factors of production in the same proportion as they are used production. Specifically, the fixed entry cost for industry i is $F_{iE}W$. Exporters in industry i also bear an iceberg-type transportation cost τ_i, regardless of the country in which they are based.

The representative consumer is the same in both countries, and has preferences represented by utility $U = V_1^{\alpha_1} V_2^{\alpha_2}$ $(\alpha_1 + \alpha_2 = 1)$ where $V_i = \left[\sum_i v_i^{(\sigma-1)/\sigma} \right]^{\frac{\sigma}{\sigma-1}}$ $[i = \{1, 2\}]$. Consumers spend a share α_i of their total income on good i. National income is R in the home country and R^* in the foreign country.

The trading equilibrium

The price that home-based exporters in industry i set in their local market is p_{il}; the price they set in their export market is p_{ix}. Because markets are segmented, profit maximization entails:

$$p_{il}(\varphi) = (W_i/\varphi)(\sigma/\sigma - 1) \quad \text{and} \quad p_{ix}(\varphi) = \tau_i p_{il}(\varphi) \quad i = \{1, 2\} \tag{9.31}$$

Upon letting P_i and P_i^* denote the home and foreign price indices of industry $i (i = \{1, 2\})$, firm φ's revenue from local sales (r_i) and export sales (r_{iX}) can be expressed as:

$$r_1(\varphi) = \alpha R \left[\frac{\sigma - 1}{\sigma} \frac{\varphi}{W_1} P_1 \right]^{\sigma-1} \quad \text{and} \quad r_2(\varphi) = (1 - \alpha) R \left[\frac{\sigma - 1}{\sigma} \frac{\varphi}{W_2} P_2 \right]^{\sigma-1}$$

and

$$r_{1X}(\varphi) = \alpha R^* \left[\frac{\sigma - 1}{\sigma} \frac{\varphi}{W_1} P_1^*/\tau_1 \right]^{\sigma-1} \quad \text{and} \quad r_{2X}(\varphi) = (1 - \alpha) R^* \left[\frac{\sigma - 1}{\sigma} \frac{\varphi}{W_2} P_2^*/\tau_2 \right]^{\sigma-1} \tag{9.32}$$

Since (9.32) holds for all φ, the marginal exporter's ratio of export revenue to domestic revenue satisfies the conditions:

$$\left[\frac{P_i^*}{\tau_i P_i} \right]^{\sigma-1} \frac{R^*}{R} = \frac{r_{iX}(\varphi_{iX})}{r_i(\varphi_{iX})} = \frac{r_i(\varphi_{iD})F_{iX}/F_i}{r_i(\varphi_{iX})} = \frac{r_i(\varphi_{iX})(\varphi_{iD}/\varphi_{iX})^{\sigma-1}F_{iX}/F_i}{r_i(\varphi_{iX})} \tag{9.33}$$

The first equality in (9.33) follows from (9.32), the second from (9.16), and the third from (9.2).

The conditions (9.33) imply:

$$\varphi_{iX} = \Lambda_i \varphi_{iD} \quad \text{where} \quad \Lambda_i \equiv \tau_i \frac{P_i}{P_i^*} \left(\frac{F_{iX}}{F_i} \frac{R}{R^*} \right)^{1/(\sigma-1)} \tag{9.34}$$

Condition (9.34) shows that the home export threshold is higher relative to the home survival threshold when the home price index is higher relative to the foreign index, and when the home market is larger relative to the foreign market. Bernard *et al.* (2007) assume that Λ_i (and Λ_i^* for the foreign country) exceeds one. This ensures consistency with the observation that only a portion of active firms in an industry export.

The home price index P_i depends on the prices set by local firms and the delivered prices of foreign exporters. It is given by:

$$P_i = \left\{ M_i \left[p_{iL}\left(\tilde{\varphi}_i\right) \right]^{1-\sigma} + \frac{1 - G(\varphi_{iX}^*)}{1 - G(\varphi_{iD}^*)} M_i^* \left[\tau_i \, p_{iL}^*\left(\tilde{\varphi}_i^*\right) \right]^{1-\sigma} \right\}^{1/(1-\sigma)} \qquad (9.35)$$

where M_i and M_i^* respectively denote the number of home and foreign firms in industry i and $\tilde{\varphi}_i$ and $\tilde{\varphi}_i^*$ denote their average productivity. The term $1 - G(\varphi_{iX}^*)/1 - G(\varphi_{iD}^*)$ is the *ex ante* probability of exporting, conditional on successful entry.[14] Conditions that match (9.31) to (9.35) apply to the foreign country.

Freedom of entry into the home industry i means that:

$$\frac{1 - G(\varphi_{iD})}{\delta} \left\{ \pi_i\left(\tilde{\varphi}_{iL}\right) + \frac{1}{1 - G(\varphi_{iX})} \pi_{iX}\left(\tilde{\varphi}_{iX}\right) \right\} - F_{iE}\, W = 0.$$

Using the fact that $\pi\left(\tilde{\varphi}\right) = \left(\tilde{\varphi}/\varphi_D\right)^{\sigma-1} \pi(\varphi_D)$ and $\pi\left(\varphi_D\right) = r(\varphi_D)/\sigma = F_i W$, we can restate the free entry conditions as:

$$\frac{F_i}{\delta} \int_{\varphi_{iD}}^{\infty} \left[\left(\varphi/\varphi_{iD}\right)^{\sigma-1} - 1 \right] g(\varphi)\, d\varphi + \frac{F_{iX}}{\delta} \int_{\varphi_{iX}}^{\infty} \left[\left(\varphi/\varphi_{iX}\right)^{\sigma-1} - 1 \right] g\left(\varphi\right) d\varphi = F_{iE}$$

$$(9.36)$$

Condition (9.36) expresses the expected value of entry as the sum of the expected value under autarky and the expected value of profits from serving the export market. For given home and foreign price indices, conditions (9.33) and (9.36) pin down the survival and export thresholds.[15]

Equilibrium in the goods market in the home country requires that expenditure of the home and foreign consumers on the varieties produced by each industry equals that industry's revenue. The latter equals the industry's payments to factors of production since profits are zero. Therefore:

$$R_i = (\alpha_i R) M_i \left[\frac{p_{iL}\left(\tilde{\varphi}_i\right)}{P_i} \right]^{1-\sigma} + (\alpha_i R^*) M_i \frac{1 - G(\varphi_{iD})}{1 - G(\varphi_{iX})} \left[\frac{\tau_i \, p_{iL}\left(\tilde{\varphi}_i\right)}{P_i^*} \right]^{1-\sigma} = w_S S_i + w_L L_i$$

$$(9.37)$$

where S_i and L_i respectively denote the quantity of skilled and unskilled labor used by home industry i in production, in entry, and in exporting activities. The first equality in (9.37) states that total spending by home and foreign consumers on the varieties produced by the home industry i equals that industry's revenue. The second equality states that the industry's revenue equals its payments to factors of production. An equivalent condition holds for the foreign country. Jointly, the conditions (9.37) state that good markets clear at the world level.

Finally, the requirement that factor markets clear constrains factor usage in each country to be equal to its factor endowments:

$$S_1 + S_2 = \overline{S} \qquad S_1^* + S_2^* = \overline{S}^* \text{ and } L_1 + L_2 = \overline{L} \qquad L_1^* + L_2^* = \overline{L}^* \qquad (9.38)$$

The conditions (9.31) to (9.38) jointly determine the survival and export cut-offs in each country. They also determine prices, factor usage, factor prices and income.

We determine the values for the endogenous variables using a stepwise procedure. First, we set the home skilled wage as the numeraire ($w_S = 1$) and then determine the equilibrium allocation of factors to industries as a function of factor prices. Second, we calculate the $W_i's$ and use (9.31) to derive product prices in both countries as a function of their factor prices. Third, we determine total home income R_i for industry i using (9.37), and set $R = R_1 + R_2$. We carry out the same operation for the foreign country. Fourth, once R and R^* are determined, we use (9.33) and (9.36) to calculate the survival and export cut-offs as a function of factor prices. Fifth, we derive the average productivities from the thresholds productivities. Sixth, we obtain the number of firms from $M_i = R_i/r(\tilde{\varphi}_i)$ and $r(\tilde{\varphi}_i) = \left[\tilde{\varphi}_i/\tilde{\varphi}_{iD} \right]^{\sigma-1} \sigma F W_i^j$. Seventh, we calculate the price indices using (9.35). At this stage, all firm and industry level variables are still expressed as functions of factor prices. As the final step, we use the second equality in (9.37) to pin down factor prices.

From autarky to free trade

The effects of a transition from autarky to free trade depend on transportation costs and can be derived from conditions (9.31) to (9.38). We consider two cases: zero transport costs and positive transport costs.

Costless trade

The skill abundance of the home country brings about a lower autarkic relative wage for skilled labor and a lower price of the skill-intensive good. When borders open, goods prices converge. The relative wage of skilled workers increases in the skill abundant home country and falls in the foreign country; home production of the skill-intensive good increases in response to the increase in its price. The Rybczynski, Heckscher–Ohlin, Stolper-Samuelson and Factor Price Equalization theorems apply, with minor changes that capture monopolistic competition, firm heterogeneity and increasing returns to scale.

The move from autarky to free trade leaves the survival productivity cut-off and the average industry productivity unchanged in both industries. Indeed, when $F_X \to 0$ and $\tau_i \to 0$, (9.36) shrinks to $(F_i/\delta) \int_{\varphi_{iD}}^{\infty} \left[(\varphi/\varphi_{iD})^{\sigma-1} - 1 \right] g(\varphi)\, d\varphi = F_{iE}$. This is also the free entry condition that obtains under autarky. Since this condition pins down the survival cut-off we conclude that the survival cut-off is unresponsive to the move from autarky to free trade. The intuition is that when borders are open to costless trade, all active firms export. Consequently, all enjoy proportionately in the extra demand on the part of consumers located in the other country, but they also suffer proportionately from the reduced demand on the part of consumers located in their own country.[16] The number of home firms in industry (i) 1 expands at each level of productivity relative to industry 2 because production realigns according to comparative advantage. In the foreign country, it is the number of firms in industry 2 that expands.

Costly trade

When trade is costly, exporters' *ex post* profits increase and non-exporters' profits fall when the economy moves towards free trade. The reason is that all firms face import competition in the open economy, but only the more productive among them gain access to the other country's market. The extra profit opportunities enjoyed by the more productive firms raise the expected value of entry into each industry due to the higher *ex ante* probability of drawing a productivity that allows an entrant to earn profits from exporting. This boosts entry and reduces further the *ex post* profits earned by firms that only sell locally. Some of these firms exit because they can no longer cover their fixed production costs. The joint effect of entry and exit is to raise the survival productivity thresholds and the average productivity in both industries.

When there is no cross-industry difference in transport costs – or in the ratio of fixed production cost to fixed export cost – the increase in average productivity is larger in the industry that enjoys the comparative advantage. The reason is that profits earned in export markets relative to profits earned from home sales are larger in that industry. As a result, exporters' *ex post* profits rise more sharply in the comparative advantage industry and, as a consequence, the expected value of entry increases more in that industry than in the other industry. The conclusion is that more entry is induced into the comparative advantage industry, which brings forth a larger increase in that industry's survival threshold and in its average productivity.

The change in the average firm's output in response to the move towards free trade is determined by the combination of lower demand at home and the new demand on the part of foreigners. As the survival threshold increases, it lowers the probability of drawing a productivity level sufficient to become an active producer. Because in equilibrium the expected value of entry must equal the entry cost, the average profit conditional on being active is higher than in autarky. Moreover, since the survival threshold increases more in the comparative advantage industry, the increase in output of that industry's average firm is larger than the increase in output of the average firm in the other industry.

There is an alternative way of understanding the pattern of change induced by a move to free trade. The opening of borders increases the demand for labor on the part of firms endowed with the superior technologies that bring profitable export opportunities. Because exporters' extra demand for skilled and unskilled labor is largest in the comparative advantage industry, the price of the factor used intensively by that industry increases relative to the price of the other factor. As a result, the cost of production in the comparative advantage industry increases relative to the cost of production in the other industry. In addition, the survival threshold increases most in the comparative advantage industry. Since the average productivity is an increasing function of the threshold productivity, and because the autarky thresholds in each industry are the same in both countries, it follows that in the trading equilibrium each country has higher average productivity in the industry that intensively uses the country's abundant factor.

Welfare and factor rewards

By triggering an increase in the average productivity which is larger in the comparative advantage industry, the transition to free trade gives rise to a Ricardian productivity gap at the industry level that magnifies the Heckscher-Ohlin-based source of comparative advantage. In addition, by increasing the demand for a country's comparative advantage good the transition to an open economy raises the relative demand for a country's abundant factor. This gives rise to a Stolper-Samuelson effect (See Chapter 4).

By increasing the average productivity in both industries, the transition to free trade lowers the price index of both goods. There is also an adjustment in the mass of consumed varieties. Consumers gain access to foreign varieties, and this reduces the price indices further. However, the total mass of varieties available for consumption does not necessarily increase because the mass of domestically produced varieties falls.

When the combined welfare gains from productivity improvements and from the change in the mass of available varieties are sufficiently large, the transition to free trade *may* increase the real reward of the scarce factor. This outcome, which stands in stark contrast to the standard Heckscher–Ohlin prediction, is more likely the less the disparity in endowments between countries.

9.4 The diversity of export destinations

Bernard *et al.* (2003) propose a different approach to the questions of why a small proportion of firms in an industry export, and why those that export are considerably more productive than those that only sell into the local market. They address these questions within the framework of a model that emphasizes the role of intra-industry cost differences and geographical barriers. Their model addresses more directly the question of why the more productive of exporting firms generally sell to a larger number of foreign markets.

The Bernard *et al.* (2003) framework assumes a representative consumer whose CES utility is defined over a continuum of goods or varieties within the interval [0,1]. The elasticity of substitution is the same for all pairs of goods. There are N countries, which gives each country $N-1$ potential trading partners. In all countries there is a continuum of potential producers for every good. A firm's efficiency, which is the output it can produce from a given bundle of inputs, is the realization of a random variable. The technology exhibits constant returns to scale.

Exporters incur an iceberg-type transportation cost $\tau_{is} \geq 1$, which is the number of units they must ship from country s to ensure that one unit arrives in country i. It is assumed that $\tau_{is} = \tau_{si}$, $\tau_{ii} = 1$, and that the triangle inequality, $\tau_{hi} \leq \tau_{hk}\tau_{ki}$ holds for all countries i, h and k. This inequality states that the cost of moving a good directly from one country to any other country is never larger than the cost of moving that good from the same origin to the same destination via a third country.

Firms engage in Bertrand price competition. Because they draw their productivity from a continuous distribution, the probability that any two firms produce at the same cost is zero.

In an open economy, consumers purchase from the firm (local or foreign) that delivers at the lowest price. Because transportation costs vary across country pairs, the lowest cost supplier to one country need not be the lowest cost supplier to another country. The number of countries that are the lowest price suppliers to some destinations is an increasing function of transportation costs.

We have shown in Section 8.1 of Chapter 8 that the profit maximizing price at which the lowest-cost supplier sells in a market is the lower of two values: 1) the cost at which the second lowest cost supplier to that market can deliver the good; 2) the monopoly price the firm would set if no other potential supplier existed.

Given this, let $\varphi_{1h}(j)$ denote the efficiency of the most efficient producer of good j based in country h and let w_h denote the cost of an input bundle in country h. Condition (9.39) ensures that the lowest cost firm based in country h supplies its local market. It does so because its production cost is lower than the delivered cost to country h from all other countries:

$$w_h/\varphi_{1h}(j) \leq w_k\tau_{hk}/\varphi_{1k}(j) \Leftrightarrow w_h/w_k\tau_{hk} \leq \varphi_{1h}(j)/\varphi_{1k}(j) \text{ for all countries } k \neq h$$

(9.39)

The same firm will supply country y if the following condition holds:

$$w_h\tau_{yh}/\varphi_{1h}(j) \leq w_k\tau_{yk}/\varphi_{1k}(j) \Leftrightarrow w_h\tau_{yh}/w_k\tau_{yk} \leq \varphi_{1h}(j)/\varphi_{1k}(j) \text{ all countries } k \neq h$$

(9.40)

This condition states that the delivered cost from country h to country y must be lower than the delivered cost of exports from any other country.

Conditions (9.39) and (9.40), and the triangle inequality, jointly imply that exporting requires a higher level of efficiency than selling locally. It implies that exporters enjoy a higher productivity on average than firms which serve only their local market. And, for given transportation costs, the number of foreign markets served by a firm relates positively to its level of efficiency.

To account for the effects arising from entry and exit, the model assumes that firms draw their technology from a Fréchet distribution $F(\varphi) = e^{-T\varphi^{-\theta}}$. The mean of this distribution is increasing in T and its variance relates negatively to $\theta > 1$. Bernard *et al.* (2003) assume that T varies across countries but not across goods, and that θ is the same across goods and across countries. T_i captures country i's technological level while θ is indicative of the scope of the gains from trade. This is because a smaller θ signifies more heterogeneity in terms of efficiency, which gives a higher probability that the foreign supplier with the lowest delivered cost will be more efficient than the most efficient local firm.

The assumption that firms draw their efficiency levels from Fréchet distributions is convenient because the joint distribution of the maximum of two independent draws from Fréchet distributions with common θ is itself a Fréchet distribution. This allows us to write the joint distribution c_1 the cost of the lowest delivered cost supplier to country y, and the delivered cost of the second lowest cost supplier (c_2), as:[17]

$$K_y(c_1, c_2) = 1 - e^{-\Phi_y c_2^{\theta}} - \Phi_y c_1^{\theta} e^{-\Phi_y c_2^{\theta}} \text{ where } \Phi_y = \sum_{i=1}^{N} T_i(w_i \tau_{yi})^{-\theta} \qquad (9.41)$$

The term Φ_y condenses the parameters of: 1) the productivity distribution in all countries; 2) countries' input costs; 3) trade costs around the world. The distribution of c_2 conditional on c_1 is:

$$H_y(c_2 | c_1) = 1 - e^{-\Phi_y(c_2^{\theta} - c_1^{\theta})} \qquad (9.42)$$

Since $\Phi_y > 0$, the conditional distribution increases stochastically in c_1. Thus, the expected delivered cost of the second-lowest-cost supplier is smaller the lower is the delivered cost of the lowest-cost supplier. The implication of this is that greater efficiency by an exporting firm is associated with a lower price in its home market and in its export markets. The reason is that the price is bound from above by the lower expected delivered cost borne by the second-lowest-cost supplier, and by a lower monopoly price.

Bernard *et al.* (2003) then show that in every country the mark-up is the realization of a draw from a Pareto distribution. A greater disparity in efficiency increases the probability of higher mark-ups. This is expected because the greater disparity in efficiency entails a greater probability of a large gap between the costs of the two most efficient firms.

A reduction in transportation costs increases the number of potential suppliers to every country. This leads to a decrease in the mark-up of firms that survive competition. However, that decrease is exactly offset by the exit of higher cost producers with the lowest mark-ups. The distribution of mark-ups across active suppliers remains unchanged. Hence, there is an increased probability that the surviving firms, whose costs are expected to be lower, set lower prices. If so, then they will also sell a larger quantity.

Bernard *et al.* (2003) calculate that a 5 percent fall in worldwide trade barriers would raise overall US labor productivity in manufacturing by 4.7 percent. The largest portion of this gain would come from a decline in the price of intermediate goods, as cheaper imports would replace domestically produced inputs. They also calculate that over 3 percent of plants would exit, and that this would contribute the remaining 0.8 percent to the productivity gain. They also determine that the US wage relative the other countries would increase by 10 percent.[18]

9.5　Measuring the impact of trade costs

The models in Bernard *et al.* (2003), Melitz (2003) and Melitz and Ottaviano (2008) predict that a symmetric reduction in the cost of importing would set in motion a process that causes productivity to increase at the industry level, increases exit, increases the probability that a firm becomes an exporter, increases export sales by firms that already exported and reduces the share of sales to local buyers.

Bernard *et al.* (2006) test these predictions by examining the responses of US manufacturing industries and plants to changes in industry-level trade costs from 1982 through 1992. They define an industry's trade cost (TC) as the sum of two components: 1) the weighted average of *ad valorem* duties on imports of all goods produced by the industry; 2) the weighted average of the *ad valorem* transportation costs of these goods.[19]

The *ad valorem* duty rate on industry i in year t – denoted d_{it} – is the amount of duty collected on products made by the industry, relative to their free on board (f.o.b.) value [$d_{it} = duties_{it}/fob_{it}$]. The *ad valorem* freight rate of industry i at time t – denoted f_{it} – is the mark-up of the cost insurance freight (*cif*) value over *fob* value, that is $f_{it} = (cif_{it} - fob_{it})/fob_{it}$.

The change in trade costs is then defined as $\Delta TC_{it} = \left[(d_{it} + f_{it}) + (d_{it-5} + f_{it-5})\right]/5$.[20] Bernard *et al.* calculate that the weighted average US tariff on 39 two-digit manufacturing industries declined from 4.8 percent to 4.2 percent in the ten-year period ending in 1992. The average freight rate fell from 5.6 percent to 4.1 percent of the *fob* value.

The estimating equations used to assess the effect of trade costs are:

$$y_{it} = c_t + \beta \Delta TC_{it} + \delta_i + \delta_t + \varepsilon_{it} \tag{9.43}$$

and

$$y_{it} = c_t + \beta \Delta TC_{it} + \gamma Z_{it} + \delta_i + \delta_t + \varepsilon_{it} \tag{9.44}$$

where δ_i and δ_t are industry and time fixed effects. Z_t is a vector of industry or plant variables whose elements change according to the choice of dependent variable. The Z_t vector also captures interactions between the change in trade costs and plant-level variables. Bernard *et al.* refer to (9.43) as the basic equation, and to (9.44) as the expanded equation. In all but one estimating equation, y is a plant-level variable. When it is an industry-level variable, only the basic equation (9.43) is estimated.

Table 9.1 reports the estimated β's and the coefficients of the interaction variable between ΔTC and plant relative productivity (*PRP*). The latter is defined as the percentage difference between a plant's productivity and the productivity of the plant with mean productivity in its four-digit industry. Column 2 displays the estimated β's from the basic equation (9.43), while column 3 shows the estimated coefficients from the broadest of the expanded equations. Column 4 gives the estimated coefficient on the interaction term in the broadest of the expanded estimating equations.

The first line of Table 9.1 presents the estimated impact of lower trade costs on total industry productivity. The dependent variable $\Delta TFP_{industry}$ is the average annual percent variation in an industry's total factor productivity from year t to year $t + 5$. The sign of the estimated β's fits the predictions of all three models, and suggests that a decline in trade costs of one standard deviation yields an annual industry productivity growth of 0.2 percent.

While all the models examined in this chapter predict a change in productivity via entry, exit and a reshuffling of output shares, one cannot dismiss the possibility that the measured effect at the industry level also captures productivity change at the plant level. To check for this possibility, Bernard *et al.* also estimate equations that have *individual* exporters' relative total factor productivity growth as the dependent variable ($y = \Delta TPF_{plant}$). Row 2 of

Table 9.1 Effects of changing trade costs on selected measures of performance

Dependent variable Y	Estimated β Basic equation	Estimated β Expanded equation	Coefficient interactive term ($\Delta TC * PRP$)
$\Delta TFP_{industry}$	−0.190*		
ΔTFP_{plant}	−1.027	−2.321*	0.545
Prob (new exporter = 1)	−8.933*	−8.621*	1.359
Prob (death = 1)	−5.664*	−6.669**	12.178**
Domestic market share	0.0008	−0.0043	0.0162*

*p < 0.10; **p < 0.05; ***p < 0.01.
Source: Bernard *et al.* (2006).

the estimation yields a statistically significant β provided one controls for plant attributes such as age, multinational status and capital intensity. Overall, the estimated coefficients suggest that productivity adjustments at surviving plants have some influence on the response of industry productivity to changing trading costs.

Row 3 in Table 9.1 shows the estimated impact of trade cost on the logit of the probability that a non-exporting plant would become an exporter. The estimated coefficients indicate, in accordance with the theory, that this probability increases when trade costs fall. A decline in trade costs of one standard deviation increases the probability of exporting by 0.6 percent. Bernard *et al.* also find that high productivity firms are more likely to enter export markets. However, the finding of a non-significant coefficient for the interaction term seems to challenge the idea that lower trade costs draw the most productive firms into foreign markets. Tybout (2006) considers the possibility that the absence of a significant coefficient may reflect the absence of an effect of lower trading costs on the export decision of the most productive *and* the least productive firms. The former may have become exporters in any case; their change of status from non-exporter to exporter is unrelated to the trade cost. The latter may not have been influenced by the fall in trade costs because their productivity handicap was too large. That leaves firms with intermediate productivity as the only group whose decision to enter foreign markets is responsive to trade costs. But then a significant coefficient for the interaction term would merely indicate that the firms in question were either above or below the average productivity; the estimated coefficient suggests they were neither.

To assess the effect of a change in trade costs on exit, Bernard *et al.* (2006) specify a logistic equation that relates the change in trade costs in the period $(t − 5, t)$ to the probability of a plant's death in period $(t, t + 5)$. The estimated coefficient displayed in Row 4 of Table 9.1 shows that a decline in trade costs equal to one standard deviation increases the probability of a plant's exit by approximately 5 percent. The coefficient of the interaction term indicates that the probability of exit in the face of falling trade costs is lower for more productive plants.

Bernard *et al.* (2006) find no evidence to support the hypothesis that the domestic share of sales correlates positively with trade costs. While the interaction term has the expected sign and is significant, its estimated impact is very small: a decline of one standard deviation in trade costs appears to increase the domestic share of the typical exporter by only 0.005 percent. The authors note that this finding stands in contrast to the literature on developing countries, which typically report that trade liberalization is associated with a fall in domestic sales.

9.6 Concluding remarks

This chapter has discussed the gains from trade that arise from a selection process that involves the replacement of less efficient by more efficient producers. Low productivity firms exit an industry in response to the transition to an open economy and high productivity firms expand into export markets. This replacement effect takes place in industries that are net importers as well as net exporters. Empirical research (e.g., Pavcnik, 2002 and Tybout, 2003) much of which looks at developing countries, finds that these within-industry reallocations of output are larger than the across-industry reallocations predicted by classical comparative advantage models.

One issue this chapter did not emphasize is productivity change at the firm level. There is some evidence in support of the argument that trade makes firms more productive. Van Biesebroeck (2005), for example, finds that sub-Saharan exporters increased productivity after entry into export markets. There is also evidence that buttresses the claim that the contribution to industry productivity from plant-level gains is smaller than the contribution from the reallocation of output across firms. Trefler (2003), for example, finds that the growth in productivity of Canadian industries following the Canada-US free trade agreement was roughly twice as large as the gains in plant productivity.

Problems

9.1 Make use of conditions (9.29) and (9.30) to determine the long-term and short-term effects of a lower τ^* on c_D and N.

Notes

1. Bernard *et al.* (2007).
2. See condition (A8.6) in the appendix of Chapter 8.
3. Roberts and Tybout (1997) determine that those costs are quite significant in the case of Colombian and Moroccan firms. Clerides *et al.* (1998) find that a firm's investment in export development relates negatively to the number of producers who have already made that investment.
4. The superscript "a" is used here to emphasize that condition (9.9) holds under autarky.
5. The realized profits of all *active* firms with the exception of the firm(s) indexed φ_D are strictly positive.
6. An appendix to Melitz (2003) shows the existence of the equilibrium which is unique when $\varphi g(\varphi)/1 - G(\varphi)$ is increasing. The latter is satisfied by commonly used distributions.
7. Baldwin and Forslid (2006) let firms draw from Pareto distributions, and let countries differ in size. Demidova (2005) does not assume a specific functional form of the productivity distribution. She assumes that that the home country's technology enjoys a hazard rate stochastic dominance. This means that for any given productivity level φ, entrants in the home country have a better chance of drawing a higher φ than entrants in the foreign country. Falvey *et al.* (2006) assume first order stochastic dominance on part of the home country's distribution over the range of productivities observed under autarky in the foreign country. This means that the probability of a home entrant drawing a better technology than a foreign entrant is not lower for any technology in the range, and higher for at least some technology.

8. Note the similarity with (9.16) and recall that exporters' delivered cost to the home market is $\tau c^* = \tau/\varphi^*$

9. Whether both countries will in fact produce the differentiated good depends on the magnitude of the gap in technology. Falvey *et al.* (2006) show: 1) that the gap which allows the differentiated industry to exist in the smaller country is larger when that country has better technology; 2) that the larger country may not have a differentiated industry if the technology of the smaller country is much better.

10. The hypothesis that a Pareto distribution fits the dispersal of productivity across sectors and countries finds support in Del Gatto *et al.* (2006). For $k = 1$, $G[c]$ is uniform and $\bar{c} = c_D/2$. As k increases the cost distribution becomes more concentrated at higher cost levels.

11. Note that when $\tau \to \infty$ and $\tau^* \to \infty$ both thresholds converge to the threshold of the closed economy.

12. The lower survival cut-off triggers exit, driven by a disappearance of the gap between price and marginal cost. In contrast to Melitz (2003) the narrowing of this gap does not hinge on an increase of the wage. Any extra demand for labor by the differentiated industry can be met via a release of workers by the homogeneous industry provided the latter is sufficiently large.

13. The remainder of this section follows Chen *et al.* (2009).

14. $1 - G(\varphi_{iD}^*)$ is the *ex ante* probability of successful entry.

15. The conditions do not contain W. This is because the model assumes that entry activities and production use inputs in the same proportion.

16. Note that the thresholds remain the same under costless trade because the production and entry processes share the same factor intensity. If they did not, the term W would appear in the free entry condition, and thresholds would change in response to the move towards free trade. We also note that the absence of W from the free entry condition in autarky implies that the autarkic survival threshold is the same in the home and foreign country, even though endowments are different.

17. The derivation of the distributions used in Bernard *et al.* (2003) is given in a mathematical appendix available at http://www.aeaweb.org/aer/contents/.

18. Alvarez and Lucas (2007) use a similar framework to explore the gains that would result from a word-wide elimination of tariffs.

19. To match products to industries they use Feenstra's (2002) concordance. They stress that changes in the composition of products or importers within industries can affect the calculated *TC*s, even when the actual statutory tariffs and transportation costs do not change.

20. The five-year gap corresponds to the interval between US manufacturing censuses.

References and additional reading

Within industry heterogeneity

Alvarez, F. and Lucas R.E. (2007), "General Equilibrium Analysis of the Eaton-Kortum Model of International Trade," *Journal of Monetary Economics*, 54, 1726–1768.

Baldwin, R.E. and Forslid, R. (2004), "Trade Liberalization with Heterogeneous Firms," CEPR Discussion paper, No. 4635.

Bernard, A.B., Eaton, J., Jensen J.B., and Kortum S., (2003), "Plants and Productivity in International Trade," *American Economic Review*, 93 (4), 1268–1290.

Bernard, A.B. and Jensen J.B. (2004), "Why Some Firms Export," *The Review of Economics and Statistics*, 86 (2), 561–569.

Bernard, A.B., Redding, S.J. and Schott P.K. (2007), "Comparative Advantage and Hedterogeneous Firms," *Review of Economic Studies*, 74 (1), 31–66.

Bernard, A.B, Jensen J.B., Redding S.J. and Schott P.K. (2007), "Firms in International Trade," *Journal of Economic Perspectives*, 21 (3), 105–130.

Chen N., Imbs J. and Scott, A. (2009), "The Dynamics of Trade and Competition," *Journal of International Economics*, 77, 50–62.

Demidova, S. (2008), "Productivity Improvements and Falling Trade Cost: Boon or Bane?" *International Economic Review*, 49 (4), 1437–1462.

Eaton, J. and Kortum, S. (2002), "Technology, Geography and Trade," *Econometrica*, 70 (5), 1741–1779.

Eaton J., Kortum, S. and Kramarz, F. (2004), "Dissecting Trade: Firms, Industries, and Export Destinations," *American Economic Review, Papers and Proceedings*, 93, 150–154.

Falvey, R., Greenaway, D., and Yu, Z. (2006), "Extending the Melitz Model to Asymmetric Countries," The University of Nottingham Research paper.

Helpman, E. and Krugman, P. (1985), *Market Structure and Foreign Trade* (Cambridge, MA: MIT Press). Melitz, M.J. (2003), "The Impact of Trade on Intra-Industry Reallocations and Aggregate Industry Productivity," *Econometrica*, 71 (6), 1695–1725.

Melitz, M.J. and Ottaviano, G. (2008), "Market Size, Trade and Productivity," *Review of Economics Studies*, 75, 295–316.

Ottaviano, G., Tabushi T., and Thisse, J.-F. (2002), "Agglomeration and Trade Revisited," *International Economic Review*, 43, 409–436.

Empirical

Alvarez, R. and Lopez, R.A. (2005), "Exporting and Performance: Evidence from Chilean Plants," *Canadian Journal of Economics*, 38 (4), 1384–1400.

Bernard, A.B., Jensen, J.B., and Schott, P.K. (2006), "Trade Costs, Firms and Productivity," *Journal of Monetary Economics*, 53, 917–937.

Clerides, S., Lack S. and Tybout, J.R. (1998), "Is Learning by Exporting Important Micro-dynamic Evidence from Colombia, Mexico and Morocco?" *Quarterly Journal of Economics*, 113 (3), 903–948.

Del Gatto, M., Mion, G., and Ottaviano, G. (2006), "Trade Integration, Firm Selection and the Costs of Non-Europe," CEPR Discussion Paper, No. 5730.

Feenstra, R.C., Romalis, J., and Schott, P.K. (2002), "US Imports, Exports, and Tariff Data, 1989–2001," NBER Working Paper 9387. Cambridge, MA: NBER.

Greenaway, D., Hine, R., and Milner, C. (1995), "Vertical and Horizontal Intra-Industry Trade: A Cross Industry Analysis for the United Kingdom," *Economic Journal*, 105, 1505–1518.

Lawrence, R.Z. (2000), "Does a Kick in the Pants get you going or does it just Hurt? The Impact of International Competition on Technological Change in US Manufacturing," in R.C. Feenstra (Ed.), *The Impact of International Trade on Wages* (Chicago: University of Chicago Press), 197–224.

MacDonald, M.J. (1994), "Does Import Competition Force Efficient Production?" *Review of Economics and Statistics*, 76 (4), 721–727.

Pavcnik, N. (2002), "Trade Liberalization, Exit, and Productivity Improvement: Evidence from Chilean Plants," *Economics Studies*, 69 (1), 245–276.

Roberts, M.J. and Tybout, J. (1997), "The Decision to Export in Colombia: An Empirical Model of Entry with Sunk Costs," *The American Economic Review*, 87 (4), 545–564.

Tybout, J.R. (2003), "Plant- and Firm Level Evidence on the "New" Trade Theories," in E. Kwan Choi and L. Harrigan (Eds.), *Handbook of International Trade,* ch. 13 (Malden MA and Oxford: Blackwell Publishing)

Tybout, J.R. (2006), "Comments on: Trade Costs, Firms and Productivity," *Journal of Monetary Economics*, 53, 939–942.

Van Biesebroeck, J. (2005), "Exporting Raises Productivity in Sub-Saharan African Manufacturing Plants," *Journal of International Economics,* 67 (2), 373–391.

10

Trade policy in imperfectly competitive markets

The welfare consequences of trade policy in oligopolistic markets differ radically from the effects that the same policies bring about in competitive environments. Small countries may gain from levying tariffs or export taxes. They may also gain from granting export subsidies. The welfare benefits derive from strengthening home firms' monopoly power in foreign markets, or from allowing home firms to capture rents that would otherwise be earned by their foreign rivals.

Then again, the welfare effects that trade policy generates in imperfectly competitive markets are very much dependent on the particular form of oligopolistic interaction. Also, their short-term effects may run counter to their long-term effects.

The primary objective of this chapter is to underscore policy issues stemming from market power. For that reason the chapter does not discuss asymmetries that exist across countries and across firms. It conducts the analysis in a partial equilibrium framework and considers the effects of pure trade policy instruments, ignoring possible interactions with other policies, such as antitrust.

The analysis proceeds from simple to more complicated. It starts with an exploration of import tariffs and export subsidies when policy makers face no trade-off between consumer and producer interests. The early findings serve as building blocks in subsequent sections, which address trade policy issues in settings that more closely reflect real-world markets.

Section 1, the longest of this chapter, looks at import tariffs and export subsidies. Section 2 analyzes quotas and voluntary export restraints. It shows why equivalences between tariffs and quotas that hold in competitive environments cease to exist under monopoly and oligopoly. It explains why quality upgrading takes place in response to quantitative restrictions, and shows how such upgrading is captured empirically. The final section considers the effects of contingent protection in the form of anti-dumping and anti-subsidy measures.

10.1 Rivalry in a single market

This section begins by exploring the welfare effects of a home tariff when a foreign oligopoly serves the home market. It then turns to the question of how export taxes and subsidies determine home welfare when home exporters enjoy oligopoly power in a foreign market. The section concludes by contrasting the welfare effects of using unilateral versus bilateral trade policy instruments.[1]

A foreign oligopoly serving the home market

A foreign oligopoly comprised of n^* firms serves the home market and encounters no competition from home-based producers.[2] The home market is segmented and exporters' marginal costs are constant. Thus, foreign firms maximize profits in the home country independently. Without loss of generality, we equate the foreign firms' export volume to its total output, that is $q_x^* = q^*$. Hence $Q_x^* = Q^* = n^* q^*$ where upper case Q denotes total industry sales. The cost borne by individual oligopolists is $C^*(q^*) = F^* + c^* q^*$.

Let p denote the price that home consumers pay when the home country levies an *ad valorem* tariff τ. The net of duty price received by exporters is then $p(Q^*)/(1+\tau)$. All foreign firms earn a profit $\pi^* = [p(Q^*)/(1+\tau)] - F^* - c^* q^*$.

Under Cournot competition, first-order conditions are then given by:

$$\left\{ p(Q^*) + q^* \frac{dp(Q^*)}{dQ^*} \frac{dQ^*}{dq^*} \right\} = \left\{ p(Q^*) + \frac{Q^*}{n^*} \frac{dp(Q^*)}{dQ^*} \right\}$$

$$= \left\{ \frac{1}{n^*} MR(Q^*) + \left[1 - \frac{1}{n^*} \right] p(Q^*) \right\} = mr(Q^*, n^*) = (1+\tau)c^* \qquad (10.1)$$

where $MR(Q^*) \equiv p(Q^*) + Q^* dp(Q^*)/dQ^*$ denotes industry marginal revenue. Equation (10.1) expresses the marginal revenue perceived by the individual firm – denoted mr – as a weighted average of price and industry marginal revenue. Differentiation of Equation (10.1) yields:

$$\frac{dQ^*}{d\tau} = c^* \left\{ \frac{1}{n^*} MR'(Q^*) + \left[1 - \frac{1}{n^*} \right] p'(Q^*) \right\}^{-1} \qquad (10.2)$$

The right-hand side of Equation (10.2) is negative when MR is downward sloping, which is normally assumed. We also have:

$$\frac{d(p/(1+\tau))}{d\tau} = -c^* \left\{ \frac{MR'(Q^*) - p'(Q^*)}{MR'(Q^*) + (n^* - 1)p'(Q^*)} + \frac{p(Q^*) - c^*}{c^*} \right\} \qquad (10.3)$$

Because price exceeds marginal cost, the condition $MR'(Q^*) < p'(Q^*)$ (that is, industry marginal revenue is more negatively sloped than demand) ensures that the price received by exporters falls when the tariff increases.

Home welfare – denoted W – is the sum of consumer welfare and tariff revenue:

$$W = \left[\int_0^{Q^*} p(\upsilon)d\upsilon - p(Q^*)Q^* \right] + p(Q^*)Q^* \tau/(1+\tau)$$

Differentiation of this expression gives:

$$\frac{dW}{d\tau} = -Q^* \frac{dp(Q^*)}{dQ^*} \frac{dQ^*}{d\tau} + \frac{1}{1+\tau} \left\{ \frac{p(Q^*)Q^*}{1+\tau} + \tau \frac{dp(Q^*)Q^*}{d\tau} \right\} \tag{10.4}$$

In (10.4), the first term is negative and captures the effect of the tariff change on consumer welfare. The sign of the second term is uncertain as, for any given value of imports, tariff revenue increases in the tariff rate while the value of imports falls.

A small tariff raises welfare above its free trade level through an improvement in the home country's terms of trade. This is shown by setting $\tau = 0$ in Equation (10.4).

$$\left. \frac{dW}{d\tau} \right|_{\tau=0} = -Q^* \frac{dp/(1+\tau)}{d\tau} > 0 \tag{10.5}$$

Figure 10.1 illustrates how a tariff affects the free trade equilibrium. The demand that exporters face under free trade is shown as p and their perceived marginal revenue is shown as mr. Under free trade, the home country imports quantity Q_1^*. When it levies a tariff, the demand shifts to $p/(1+\tau)$, the perceived marginal revenue shifts to $mr/(1+\tau)$, exports fall to Q_2^*, and consumer surplus falls by an amount represented by the sum of areas A and B.

Tariff revenue is represented by the sum of the lighter-shaded area A and the darker-shaded area C. The change in welfare due to the tariff is represented by area C less area B. The gain in welfare derives from the capture of exporter surplus (area C) in the form of tariff revenue. This gain is set against the loss due to a widening of the gap between the price home consumers pay for imports and the external world cost of the imports to the home country. A tariff increase always expands area B, but it may increase or decrease the size of area C. A small tariff will increase area C by more than area B since area B is proportional to τ^2 whereas area C is proportional to τ.

Home welfare is highest when a marginal increase in the tariff adds as much to area B as it adds to area C. As in the case of the fully competitive large economy (see Chapter 5), the welfare maximizing τ is lower than the revenue maximizing tariff since home welfare includes consumer surplus which decreases monotonically in the tariff.

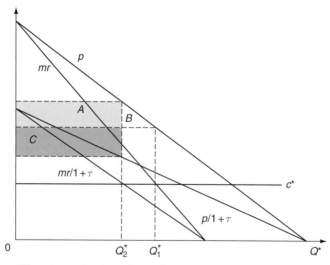

Figure 10.1 A tariff against a foreign oligopoly

Finally, we note that area C decreases relative to area B when n^* increases, and as n^* becomes very large area C vanishes as firms' marginal revenue approaches price. In the limit, the effect of the tariff is the same as in a competitive market.

A home oligopoly serving a foreign market

Consider now the case of a home-based oligopoly that serves a segmented foreign market. There are n home firms, all having the same cost function $C(q) = F + cq$. Home firms face no competition in the foreign market. In the absence of home consumption, the entire production by home firms is then consumed in the foreign country, that is, $q_x = q$ and $Q_x = Q = nq$.

When the home country levies an *ad valorem* export tax θ, home firms receive a price $p^*(Q)/(1+\theta)$, and their net profit can be expressed as $\pi = [p^*(Q)/(1+\theta) - c]q - F$. Cournot competition therefore entails:

$$p^*(Q) + q\frac{dp^*(Q)}{dQ} = p^*(Q) + \frac{Q}{n}\frac{dp^*(Q)}{dQ} = (1+\theta)c \tag{10.6}$$

Since Equation (10.6) has the same form as Equation (10.1), it follows that in qualitative terms a change in θ affects price and quantity in the same way as a change in the tariff. That is, $dQ/d\theta < 0$ and $d[p^*/(1+\theta)]d\theta < 0$.

In the absence of home consumption, home welfare equals gross industry profits as given by $[p^*(Q) - c]Q - nF$. Therefore, we can express the change in welfare as:

$$\frac{dW(\theta)}{d\theta} = [p^* + Qp^{*'} - c]\frac{dQ}{d\theta} = [MR^* - c]\frac{dQ}{d\theta} \tag{10.7}$$

When $n > 1$ and $\theta = 0$, condition (10.5) implies $p^*(Q) + Q\frac{dp^*(Q)}{dQ} \equiv MR^* < c$. Since $dQ/d\theta < 0$, we conclude that home welfare is higher under a small export tax than under free trade. The optimal export tax induces the home industry to export a quantity smaller than it would have if home firms maximized joint profits. The reason that Cournot firms export a larger quantity is that they do not internalize the effect of their quantity decisions on their rivals' profits. The optimal export tax induces each firm to set quantity as if these effects were internalized.

Figure 10.2 illustrates the welfare effect of the export tax. The free trade demand faced by the home industry is shown as p^* and the marginal revenue perceived by individual firms is shown as mr^*. Industry marginal revenue is MR^*. Under the export tax, the average revenue is $p^*/(1+\theta)$ and the perceived marginal revenue is $mr^*/(1+\theta)$.

The optimal export tax reduces exports from Q_1 to Q_2 where Q_2 is the quantity for which $MR^* = c$. The export tax also lowers exporters' after-tax profits by an amount equal to the difference in areas $NRUW$ and $TSVW$ shown in Figure 10.2. The area $KLST$ is tax revenue that accrues to the home country. A portion $KLMN$ of this area is the amount of surplus transferred from foreign consumers to the home country. The tax therefore increases home welfare by an amount represented by area VUZ.

Home and foreign oligopolies competing in a third country

We now let the home firms compete with foreign firms in a third country. First, we examine how trade taxes and subsidies affect home welfare when only the home country

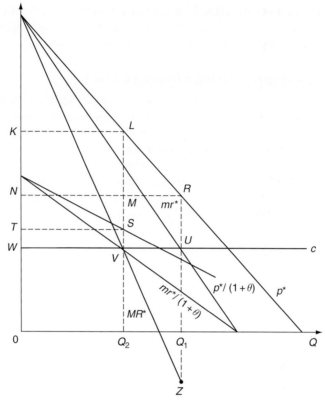

Figure 10.2 An export tax on home oligopoly

adopts an interventionist trade policy. Then we look at the welfare consequences when both countries pursue such policies. To facilitate a comparison with earlier findings, we maintain the assumption that the home and foreign industries export their entire production.

Home country adopting an activist trade policy: firms competing in quantity

There are n identical home firms that produce at marginal cost c and bear a fixed cost F. Similarly, there are n^* identical foreign firms with marginal cost c^* and fixed cost F^*. The home and foreign industries sell into a third country, where inverse demand is given as $\tilde{p} = \tilde{p}(Q + Q^*)$. The home country levies an *ad valorem* export tax θ, or grants an *ad valorem* subsidy σ. We define $\varphi \equiv (1+\theta)/(1+\sigma)$, where either $\sigma = 0$ and $\theta \geq 0$, or $\theta = 0$ and $\sigma \geq 0$. Given this, the profits of home and foreign firms can be expressed as:

$$\pi = \left[\frac{1}{\varphi}\tilde{p}(Q+Q^*) - c\right]q - F$$

and

$$\pi^* = \left[\tilde{p}(Q+Q^*) - c^*\right]q^* - F^*$$

Under Cournot competition, the first order conditions for profit maximization are:

$$\tilde{p}(Q+Q^*) - \frac{Q}{n}\tilde{p}'(Q+Q^*) - \varphi c = 0 \tag{10.8a}$$

$$\tilde{p}(Q+Q^*) - \frac{Q^*}{n^*}\tilde{p}'(Q+Q^*) - c = 0 \tag{10.8b}$$

We remark that a home export tax is formally equivalent to a transport cost, and it therefore lowers the amount of output the home industry produces for any given output chosen by the foreign industry. In terms of Figure 8.1. in Chapter 8, the tax shifts the home industry's best response function downward; an export subsidy would instead move the best response function upward. Thus, in equilibrium, home exports are smaller under an export tax and larger under the export subsidy.

In the absence of local consumption, home country welfare W is:

$$W[Q,Q^*] = \left[\frac{1}{\varphi}\tilde{p}(Q+Q^*) - c\right]Q + \left[\left(1 - \frac{1}{\varphi}\right)\tilde{p}(Q+Q^*)Q\right]$$

$$= \left[\tilde{p}(Q+Q^*) - c\right]Q$$

where the first term represents the home industry's profits and the second term captures government revenue under the tax, or expenditure under the subsidy. The welfare effect of a small change in φ is then given as:

$$\frac{dW(Q,Q^*)}{d\varphi} = \frac{\partial W}{\partial Q}\frac{dQ}{d\varphi} + \frac{\partial W}{\partial Q^*}\frac{dQ^*}{d\varphi}$$

$$= \left[\widetilde{MR}(Q+Q^*) - c\right]\frac{dQ}{d\varphi} + Q\tilde{p}'(Q+Q^*)\frac{\partial Q^*}{\partial Q}\frac{dQ}{d\varphi} \tag{10.9}$$

where $\widetilde{MR}$ stands for the home industry's marginal revenue. The term in square brackets has the same form as in (10.7), and is similarly interpreted.

Because free trade entails $\widetilde{MR} - c < 0$ under Cournot competition, and because $dQ/d\varphi < 0$, we can conclude that the first term in (10.9) is positive when $\varphi = 1$. The second term captures the so-called "strategic effect" which is the impact of the home country's trade intervention on the foreign firms' exports. The strategic effect is negative because $dQ^*/dQ < 0$, and because $dQ/d\varphi < 0$ and $\tilde{p}' < 0$. The sign $dW/d\varphi$ is therefore ambiguous.

Thus, it appears that the use of some trade instrument improves welfare, but that instrument could be an export tax or an export subsidy. To determine which instrument improves welfare we set $dW/d\varphi = 0$ and use (10.8a) to derive $sign\,(\varphi^0 - 1) = sign\left(1 - \frac{1}{n} + \frac{dQ^*}{dQ}\right)$, where φ^0 denotes the optimal tax or subsidy. Because $-1 < dQ^*/dQ < 0$, we conclude that the strategic effect dominates when $n = 1$ and is dominated when n is large. The reason is that, when $n = 1$, the local firm fully internalizes the effects of its quantity choices on industry profits. Therefore, a subsidy that expands the home industry's output will increase home welfare. By contrast, when n is large, the home industry produces too much output from the perspective of home welfare since the price in the export market is lower than the monopoly price. An export tax increases home welfare by bringing the foreign price closer to its monopoly level. The foreign industry gains from the home export tax.

Figure 10.3 shows the free trade duopoly equilibrium at point R where the free trade best response functions r_f and r_f^* intersect. Home profits are maximized when the home government grants an export subsidy that shifts the home firm's best response line from r_f to r such that it intersects r_f^* at S the point where r_f^* is tangent to a home firm iso-profit curve.

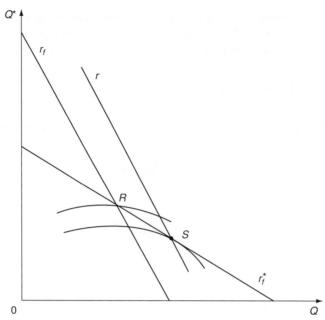

Figure 10.3 An export subsidy under Cournot competition

The equilibrium at this tangency point is a Stackelberg equilibrium. It is the equilibrium that would have emerged in the absence of a subsidy if the home firm could commit to a quantity *before* the foreign firm chose its own quantity. In this instance the home government rather than the home firm makes the commitment. The subsidy confers on the home firm an advantage akin to that of a first-mover, even though both firms choose their quantity simultaneously.

Because the line r_f^* is flatter than a 45° line, we know that total exports are larger at S than at R. Thus, the equilibrium price in the importing country is lower than under free trade. Foreign profits are lower than under free trade because both the price in the export market and the volume of exports by the foreign industry is lower. The subsidy increases the net of subsidy home profits at the expense of foreign profits. The literature refers to this effect as "profit shifting."

The joint profits of the home and foreign firm are lower with the subsidy than under free trade. This is because the total quantity exported is larger at S than at R, and because total exports at R already exceed the volume of exports that the two firms would choose if they maximized joint profits.

The shift in equilibrium brought about by an export subsidy can also be attained by other measures that induce the home firm to expand output. For example, Irwin (1992) argues that the Dutch United East India Company came out ahead of the English East India Company and gained dominance in the seventeenth-century spice trade in part because its charter contained a clause under which managers were compensated on the basis of profit and revenue. This gave them a direct stake in increasing turnover, and it committed the firm to a trading volume that exceeded the volume that it would have chosen if managers' income depended only on profits, which was the case for the English East India Company.

A home country adopting an activist trade policy: Firms competing in price

When firms set price rather than quantity, welfare maximization calls for an export tax even when $n = 1$. To see why, consider a market in which the home and foreign firm produce different varieties of a differentiated good. Let the demand for each variety in the export coun-try be $Q = \tilde{d}(p, p^*)$ and $Q^* = \tilde{d}^*(p, p^*)$, where $dQ/dp < 0, dQ/dp^* > 0, dQ^*/dp$ and $dQ^*/dp^* < 0$. Assuming that $c = c^*$, home and foreign profits can be expressed as:

$$\pi = \left[\frac{p}{\varphi} - c\right]\tilde{d}(p, p^*) - F \text{ and } \pi^* = \left[p^* - c\right]\tilde{d}^*(p, p^*)$$

If each firm sets its price assuming that the price set by the other firm is given, the first-order conditions are:

$$\tilde{d}(p, p^*) + p\frac{\partial\tilde{d}(p, p^*)}{\partial p} - \varphi c\frac{\partial\tilde{d}(p, p^*)}{\partial p} = 0 \tag{10.10a}$$

$$\tilde{d}^*(p, p^*) + p^*\frac{\partial\tilde{d}^*(p, p^*)}{\partial p^*} - c\frac{\partial\tilde{d}^*(p, p^*)}{\partial p^*} = 0 \tag{10.10b}$$

These conditions implicitly define upward sloping best response functions. As shown in Figure 10.4, these best response functions are linear since the demands for each variety are linear in p and p^* and marginal costs are constant.[3] Figure 10.4 also shows a number of home firm iso-profit curves. The more distant an iso-profit curve is from the horizontal axis the larger the profits of the home firm.[4] Thus, the home firm's profits at S are higher than its profits at the free trade equilibrium R.

The equilibrium which maximizes home welfare is located at S, the point where a home iso-profit curve is tangent to r_f^*. Point S is the equilibrium of a simultaneous price game when the home government levies an export tax which shifts the home firm's free trade best response function outward towards r. The tax is formally equivalent to an increase in the home firm's marginal cost.

When $\tilde{d}(p, p^*) = \tilde{d}^*(p, p^*)$, T is the mirror image of S. Foreign profits at S equal home profits at T. The latter are clearly higher than home profits at S. The implication is that a home export

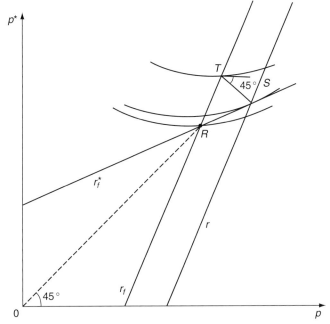

Figure 10.4 An export tax under Bertrand rivalry

tax that moves the equilibrium from R to S increases foreign profits by more than it increases home profits.

When several home firms are active, the home country has an added incentive to tax exports. This arises from the absence of internalization by home firms. That is, home firms set their price without taking into account that they will increase rivals' profits when they raise their own price. The implication is that, unlike quantity competition, which may call for an export tax or an export subsidy depending on the number of home firms, price competition always calls for an export tax.

Home and foreign countries adopting an activist trade policy

Consider the following two-stage game. At the first stage both governments simultaneously commit to an export tax or subsidy. At a second stage, firms engage in Cournot or Bertrand competition, taking the decisions of their governments as given.

Cournot competition

When both countries adopt an activist stance, profit maximization by the home and foreign firm entails:

$$\tilde{p}(Q+Q^*) - Q\tilde{p}'(Q+Q^*) - c/(1+\sigma) = 0$$

and

$$\tilde{p}(Q+Q^*) - Q^*\tilde{p}'(Q+Q^*) - c^*/(1+\sigma^*) = 0$$

where σ and σ^* denote the home and foreign subsidy rates. Because each government subsidizes exports, the two best response functions in Figure 10.5 shift to the right. Specifically, r_f shifts outward towards r, and r_f^* shifts towards r^*. When the subsidies are set to maximize the profit of the local firm, these shifts ensure that each firm's response function is tangent to an iso-profit curve of the other firm. The equilibrium with subsidies is therefore at point T in Figure 10.5.

When the countries are identical, both home and foreign firms export more than in the free trade equilibrium at R. Because joint exports at R are larger than the volume of exports that maximizes joint profits, it follows that total profits are lower at the equilibrium T than under free trade. Both countries would be better off if they agreed to tax their exports and bring the equilibrium closer to M, the point at which joint profits are highest.[5]

Price competition

When both countries set export taxes the best response functions shift outward. When governments set the taxes to maximize the profits earned by their domestic firm the best response functions intersect at a point where each is tangent to an iso-profit locus of the other firm. The taxes shift the price equilibrium from R to T in Figure 10.6. In the new equilibrium each exporter earns a higher profit than under a unilateral export tax. This arises since one firm's price increase raises the profit earned by the other firm. Even so, joint profits are still not maximized when the two countries tax exports. Instead, they are highest when the equilibrium is at M, the point where iso-profit curves of the two firms are tangent to each other. This cannot happen at T because at that point each firm's iso-profit curve is tangent to the best response

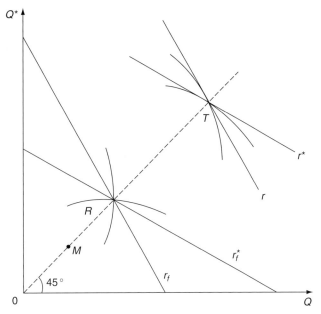

Figure 10.5 Nash equilibrium in subsidies under Cournot competition

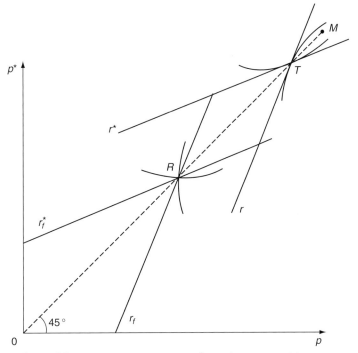

Figure 10.6 Nash equilibrium in export taxes under price competition

function of the other firm, and at that point the best response lines intersect. Again, the failure of governments to maximize joint profits by unilaterally setting taxes derives from their not taking into account the effect that taxes have on the profits earned by the firm located in the other country.

10.2 Extensions

Trade policy and the environment: A digression

Subsidizing home exports is not the only available means of shifting profits towards the home industry. Any measure that effectively reduces the home industry's marginal cost will have the same effect. This observation may be the source of the claim that governments are reluctant to impose environmental standards on firms that compete in imperfectly competitive international markets.

Barret (1994) and Neary (2006) examine how pollution taxes set by a home government affect home welfare when a single home firm competes with a single foreign firm in a third market. Assume the firms' exports are Q and Q^*, respectively, and that the home country does not consume the product in question. The manufacturing process pollutes the environment in the country where it takes place. A quantity of emissions z creates an environmental damage $D(z)$, where $D'(z) > 0$ and $D''(z) > 0$.

If the cost of home production is $C(Q, z)$, with $\partial C/\partial z < 0$ and $\partial C/\partial Q > 0$, then home profit can be expressed as $\Pi = R(Q, Q^*) - C(Q, z) + \sigma Q - tz$, where $R(Q, Q^*)$ denotes home revenue, while σ and t are a per unit export subsidy and a per unit tax on pollution. It is assumed that $\partial^2 C/\partial z^2 > 0$ $\partial^2 R/\partial Q^2 < 0$, $\partial R/\partial Q^* < 0$ and $\partial^2 R/\partial Q \partial Q^* > 0$. The last of these conditions implies that the two firms produce strategic substitutes, which means that their best response functions slope downwards.

Profit maximization by the home firm entails:

$$\frac{\partial \Pi}{\partial Q} = \frac{\partial(R - C)}{\partial Q} + \sigma = 0 \tag{10.11a}$$

$$\frac{\partial \Pi}{\partial z} = -\frac{\partial C}{\partial z} - t = 0 \tag{10.11b}$$

Since the home industry exports its entire output, home welfare can be expressed as:

$$W = R(Q, Q^*) - C(z, Q) - D(z)$$

In the first period the home government chooses t and σ to maximize W. It takes into account the effects of the tax and subsidy on the output and pollution levels that the two firms choose simultaneously in the subsequent period. In this case, the optimal export subsidy and pollution tax satisfy the conditions:

$$\frac{\partial W}{\partial \sigma} = \left[\frac{\partial(R - C)}{\partial Q} + \frac{\partial R}{\partial Q^*} \frac{\partial Q^*}{\partial Q} \right] \frac{\partial Q}{\partial \sigma} = 0 \tag{10.12a}$$

$$\frac{\partial W}{\partial t} = \left[\frac{\partial(R - C)}{\partial Q} + \frac{\partial R}{\partial Q^*} \frac{\partial Q^*}{\partial Q} \right] \frac{\partial Q}{\partial t} - \left[\frac{\partial C}{\partial z} + \frac{dD}{dz} \right] \frac{\partial z}{\partial t} = 0 \tag{10.12b}$$

The expressions (10.11a) and (10.12a) show that the optimal subsidy is positive and satisfies the condition $-\sigma = \frac{\partial R}{\partial Q^*} \frac{\partial Q^*}{\partial Q}$. But since (10.12a) implies that the first term on the right-hand-side of (10.12b) is zero, that condition can hold only if the tax equalizes at the margin the effect of pollution on cost and on environmental damage. This is the standard optimality rule in environmental economics.

Consider now the case where σ is constrained to be zero and the only available instrument is t. From (10.11b) and (10.12b), it is immediately apparent that the welfare maximizing t satisfies the first order condition $\frac{\partial R}{\partial Q^*} \frac{\partial Q^*}{\partial Q} \frac{\partial Q}{\partial t} - \left[\frac{\partial C}{\partial z} - \frac{dD}{dz} \right] \frac{\partial z}{\partial t} = 0$. Since the first term in this expression is negative by assumption, and since $\partial z/\partial t < 0$, the condition can only be satisfied if $-\partial C/\partial z < dD/dz$. This means less protection for the environment than under the standard rule found in environmental economics textbooks.

The intuition for this result is as follows. When the subsidy tool is available it can be used to generate a Stackelberg equilibrium in quantities. The only objective served by the tax is to reduce the environmental damage. Tax is set to ensure that, at the margin, the reduction in the damage from pollution equals the increase in production cost. But when the government loses the subsidy tool, it responds optimally by reducing the pollution tax in order to lower the home firm's marginal cost and capture rents from the foreign firm. This entails an environmental sacrifice. Under the optimal tax, with no subsidy the home firm produces a smaller quantity than a Stackelberg leader.

Again, making the assumption that firms compete in price rather than quantities changes things radically. The optimal pollution tax abides by the standard rule of environmental economics when the home government can also tax exports. When it cannot, it sets a pollution tax that also serves to reduce exports. In this case, the optimal pollution tax is higher than when both instruments are available.

Cournot competition with heterogeneous home firms

Until now our analysis has proceeded under the assumption that all firms in a country produce at the same cost. When this condition is not met, trade policy affects welfare via a channel not yet encountered: a reallocation of production among firms that incur different costs. We illustrate this for an export tax levied on an industry with n firms.

Assume that the export market is segmented and that changes in the tax rate have no effect on the number of exporters. With c_j and F_j denoting the marginal and fixed cost borne by firm j, home welfare can be expressed as:

$$W(\theta) = p^*(Q)Q - \sum_{j=1}^{n} [c_j q_j + F_j] = [p^*(Q) - \phi] Q - \sum_{j=1}^{n} F_j$$

where $\phi \equiv \sum_{j=1}^{n} c_j \frac{q_j}{Q} = \sum_{j=1}^{n} c_j m_j$ represents the weighted average marginal cost of the industry. From this it follows that $\dfrac{dW}{d\theta} = [p^*(Q) + Qp^{*\prime}(Q) - \phi] \dfrac{\partial Q}{\partial \theta} + Q \sum_{j=1}^{n} \dfrac{\partial \phi}{\partial m_j} \dfrac{\partial m_j}{\partial \theta}$.

Given this, we now show that an identical increase in the marginal cost of all firms lowers the market share of firms with lower than average market share ($m_j < 1/n$) provided that $dMR^*(Q)/dQ < dp^*(Q)/dQ$. We begin by noting that under Cournot competition the first order conditions $p^* + m_j Qp^{*\prime}(Q) = c_j$ imply:

$$\left[(1 - m_j) p^{*\prime} + m_j MR^{*\prime} \right] dQ + Qp^{*\prime} dm_j = dc_j \quad j = 1 \ldots \ldots n \qquad (10.13)$$

Summing the n equalities over all j and dividing by their sum yields: $\left[(1 - 1/n) p^{*\prime} + MR^{*\prime}/n \right] dQ = (1/n)d \sum_{j=1}^{n} c_j$. This expression can be solved for dQ, which can then be inserted into (10.13) to give:

$$dc_j = \{[(1-m_j)p^{*'} + m_j MR^{*'}]/[(1-1/n)p^{*'} + MR^{*'}/n]\}$$

$$\times \left[(1/n)d\sum_{j=1}^{n}c_j\right] + Qp^{*'}dm_j \qquad (10.14)$$

Condition (10.14) implies that an identical change in marginal cost of all firms yields:

$$dm_j/dc = [(1/n - m_j)(MR^{*'} - p^{*'})]/[(1-1/n)p^{*'} + MR^{*'}/n]Qp^{*'} \qquad (10.15)$$

This means that if industry marginal revenue is steeper than demand then: $sign[dm_j/dc] = sign[m_j - 1/n]$. We conclude that a policy that raises the effective marginal costs of all firms equally increases the market share of the firms with above average market shares (the low-cost producers) and lowers the market shares of firms with lower than average market shares (the high-cost producers). By tilting market shares in favor of the lower cost producers the export tax saves resources in production. This generates a welfare gain that comes in addition to the gain from internalization.

Note that the reallocation of production towards more efficient producers is even more pronounced under an *ad valorem* export tax because the latter induces the same effect on outputs as an equi-proportional increase in the marginal costs of all firms.

10.3   Rivalry across markets

We now consider the empirically more relevant case where home and foreign firms sell locally as well as into each other's markets. We distinguish the case where the two markets are segmented from the case where they are connected. We also set apart the case where the number of firms is fixed from the case where the number of firms is determined by a free entry condition.

Segmented markets and fixed numbers of firms

As indicated earlier, a tariff imposed by the home country does not influence the equilibrium in the foreign market when marginal costs are constant, markets are segmented, and the number of producers is given. In this case, the effect of a home tariff on home welfare is as shown by (10.6). One can therefore focus on the effects of a tariff on the equilibrium in the importing country.

The home welfare function is now:

$$W(\tau) = \left[\int_0^{Q+Q^*} p(v)dv - p(Q_l + Q_x^*)[Q_l + Q_x^*]\right] + \frac{\tau}{1+\tau}Q_x^* p(Q_l + Q_x^*)$$

$$+ \left[p(Q_l + Q_x^*) - c\right]Q_l + [p^*(Q_x + Q_l^*) - c]Q_x - nF$$

In this expression, the first and second terms are consumer surplus and tariff revenue, the third and fourth terms are home industry profits from local sales and exports. Differentiation of this expression yields:

$$\frac{dW(\tau)}{d\tau} = -\left[(Q_l + Q_x^*)\frac{dp}{d\tau}\right] + \frac{d}{d\tau}\left[\frac{\tau}{1+\tau}pQ_x^*\right] + \left[(p-c)\frac{dQ_l}{d\tau} + Q_l\frac{dp}{d\tau}\right]$$

$$(10.16)$$

Note that the second component of the third term cancels out the first component of the first term. This represents the part of the decline in consumer surplus that is recouped in the form of higher profits by home firms. At the free trade equilibrium we have:

$$\left.\frac{dW(\tau)}{d\tau}\right|_{\tau=0} = -Q_x^* \frac{d}{d\tau}\left[\frac{p}{1+\tau}\right] + [p-c]\frac{dQ_l}{d\tau} > 0 \qquad (10.17)$$

The first term of this expression is the same as that in (10.5). This term is positive provided $MR' - p' < 0$, which is generally assumed. The second term is also positive because a tariff increase shifts the foreign best response function downward. This increases Q_l and lowers Q_x^*. We note that the presence of a home industry does not modify our earlier finding that a small tariff benefits home welfare. However, when the importing country also produces the imported good then the optimal tariff rate is higher that when it does not. The reason is that the tariff increases the profits of the home firms.

The change in foreign profits due to the home tariff is:

$$\frac{d\pi^*}{d\tau} = \left[\frac{p(Q_l + Q_x^*)}{1+\tau} - c^*\right]\frac{dQ_x^*}{d\tau} + \frac{Q_x^*}{1+\tau}\frac{d}{d\tau}\left[\frac{p}{1+\tau}\right] < 0 \qquad (10.18)$$

The first term in (10.18) captures the effect from the change in the volume of foreign exports; the second term is the effect of the tariff on the net price received by foreign exporters. Using (10.17) and (10.18), we find the following effect on world welfare:

$$\frac{d(W+\pi^*)}{d\tau} = [p-c]\frac{dQ_l}{d\tau} + [p-c^*]\frac{dQ_x^*}{d\tau}$$

$$= [p-c]\frac{d(Q_l + Q_x^*)}{d\tau} + [c-c^*]\frac{dQ_x^*}{d\tau} \qquad (10.19)$$

Because the home industry's best response function is steeper than -1, it follows that $d(Q_l + Q_x^*)/d\tau < 0$. Thus, the home tariff lowers world welfare when $c = c^*$. Because $dQ_x^*/d\tau < 0$, the home tariff also lowers world welfare when $c > c^*$. However, when $c < c^*$, a higher home tariff may raise world welfare. The reason is that the share of output produced by the lower-cost home firms increases.

Segmented markets and free entry

We now allow firms to enter and exit the industry in response to profit incentives. One country's trade policies now affect the number of active firms in both countries. For example, when a home tariff reduces profits earned by exporters to the home country some firms will exit the foreign industry.

Venables (1985) shows that the price and welfare effects of trade policy differ drastically from those derived in the section above. He assumes that the home and foreign inverse demand are $Q = Q(p/\lambda)$ and $Q^* = Q(p^*/\lambda^*)$, where λ and λ^* measure market size. All home firms bear a marginal cost c and a fixed cost F. Starred variables denote the same for foreign producers. Exporters bear a transport cost τ per unit exported. Local sales and export sales by individual home firms are q_l and q_x while q_l^* and q_x^* denote the same for foreign firms. Given this, profits can be expressed as:

$$\pi = (p-c)q_l + (p^*-c-\tau)q_x - F \text{ and } \pi^* = (p^*-c^*)q_l^* + (p-c^*-\tau)q_x^* - F^*$$

Letting n and n^* denote the number of home and foreign producers allows us to state the total quantities sold into each market as:

$$Q = nq_l + n^*q_x^* = Q_l + Q_x^* \text{ and } Q^* = n^*q_l^* + nq_x = Q_l^* + Q_x \qquad (10.20)$$

Because markets are segmented, firms set quantities independently in each country. Under Cournot competition the optimal quantities will satisfy the first order conditions:

Home firms: $p + q_l p'(Q_l + Q_x^*) - c = 0$ and
$$p^* + q_x p^{*\prime}(Q_l^* + Q_x) - (c + \tau) = 0 \qquad (10.21a)$$
Foreign firms: $p^* + q_l^* p^{*\prime}(Q_l^* + Q_x) - c^* = 0$ and
$$p + q_x^* p'(Q_l + Q_x^*) - (c^* + \tau) = 0 \qquad (10.21b)$$

Using (10.20) and (10.21), the zero profit conditions can be expressed as:

$$\pi = \frac{1}{p'}(p - c)^2 + \frac{1}{p^{*\prime}}(p^* - c - \tau)^2 - F = 0 \qquad (10.22a)$$

$$\pi^* = \frac{1}{p'}(p - c^* - \tau)^2 + \frac{1}{p^{*\prime}}(p^* - c^*)^2 - F^* = 0 \qquad (10.22b)$$

Conditions (10.20) to (10.22) jointly determine the local and export sales of individual firms in each country. They also determine the number of firms, the total sales in each country and the prices p and p^*. For the particular case where demands have the form $p = a - Q/\lambda$ and $p^* = a - Q^*/\lambda^*$, the zero profit conditions can be written:

$$\pi = \lambda(p - c)^2 + \lambda^*(p^* - c - \tau)^2 - F = 0 \qquad (10.23a)$$

and

$$\pi = \lambda(p - c^* - \tau)^2 + \lambda^*(p^* - c - \tau)^2 - F^* = 0 \qquad (10.23b)$$

Figure 10.7 displays these zero profit conditions for the particular case where $c = c^*$ and $\lambda = \lambda^*$. The locus of combinations of prices p and p^* for which home firms earn zero profits is given by the segment of a circle with radius $\sqrt{F/\lambda}$ centered at A. This locus is labeled $\pi = 0$ in Figure 10.7. Similarly, $\pi^* = 0$ represents the locus of price combinations for which foreign firms earn zero profits. That locus is the segment of a circle centered at A^*.

In order to preserve zero profits, a higher price in one country must be accompanied by a lower price in the other country. This explains why the zero profit loci are downward sloping. The slopes are $\dfrac{dp^*}{dp}\bigg|_{\pi=0} = -\dfrac{q_l}{q_x}$ for the home country and $\dfrac{dp^*}{dp}\bigg|_{\pi^*=0} = -\dfrac{q_x^*}{q_l^*}$ for the foreign country.[6] Thus, at point E (which is the intersection of the zero profit loci) the slope of the $\pi = 0$ locus is steeper than the slope of the $\pi^* = 0$ locus. The reason for this is that symmetry of demands and positive transportation costs means that firms have larger local sales relative to export sales. If so, a smaller increase in the local price is required to compensate for a decline in price in the export market.

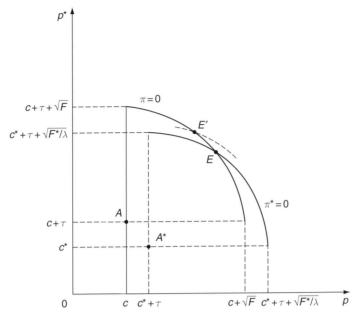

Figure 10.7 Tariff under freedom of entry

Tariffs, export taxes and export subsidies

From the perspective of firms, an import tariff levied by the home country or an export tax levied by the foreign country is equivalent to an increase in the cost of transporting a product from the foreign country to the home country. Hence, an import tariff brings about a shift of the $\pi^* = 0$ locus which moves the intersection with (of the zero profit loci to E') the $\pi = 0$ locus from E to E'.

In the new equilibrium, the home price is lower and the foreign price higher. This change can be explained as follows. By lowering the profits that foreign firms earn in the home market, a home tariff and a foreign export tax induce the exit of foreign firms. This causes price in the foreign country to increase. The increase in the foreign price enhances the export profits of home firms which in turn brings forth new entry in the home market. This, and the fact that the marginal cost incurred by home firms in their local market is lower than their marginal delivered cost to the foreign market, brings down the home price in a way that ensures that the profit of home firms remains zero.

The implication of this effect is that home consumers gain from a home tariff as well as from a foreign export tax. Because industry profits are zero, the effect of the export tax on home welfare is the same as its effect on consumer welfare. Home welfare increases with the foreign export tax as long as it is not prohibitive.

Regarding the home country's welfare, the desirability of a tariff appears even greater in view of the fact that tariff revenue is part of home welfare. The latter does not imply that the tariff that maximizes home welfare is prohibitive. The reason is that government revenue falls when the tariff rate crosses a threshold.[7]

Consider now the welfare effects of an export subsidy. Because the subsidy is formally equivalent to a fall in transport cost it brings a about a downward shift of the $\pi = 0$ locus. The new equilibrium therefore involves a lower p and a higher p^*. The intuition for these price changes is that, all else being equal, the export subsidy increases the profits of home firms. The home price must therefore fall to re-establish zero profits for home firms. The extra home exports generated by the subsidy lower the profits foreign firms earn on their local sales. To restore their profits to zero an increase in p^* is required. This price increase then lowers foreign consumer surplus and foreign welfare.

Venables (1985) shows that a small subsidy increases the welfare of the country that grants the subsidy when the quantity sold in each market by local firms exceeds the quantity sold into that market by exporters.

Connected markets and free entry[8]

As indicated in Chapter 8, firms do not independently maximize profits in countries when markets are connected. This changes the welfare consequences of trade policies. To see why, consider again the case of linear demands. Assume the home and foreign firms produce different varieties of a differentiated good. Let the inverse demands for the home variety in the home and foreign country be:

$$p = a - bQ_l - kQ_x^* \quad \text{and} \quad \bar{p} = a - b(Q_x/\lambda) - k(Q_l^*/\lambda)$$

where Q_l and Q_x denote respectively the home industry's local sales and export sales, while Q_l^* and Q_x^* denote the same for the foreign country. λ is the size of the foreign country relative to the home country and $b \geq k > 0$.[9] The inverse demands for the foreign variety in the foreign and the home country are $p^* = a - b(Q_l/\lambda) - k(Q_x^*/\lambda)$ and $\bar{p}^* = a - bQ_x^* - kQ_l$.

When transportation costs are zero and trade is free, the connectedness of markets entails $p = \bar{p}$ and $p^* = \bar{p}^*$. To ensure the preservation of these two equalities, the home country absorbs a fraction $1/1 + \lambda$ of each additional unit of output produced and the foreign country absorbs the fraction $\lambda/1 + \lambda$.

The home and foreign inverse demands can then also be expressed as:

$$p = a - b\frac{Q}{1+\lambda} - k\frac{Q^*}{1+\lambda} \quad \text{and} \quad p^* = a - b\frac{Q^*}{1+\lambda} - k\frac{Q}{1+\lambda} \tag{10.24}$$

where $Q^* = Q_l^* + Q_x^*$ and $Q = Q_l + Q_x$. When the home country levies a tariff τ, and the foreign country remains a free trader, connectedness of the markets entails $p = \bar{p}$ and $\bar{p}^* = (1+\tau)p^*$. The foreign inverse demand is then $p^* = a\frac{1+\lambda}{1+\lambda+\tau} - b\frac{Q^*}{1+\lambda+\tau} - k\frac{Q}{1+\lambda+\tau}$ and the home inverse demand remains as in (10.24).

Using $q = Q/n$ and $q^* = Q^*/n^*$, the first order conditions can then be expressed as:

$$a - b\frac{(n+1)q}{1+\lambda} - k\frac{n^*q^*}{1+\lambda} = p - \frac{bq}{1+\lambda} = c \tag{10.25a}$$

$$a\frac{1+\lambda}{1+\lambda+\tau} - b\frac{(n^*+1)q^*}{1+\lambda+\tau} - k\frac{nq}{1+\lambda+\tau} = p^* - \frac{bq^*}{1+\lambda+\tau} = c^* \tag{10.25b}$$

Free entry ensures that price equals average cost, that is:

$$p = c + F/q \text{ and } p^* = c^* + F^*/q \tag{10.26}$$

Jointly, conditions (10.25) and (10.26) yield:

$$q = \sqrt{F(1+\lambda)/b} \quad \text{and} \quad q^* = \sqrt{F^*(1+\lambda+\tau)/b} \tag{10.27}$$

The expressions (10.27) show that output per home firm is unaffected by the tariff. The implication is that any change in the total output of the home variety occurs exclusively via an adjustment of the number of home firms. Moreover, since output per home firm remains the same, the average cost and price of the home variety are unchanged.

The average cost of foreign firms is reduced by the home tariff because q^* increases. The price of the foreign variety must then fall. This improves the home country's terms of trade. Home consumers pay $(1+\tau)p^* = (1+\tau)\sqrt{b/F^*(1+\lambda+\tau)}$ for the imported variety. That price increases the tariff.[10] As home profits are always zero, the welfare effect of a tariff change is fully captured by the change of consumer surplus and tariff revenue. Clearly, the surplus of home consumers declines with the tariff. Tariff revenue increases with τ as long as τ is low but decreases when the tariff crosses a threshold. As in section 10.1, it is possible to show that a small tariff increases home welfare.

When the home country levies an *ad valorem* export tax θ, the connectedness of markets implies $p = \bar{p}/(1+\theta)$ and $p^* = \bar{p}^*$. The welfare effects of the tax can be analyzed along the lines followed above for the tariff. Specifically, the price of the foreign variety is the same as under free trade. The tax lowers the price at which the home variety sells in the home country and it increases the price at which it sells in the foreign country. The change in home welfare is captured by the change of consumer surplus plus tax revenue. A small export tax unambiguously increases home welfare.

Because an export subsidy is a negative export tax, it has the opposite effect on prices. But, since the subsidy involves home government expenditure, it unambiguously reduces home welfare.

Finally, note that, when the home and foreign goods are perfect substitutes (i.e., $b = k$), an arbitrarily small home tariff or export subsidy eradicates the foreign industry. This knife-edge outcome is due to the fact that when the home and foreign firms earn zero profits under free trade, foreign profits can only be negative when home profits are zero under the tariff.

Connected markets and fixed numbers of firms

Markusen and Venables (1988) examine how trade policy affects prices and welfare when markets are connected and the number of firms is fixed. They assume demands are linear and identical in the two countries except for scale. The home and foreign industry produce different varieties of a product. There is product differentiation within each country. All firms bear a constant marginal cost and a fixed cost.

An import tariff levied by the home country raises the consumer price of the imported variety and it lowers the price foreign firms receive in the home market. However, the lower price foreign firms receive on export sales spills over to the price they obtain in their local market. This spillover dilutes the effect of the tariff on the home price of the imported variety.

The increase in price that home consumers pay for the imported variety causes a shift in demand in favor of the home variety. This raises the quantity produced by the home industry. Home welfare increases because the home country's terms of trade improve, and because the output of the home industry expands.

A foreign export tax has the same effect as a home import tariff on home prices, foreign prices and on quantities. However, the effect on home welfare is not the same since the home government collects revenue under a tariff but not under a foreign export tax. Markusen and Venables (1988) show that a home tariff raises home welfare whereas a foreign export tax has an ambiguous effect of home welfare. A home tariff also lowers foreign welfare.

10.4 Quantitative restrictions

This section explores the effects of an import quota in a market served by a single domestic firm as well as by a competitive fringe of foreign exporters. It then considers how an import quota affects welfare when firms in the importing country are price takers and market power resides solely with a single foreign exporter. Lastly, it examines the welfare consequences of a quota in a duopoly setting where a single firm located in the importing country faces a single foreign exporter.

Domestic market power

Bhagwati (1965) shows that a tariff and a quota that allow the same volume of imports does not affect welfare equally in an importing country served by a single local firm. This is shown in Figure 10.8, which displays consumer demand in the importing country as DD' and the marginal cost of the single domestic producer as MC. Foreign supply is infinitely elastic at the world price p^*. The quota allows a volume of imports equal to the volume imported under a tariff.

Imposing the *ad valorem* tariff τ raises the home price to $(1+\tau)p^*$ and increases home production from Q_1 to Q_2. Under the tariff, the residual demand faced by the home firm (market demand *minus* foreign supply) is shown as the kinked line VND which is infinitely elastic at the price $(1+\tau)p^*$.

If the tariff is replaced by a quota that limits imports to the quantity imported under the tariff, the demand faced by the local firm is the market demand at prices lower than p^*. At higher prices, the firm faces the residual demand shown as $DSTZ$, which is market demand less the volume of imports allowed under the quota. The marginal revenue associated with this residual demand intersects MC at J. Thus, profit maximization by the local firm entails output Q_3, which is lower that the output produced under the tariff and, accordingly, the consumer price is higher. The local firm sets a higher price than $(1+\tau)p^*$ because under the quota consumers

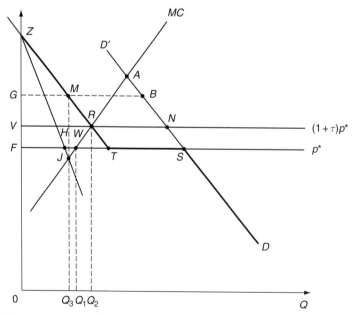

Figure 10.8 Quota-restricted imports and domestic market power

cannot import unlimited quantities. It follows from continuity that a quota which allows imports somewhat in excess of free trade imports also raises the domestic price above p^*.

Domestic welfare is lower under the quota than under the tariff. The tariff lowers home welfare by amount represented by the area RTW. The quota lowers consumer welfare by an amount shown as area $GBSF$. The rent earned by importers (or by the government in the form of revenue earned from the sale of import licenses) is given by area $MBST$. The increase in home firm profits due to the quota is shown as area $GMHF$ minus area HWJ. We conclude that replacing the tariff with a quota that allows the same volume of imports lowers welfare by an amount represented by the area JRM.

Foreign monopoly

Shibata (1968) considers the case of an importing country served by a fringe of competitive home producers and by a single dominant foreign firm. The foreign firm produces at a marginal cost MC^* and faces the residual demand shown as D in Figure 10.9. Imports are initially subject to an *ad valorem* tariff τ which lowers the demand faced by the foreign seller to $D/(1+\tau) \equiv D_\tau$. The imported quantity is then Q_τ. This is the quantity at which the marginal revenue associated with D_τ equals the exporter's marginal cost. Home consumers pay the price $\hat{p}_\tau$ and the foreign firm receives p_τ per unit exported.

When a quota that admits a volume of imports Q_τ replaces the tariff, the foreign firm faces a residual demand shown as the kinked line ABQ_τ in Figure 10.9. The marginal revenue line MR associated with the downward sloping segment of this demand is larger than MC^* for all $Q < Q_\tau$. Since the volume of exports remains as under the tariff the price home consumers pay is the same as under the tariff. The difference between the tariff and the quota is that under the quota the foreign exporter sells at $\hat{p}_\tau$, the price that consumers pay under the tariff.

Home and foreign market power

Hwang and Mai (1988) examine the consequences of a quota when one local firm and one foreign firm serve the country which restricts imports. Figure 10.10 displays the firms' free trade

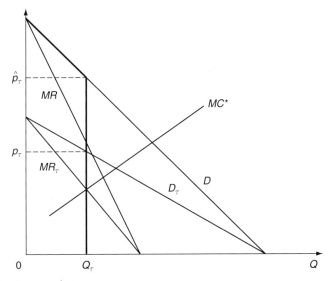

Figure 10.9 Foreign market power

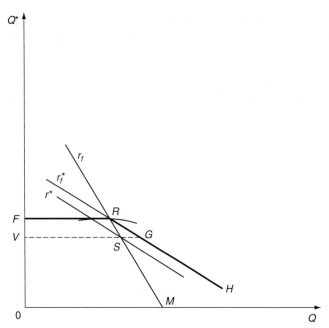

Figure 10.10 Cournot competition with a VER

best response functions as r_f and r_f^* and the Cournot equilibrium R. When the home country restricts imports by a quota which allows a volume of imports equal to the volume imported under free trade – represented by the length of the segment OF – the foreign best response function becomes the kinked line FRM. The equilibrium remains as under free trade. This may seem rather startling in light of the earlier finding that a quota which admits the free trade volume of imports reduces home output. Note though, that there is an important difference in assumptions. The earlier finding is contingent on the assumption that the home firm is a Stackelberg leader, that is, it chooses quantity taking into account the response of imports to that choice. Under Cournot competition, by contrast, the home firm takes the quantity sold by its rival as a given. The implication is that when the quota-constrained exporter sells the same amount as under free trade, the optimal response of the home firm is to produce the free trade quantity.

A more restrictive quota shifts the horizontal segment of the foreign best response function downward, for example towards VGH as shown in Figure 10.10. This generates about the same equilibrium as an import tariff that lowers the response function from r_f^* to r^*. We can therefore conclude that under Cournot competition the substitution of a tariff for a quota that allows the same volume of imports has no effect on price.

Since a more restrictive quota slides the equilibrium point downward along the response function r_f, it increases the home firm's equilibrium quantity and lowers the exporter's quantity. Under the standard assumptions, which ensure that r_f has a slope steeper than a 45° line, the total quantity sold in the home market declines as the quota is tightened. The sum of profits earned by the two firms increases as the equilibrium approaches the monopoly quantity M.

The profits earned by the foreign firm are lower under the quota. Indeed, G lies on a foreign iso-profit curve that is more distant from the vertical axis. This suggests that foreign producers engaged in quantity competition will oppose a quantitative restriction of their exports.

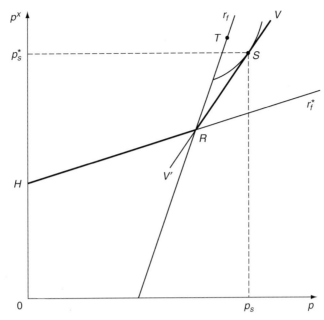

Figure 10.11 Price competition with a quota or VER

When firms compete in price the very same quantitative restriction may increase the profits of the home firm *and* of the foreign firm. Harris (1985) considers a market into which a home and a foreign firm sell imperfect substitutes. Consumer demands in the importing country for the home and foreign variety are $q = a - \alpha p + \gamma p^*$ and $q^* = a^* - \alpha p^* + \gamma p$, where $\alpha > \gamma$. Figure 10.11 displays the free trade best response functions r_f and r_f^* for the case where marginal costs are constant and identical for both firms.

If the home country restricts imports to $\bar{q}^*$, prices must change to satisfy the constraint $a^* - \alpha p^* + \gamma p \leq \bar{q}^*$. This means that firms' pricing decisions are no longer independent. Specifically, for any p chosen by the home firm, the foreign firm must set p^* to ensure that it does not export more than the volume allowed under the quota. This turns the foreign firm into a price follower.

The locus of price combinations p and p^* for which the volume imports equal the free trade level of imports is displayed as the line VV'. Clearly, VV' passes through R when the quota allows the free trade volume of imports. VV' is flatter than r_f. To see why, it is sufficient to note that an upward move in prices along r_f lowers the imported quantity since the increase in foreign price exceeds the increase in the home price. This means that in order to maintain the free trade volume of imports the increase in p that accompanies the increase p^* must be larger than the increase corresponding to the slope of r_f. The same argument explains why VV' is steeper than r_f^*.

When the home country sets a quota or imposes a voluntary export restraint (VER) that limits exports to their free trade level, the foreign best response function becomes the kinked line HRV.

If the home firm sets its price p first (i.e. acts as a Stackelberg leader), the foreign firm chooses p^* on HRV to ensure that it exports the quantity allowed under the VER. Given that, the home firm chooses a price that yields an equilibrium at S, the point where a home isoprofit curve is tangent to HRV. Clearly the two equilibrium prices are higher at S than at the free trade equilibrium R.

The home and foreign profits are also higher than under free trade. The foreign firm profits are higher because it exports the same quantity as under free trade but sells at a higher price.

By virtue of continuity it must also be true that a VER that restricts exports somewhat below the free trade level increases the foreign firm's profits. Hence Harris's (1985) contention that a voluntary export restraint may indeed be voluntary.

Quotas and quality

Quotas give firms an incentive to upgrade the quality of the goods they export to the restricted market. This comes about through two channels. The first channel operates via a change in the composition of individual products within the quota-restricted product category. The quota shifts consumer demand within the restricted product category away from lower quality products that sell at a lower price, toward higher quality products that sell at a higher price. This upgrading takes place because the quota raises the cost of each variety by an amount equal to the quota rent. Thus, the prices of the higher priced varieties fall relative to those of the lower priced varieties. This change in prices tilts demand in favor of the higher quality varieties. The second channel involves a change in the quality of individual products within the restricted category.

The VER on Japanese car exports: Measuring quality change

Imports quotas and VERs produce welfare effects through their effect on quality. That effect can be quantified, as Feenstra (2003) shows for the case of Japanese automobiles.[11]

Japanese automobile exports to the US were subjected to a VER in 1981. The so-called 'voluntary' agreement followed earlier accords with the United Kingdom (UK) (1976) and France (1980). It preceded similar restrictions on Japanese exports of automobiles to the Benelux countries, West Germany and Sweden.[12]

Table 10.1 shown in Feenstra (1988) summarizes the impact of the VER on quality. The first row displays the suggested average retail prices of Japanese passenger vehicles from 1980 through to 1985. The numbers are weighted averages of suggested retail prices of base models where quantities actually sold serve as weights. The numbers show a 55 percent increase from 1980 through 1985. The increase reflects the result of three distinct price effects: a first effect due to the VER and other factors such as inflation; a second effect attributable to a change in

Table 10.1 US imports of Japanese cars and trucks, 1980–85

	1980	1981	1982	1983	1984	1985
Cars						
Unit value	5175	6211	6834	7069	7518	8038
Price index	100.0	119.8	129.1	131.2	138.8	148.3
Unit quality	5124	5511	5896	6257	6488	6709
Quality index	100.0	107.4	112.8	117.3	121.3	125.4
Trucks						
Unit value	4937	6298	6419	6089	6261	6339
Price index	100.0	127.5	131.8	125.3	127.3	129.7
Unit quality	4943	5041	5275	5276	5274	5620
Quality index	100.0	102.1	106.4	105.5	104.7	112.3

Source: Feenstra (1998, 2003).

the quality of individual models; a third effect which derives from a shift in the composition of demand from lower priced to higher priced models.

In reality, price changes are more accurately measured by an index that uses constant weights between consecutive years. Such an index, reported in row 2 of the table, shows a 48 percent increase from 1980 to 1985, with 60 percent of that increase taking place during the period 1980–82. The index still reflects the three aforementioned effects.[13]

To determine the portion of the price increase due to quality upgrading Feenstra (1988) uses hedonic regression. Hedonic regression is an econometric technique that relates the evolution of the price of a product to measurable changes in its characteristics. In the case of automobiles the characteristics are: horsepower, length, weight, gas mileage, width and so on. The basic idea behind hedonic regression is that prices ultimately depend on the services provided by a product, and the range and quality of the services are to some extent measurable. Hedonic regression extracts the effect of quality on price by identifying the variation in price explained by the variation in quality characteristics. The residual part is attributed to other factors, possibly movements in exchange rates and production cost changes.

The estimating equation is:

$$p_m^t = \alpha^t + \exp(\beta^t + \sum_h \gamma_h^t Z_{mh}^t) + \varepsilon_m^t$$

where p_m^t represents the list price of model m in year t and, Z_{mh}^t is a measure of characteristic h possessed by model m in year t. This specification disentangles the *specific* price increase due to the quota and captured by α^t, from the *percentage* change in price resulting factors such as fluctuations in cost and exchange rates that are picked up β^t.

Trucks, unlike passenger cars and utility vehicles, were not subject to a quantitative restriction. In 1981, however, the tariff rate on nearly all Japanese trucks increased from 4 percent to 25 percent as a result of lightweight cab/chassis vehicles being reclassified as complete trucks. Since the wholesale price accounts for about three quarters of the suggested retail value, the ensuing tariff increase should have boosted the retail price of trucks by 16 percent. Because there was no quantitative restriction of trucks, the α^t variable can be omitted from the estimating equation for trucks.

Table 10.2 displays in columns (1) and (2) the initial estimation results for cars and trucks. The coefficients at the top of the table are estimates of the β's. They show that an increase in horsepower of 100 was associated with a price increase of $e^{0.69} = 2$, that is, it led to a doubling of the price. The lower part of the table displays the proportional and specific price increases relative to the years 1979 and 1980.

Because of collinearity between variables α_t and s_t, the standard errors of their coefficients are high. To address this problem, Feenstra (2003) pools the data for cars and trucks allowing different coefficients on characteristics and on proportional price increases. Then he tests the hypothesis that the proportional increase for trucks from 1981 through 1985 was larger than for cars in a proportion of 0.16. The estimation results show that this hypothesis can be accepted for the period 1980–84 but not for the year 1985.

A re-estimation of the model with a 0.16 difference in the coefficients of the proportional changes imposed as a constraint for the period 1981–84, yields the results that Table 10.2 displays in columns (3) and (4). The coefficients reveal that by 1984–85 the VER had increased the retail price of Japanese cars in the US by about 1000 dollars.[14]

The estimated coefficients serve to determine the quality of *individual models* in each year by calculating the sum $\beta^{1980} + \sum_h \gamma_h^t Z_{mh}^t$. The unit qualities shown in Table 10.1 can then be obtained as a weighted average across models, using the quantities sold each year as weights. The quality index – also reported in Table 10.1 – is determined in the same way,

Table 10.2 Hedonic regression with price as dependent variable

	Cars	Trucks	Cars	Trucks
Constant	6.33*	7.71*	5.83*	6.63
Weight (tons)	0.03	0.41*	0.05	0.48*
Width (feet)	0.36*	0.01	0.39*	0.21
Height (feet)	−0.06	0.01	−0.06*	−0.03
Horsepower (100)	0.69*	0.20	0.81*	0.24
Transmission (5-speed or auto)	0.14*	0.03	0.18*	0.05
Power steering	0.06*	0.09	0.07*	0.06
Air conditioning	0.15*		0.16*	
Four-wheel drive	0.22*		0.30*	
Proportional				
α^{1980}	0.01	0.004	0.01	0.01
α^{1981}	0.05	0.21*	0.07	0.23*
α^{1982}	0.09	0.23*	0.07	0.23*
α^{1983}	0.02	0.17*	−0.001	0.16*
α^{1984}	0.09	0.19*	0.02	0.18*
α^{1985}	0.22*	0.18*	0.10	0.11
Specific				
s^{198}	410		367	
s^{1982}	378		600*	
s^{198}	770		887*	
s^{1984}	624		1,104*	
s^{1985}	−123		856*	
# of Obs	179	75	254	254

Source: Feenstra (2003). Starred variables are significant at the 95 percent level.

using constant weights from year to year. Finally, the ratio of the change of unit quality to the quality index serves as indicator of the evolution of the product mix.

The fact that unit quality increased proportionately more than the index in the period 1980–85 shows that while individual models were upgraded, consumers also shifted to more expensive models. The table reveals that over the period 1980–85, the increase in the quality of individual models accounted for about half of the increase in price. The largest increase took place in the immediate aftermath of the restriction of exports.

The quality of trucks also increased but not as much. This suggests that the VER may not have been the only factor explaining the quality upgrading of cars.

10.5 Contingent protection

This section begins with a short description of the dissemination of anti-dumping legislation. It then looks at the causes and consequences of dumping. Finally it examines the effects of anti-subsidy measures that target products that have benefitted from subsidies in the exporting country.

The dissemination of anti-dumping legislation

Canada enacted the first anti-dumping law in 1904. The US followed in 1916. As recently as the 1980s, 95 percent of all anti-dumping cases were initiated in five jurisdictions: Canada, New Zealand, Australia, US and the European Community. More recently there has been an explosion in demand for anti-dumping protection.[15] By 2003, 98 countries had enacted anti-dumping laws, although not all chose to use them.[16] Feinberg and Reynolds (2006) report that in the period 1995–2003, most anti-dumping cases were filed in India, the US, the European Union (EU), Argentina and South Africa.

The proliferation of anti-dumping legislation has coincided with a fall in most-favoured-nation tariffs, possibly because the availability of the anti-dumping option softened resistance to a lowering of conventional tariffs. Finger (1993) conjectures that enactment of anti-dumping legislation has been a tit-for-tat strategy motivated by the desire to protect one's exporters from abusive use of anti-dumping measures by trading partners.

Prusa and Skeath (2001) along with Feinberg and Reynolds (2006) view the rise in anti-dumping filings primarily as retaliation for past anti-dumping action taken by others and as a deterrent against future action by trading partners. Blonigen and Bown (2003) put forward the idea that the rising threat of retaliatory action by trading partners may in fact dampen anti-dumping activity. Their analysis of US cases in the period 1980–98 shows that petitioning industries were less likely to target imports from countries where their own exposure to retaliatory action was significant. It also shows that US agencies were less likely to rule affirmatively against these countries.

Why do firms dump?

Dumping in competitive markets

Pricing below average cost is a common short-run response to depressed demand. When firms' costs are partially sunk, profit maximization may actually call for pricing below average total cost in periods of low demand. The costliness of adjusting production rates in response to demand fluctuations – possibly because of a high cost of hiring and firing – encourages the smoothing of output over the business cycle. This increases the likelihood of a finding of dumping.[17]

A finding of dumping may also ensue from exchange rate fluctuations. To determine the margin of dumping, the agency converts the price at which the exporting firm sells in its local market into the currency of the importing country. The conversion process may lead to determination of dumping. To see how, consider the case of a Canadian exporter who makes a commitment in January with regard to the price at which he will offer a product for the next 12 months in Canada and the US. The price quoted to American buyers is in US dollars. Assume that the price in Canadian dollars equals the price in US dollars at the exchange which prevails early in the year. By August, the Canadian dollar has appreciated. If the US authorities use the August exchange rate to compare prices, they will find a positive margin of dumping.[18]

Dumping to exploit or create market power

Viner (1923) views dumping as a form of third degree price discrimination. In a two-country world, such discrimination unambiguously raises world welfare if the firm refrains from serving one country when it is constrained to price uniformly. When the firm serves both markets under uniform pricing, discrimination has an ambiguous effect on world welfare. The opening of a price gap across markets has an adverse effect on welfare, but it may also bring about an increase in total output. And, when total output increases, its welfare enhancing effect just might surpass the welfare loss ensuing from the gap in prices.

Malueg and Schwarz (1994) examine the welfare effects of price discrimination when a monopolistic firm sells into a continuum of markets, with linear demands. The demands have a common horizontal intercept and their vertical intercepts are distributed uniformly across markets. Malueg and Schwarz (1994) find that third degree discrimination yields higher global welfare than uniform pricing when the dispersion of the vertical intercepts is large, and its lowers global welfare when the dispersion is small. The reason is that when the dispersion is large, too many markets are not served when the firm prices uniformly. A mixed system under which the firm discriminates across groups of countries with similar demands, and prices uniformly within each group yields a higher welfare than either uniform pricing and unrestricted discrimination. The reason is that under the mixed system there is sufficient discrimination to ensure that all markets are served, but not enough to engender significant losses from output-misallocation across markets.

At times dumping has been viewed as a predation strategy. Predation refers to conduct designed to drive competitors out of the market or discipline them. The common feature of practices deemed predatory is that one firm – the predator – engages in conduct harmful to itself for no other reason than to injure a competitor. The goal is to induce the competitor to exit the market, or to adopt a stance more accommodating to the predator. The firm that engages in predatory conduct calculates that such a response by the targeted firm will eventually enhance its market power and allow it to earn extra profits over the long term that will outweigh the losses suffered during the predation period.

An extensive literature examines whether a predator can attain this objective by pricing below short-run marginal cost. To maintain positive sales the targeted firm has to match the low price. If it does, and its cost is not significantly lower than that of the predator, both firms incur losses. The predator bets that the targeted firm will exit before long, allowing it to recoup its losses. However, the bet cannot pay off unless predator has sufficient capacity to meet demand at the low price, can sustain losses for a longer time that the prey, and has reason to believe that the targeted firm, or another producer, will not re-enter the market in the post-predation period. The stringency of these conditions explains why economists consider that predatory pricing is rare. Willig (1998) suggests that in nearly all US cases he examined, there appears to have been no need to intervene to protect competition from international predation, or to protect competition at all.[19]

Prusa (1992) argues that the initiation of anti-dumping proceedings may be a first step in action that leads to collusive arrangements between local firms and exporters. He notes that a substantial proportion of cases are resolved with negotiated agreements. The agreements involve settlements under which exporting firms and the rivals in the importing country earn profits unattainable in a non-cooperative trade environment. This suggests that the parties involved in an anti-dumping proceeding always aim for a negotiated agreement. Yet, only about one fifth of all petitions filed in the US are withdrawn upon reaching an agreement. Zanardi (2000) attributes this to the cost of bargaining – which may well correlate with the number of actors – and to asymmetry in bargaining power between exporters and local producers.

The destruction, diversion and deflection of trade

Anti-dumping action reduces the volume of subject imports from countries whose firms have been found to engage in injurious dumping. This reduction is referred to as trade destruction. Anti-dumping measures may also induce additional imports from non-subject countries. Bown and Crowley (2007) call this trade diversion. Finally, they may also encourage shipments from the subject country to third countries to make up for lost sales to the country that takes anti-dumping measures. This is called trade deflection.[20]

Prusa (2001) finds that US anti-dumping action from 1980 through 1994 has lowered imports from subject countries by 50 percent on average; it increased imports from non-subject sources by 40–60 percent.[21] Bown and Crowley (2007) determine that the US anti-dumping duties imposed on Japanese imports from 1992 through 2001 increased Japanese exports to third countries by 11–22 percent

While the aforementioned studies examine trade flows within the targeted product class, Vandenbussche and Zanardi (2010) look at the effect of anti-dumping action on aggregate flows. Their estimating equation is:

$$\ln(X_{ijt}) = \alpha_i + \alpha_j + \beta_1 (adoption)_{jt} + \beta_2 (overall\, AD\, use_{jt-1}) + \sum_k \gamma_k X_k$$
$$+ \sum_k \theta_k (trade\, policy_k) + \delta_t (year\, dummy) + \varepsilon_{ijt}$$

where X_{ijt} denotes the real value of total exports from country i to country j in period t. Adoption$_{jt}$ is a dummy variable equal to zero before enactment of country j's anti-dumping law and equal to 1 thereafter. The variable $ADuse_{jt-1}$ measures the number of anti-dumping initiations and anti-dumping measures by country j in the year $t-1$. X_k is a vector of explanatory variables commonly found in gravity equations. It includes the GDPs of countries i and j, the distance that separates them, their openness to trade, and dummy variables that indicate whether a country pair shares a language or a border. The impact of trade policy is controlled by dummy variables which denote whether country j was a member of the World Trade Organization (WTO) in year t, and whether countries j and i belonged to a regional free trade zone in year t. Also included among the list of regressors is an index that captures the openness to trade index of country j in year t. Finally, year dummies control for the time variation in the trade relationship.

The sample consists of annual trade flows from a large set of countries from 1980 through 2000. Estimation results reveal that the mere adoption of anti-dumping legislation has had no significant effect on countries' aggregate imports. However, the overall use of anti-dumping – rather than its bilateral use – appears to have curbed trade. That is, even when the exporting country did not face anti-dumping measures against itself in an importing country, its exports to that country are curtailed by the latter's overall use of anti-dumping measures. This reduction in trade does not relate to the number of anti-dumping cases initiated but to the number that have resulted in import restrictions. The estimation results also reveal that the spillover from subject products to other products occurs primarily within the broad sector to which the subject products belong.

The estimated coefficients suggest that Mexico's anti-dumping caseload caused a 7.2 percent reduction in its aggregate imports which, in the view of authors, undid an important part of what had been accomplished by the trade liberalization initiated in 1985.

Subsidies and countervailing

Countervail has received less theoretical attention than anti-dumping. The literature has focused on two questions: does the use of countervail eliminate the incentive to subsidize exports? What is the optimal countervailing duty? Dixit (1988) shows that partial rather than full countervailing is optimal. Collie (1991) analyzes retaliation against an export subsidy by an importing country within a three-stage framework. In the first stage the foreign exporting country sets a per unit export subsidy to maximize its national welfare. In the second stage the home country responds with a combination of a specific import tariff and a specific production subsidy, or just an import tariff. It sets the tariff and subsidy to maximize home welfare. In the third and final stage, home and foreign firms engage in Cournot competition. Collie (1991) finds that the importing country can make use of the tariff to extract foreign rents and avail itself of a production subsidy to counter the domestic distortion that derives from foreign oligopoly power in the home market. The foreign export subsidy brings about an increase in the home import tariff and lowers the home production subsidy.[22] The reason is that the export subsidy increases the amount of foreign rent available for extraction by means of the tariff. Nevertheless, the optimal countervailing tariff is lower than the export subsidy.

Welfare in the importing country is increased by the foreign export subsidy when the importing country sets the countervailing tariff and production subsidy to maximize its welfare. Welfare in the exporting country falls as a result of the home tariff response, which shifts exporters' profits to the home country and worsens the foreign country's terms of trade.

When the home country refrains from subsidizing production, the response to the foreign export subsidy may call for an increase or a decrease of the tariff. However, full countervail remains suboptimal even when the response calls for an increase in the tariff.

Qiu (1995) finds that a country may benefit from subsidizing its exports when countervail is sufficiently delayed. The optimal subsidy rate relates positively to the amount of delay. More recent models – reviewed in Baylis (2007) – consider the effects of uncertainty. Ishikawa and Komoriya (2007) explore the impact of subsidies and countervail when exporting countries have different unit costs.

10.6 Concluding remarks

Intuitions gained from the analysis of trade policy in perfectly competitive settings are often misleading when applied to oligopolistic environments. Having worked one's way through a number of sections that underscored why countries need not be large to derive a benefit from import tariffs, export taxes or subsidies one may ask whether government intervention in the trade arena now enjoys theoretical support. Since much trade is conducted by corporations enjoying market shares suggestive of market power, this chapter's findings raise the more general question of whether free trade as a guiding principle of policy has been significantly weakened.

The majority consensus emerging from the literature is that the case for interventionism is hardly strengthened by the findings summarized in this chapter.[23] The fundamental nature of the argument is that, while the existence of a welfare improving policy prescription within the framework of a model is necessary to recommend a deviation from free trade, it is not a sufficient condition.

There is first and foremost the issue of robustness. None of the models examined in this chapter captures oligopolistic competition in all its complexity, but even a comparison of the simplest models reveals that policies suggested by models that assume quantity competition can be radically different policies hinted at by models which assume price competition. And, even under quantity competition, opposing policy prescription results from changing assumptions regarding freedom of entry or market segmentation. The welfare effect of export subsidies, for example, depends crucially on whether markets are segmented or connected. It is rarely straightforward to determine in a particular instance the extent to which prices are equalized across markets.[24] And, while it is common to treat entry as free in the long run and somewhat limited in the short run, it is far from obvious how one determines in a particular instance the period of time it takes to observe the long-term effects of a policy. The design of a policy that fits the circumstance of a particular industry so that it improves welfare with a high degree of probability imposes information requirements unlikely to be met in practice. And, if a government somehow resolved the information problems, its trade policies may still fail to produce the intended effects if trading partners used similar instruments.

There is also a danger of targeting the wrong industry. A policy designed to expand the production of one oligopolistic industry could lower overall welfare when binding endowment constraints lead to a contraction of output by other industries that enjoy positive price cost margins.[25] The likelihood that trade taxes or subsidies will increase welfare is reduced further when trade policy is determined one industry at a time, as is probable in practice.

Commitment problems cannot be overlooked. Consider the case of a subsidy designed to bring forth investments to expand production capacity and allow home firms to capture a larger share of the world market. If a government cannot credibly commit to terminating the subsidy program at the set date, the beneficiaries of the program may refrain from increasing capacity by the amount necessary to capture the intended market share. They may reckon that the subsidy will be renewed if the government's objective is not fully attained upon expiry of the current program.[26]

Political economy considerations also weigh heavily against selective interventionism. Lobbying entails a resource cost that ought to be set against possible gains from intervention. A government's readiness to use strategic trade policy is likely to induce greater spending on lobbying. Because trade policy is made through a political process, small groups with a keen appreciation of the gains they can obtain from selected measures will likely be more successful in influencing governments than larger groups with more diffuse stakes.

Finally, one cannot overlook the fact that by drawing a sharp delineation between home and foreign firms, this chapter has passed over the policy implications of cross-ownership. Total or partial ownership of firms located in one country by residents of another country complicates the welfare implications of trade policy. The profits accruing to firms located in the home country are no longer in their entirety part of home welfare, and a portion of the profits of firms operating in foreign markets are part of home welfare.[27] Foreign shareholding also raises the possibility that firms located in different countries operate under common management, and for that reason alone they respond differently to policy interventions than independent profit maximizers. This raises a new set of issues that are taken up in the next chapter.

Problems

10.1 Show that a small tariff levied by a country whose market is served by a foreign oligopoly improves the importing country's terms of trade. Examine how that improvement depends on the number of foreign oligopolists. Assume that the exporters engage in Cournot competition in the importing country.

10.2 Countries 1 and 2 have a single firm each. Both produce at a unit cost $c = 1$. Neither consumes the good. They export their output to a third country which cannot produce the good, and whose inverse demand is $p = 12 - (Q^1 + Q^2)$ where Q^i denotes the export volume of country i. Determine how world welfare changes when each country grants an export subsidy that maximizes the profits of its domestic exporter.

10.3 A single home and a single foreign firm serve a segmented third market. The home country does not sell in its local market. The demands for home and foreign products in the third country are respectively $Q = a - p - kp^*$ and $Q^* = a - p^* - kp$ $(k < 1)$ where p and p^* respectively denote the prices at which the home and foreign firm sell in the third country. Q and Q^* denote the quantities demanded of each variety. The unit cost of the home variety is $c/(1+z)$ where z denotes the amount of pollution created per unit of output. The environmental damage in the home country is $z + bz^2/2$. Assume that the home government sets a unit tax t on pollution to maximize home welfare. Compare the welfare maximizing t

when the tax is the only instrument used by the home government to the welfare maximizing t when the government also grants an export subsidy. Verify how the welfare maximizing t evolves as a function of the subsidy.

10.4   Two firms based in the home country and one firm based in the foreign country produce the same homogeneous good and export it to a third country. The importing country does not produce the good. The foreign firm produces at the marginal cost c^*. The first home firm produces at the same marginal cost as the foreign firm, that is, $c_1 = c^*$; the second home firm produces at marginal cost $c_2 = \alpha c_1 (\alpha > 1)$. Assume that the demand in the third country is linear and examine how the optimal home export tax or subsidy changes as a function of α when the other countries are free traders.

10.5   A home firm holds a patent in a home country (h) where it is based, and in a foreign country (f). The patented technology allows it produce at zero cost. The markets are segmented. The patent expires in the foreign country before it expires in the home country. Upon expiry of the patent a single firm which produces at unit cost c enters the industry in country 2 and produces a different variety of the good. Upon entry, both the incumbent and entrant engage in price competition. The inverse demand for variety i is
$$q_i = \frac{5}{n+\gamma} - \frac{p_i}{\gamma} + \frac{n}{n+\gamma}\frac{\bar{p}}{\gamma}$$ in both countries, where n denotes the number of varieties sold
in the market, $\gamma = 1/2$ and $\bar{p} = (1/n)\sum_{j=1}^{n} p_j$. Country 2 levies an antidumping duty equal a fraction "a" of the margin of dumping. Compare the prices at which the incumbent sells into each market before and after expiration of the patent.

Notes

1. This section draws primarily on Brander and Spencer (1984, 1985), Eaton and Grossman (1986) and Helpman and Krugman (1989).
2. The analysis proceeds along the same lines when the market is also served by a competitive fringe of home firms.
3. To show that the slopes of the response functions are positive differentiate Equation (11.9) and use the second order conditions.
4. To see why, it is sufficient to note that for any given p the home firm sells a larger quantity when p^* is higher.
5. de Meza (1986) and Neary (1994) provide an analysis of the effects of subsidies under alternative assumptions.
6. These slopes follow from differentiation of (11.23), upon using $q_l = \lambda(p - c), q_x^* = \lambda(p^* - c - \tau)$ and the corresponding condition for the foreign country.
7. Venables (1985) proves these results for general demands.
8. This section draws on Horstmann and Markusen (1986).
9. $b = k$ when the home and foreign varieties are perfect substitutes.
10. An increase in the foreign export tax produces the same effect.
11. He assumes that consumer utility can be represented by a CES function and that marginal cost does not depend on quantity. Krishna (1987) shows that the quality effect is ambiguous for more general forms of utility.
12. The initial restriction to 1.68 million cars was raised to 2.02 million in 1984 and subsequently to 2.51 million. The VER was lifted in 1992.

13. The price index is the Fisher Ideal index of change for each pair of years, that is, the geometric mean of the Laspeyres index which uses first year quantities as weights, and the Paasche index which uses second year quantities as weights.
14. Thus, the quota rent accruing to Japanese firms was roughly 2.2 billion dollars as they exported about 2.2 million cars to the US during that period. Total quota rents transferred abroad were in fact higher as European exporters also raised their prices. The welfare loss would also include the deadweight loss from the reduction in quantity due to an increase in the price of imported and locally produced vehicles. The price response of non-Japanese sellers is consistent with the hypothesis that a quota facilitates collusive behavior.
15. See Prusa (2001).
16. See Falvey and Nelson (2006). Finger (1993) reviews the political considerations that led to the enactment of the first anti-dumping law.
17. In Ethier (1982) the fixed labor input is managerial workers.
18. Other explanations for dumping include incomplete pass-through of exchange rate fluctuations (Leidy and Hoekman, 1988; Feinberg, 1989).
19. Eaton and Mirman (1991) examine predatory dumping in an environment where information in imperfect; Hartigan (1996) looks at how predatory dumping emerges when capital markets are imperfect.
20. Trade deflection is observable only when the country taking anti-dumping measures is large.
21. Remarkably, Prusa also finds that imports suffered a fall when petitions for anti-dumping measures were unsuccessful. This may be due to temporary duties levied while the investigation was ongoing, and from the dampening effect of uncertainty about the outcome of the proceedings.
22. Collie (1994) provides a formal proof for the case of linear demands.
23. Of particular interest in this regard are Brander (1986), Grossman (1987), Krugman (1993) and McCulloch (1993).
24. Also, the domestic market may be connected to some foreign markets but not others.
25. See Dixit and Grossman (1986).
26. Tornell (1991) examines this issue in detail.
27. Using data on the foreign ownership of US industries, Dick (1993) shows that optimal subsidies are lower than when cross-ownership is ignored.

References and additional reading

General

Feenstra, R. (Ed.) (1988a), *Empirical Methods for International Trade* (Cambridge, MA: MIT Press).
Feenstra, R.C. (2003), *Advanced International Trade: Theory and Evidence* (Princeton: Princeton University Press).
Helpman, E. and Krugman, P.R. (1989), *Trade Policy and Market Structure* (Cambridge, MA and London: MIT Press).
Jackson, J. (1989), *The World Trading System: Law and Policy of International Economic Relations* (Cambridge, MA and London: MIT Press).
Krugman, P.R. (1993), "The Narrow and Broad Arguments for Free Trade," *American Economic Review*, 83 (2), 362–366.

Krugman, P.R. and Smith, A. (Eds.) (1994), *Empirical Studies of Strategic Trade Policies* (Chicago and London: University of Chicago Press).

McCulloch, R. (1993), "The Optimality of Free Trade: Science or Religion?" *American Economic Review*, 83 (2), 367–371.

Seade, J. (1980), "On the Effects of Entry," *Econometrica*, 48 (2), 479–489.

Tirole, J. (1988), *The Theory of Industrial Organization* (Cambridge, MA and London: MIT Press).

Tariffs and subsidies

Barrett, S. (1994), "Strategic Environmental Policy and International Trade," *Journal of Public Economics,* 54, 325–338.

Brander, J.A. (1986), "Rationales for Strategic Trade and Industrial Policy"' in Krugman, P.R.(Ed.), *Strategic Trade Policy and the New International Economics,* (Cambridge, MA: MIT Press), 213–46.

Brander, J.A. (1995), "Strategic Trade Policy," in G. Grossman.and K. Rogoff (Eds.), *Handbook of International Economics, Volume 3* (Amsterdam: North-Holland), 1395–1455.

Brander, J. and Spencer, B.J. (1984), "Tariff Protection and Imperfect Competition," in H. Kierzkowski (Ed.), *Monopolistic Competition and International Trade* (Oxford: Oxford University Press).

de Meza, D. (1986), "Export Subsidies and High Productivity: Cause or Effects," *Canadian Journal of Economics*, 19, 347–350.

Dick, A.R. (1993), "Strategic Trade Policy and Welfare," *Journal of International Economics*, 35, 227–249.

Dixit, A.K. and Grossman, G.M. (1986), "Targeted Export Promotion with Several Oligopolistic Industries," *Journal of International Economics*, 21, 233–250.

Dixit, A.K. and Kyle, A.S. (1985), "The Use of Protection and Subsidies for Entry Promotion and Deterrence," *American Economic Review*, 75, 139–152.

Dixit, A.K. (1984), "International Trade Policy for Oligopolistic Industries," *Economic Journal Conference Papers*, 94, 1–16.

Eaton, J. and Grossman, G.M. (1986), "Optimal Trade and Industrial Policy under Oligopoly," *Quarterly Journal of Economics*, 101, 383–406.

Grossman, G.M.(1987), "Strategic Export Promotion: A Critique", in P.R. Krugman (Ed.), *Strategic Trade Policy and the New International Economics* (Cambridge, MA: MIT Press), 213–246.

Hatzipanayotou, P., Lahiri, S., and Michael, S.M. (2002), "Can Cross-Border Pollution Reduce Pollution?" *Canadian Journal of Economics*, 35 (4), 805–818.

Irwin, D.A., (1992), "Strategic Trade Policy and Mercantilist Trade Rivalries," *American Economic Review, Papers and Proceedings*, 82 (2), 134–139.

Krugman, P.R. (1993), "The Narrow and Broad Arguments for Free Trade", *American Economic Review*, 83 (2), 362–366.

Markusen, J.R. and Venables, A.J. (1988), "Trade Policy with Increasing returns and Imperfect Competition: Contradictory Results from Competing Assumptions", *Journal of International Economics*, 24, 299–316.

Neary, P.J. (2006), "International Trade and the Environment: Theoretical and Policy Linkages," *Environmental & Resource Economics*, 33, 95–118.

Romer, P.M. (1994), "New Goods, Old Theory, and the Welfare Cost of Trade Restrictions," *Journal of Development Economics*, 43, 5–38.

Tornell, A. (1991), "On the Ineffectiveness of Made-to-Measure Protectionist Programs", in Helpman E. and Razin, A. (Eds). *International Trade and Trade Policy* (Cambridge, MA and London: MIT Press), 66–79.

Venables, A.J. (1985), "Trade and Trade Policy with Imperfect Competition: The Case of Identical Products and Free Entry," *Journal of International Economics*, 19, 1–19.

Quotas and VERs

Aw, B. and Roberts, M. (1986), "Estimating Quality Change in Quota Constrained Markets: The Case of US Footwear," *Journal of International Economics*, 21, 45–60.

Bhagwati, J.N. (1965), "On the Equivalence of Tariffs and Quotas," in R.E. Baldwin *et al.* (Eds.), *Trade Growth and the Balance of Payments – Essays in Honor of Gottfried Haberler* (Chicago: Rand McNally), 53–67.

Bhagwati, J.N. (1968), "More on the Equivalence of Tariffs and Quotas," *American Economic Review*, 58, 481–485.

Boorstein, R. and Feenstra, R.C. (1991), "Quality Upgrading and its Welfare Cost in US Steel Imports, 1969–1974," in E. Helpman and A. Razin (Eds.), *International Trade and Trade Policy* (Cambridge, MA: MIT Press), 167–186.

Chen, K.-M.and Lin, C.C. (2007), "The Impact of Exchange Rate Movements on Dumping Activity: Theory and Evidence," presented at Third Annual APEA Conference, Hong Kong University of Science and Technology, Hong Kong, China, July 25–26 2007.

Clarida, R. (1993), "Entry, Dumping and Shakeout," *American Economic Review*, 83, 180–202.

Collie, D. (1991), "Export Subsidies and Countervailing Tariffs," *Journal of International Economics*, 31, 309–324.

Collie, D. (1994), "Strategic Trade Policy and Retaliation," *Japan and the World Economy*, 6, 75–88.

Das, S.R and Donnenfeld, S. (1987), "Trade Policy and its Impact on Quality of Imports," *Journal of International Economics*, 23, 77–95.

Das, S.R. and Donnenfeld, S. (1989), "Competition and International Trade: Quantity and Quality Restrictions," *Journal of International Economics*, 27 (4), 299–318.

de Melo, J. and Messerlin, P.A. (1988), "Price, Quality and Welfare Effects of European VERs on Japanese Autos," *European Economic Review*, 32, 1527–1546.

de Melo, J. and Winters, L.A. (1993), "Price and Quality Effects of VERs Revisited: A Case Study of Korean Footwear Exports," *Journal of Economic Integration*, 8 (1), 33–57.

Faini, R. and Heimler, A. (1991), "The Quality of Production of Textiles and Clothing and the Completion of the Internal Market," in L.A. Winters and A. Venables (Eds.), *European Integration: Trade and Industry* (Cambridge: Cambridge University Press).

Falvey, R. (1979), "The Comparison of Trade within Export-Restricted Categories," *Journal of Political Economy*, 87 (5), 1142–1165.

Feenstra, R.C. (1985), "Automobile Prices and Protection: The US-Japan Trade Restraint," *Journal of Policy Modeling*, 7 (1), 49–68.

Feenstra, R.C. (1988), "Quality Change under Trade Restraints in Japanese Autos," *Quarterly Journal of Economics*, 33 (1), 131–146.

Harris, R. (1985), "Why Voluntary Export Restraints are 'Voluntary,'" *Canadian Journal of Economics*, (4), 799–809.

Hwang, H. and Mai, C.-C. (1988), "On the Equivalence of Tariffs and Quotas under Duopoly: A Conjectural Variations Approach," *Journal of International Economics*, 24, 373–380.

Krishna, K. (1987), "Tariffs versus Quotas with Endogenous Quality," *Journal of International Economics*, 23, 97–122.

Krishna, K. (1990a), "The Case of Vanishing Revenue: Auction Quotas with Monopoly," *American Economic Review*, 80 (4), 828–837.

Krishna, K. (1990b), "Protection and the Product Line," *International Economic Review*, 31 (1), 87–102.

Rodriguez, C. (1979), "The Quality of Import and the Differential Welfare Effects of Tariffs, and Quality Controls as Protective Devices," *Canadian Journal of Economics*, 22 (3), 439–449.

Shibata, H. (1968), "A Note on the Equivalence of Tariffs and Quotas," *American Economic Review*, 58, 137–142.

Contingent protection

Baylis, K. (2007), "Countervailing Duties," in J.D. Gaisford and W.A. Kerr (Eds.), *Handbook of International Trade Policy* (Cheltenham, UK: Edward Elgar Publishing).

Bellis, J-F. (1990), "The EEC Antidumping System," in J.H. Jackson and E.A. Vermulst (Eds.), *Antidumping Law in Practice: A Comparative Study* (London: Harvester Wheatsheaf).

Blonigen, B.A. and Bown, C.P. (2003), "Antidumping and Retaliation Threats," *Journal of International Economics*, 60, 243–279.

Boltuck, R. and Litan, R.L. (Eds.) (1991), *Down in the Dumps: Administration of the Unfair Trade Laws* (Washington, DC: Brookings Institution).

Bown, C.O. and Crowley, M.A. (2007), "Trade Deflection and Trade Depression," *Journal of International Economics*, 72, 176–201.

Brander, J. A. and Krugman, P. (1983), "A 'Reciprocal' Dumping Model of Trade," *Journal of International Economics*, 15 (3/4), 313–323.

Deardorff, A. (1990), "Economic Perspectives on Antidumping Law," in J.K. Jackson and E.A. Vermulst (Eds.), *Antidumping Law and Practice: A Comparative Study* (Ann Arbor: Harvester Wheatsheaf).

Dixit, A. (1988), "Anti-Dumping and Countervailing Duties under Oligopoly," *European Economic Review*, 32, 55–68.

Eaton, J., and Mirman, L.J. (1991), "Predatory Dumping as Signal Jamming," in A. Takayama, M. Ohyama, and H. Ohta (Eds.), *Trade, Policy, and International Adjustments* (New York: Academic Press) 60–76.

Ethier W. (1982), "Dumping," *Journal of Political Economy*, 90 (3), 487–506.

Ethier, W.J. and Fisher, R.D. (1987), "The New Protectionism," *Journal of Economic Integration*, 2 (2), 1–11.

Falvey, R. and Nelson, D. (2006), "Introduction: Special Issue on 100 years of Antidumping," *European Journal of Political Economy*, 545–553.

Feinberg, R.M. (1989), "Exchange Rates and 'Unfair Trade,'" *Review of Economics and Statistics*, 71, 704–707.

Feinberg, R.M. and Reynolds, K.M. (2006), "The Spread of Antidumping Regimes and the Role of Retaliation in Filings," *Southern Journal of Economics*, 72 (4), 877–890.

Finger, J.M. (1993), "The Origins and Evolution of Antidumping Regulation," in J.M. Finger (Ed.), *Antidumping: How it Works and Who gets Hurt* (Ann Arbor: Michigan University Press).

Fischer, R.D. (1992), "Endogenous Probability of Protection and Firm Behavior," *Journal of International Economics*, 32, 149–163.

Flam, H. (1987), "Reverse Dumping," *European Economic Review*, 31, 82–88.

Gruenspecht, H.K. (1988), "Dumping and Dynamic Competition," *Journal of International Economics*, 25, 225–248.

Hartigan, J.C. (1996), "Predatory Dumping," *Canadian Journal of Economics*, 29 (1), 228–239.

Ishikawa, J. and Komoriya, Y. (2007), "Subsidies and Countervailing Duties with Firm Heterogeneity," *Asia-Pacific Journal of Accounting & Economics*, 14, 279–291.

Jackson, J.H. and Vermulst, E.A. (Eds.) (1990), *Antidumping Law and Practice: A Comparative Study* (London: Harvester Wheatsheaf).

Leidy, M.P. and Hoekman, B.M. (1988), "Production Effects of Price- and Cost-Based Anti-Dumping Laws under Flexible Exchange Rates," Discussion Paper 224, Research Seminar in International Economics (University of Michigan).

Marvel, H.P. and Ray, E.J. (1995), "Countervailing Duties," *The Economic Journal*, 105, 1576–1593.

Messerlin, P. (1990), "Anti-Dumping Regulation or Pro-Cartel Law? The EC Chemical Cases," *World Economy*, 13 (4), 465–492.

Messerlin, P. and Reed, G. (1995), "Antidumping Policies in the United States and the European Community," *Economic Journal*, 105, 1565–1575.

Malueg, D.A. and Schwartz M. (1994), "Parallel Imports, Demand Dispersion, and International Price Discrimination," *Journal of International Economics*, 37, 167–195.

Moraga-Gonzalez, J.L. and Viaene, J.-M. (2004), "Anti-dumping, Intra-industry Trade and Quality Reversals," *Tinbergen Institute Discussion Paper*, 04-124/2.

Prusa, T.J. (1992), "Why Are So Many Antidumping Petitions Withdrawn?" *Journal of International Economics*, 33, 1–20.

Prusa, T.J. (1994), "Pricing Behavior in the Presence of Antidumping Law," *Journal of Economic Integration*, 9 (2), 260–289.

Prusa, T.J. (2001), "On the Spread and Impact of Anti-dumping," *Canadian Journal of Economics*, 34 (3), 591–611.

Prusa, T.J. and Skeath, S. (2002), "The Economics and Strategic Motives for Antidumping Filings," *Weltwirtschaftliches Archiv*, 138, 389–413.

Qiu, L.D. (1995), "Why Can't Countervailing Duties Deter Export Subsidization?" *Journal of International Economics*, 39, 249–272.

Reitzes, J.D. (1993), "Antidumping Policy," *International Economic Review*, 34 (4), 745–763.

Spencer, B.J. (1993), "Capital Subsidies and Countervailing Duties in Oligopolistic Industries," *Journal of International Economics*, 24, 45–69.

Staiger, R.W. and Wolak, F.A. (1989), "Strategic Use of Antidumping Law to Enforce Tacit International Collusion," National Bureau of Economic Research Working Paper 3016. Cambridge, MA: NBER.

Taylor, C.T. (2004), "The Economic Effects of Withdrawn Antidumping Investigations: Is there Evidence of Collusive Settlement?" *Journal of International Economics*, 62, 295–312.

Vandenbussche, H. and Zanardi, S. (2010), "The Chilling Trade Effects of Antidumping Proliferation," *European Economic Review*, 54 (6), 760–777.

Viner, J. (1923), *Dumping: A Problem in International Trade* (Chicago: University of Chicago Press).

Willig, R. (1998), "Economic Effects of Antidumping Policy," in R. Lawrence (Ed.) *Brookings Trade Forum 1998* (Washington DC: Brookings Institution).

Zanardi, M. (2000), "Antidumping Law as a Collusive Device," *Canadian Journal of Economics*, 37, 95–112.

11

Multinational production

In Chapters 8 and 9 we had to abandon the assumption that markets are perfectly competitive, in order to account for the pervasiveness of intra-industry trade. This allowed us to explain the causes and consequences of intra-industry trade. It did not, however, explain why a substantial proportion of intra-industry and inter-industry trade flows between establishments that are owned by the same entity.

Firms that own and manage establishments in more than one country are called multinational enterprises (MNEs). The controlling unit is referred to as the parent; the controlled unit as the affiliate or subsidiary. The literature distinguishes between horizontal and vertical multinationals. Horizontal multinationals produce the same product or similar products in different countries. Vertical MNEs produce intermediate products in one country and ship them for further processing to their affiliates located in other countries. Empirically, the distinction between the two types of multinationals is not straightforward. Multinationals often produce identical products in several countries and also manufacture components in one country and ship them for further processing to affiliates located in different countries.

A domestic firm can become multinational by merging with or acquiring an existing foreign firm or by establishing an entirely new entity in a foreign country. The capital that finances the acquisition of the existing foreign entity or the establishment of the new entity may originate from the country of the parent, from the country of the affiliate or from a third country. The firm is said to engage in foreign direct investment (FDI) when it exercises control over the foreign establishment in which it acquires an ownership share.

While the notions of ownership and control appear simple enough, there is in fact no theoretically based threshold of equity participation that qualifies a foreign establishment as an affiliate. Common ownership and control are instead in the nature of a continuum. Asserting common ownership is a matter of definition, not theory. Control is similarly fuzzy, as the autonomy of entities under common ownership is a matter of degree. Any percentage ownership may be combined with varying degrees of autonomy of the affiliates. However, because ownership – unlike control – is easily quantifiable, statistical agencies rely on the criterion of ownership to distinguish between multinational and purely domestic enterprises.[1]

This chapter begins by pointing to the growing importance of multinationals in the world economy. It then addresses the question of what motivates the pursuit of common ownership and control of establishments in different countries. It does so by exploring a large literature that explains the appearance of multinational firms in terms of three "advantages": ownership, location and internalization. Then it delves into oligopolistic interactions that impinge on the decision to be multinational.

Three further sections then examine the interaction between endowments, transport costs and the vertical separation of production stages. Jointly, these factors determine the breakdown of firms into strictly national versus multinational, and also whether multinational is primarily of the horizontal or vertical type.

The chapter then investigates how heterogeneity of the productivity of firms within an industry influences their choices between serving a given foreign market from their home base, from a affiliate located in the foreign country or from an affiliate located in a third foreign country.

The final section of this chapter delves more deeply into the question of why so much of international trade is between entities under common ownership. It also explores how factor endowments and the enforceability of contracts affect a firm's choice between outsourcing and the cross-border vertical integration of production.

11.1   Measuring multinational activity

The United Nations Conference on Trade and Development (UNCTAD) (2009) defines the flow of FDI as capital provided by, or received from, a foreign entity over a specific period of time (e.g., one year). FDI flows comprise equity capital, reinvested earnings and intracompany loans. What distinguishes FDI from portfolio investment is that it establishes or maintains control of the enterprise receiving the investment.

A country's inward stock of FDI is the total value of all capital invested by all foreign-based parent firms in their affiliates in that country plus the net indebtedness of their affiliates in that country. A country's outward stock of FDI is the total value of all capital invested in foreign entities owned or controlled by locally based parents. The inward or outward flows and stocks of FDI are the most widely used yardsticks of multinational activity. They are the only data on multinational activity available on a global basis that are comparable across countries.

The growth in multinational activity (FDI) has risen much faster than world trade which, as was indicated in Chapter 1, has grown more rapidly than world output. Table 11.1 displays the world outward FDI stock for selected years and presents alternative measures of MNE activity. As indicated, the world's outward stock of FDI in 2008 was 28 times larger in nominal terms than it was in 1982. Over the same period, world GDP grew 500 percent and world exports 800 percent. This remarkable growth in the stock of FDI has been accompanied by a change in its composition. From 1990 to 2007, the share of services sectors in the world inward FDI stock increased from 48.9 percent to 63.9 percent while the share of manufacturing sectors fell from 41.2 percent to 27.1 percent.[2]

Table 11.1   MNEs in the world economy (values in current prices; billions of US dollars)[a]

	1982	1990	2000	2008
FDI outward stock	579	1786	5,976	16,206
Sales of foreign affiliates	2530	6026	15,680	30,311[b]
Total assets of foreign affiliates	2036	5,938	21,102	69,771
Employment by foreign affiliates (thousands)	19,864	24,476	45,587	77,386[b]
World GDP	11,963	22,121	31,895	60,780
Exports of goods and non-factor services	2395	4414	7036	19,990

[a] These measures do not fully reflect the weight on multinational activity in individual economies because they do not account for investments in the form of retained earnings originating in the country of the affiliate. Also, stocks are appraised at the book value of assets rather than replacement value.
[b] The 2008 sales and employment numbers are obtained from a regression of sales and employment against inward FDI stock for the period 1982–2006. Not included in this table are the worldwide sales by foreign affiliates associated with their parent firms through non-equity relationships, and of the sales of the parent firms themselves. Worldwide sales, total assets and employment of foreign affiliates are estimated by extrapolating the worldwide data of foreign affiliates of transnational corporations from Austria, Canada, the Czech Republic, Finland, France, Germany, Italy, Japan, Luxembourg, Portugal, Sweden, and the US.
Source: Dunning and Lundan (2008) and UNCTAD (2009).

Table 11.2   Percentage of world FDI stock

	Inward		Outward	
	1990	2008	1990	2008
France	5.0	6.6	6.3	8.3
Germany	5.7	4.7	8.5	9.0
United Kingdom	10.5	6.6	12.8	9.3
United States	20.3	14.9	24.1	19.5

Source: UNCTAD (2009).

As indicated in Table 11.2, a relatively small number of industrialized countries account for a substantial share of the world inward and outward stock of FDI, with just four countries accounting for about 50 percent of the world outward stock. According to UNCTAD (2009), developed countries accounted for 84 percent of the world outward stock of FDI in 2008 and 68 percent of the inward stock.[3]

The ratio of inward FDI stock relative to GDP is an indicator of the importance of multinational firms in a nation's economy. This ratio varies substantially across countries even among highly developed and geographically close countries. Table 11.3 illustrates the increasing role played by multinationals in the economies of India, the Republic of Korea, and the Russian Federation.[4]

It is estimated that multinational firms account for more than two thirds of world trade, and that half of that trade is intra-firm, meaning that it flows between affiliates, or between affiliates and their parent firm. Barefoot and Mataloni (2009) report that in 2006 US-based parent firms were responsible for 51.3 percent of total US exports, with intra-firm flows accounting for 38 percent of their exports and 37 percent of their imports. Anderson and Zeile

Table 11.3 Inward stock of FDI as a percentage of GDP

	1990	2000	2007
Belgium and Luxembourg	27.8	78.7	132.3[a]
Netherlands	23.3	65.8	87.9
France	3.4	19.6	39.6
Germany	6.7	14.5	19.0
Italy	5.4	11.3	15.6
United Kingdom	20.6	30.5	48.6
Canada	19.7	29.8	39.2
United States	6.9	12.9	15.2
China	5.4	17.9	10.2
India	0.5	3.8	6.5
Rep. of Korea	2.0	7.3	12.3
Russian Federation	na	12.4	25.1
Australia	23.7	28.70	38.0
Japan	0.3	1.1	3.0
Brazil	8.5	17.1	25.0

[a]Year 2005
Source: Dunning (2008); UNCTAD (2008); The Economist (2010).

(2009) claim that in the same year 19.1 percent of US imports went to US-based affiliates of non-US parents and slightly more than half of these imports flowed intra-firm.

Kiyota and Urata (2008) find that Japanese MNEs accounted for 93.6 percent of Japanese exports and 81.2 percent of imports in 2000.[5] For France, multinational firms accounted for 73 percent of total industrial exports and 64 percent of total imports in 1999.[6] In 2005, 34 percent of Canadian exports and 25 percent of imports were classified as intra-firm. Nearly half of that trade was in transportation equipment, an industry dominated by large American companies that operate on both sides of the border.[7]

11.2 Why multinational? The OLI framework

After settling on a definition, discussion of the MNE naturally turns to the question: "Why multinational?" Why carry out production in an establishment controlled by an entity domiciled in a different country? That such a question is even raised attests to the widely held belief that familiarity with a country's business practices and its legal and cultural norms gives a firm a significant competitive edge. Why then should production take place in a plant at least partially run by foreigners, rather than in a native firm? After all, indigenous firms are presumably better integrated into local networks, more familiar with local tastes, and more knowledgeable about local written and unwritten rules.

A considerable literature holds that intangible capital is the key asset that allows foreign transplants to offset the handicap resulting from a shallower understanding of a foreign business environment (Johnson,1970; Hymer,1976).[8] Multinational firms are said to possess *knowledge-based assets* that allow them to produce better, more distinctive and possibly cheaper products than local producers. The knowledge may be patented or copyrighted. It may derive from research and development,(R&D) superior entrepreneurial capacity or superior organizational skills. These knowledge-based advantages are often supported by a reputation for quality and reliability built on advertising, branding, and trademarking.

Knowledge-based assets are public goods in the sense that the cost of their deployment outside the home country is low compared with the cost of their development in the parent's home country. This explains why their use in foreign affiliates *can* be profitable. However, it leaves open the question why a firm establishes a foreign subsidiary when other alternatives to supply foreign markets, such as exporting, licensing and joint venture, are available.

This is the very question the literature addresses by a framework known as "OLI." This acronym, which stands for ownership, location and internalization, encapsulates the three conditions deemed necessary for the emergence of a multinational firm. These three conditions are: (1) the enjoyment of advantages derived from the *ownership* of knowledge which allow the firm to survive and thrive in an unfamiliar environment; (2) the existence of *locational* advantages which determine that the knowledge-based assets are more profitably exploited by producing in the foreign environment than by concentrating all production in the home country; (3) the existence of *internalization* advantages, which make the exploitation of the locational advantages more profitable when producing in an affiliate than contracting out production to local firms.

Ownership advantages

A large body of empirical work supports the key role of knowledge-based assets. Caves (1974), Pugel (1978), Lall (1980), Bergsten *et al.* (1978) and Grubaugh (1987) find a positive and significant relationship for US firms between their level of outward multinational activity (FDI) and their research and advertising intensity.[9] Caves (1974) finds that the percentage of industry sales accounted for by foreign subsidiaries in the UK relates positively to the R&D intensity of the matching US industry.[10] He also finds that the share of UK industries' output accounted for by foreign owned firms is positively related with US *and* UK industry advertising intensities.

Lall and Siddarthan (1982) determine that neither the research intensity nor advertising intensity across US industries correlates significantly with the cross-industry variation in manufacturing shares accounted for by US-based affiliates of non-US parents. They attribute this finding to the supremacy of US firms in terms of differentiation advantages. Specifically, they argue that foreign rivals might well possess intangible advantages in differentiation, but that these advantages are found only in areas too narrow to have an impact on the share of affiliate production at the three-digit industry level.

Doms and Jensen (1998) observe that US-based foreign-owned plants are more productive than domestically owned US plants even after controlling for plant age and size. Similarly, the plants of US multinationals abroad are also more productive than are locally owned plants.[11] Criscuolo and Martin (2009a, 2009b) find that the productivity leadership of UK-based affiliates of US parents over British firms derives from the purchase of technologically superior local producers.[12]

Cantwell (1989) theorizes that a country's knowledge-based assets may serve to attract foreign firms intent on learning about the host country's technologies. This hypothesis is supported by Kogut and Chang (1991), who find that Japanese firms are more likely to invest in the US when Japanese R&D intensity is lower than the R&D intensity in the matching US industry. Pugel *et al.* (1996) provide further evidence in this regard. They argue that a country's possession of important intangible assets can be either a repellent or a lure for FDI. Their finding of no significant correlation between the R&D intensity of US industries and levels of Japanese FDI in the US suggests to them that neither the repelling influence nor the access to technology influence dominates across their sample. This contrasts with the significant negative correlation they find for US advertising intensity, a finding that they suggest reflects that the strong marketing capabilities of local US producers deters Japanese FDI in the US.

Kogut and Chang (1991) argue that the investment motive can be inferred from the difference in R&D intensity of the parent and host countries. A positive association of outward multinational activity with R&D intensity in the donor country minus R&D intensity in the host country suggests an exploitation of a technological advantage. By contrast, a negative association points to a quest for technological sourcing. Neven and Siotis (1995) rely on this approach and find some corroboration of a technological sourcing motive for Japanese and US foreign direct investment in France, Germany, Italy, and the UK. However, they find no such evidence in the case of intra-European Community (EC) investments.

Belderbos and Sleuwaegen (1996) argue that the ownership of knowledge-based advantages should be most apparent in the case of FDI taking place in countries least familiar to the parent firm. To test this hypothesis, they compare Japanese multinational activity in Asia and in Western countries. They argue that the presence of Japanese trading houses in South Asian countries gives Japanese firms advantages in terms of market intelligence that they do not enjoy in Western markets. Also, host country government support and the absence of strong local competition in South Asian countries suggest a lesser role for firm-specific advantages than in Western markets. Therefore, the ownership of knowledge-based assets should be less important for Japanese FDI in Asian countries than in Western countries. They find support for this hypothesis. Specifically, they show that the R&D intensity, sales cost intensity and human resource intensity of Japanese firms correlate positively with the probability that they invest in Western countries rather than Asian countries.[13]

Locational advantages

As indicated, the mere possession of knowledge-based assets does not imply that the best way to exploit them is by going multinational. The owners of these assets might well earn higher profits by concentrating production in their home base and then serving other markets by just exporting.

The following example illustrates the trade-off between the decisions to concentrate production in a single country versus fragmenting production across countries. Let the demands for the firm's product in the home country and foreign country be $q = L(a - p)$ and $q^* = L^*(a - p^*)$, where q, p and L denote the quantity sold in the home country, the home price and size of the home market. Let starred variables denote the same variables for the foreign country. Assume that the two markets are segmented, that marginal production cost c is the same in both countries, and that per plant fixed costs are F and F^*. The corporate tax burden in the home and foreign country are T and T^*. Subsumed in T and T^* are regulations regarding tax rates, depreciation schedules, deferral and tax conventions among countries. The transport cost between countries is τ. The firm may serve both countries from the home base or from the foreign base or, alternatively, it may serve each market from a local establishment. We now explore what determines the choice of these different options.

Profits under each of the three possible forms of organizing production are:

(a) Producing in a home plant only:

$$\Pi = (1 - T) \left\{ [(a - c)^2 L + (a - c - \tau)^2 L^*]/4 - F \right\} \tag{11.1}$$

(b) Producing in a foreign plant only:

$$\Pi^* = (1 - T^*) \left\{ [(a - c - \tau)^2 L + (a - c)^2 L^*]/4 - F^* \right\} \tag{11.2}$$

and (c) Producing in a home plant and in a foreign plant:

$$\Pi^{MNE} = (1 - T) \left\{ (a - c)^2 L/4 - F \right\} + (1 - T^*) \left\{ (a - c)^2 L^*/4 - F^* \right\} \tag{11.3}$$

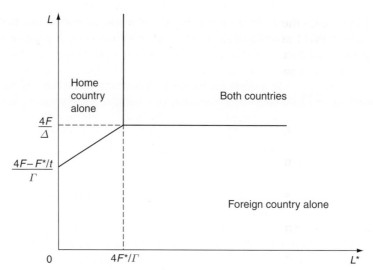

Figure 11.1 Transportation cost and the choice of production sites

Defining $t \equiv (1 - T)/(1 - T^*)$ and $\Delta \equiv \left[(a - c)^2 - t(a - c - \tau)^2 \right]$, one can easily check that $\Pi^{MNE} > (<) \Pi$ when $F^* < (>) L^* \Delta / 4$. Similarly, defining $\Gamma \equiv \left[(a - c)^2 - (a - c - \tau)^2 / t \right]$, one can check that $F < (>) L \Gamma / 4$ ensures $\Pi^{MNE} > (<) \Pi^*$.

A first implication of these results is that the firm does not produce in both countries if either Δ or Γ is negative.

Figure 11.1 indicates the firm's profit maximizing choice for the location of production for the case where $\Delta > 0$, $\Gamma > 0$ and $F - F^*/t > 0$. Production takes place in two plants when both markets are sufficiently large. The reason is that the fixed per plant cost can then be spread over a larger number of units. Because $d\Delta/d\tau > 0$ and $d\Gamma/d\tau > 0$, it also follows that the profit from multi-plant production increases relative to the profit from producing in a single plant as τ becomes larger.

Transfer pricing

According to internationally agreed principles, a product's *value for duty* should be based on the actual value of the product on which duty is assessed. GATT Article VII.2 stipulates that "actual value" should be the price at which such or like merchandise is sold or offered for sale in the ordinary course of trade under fully competitive conditions. Nonetheless, exporters have some flexibility when declaring value for duty. This can arise because comparable arm's length prices may not exist or, if they do exist, customs authorities are unable or unwilling to find out what these prices are. Declaring a high value for duty means the exporter will increase the amount of duty to be paid. However, since a higher declared import price shifts profits from the importing country to the exporting country, total taxes paid by the firm can fall when profits declared in the importing country are more heavily taxed than profits declared in the exporting country. Whether the exporter is better off declaring a low or a high value for duty therefore depends on the rate of duty relative to the difference in taxation rates between countries.[14]

We now examine the effect of tariffs and taxes on the choice of price at which a firm will transfer output between affiliates in different countries. Denote the *ad valorem* tariff rates in the home and foreign country as τ and τ^*. Denote the transfer price set by the firm as R, which we assume is a value inside the interval $[R_{min}, R_{max}]$, where this interval constraint is such that pricing outside the interval would trigger an investigation by customs authorities that would impose a heavy burden on the firm.[15]

If marginal cost equals c in all countries, the net of tax profits associated with the three production location options are:

(a) For a home plant alone:

$$\Pi = (1 - T)\left[(p - c)q + (R - c)q^* - F\right] + (1 - T^*)\left[p^* - R(1 + \tau^*)\right]q^*$$

(b) For a foreign plant alone:

$$\Pi^* = (1 - T)\left[p - R^*(1 + \tau)\right]q + (1 - T^*)\left[(R^* - c)q + (p^* - c)q^* - F^*\right]$$

(c) For two plants:

$$\Pi^{MNE} = (1 - T)\left[(p - c)q - F\right] + (1 - T^*)\left[(p^* - c)q^* - F^*\right]$$

We will only compare options (a) and (c).[16] Differentiation of Π shows that the optimal transfer price is:

$$R = \begin{cases} R_{\max} & when \quad (1 + \tau^*) < (1 - T)/(1 - T^*) \\ R_{\min} & when \quad (1 + \tau^*) > (1 - T)/(1 - T^*) \end{cases}$$

Quantities are optimally chosen when:

$$MR(q) = c \quad and \quad MR^*(q^*) = c\frac{1 - T}{1 - T^*} - R\left[\frac{1 - T}{1 - T^*} - (1 + \tau^*)\right]$$

Since differentiation of Π and Π^{MNE} with respect to q will yield the same expression, we know that the quantity sold in the home market is the same under options (a) and (c).

We now compare profits under options (a) and (c) for the general case where $T \neq T^*$. We start by solving the first-order conditions for q and q^* for the particular case where demands are $q = L(a - p)$ and $q^* = L^*(a - p^*)$. Upon defining $t \equiv (1 - T)/(1 - T^*)$, the first order conditions yield the following expressions for profits under options (a) and (c) respectively:

$$\Pi = (1 - T)\left[(a - c)^2 L/4 - F\right] + (1 - T^*)\left[(a - tc) - R(1 + \tau^* - t)\right]^2 L^*/4$$
$$\Pi^{MNE} = (1 - T)\left[(a - c)^2 L/4 - F\right] + (1 - T^*)\left[(a - c)^2 L^*/4 - F^*\right]$$

In contrast to what we found in the section above, a zero fixed cost no longer calls for local production in each market. To make that point clear, we focus on the case where $F^* = 0$. For this case, we obtain the condition:

$$\Pi^{MNE} > \Pi \quad if \quad c(1 - t) - R(1 + \tau^* - t) < 0$$

Now consider Figure 11.2 which displays the optimal transfer price as a step function bounded by R_{min} and R_{max}. We can discern three cases: Case 1, where $t < 1$, is shown as area I. Case 2, where $1 < t < (1 + \tau^*)$ is shown as area II. Case 3, where $1 + \tau^* < t$, is shown as area III. Given this, the plant location and transfer price are case-specific.

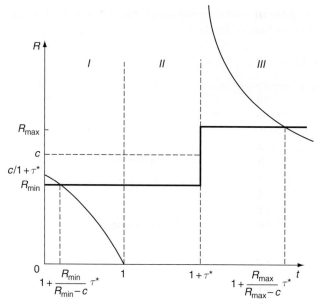

Figure 11.2 Location choice and transfer pricing

Case 1: when $t < 1$, the condition $c(1-t) - R(1+\tau^* - t) < 0$ holds for all the pairs (R, t) with coordinates put them above the downward-sloping curve (a branch of a hyperbola) shown in area *I*. The firm produces in a home plant only when $t < 1 + [R_{\min}/(R_{\min} - c)]\tau^*$. The latter condition holds provided $c/1 + \tau^* > R_{\min}$. When $t > 1 + [R_{\min}/(R_{\min} - c)]\tau^*$ the firm earns a higher profit when it establishes a plant in each country.

Case 2: when $1 < t < (1 + \tau^*)$, the condition $c(1-t) - R(1+\tau^* - t) < 0$ holds for any R. The two-plant solution is always profit maximizing when t belongs to area *II*.

Case 3: when $1 + \tau^* < t$, the condition $c(1-t) - R(1+\tau^* - t) < 0$ holds for all the pairs (R, t) with coordinates that put them below the curve (the second branch of the hyperbola) shown in area *III*. Specifically, the two-plant option is preferred when $t < 1 + [R_{\max}/(R_{\max} - c)]\tau^*$

We conclude that, when the taxation of profits earned in the home county is low compared with the taxation of profits earned in the foreign country, a home plant alone is profit maximizing. As tax burdens converge, profit maximization calls for a plant in each location. However, a very high tax burden in the home country may lead to a concentration of production in the home country. This peculiar outcome arises when the firm can show losses on exports by setting a sufficiently low transfer price. These losses compensate for the profits earned from local sales.

Grubert and Mutti (1991) examine US MNE activity across 33 countries and find evidence of income shifting to low tax countries. Host country corporate income tax rates appear to have a large and significant negative impact on export sales by local US-owned subsidiaries to third countries, but not on local sales.

Internalization

We now consider the question of why owners of knowledge-based assets would forgo the opportunity to have indigenous firms exploit these assets given that indigenous firms are more knowledgeable about the local environment. We discuss two factors that merit particular attention among the factors that determine the profitability of outsourcing production relative to in-house production.

Dissipation of knowledge and loss of reputation

One factor in the decision on whether to outsource or undertake in-house production is the cost of transferring knowledge. There is evidence that transferring knowledge among establishments under common ownership is less costly than transferring them at arm's length via the market. Teece (1977) infers from survey data that a technology transfer to a joint venture partner is on average 5.1 percent more costly than a transfer to a wholly owned subsidiary. He also determines that a technology transfer to an independent licensee costs on average about 8.7 percent more than a transfer to a subsidiary.

In addition to its potentially higher cost, arm's length licensing of technology entails risks. One is that the prospective licensor may have to reveal to potential competitors aspects of the technology, and may not have the resources to enforce nondisclosure agreements entered into with them.

The desire to preserve a reputation for quality also encourages in-house production. Horstmann and Markusen (1987) explore the consequences of a misalignment of incentives in this respect. Horstmann and Markusen assume that a potential licensor owns a technology that makes it possible to produce a product with either high or low quality, with the former costing more than the latter. In the absence of a technology transfer, potential licensees – of which there are many – can only produce the low-quality product. Prior to purchase, consumers are unable to detect whether any given seller is offering the high or low-quality product. However, consumers can become aware that a particular seller offers the high-quality product if the seller has been licensed to use the licensor's well-known brand. Given this, consumers are willing to pay a higher price for the branded product so long as the licensee maintains a reputation as a high-quality producer (seller). If in any given time period the licensee violates the commitment not to skimp on quality then consumers will find this out in the subsequent period and the licensee's reputation as a high-quality producer is then lost forever. We now consider this more formally.

Let π_h denote by the licensee's per period profit derived from the production of high quality and let π_l be the licensee's profit in the single period during which he produces low quality (while maintaining the reputation as a high-quality producer). Because in that single period the licensee sells at the higher price but incurs lower costs, it must be true that $\pi_h < \pi_l$. In the subsequent period the licensee's profits fall to zero since consumers discover the producer is not a high-quality producer. Given this, the following inequality must hold to ensure that the licensee does not default on being a high-quality producer:

$$\frac{\pi_h - g}{i} > \pi_l - g \qquad (11.4)$$

where i denotes the discount rate and g represents the fixed per period payment to the licensor. In (11.4), the term on the left is the present value of the infinite stream of profits earned in the absence of defecting. The term on the right is the one-period profit from defecting. It is clear that when $g = \pi_h$, the licensee earns a higher profit by defecting. Only when the licensee's production cost is lower than that licensor's cost can licensing be the more profitable option.

Denoting by Π the profits from in-house exploitation of the technology allows one to express the condition that licensing is the preferred option as $\Pi < g$. Because (11.4) is necessary to avert skimping, it follows that licensing is the more profitable route of exploiting the technology when $\dfrac{\pi_h - i\pi_l}{1 - i} > g > \Pi$.

Incomplete contracts and opportunistic behavior

A firm that transacts in spot markets can adjust the quantity it purchases or sells (almost) costlessly in response to changing market conditions. The firm can also easily switch trading partners. Locking itself into long-term contracts must therefore confer advantages to a firm that outweigh the loss of flexibility.

One instance where gains from trade cannot be achieved by spot transactions (as opposed to a long-term contract) is when one party must make a relationship-specific investment that cannot be recouped if the other party reneges on the deal. Consider a situation where a seller can only serve a buyer by building a machine designed to the buyer's specifications. The machine is "unique", and it cannot be produced according to a different specification. The cost of the machine is therefore sunk as soon as it is incurred.

In the absence of a contract which commits the buyer to purchasing a sufficient quantity at a price that allows recovery of the sunk cost, no supplier will be willing to build the machine. If the parties instead write a contract, they are likely to ensure that it spells out each side's obligations, their responses to different possible contingencies and the penalties for non-performance. The costs of anticipating future contingencies, negotiating and drafting terms, monitoring and enforcing performance are called transaction costs. If transaction costs are zero, the parties could enter into contracts that specify what each party will do for every conceivable state of affairs. Such contracts – called complete contracts – would never need revision, and all parties would honor them regardless of the circumstances that occur. Yet, in practice, transactions costs are always positive, and they are larger the more complex the deal and the less certain the future. For these reasons, real world contracts spell out only a limited number of contingencies; real world contracts are also somewhat nebulous as to what constitutes adequate performance.

The incompleteness of real world contracts opens the door to opportunistic behavior. To see why, consider a transaction that requires a supplier S to acquire a customer-specific intermediate input that has no value outside the relationship with buyer B. Let F be the cost of producing the input and assume the contracted price of the input is also F. Let R denote firm B's expected revenue from the sale of the final product and let G be the cost of other inputs that firm B must combine with the tailor-made input supplied by supplier S. Once the input is produced, the aggregate gain from the trade is $W = R - G$. If the parties do not trade upon completion of the production process then firm B's best option is to contract with another supplier at the same price F. If the cost of searching for another supplier is H then firm B's return is $W - F$ if the deal goes through and it is $W - (F + H)$ if the deal does not go through. Assume that firm S's best alternative is to throw away the specialized input at zero cost. Then firm S receives F if the deal goes through and obtains zero if the deal does not go through. The aggregate surplus from termination of the relationship is therefore $(W - (F + H) + (0))$.

The parties' joint advantage from maintaining the relationship (called the quasi-rent) equals $[W - F] - [W - (F + H)] = H$. The quasi-rent is also the amount that the parties will try to appropriate when they act opportunistically. For example, the buyer will likely invoke a change in the environment (for example, an unforeseen drop in the demand for the buyer's final product) to justify a demand for a lower price. The buyer will do this knowing that the seller's best option if renegotiation breaks down is the salvage value of zero. On the other hand, supplier S will seek to impose a price above F, possibly alleging an unforeseen increase in cost.

The literature refers to the predicament that arises from such opportunistic behavior as the *holdup problem*. The expectation of a holdup problem affects contractual performance since a supplier may skimp on quality when doing so is not immediately detectable. Such opportunistic behavior reduces the expected joint surplus from cooperation. In such cases, the integration of input production and final output production within the same firm (vertical integration) may be the preferred mode of organizing production.

It is important to stress that such integration does not necessarily eradicate opportunistic behavior. Grossman and Hart (1986) argue that it merely substitutes opportunistic self-interested owners for equally opportunistic self-interested employees. Specifically, the authors argue that the managers of divisions that produce inputs will act opportunistically by not providing optimal (unobservable) effort when a portion of the surplus generated by their effort accrues to the owners of the firm.

The crucial difference between in-house production and arm's length contracting resides in the ownership of the inventory of inputs. Ownership confers rights of control called residual rights. These rights allow the owner to retain control of the inventory of inputs when he fires the manager for inadequate performance. Unlike the independent supplier, the manager cannot threaten to withhold the input. The implication is that a manager's potential gain from *ex post* bargaining is lower than that of an independent supplier.[17] This carries implications for the manager's *ex ante* incentives. In addition, because the allocation of residual rights affects incentives, it also determines the size of the surplus to be distributed.

The optimal choice between vertical integration and arm's length contracting with an input supplier is that which minimizes the distortions in terms of effort and other investments by all parties. Grossman and Hart (1986) argue that when a final good firm owns the assets of the party that produces the input it will secure a larger share of the *ex post* surplus than when an independent seller owns the assets. The final good producer will then overinvest, and the producer of the input will underinvest. The converse arises when the producer of the input owns the assets. The implication is that vertical integration is more likely to arise when the investment required from one party is very important relative to the investment by the other party. The preferred option is more likely to be arm's length contracting when the required investments of the two parties are similar.

The industry-specific factors that determine the choice between in-house production versus arm's length contracting play out in the same way whether the outside supplier is a home or foreign firm.[18] From an international trade perspective, the primary question of interest is how these industry-specific factors interact with country characteristics and trade barriers. This topic will be taken up below in section 11.8.

11.3 Oligopolistic interaction

Oligopolistic interaction adds a further twist to the decision of whether to serve a foreign market through exports or a local plant. The deterrence of entry by rival producers may call for production in a foreign market even when transport costs and tariffs are low in relation to the fixed cost of operating a foreign affiliate. Also, serving a foreign market by exporting *and* by local production may offer an advantage that cannot be obtained from producing in a single location.

Entry deterrence under Cournot competition

Consider a home firm that has already incurred a firm-specific fixed cost *and* a plant-specific fixed cost in its home market. The firm-specific cost, which could include the cost of management, marketing and R&D, is borne by headquarters and is invariant to the number of plants. The plant-specific cost is proportional to the number of plants. The firm now considers whether to enter a foreign market by exporting or by producing in a foreign affiliate. The home and the foreign markets are segmented. Exporting entails a transport cost τ per unit exported. Production in an affiliate carries a marginal cost c, which is the same as the marginal production cost in the home market. It also entails a plant-specific fixed cost F.

The home firm knows that, following its entry into the foreign market, there may be entry by a local firm. Assume for simplicity that the local entrant's costs are the same as the costs borne by the home firm. Also assume that if local entry does takes place, the two firms will compete as Cournot duopolists.[19] The game unfolds in two stages. In a first stage the home firm decides whether or not to establish a subsidiary in the foreign country; in the second stage the foreign firm decides whether or not to enter.

Because markets are segmented, one can limit the analysis to the foreign country. The quantities produced by the incumbent and the local entrant are respectively denoted q and q^*. Figure 11.3 displays the firms' best response functions. The home firm's response function is r_E when it exports and r_{MNE} when it serves the foreign market through a local affiliate. The response function r_E is situated below the response function r_{MNE} because the marginal delivered cost of export sales, equal to $c + \tau$, is larger than the marginal production cost c. The foreign firm's best response function is r^*. If the foreign firm enters and the home firm serves the foreign market by exporting, the duopoly equilibrium is at point H. If the home firm instead serves the foreign market through a local affiliate the duopoly equilibrium is at point J.

Let π_I and π_I^* denote the values of incumbent's and the entrant's profits when the equilibrium is at point I (where $I = \{H, J\}$) in Figure 11.3, Let $\tilde{\pi}_I$ and $\tilde{\pi}_I^*$ denote the variable profit – the difference between revenue and variable cost – earned by the home and foreign firm when the equilibrium is at point I. If the local firm enters, its profit is $\pi_I^* = \tilde{\pi}_I^* - F - \textit{firm specific cost}$. Clearly, $\pi_H^* > \pi_J^*$ in view of the fact that the home firm produces a smaller quantity when the duopoly equilibrium is at H than when it is at J. Since total industry output is smaller at H than at J the price at the equilibrium H is higher than the price at the equilibrium J.

Consider now the question of under what conditions the home firm prefers to supply the foreign market via a foreign affiliate rather than by exporting. Note first that when $\pi_J^* > 0$, entry will take place regardless of the channel through which the home firm serves the foreign market. Given this, the profit maximizing strategy of the home firm is to export if $\tilde{\pi}_J - F \leq \tilde{\pi}_H$

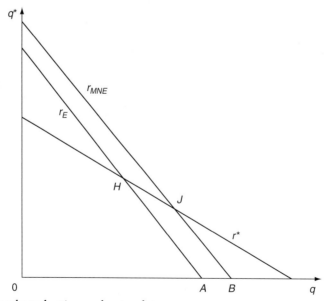

Figure 11.3 Local production and entry deterrence

and to set up a local plant otherwise. Conversely, when $\pi_H^* < 0$, the foreign firm will not enter even when the home firm chooses to export. If so, the home firm will serve the foreign market via the channel that maximizes its profit as a monopolist. Specifically, it will choose to export if $\tilde{\pi}_A \geq \tilde{\pi}_B - F$ and it will choose to produce in a foreign affiliate if $\tilde{\pi}_A < \tilde{\pi}_B - F$.

The interesting case arises when $\pi_H^* > 0 > \pi_f^*$ and $\tilde{\pi}_B - F \leq \tilde{\pi}_A$. That is, when the local firm can earn positive profits by entering, but only if the home firm exports. At the same time, exporting is the more profitable option for the home firm when foreign entry does not take place. Under these conditions, the home firm is better off choosing the export option when $\tilde{\pi}_B - F \leq \tilde{\pi}_H$; it is better off serving the foreign market via a local affiliate when $\tilde{\pi}_B - F > \tilde{\pi}_H$.

Softening price competition

Section 11.2 showed that when marginal cost is constant the firm serves a market either by producing locally or by exporting; the firm will never do both. However, with increasing marginal cost dual sourcing can be profit maximizing (Horst, 1971). Dual sourcing may also yield higher profits when marginal cost is constant but uncertain (Kogut and Kulatilaka, 1994), and when investment in capacity is irreversible and foreign demand is uncertain (Rob and Vettas, 2003).[20]

Choi and Davidson (2006) argue that dual sourcing can be more profitable in an oligopolistic environment when the home firm faces uncertain marginal costs in the foreign country. To show this, they assume that marginal cost in the home country is c but that there is uncertainty about the foreign cost, which can be either $\bar{c}$ or $\underline{c}$, where $\bar{c} > c > \underline{c}$. Given this, the firm considers the following options: 1) to serve the foreign market from its home base; 2) to serve the foreign country by producing in a local affiliate that has sufficient capacity to meet local demand regardless of the realization of local cost; 3) to serve the foreign country from two plants: one located in the home country, the other in the foreign country.

Choi and Davidson (2006) assume that the firm chooses a production capacity, with the cost of a small capacity denoted as $\underline{F}$ and the cost of larger capacity denoted as $\overline{F}$; it is assumed that $\overline{F} < 2\underline{F}$. A large capacity is sufficient to meet foreign market demand even when the price is low as result of a low foreign cost realization. A small capacity plant cannot meet foreign market demand even if the price is high as a result of a high foreign cost realization. However, two small plants have sufficient capacity to meet foreign market demand regardless of cost.

A monopoly chooses to export from the home country when the probability of $\underline{c}$ is sufficiently low. It serves the foreign market from a local affiliate exclusively when the probability of $\underline{c}$ is sufficiently high. For intermediate probabilities it chooses to supply the foreign market from two plants. To be exact, it produces up to capacity in the lower cost country, and satisfies the remainder of the demand from a plant located in the higher cost country. Its marginal cost is then c or $\bar{c}$; its infra-marginal cost is c or $\underline{c}$. The important feature under dual sourcing is that the firm's marginal cost is higher on average than when it produces only at home or only in the foreign country, but its average cost is lower.

Consider now the situation where the home firm faces price competition in the foreign market from a local firm endowed with unlimited production capacity. The higher marginal cost associated with dual sourcing allows the home firm to make a credible commitment to set a higher price. When response functions are upward-sloping, this commitment elicits a higher price on the part of the competitor. This benefits the home firm.

The existence of price competition weakens the conditions under which dual sourcing is profit maximizing for the home firm, and it expands the range of probabilities of $\underline{c}$ for which the firm chooses to serve the foreign market from a local affiliate *and* its home base. Choi and Davidson (2006) argue that similar uncertainty may account for the prevalence of two-way FDI flows between developed countries.

11.4 Endowments and the fragmentation of production

We now consider the question of how cross-country differences in absolute and relative endowments influence the composition of firms in an industry as being either national or multinational. We look first at horizontal fragmentation. We then examine how endowments and factors intensities jointly determine the extent to which firms undertake the geographical separation of vertically related productions stages.

Horizontal fragmentation[21]

Two countries, called home (h) and foreign (f), are endowed with L^i units of labor and K^i units of capital $[i=h,f]$. They can produce the same two goods, using the same technologies. One good, z, is homogeneous, freely tradable and produced by a perfectly competitive industry. This good serves as the numeraire. Its unit cost in country i is $c(r_i, w_i)$, where w_i and r_i denote the local wage and rental rate. Competition in the homogeneous industry entails:

$$c(r_i, w_i) \geq 1 \text{ and } z_i \geq 0 \quad i = h,f \tag{11.5}$$

The second good is differentiated and produced by a monopolistically competitive industry. Preferences for that good are represented by the Dixit-Stiglitz sub-utility $V \equiv \left[\sum_{k=1}^{n} v_k^\rho \right]^{1/\rho}$, where v_k denotes consumption of variety k, and $\rho \equiv (\sigma - 1)/\sigma < 1$ with $\sigma > 1$ denotes the elasticity of substitution between varieties. The representative consumer, assumed to be identical in both countries, has a Cobb-Douglas utility $U = Z^{1-\alpha} V^\alpha$ $[0 < \alpha < 1]$, where Z stands for consumption of the homogeneous good. As indicated in Chapter 8, a consumer with this type of utility function will spend a fixed portion α of income on the differentiated good.

The differentiated good may be produced by national or multinational firms. Each firm produces a single variety. No variety is produced by more than one firm. Multinationals operate one plant in country h and another in country f. Each plant serves only the local consumers. National firms operate a single plant which serves local consumers, and possibly foreign consumers.

National and multinational firms incur the same marginal cost $b(w_i, r_i) \equiv b_i$. The price p_i of the differentiated good in the home country therefore satisfies the condition:[22]

$$p_i = [\sigma/\sigma - 1]b(w_i, r_i) \tag{11.6}$$

Only a fraction $1/\tau \leq 1$ of an exported differentiated good arrives at its destination; the rest "melts" in transport. Since the marginal delivered cost of exports from country i is $\tau b(w_i, r_i)$, it follows that a variety that sells at the price p_i in country i (where it is produced) will sell at the price τp_i in foreign country j $(j \neq i)$.[23] Because the multinational firm incurs the same marginal cost as a national firm, it sells locally at the same price as a national firm.

Denote the number of multinationals as $\tilde{n}$ and the number of national firms based in country i as n_{i}. Then we can express the price index of the differentiated industry in country i as:

$$P_i = \left[n_i p_i^{1-\sigma} + n_j (\tau p_i)^{1-\sigma} + \tilde{n} p_i^{1-\sigma} \right]^{\frac{1}{1-\sigma}} \quad i,j = h,f; \quad i \neq j \tag{11.7}$$

By letting $\tilde{q}_i$ denote the quantity sold by a multinational firm in country i, and letting q_{ij} denote the quantity sold in country j by a national firm based in country i, we can state the demands faced in countries i and j by firms based in country i and producing a differentiated product as:

$$q_{ii} = \tilde{q}_i = p_i^{-\sigma} P_i^{\sigma-1} E_i \text{ and } q_{ij} = \tau^{1-\sigma} p_i^{-\sigma} P_i^{\sigma-1} E_i \qquad (11.8)$$

where E_i denotes country i's expenditure on the differentiated good.

All national and multinational firms incur a firm-specific cost that reflects the use of capital and labor in the production of headquarter services.[24] Markusen and Venables (2000) assume that these inputs enter fixed cost in the same proportion as in variable costs. Since national firms incur their fixed costs locally, these costs are $b_i F$. In contrast, multinationals' firm-specific fixed costs are at least partially footloose. The multinational firm can bear them partially in the country where this cost is lowest. To be exact, a multinational firm's fixed cost is $\Psi[b_h, b_f]\tilde{F}$, where Ψ is a symmetric function homogeneous of degree 1, and $\Psi = b_h = b_f$ when $b_h = b_f$. The assumption that $\tilde{F} > F$ captures the idea that there is an additional fixed cost for the multinational firm's second plant.

Given the above, the profits earned by national and multinational firms are:

$$\pi_i = [p_i - b(w_i, r_i)](q_{ii} + q_{ij}) - b(w_i, r_i)F \quad i,j = h,f \quad \text{and} \quad i \neq j \qquad (11.9)$$

$$\tilde{\pi} = [p_h - b(w_h, r_h)]\tilde{q}_h + [p_f - b(w_f, r_f)]\tilde{q}_f - \Psi[b_h, b_f]\tilde{F} \qquad (11.10)$$

Freedom of entry and exit implies that profits are non-positive in equilibrium, which can be stated as $\sigma b_i F \geq p_i (q_{ii} + q_{ij}) = b_i (\sigma/\sigma - 1)(q_{ii} + q_{ij})$. Given this, the following must be true:

For national firms: $\quad \sigma F \geq q_{ii} + q_{ij} \quad n_i \geq 0 \quad i,j = h,j \quad \text{and} \quad i \neq j \qquad (11.11)$

For MNE's: $\quad \sigma \psi [b(w^h, r^h), b(w^f, r^f)]\tilde{F} \geq p_h\tilde{q}_h + p_f\tilde{q}_f \quad m \geq 0 \qquad (11.12)$

Again, we stress that if $n_i > 0$ then the first expression in (11.11) holds with equality; and if $m > 0$ then the first expression in (11.12) holds with equality.

Using Shephard's lemma, the factor market clearing conditions can be expressed as:

$$L_i = z_i \frac{\partial c(w_i, r_i)}{\partial w_i} + n_i \left[q_{ii} + q_{ij} + F\right]\left[\frac{\partial b(w_i, r_i)}{\partial w_i}\right]$$
$$+ m\left[\tilde{q}_i + \tilde{F}\frac{\partial \Psi(b_h, b_f)}{\partial b_i}\right]\left[\frac{\partial b(w_i, r_i)}{\partial w_i}\right] \qquad (11.13)$$

$$K_i = z_i \frac{\partial c(w_i, r_i)}{\partial r_i} + n_i \left[q_{ii} + q_{ij} + F\right]\left[\frac{\partial b(w_i, r_i)}{\partial r_i}\right]$$
$$+ m\left[\tilde{q}_i + \tilde{F}\frac{\partial \Psi(b_h, b_f)}{\partial b_i}\right]\left[\frac{\partial b(w_i, r_i)}{\partial r_i}\right] \qquad (11.14)$$

The first, second and third terms in (11.13) and (11.14) represent factor demand by the homogeneous sector, and by the national and multinational firms in the differentiated sector.

Conditions (11.5) to (11.14) characterize the equilibrium. They allow us to investigate how the allocation of production between national and multinational firms respond to changes in fixed costs, transportation costs and endowments. However, in this instance, comparative statics techniques are not helpful due to the dimensionality of the model, and to the complications that arise from the fact that some equilibrium conditions are inequalities for certain values of the exogenous variables and equalities for other values. Markusen and Venables (2000) therefore rely on a numerical technique to obtain results.

They find that multinationals are more likely to emerge under the following conditions: 1) countries' incomes and endowments of capital per worker are close to each other; 2) the fixed cost borne by multinationals is not markedly higher than the fixed cost incurred by national firms; 3) transportation costs are high; 4) varieties are close substitutes.

Then they consider how perturbations of exogenous variables affect profits. First they establish baseline equilibria in which active firms are only multinational, or multinationals and national firms coexist. These equilibria are obtained by imposing identical endowments and calibrating the transportation cost and the fixed cost. Then they examine how the equilibrium configuration of firms changes when the endowment point moves inside the world endowment box, or when the size of the world endowment box varies.

They find that an equal increase in the income of both countries ($dE_h = dE_f > 0$) does not affect mark-ups or the quantity that individual firms produce since prices do not change (see appendix of Chapter 8). Instead, the income changes lead to a proportionate increase in the number of national and multinational firms.

Markusen and Venables (2000) then explore the consequences of a change in the cross-country distribution of income that keeps world income fixed ($dE_h = -dE_f > 0$). This corresponds to a move away from the midpoint of the world endowment box along the main diagonal. This change benefits active national firms based in the country whose income rises because it increases the portion of sales on which they bear no transport cost. Active national firms based in the other country are affected adversely. Multinational firms are not affected because they do not incur any transport costs, and because the demand they face is unchanged since world income is also unchanged.[25] The change in the cross-country distribution of income therefore increases the number of national firms in the country whose size increases. If there are no such firms in the country initially, the change brings about the emergence of national firms. The opposite effect takes place in the other country. The change in the number of multinational firms is not as significant. When the income distribution becomes very asymmetric, national firms re-emerge in the smaller country. The reason is that the increase in the number of national firms in the large country and the concurrent decline in the number of multinational firms makes room for national firms based in the smaller country.

Finally, Markusen and Venables (2000) consider the effects of an increase in marginal cost in one country, accompanied by a decrease in marginal cost of equal magnitude in the other country ($db_h = -db_f > 0$). These changes occur as the endowment point moves in the southeast or north-west direction inside the world endowment box. This change clearly benefits national firms based in the country where cost has fallen. It should therefore increase the number of national firms in that country. The impact on multinationals is smaller because these firms operate in both countries and because they can allocate a portion of their fixed costs to the country where cost has decreased. Still, the number of multinational firms falls because their costs increase relative to the costs of national firms based in the country in which marginal cost declines. The latter also explains why multinational production does not take place when the disparity in relative endowments, and hence the disparity in production costs, is substantial.

Vertical fragmentation

We now consider the question of how endowments influence whether firms fragment vertically across borders – that is, whether they undertake different stages of a production process in different countries. We first examine the basic framework developed in Helpman (1984) and Helpman and Krugman (1985). We then address the question of why, in apparent opposition to the predictions of the basic model, the number of labor–intensive affiliates in the least developed countries remains small.

The key difference between the model we will now study and the model studied in section 3 of Chapter 8 is that the manufacture of the differentiated product can be fragmented into stages that use inputs in different proportions. The first stage involves production of head-quarter services by means of capital and labor. The second stage uses capital and labor along with headquarter services to produce a final good.[26] The production of headquarter services is more capital intensive than the production of the final good. Headquarters services serve as inputs in the country where they are produced, or in a different country. These services are tailored to a particular variety of the differentiated good. That is, headquarter services produced by one firm cannot serve as inputs in the production of another firm's final good. The implication is that any international trade in headquarter services must stay within the confines of a single firm.

It is assumed that there is a minimal cost of vertically separating the two stages of produc-tion. This assumption ensures that vertical fragmentation does not take place when it does not reduce the sum of the first and second stage costs.

Trade in headquarter services and factor price equalization

Consider Figure 11.4 in which the area OQO^*Q' is the parallelogram first seen in Figure 8.3. As was indicated for Figure 8.3, the coordinates of Q with O as origin represent factor usage by the differentiated industry in the integrated economy. Units of output are chosen to ensure that the vector $\overline{OQ}$ represents the world output of the differentiated industry. The coor-dinates of H show factor use in the production of headquarter services in the integrated economy. Factor use in manufacturing is obtained by subtracting the coordinates of Q from the coordinates of H. Because the first stage of manufacturing is more capital-intensive, OH is steeper than HQ. Note that Figure 11.4 is drawn under the assumption that the second stage production process is more capital intensive than the production of the homogeneous good.

In Chapter 8 it was shown that free trade will equalize factor rewards when country endowments lie inside the parallelogram OQO^*Q'. Chapter 8 also established that for such an allocation of factors, trade in final products will replicate the equilibrium of the inte-grated economy. In this section we will show that vertical fragmentation combined with trade equalizes factor prices for endowments in the larger area $OHQO^*H'Q'$.

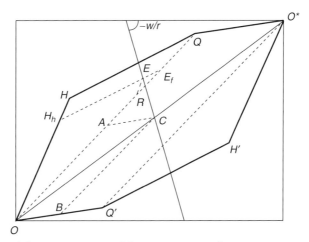

Figure 11.4 Vertical fragmentation and factor price equalization

Consider the endowment point E displayed in Figure 11.4. Home-based firms use local capital and labor to produce $\overline{OH_h}$ units of headquarter services. They use the quantity $\overline{H_h E}$ of home country factors and the quantity $\overline{EE_f}$ of foreign factors in the second stage of production.[27] The foreign factors are used in a foreign affiliate owned by the home-based parent. Finally, let the foreign firms produce a quantity O^*Q of the homogeneous good and a quantity QE_f of the differentiated good.

The outputs of the differentiated and homogeneous goods are $\overline{OQ}$ and $\overline{QO^*}$ respectively. Each good uses factors in the same proportion as in the integrated economy and all prices are those of the integrated economy. Because both countries produce and consume the differentiated good, there is intra-industry trade. Part of this trade is carried out by multinational firms headquartered in the home country.

The home country is a net exporter of differentiated products. This is seen in Figure 11.4 by comparing the home country's production of the differentiated good to its consumption of this good. Production of the differentiated good is given by the vector $\overline{OR}$ where R lies at the intersection of OQ with the line parallel to OH going through E. The consumption point C lies at the intersection of the main diagonal OO^* with the line through E with slope equal to the ratio of factor prices (i.e., $-w/r$). This line can be interpreted as a budget constraint. The coordinates of consumption point C with respect to the origin O represent factor usage in the production of the bundle consumed in the home country; its coordinates with respect to O^* show the same for the foreign country.

To derive the home country's consumption of each good, we first draw a line going through C and parallel to OQ. Point B is the intersection of this line with OQ'. We then draw a second line through C that is parallel to OQ' and denote its intersection with OQ as the point A. The length of the vectors $\overline{OA}$ and $\overline{OB}$ now represent home consumption of the differentiated and of the homogeneous good. Since $\overline{OR} > \overline{OA}$, we conclude that the home country is a net exporter of the differentiated good. Its net exports are given by $\overline{AR}$. Clearly, the home country exports capital services and imports labor services as predicted by the Heckscher-Ohlin theory.

There may also be an equilibrium in which the home country is a net importer of the differentiated *and* the homogeneous good. In this case it pays for these imports by exporting headquarter services. Such an equilibrium arises when the endowment point is slightly below the boundary HQ of the factor price equalization set.

Finally, we note that the existence of the vertical fragmentation equilibrium does not hinge on the existence of transport costs. However, when there are transport costs for components and final assemblies their magnitude determines the range of production cost differences that bring about vertical fragmentation.

Hummels *et al.* (2001) estimate that the trade in inputs used to produce goods that are subsequently exported accounted for 30 percent of world exports in 1995, having grown by 40 percent over the preceding 25 years.[28] They attribute this growth, in particular the expansion of trade which involves the movement of components and subassemblies back and forth across borders, to the fall in transport costs and tariffs over the period.

Multiple production stages

Consider now the possibility of separating production into three or more stages. Assume the production of headquarter services is most capital intensive, followed by the manufacture of components, and then by the assembly of components as the least capital-intensive stage. Using the same analytical tool as above, Helpman and Krugman (1985) determine that trade alone equalizes factor prices when relative endowments are not too far apart. When they are sufficiently close to each other there is no vertical separation of production stages. When the gap in relative endowments crosses a threshold, firms in the capital abundant country transfer the assembly stage to the labor abundant country. As the disparity in endowments grows further, it eventually crosses a second threshold. At that point the home firms transfer all assembly and part of component production to the foreign country. When the gap crosses a third threshold the capital abundant country specializes in headquarter services and exports these to its foreign affiliates in exchange for imports of both final goods.

Convergence and divergence of factor prices

Fragmentation of the production process does not necessarily equalize factor prices, or even bring about a convergence of factor prices. Venables (2004) explains why. He considers a baseline trading equilibrium in which a homogeneous good is produced in the home and in the foreign country. The foreign country is abundant in labor, has a lower wage to rental ratio than the home country, and uses less capital per worker to produce the homogeneous good. Fragmentation is possible for a second good. The home firms that produce the second good transfer the labor-intensive stage of manufacturing to the foreign country.

We consider first the case where the relocated stage of manufacture is more labor-intensive than is production of the homogeneous good in *both* countries. In this case, the relocation of production releases home capital and labor in a proportion that exceeds the home country's labor to capital usage in its homogeneous industry. The home country's homogeneous industry must then become more labor-intensive to absorb the factors of production released by the other industry. This brings about a fall in the home country's wage-rental ratio. The opposite change takes place in the foreign country. Because the relocated second stage of production uses more labor per unit of capital than the homogeneous sector in the foreign country, the other sectors in that country must release more labor per unit of capital than they used before the transfer; that is, these sectors become more capital-intensive. This requires an increase in the foreign wage-rental ratio. We conclude that the vertical fragmentation of production by home firms brings about a convergence of factor prices.

Next we consider the case where the relocated stage is more capital-intensive than the homogeneous sector in the foreign country, but less capital-intensive than the homogeneous sector in the home country. The factors that the relocation of production releases in the home country can only be absorbed by the rest of the home economy if home production becomes more labor-intensive. This requires a decline in the home country's wage-rental ratio. However, the homogeneous sector in the foreign country must also become more labor-intensive since the relocated stage of production uses more capital per worker than the other sectors in the foreign country. These sectors will release the factors of production required by the relocated stage in the right proportion when the foreign local wage-rental ratio falls by a sufficient amount. Since both countries' wage-rental ratios now move in the same direction, the gap between them could widen in response to the relocation of production.

Venables (2004) suggests that the latter may actually have happened when American firms responded to the formation of the North American Free Trade Area by transferring highly unskilled labor-intensive production stages to Mexico. If true, these transfers may have played a part in increasing the gap between skilled and unskilled wages in both countries.

Affiliates in poor small countries

Zhang and Markusen (1999) note that, if firms truly fragment vertically to benefit from cross-country factor price differences, much of the unskilled labor-intensive production should migrate to the countries abundant in unskilled labor. In fact, one observes the opposite. The share of world FDI that flows to the group of least developed countries is smaller than that group's share of world GDP and population. Also, inward per capita FDI flows are significantly lower for the smaller countries in that group. The Helpman and Krugman (1985) model is inconsistent with the first of these facts and it cannot account for the second one.

Zhang and Markusen (1999) solve the puzzle by way of a slight change in the Helpman and Krugman (1985) framework. They consider a production process which involves the manufacture of an intermediate product by skilled workers, followed by assembly that uses unskilled labor. The key difference from Helpman and Krugman (1985) is the assumption that assembly, although unskilled, requires a minimal contribution from skilled workers in the country where assembly takes place.

The latter requirement makes the relationship between the gap in relative endowments and vertical fragmentation non-monotonic. When countries' endowments are similar, the difference in cost is small relative to the cost of shipping components for assembly to the poor country, and the cost of shipping final assemblies to the rich country. Therefore, firms do not fragment vertically. When the disparity in endowments becomes sufficiently large, the country abundant in unskilled labor becomes host to affiliates that specialize in assembly. But when skilled workers in the poorer country become very scarce, local assembly ceases.

Transport costs contribute to the dearth of assembly in small countries. The reason is that firms incur a lower transport cost when they locate in a larger country because this is where they sell most of their final output.

Fragmenting production: the evidence

Brainard (1997) examines the extent to which US firms' fragmentation decisions reflect a trade-off between minimization of the cost of production cost and trade friction.[29] She examines how this trade-off, as well as other factors, affects the decision whether to establish a foreign affiliate, and how it influences the composition of the total sales by US industries in a foreign market into export sales from a US base versus local sales by affiliates of US parents. Her data set consists of US export sales to 27 countries in 63 primary and manufacturing industries, and the sales by majority-owned affiliates of US parents located in these countries.[30]

Brainard's (1997) explanatory variables fall into three categories. The first contains proximity variables that include FREIGHT and the TARIFF. TARIFF is defined as the average tariff of country i levied on goods made by industry j. FREIGHT is calculated as the sum of freight and insurance charges from the US to country i of products made by industry j, divided by their import values. To account for the effect of non-tariff barriers, Brainard's (1997) equation includes the variables TRADE and FDI to capture the recipient countries' openness to imports and FDI.[31]

Two other explanatory variables pick up the influence of scale economies: PSCALE is the number of production workers in the industry's median-sized plant while CSCALE proxies for firm-level scale economies. CSCALE is defined as the number of non-production workers in the average sized US-based firm. Inclusion of the recipient country's GDP among the explanatory variables makes it possible to determine if a country is more likely to host foreign affiliates when it absorbs a large volume of output.

The second category of variables relates explicitly to cross-country cost differences. PWGDP is defined as the difference between GDP per worker in the US and country i and proxies for the gap in relative endowments. Brainard (1997) stresses that exports and affiliate sales of differentiated products should relate negatively to PWGDP if one of the following conditions holds: 1) the differentiated industries are more capital intensive than the other sectors of the economy; 2) the differentiated industries produce goods with higher income elasticity. If affiliate sales concentrate in differentiated industries, it also follows that the share of exports in a country's total purchases from US-owned firms should relate positively to its income differential with the US.

A third and more eclectic category of explanatory variables includes *TAX*, defined as the average corporate tax rate in a potential host country. Exports should be the preferred mode of serving high tax countries as profits earned by local affiliates are taxed more heavily. A shared language with the US may influence the ratio of affiliate sales to total sales if exporting requires less communication than operating a local affiliate. To assess the impact of a shared language Brainard (1997) uses the dummy variable *LANG* which equals 1 for English-speaking trading partners, and is zero for other countries. A second dummy variable, labeled *ADJ*, equals 1 for countries that share a border with the US. The dummy variable *COUP* proxies for political risk and takes the value of 1 for countries that experienced a *coup d'état* in the preceding decade.

Membership in the EC gives a country preferential access to other member states. This contributes to its attractiveness as host of foreign affiliates. Membership is captured by the dummy variable *EC*. The estimating equations also include an R&D intensity variable that links the empirical model to the vast literature that stresses the key role of knowledge-based assets.

Because the dependent variable is censored at 0 and 1, Brainard (1997) uses both OLS and Tobit techniques. Table 11.4 displays the results from Tobit estimation. The dependent

Table 11.4 Presence of affiliates and share of outward affiliate sales[a]

Explanatory variables	Dependent variables	
	$outd_i^j$	$outsh_i^j$
$FREIGHT_i^j$	−0.798***	0.204
$TARIFF_i^j$	0.127**	0.207***
$TRADE_i$	−0.462	−0.940***
FDI_i	−0.294	1.050*
$LANG_i$	0.450***	9.241*
ADJ_i	0.796**	−0.254
$PSCALE^j$	−0.175***	−0.253***
$CSCALE^j$	0.900	0.181***
$PWGDP_i$	−0.395***	−0.351***
TAX_i	−0.4848	0.810*
$COUP_i$	−0.6520*	−1.834***
EC_i	0.893***	0.283
Constant	−0.284	−0.284
GDP	0.319***	
RD	15.104***	

***$p < 0.01$; **$p < 0.05$, *$p < 0.10$.
[a]Number of observations = 1035; positive observations = 760; Log likelihood = −1551.
Source: Brainard (1997).

variable in the first column ($outd_i^j$) is a dummy indicating the presence or absence of US affiliate sales of industry j in country i. The dependent variable in the second column ($outsh_i^j$) is the share of affiliate sales in total sales by industry j in country i.[32]

Estimation results yield a positive sign for the *TARIFF* variable in both columns. This is expected when fragmentation is horizontal. The estimated effect of *FREIGHT* is not as clear-cut. The variable relates positively and significantly to the probability of a country being served by one or more affiliates, but it does not correlate significantly to the share of industry sales originating in affiliates. The coefficients of the *TRADE* and *FDI* variables are not significant, or have signs contrary to predictions.

The estimated coefficients of *PSCALE* and *GDP* are significant in both columns. Their signs accord with theory for the case of horizontal fragmentation. Firm-level scale economies *(CSCALE)*, by contrast, are shown to influence the share of total sales originating in affiliates but not the decision to establish a foreign affiliate. A common language and a shared border *(LANG* and *ADJ)* increase the probability that a US firm will produce in foreign affiliates, but they do not seem to influence significantly the share of total sales originating in the foreign affiliates.

The coefficient of per capita income *(PWGDP)* is negative and significant in both equations. This result lends support to the hypothesis that firms are less inclined to establish affiliates in poorer countries, and have a greater propensity to serve these countries via exports even when they have a local affiliate.

Political stability *(COUP)* relates negatively to the probability that a country will host US affiliates, or will be served primarily by the affiliates it hosts. *EC* membership relates positively to the probability that a country will host US affiliates. The tax rate in the destination country *(TAX)* correlates positively with the extent to which US firms penetrate its markets via affiliate sales. This is unexpected. Brainard (1997) suggests that the positive sign may derive from a positive correlation between *TAX* variable and macroeconomic indicators such as public investment and income.

Overall, the findings reported in Table 11.4 lend some support to the claim that avoiding trade frictions is the prime motivation behind the decision of US firms to undertake production in foreign affiliates.

11.5 The knowledge-capital model

The models examined in section 11.4 allowed a binary fragmentation choice. Firms chose either between strictly national production and horizontal fragmentation or between strictly national production and vertical fragmentation. The knowledge-capital model developed in Markusen *et al.* (1996), Markusen (2002), Markusen and Venables (1998, 2000), and Markusen and Maskus, (2001, 2002) expands the range of fragmentation options. It allows firms to choose between all three fragmentation types. The model also explains under what conditions horizontally fragmented firms, vertically fragmented firms and strictly national firms coexist in equilibrium.

Jointness of inputs and the separability of production stages

The knowledge-capital model builds on three key assumptions: 1) firms can geographically separate manufacturing from the production of knowledge-based inputs used in manufacturing; 2) the production of the knowledge-based inputs is skilled-labor intensive relative to manufacturing; 3) the knowledge-based inputs are at least partially joint – that is, their concurrent use in multiple plants is only slightly more costly than their use in a single plant.[33] Also, the additional cost of setting up an extra plant in another location is small relative to the cost of establishing a wholly new firm in that location.

Assumptions 1 and 2 imply that a disparity in relative endowments motivates the separation of unskilled-labor intensive manufacturing from the production of knowledge-based inputs labeled headquarter services. The jointness of inputs induces horizontal fragmentation in the presence of trade friction.

The home (h) and foreign (f) markets are segmented. Each country may produce two homogeneous goods (X and Y). The representative consumer is the same in both countries and has Cobb-Douglas preferences. Workers are mobile between industries and immobile between countries. Competitive firms use skilled and unskilled workers to produce the good Y which serves as numeraire. They produce this good by means of a constant elasticity of substitution CES technology which is identical across countries. The X industry is composed of Cournot firms which may produce headquarter services in one country and engage in final manufacturing in the other country. Both production stages draw on the local labor pool. Firms in the X industry choose between a strictly national structure and a vertical or horizontal multinational structure. Freedom of entry ensures that in equilibrium profits are zero or negative regardless of the structure chosen.

Six configurations are a priori possible in equilibrium: 1) horizontally fragmented firms producing headquarter services and final output in both countries; the parent may be based in either country; 2) vertically fragmented firms producing headquarter services in one country (h or f), and undertaking final production in the other country (f or h); 3) strictly national firms concentrating all stages of production in country h, or in country f.

Firms in the X industry incur firm-specific as well as plant-specific fixed costs. National firms bear a single firm-specific cost and a single plant-specific cost fixed cost. Vertically fragmented firms incur a firm-specific cost in the country where they produce headquarter services (h or f), and a plant-specific cost in the country that hosts their final production facility (f or h). Horizontally fragmented firms sustain a firm-specific cost and a plant-specific cost in both countries.

The labor that enters the firm-specific fixed cost is skilled, whereas the labor that accounts for the plant-specific fixed cost is unskilled. The joint nature of headquarter services is captured by assuming that the labor requirement that gives rise to the fixed firm-specific cost of a horizontally fragmented firm is less than twice the requirement of two national firms. It is larger though than the firm-specific requirement of a single national firm.

Horizontal fragmentation creates an extra demand for skilled workers that firms must meet partly in the parent country and partly in the host country. Also, the firm-specific fixed labor requirement of a horizontally fragmented firm exceeds the requirement of a vertically fragmented firm. The latter is larger than the requirement of a national firm. Thus, vertical unbundling is not costless.

Headquarter services are more skill-intensive than manufacturing, and manufacturing of the X good is more skill-intensive than the Y good. Horizontally fragmented firms are more skill-intensive than national firms and vertically fragmented firms. This is consistent with the hypothesis that horizontal fragmentation is contingent on the use of some skilled labor in overseas affiliates.

Variable production costs and transport costs in the X industry derive from fixed coefficient technologies. Transportation across borders relies on unskilled workers.

Endowments and firm type

A model that admits such a large number of possible configurations of firms contains a great many equations and inequalities. Since this precludes solving the model analytically, numerical techniques are used instead. The basic process is as follows. First, one calibrates parameter values to ensure that when countries are equally abundant in skilled and unskilled work-ers, the only active firms are horizontally fragmented multinationals. The equilibrium is then perturbed by changing endowments and transportation costs.

Horizontally fragmented firms dominate the X industry when countries are similar in size and in relative endowments, and when transport costs are high. In fact, horizontally frag-mented firms may be the only active producers when endowments are at the center of the box. As one moves away from this center point, horizontally fragmented firms become less domi-nant and may coexist with national firms, with vertically fragmented firms, or with both. The direction of the move in endowments determines whether national or vertically fragmented firms gain at the expense of horizontally fragmented producers.

Moving the endowment point along the main diagonal of the world endowment box leaves relative endowments unchanged, providing no incentive for firms to vertically fragment; national firms therefore become more pervasive as the endowment point moves along the main diagonal in either direction. This arises because, as countries become more unequal in size, the savings in fixed plant costs from not producing final output in the smaller country increases relative to costs of transporting output from the larger country to the smaller coun-try. Consequently, national firms headquartered in the home (foreign) country dominate the industry in the home (foreign) country when either: a) the home (foreign) country is large and skill abundant or b) the two countries are similar in size and relative endowments and transport costs are low.

When the endowment point is positioned some distance from the main diagonal of the world endowment box, and countries are about equally sized, producers have an incen-tive to fragment the stages of production. The cost differential encourages them to locate headquarters in the skill-abundant country and to engage in final production in the other, unskilled-abundant country. Even so, firms refrain from vertical separation of production stages as long as the gap in relative endowments remains small. The reason is that the cost of fragmentation outweighs the savings in production costs achievable from a relocation of a production stage. As long as the gap in relative endowments remains small, the only active firms in equilibrium are horizontal multinationals and strictly national producers based in the skilled-labor abundant country. National firms pay a transport cost that horizontal multinationals do not pay, but they save the fixed plant-specific cost.

When the gap in relative endowments between countries crosses a threshold, vertical firms emerge. They gain in importance as the gap grows. A reversal occurs when skilled labor becomes very scarce in the country that hosts final production. The reversal is due to the increase in the skilled wage attributable to the lack of skilled workers in one coun-try. This increase raises the cost of manufacturing in that country because skilled labor enters fixed plant-specific cost. When the skilled wage increases beyond a second threshold, purely national firms start to gain at the expense of vertically fragmented producers.

As endowments move away from the diagonal in a way that points to an increase in the rela-tive abundance of skilled labor in the large country, the share of national firms in that country increases relative to the other firm types. In contrast, an increase in the relative skill abun-dance of the small country increases the number of vertically fragmented firms headquartered in that country.

Vertically fragmented firms headquartered in the home (foreign) country dominate when the home (foreign) country is small, skill abundant and when the cost of shipping from the host country to the parent country is not too high. Markusen (2002) observes that the latter is consistent with the pervasiveness of multinational firms headquartered in small countries such as Sweden, the Netherlands, and Switzerland that are rich in skilled labor.

The configuration of firm types determines the extent of affiliate production. Affiliate production is highest when one country is small and skill-abundant. The reason is that headquarters cluster in the small country, and final good production is undertaken by affiliates located in the large country. Conversely, affiliate production is smallest when national firms headquartered in the large country dominate.

Trade and investment barriers influence affiliate production in a non-monotonic way. When horizontal fragmentation dominates, a reduction in transport cost reduces affiliate production as national firms grow at the expense of horizontally fragmented multinationals.

Trade and affiliate production are substitutes when endowments give rise to a configuration in which horizontal MNEs and national firms dominate. Lower transport costs increase the presence of vertically fragmented firms headquartered in the smaller country at the expense of horizontally fragmented firms. The reason is that it is now less costly to ship output across borders.[34] Lower transport costs also increase world output by affiliates as the production of headquarter services concentrates in the smaller country, and final production, which is increasingly affiliate production, moves to the large country. Because the direction of change in total trade and in total affiliate production is now the same, trade and affiliate production can be said to be complements.

A surprising finding of the model is that lifting a ban on the establishment of foreign affiliates may reverse the direction of trade. To see why, imagine a baseline equilibrium in which a country abundant in unskilled workers prohibits the establishment of foreign plants on its territory. The other country, which is moderately sized and abundant in skilled labor, is a net exporter of X products. Lifting the ban turns the first country into an attractive host of affiliates who specialize in the unskilled final stage of production. These affiliates export final output to the country relatively abundant in skilled workers. That country then becomes a net importer of X-products.

Estimating the knowledge-capital model

Estimating equations must have quadratic and interactive terms in order to capture the relationships that the model predicts. In this section we contrast the empirical approach pioneered by Carr *et al.* (2001) with the more recent empirical method developed in Braconier *et al.* (2005).

Carr *et al.* (2001) look at the determinants of sales by US-owned affiliates and the sales by US-based affiliates of overseas parents. Braconier *et al.* (2005) focus on outward and inward FDI of the US, Germany and Italy, and on the outward FDI of Sweden and Japan. In both studies the dependent variable is real total sales by majority-owned manufacturing affiliates.[35]

The two studies capture the combined size of the recipient and donor country as a sum of their real gross domestic products *(SUMGDP)*. They differ from each other with regard to the measure of the asymmetry in country sizes. Carr *et al.* (2001) use the squared difference of the *GDPs* of the parent and host country (*GDPDIFFsquare*). Braconier *et al.* (2005) use $SIZE_i \equiv \sqrt{(S_i/(S_i + S_j))^2 + (U_i/(U_i + U_j))^2}$, where $S_i(S_j)$ and $U_i(U_j)$ respectively denote country $i(j)$'s endowments of skilled and unskilled workers.[36] This measure is the normalized Euclidian distance between the endowment point in the world endowments box and the origin. The Braconier *et al.* (2005) equation also includes the square of $SIZE_i$, denoted *SIZEsquare,* among explanatory variables.

Carr *et al.* (2001) proxy skill abundance through $SKILLDIFF_i \equiv (S_i/N_i) - (S_j/N_j)$ where $S_i(S_j)$ is as above and $N_i(N_j)$ denotes the population of country $i(j)$. Braconier *et al.* (2005) measure country i's skill abundance as $SKILL_i \equiv (S_i/(S_i + S_j))/(U_i/(U_i + U_j))$.[37] Since the knowledge-capital model predicts that headquarters locate in the more skill-abundant country, the two measures should correlate positively with affiliate production. Both studies interact their measure of skill abundance with the gap in country sizes (*GDPDIFF* SKILLDIFF* in Carr *et al.* and $SIZE_p$*SKILL$_p$* in Braconier *et al.*).

The variables $INVCOST_h$ and $TRADCOST_h$ account for investment and trade barriers in the host country. One expects a negative coefficient for $INVCOST_h$ while a positive coefficient is expected for $TRADCOST_h$ since trade friction encourages horizontal fragmentation. Inclusion of the interaction terms ($TRADCOST_h^* SKILLDIFFsquare$ in Carr et al. (2001) and $TRADCOST_*SKILLsquare$ in Braconier et al. (2005)) makes it possible to assess whether horizontal fragmentation is more responsive to trade friction when relative endowments are similar. Because trade barriers in the parent country $(TRADCOST_p)$ increase the parent's cost of importing from the foreign affiliate they lessen incentives to fragment vertically. One therefore expects a negative coefficient on this variable.

The two studies also consider the effect of geographic distance *(DISTANCE)* between the parent and host country. The effect is *a priori* ambiguous because distance may similarly affect the cost of exporting and the cost of monitoring overseas production. Equally ambiguous is the expected sign of the coefficient of a dummy variable labeled *ADJACENT* which indicates whether the parent and host country share a border.

Table 11.5 presents the results of weighted least squares estimations with country fixed effects.[38] The coefficients of variables that capture size and skill have the expected signs and are significant in both regressions. However, the data do not show much evidence in support of an impact for trade and investment barriers.

Table 11.5 Estimating the knowledge-capital model[a]

	Carr, Markusen and Maskus (2001)	Braconier, Norbäck and Urban (2005)
SUMGDP	13.72***	100.00**
GDPDIFFsquare	−0.001***	
$SIZE_p$		454.91***
$SIZEsquare_p$		−390.71***
$SKILL_p$		81.74***
SKILLDIFF	15.04*	
$GDPDIFF \times SKILLDIFF$	−4.44**	
$SIZE_p \times SKILL_p$		−110.24***
$INVCOST_h$	−173.2*	0.22
$TRADCOST_h$	69.4	0.26
$TRADCOST_h \times SKILLDIFFsquare$	−811.6	
$TRADCOST_h \times SKILLsquare$		−0.04
$TRADCOST_p$	−75.5*	0.31
DISTANCE	−0.87	−0.0002***
ADJACENT		28.74***
INTERCEPT	−24.55	95.05
Adj. R^2	0.87	0.79
Number of observations	509	1122

***$p < 0.01$; **$p < 0.05$, *$p < 0.10$.
[a] The subscript p indicates that the variable pertains to the country of the parent; the subscript h indicates that it pertains to the country that hosts the affiliate.
Source: Braconier et al. (2005) and Carr et al. (2001).

To examine the nature of non-linear influences one differentiates the estimated equation. For example, one can use the Carr *et al.* (2001) results to calculate the following effect of a change in relative skilled-labor abundance in the parent country:

$$\partial sales / \partial SKILLDIFF = 15.04 - 4.4 \times (GDPDIFF)$$

$$- 2 \times 811.6 \times (TRADECOST_h \times SKILLDIFF)$$

This derivative is generally positive for similar countries, but its magnitude is reduced by an increase in the gap in *GDPs*. The reason is that greater asymmetry in country sizes leads to the replacement of vertically fragmented firms by national firms headquartered in the larger country. The effect of a gap in skill difference is also weaker when the host country's trade cost is larger, but the estimate of that effect is not significant.

The estimation results imply that an increase in *host-country* skill-abundance increases inward investment if the host country is sufficiently small relative to the parent country. The results are also consistent with the aforementioned finding that the poorest countries receive a much smaller share of world investment than their share of world income.

11.6   Heterogeneous firms: exporting versus FDI

In Chapter 9 we pointed to productivity differences between firms within industries as the source of differences in firms' propensity to export. In this section we explore how productivity differences can account for the decomposition of industries between national and multinational firms. We do so in a two-country framework that is a simplified version of the more general model found in Helpman *et al.* (2004).

Each country produces a homogeneous good and a differentiated good using labor as the only input. The homogeneous industry is perfectly competitive, and it produces one unit of output using one unit of labor. Firms in the differentiated goods industry engage in monopolistic competition. Entry in the differentiated goods industry is contingent on the payment of an entry fee F_E which entitles the potential entrant to a draw a labor per unit of output coefficient c from a distribution $G(c)$. Firms that draw a productivity value $1/c$ which allows them to earn a variable profit at least as large as their fixed production cost F_D become active. When the wage in country $i(i=h,f)$ is w^i the firm that draws c incurs a marginal cost cw^i when it produces in country i. To export requires an additional fixed cost F_X, while serving the foreign country's consumers through a local affiliate requires an extra fixed cost F_I.[39] Exporting the differentiated good also entails an iceberg transport cost $\tau > 1$.

The representative consumer's preference for varieties is the standard CES form, and the upper tier utility is the same Cobb-Douglas function that we examined in the appendix of Chapter 8. Consumers in country i spend a portion α of the country's income E_i on the differentiated good. The variable profit from local sales by the firm which bears the marginal cost cw^i is then $\alpha E^i \left[\dfrac{cw^i(\sigma/1-\sigma)}{P^i} \right]^{1-\sigma}$ where σ is the elasticity of substitution between varieties and P^i denotes the price index of the differentiated good in country i.

Since the homogeneous good can be transported at zero cost we have $w^h = w^f$ if both countries produce the homogeneous good. Given this, we can normalize both wages to 1. Defining $B^i \equiv \left[\dfrac{\sigma}{1-\sigma} \dfrac{1}{P^i} \right]^{1-\sigma} \alpha E^i$, we can then express the firm's operating profit from domestic sales as $\pi^i(c) = c^{1-\sigma} B^i - F_D$ where $i=h,f$. Since the marginal *delivered* cost of export sales is $c\tau$, the *additional* operating profit from exports is $\pi_X^i(c) = (\tau c)^{1-\sigma} B^j - F_X$, where $i,j=h,f$ and

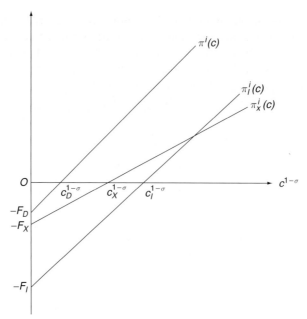

Figure 11.5 Firm heterogeneity, exports and affiliate production

$i \neq j$. Similarly, the firm's *additional* operating profit from affiliate production in the foreign country is $\pi_I^i(c) = c^{1-\sigma} B^j - F_I$ where $i, j = h, f$ and $i \neq j$.

Figure 11.5 displays the profits $\pi^i(c)$, $\pi_X^i(c)$, and $\pi_I^i(c)$ as linear functions of $c^{1-\sigma}$ for the particular case where $B^h = B^f$. The term $c^{1-\sigma}$ decreases in c since $1 - \sigma < 0$. Thus, each of the three profit functions is decreasing in c. The lines $\pi^i(c)$ and $\pi_I^i(c)$ have the same slope when $B^h = B^f$. Finally, because $\tau > 1$ and $\sigma > 1$, the line $\pi_X^i(c)$ is not as steep.

It is clear from Figure 11.5 that only firms whose technology draw puts them to the right of $c_D^{1-\sigma}$ will be active. Firms with $c^{1-\sigma} \in [c_D^{1-\sigma}, c_X^{1-\sigma}]$ will be active only in their local market. Firms for which $c^{1-\sigma} > c_X^{1-\sigma}$ also serve the foreign country and, among these firms, the subset that has $c^{1-\sigma} \in (c_X^{1-\sigma}, c_I^{1-\sigma})$ export. The most productive firms with $c^{1-\sigma} > c_I^{1-\sigma}$ could also earn positive profits from exporting but they are better off by serving the foreign country through a local affiliate.[40]

When $B^h = B^f = B$ the cut-offs are the same in both countries and satisfy the following conditions:

$$c_D^{1-\sigma} B - F_D = 0 \tag{11.15}$$

$$(\tau c_X)^{1-\sigma} B - F_X = 0 \tag{11.16}$$

$$(\tau c_I)^{1-\sigma} B - F_X = c_I^{1-\sigma} B - F_I \tag{11.17}$$

Freedom of entry ensures equality between the expected operating profit and the cost of entry:

$$\int_0^{c_D} \left[c^{1-\sigma} B - F_D \right] dG(c) + \int_{c_I}^{c_X} \left[(\tau c)^{1-\sigma} B - F_X \right] dG(c)$$

$$+ \int_0^{c_I} \left[c^{1-\sigma} B - F_I \right] dG(c) - F_E = 0 \tag{11.18}$$

Conditions (11.15) to (11.18) determine c_D, c_X and c_I and B. Neither the cut-off marginal costs nor B depend on country size. The first term in (11.18) is the expected operating profit from being an active firm which is conditional on a draw of $c < c_D$. The second term in (11.18) is the expected operating profit from exporting, an activity only undertaken by firms that draw a marginal cost between c_I and c_X ($c_I < c_D$). The third term in (11.18) represents the expected operating profit from affiliate production which is only carried out by firms with $c < c_I$.

Because profits are zero we can write $E^i = w^i L^i$ and, since $w^i = 1$ for $i = h, f$ this zero profit condition reduces to $E^i = L^i$. Given this, the price index is implicitly determined by

$$B = \left[\frac{\sigma}{1-\sigma} \frac{1}{P^i} \right]^{1-\sigma} \alpha L^i \text{ for } i = h, f.$$ Since firms with labor coefficient c sell at the price $c\sigma / (1 - \sigma)$

in the market where they produce, and sell at the price $\tau \, c\sigma / (1 - \sigma)$ in their export market, the number of active firms in country i (denoted as n^i $(i = h, f)$), follows from:

$$P^i = \left[n_E^i \int_0^{c_D} \left[c\sigma / (1 - \sigma) \right]^{1-\sigma} dG(c) + n_E^j \left\{ \int_{c_I}^{c_X} \left[\tau \, c\sigma / (1 - \sigma) \right]^{1-\sigma} dG(c) \right. \right.$$
$$\left. \left. + \int_0^{c_I} \left[c\sigma / (1 - \sigma) \right]^{1-\sigma} dG(c) \right\} \right]^{1/1-\sigma} \quad i, j = h, f \text{ and } i \neq j. \qquad (11.19)$$

Helpman *et al.* (2004) show that the two countries will have the same wage, the same cut-offs, and the same *B*'s provided they do not differ too much in size and they draw their technology from the same distribution. Moreover, the larger country will have a larger number of entrants per capita, and its consumers will enjoy greater product variety. Also, the larger country will be served disproportionately by locally based firms. When $G(c)$ is a Pareto distribution, a larger dispersion of productivity will lower export sales relative to affiliate sales; Helpman *et al.* (2004) provide empirical support for this prediction of their model.

11.7 A multi-country setting

In a setting that has three or more countries the key questions become: 1) In which country or countries, if any, will a parent firm establish affiliates? 2) Which affiliates will produce final output, and which will produce inputs? 3) Which country, or countries, will each affiliate serve?

The number of possible fragmentation regimes grows rather dramatically when the number of potential host countries increase. To see why, consider a framework in which a firm headquartered in country p has the option of setting up affiliates in countries i and j. Possible strategies include, but are not limited to, the following: 1) undertaking identical production types in countries p and i (or j), and serving country j (or i) from country p; 2) setting up plants in countries p, i and j and have each serve its local market; 3) setting up plants that assemble components in country i or/and j and export the assembled product to country p and/or country j and i; 4) establishing plants that produce components in country i for assembly in country j and shipment of final output from country j to country p; 5) producing components in country i, shipping them for final assembly to countries p and j, and exporting a portion of final assemblies to country i.

When selecting a regime the firm must consider the attractiveness of a potential host country relative to the country of the parent, and relative to third countries. This section starts by showing how the establishment of a foreign affiliate in one country encourages multinational activity in another country. It then reports econometric results on the determinants of the composition of affiliates' sales between sales to the host country and export sales. The section concludes with a short description of a method that may serve to show whether the attractiveness of a country as a host of foreign affiliates is influenced by characteristics of neighboring countries and by the multinational activity in these countries.

Cross-country interdependence and complex fragmentation

Yeaple (2003) considers a three-country framework, in which firms headquartered in a northern country called West (W) may establish production facilities in a second northern country called East (E), or in a country called South (S), or in countries East and South. Firms choose between four production regimes: 1) remaining national and producing only in West; 2) fragmenting horizontally and producing in West and in East; 3) fragmenting vertically and producing in West and in South; 4) undertaking complex fragmentation by producing in West, East and South.

All firms produce a single variety of a differentiated good by costless assembly of two components. The first component is manufactured by skilled labor only, the second by unskilled labor only. Skilled workers reside only in the North. They earn a wage r_N. The unskilled wage is w_N in the North and $w_s = 1$ in the South. Units of output are defined to ensure that the marginal production cost of the component produced by skilled workers – called the first component – is r_N. The cost of the second component, produced by unskilled labor, is either w_N or 1, depending on the location of its production. The marginal production cost of an assembled product is therefore $z^\lambda r_N^{1-\lambda}$ where $z = w_N$ or $z = 1$, depending on whether workers in the North or the South produce the unskilled component. The parameter λ captures the cost share of the unskilled component.

All firms employ a fixed number G of skilled workers. There is also a fixed skilled labor requirement per affiliate which is f_N in the North and f_s in the South. Furthermore, $G > \max[f_N, f_s]$.

Firms that ship output between countries bear an iceberg-type transportation cost $\tau > 1$ which is the same for components as for final assemblies. Thus, the *delivered* marginal cost of an unskilled component sent for final assembly to a northern country is $\tau^\lambda r_N^{1-\lambda}$.

Transportation cost creates a motive for horizontal fragmentation, but blunts incentives for vertical fragmentation. Yeaple (2003) assumes $\tau < w_N$. This ensures that the delivered cost in the North of an unskilled component produced in the South is lower than the production cost of that component in the North.

Only the two northern countries (assumed to be identical) consume the differentiated product. This assumption limits the number of fragmentation regimes one must examine. The assumption that northern countries are identical ensures that fragmentation across northern countries, if it takes place, is horizontal. By assuming that the South does not consume the differentiated good, one rules out horizontal fragmentation to serve the South from a local affiliate.

Consumer preferences for the differentiated product derive from a CES utility. Freedom of entry ensures the absence of positive profits under any fragmentation regime. Typically, profits are zero under one regime and negative under the other regimes.

Upon defining $A \equiv (\alpha E / \sigma) [(\sigma - 1)/\sigma P]^{1-\sigma}$ where αE is the income spent on the differentiated good, σ is the elasticity of substitution among varieties, and P is the price index of the differentiated industry, Yeaple (2003) expresses the profits associated with each of the aforementioned fragmentation regimes as (11.20)–(11.23) below:[41]

$$\text{Strictly national production: } \pi_n = A\left[(w_N^\lambda r_N^{1-\lambda})^{1-\sigma} + (\tau w_N^\lambda r_N^{1-\lambda})^{1-\sigma}\right]$$
$$- r_N F \leq 0 \qquad\qquad (11.20)$$

$$\text{Horizontal fragmentation: } \pi_{hf} = A\left[(w_N^\lambda r_N^{1-\lambda})^{1-\sigma} + (w_N^\lambda r_N^{1-\lambda})^{1-\sigma}\right]$$
$$- r_N(F + f_N) \leq 0 \qquad\qquad (11.21)$$

$$\text{Vertical fragmentation: } \pi_{vf} = A\left[(\tau^\lambda r_N^{1-\lambda})^{1-\sigma} + (\tau\,\tau^\lambda r_N^{1-\lambda})^{1-\sigma}\right]$$
$$- r_N(F+f_s) \leq 0 \tag{11.22}$$

$$\text{Complex fragmentation: } \pi_{cf} = A\left[(\tau^\lambda r_N^{1-\lambda})^{1-\sigma} + (\tau^\lambda r_N^{1-\lambda})^{1-\sigma}\right]$$
$$- r_N(F+f_N+f_s) \leq 0 \tag{11.23}$$

In the above expressions, the first term appearing in the square brackets stands for the delivered marginal cost of a final assembly to the parent country West. The second term is the delivered marginal cost to country East.[42] Conditions (11.20) and (11.21) imply that the gain from horizontal fragmentation, starting from a position of no fragmentation, is $B_{NH} \equiv \pi_{hf} - \pi_n = A(w_N^\lambda s_N^{1-\lambda})^{1-\sigma}(1-\tau^{1-\sigma}) - r_N f_N$. Likewise, (11.22) and (11.23) show that the gain from a move from vertical fragmentation to complex fragmentation is $B_{VC} \equiv \pi_{cf} - \pi_{vf} A(w_N^\lambda s_N^{1-\lambda})^{1-\sigma}$ $(1-\tau^{1-\sigma}) - r_N f_N$. Clearly, $B_{VC} > B_{NH}$ since $\tau < w_N$ and $\sigma > 1$. The implication is that horizontal fragmentation of an already fragmented vertically fragmented firm produces a larger gain than the horizontal fragmentation of a strictly national firm. The intuition behind this complementarity is a simple one. By fragmenting horizontally a firm trades off the fixed cost of an extra plant against the benefit of a lower delivered variable cost to country East. Production of the unskilled component in the South ensures that the delivered marginal cost to the North is lower than the cost of producing the unskilled component in the North. Therefore, local sales in the North are larger. This makes horizontal fragmentation more profitable as the fixed cost of the affiliate in East can be spread of a larger volume of sales.

Likewise, a move from horizontal to complex fragmentation makes a greater contribution to profits than a move from strictly national production to vertical fragmentation. The reason is that the increase in sales of the final good in the northern country hosting the affiliate increases the demand for the component produced by unskilled labor. As a result, the fixed cost of the southern subsidiary can be spread over a larger number of units than would be the case if the firm was strictly national.

The fragmentation regime that emerges in equilibrium depends on the wage gap between the North and the South, and on the industry characteristics $(\tau, \sigma, \lambda, f_N, f_s, F)$. Figure 11.6 displays the impact of transportation cost τ and the northern wage regime, on the fragmentation regime for the particular case where λ is sufficiently high.

When the northern wage is only moderately larger than the southern wage, firms are either strictly national or vertically fragmented, provided that the transportation cost is lower than

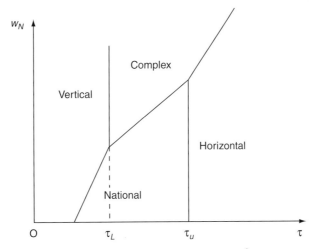

Figure 11.6 Fragmentation regimes, transportation costs, and wages

a threshold value $\tau_U = \left[\left(1 + f_N/F \right) / \left(1 - f_N/F \right) \right]^{1/\sigma - 1}$. This is the transportation threshold cost for which the profits from horizontal fragmentation equal the profits from strictly national production. For a higher transportation cost, firms are fragmented horizontally. A larger wage gap gives rise to vertical fragmentation if transportation cost is smaller than a second threshold value $\tau_L = \left[1 + \dfrac{2f_N/F}{1 + f_S/F - f_N/F} \right]$ which equalizes the profits from vertical and complex fragmentation. The inequality $\tau_L < \tau_U$ follows from $G > \max \left[f_N, f_S \right]$.

When transportation cost exceeds τ_L and the northern wage is high relative to the southern wage fragmentation is either complex or horizontal. The latter type of fragmentation becomes more likely when transport cost increases sufficiently relative to the northern wage. When $\tau \in (\tau_L, \tau_U)$, and the northern wage is sufficiently high compared with the southern wage, complex fragmentation is the only regime that survives in equilibrium.

To determine how multinational activity depends on factor endowments, Yeaple (2006) embeds the differentiated sector in a two-sector economy. He finds that employment in the South falls when endowments in the North and the South become more similar. In the North, employment of skilled and unskilled workers falls when $\tau \in (\tau_L, \tau_U)$, and rises when $\tau > \tau_U$.

In subsequent work, Grossman et al. (2006) explore complex fragmentation when firms are not equally productive.[43] They find that more productive firms have a higher propensity to fragment. Specifically, they determine that the least productive firms concentrate all production in their home country. This is because they do not sell a sufficient volume to cover the fixed cost of affiliate production. Highly productive firms, by contrast, carry out all production stages in the South. Since their variable cost is low, their output is sufficiently large to cover the fixed cost of overseas production. Firms with intermediate productivity export final assemblies from their northern home base or from their southern affiliate to the other northern country. These are the firms that engage in intra-firm trade.

Affiliates and their destination markets

Hanson et al. (2001) agree with Brainard (1997) that cheaper access to local consumers may have been the predominant motive behind US multinational activity in the 1980s. They also hold the view that other motives gained prominence in the 1990s. Hanson et al. focus on the role of affiliates as export platforms to the parent country and to third countries. Their study is based on a sample of US affiliate activities in 58 host countries in the years 1982, 1989 and 1994. The affiliates belong to 12 two-digit industries, including seven industries in manufacturing.

Table 11.6 reports the coefficients from OLS estimations for the subsample of manufacturing industries. The explanatory variables that appear in column (1) have as many as three subscripts. The subscript i denotes the industry, subscript j indexes the host country, and subscript t indexes the year. For example, $TRANSPORT\ COST_{ijt}$ is the cost of transporting goods made by industry i from the US to country j in year t. It is calculated as the gap between cost insurance freight (cif) and free on board (fob) values of US imports divided by the customs value of the imports. Skill intensity is proxied by the ratio of college-educated workers to high-school educated workers in the US industry. Scale economies are captured by the average affiliate employment in the US industry. Host country j's effective corporate income-tax rate in year t is denoted TAX_{jt}. That variable enters the estimating equations as $(1 - TAX_{jt})$. English and non-tariff barrier (NTB) dummies indicate whether the host country is English-speaking, and whether it restrains imports by a set of non-tariff barriers. All non-categorical variables are expressed in logs.

Table 11.6 Affiliates' exports, local sales and total sales

(1)	(2)	(3)	(4)	(5)
Variables	Affiliates' exports	Affiliates' exports/Affiliates' local sales	Affiliates' imports for processing	Affiliates' imports for processing/ affiliate total sales
GDP_{jt}	0.887***	−0.112	0.711***	−0.127**
$GDP_{jt}/POPULATION_{jt}$	1.078***	0.341**	0.433***	−0.539***
$1 - TAX_{jt}$	3.819***	2.736***	1.299***	−0.299
$DISTANCE\ US_j$	−0.329**	0.240*	−0.717***	−0.273***
$ENGLISH\ DUMMY_j$	0.812***	0.243	1.115***	0.287
$SKILL\ INTENSITY_{it}$	0.764***	−0.311	1.121***	0.104
$SCALE_{it}$	−0.346	0.458*	0.159	0.812***
$TRANSPORT\ COST_{ijt}$	−4.744**	−6.396***	−3.626*	2.454
$TARIFF_{ijt}$	−4.171**	−1.150	−2.883*	−1.359
$NTB\ DUMMY_{ijt}$	−0.802***	−0.493**	−0.367*	0.102
$\bar{R}^2$	0.42	0.50	0.47	0.44
# observations	455	455	436	436

*$p < 0.10$; **$p < 0.05$; ***$p < 0.01$.
Source: Hanson *et al.* (2001).

Columns (2) and (3) show how the aforementioned variables relate to the dollar value of affiliates' exports and to exports as a share of affiliates' total sales. Columns (4) and (5) show how they relate to the dollar value of affiliates' imports for further processing, and to the share of these imports in total affiliate sales.

The positive sign of the *GDP* coefficient in columns (2) and (4) reflects the fact that larger countries host a greater number of affiliates, and that their affiliates are larger in size. Interestingly, country size does not appear to influence the composition of affiliate sales as between exports and local sales.[44] The negative coefficient of *GDP* in column (5) is consistent with the idea that smaller destination markets make outsourcing more attractive relative to production for the local consumption. Column (3) indicates that affiliates located in countries that enjoy a higher per capita GDP are more export oriented.

Taxes correlate negatively with the value of affiliates' exports, with the value of affiliates' imports for further processing and with affiliates' exports as a share of their total sales.[45] This is consistent with the hypothesis that a low tax country is more attractive as an export platform and more appealing as a host of plants that process inputs imported from the parent firm. It does not appear, however, that importing for further processing is more responsive to taxation than other forms of affiliate activity.

Affiliates in English-speaking countries, and in countries geographically close to the US, appear more export-oriented than affiliates located in more distant countries. They also import more goods for further processing. There is no strong evidence that being English-speaking and more distant from the US are conducive to a greater export orientation.

Even so, column (5) indicates that importing for further processing plays a greater role relative to affiliates' other activities in countries geographically close to the US.

The estimated coefficients also reveal that affiliates belonging to skill-intensive industries are more engaged in exports and have a greater propensity to import goods for further processing. This is expected if skill intensity correlates positively with multinational activity. Still, the coefficients in columns (3) and (5) show that, in manufacturing industries, skill intensity does not influence the share of affiliates' activities devoted to exporting, or to processing imported inputs.[46] The weakly significant effect of scale on export orientation may reflect the incentive to concentrate production activities characterized by scale economies, in fewer locations.

The trade cost variables relate negatively to the value of affiliates' exports and to exports as a share of their total sales. Hanson *et al.* (2001) conjecture that this reflects the greater profitability of selling in a host country protected by import barriers. Alternatively, the negative sign may capture the increased cost of importing inputs which reduces the competitiveness in world markets of the goods produced by the local affiliates.

Host countries and their surrounding markets

Blonigen *et al.* (2007) address the question of how the attractiveness of a country as a potential host of affiliates is affected by the size of surrounding countries and by the multinational activity taking place in these countries. They examine the third country effect on the FDI of US firms in 35 host countries during the period 1983–98. The approach rests on a comparison of the coefficients and explanatory power of a baseline estimating equation and an expanded equation that includes variables that capture third country effects.

The explanatory variables in the baseline equations are host country GDP, population, trade and investment barriers, and distance to the US. Additional explanatory variables are proxies for political and financial risk. The expanded equation includes two additional regressors. The first is a measure of surrounding market potential. It is defined as the sum of inverse-distance-weighted GDPs of the other countries in the sample.[47] The second additional regressor is a spatial autoregressive term defined as the weighted sum of FDI in other host countries over a number of years. The weights are proportional to the inverse of the distance to the host country under observation. The autoregressive term is designed to capture the interdependence of FDI flowing to different countries.

A comparison of estimated coefficients from the baseline and expanded estimation equation reveals the following: 1) the hypothesis that the host country GDP and surrounding market potential exert an equal pull on FDI is rejected; 2) the spatial lag variable is positive and significant at the 1 percent level. It reveals that multinational activity in a country increases by approximately 5 percent when the distance-weighted activity in the surrounding countries increases by 10 percent; 3) when the expanded equation is re-estimated with country-level dummies included, the coefficient that captures the surrounding market potential is no longer significantly different from zero. The coefficient of the spatial lag variable falls by a factor of 3 but remains statistically significant at the 10 percent level.

Estimation results also reveal that the coefficients of the traditional control variables change much more when country dummies are included than when the surrounding market potential variable and FDI activity in other markets are included. The implication is that the bias from omitting the aforementioned third-country variables from the estimating equation is quite small.

11.8 Endowments and intra-firm trade

Until now we have dealt primarily with the question of whether firms undertake production in the home country or in a foreign country. We now explore how industry and country characteristics interact to determine whether the production undertaken in a foreign country is carried out in affiliated establishments or contracted out to independent foreign firms.

First though, we will clarify some terms that we use throughout this section. We say that a firm *outsources* when it procures an input from an independent supplier. We say that it *offshores* when it procures the input from a foreign country; a firm that offshores may obtain the input from an independent foreign supplier or from a foreign affiliate. When it does the latter it is a *vertically fragmented multinational*. When it contracts with an independent foreign supplier it engages in *foreign outsourcing*. Similarly, a strictly national firm may produce an intermediate product in-house, or acquire it from an independent supplier located in the same jurisdiction. The firm engages in *domestic outsourcing* when it does the latter.

Capital-intensity and the allocation of residual rights

Antràs (2003) observes that intra-firm imports as a share of total US imports are larger when the exporting industries are more capital intensive. He also notes that the share of intra-firm imports is larger when the exporting country is capital abundant. To explain these relationships he combines the Krugman-Helpman apparatus of international trade with the aforementioned Grossman and Hart (1986) model.

The model assumes a world inhabited by identical consumers who spend their income on a continuum of differentiated varieties of two final goods, labeled Y and Z. Their preferences can be represented by the function $U = \left[\int_0^{n_Y} y(i)^\rho di \right]^{\alpha/\rho} \left[\int_0^{n_Z} z(i)^\rho di \right]^{(1-\alpha)/\rho}$ where $y(i)$ and $z(i)$ denote the consumption of variety i of the good Y and Z respectively, and $1/(1-\rho) \equiv \sigma > 1$ is the elasticity of substitution between any two varieties.

The endogenously determined measures of variety of goods Y and Z are n_Y and n_Z. Each firm produces a single variety using tailor-made intermediate goods, which is denoted $x_Y(i)$ for variety i of the Y good, and $x_Z(i)$ for variety i of the Z good. The intermediate goods must be of high quality to serve as inputs. When they are not, the output of the final good is zero. Production of the final good entails no cost besides that of the intermediates. Quantities are measured in a way that ensures $y(i) = x_Y(i)$ and $z(i) = x_Z(i)$.

There are potentially two types of firms: Final good producers, and producers of the intermediate inputs. Before any investment is made, final good producers determine whether they obtain the intermediate input from an independent supplier, or produce it in-house. A firm that chooses the latter route can fire the manager of the division that produces the input at any time. It can also seize the physical assets, including the inventory of the intermediate input. The final good firm cannot do the same when it purchases the input from an independent supplier.

There is free entry into each sector. This ensures zero expected profits, whether or not firms integrate vertically. Production of a high-quality intermediate input uses capital and labor. The variable cost of a high-quality input originates from a production function $x_k(i) = \left[K_k(i)/\beta_k \right]^{\beta_k} \left[L_k(i)/1-\beta_k \right]^{1-\beta_k}$ where $K_k(i)$ and $L_k(i)$ respectively denote capital and labor utilization in the production of variety i of good $k \in \{Y, Z\}$. Production also requires firms to bear a fixed cost $Fr^{\beta_k} w^{1-\beta_k}$ $[k \in \{Y, Z\}]$ where r and w respectively denote the rent and the wage.[48] A fixed cost is incurred in final good production and in input production. That cost is the same whether the input is produced in an integrated firm, or by an independent supplier. Production of good Y is more capital intensive than production of good Z, that is, $1 \geq \beta_Y \geq \beta_Z \geq 0$. The cost of a low-quality intermediate input is negligible.

The production of the inputs calls for non-contractible *ex ante* investments in capital and labor. That is to say, no outside party can discern the quality of the intermediate input, or verify capital and labor utilization. No enforceable contract contingent on revenue from the sale of final product can be drafted.

As indicated in section 11.2, efficiency requires that residual rights be held by the party that makes the *ex ante* investment. A problem arises, however, when that party has low bargaining power. In that instance, the ownership of residual rights may not suffice to bring forth the adequate level of investment. To mitigate the adverse effects on incentives resulting from the hold-up problem, the other party may share in the investment. Antràs (2003) sees evidence of such sharing in the occasional provision by buyers of used machinery and specialized tools to independent suppliers.[49]

The problem is that such sharing exposes input buyers to risk. The vulnerability to opportunistic behavior becomes two-sided. Moreover, if the required sharing is substantial, *ex ante* efficiency may dictate that residual rights be held by the input user. This circumstance is likelier when the production of the input is more capital-intensive.

In such an environment the organizational form of production emerges as equilibrium of the following game: at time t_0 a final good firm determines whether or not to enter the market, and whether to produce the input in-house or purchase it from an independent supplier. The extent of cost-sharing is also decided at $t = t_0$. At time t_1 producers make the required investments in capital and labor. At t_2 the final output producer hands the specifications of the input (and possibly the capital stock) to the party producing the input. That party is either a division of the firm, or an outside supplier. Inputs are produced. At time t_3 the quality of the input becomes observable, and the two parties engage in generalized Nash bargaining which leaves the final good producer with a fraction $1 > \phi > 1/2$ of the *ex post* gain from trade. Finally, at $t = t_4$ the final good is produced and sold if the quality of the input is adequate.

The closed economy

Consider industry Y which claims a share α of consumers' revenue. The demand for variety i produced by that industry is:

$$y^S(i) = A_Y p_Y^s(i)^{-\sigma} \text{ where } A_Y = \alpha E \Big/ \left[\int_0^{n_Y^V} p_Y^V(j)^{1-\sigma} dj + \int_0^{n_Y^O} p_Y^O(j)^{1-\sigma} dj \right] \quad (11.24)$$

where E denotes consumers' revenue and $p_Y^S(i)$ is the price of variety i when the producer opts for the organizational form $S = \{V, O\}$ where $V =$ vertical integration and $O =$ outsourcing.

The vertically integrated firm

When the intermediate input is of high quality, revenue from the sale of final output is $R_Y(i) = p_Y^V(i) y^V(i)$ provided the parties come to an agreement in *ex post* bargaining. When they do not reach a settlement, the final-good producer seizes a fraction $\delta \in (0,1)$ of the input, sells a quantity $\delta y(i)$ of output, and earns the revenue $\delta^\rho R_Y(i)$. The *ex post* gains from trade are therefore $[1 - \delta^\rho] R_Y(i)$.

Under generalized Nash bargaining the owners of the integrated firm get $\delta^\rho R_Y(i) + \phi \left[(1 - \delta^\rho) R_Y(i) \right]$ which is the sum of their default option, and of a fraction ϕ of the quasi rent. The division that has already produced the input gets $0 + (1-\phi)\left[(1 - \delta^\rho) R_Y(i) \right]$ because its default value is zero. The condition $(1 - \phi)(1 - \delta) > 0$, entails that the input division never produces low quality in equilibrium.

Final good producers choose the quantity of capital to maximize $\overline{\phi}R_Y(i) - rK_Y(i)$ where $\overline{\phi} = \delta^\rho + \phi(1-\delta^\rho) > \phi$. The managers of the input division choose the quantity of labor to maximize $(1-\overline{\phi})R_Y^V(i) - wL_Y^V(i)$. This yields an equilibrium in which the quantities of capital and labor that enter variable cost are given by (11.25) below:

$$K_Y^V(i) = \frac{\alpha}{r}\beta_Y\overline{\phi}p_Y^V(i)y^V(i) \text{ and } L_Y^V(i) = \frac{\alpha}{w}(1-\beta_Y)(1-\overline{\phi})p_Y^V(i)y^V(i) \qquad (11.25)$$

where $p_Y^V(i) = \left[\dfrac{r^{\beta_Y}w^{1-\beta_Y}}{\rho\overline{\phi}^{\beta_Y} + (1-\overline{\phi})^{\beta_Y}}\right]$ and $y^V(i)$ is given by (11.24).

The final good producer (FG) and the input division (S) also choose the quantities of capital and labor that enter fixed cost. They are respectively given by:

$$\tilde{K}_{Y,H}^V(i) = \beta_Y F_H [w/r]^{1-\beta_Y} \text{ and}$$
$$\tilde{L}_{Y,H}^V(i) = (1-\beta_Y)F_H [w/r]^{-\beta_Y} \text{ where } H = \{FG, S\} \qquad (11.26)$$

These conditions yield the following expression for the profits earned by integrated final good producers:[50]

$$\pi_Y^V(i) = \left[1 - \rho(1-\beta_Y) + \rho\overline{\phi}(1-2\beta_Y)\right]A_Y(p_Y^V)^{1-\sigma} - Fr^{\beta_Y}w^{1-\beta_Y} \qquad (11.27)$$

The non-integrated firm

Final good producers' *ex post* opportunity cost is zero because they cannot seize the input when they do not reach an agreement with their suppliers. The *ex post* opportunity cost is also zero for suppliers because the input has zero salvage value. Therefore the quasi-rent is $R_Y(i)$. The final good producer and the supplier respectively maximize $\phi R_Y^O(i) - rK_Y^O(i)$ and $(1-\phi)R_Y^O(i) - wL_Y^O(i)$. By following the same steps as above, one shows that the profits of the non-integrated final good firm are:

$$\pi_Y^O(i) = \left[1 - \rho(1-\beta_Y) + \rho\phi(1-2\beta_Y)\right]A_Y(p_Y^O)^{1-\sigma} - Fr^{\beta_Y}w^{1-\beta_Y} \qquad (11.28)$$

where $p_Y^V(i) = \left[\dfrac{r^{\beta_Y}w^{1-\beta_Y}}{\rho\phi^{\beta_Y}(1-\phi)^{\beta_Y}}\right]$

Vertical integration or outsourcing

Because the fixed costs are the same for both types of organization, it follows from (11.27) and (11.28) that firms choose integration when the ratio $\Theta = \dfrac{\left[1 - \rho(1-\beta_Y) + \rho\overline{\phi}(1-2\beta_Y)\right](p_Y^V)^{1-\sigma}}{\left[1 - \rho(1-\beta_Y) + \rho\phi(1-2\beta_Y)\right](p_Y^O)^{1-\sigma}}$
is larger than 1. Substituting for prices, Antràs (2003) shows that $\partial\Theta/\partial\beta_Y > 0$ and $\Theta < 1$ for low enough β_Y, and $\Theta > 1$ otherwise.[51] Since Θ is continuous in β_Y, there exists a threshold value $\hat{\beta} \in (0,1)$ such that integration comes about when $\beta_Y > \hat{\beta}$, and outsourcing takes place when $\beta_Y < \hat{\beta}$.

This finding is consistent with the Grossman and Hart (1986) claim that residual rights should reside with the party that makes the more important contribution to investment. And, if capital-intensity relates positively to vertical integration, it also entails that intra-firm trade should be more common in capital-intensive industries.

Because firms are symmetric, it must be true that either $n_Y^V = 0$ or $n_Y^O = 0$, except in a knife-edge situation when $\beta_Y = \hat{\beta}$. Thus, $A_k = \alpha E(p^S)^{\sigma-1}/n_k^S$ with $k = \{Y,Z\}$ and $S = \{V,O\}$ where

$V = vertical\ integration$ and $O = outsourcing$ when $k = Z$. Plugging the latter into (11.27) and (11.28) and setting profits to zero, yields (11.29) below, which expresses the mass of varieties produced under integration and under outsourcing as a function of total expenditure:

$$n_Y^V = \frac{1 - \rho(1 - \beta_Y) + \rho\phi^V(1 - 2\beta_Y)}{f r^{\beta_Y} w^{1 - \beta_Y}} \alpha E \quad \text{and}$$

$$n_Y^O = \frac{1 - \rho(1 - \beta_Y) + \rho\phi^O(1 - 2\beta_Y)}{f r^{\beta_Z} w^{1 - \beta_Z}} \alpha E \tag{11.29}$$

Equilibrium in the closed economy

When $\beta_Y > \hat{\beta} > \beta_Z$, integration is universal in the Y-industry and outsourcing is the sole organizational form in the Z-industry. This allows a simplification of notation by dropping the superscript V from all variables pertaining to the Y- industry and, similarly, eliminating the superscript O for the Z-industry.

The model can now be closed. The zero profit conditions imply that total expenditure equals total factor income. Letting L and K denote the economy's endowment of labor and capital, the equality can be stated as:

$$E = wL + rK \tag{11.30}$$

Also, equilibrium in the labor market requires:[52]

$$L = n_Y L_Y + n_Z L_Z \tag{11.31}$$

where L_y and L_z denote the sum of labor inputs that enter variable and fixed costs of the final and intermediate good of the Y and Z industries. Jointly, conditions (11.29) and (11.30) yield:

$$wn_Y L_Y = (1 - \beta_Y)\left[1 - \rho\beta_Y(2\bar{\phi} - 1)\right]\alpha(rK + wL)$$

$$wn_Z L_Z = (1 - \beta_Z)\left[1 - \rho\beta_Z(2\phi - 1)\right]\alpha(rK + wL) \tag{11.32}$$

The latter, jointly with (11.25) and (11.26) determine factor prices.

The open economy

The economy just described is now carved up into a number $J \geq 2$ of distinct countries, identical to each other in all respects except for the endowments of labor and capital. The countries may trade in intermediate inputs at zero cost, but neither final output nor capital or labor crosses national borders.

Also, individual country endowments are sufficiently close to each other to ensure factor price equalization and make certain that final good prices and aggregate allocations are identical to those of the integrated economy. It then follows from the definition of Θ and from (11.29), that the cutoff value $\hat{\beta}$ is the same in all countries. If so, the $Y-$ industry is integrated vertically in all countries, and the Z-industry is integrated in no country. Factor price equalization across countries must then imply that the cross-country differences in the Y-industry are limited to differences in the number of producers.

Denote by K_k^j and L_k^j be the total quantities of capital and labor per variety in industry $k = \{Y, Z\}$. Letting K^j and L^j represent county j's endowment of capital and labor, makes it possible to express factor market clearing in country j as:

$$n_Y^j K_Y^j + n_Z^j K_Z^j = K^j \quad \text{and} \quad n_Y^j L_Y^j + n_Z^j L_Z^j = L^j \tag{11.33}$$

Substituting (11.25) and (11.26) into (11.33) yields the share of Y and Z varieties produced in country j.

The share of varieties of intermediate inputs used by industry Y and produced in country j is an increasing function of $K^j / \sum_{j \in J} K^j$, and a decreasing function of $L^j / \sum_{j \in J} L^j$. The converse is true with respect to country j's share of production of intermediate inputs of varieties of industry Z. That share decreases in $K^j / \sum_{j \in J} K^j$ and increases in $L^j / \sum_{j \in J} L^j$. Also, the world share of varieties of good Y produced in country j, is larger (smaller) than the country's share of world income if K^j / L^j, that is, the ratio of the endowments in country j, is larger (smaller) than K/L which is the endowment ratio at the world level.

Because preferences are homothetic and prices are the same everywhere, country j's share of world consumption of the Y and of the Z good is $s^j \equiv (rK^j + wL^j)/(rK + wL)$. And, since intermediate inputs are the only products traded, it follows that country j exports (imports) the inputs produced by the Y industry and imports (exports) intermediate goods produced by the Z industry if and only if K^j / L^j is larger (smaller) than K/L. Since firms in the Y sector are vertically integrated, whereas those in the Z sector are not, it also follows that exports sales originating in capital-rich countries circulate within the confines of firms, whereas exports originating in capital-poor countries flow between unrelated parties.

Heterogeneous firms and intra-firm trade

Antràs' (2003) model suggests that integrated and non-integrated firms only coexist on a knife edge in parameter space. In the real world though, such coexistence is common. To account for that fact, Antràs and Helpman (2004) incorporate features of the Antràs' (2003) model in a Melitz (2003) framework.

The model assumes that final output and headquarter services are produced in the North, whereas components may be manufactured either in the North or in the South. Labor is the only input used in the manufacture of components. The production technology is the same in the North as in the South, but the northern wage exceeds the southern wage. Contracts between a final-good firm and an input producer are incomplete.

Final good producers choose between four organizational forms: 1) vertical integration with component production taking place in the North; 2) vertical integration with component production taking place in a southern affiliate; 3) outsourcing of component production to an independent northern supplier; 4) outsourcing of components to an independent southern supplier.

Final good firms bear a fixed organizational cost which is higher in the South than in the North regardless of ownership structure. To justify this assumption Antràs and Helpman (2004) evoke the higher cost of search, monitoring and communication in a foreign country. They also assume that for *any given* location, the integrated firm incurs a higher fixed cost than the non-integrated firm. The latter reflects the perception that managerial overload associated with in-house production carries a cost that outweighs the benefits from scope economies in the integrated firm.

Thus, final good firms face the following tensions: 1) by locating in the South they enjoy lower variable costs but sustain higher fixed costs; 2) by integrating vertically they earn a higher share of revenue but incur a higher fixed cost, and they lessen the incentives given to the producer of the input.

Figure 11.7 displays the pattern of organization of production as a function of the productivity θ when production is intensive in headquarter services. The most productive firms produce inputs in southern affiliates. Somewhat less productive firms secure inputs from independent suppliers in the South. Firms with even lower productivity are vertically integrated

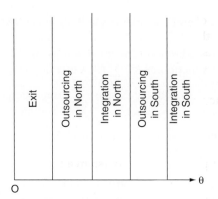

Figure 11.7 Productivity and organizational forms

and produce in the North. Finally, the least productive firms procure their inputs from independent northern suppliers.

The more productive firms sell larger quantities and therefore derive greater savings in variable cost from offshoring. This explains why they have a greater propensity than their less productive rivals to bear the fixed cost of producing in a southern location.[53]

Contractibility and the product cycle

In the years that immediately follow its launch a product is usually manufactured in the country where it has been developed. Typically it is in a northern country. Only in later years is relocation of manufacture to a lower wage country contemplated. Vernon (1966) explains that this is because in the early years of a product's life, proximity between the manufacturing and engineering division is essential as it allows a quicker response to production snags and design problems. The standardization of manufacturing makes it less skill-intensive, and only then does relocation to a country abundant in unskilled labor provide a cost advantage.

Vernon's so-called product cycle hypothesis is formalized and extended in Antràs (2005). Antràs assumes that a final good is created by combining a product development input with a low-tech input. Product development – a general term for ideas relating to product improvement and marketing – is a high-tech input. Product development always originates in the North and remains a necessary input throughout the entire life of the product. However, its contribution to final output falls over time.

Contracts between a northern and a southern party are incomplete but contracts between northern partners are complete. Thus, relocation of production to the South entails a trade-off. A firm that relocates enjoys a lower southern wage, but also bears a burden due to incomplete contracting. The dynamic that this trade-off produces is similar to that of Vernon's life cycle. Specifically, relocation of production to the South does not pay as long as the product is new and uses the product development input intensively. As the product matures and becomes less intensive in the high-tech input, the gains from a lower southern wage increase relative to the costs resulting from incomplete contracting. When the wage gap between North and South is sufficiently large, manufacturing is eventually relocated to the South. First it is transferred to an independent southern firm, or a southern subsidiary, and possibly later to an unaffiliated southern producer.

Partial contractibility

Antràs and Helpman (2008) extend the analysis to partial contractibility. They assume that manufacture of the input involves a range of production activities, some of which are contractible, others not. The contractible portion of activities defines the degree of contractibility of the input. Contractibility varies across countries. It reflects a country's performance in terms of enforcement of contracts. The interaction between input-specific and country-specific contractibility determines the organization of production.

In equilibrium there is underinvestment in non-contractible activities and overinvestment in contractible activities. Final good firms produce headquarter services and are based in the North. They may outsource the production of an input to an independent northern supplier or to a southern supplier. They may also produce the input in-house in a northern or in a southern country. The wage is lower in the South, but the North has better contracting institutions. Thus, final-good producers who outsource trade off a lower variable cost against contract incompleteness.

Figure 11.8 illustrates the relationship between productivity, contractibility and organizational form. The firm with productivity θ and organizational form $k = \{V, O\}$ where $V =$ *vertical integration* and $O =$ *outsourcing*, earns a profit $\pi_k(\theta) = \theta^{\alpha/(1-\alpha)}\pi_k(1) - F_k$, where $\pi_k(1)$ denotes the profit of a firm whose $\theta = 1$, and F_k is the fixed cost of offshoring under the organizational form k. Profits are linear functions of $\theta^{\alpha/(1-\alpha)}$. The line $\pi_V(\theta)$ in Figure 11.8 is steeper than the line $\pi_O(\theta)$ if production is intensive in headquarter services; it is flatter otherwise.

It is apparent from panel (b) that firms whose productivity puts them to the right of point B integrate vertically. Firms whose productivity puts them between A and B outsource, and firms with productivity to the left of point A concentrate all production in their home market. Panel (a) illustrates a situation where all the firms that engage in offshoring also outsource.

Consider now the effect of an improvement in contractibility in the South. The improvement increases $\pi_V(1)$ and $\pi_O(1)$, and it produces a counterclockwise rotation of the lines $\pi_V(\theta)$ and $\pi_O(\theta)$ around their vertical intercepts. This is indicated by the arrows in panel (b). The rotation shifts points A and B to the left, increasing the range of productivities for which firms integrate vertically. The impact of the rotation on the range of θ's for which firms prefer outsourcing is ambiguous because A *and* B shift to the left. Whether that range expands or contracts depends on relative magnitude of the two shifts. It is clear, however, that the range of productivities for which all production is concentrated in the North narrows. The upshot is that lower contractual friction in the South encourages offshoring to the South.

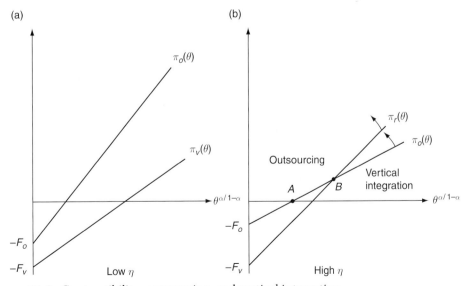

Figure 11.8 Contractibility, outsourcing, and vertical integration

Market thickness and matching

The models we examined above assume that there is an infinitely elastic supply of independent firms capable of producing the customized input. In reality, final good firms may not easily find a supplier. Similarly, independent suppliers may not readily hit upon an alternative buyer of the input if negotiations with the projected buyer break down.

McLaren (2000) and Grossman and Helpman (2003, 2005) examine how the difficulty of finding a fitting partner affects the organization of production. The set-up they imagine assumes that the final good firm needs a fully or partially customized input. It can produce the input in-house or acquire it from an outside supplier. The final good firm cannot contractually commit to purchasing the input at a predetermined price. Because the cost of the input is at least partially sunk, the supplier – who must invest in the input – faces a risk of hold-up. The supplier responds optimally by providing less than optimal investment. This entails a cost that the final good producer can avoid by integrating vertically. The problem is that production cost is higher in the integrated firm.

In McLaren (2000) suppliers choose not to tailor the input fully to the needs of the intended buyer. The reason is that the prospects of finding an alternative buyer are better when the input is not fully tailored to the needs of the projected buyer. As a result, the supplier enjoys a better threat point in bargaining. This increases his *ex post* payoff and the attractiveness of purchasing the input relative to in-house production.

A first implication is that vertical integration by one firm lowers the attractiveness of outsourcing to other firms. This comes about because a reduction in the number of potential secondary buyers makes the market for incompletely specialized inputs thinner. The opening of borders to international trade, on the other hand, thickens the secondary market. This increases the attractiveness of arm's length arrangements relative to vertical integration. This is a gain from trade unrelated to specialization, to a lessening of market power or to enhanced variety. It derives solely from a lowering of production cost through outsourcing, and better fine-tuning of inputs to the buyers' requirements.

In Grossman and Helpman (2002) it is the probability of finding the initial partner that plays the key role. That probability is a function of the number of final good firms relative to the number of independent input suppliers. As in McLaren (2000), vertical integration by one firm reduces the attractiveness of arm's length contracting for other firms. In this instance though, it happens by way of a reduced probability of finding the initial match.

Grossman and Helpman (2003) consider the problem of a northern industry which produces a final good. It decides whether to source an input from an independent southern firm, or to have its own affiliate in the South produce the input at a lower cost. The cost of the input is lower when it is produced by an independent supplier. Even so, an independent supplier – in contrast to an integrated firm – incurs a fixed cost of customization of the input to the buyer's needs. The amount of fixed cost is an increasing function of the distance in characteristic space that separates the buyer from the seller.[54]

There is freedom of entry for input suppliers and final good producers. Final good producers who choose to outsource negotiate the terms with the supplier closest to them in characteristic space. There is only time for negotiation with one supplier.

When the development cost has been sunk and a prototype has come into existence, the parties negotiate the terms of an order. If they reach an agreement each party captures half of the joint profits. When they do not, the supplier has no alterative use for the prototype, and the final producer has no substitute source of supply.

Grossman and Helpman (2003) determine that firms located below a threshold distance from an input supplier secure their customized input via an arm's length contract, whereas firms farther away integrate vertically. The threshold distance increases when the cost of production borne by the independent supplier declines relative to the production cost of the integrated firm. Also, the market share of firms that outsource relates positively to the income spent of the final product. The reason is that an increase in spending elicits entry by final good producers, and by doing so, boosts the derived demand for inputs. The latter encourages entry by input producers, and a thicker market for inputs helps final good producers find suppliers whose expertise matches their need more closely. One implication is that, all else being equal, outsourcing should be more common relative to affiliate production in larger countries.

11.9   Intra-firm trade and outsourcing: the evidence

Antràs (2003) looks at the share of intra-firm imports in total US imports. He defines intra-firm imports as the sum of imports by US-based parents from their majority-owned affiliates and imports shipped by foreign multinationals to their US affiliates. His panel has 23 manufacturing industries and four years of data. The estimating equation has industry intra-firm imports as a share of total US imports as a dependent variable. The key explanatory variable is the capital intensity *(CAPINT)* of the importing industry, measured as the ratio of the industry's capital stock relative to the total employment of the industry. According to theory the relevant intensity should be that of the industry in the exporting country but Antràs (2003) utilizes the intensity of the matching US industry.

The remaining independent variables serve as controls for other industry-specific determinants of the decision to integrate. They include skill intensity *(SKILINT)* measured as the ratio of non-production to production workers, advertising intensity *(ADVINT)* and R&D intensity *(RDINT)*. To account for the possibility that scale economies might be a cause of integration, the model incorporates a scale variable *(SCALE)* defined as the industry's average capital stock per establishment. The final explanatory variable is industry value added relative to industry sales *(VALADINT)*. This variable picks up the importance of unaffiliated suppliers in the industry's value chain. Dependent and explanatory variables are in expressed in logs.

Column (1) of Table 11.7 displays the results of random effects estimation. The estimated elasticity of the share of intra-firm imports with respect to the capital–labor ratio is highly significant. It shows that intra-firm imports as a share of total imports increases by 0.72 percent when the capital–labor ratio increases by 1 percent. Among control variables, only R&D intensity displays a significant coefficient. The sign of the coefficient accords with the hypothesis that knowledge-based assets are a determinant of multinational activity. Antràs (2003) also finds a positive and significant association between the ratio of intra-firm imports to total imports originating in a country, and that country's endowment of capital relative to labor.

Yeaple's (2006) revisits the role of factor intensity. His dependent variable is US parents' imports from their majority-owned foreign affiliates, as a share of total US imports. The explanatory variables match those of Antràs (2003) but include an additional variable labeled *DISPERSION* which measures the disparity of productivity within an industry.[55] The estimated coefficient displayed in column (2) supports the theoretical prediction of a positive relationship between *DISPERSION* and the share of imports that flow intra-firm.

A partition of the sample into developed countries, emerging countries and less developed countries reveals an additional relationship. The *CAPINT* coefficient is positive in all subsamples but its size is inversely related to the level of development of the country grouping. The coefficient is not significantly different from zero for the cluster of developed countries. The coefficients of the *DISPERSION* variable follow a similar pattern. They are positive for all groupings but their size is inversely related to the level of development. Only for the least developed countries and emerging countries are the coefficients significantly different from zero.

Interestingly, the coefficients of *RDINT* display the opposite pattern. They are positive for all three subsamples, but statistically significant only for the group of developed countries.

Table 11.7 Factor intensity and intra-firm share

Variable	(1) Antràs (2003)	(2) Yeaple (2006)	(3) Nunn & Trefler (2007)
CAPINT	0.723***	0.74***	0.61***
SKILINT	−0.081	0.21	0.079***
RDINT	0.421***	0.24	
ADVINT	0.035	0.06	
SCALE	0.100	−0.53***	
VALADINT	0.403	−0.17	
DISPERSION		1.42***	
$\overline{R}^2$	0.43	0.11	0.17
# observations	92	51	370

*$p < 0.10$; **$p < 0.05$; ***$p < 0.01$.
Source: Antràs (2003), Yeaple (2006), Nunn and Trefler (2007).

Yeaple (2006) holds that these patterns bring to light the fact that the least developed countries do not on average produce goods that require knowledge inputs; their goods require physical inputs produced by US multinationals.

Nunn and Trefler (2008) use a substantially expanded sample. Their dependent variable is built from shipment records at the six-digit Harmonized System level. They classify shipments as intra-firm when one party to the transaction owns at least 6 percent of the other party.[56] Their import data on 5423 products exported by 210 countries are allotted to 370 industries. Their definitions of capital and skill intensity are as in Antràs (2003).

Column (3) of Table 11.7 displays their baseline estimation results. They bear out the positive association of intra-firm trade with capital intensity. But, in contrast to Antràs (2003) and Yeaple (2006), skill intensity relates positively and significantly to the dependent variable.[57]

Because at the Harmonized System six-level goods originating in poor countries may be very different from goods exported by rich countries, Nunn and Trefler (2008) also calculate the ratio of intra-firm imports to total imports for individual exporting countries. They pool across industries and countries and re-estimate the equation, allowing for country fixed effects. The estimated coefficients of *CAPINT* and *SKILINT* remain positive, but are smaller than those shown in Table 11.7.

To determine how heterogeneity of productivity within industries affects the intra-firm share of imports, they partition the sample industries into five quintiles ranked in increasing order of headquarter intensity, skill intensity or capital intensity. Then they estimate the equation:

$$\frac{M_{gc}^V}{M_{gc}^V + M_{gc}^O} = \gamma_c + \gamma_{CAP}\ln(CAPINT_g) + \gamma_{SKIL}\ln(SKILINT_g)$$

$$+ \sum_{p=1}^{5}\gamma_{\eta p}I_{gp}^\eta + \sum_{p=1}^{5}\sum_{p=1}^{5}\gamma_{\theta\eta p}\,(x_g^\theta I_{gp}^\eta) + \varepsilon_{gc}$$

where M_{gc}^k denotes intra-firm or arm's length imports $[k = \{V = \text{intra-firm}, O = \text{arm's length}\}]$ of industry g goods from country c. The variable x_g^θ denotes the standard deviation of sales in industry g and proxies for the dispersion of firms' productivities. The dummy variable I^{η}_{gp} equals 1 if industry g belongs to quintile p, and zero otherwise. Finally γ_c captures the country fixed effect.

The coefficient of primary interest is $\gamma_{\theta\eta p}$. According to theory it should be zero for industries that are low in headquarter intensity, skill intensity and capital intensity. It should be positive otherwise. The estimated $\gamma_{\theta\eta p}$, displayed in row 1 of Table 11.8, bear out this prediction. An F-test does not reject the hypothesis of equality of any pair of coefficients $\gamma_{\theta\eta 2}$ to $\gamma_{\theta\eta 5}$ but it clearly rejects the hypothesis of equality between $\gamma_{\theta\eta 1}$ and any other coefficient. Overall, the estimated relationship suggests that above a fairly low threshold of headquarter intensity, greater productivity increases the share of intra-firm imports.

Nunn and Trefler (2008) then consider the effects of partial contractibility. To capture the combined effect of the foreign country's contracting environment and the relationship-specific character of the investment, they construct the interactive variable $x^{\mu}_g \equiv r_c \times (1 - z_g)$, where z_g stands for the proportion of industry g's intermediate inputs that is relationship-specific, and therefore prone to contracting problems.[58] The variable r_c, taken from Kaufman et al. (2005) captures the quality of contract enforcement in country c. The sample is again partitioned in quintiles ranked in increasing order of headquarter intensity.

The estimating equation is:

$$\frac{M^V_{gc}}{M^V_{gc} + M^O_{gc}} = \gamma_g + \gamma_c + \sum_{p=1}^{5} \gamma^{\mu}_{\eta p}(x^{\mu}_g I^{\eta}_{gp}) + \varepsilon_{gc}$$

where $I^{\eta}_{gp} = 1$ when industry g is in quintile p and $I^{\eta}_{gp} = 0$ otherwise. The coefficients γ_g and γ_c capture industry and country fixed effects.

Row 2 of Table 11.8 displays the estimated $\gamma^{\mu}_{\eta p}$'s. While the estimates lack precision, they nevertheless reflect the absence of a contractibility effect in the case of low headquarter-intensive industries.

Defever and Toubal (2007) and Corcos et al. (2008) explore the determinants of intra-firm imports at the individual firm level. The general form of the estimating equations is $y_{ipc} = \beta_0 + X_i\bar{\beta}_i + X_p\bar{\beta}_p + X_c\bar{\beta}_c + \varepsilon_{ipc}$ where X_i represents a row vector of firm characteristics, X_p is

Table 11.8 Productivity dispersion and contractual completeness as determinants of the share of intra-firm imports in total US imports[a]

	$P=1$	$P=2$	$p=3$	$P=4$	$P=5$
Productivity dispersion interactions	0.03***	0.13***	0.12***	0.09***	0.11***
Contractual completeness Interaction	−0.12	−0.05	−0.04** .	0.10**	0.11**

*$p < 0.10$; **$p < 0.05$.
[a]In the absence of firm-level data, productivity dispersion is calculated from the dispersion of sales from different US locations from which exports are shipped. The numbers reported in Table 11.5 pertain to the case when quintiles are determined on the basis of capital intensity. The size, significance and pattern of estimated coefficients are similar when the selection criterion is skill intensity.
Source: Nunn and Trefler (2008).

a row vector of product characteristics and X_c is a row vector of country characteristics. The dependent variable $y_{ipc} = 1$ if the imports by firm i of product p from country c are intra-firm, and $y_{ipc} = 0$ if they are at arm's length.[59]

Both studies relate the import category to the productivity and factor intensity of the individual firm rather than the industry. This is a desirable feature for two reasons: 1) the theoretical models speak about organizational decisions made by firms, not by industries; 2) more importantly, there is significant heterogeneity with regard to productivity and factor intensity within industries, even within finely defined industries.

Logit estimation reveals that the likelihood of intra-firm imports relates positively to firm-level productivity, capital intensity, skill intensity and headquarter intensity. Corcos *et al.* (2008) also show that trade is more likely to flow within the confines of the firm when imports originate in countries that enjoy better functioning judicial institutions, and when both the final output and the input are complex products. Surprisingly perhaps, they also find that capital-intensive firms tend to import labor-intensive goods from related parties in labor–abundant countries.

11.10 Concluding remarks

Multinationals are normally the largest and the most productive firms in their industry. This agrees with the hypothesis that the ownership knowledge-based assets are indispensable to overcome the competition from host country producers. It is also consistent with the finding that cross-industry variation in multinational activity correlates with R&D intensity and advertising intensity.

In the case of the largest and most technologically advanced economies, a high R&D intensity may well reflect an industry's advantage at the world level. Also, because of the uncertainty of payoffs on R&D spending, a high R&D intensity may relate positively to the dispersion of productivity within industries. And, because the most productive firms sell larger quantities, they are willing to bear the extra fixed costs of operating in different countries. While empirical studies support the theoretical prediction that tariffs and transportation cost affect affiliate activity, the measured impacts reflect the conflicting effects of trade barriers on horizontal and vertical fragmentation.

Internalization is what distinguishes multinational activity from unadorned outsourcing. Firms' desire to avoid exposure to opportunistic behavior is the key motive behind internalization. This explains why the quality of a country's contract enforcement determines whether that country is more likely to be served via exports or affiliate production. It also explains why trade in goods prone to contracting problems is more likely to flow within the confines of a single organization.

Problems

11.1 Examine how a decrease in home country's tax burden in the home changes Figure 11.1.

11.2 Refer to Figure 11.1, assume that that $T = T^* = 0$ and show that the set of (L, L^*) values for which production in two plants maximizes joint welfare of both countries is larger than the set that maximizes profits. Explain why this is so.

11.3 A home firm faces a demand $q^* = 10 - p^*$ in foreign country. It produces in the home country and ships output to its distribution affiliate in the foreign country. The foreign country levies a tariff τ^* on the value of imports. Tax rates on profits earned in the home and the foreign country are respectively T and T^*. The price at which the home plant transfers product to the distribution affiliate is R. The transfer price must lie in the interval $[\underline{R}, \overline{R}]$. Otherwise the firm incurs a steep penalty. Unit production cost is c. Determine the profits maximizing values of p^* and R.

11.4 When a home produces locally and exports to the foreign country it bears a unit production cost c and pays a specific tariff τ. When it produces in the foreign country it bears a unit cost c_1 in the first period, and then, as a result of gaining experience in the foreign market its unit cost of producing in that market falls to c_2. Specifically, assume that $\overline{c} > c + \tau > \underline{c}$. The firm knows in period 1 that in the period 2 a foreign firm will enter the foreign market and will be produce at a unit cost c_2. It is also known that upon entry the two firms will engage in Cournot competition. Determine under what condition the home firm prefers setting up a foreign plant to exporting. Suppose that the market operates only two periods, and that the discount rate is r. The inverse demand in the foreign market is $p^* = 12 - Q^*$ where Q^* is the total quantity sold in that market.

11.5 Show that when the endowment point is slightly below the boundary HQ of the factor price equalization set shown in Figure 11.4, the home country is a net importer of the differentiated good.

Notes

1. While the definition of FDI as investment to a minimum equity stake of 10 percent has been largely standardized, variations remain across countries, and the distinction between portfolio investment and FDI is sometimes difficult to establish.
2. UNCTAD (2009).
3. UNCTAD (2009) Table B.2.
4. The changes over time in Table 11.3 also reflect movements in exchange rates.
5. OECD (2005).
6. See OECD (2005).
7. Source: Canada (2009).
8. Implicit in that contention is the assumption that the handicap of a shallower knowledge of the foreign environment is substantial and that potential competition from local firms is intense.
9. R&D intensity is defined as expenditure on research and development per dollar of sales, or as employment of scientists and engineers as a share of total employment. Advertising intensity is spending on advertising per dollar of sales.
10. It relates negatively to the share of royalty payments accruing to the industry's UK-based firms. This finding is hardly unexpected if one holds the view that the key determinant is the technological rank of the host country industry relative to the rank of same industry in the country of the parent.
11. Earlier work by Globerman *et al.* (1994) found that the higher productivity of Canadian-based foreign affiliates over Canadian-owned plants disappears when the estimating equations account for differences in size, capital intensity, share of non-production workers and share of male workers.
12. They also establish that firms which are globally engaged use more knowledge, and that the knowledge they use originates from outside and inside the firm, in particular from establishments under common ownership.

13. Sales cost intensity is the sum of advertising and sales force expenditure as a percentage of sales. Human resource intensity is the labor cost of non-factory employees as a fraction of total labor cost.

14. Strictly speaking, under- and over-involving does not require that the transaction take place among affiliates of the same enterprise. However, common ownership and management reduces the risk that deviations from arm's length pricing will be detected.

15. We assume that the bounds are exogenous for simplicity's sake. Samuelson (1982) and Eden (1985) present a model in which the bounds are determined endogenously. Kant (1988) assumes that the probability that penalties will be imposed for over- and under-invoicing increases with the distance between the transfer price and the arm's length price. The latter allows outcomes where the transfer price is in the interior rather than at a boundary of the admissible interval.

16. Problem (11.3) addresses the question how adding option (b) affects the firm's location decision.

17. The consequences become apparent considering the following example. Assume that the final producer can seize the intermediate input and hire a new manager at a cost $c < H$. The best price, the seller can hope for when he renegotiates is then $F + c$ rather than $F + H$. This improves the bargaining position of the user of the intermediate input and may reduce the likelihood of opportunistic conduct on the part of the seller.

18. A list of factors that favor vertical integration appears in Church and Ware (2000), Carlton and Perloff (2005) and in most other industrial organization textbooks.

19. The problem is examined in Horstmann and Markusen (1987) and Smith (1987). This section is based on Smith.

20. In such environments the use of both channels mitigates the firm's risk. When cost fluctuates using both channels allows the firm to shift production to the lower cost location. When demand is uncertain in one country it reduces the risk of winding up with excess capacity in that country if demand turns out to be unexpectedly low.

21. This section draws on Markusen and Venables (2000) and Markusen (2002).

22. Expression (11.6) is developed in the appendix of Chapter 8.

23. Still the exporting firm based in country i receives only p_i per unit consumed in country j since it must export τ units to ensure that one unit arrives in country j.

24. Headquarter services are a convenient label for inputs such as R&D and general management.

25. Recall that the factor price equalization set is one-dimensional when transportation costs are positive.

26. Alternatively one may consider that the first stage involves the manufacture of components, while the second stage consists of assembly of these components.

27. The points H_h and E_f are located at the intersections with OH and OQ of a line passing through E and parallel to HQ.

28. This is trade by all firms not just MNE's.

29. Earlier studies addressing the same question are Horst (1974) and Swedenborg (1979).

30. She also examines the determinants of foreign multinational activity in the US. Her findings in this regards are not reported here.

31. The data derived from a survey can be found in World Competitiveness Report (1992).

32. Columns 3 and 4 are found in Table 2 of Brainard (1997). The explanatory variables as well as the dependent variable in the second column are expressed in logs.

33. They are fully joint when the cost of using the input in multiple plants is the same as the cost of using it in a single plant.

34. Interestingly, when countries are moderately asymmetric in size and in relative endowments and the smaller country is richer in skilled labor, the very same fall in transportation cost may stimulate affiliate production if the industry is primarily composed of horizontal and vertical MNEs.

35. Real sales are calculated by converting local sales into US dollars and dividing by a wholesale price index.

36. Clearly, $SIZE_i \in \left(0, \sqrt{2}\right)$. When the parent and host country are equally sized, $SIZE_i = \sqrt{1/2}$.

37. Thus, $SKILL_i$ represents the slope of the line through the country i's point of origin and its endowment point.

38. In the Carr *et al.* (2001) estimation, the country dummies pertain only to the host country as the parent country is always the US. Both studies report that most country dummies are significant.

39. The fixed cost of exporting presumably includes the cost of forming an overseas distribution and servicing network. F_I also includes the latter and a cost of operating a subsidiary.

40. The assumption $\left[\dfrac{w^f}{w^h}\right]F_I > \tau^{\sigma-1}F_X > F_D$ ensures the existence of these three classes of active firms.

41. See appendix of Chapter 9.

42. Note that in the case of vertical fragmentation the delivered cost to the parent country includes the cost of shipping the component manufactured in the south. The delivered cost to the other northern country includes the cost of shipping the southern component to the country of the parent and the cost of shipping the final assembly from the parent country *(W)* to the other northern country *(E)*.

43. Ekholm *et al.* (2007) explore complex fragmentation in a duopoly framework where each northern country is the home base of a single firm.

44. However, the regression based on the larger sample of 12 sectors indicates that affiliates located in smaller markets have a stronger outward orientation.

45. Contrast this with Brainard's (1997) findings on the effect of taxes.

46. They do when non-manufacturing industries are included in the sample.

47. Bloningen *et al.* (2007) retain host country GDP as a separate regressor, noting that while the host country GDP and surrounding market potential are likely to determine horizontal fragmentation and export platform activity, only surrounding market potential matters for the latter.

48. The assumption that factor use has the same intensity for the fixed and variable component of cost, entails a homothetic total cost.

49. Dunning (1993) and Milgrom and Roberts (1993) mention these practices. They also point out that buyers will occasionally provide assistance in obtaining capital equipment.

50. To derive Equation (11.27), write profit as $\overline{\phi}R_Y^V - rK_Y - F_{FG} + T = \overline{\phi}R_Y^V - \rho\beta_Y\overline{\phi}R_Y^V - F_{FG} + T^V$, where T^V is the transfer payment made by the input division. Because the transfer ensures that the input division earns zero profits, we have $T^V = (1 - \overline{\phi})[1 - \rho(1 - \beta_Y)]A_Y(p_Y^V)^{1-\sigma} - F_{IS}r^{\beta_Y}w^{1-\beta_Y}$. Plugging this expression into the profit equation and using $F = F_{FG} + F_S$ then yields Equation (11.27).

51. The formal proof appears in appendix II of Antràs (2003). The assumption that technology is Cobb-Douglas ensures that Θ is not a function of factor prices.

52. As indicated in Chapter 8 the capital market clears when the other markets clear.

53. It should be stressed though, that the ranking of organizational forms displayed in Figure 11.7 is contingent on the assumed ordering of fixed costs. Also, the equilibrium

may not display all four types of organization. Whether it does, depends on the gap that separates the northern and southern wage. Still, the ranking of the types that do exist in equilibrium follows the pattern shown in Figure 11.7.

54. The model assumes that final good producers are distributed uniformly on a circle. A finite number of independent suppliers are located at equally spaced points on a circle. It is the distance between the location a final-good firm and a supplier which determines the fixed cost the latter must incur to develop the prototype that meets the needs of that particular final-good firm.

55. *SKILINT* is now defined as the share of workers in the industry that have no less than a high school education, and *SCALE* is now defined as the industry's average plant size.

56. The hypothesis is that control requires a 6 percent stake.

57. Because the data do not distinguish between imports by US parents from their foreign affiliates and imports by affiliates of foreign parents, separate regressions are run on a restricted subsample of countries for which at least two-thirds of intra-firm imports originate in US-owned parents. Both coefficients are substantially smaller in the restricted sample but they remain significant.

58. The measure is based on Rauch's (1999) classification of goods according to whether they are sold on an organized exchange, reference priced or neither. It is in the latter group that one presumably finds the intermediate inputs which are most relationship-specific. Price reference goods are intermediate in terms of susceptibility to opportunism. Goods that belong to the remaining group are least susceptible to hold-up. Nunn (2007) calculates r_c indices for each industry as the weighted sum of the ranking of their inputs in terms of vulnerability to opportunism, the weights being the share of each input in the total value of inputs used by the industry.

59. Their primary data are constructed from balance sheet information on all French firms that employ at least 20 workers. This data is matched up with data from a survey of imports by firms that trade more than 1 million euros, and are owned by manufacturing groups that control at least 50 percent of the equity capital of a foreign entity. The import data are broken down by product, country of origin and sourcing mode. Imports not reported in the survey are assumed to flow between unrelated parties.

References and additional reading

Extent of multinational activities

Anderson, T. and Zeile, W.J. (2009), "Operations of US Affiliates of Foreign Companies," Preliminary Results from the 2007 Benchmark Survey, Survey of Current Business, at: http://www.bea.gov/scb/pdf/2009/11%20November/1109_foreign.pdf.

Bardhan, A. (2009), "A Note of Intra-firm Trade & Offshoring in Manufacturing and Services," available at http://www.atdforum.org/IMG/pdf_FTA_on_intra_firm_Sufian.pdf.

Bloningen, B.A., Davies, R.B., Waddell, G.R., and Naughton, H.T (2007), 'FDI in Space: Spatial Autoregressive Relationships in Foreign Direct Investment', *European Economic Review*, 51, 1303–1325.

Canada, Foreign Affairs and International Trade (2009), "Canada's State of Trade and Investment Update 2008 – including a special feature on Canadian Direct Investment Abroad," available at http://www.international.gc.ca/economist-economiste/performance/state-point/2008.aspx?lang=eng#a1.

Mataloni, R.J. (2008), "US Multinational Companies Operations in 2006, Survey of Current Business," available at http://www.bea.gov/scb/pdf/2008/11%20November/1108_mnc.pdf.

OECD (Organisation for Economic Co-operation and Development) (2005), *Measuring Globalisation: OECD Economic Globalisation Indicators*.

UNCTAD (2009), *World Investment Report* (Geneva: United Nations) available at http://unctad.org/en/docs/wir2009_en.pdf.

United Nations, Centre for Transnational Corporations (1992), *The Determinants of Foreign Direct Investment: A Survey of the Evidence* (New York: United Nations).

US Bureau of Economic Analysis (1990), *Foreign Direct Investment in the US: Operations of US Affiliates, Revised 1989 estimates* (Washington, DC: US Bureau of Economic Analysis).

US Bureau of Economic Analysis (1990), *US Direct Investment Abroad, Revised 1989 Estimates* (Washington, DC: US Bureau of Economic Analysis).

US Bureau of the Census, Annual Survey of Manufactures (1989), *Statistics for Industry Groups and Industries* (Washington, DC: US Bureau of the Census).

World Economic Forum (1992), *World Competitiveness Report*, International Institute for Management Development.

OLI and imperfect competition

Baltagi, B.H., Egger, P., and Pfaffermayr, M. (2007), "Estimating Models of Complex FDI: Are there Third-Country Effects?" *Journal of Econometrics*, 140, 260–281.

Barefoot, K.B. and Mataloni Jr., R.J. (2009), "US Multinational Companies, Operations in the United States and Abroad in 2007," *Survey of Current Business*, available at http://www.bea.gov/scb/pdf/2009/08%20August/0809_mnc.pdf.

Belderbos, R. and Sleuwaegen, L. (1996), "Japanese Firms and the Decision to Invest Abroad: Business Groups and Regional Core Networks," *Review of Economics and Statistics*, 28 (2), 214–221.

Bergsten, C.F., Horst, T., and Moran, T. (1978), *American Multinationals and American Interest* (Washington DC: Brookings Institution).

Bloningen, B.A. (1997), "Firm-Specific Assets and the Link between Exchange Rates and Foreign Direct Investment," *American Economic Review*, 87, 447–466.

Bloningen, B.A., Davies, R.B., Waddell, G.R., and Naughton, H.T. (2007), "FDI in Space: Spatial Autoregressive Relationships in Foreign Direct Investment," *European Economic Review*, 51, 1303–1325.

Brainard, S.L. (1997), "An Empirical Assessment of the Proximity-Concentration Trade-Off between Multinational Sales and Trade," *American Economic Review*, 87 (4), 520–544.

Cantwell, J. (1989), *Technical Innovation in Multinational Corporation* (Oxford: Basil Blackwell).

Carlton, D.W. and Perloff, J.M. (2005), *Modern Industrial Organization* (Boston: Pearson-Addison Wesley).

Caves, R.E. (1974), "Causes of Direct Investment: Foreign Firm's Shares in Canadian and United Kingdom Manufacturing Industries," *Review of Economics and Statistics*, 56 (3), 279–290.

Caves, R.E. (1971), "International Corporations: The Industrial Economics of Foreign Investment," *Economica*, 38 (149), 1–27.

Church, J. and Ware, R. (2000), *Industrial Organization: A Strategic Approach* (Boston, MA: Irwin- McGraw Hill).

Choi, J.P. and Davidson, C. (2006), "Strategic Second Sourcing by Multinationals," *International Economic Review*, 45 (2), 579–600.

Criscuolo, C. and Martin, R. (2009a), "Multinationals and US Productivity: Evidence from Great Britain," *Review of Economics and Statistics*, 91 (2), 263–281.

Criscuolo, C. and Martin, R. (2009b), "Global Engagement and the Innovation Activities or Firms," *International Journal of Industrial Organization*, 28 (2), 191–202.

Dixit, A.K. and Stiglitz, J.E. (1977), "Monopolistic Competition and Optimum Product Diversity," *American Economics Review*, 67, 297–308.

Doms, M.E. and Bradford Jensen J. (1998), "Comparing Wages, Skills, and Productivity between Domestically and Foreign-Owned Manufacturing Establishments in the United States," in R.E. Baldwin, R.E. Lipsey and J.D. Richardson (Eds.), *Geography and Ownership as Bases for Economic Accounting* (Chicago: University of Chicago Press).

Dunning, J.H. (1993), *Multinational Enterprises and the Global Economy* (Addison Wesley Longman, Inc.).

Dunning, J. and Lundan, S.M. (2008), *Multinational Enterprises and the Global Economy*, 2nd ed. (Cheltenham, UK: Edward Elgar).

Eden, L. (1985), "Microeconomics of Transfer Pricing, in Rugman, A.M. and Eden L. (Eds.), *Multinationals and Transfer Pricing,* (New York: St Martin's Press), 13–46.

Ekholm, K., Forslid R., and Markusen J.R. (2007), "Export-Platform Foreign Direct Investment," *Journal of the European Economic Association*, 5 (4), 776–795.

Globerman, S., Ries J., and Vertinsky, I. (1994), "The Economic Performances of Foreign-Owned Subsidiaries in Canada," *Canadian Journal of Economics*, 27 (1) 143–156.

Grubaugh, S.G., (1987), "Determinants of Foreign Direct Investment," *Review of Economics and Statistics*, 69, 149–52.

Grubert, H. and Mutti, J. (1991), "Taxes, Tariffs, and Transfer Pricing in Multinational Corporate Decision Making," *Review of Economics and Statistics*, 79, 285–293.

Gupta, V.K. (1983), "A Simultaneous Determination of Structure, Conduct and Performance in Canadian Manufacturing," *Oxford Economic Papers*, 35 (2), 281–301.

Hanson, G.H., Mataloni, R.J. and Slaughter, M.J. (2001), "Expansion Strategies of US Multinational Firms," *Brookings Trade Forum*, 245–295.

Helpman, E., and Krugman P.R. (1985), *Market Structure and Foreign Trade: Increasing Returns, Imperfect Competition, and the International Economy* (Cambridge, MA and London : MIT Press).

Helpman, E., Melitz, M., and Yeaple, S.R. (2004), "Export versus FDI with Heterogeneous Firms," *American Economics Review*, 94 (1), 300–316.

Horst, T. (1971), "The Theory of the Multinational Firm: Optimal Behavior under Different Tariff and Tax Rates," *Journal of Political Economy*, 79, 1059–1072.

Horst T. (1974), "The Industrial Composition of US Exports and Subsidiary Sales to the Canadian Market," *American Economic Review*, 62 (1), 37–45.

Horst T. (1972), "Firm and Industry Determinants of the Decision to Invest Abroad: An Empirical Study," *Review of Economics and Statistics*, 54, 258–266.

Horstmann, I.J. and Markusen, J.R. (1987), "Licensing versus Direct Investment: A Model of Internalization of the MNE," *Canadian Journal of Economics*, 20, 464–481.

Horstmann, I.J. and Markusen, J.R. (1987), "Strategic Investments and the Development of Multinationals," *International Economic Review*, 28 (1), 109–121.

Hymer, S. (1976), "The International Operations of National Firms: A Study of Foreign Direct Investment," PhD dissertation (Cambridge, MA: MIT Press).

Johnson, H.G. (1970), "The Efficiency and Welfare Implications of the International Corporation," in C.P. Kindleberger (Ed.), *The International Corporation* (Cambridge, MA: MIT Press).

Kant, C. (1988), "Endogenous Transfer Pricing and the Effects of Uncertain Regulation," *Journal of International Economics,* 24, 147–57.

Kiyota, K. and Urata S. (2008), "The Role of Multinational Firms in International Trade: The Case of Japan," *Japan and the World Economy,* 20 (3), 338–352.

Kogut, B. and Chang, S.J. (1991), "Technological Capabilities and Japanese Foreign Direct Investment in the United States," *The Review of Economics and Statistics,* 73 (3), 401–413.

Kogut, B. and Kulatilaka, N. (1994), "Operating Flexibility, Global Manufacturing, and the Option Value of a Multinational Network," *Management Science,* 40, 123–139.

Kumar, N. (1998), "Multinational Enterprises, Regional Economic Integration, and Export-Platform Production: An Empirical Analysis for the US and Japanese Corporations," *Weltwirtschaftliches Archiv,* 134 (3), 450–483.

Lall, S. (1980), Monopolistic Advantages and Foreign Involvement by US Manufacturing Industry, *Oxford Economic Papers,* 32, 102–122.

Lall, S. and Siddharthan, N.S. (1982), "The Monopolistic Advantages of Multinationals: Lessons from Foreign Investment in the US," *Economic Journal,* 92 (367), 668–683.

Melitz, M. (2003), "The Impact of Trade on Intra on Intra-Industry Reallocations and Aggregate Industry Productivity," *Econometrica,* 71 (6), 1695–1725.

Neven, D. and Siotis, G. (1996), "Technology Sourcing and FDI in the EC: An Empirical Evaluation," *International Journal of Industrial Organization,* 14, 543–560.

Pugel, T.A. (1978), *International Market Linkages and US Manufacturing: Prices, Profits, and Patterns* (Cambridge, MA; Ballinger).

Pugel, T.A., Krages, E.S., and Kimura, Y. (1996), "Further Evidence of Japanese Direct Investment in US Manufacturing," *Review of Economics and Statistics,* 78 (2), 208–213.

Rob, R., and Vettas, N. (2003), "Foreign Direct Investment and Exports with Growing Demand," *Review of Economic Studies,* 70, 629–648.

Samuelson, L. (1982), The Multinational Firm with Arm's Length Transfer Price Limits, *Journal of International Economics,* 13, 365–74

Smith, A. (1987), "Strategic Investment, Multinational Corporations and Trade Policy," *European Economic Review,* 31, 89–96.

Swedenborg, B. (1979), *The Multinational Operations of Swedish Firms* (Stockholm: Industrial Institute for Economic and Social Research).

Teece, D.J. (1977), "Technology Transfer by Multinational Enterprise: an Assessment," *Economics Journal,* 87, 242–261.

Economist, The (2010), *Pocket World in Figures,* 2010 Edition.

Tomiura, D. (2007), "Foreign Outsourcing, Exporting and FDI: A Productivity Comparison at the Firm Level," *Journal of International Economics,* 72, 113–127.

Yeaple, S.R. (2003), "The Complex Integration Strategies of Multinationals and Cross Country Dependencies in the Structure of Foreign Direct Investment," *Journal of International Economics,* 60, 293–314.

Yeaple, S.R. (2006), "Offshoring, Foreign Direct Investment, and the Structure of US Trade," *Journal of the European Economic Association,* 6, 602–611.

Endowments

Braconier, H., Norbäck, P.-J., and Urban, D. (2005), "Reconciling the Evidence on the Knowledge-Capital Model," *Review of International Economics,* 13 (4), 770–786.

Carr, D., Markusen, J.R., and Maskus, K.E. (2001), "Estimating the Capital-Knowledge Model of the Multinational Enterprise," *American Economic Review,* 91, 693–708.

Grossman, G.M., Helpman, E., and Szeidl, A. (2006), "Optimal Integration Strategies for the Multinational Firm," *Journal of International Economics*, 70, 216–238.

Helpman, E. (1984), "A Simple Theory of International Trade with Multinational Corporations," *The Journal of Political Economy*, 92 (3), 451–471.

Hummels, D., Jun Ishii and Kei-Mu Yi (2001), "The Nature and Growth of Vertical Specialization in World Trade," *Journal of International Economics*, 54 (1), 75–96.

Markusen, J.R. (2002), *Multinational Firms and the Theory of International Trade* (Cambridge, MA: MIT Press).

Markusen, J.R. and Maskus, K.E. (2002), "Discriminating among Alternative Theories of the Multinational Enterprise," *Review of International Economics*, 10 (4), 694–707.

Markusen, J.R., Venables, A. J., Eby Konan, D., and Zhang, K.H. (1996), "A Unified Treatment of Horizontal Direct Investment, Vertical Direct Investment, and the Pattern of Trade in Goods and Services," National Bureau of Economic Research Working Paper 5696. Cambridge, MA: NBER.

Markusen, J.R., and Maskus, K.E. (2001), "Multinational Firms: Reconciling Theory and Evidence," in M. Blomstrom and L.S. Goldberg (Eds.), *Topics in Empirical International Economics: A Festschrift in Honor of Robert E. Lipsey* (Chicago: University of Chicago Press).

Markusen, J.R. and Venables, A.J. (1998), "Multinational Firms and the New Trade Theory," *Journal of International Economics*, 46, 183–203.

Markusen, J.R. and Venables, A.J. (2000), "The Theory of Endowment, Intra-Industry and Multinational Trade," *Journal of International Economics*, 52, 209–235.

Venables, A.J. (2004), "Vertical Foreign Direct Investment: Input Costs and Factor Prices," in Barba Navaretti, G., and Venables, A.J. (2004), *Multinational Firms in the World Economy* (Princeton: Princeton University Press).

Zhang, K.H. and Markusen, J.R. (1999), "Vertical Multinationals and Host Country Characteristics," *Journal of Development Economics*, 59, 233–252.

Contracting

Antràs, P. (2003), "Firms, Contracts and Trade Structure," *Quarterly Journal of Economics*, 118, 1375–1418.

Antràs, P. (2005), "Incomplete Contracts and the Product Cycle," *American Economic Review*, 95 (3), 1054–1073.

Antràs, P. and Helpman, E. (2004), "Global Sourcing," *Journal of Political Economy*, 112 (3), 552–580.

Antràs, P. and Helpman, E. (2008), "Contractual Frictions and Global Sourcing," in E. Helpman, D. Marin, and T. Verdier (Eds.), *The Organization of Firms in a Global Economy* (Cambridge, MA: Harvard University Press).

Corcos, G., Irac, D.M., Mion G. and Verdier, T. (2008), "The Determinants of Intra-Firm Trade," Centra Studi d'Agliano, Development Studies Working Papers, No. 267.

Defever, F. and Toubal, F. (2007), "Productivity and the Sourcing Modes of Multinational Firm: Evidence from French Firm-Level Data," CEP Discussion Paper No. 842.

Grossman, G.M. and Helpman, E. (2003), "Outsourcing versus FDI in Industry Equilibrium," *Journal of the European Economic Association*, 1 (2–3), 317–327.

Grossman, G.M. and Helpman, E. (2005), "Outsourcing in a Global Economy," *Review of Economic Studies*, 72, 135–159.

Grossman, S.J. and Hart, O.D. (1986), "The Costs and Benefits of Ownership: A Theory of Vertical and Lateral Integration," *Journal of Political Economy*, 94 (4), 691–619.

Helpman, E., Marin, D., and Verdier, T. (Eds.) (2008), *The Organization of Firms in a Global Economy* (Cambridge, MA: Harvard University Press).

Kaufman, D., Kraay, A., and Mastruzzi, M. (2003), "Governance Matters: Governance Indicators for 1996-2005," *Working paper 3106, World Bank.*

McLaren, J. (2000), " 'Globalization' and Vertical Structure," *American Economic Review,* 90 (5), 1239–1254.

Milgrom, P. and Roberts, J. (1992), *Economics, Organization and Management,* (Englewood Cliffs, NJ: Prentice Hall).

Nunn, N., (2007), "Relationship Specificity, Incomplete Contracts and the Pattern of Trade," *Quarterly Journal of Economics,* 122, 569–600.

Nunn, N. and Trefler, D. (2008), "The Boundaries of the Multinational Firm: an Empirical Analysis," in E. Helpman, D. Marin, and T. Verdier (Eds.), *The Organization of Firms in a Global Economy* (Cambridge, MA: Harvard University Press).

Rauch, J. E. (1999), "Networks versus Markets in International Trade," *Journal of International Economics,* 48, 7–35.

Vernon, R. (1966), "International Investment and International Traded in the Product Cycle," *Quarterly Journal of Economics,* 80 (2), 190–207.

Special topics

12

Economic integration

Since the mid-1980s there has been a surge of regional trade agreements (RTAs) around the world as subsets of countries have sought deeper integration among themselves. To date, the best known examples of RTAs include Mercosur, the North American Free Trade Agreement (NAFTA), and the accession of 12 additional countries into the European Union (EU). Agreements such as these are the most notable, but many other initiatives for special association agreements within Europe, Asia and the two American continents have been concluded. Recent examples include:

▲ European Monetary Union (EMU) in 1999;

▲ bilateral free trade agreements between the Association of Southeast Asian Nations (ASEAN) and China, and ASEAN and Japan;

▲ the extension of the Mercosur agreement to include services (besides goods);

▲ a series of bilateral free trade agreements between the US and Australia, Bahrain, Chile, Jordan, Morocco, Oman, Peru, and Singapore.

Through an RTA, a group of countries agree to enjoy freer international economic relations among themselves. In the extreme, this allows for the free movement of goods and services, capital and labor within the integrated area. However, the institutional arrangements under which countries open their borders will differ in reality. The following describes in increasing degrees of intensity the various schemes of integration.

In a *preferential trade agreement*, participating countries offer reciprocal preferred treatment by reducing tariffs and other trade barriers in some categories of goods and services. In 2009 Chile adopted legislation to eliminate tariffs on imports of goods from India. Agreements can be non-reciprocal as well when countries are at different stages of economic development, such as in the US-Caribbean Basin Recovery Act. The legal cover for preferential agreements is the so-called Enabling Clause.

In *a free trade area* (FTA), member countries eliminate tariffs among themselves but maintain individual tariff schedules on imports from non-member countries. As members maintain their own external tariff, imports can enter through the member country with the lowest tariff and then be re-exported to other members. Member countries therefore agree to "rules of origin" that determine whether a good is eligible for a tariff-free treatment. These rules often require that goods contain a high percentage of domestic content to prevent the simple repackaging of goods. The NAFTA fits this definition.[1]

In a *customs union* (CU), members also eliminate tariffs among themselves but establish a common external tariff (CET) against non-members. Customs revenues accrue either to a common fund or to each member's Treasury. Article XXIV of the General Agreement on Tariffs and Trade (GATT) and Article V of the General Agreement on Trade in Services (GATS) spell out the principles for both customs unions and free trade areas.

A *common market* allows the free movement of capital and persons in addition to the requirements of a customs union. The European Union (EU) comes closest to this definition.

Finally, in an *economic union*, members of a common market unify all other economic (fiscal, monetary) and socio-economic (labor, social security) policies. While this is the ultimate goal of the EU, only the "Eurozone" has unified its monetary policy. The US is an economic union.

As of mid-May 2011, some 489 RTAs have been notified to the World Trade Organizaiton (WTO).[2] Of existing RTAs, customs unions account for less than 10 percent while the majority adopts the status of a FTA. Geographically, free trade initiatives are unevenly distributed across various parts of the world. On average, each trading nation is currently a member of six preferential agreements. However, the typical developed country of the northern hemisphere is on average a member of 13 agreements (World Bank, 2005). Given this, the image that emerges from these observations is that of a "spaghetti bowl" of preferential treatments (Bhagwati, 2002). The global economy looks complex beyond comprehension, with a web of treaties and rules whose prospects of a reallocation of global production are fundamental, but not yet fully understood.

The objective of this chapter is to shed some light into the pros and cons of economic integration. It seems a priori that RTAs are a good thing because they represent a move toward freer trade. However, a common feature of these agreements is the discriminatory treatment that favors members relative to non-members. For example, goods imported from member countries face a zero tariff while similar goods imported from non-member countries face a positive tariff. Therefore, the analysis of Section 12.1 focuses on the concepts of the theory, each with different welfare implications. Building upon these results, Section 12.2 outlines the main reasons for economic integration. For example, Kemp and Wan (1976) have proved one of the main theorems in the field to give a rationale for the gradual enlargement of a customs union until all countries of the world are included. Section 12.3 addresses the question whether RTAs are a stumbling or a building block to multilateral trade liberalization. Section 12.4 extends the analysis to include factor markets and examines the empirical evidence. In Section 12.5, we use the theory to highlight the empirics of integration, including simulation results on NAFTA.

12.1 Basic concepts

Trade creation and trade diversion

The traditional treatment of economic integration considers a customs union[3] and focuses on two central concepts: trade creation and trade diversion.[4] Trade creation is the trade created within the CU when production in member countries is replaced by imports from a more efficient producer in the union. Trade diversion is the amount of trade diverted by the CU when imports from an outsider are replaced by imports from a less efficient union producer.

The trade creating and trade diverting effects of a CU are illustrated in Figures 12.1 and 12.2, respectively. The exposition builds on a method of analysis already set out in Chapter 5. Consider a single good and three countries: the home country (H), the partner country (P) and the outside world (W). The home country, assumed small compared with P and W, faces infinitely elastic supply at prices p_p and p_w, respectively. The home country's supply is indicated by the line qq_h in each figure while the line dd_h represents the home country's demand for the commodity. Before H forms a CU with P, H is assumed to have imposed a non-prohibitive, non-discriminatory, *ad valorem* tariff τ on imports from both P and W.

Assume that P is the least-cost supplier (that is, $p_p < p_w$). Before the formation of the CU, the domestic price of imports from P is $p_h = p_p(1 + \tau)$. From Figure 12.1, it is clear that at this price, H produces q_0, consumes d_0 and imports $(d_0 - q_0)$ from P. Now let H form a CU with P. The price of imports from P now drops to p_p and implies a fall in home's production to q_1, an increase in home's consumption to d_1 and a rise in its imports from P to $(d_1 - q_1)$. The sum of the distances q_0q_1 and d_0d_1 represents the amount of trade created by the CU. The welfare

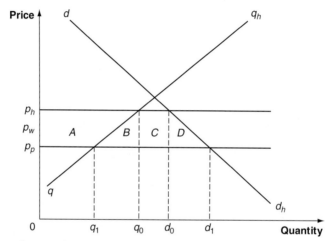

Figure 12.1 A trade-creating customs union

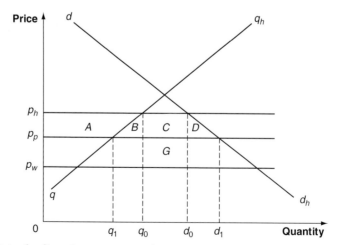

Figure 12.2 A trade-diverting customs union

implication is a loss in the surplus of home producers equal to area A, a loss in tariff revenue measured by area C, and a gain in consumers' surplus measured by area $[A + B + C + D]$. The net welfare gain is therefore area B and D which is positive. Hence, a trade creating CU benefits the home country. The more elastic are the lines qq_h and dd_h and the higher is τ, the larger are areas B and D and the larger the net welfare gain from joining the union.

If W is instead the least-cost source of foreign supply ($p_w < p_p$), the CU will be trade diverting. This is shown in Figure 12.2. This figure is similar to Figure 12.1 except that the roles of prices p_p and p_w have been reversed. Before the formation of a CU, the domestic price of imports from W is $p_h = p_w(1 + \tau)$, the home country consumes d_0 of which q_0 is domestically produced and $(d_0 - q_0)$ is imported from W. If a CU is now formed between H and P, then all imports previously supplied by W will be imported from P at the lower price p_p. This is the pure trade diverting effect of the CU. However, since $p_p < p_w(1 + \tau)$ the volume of imports increases from $q_0 d_0$ to $q_1 d_1$. Hence, there is also trade creation. The decline in the price decreases the producer surplus of home producers by area A, but increases consumer surplus by the amount equal to area $[A + B + C + D]$. Areas C *plus* G show the loss of tariff revenue formerly collected on imports from W. The net effect on the home country's welfare is then area B and D *minus* G which is indeterminate. Hence, a net welfare loss occurs if area G is larger than area B and D. If it is not so then we have an example in which a trade diverting CU is beneficial to the home country.

Trade modification

Trade modification means the change in trade with non-member countries due to the elimination of tariffs on goods traded only within the CU.[5] Assuming that imported goods into the CU are different from those produced within the CU, trade modification claims that the trade flows between member countries could be complementary to those from non-member countries, instead of perfect substitutes as assumed in trade diversion.

Trade modification departs from trade diversion in the following way. Suppose, as an example, that H imports automobiles from P and tyres from W. Upon the abolition of tariffs between H and P, home automobile imports from P increase and tyre imports from W are likely to rise as well. As a result, the bilateral trade flow between H and P is complementary to that between H and W. Call this positive trade modification.

Trade modification resembles trade diversion as follows. Suppose that H imports compact cars from P and full size cars from W. If H abolishes its tariffs on cars from P, imports of compact cars from P increase, partly at the expense of full size cars from W. As a result, the bilateral trade flow between H and P is a substitute for that between H and W as in trade diversion (but for different reasons). Call this negative trade modification.

Quantification: A search for trade diversion

Figure 12.2 has illustrated that the economic desirability of a CU depends on the extent of trade diversion. Measurement of the latter is therefore an important empirical question. Many empirical studies took on the issue, four of which – each with a different emphasis – will be discussed here.

The Johnson approach

Measuring the net welfare effects of a CU is easily done for a single commodity. As shown in Figure 12.2, the negative effect of pure trade diversion are given by area G, which can be estimated as:

$$\text{Area } G = (p_p - p_w)(d_0 - q_0) \tag{12.1}$$

Likewise, the positive welfare effects of trade creation may be approximated by:

$$\text{Area } B = \frac{(p_h - p_p)(q_0 - q_1)}{2} \equiv \varepsilon q_0 \frac{(p_h - p_p)^2}{2} \tag{12.2}$$

$$\text{Area } D = \frac{(p_h - p_p)(d_1 - d_0)}{2} \equiv \eta d_0 \frac{(p_h - p_p)^2}{2} \tag{12.3}$$

where $p_h = p_w(1 + \tau)$ is assumed to be unity, ε is the price elasticity of supply ($\varepsilon > 0$), and η is the price elasticity of demand (defined positively, $\eta > 0$). Adding (12.2) and (12.3) and subtracting (12.1), we can write:

$$\begin{aligned}\text{Area } (B + D - G) = [p_w\tau - (p_p - p_w)]^2(\varepsilon q_0 + \eta d_0)/2 \\ - (p_p - p_w)(d_0 - q_0)\end{aligned} \tag{12.4}$$

Several inferences can be made from (12.4) about the likelihood that a trade-diverting CU is welfare improving. Welfare is increasing in a number of parameters: (1) the more elastic is the demand and supply curve; (2) the lower the difference in production efficiency between P and W (the closer p_p is to p_w); (3) the higher is τ, and (4) the lower the pre-union level of outside imports ($d_0 - q_0$) relative to domestic demand or supply. Johnson (1958) contributed to the analysis of CU by using this method to approximate the sectoral effects of the UK accession to the European Free Trade Agreement (EFTA).[6] Likewise, Bhagwati (1971) showed that to rule out welfare deterioration from a trade-diverting CU the elasticity of supply from P and W must be infinite and more importantly the import elasticity in H must be infinite as well – that is, setting $\varepsilon = \infty$ or $\eta = \infty$ in (12.4).

Apparent consumption

Trade creation and diversion can also be estimated by looking at changes in the sources of supply of goods for a nation that is member of an RTA. It is a matter of computing a country's apparent consumption (d) as the sum of its three components: domestic production net of exports ($q - x$), intra-union imports (m^i) and extra-union imports (m^*). Taking ratios, we obtain the following identity:

$$\frac{(q - x)}{d} + \frac{m^i}{d} + \frac{m^*}{d} = 1 \tag{12.5}$$

(12.5) simply adds the share of each component of apparent consumption: the domestic share (production *minus* exports), a partner share (second term) and an outside share (third term).

Jacquemin and Sapir (1988) compute formula (12.5) for total manufactures in a sample of three EU countries (Germany, France and the UK) over the period 1973–84. The empirical counterpart of (12.5) is given in Table 12.1. Trade creation should be reflected by a fall in the share of consumption that is supplied by a country's domestic producers. Column (1) of Table 12.1 shows that this is the case for all countries, although the evolution as well as the starting and ending percentages vary across countries. Column (2) indicates that the share of intra-union trade rises for all countries. Trade diversion should be reflected by a decrease in the share of EU imports from countries outside the EU. The values in column (3) of Table 12.1 indicate that just the opposite occurred for Germany and France. The UK shows an erratic pattern but no indication of a decrease. Overall, the results are indicative of trade creation with member countries and positive trade modification with non-member countries and again exclude trade diversion on the aggregate.

Table 12.1 Components of apparent consumption, 1973–84[1]

Year	Germany			France			UK		
	(1)	(2)	(3)	(1)	(2)	(3)	(1)	(2)	(3)
1973	85.2	8.7	6.2	81.6	12.3	6.1	78.7	7.5	13.8
1974	84.8	8.8	6.4	79.5	13.2	7.3	75.7	9.2	15.1
1975	84.2	9.2	6.5	81.5	12.1	6.4	79.4	8.4	12.3
1976	82.8	9.8	7.3	79.1	13.7	7.2	77.2	9.5	13.3
1977	82.2	10.1	7.7	78.5	13.9	7.5	76.8	10.0	13.2
1978	81.8	10.3	7.9	78.4	14.1	7.4	76.3	10.3	13.4
1979	80.9	10.7	8.4	77.2	14.7	8.2	75.2	11.2	13.6
1980	79.5	11.0	9.5	76.8	14.4	8.8	74.8	10.8	14.4
1981	78.5	11.1	10.4	76.0	14.7	9.3	76.5	11.2	12.3
1982	77.8	11.6	10.6	74.9	15.5	9.6	75.5	11.9	12.6
1983	77.5	11.8	10.8	74.4	15.7	9.9	73.4	13.1	13.5
1984	75.9	12.1	12.0	73.1	16.3	10.6	71.4	13.7	14.9

[1] column (1) = Domestic production; column (2) = Intra-EU imports; column (3) = Extra-EU imports. Numbers are % (scale 100) of apparent consumption.
Source: Jacquemin and Sapir (1988).

Complementarities among bilateral trade flows

Although the above method of measurement is useful, it assumes that imports and domestic production are perfect substitutes. However, in a world of many commodities, goods might be imperfect substitutes and trade diversion for some commodities could be offset by positive trade modification for the others. There is therefore the empirical question of whether trade flows within the CU are substitutes for, or complementary to, those from outsiders. If complementarities are found, then the negative welfare effects of trade diversion may not exist.

To examine whether bilateral trade flows are substitutes or complements, Viaene (1982) estimates the following system of equations for Spain's bilateral import flow from seven EU countries and the rest of the world (ROW)[7]:

$$m_{lt} = \beta_l^1 \, AV_t + \beta_l^2 \, CAP_t + \beta_l^3 \, p_{lt} + \alpha_l \sum_{i \neq l} m_{it} + u_{lt}, \qquad (12.6)$$

where

m_{lt} = Spain's real aggregate imports from country l at time t

m_{it} = Spain's real aggregate imports from country i $(i \neq l)$

AV_t = Spain's real gross value added in agriculture and industry (a measure of aggregate activity)

CAP_t = rate of capacity utilization of the Spanish economy (pressure of demand variable)

p_{lt} = region l's export price (including tariffs) relative to Spain's domestic price

u_{lt} = disturbance term.

Table 12.2 Substitution and complementarity of Spain's bilateral import flows, 1961–77

Country/ Region	Value	Elasticity
Belgium–Luxembourg	0.0117 (2.795)	0.528
Denmark	0.0027 (1.539)	0.397
France	0.0293 (2.750)	0.281
Germany	0.0393 (2.159)	0.287
Italy	0.0163 (1.960)	0.286
Netherlands	0.0230 (4.883)	0.786
UK–Ireland	−0.0145 (−1.616)	−0.191
Rest of World	0.7708 (3.278)	0.505

t-statistics in parentheses.
Source: Viaene (1982).

Parameter α_l measures the dependency of Spain's bilateral import flow from country l with the sum of all other bilateral import flows $(\sum m_i)$. If the effect of a change of $(\sum m_i)$ on m_l is positive $(\alpha_l > 0)$, the flows are complementary and if negative $(\alpha_l < 0)$, the flows are substitutes.

The system of eight bilateral import equations was estimated using Three Stage Least Squares (3SLS) on annual data for the period 1961–77. Table 12.2 presents the estimates of α_l and the implied elasticity values. The results show evidence of interdependencies in Spain's imports from all sources. The positive values (except for UK-Ireland) indicate that each country's bilateral exports to Spain are complementary with respect to the aggregate of the other bilateral flows. Most notably, Spain's imports from the ROW are complementary with those from EC countries. Hence, if trade between Spain and the EC expands as a result of a CU then Spain's imports from the ROW would also expand. The possibility of trade diversion is therefore not supported by the data.

Endogenous tariff determination

The literature on endogenous tariff formation within integrated areas introduces political economy considerations into the traditional analysis. Besides social welfare, governments' objective function gives weight to political variables. For example, when producers form lobbies in a lobbying framework of the sort originated by the "protection for sale" literature, Grossman and Helpman (1995a) show that the RTAs most likely to arise are those with partners that are relatively inefficient. Higher production costs for P imply a higher price p_p which in the light of (12.4) increases the likelihood of trade diversion.

Richardson (1993) challenges the idea that RTAs exacerbate inefficiencies and proposes the counter-intuitive prediction that trade diversion is expected to decrease endogenously. The reason is that the home country could lower its tariff against the non-partner. Why? Let us outline the argument by referring to Figure 12.2. Area G can be avoided if home switches its imports back to W. This can only be obtained if H lowers its external tariff τ to the level where the non-partner's tariff-ridden price $p_w(1+\tau)$ is just below p_p, the tariff-free price of the partner. Trade diversion is then eliminated. The home country would even obtain tariff revenues without causing any harm to consumers and import-competing firms since $p_w(1+\tau) \approx p_p$. This decrease in the external tariff is endogenous however. If the level τ is determined by some political influence of the industry, as domestic production may reduce from q_0 to q_1, the political support for protection and therefore τ may decrease with integration. Bohara *et al.* (2004) test the Richardson hypothesis using detailed cross-industry data on Argentinian tariffs before and after the formation of Mercosur in 1991. In support of the Richardson hypothesis, the main empirical finding is that an increase in the ratio of intra-union imports to value added does indeed lead to a decline in the external tariff. This makes a case for regional integration.

12.2 Rationale for trade agreements

This section outlines the main reasons for economic integration. These include the optimal tariff whereby an RTA reaches a maximum welfare gain for an integrated area as a whole. This is followed by various models including scale economies. Finally, the theorem by Kemp and Wan (1976) is introduced. This is one of the most important theorems in this field since it gives a rationale for the gradual enlargement of a customs union until all countries of the world are included.

Optimal tariff

Though the implications of terms of trade changes are relevant for individual countries as well, the focus of our analysis is on the setting of an optimal common external tariff (CET) for a customs union. The exposition builds on a method of analysis already set out in Chapter 5. Consider the following two-good economies: H(home), P (partner) and W (the rest of the world). The international equilibrium for good 2 is depicted in Figure 12.3. The curve x_w is non-CU supply of good 2 and the curve m_{cu} is the sum of both home and partner import

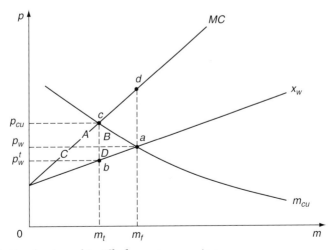

Figure 12.3 Optimal external tariff of a customs union

demands for good 2. Hence, the equilibrium is at point a, with imports m_f from W and price p_w (relative price of good 2).

Though in isolation H and P are assumed too small to affect their terms of trade with W, together in the CU they may have enough market power to affect the equilibrium price. This case is illustrated in Figure 12.3. Because x_w is upward sloping, the marginal cost of imports to the CU exceeds the supply price. This is so because if the CU were to import one less unit, it would save its price p_w. But it would also force down this price and save on what is still imported, the saving being represented by the distance ad.

This is formally shown by writing the supply curve in inverse form as $p = p(x_w)$. Then the cost of imports equals $x_w p(x_w)$. The marginal cost of imports is $p(x_w) + x_w[dp(x_w)/dx_w]$, and can be rewritten as:

$$MC = p(x_w)[1 + (x_w/p(x_w))(dp(x_w)/dx_w)] = p(x_w)[1 + 1/f^*] \qquad (12.7)$$

where f^* is the elasticity of export supply that varies between 0 and ∞. This marginal cost of imports to the union is shown as the MC curve in Figure 12.3. At point a, the import price p_w is less than the marginal cost of m_f units. Hence, by restricting its demand for imports, the CU reduces the equilibrium relative price of imports and will continue to restrict its demand until point c where the internal price in the union equals the marginal cost.

One way to restrict trade is with an *ad valorem* tariff τ. The internal price of the union is then $p_{cu} = p_w(1 + \tau)$. The solution for τ is obtained by setting the internal price p_{cu} equal to the marginal cost of imports in (12.7):

$$\tau = \frac{1}{f^*} \qquad (12.8)$$

The solution for τ is the optimum tariff formula: $\tau = 0$ when the foreign supply is perfectly elastic ($f^* = \infty$), that is when the CU is too small to have market power, and $\tau > 0$ otherwise. It is therefore optimal for a CU to restrict trade with respect to outsiders if $f^* > 0$ and to do it by imposing a CET that corresponds to the inverse export supply elasticity. The CU then achieves a maximum welfare gain for the CU as a whole. Building on the analysis set out in Chapter 5, the welfare gain of this policy to the CU is measured by area C *minus* area B. The welfare loss to W equals area C and D. The net loss in world welfare equals the sum of areas B and D.

Empirical findings

The inverse relationship (12.8) between optimal tariffs and export elasticities holds in broader contexts as well. In Broda *et al.* (2008) social welfare is the sum of individual indirect utilities and governments' maximization of this social welfare function leads to (12.8). The inverse relationship also holds if the government's objective includes political components as well. In Grossman and Helpman (1995a) policymakers maximize a weighted sum of social welfare and contributions from organized lobbies representing factor owners. The solution is an optimal tariff for each of the J sectors of the economy:

$$\tau_j = \frac{1}{f_j^*} + \frac{I_j - \alpha}{a + \alpha} \frac{1}{P_j e_j} \quad j = 1, 2, \dots, J \qquad (12.9)$$

While the first term is the standard terms of trade motive of a tariff the second is the lobby motive. Parameter a is the weight to social welfare in the government's objective function ($a \geq 0$) and reduces the lobby motive to zero when it becomes infinite. Parameter α is the fraction of voters that are represented by a lobby ($0 \leq \alpha \leq 1$) and any increase in α reduces the lobby motive as well. I_j is a binary variable that equals 1 if industry j is politically organized and zero otherwise ($I = 0$ or $I = 1$); P_j is the import penetration ratio – that is, the ratio of imports over domestic production, both in value terms ($0 \leq P_j \leq 1$); e_j is the elasticity of the import demand function that is related to the deadweight loss of a tariff.

Given this, the contribution of Broda *et al.* (2008) is twofold. First they estimate the inverse export supply elasticities ($1/f_j^*$) for 15 counties and goods at the six-digit Harmonized System (HS) level for time periods during which these countries were not member of either GATT or WTO. Second they estimate a relationship like Equation 12.9 to derive terms of trade effects associated with the market power of each country in the sample.

Table 12.3 shows estimates of the inverse export supply elasticity for countries in the sample. The table reports the median of all estimates in any country. For example, the median across all 739 goods in Algeria is 2.8. Hence, the median export supply elasticity in Algeria is 0.357, that is, a 10 percent increase in price increases the export supply of the median good by 3.57 percent. For the full sample, the median inverse export supply elasticity is 1.6, implying a median export supply elasticity of 0.63. Turning now to the estimates of Equation 12.9, the finding is that countries set import tariffs 9 percent higher on inelastically supplied goods relative to those supplied elastically.

Internal economies of scale: Cost reduction and trade suppression

The question of this section is whether economies of scale, assumed to be internal to firms, strengthen the argument in favor of economic integration. The scale economies treatment of a customs union is not very different from that of trade policy of Chapter 10. Results are usually specific to particular models that are representative of particular market structures. Given this, our aim is to construct a minimal model where the concepts relevant to scale economies are introduced (Corden, 1972).[8] Particularly relevant in this context is the way countries adjust their external tariffs to sustain particular market structures after trade integration. Although the evidence is indicative of lower external tariffs, Panagariya (1996) notes that Mexico, Israel and Mercosur raised some of their external tariffs after entering an RTA.

Table 12.3 Inverse export supply elasticity of 15 countries[1,2]

Country	Estimated ($1/f_j^*$): median	Country	Estimated ($1/f_j^*$): median
Algeria	2.8	Lithuania	1.2
Belarus	1.5	Oman	1.2
Bolivia	2.0	Paraguay	3.0
China	2.1	Russia	1.8
Czech Republic	1.4	Saudi Arabia	1.7
Ecuador	1.5	Taiwan	1.4
Latvia	1.1	Ukraine	2.1
Lebanon	0.9	*Median*	1.6

[1] The number of products for which elasticities are estimated varies between 511 for Paraguay and 1125 for China. The table reports the median over each countries' estimates.
[2] Median in the table is the median over all countries and all products.
Source: Broda *et al.* (2008, Table 3A, column 'Medium').

The exposition builds on the method of analysis already set out in the previous section. Consider the market for a single homogeneous good in our three-country model, that is, H, P, which will form a union, and country W. Assume the good is initially or potentially supplied by a single firm in each of the union countries. Country W can supply units of this good at fixed price p_w, the constancy of p_w implying insignificant economies of scale in W resulting from the union. The average cost curve of each firm in each union country is assumed to lie above p_w so that no firm exports to W. In this framework we now explore the concepts of cost reduction and trade suppression associated with market integration. The single-country analysis of these effects is illustrated in Figure 12.4; the two-country analysis, involving H and P, is in Figure 12.5.

Figure 12.4 shows the declining average cost curve of the home producer where point M defines the minimum efficient size. Home demand before and after the formation of the CU is denoted, respectively, as dd_h and dd_{cu}. The latter is the sum of H and P demand.

As $AC_h > p_w$ everywhere, production is profitable only if the country levies a tariff. The tariff rate is "made-to-measure" such that the tariff inclusive import price just equals the average cost. This tariff inclusive price is also the price p_h the profit maximizing firm charges in order to prevent imports. If $p_h < AC_h$ the firm would exit the market and the whole of home's consumption would be imported. If $p_h > AC_h$, the firm would potentially earn positive profits but there would be imports and no domestic production. Without integration, equilibrium is at point a with d_0 being the quantity consumed and produced by the home firm. With integration, equilibrium occurs at the intersection of AC_h and dd_{cu} at the equilibrium price p_{cu}. The CET that guarantees CU production can be lower than before integration. The welfare gain to home consumers corresponds to the area A and B. This gain arises from the cost reduction resulting from a larger internal market. The initial consumption d_o is now obtained at the lower price p_{cu}, the associated gain corresponding to area A. An extra quantity is also purchased at this lower price, on which area B of consumer surplus is obtained.

Firm entry

Consider now the case where a tariff lower than the made-to-measure tariff is applied. Equilibrium is initially at point b with d_2 imported from W at the tariff inclusive price $p_w^t = p_w(1 + \tau)$. Upon market integration, the equilibrium price is p_{cu}, provided the made-to-measure CET is

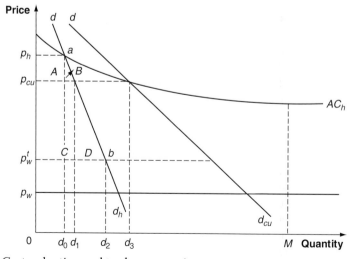

Figure 12.4 Cost reduction and trade suppression

(a)

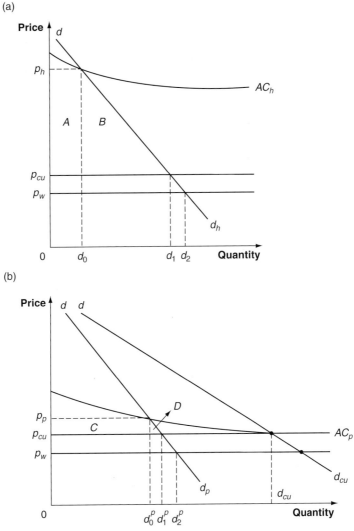

(b)

Figure 12.5 Customs union and internal economies of scale

increased. A home producer could enter the market, produce d_1 for the home country and export $d_1 d_3$ to P. If so, cheaper imports from W will be replaced by more expensive domestic production, which leads to a loss in domestic consumer surplus equal to area C and D. This is the trade suppression effect.

Firm exit

Consider now the case of two firms in two member countries. The H and P markets are represented by panels (a) and (b) of Figure 12.5, respectively. In Figure 12.5, H's demand is dd_h, P's demand is dd_p and the union demand is dd_{cu}, the horizontal sum of dd_h and dd_p. Both H and P are assumed to face price p_w from W. The home firm is assumed to be the least efficient producer.

Given this, the welfare consequences of a CU depend on the pre-union market structure. Of the several cases that can arise, we investigate here the one in which there is initial production in both union countries. This is only possible if both countries initially levy made-to-measure tariffs, H's tariff being larger than P's. Market structures that generate less favorable outcomes are left as an exercise (see Problems 12.2 and 12.3).

The post-union equilibrium is given by the intersection of AC_p and the union's aggregate demand dd_{cu}. Total union production and consumption is d_{cu} at the internal union price p_{cu}. The CET can be less than the two initial tariffs and since $p_{cu} < AC_h$, the home firm exits the union market which is then captured by P's firm.

Home's initial production d_0 is replaced by cheaper imports from P which generates the familiar trade-creation gain equal to area A. The lower union price p_{cu} induces increased consumption $d_0 d_1$ and a welfare gain equal to area B. The total home gain equals area A and B. The partner country's welfare gain corresponds to the area C and D which is the gain from cost reduction.

Welfare

Kemp and Wan (1976) provide conditions under which a set of countries may form a Pareto-improving CU. The result is appealing because it gives an incentive for the gradual enlargement of a CU until all countries are included and hence free trade prevails in the world.

Proposition 12.1 (Kemp-Wan): There exists a common set of tariffs and a system of lump-sum compensatory payments, involving only members of the union, such that there is an associated tariff-ridden competitive equilibrium in which each individual, whether a member of the union or not, is not worse off than before the formation of the union.[9]

The analysis is a general equilibrium description of CU formation. The result assumes any number of countries and commodities and permits there to be trade restrictions and costs of transport. The theorem states that a CU, if properly defined, can potentially be world Pareto-improving. Welfare gains arise from trade creation between members of the union while avoiding trade diversion with the rest of the world. What is required is for the CU to adjust its CET so as to leave trade with the rest of the world the same as before the formation of the CU. The terms of trade and welfare of outsiders will then remain unchanged.

The Kemp-Wan result also requires income transfers between countries such that no member of the union is worse off after the union. A customs union has the ability to provide such cross-country compensatory payments among its members to compensate for the uneven distribution of gains. These payments are normally financed from revenue generated by the union's CET. Upon the formation of the EU for example, tariff revenues formally collected by individual member countries are instead channeled to a common fund. This fund is then used for redistributing income across member countries through regional development programs and various social projects. On balance, each member country can determine its net payment to the rest of the union, whether positive or negative.

Quantification

A testable hypothesis of the Kemp-Wan proposition is whether the actual system of payments within a CU ensures that each member's post-union level of satisfaction is at least equal to its pre-union level. This is precisely the question Grinols (1984) investigated for the UK's entry into the EU.

To understand Grinols's analysis, let the production possibility curve for a country considering joining a CU be given by $T_1 T_2$ in Figure 12.6. Good 1 is on the vertical axis, good 2 on the horizontal axis. Prior to joining the CU, the represented economy is assumed to have levied a non-discriminatory tariff, so that the initial tariff-ridden equilibrium involves production at point a, consumption at point a', and a level of welfare u_0.

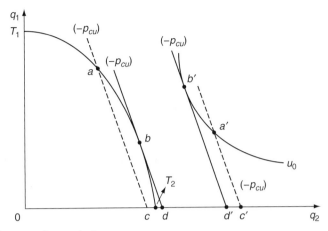

Figure 12.6 The transfer analysis

Upon joining the union, the country adopts the union's CET, which implies the new equilibrium terms of trade p_{cu}. At this price, a transfer to this economy equivalent to the distance cc' is necessary to achieve the pre-accession welfare level u_0. The CU brings, however, gains from substitution in production and in consumption. At the price p_{cu}, production shifts from good 2 to good 1 until the tangency point b. Likewise, substitution in consumption leads to the new consumption point b'. Considering these two gains, the theoretical transfer guaranteeing the welfare level u_0 is dd'. Therefore, the following difference assesses whether the UK's entrance into the EU was welfare improving:

$$T - dd' \overset{>}{\underset{<}{=}} 0$$

In this expression, T is the actual net transfer in pounds from the EU to Britain and dd' is the theoretical transfer. If the difference is positive (negative), then the welfare improved (deteriorated). Grinols computed the annual value of $(T - dd')$ over the period 1972–80. On average over the period, the loss to the UK amounts to more than 1.5 percent of its GDP. In some years, Britain would have been better off by as much as 3 to 4 percent of GDP by not entering the EU.[10]

12.3 Regionalism versus multilateralism

It is clear from Figure 12.3 that the CU's optimal tariff creates a welfare loss for the rest of the world W. We might therefore expect W to retaliate unless it consists of a number of small countries which are unable to organize. The possibility of retaliation gives rise to the debate about the overall desirability of increased regionalism. In particular two intriguing questions are raised: (1) Would the division of the world into regional blocs be expected to lead to global trade conflicts and therefore lower welfare? (2) Do regional agreements compete with or complement the multilateral trading system personified by the WTO? A large number of inspiring papers have contributed to these issues and their answers have been mixed.

Retaliation and global trade wars

The case of retaliation as a result of a CU amounts to solving a non-cooperative tariff policy game. Assume the players in the game are the policy makers of two large economic blocs: the EU and the US. The situation is a two-by-two game because each of the two governments has

Table 12.4 Prisoner's dilemma trade policy game

EU \ US	Free trade	Optimal tariff
Free trade	$(10, 10)$	$(6, 12)$
Optimal tariff	$(12, 6)$	$(9, 9)$

two possible actions in its action set: free trade and an optimal tariff. The payoffs are given by Table 12.4. The payoffs to the blocs represent the level of national welfare realized in each of the four possible scenarios. The US strategies are represented by the two columns; the EU's strategies by the two rows. For example, if the US chooses a free trade policy and EU chooses to impose an optimal tariff then the payoffs are (12, 6): 12 for the EU and 6 for the US.

The non-cooperative solution

In Table 12.4, each player has a dominant strategy. The EU's best response to the strategies chosen by the US is the strategy that yields it the greatest payoff. EU does not know which action US is choosing but if it chooses free trade, EU faces a free trade payoff of 10 and a tariff payoff of 12. Likewise, if the US chooses the optimal tariff policy, the EU faces a free trade payoff of 6 and a tariff payoff of 9. In either case, the EU does better with an optimal tariff policy. Since the game is symmetric, the US's incentives are the same. The Nash equilibrium is therefore (9, 9) – that is, when both regions choose an optimal tariff, the equilibrium payoffs are worse for both regions than free trade.[11]

The cooperative solution

What difference would it make if the two players could reach an agreement before making their decisions? In such an agreement both trading nations might establish a supranational organization like the WTO to monitor commitments and achieve solutions between them. A cooperative game is then possible – the solution would be a set of strategies that would maximize the sum total of the benefits accruing to the two governments. At this cooperative equilibrium, both regions choose a free trade strategy because total world welfare reaches a maximum of 20 units, the equilibrium payoffs being better for both regions than the non-cooperative solution. This simple trade policy game thus offers a simple explanation of the need for an international organization like the WTO.

The above results on retaliation imply that, as new RTAs form, global trade conflicts may emerge that would endanger the post-war cooperation in international trade. A number of contributions to the game-theoretic international trade literature do not, however, support the idea of a global trade war (Perroni and Whalley, 1996). Chisik (2003) shows that trade liberalization as a cooperative relationship can be achieved gradually in a non-cooperative environment. Also, a large share of the new RTAs take the form of free trade areas which, unlike a CU, do not coordinate their external tariff policy. Hence, the retaliatory power of outsiders is not exacerbated (Kennan and Riezman, 1990). Second, trade retaliation in reality is episodic and more of the form of a single retaliatory exchange while non-cooperative tariff games assume that retaliation continues until the Nash outcome is reached. Episodic trade conflict is a feature of recent work on infinitely repeated games that search for conditions under which two countries can sustain freer trade given that they determine trade policies non-cooperatively (Dixit, 1987; Riezman, 1991). In these models, even if cooperation can be sustained over time, periodic reversions to high tariffs will occur in order to provide renewed incentives for countries to cooperate.

Limits to regionalism

It was assumed in Table 12.4 that, when both regions choose an optimal tariff, their equilibrium payoffs are worse than free trade. This raises the question of whether the division of the world into regional blocs is expected to lower global welfare below the free trade level. Krugman (1991) tackles this question in a stylized but elegant model of the world using the love-of-variety utility function of Chapter 8.[12]

Consider a world that consists of N regions that are similar in all respects: same taste and same size. Each region is specialized in the production of a single good that is an imperfect substitute for other $(N-1)$ products. Each region produces one unit of the good to be shared between own consumption and exports to the $(N-1)$ trade partners. A trading bloc is a subset of the world that contains several regions, all equal in size and fully symmetric. Assume there are b such trading blocks ($b \leq N$), each including N/b regions. When $b = 1$, all regions of the world are part of a single bloc and free trade prevails. The question is how world welfare behaves when b departs from unity.

Chapter 8 gives the following measure of aggregate price when the number of consumed varieties is taken into account:

$$P = \left[\sum_{i=1}^{N} p_i^{1-\sigma} \right]^{\frac{1}{1-\sigma}}$$

where $\sigma > 1$ denotes the constant elasticity of substitution between varieties. When $p_i = p$ for all i, we have $P = N^{1/(1-\sigma)}p$: an increase in N lowers P by an amount inversely related to σ. The consumer price of a good made within a bloc is assumed to be 1, that of a good coming from outside is $(1+\tau)$ where τ is an *ad valorem* tariff, common to all regions of a single bloc. The price index in each bloc is thus:

$$P = \left[\sum_{i=1}^{N/b} 1 + \sum_{(N/b)+1}^{N} (1+\tau)^{1-\sigma} \right]^{\frac{1}{1-\sigma}} = N^{1/(1-\sigma)} \left[b^{-1} + (1-b^{-1})(1+\tau)^{1-\sigma} \right]^{1/(1-\sigma)}$$

(12.10)

Consider consumer demands in a particular bloc. Equation (A8.2) gives us the demand for a particular variety as a function of bloc income E and relative prices. Using (12.10) we obtain the demand for variety i when i is produced in the trading bloc:

$$v_i = \frac{P^{\sigma-1}}{p_i^{\sigma}} E = \frac{E}{N(b^{-1} + (1-b^{-1})(1+\tau)^{1-\sigma})}$$

For i not being produced in the trading bloc:

$$v_i = \frac{p^{\sigma-1}}{p_i^{\sigma}} E = \frac{(1+\tau)^{-\sigma} E}{N(b^{-1} + (1-b^{-1})(1+\tau)^{1-\sigma})}$$

The income level E of the trading bloc is the sum of the production value N/b and the tariff revenue levied on the value of the $N(1-b^{-1})$ varieties imported from outside the bloc. Using the equations above this implies:

$$E = \frac{N}{b} + \frac{N(1-b^{-1})\tau(1+\tau)^{-\sigma} E}{N(b^{-1} + (1-b^{-1})(1+\tau)^{1-\sigma})}$$

Solving this equation for the income level E gives:

$$E = \frac{N}{b}\left[\frac{b^{-1} + (1 - b^{-1})(1 + \tau)^{1-\sigma}}{b^{-1} + (1 - b^{-1})(1 + \tau)^{-\sigma}}\right] \tag{12.11}$$

As shown in the Appendix to Chapter 8, the welfare of a trading bloc is equal to $V = E/P$. Since there are b trading blocs in the world, world welfare is $W = bE/P$ and, using (12.10) and (12.11), has the following alternative expression:

$$W = N^{\sigma/(\sigma-1)}\frac{\left[b^{-1} + (1 - b^{-1})(1 + \tau)^{1-\sigma}\right]^{\sigma/(\sigma-1)}}{\left[b^{-1} + (1 - b^{-1})(1 + \tau)^{-\sigma}\right]} \tag{12.12}$$

The major contribution of (12.12) is to establish an important benchmark. With $b = 1$, prices are all equal and world welfare being simply $W = N^{\sigma/(\sigma-1)}$ increases in the number of varieties but decreases in the elasticity of substitution in world trade since goods then become less differentiated.

The comparative statics of (12.12) with respect to parameters other than N cannot be signed *a priori*. Therefore to see how world welfare behaves with respect to b, we perform numerical simulations to give an interpretation to global welfare. Figure 12.7 reproduces these in a two-dimensional graph combining W and b, assuming $N = 10$ and three plausible estimates of σ: $\sigma = 3$, $\sigma = 4$ and $\sigma = 6$. Simulations results are obtained in two steps. First, tariff τ is substituted away in (12.12). Blocs adjust the external tariff optimally and apply optimal tariff formula (12.8). However, in this setting, the inverse export supply elasticity changes with σ and the number of blocs as both change the market power of each bloc. In Krugman (1991), the optimal tariff is obtained as the solution to the following implicit function:

$$\tau = \frac{(1 + \tau)^{\sigma} + b - 1}{((1 + \tau)^{\sigma} + b - 2)(\sigma - 1)}$$

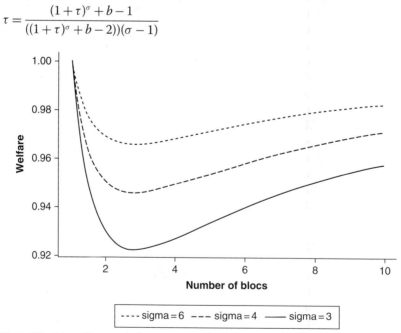

Figure 12.7 World welfare and the number of trading blocs[1,2]

Notes: (1) Numerical simulations relate world welfare W to the number of blocs b; (2) parameter values are $N = 10$ and three estimates of σ: $\sigma = 3, \sigma = 4$ and $\sigma = 6$
Source: Authors' own computations.

Second, simulated values of W are divided by the number $10^{\sigma/(\sigma-1)}$ to normalize world welfare at unity when $b = 1$.[13]

Though the model is too simple to capture a complex world, several interesting points emerge from Figure 12.7. First, the optimal number of trading blocs is 1 – that is, free trade is welfare superior to any other bloc formation. This gives a justification for our selection of payoffs in Table 12.4. Second, the relationship between welfare and the number of blocs is U-shaped, with a minimum reached at a small number of blocs. This result is about the same for different elasticities of substitution. The reason is that when blocs are formed there is a trade-off between trade creation and trade diversion. Trade creation arises because intra-bloc trade increases as tariffs vanish within the bloc. Trade diversion arises as well because, with b small, a large bloc tends to take advantage of its size to increase market power and to set a higher optimal tariff. Third, world welfare is minimized when $b = 3$. This number provides some quantification of policymakers' fear that the trading world might be divided into three zones of economic influence: China, EU and the US. Recently, new RTAs consist of individual countries or groups of countries that wish to join an existing integrated area, either the EU or the US and the fear is that China might play a similar role in the future. This has been termed the "hub and spoke" structure of integration by Wonnacott (1990).

Stumbling block or building block?[14]

The recent literature offers further insight into the question of whether the formation of RTAs helps (a *building* block) or harms (a *stumbling* block) multilateral trade cooperation. So far, answers in the theoretical literature have been mixed. Here are several examples. Ethier (1996) argues that RTAs give newcomers a marginal advantage compared with non-participating small countries in attracting foreign direct investments (FDI) which then gain access to a large market. Bagwell and Staiger (1998) show that, in a repeated game, RTAs are a stumbling block if countries are very patient and a building block otherwise. In a repeated game as well, Saggi (2006) shows that, when countries are asymmetric with respect to either market size or cost, there are circumstances where RTAs facilitate multilateral tariff cooperation. In a political-economy framework, Levy (1997) shows that bilateral free trade agreements can shift median voter preferences against subsequent multilateral free trade.

Though the theoretical literature is ambiguous, the empirical literature so far is not and supports the idea of RTAs harming multilateral trade cooperation. Limão (2006) finds evidence of a stumbling block effect in the US: its RTAs offer smaller reductions in multilateral tariffs of the good it imported from its RTAs relative to non-RTA goods. Karacaovali and Limão (2008) show evidence of a stumbling block effect in the EU as well: several preferential trade agreements of the EU have retarded multilateral trade liberalization. However, this is not the case for countries that have gained full EU membership and therefore access to intra-union transfers.

12.4 Factor markets

The previous sections have focused on the new movements of goods created by an RTA. However, a customs union can also permit factor mobility between union countries. The EU, for example, has gone beyond the idea of a customs union to allow for the overall right of establishment for capital and labor in member countries, becoming thereby a common market. The primary emphasis of this section is on international capital mobility, labor migration having been examined separately in Section 6.3.

We adopt the MacDougall-Kemp model to analyze the effects of international capital mobility. MacDougall (1960) and Kemp (1964) considered the simplest model assuming one good, two homogenous factors of production, two countries and competitive markets. More rigorous models can be found in Ruffin (1984) and in Wong (1995). Though simple, the MacDougall-Kemp model provides answers to contemporanous questions such as: what are the gains from capital mobility for participating countries? What is the effect of capital mobility on the level and distribution of income in these countries? In addition, the analysis is able to identify the group of primary factors that would favor and oppose such capital mobility and, therefore, gives a political economy interpretation to the design of various institutional agreements. Though our framework restricts itself to integrated areas, the analysis can be used to interpret the broader issues of firm relocation.

Capital mobility

Consider two countries, H and P, which will form a common market. Each country produces a single good by means of two primary factors: capital K and labor L. The production functions, $F(K_h, L_h)$ and $F(K_p, L_p)$ respectively, are neoclassical (see Section 4.1) and have similar functional forms. The national capital-labor ratios are assumed to be different, with H being relatively more capital-abundant than P, that is $(K_h/L_h) > (K_p/L_p)$. Normalizing the goods price at unity nominal (and real) returns to capital are equal to the respective value marginal product: $r_h = F_K(K_h, L_h)$ at home and $r_p = F_K(K_p, L_p)$ abroad, where $F_K(.,.)$ is the marginal product of capital.

The left and right vertical axes of Figure 12.8 measure r_h and r_p respectively. The capital stock of both countries is measured by the distance OO^* along the horizontal axis. Any point of this axis denotes an allocation of capital between the two countries. In the absence of capital mobility, OK_0 is owned by H and K_0O^* is owned by P.

The curves hh and pp, drawn with reference to origins O and O^* respectively, relate the capital stock to the physical marginal product of capital in each country. By definition, each curve is drawn holding fixed a country's stock of labor. Each curve is a decreasing function of the capital–labor ratio owing to diminishing marginal returns. Factors in each country are fully employed as long as the real rental rates equal the marginal products. The initial allocation of the factor endowments therefore implies $r_h^0 < r_p^0$ and also $w_h^0 > w_p^0$.

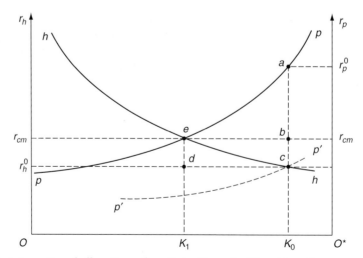

Figure 12.8 International allocation of capital with and without taxation

Total home output produced with capital OK_0 is equal to the area under the curve hh up to K_0. To see this, consider:

$$\int_0^{K_0} F_K(K_h, L_h)dK_h = F(K_0, L_h) - F(0, L_h) = F(K_0, L_h) \tag{12.13}$$

where $F(0, L_h) = 0$ since it is a property of neoclassical production functions that a single factor does not produce any output in the absence of the other. Under our assumptions, the part of output that goes to domestic capital owners equals the real rental rate times the capital stock, $(r_h^0 . OK_0)$. The part of output that goes to labor is the remaining area under each curve. The partner country's output and income distribution are obtained by analogy.

If capital mobility is allowed, capital will flow from the low return to the high return country, that is, from H to P until factor price equalization is achieved at point e in Figure 12.8. At point e, the quantity K_0K_1 of domestically owned capital has been transferred to P and the new equilibrium return to capital is r_{cm}. Given this, P production increases by:

$$\Delta Y_p = \int_{K_0}^{K_1} F_K(K_p, L_p)dK_p = \text{area } eaK_0K_1 \tag{12.14}$$

However, against this increase, there is a less than offsetting repatriation of profits paid to domestic capital owners given by the area ebK_0K_1, thus yielding a foreign gain of eab. This gain accrues exclusively to foreign workers, who also absorb the decrease in the return to foreign capital – the area $abr_{cm}r_p^0$. Clearly, the outflow of domestic capital causes a gain in foreign welfare but the gains are all reaped by foreign workers.

While this reallocation of capital raises P's production, it reduces home's production by ecK_0K_1. The net effect is an increase in union output and welfare that corresponds to area eac. Of the total gain, ebc accrues to H and eab to P. The home country's welfare gain is the income generated by K_0K_1 units of its capital now working in P, area ebK_0K_1 less the loss in domestic product caused by the displacement of these units abroad – area ecK_0K_1. Since home's capital–labor ratio decreases, its real wage rate and real rental rate move in opposite directions.

Taxation

Though some capital flows are observed between wealthy and poor countries, the bulk of capital flows are among the wealthy ones. An intriguing question is why more capital does not flow from rich countries, such as Germany and the US into poorer countries like Africa, Mexico and Latin America until capital–labor ratios, and hence wages and capital returns, are equalized. This is the so-called Lucas paradox (Lucas, 1990).

One reason advanced in the literature is that the simple framework of this section clearly overstates the actual difference in marginal products of capital. A claim is that the assumptions on technology of our model must be amended to account for differences in human capital (Lucas, 1990), institutions (Alfaro et al., 2008), political risks and corporate income taxation. The focus of our analysis is on the latter.

Corporate income tax

Table 12.5 summarizes the statutory corporate income tax rates of 20 OECD countries for 1999 and 2009. Table 12.5 suggests that there is considerable variation in these rates over time and across countries. Although over time there is a certain convergence of corporate tax

Table 12.5 Corporate income tax rates[1,2]

Country	1999	2009	Country	1999	2009
Australia	36.0	30.0	Mexico	35.0	28.0
Belgium	40.2	33.99	Netherlands	35.0	25.5
Canada	42.87	31.32	Poland	34.0	19.0
Czech Republic	35.0	20.0	Portugal	37.4	26.5
France	40.0	34.43	Slovak Republic	40.0	19.0
Germany	52.0	30.18	Spain	35.0	30.0
Greece	40.0	25.0	Sweden	28.0	26.3
Hungary	18.0	20.0	Switzerland	25.09	21.17
Ireland	28.0	12.50	United Kingdom	30.0	28.0
Japan	40.9	39.54	United States	39.39	39.1

[1] This table shows the combined central and sub-central corporate income tax rates.
[2] Percentages.
Source: OECD Tax Database (2009, Table II.1).

rates towards 30 percent, the difference in 2009 between the maximum (Japan) and minimum (Ireland) observation is still large – about 27 percent. The different tax regimes therefore introduce important distortions in the allocation of international investments.

Let us first consider the case where the foreign country P imposes a tax t_p on all capital incomes while capital is not subject to a tax in H. This will of course affect the quantity of home capital that is exported to P and let Z denote these capital exports. Private investors who react to after-tax returns are only interested in the following relationship:

$$F_K(K_h - Z, L_h) = (1 - t_p)F_K(K_p + Z, L_p)$$

Differentiating totally, we obtain:

$$\frac{dZ}{dt_p} = \frac{F_K(K_p, L_p)}{[F_{KK}(K_h, L_h) + F_{KK}(K_p, L_p)]} < 0 \tag{12.15}$$

where $F_{KK}(.,.) < 0$ is the second partial derivative of F with respect to K and where (12.15) is valued at the initial equilibrium, that is $t_p = Z = 0$. Of course, the effect of introducing a foreign corporate tax is to repatriate some domestically-owned capital from P and reduce the stock of domestic capital in the foreign economy.

Consider the graphical analysis of Figure 12.8 and suppose a tax $t_p = ac/aK_0$ is imposed in P. Private investors who react to after-tax returns consider the line $p'p'$ which is obtained by a $ac/aK_0\%$ downward shift of the curve pp. Starting from the free mobility equilibrium point e, the result of this foreign tax is the repatriation of H capital working in P until point c where the after-tax returns are equalized. An amount $Z = K_1K_0$ of domestically-owned capital returns in H. Despite free mobility of capital a differential in gross marginal products prevails and corresponds to that before capital mobility was permitted. There thus exists a finite corporate tax rate that duplicates the pre-mobility allocation of capital stocks even though capital is mobile. The global loss due to foreign taxation corresponds to area eac and completely offsets the initial gain due to the free mobility of capital. Also, deadweight losses associated with taxation are likely to arise in the foreign economy (not shown).

Optimal tax rule

The substantial flows of foreign investments create a taxation problem for both the host and source countries. Of particular importance is the derivation of the optimal tax rule on foreign investment income for a capital-exporting country and for a capital-importing country. To simplify matters we consider only the former case, capital-importing countries being analyzed by analogy. The following result has had a major impact on the field (see Ruffin, 1984).[15]

Proposition 12.2 (MacDougall-Kemp) It pays a capital exporting country that is sufficiently large to affect foreign marginal products to restrict incipiently its capital exports by raising an optimum tax rate on foreign capital income. The optimal tax is equal to the inverse foreign elasticity of demand for imported capital.

To show this result, consider national income NI_h as the sum of production and foreign capital income:

$$NI_h = L_h f\left(\frac{K_h - Z}{L_h}\right) + r_p Z$$

where the production function is expressed as in (4.3). In per capita terms:

$$ni_h = f(k_h - z) + r_p z \tag{12.16}$$

where $ni_h = NI_h/L_h$, $k_h = K_h/L_h$ and $z = Z/L_h$. Also, taxation creates a wedge between the home and foreign marginal returns: $r_h = (1 - t_h)r_p$. To obtain the optimal tax rule we set $\partial ni_h/\partial z = 0$ in (12.16) and solve for t_h:

$$t_h = \frac{1}{\varepsilon_p} \tag{12.17}$$

where $\varepsilon_p = -(\partial z/\partial r_p)/(r_p/z) > 0$. In analogy to optimal tariff formula (12.8), it is optimal for a capita-exporting country to raise a tax on foreign income that is the inverse foreign elasticity of demand for imported capital. However, when $\varepsilon_p = \infty$ the home economy is too small to affect world capital returns and sets $t_h = 0$. Of course the above framework makes the naïve assumption of no retaliation and excludes strategic interactions among countries. To date tax retaliation is one of the major areas of research.

Distribution of economic activity

The position of point e in Figure 12.8 is important because it distributes the total stock of physical capital between H and P after integration. This distribution depends on the slope and the position of the marginal product curves, both being influenced by the technology and the labor resources available to each country. Of course, each country's technology and stock of human capital are the result of current and past policies adopted by policymakers. For example Ireland, although an EU member, independently conducted in the 1980s and 1990s a number of policies (e.g., low corporate tax rate, education reforms) that differed significantly from those followed by other EU member states. These policies attracted multinationals in key sectors to Ireland, particularly from the US, and led some EU firms to relocate to Ireland.

At the same time, Ireland's share of EU-15 GDP rose from 0.6 percent in 1980 to 1.2 percent in 2000.

Bowen *et al.* (2010, 2011) demonstrate how the distribution of resources among members of an integrated economic area (IEA) is obtained. To that end, consider an IEA that consists of $n = 1, \ldots, N$ separate members, each producing a single homogenous good by means of a constant return to scale aggregate production function of the Cobb-Douglas form:

$$Y_{nt} = A_{nt} K_{nt}^{\alpha_n} H_{nt}^{1-\alpha_n} \quad n = 1, \ldots, N, \tag{12.18}$$

where Y_{nt} denotes the quantity of the single good produced, K_{nt} the stock of physical capital, and H_{nt} the stock of human capital (not labor), all for country n at time t. Here A_{nt} is a scale parameter and α_n is capital's share of total output. For simplicity we assume similar technologies across countries, implying a similar α and a similar A_t for all countries. The goods price is normalized at unity. If physical capital and labor are perfectly mobile between the N members then we would expect the (value) marginal product of each factor to be equal. From the N first order conditions of profit maximization with respect to K_n and from the equalization of rates of return to physical capital in the IEA, we obtain:

$$\frac{Y_{1t}}{K_{1t}} = \ldots = \frac{Y_{it}}{K_{it}} = \ldots = \frac{Y_{Nt}}{K_{Nt}} \tag{12.19}$$

Likewise, from the N first order conditions of profit maximization with respect to H_n and from the equalization of rates of return to human capital in the IEA, we obtain:

$$\frac{Y_{1t}}{H_{1t}} = \ldots = \frac{Y_{it}}{H_{it}} = \ldots = \frac{Y_{Nt}}{H_{Nt}} \tag{12.20}$$

The ratio of (12.19) to (12.20) gives the following relationship between ratios of human to physical capital:

$$\frac{H_{1t}}{K_{1t}} = \ldots = \frac{H_{it}}{K_{it}} = \ldots = \frac{H_{Nt}}{K_{Nt}} = \frac{\sum_{n=1}^{N} H_{nt}}{\sum_{n=1}^{N} K_{nt}} \tag{12.21}$$

Like in (12.21), we can rewrite (12.19) as:

$$\frac{Y_{1t}}{K_{1t}} = \ldots = \frac{Y_{it}}{K_{it}} = \ldots = \frac{Y_{Nt}}{K_{Nt}} = \frac{\sum_{n=1}^{N} Y_{nt}}{\sum_{n=1}^{N} K_{nt}} \tag{12.22}$$

Combining (12.21) and (12.22) yields a simple relationship between output, physical capital and human capital for reference member i of the IEA:

$$\frac{Y_{it}}{\sum_{n=1}^{N} Y_{nt}} = \frac{K_{it}}{\sum_{n=1}^{N} K_{nt}} = \frac{H_{it}}{\sum_{n=1}^{N} H_{nt}} \quad i = 1, \ldots, N \tag{12.23}$$

Hence, with perfect capital mobility and similar technology, each economy's share of total output of the integrated area, and each economy's share of total physical capital stock, at any date t equals its share of the total stock of human capital.

Identity (12.23) has an important implication. It contrasts the policies pursued in isolation by any given member with those that are instead pursued jointly (harmonized) across all members of the integrated area. To see this, assume all N economies agree to increase their human capital by a coordinated factor λ. It follows from (12.23) that all shares will remain the same. In contrast, assume that any individual economy i increases its human capital by the same factor λ. It follows that this economy's share of total IEA physical capital and share of IEA output will then increase (as long as this policy is not imitated by other members). The later argument explains Ireland's unusual success.

There are many reasons to believe that (12.23) is too simple to capture a complex world. For example, technology is likely to differ across countries. Also, many barriers to capital mobility (e.g. corporate income tax differentials, capital controls) and labor mobility (e.g. language, different pension systems) would create persistent differences in factor rates of returns between members. Other realistic situations would include the endowment of natural resources, the presence of other sectors like a non-tradable sector and so on. Hence, it is a matter of empirical verification.

It is very likely that the share prediction will not hold exactly but may hold in a statistical sense. Also, the adding-up constraint of shares within each group may imply a non-linear relationship between shares. Given this, we provide an indication of the potential validity of the equal-share relationship by examining a "weak" form of this relationship, namely, that there will be conformity between (pair-wise) rankings of the output and factor shares across members of an economic group. Table 12.6 provides evidence of this weaker proposition by

Table 12.6 Spearman rank correlations for output, physical capital and human capital shares[1]

Economic group	Output-physical capital[2]	Output-human capital	Human capital-physical capital
US States	0.987*	0.981*	0.963*
EU–14[3]	0.956*	0.82*	0.881*
Andean Community	1.0*	0.9*	0.9*
Mercosur	1.0*	0.6	0.6
Latin American Integration Association	0.988*	0.830*	0.818*
Bangkok Agreement	1.0*	0.2	0.2
Southern African Customs Union	0.2	0	0.4
Southern African Development Community	0.661*	−0.164	−0.176
World (64 countries)	0.724*	0.723*	0.464*

[1] Year 2000.
[2] *Indicates when coefficients are significantly different from zero at the 1 percent level; critical values of the tests are obtained from Zar (1972).
[3] See the WTO website for the list of member countries of each RTA.
Source: Bowen *et al.* (2010).

reporting Spearman rank correlation coefficients for pair-wise rankings of the shares across nine economic groups in year 2000. Estimated rank correlations are positive except for SADC and are significant in 18 of the 27 cases. In several cells rank correlations are close or equal to unity, indicating conformity between (pair-wise) rankings. Most correlations are high for US states, EU-14 and Latin American groupings and correlations between output and physical capital shares are higher than in the other two pair-wise computations. Altogether, these results support a "weak" form of the equal-share relationship.

12.5   Empirics of integration

From the exposition so far the integration literature seems fragmented, made piece by piece with few general conclusions. Against this background, empirical analyses of integration have gained in importance and developed essentially along two lines of research. On the one hand, part of the literature has extended the gravity model of Section 6.1 to compute the marginal effects of institutions like RTAs, the WTO and monetary unions. On the other hand, the prospect of NAFTA stimulated a large amount of research on its potential effects. The quantitative assessment of these effects was typically made using Applied General Equilibrium Models (AGE).[16] This section examines some empirical premises of the conjecture that RTAs promote trade, FDI and income of participating countries.

Gravity equations

Rose (2000) initiated a new stream in the empirical literature. He uses the gravity equation to estimate the separate effects of trade agreements and currency unions on international trade. He finds a significant effect on trade for both variables. More specifically, the conclusion is that countries with a common currency would trade three times as much as countries that do not share a common currency. These results led to numerous reactions, most of them questioning the large common currency effects on trade.

Several empirical studies have examined the hypothesis that a regional trade agreement increases members' trade and share of FDI. In a recent study of trade, Baier and Bergstrand (2007) use a gravity model and show that an RTA approximately doubles two members' bilateral trade after 10 years. The contribution of Brouwer et al. (2008) is to assess the implications of EU and EMU for member countries. Empirical results convincingly support a positive effect of EU on trade and investment, and a positive effect of EMU on investment and a non-negative effect of EMU on trade. For Slovenia, for example, the effects of EMU on foreign direct investment are estimated to be about 22 percent, those on trade about 8 percent.

Applied general equilibrium models: NAFTA

Recent decades have seen a wave of regionalism in North America starting in the Canada-US Free Trade Agreement (CUSTA) in 1988 and extended to the NAFTA in December 1992 by including Mexico. The latter agreement reduces and ultimately eliminates most of the barriers to trade and investment (but not to investments in the Mexican oil industry) among Canada, Mexico and the US.

An interesting feature of the NAFTA is that at the time of the agreement participating countries were at widely different stages of economic development and countries had different relative supplies of physical and human capital. One must therefore expect the efficiency gains brought about by free trade and investment to arise for different reasons. Between Canada and the US, gains from freer trade should reflect gains from economies of scale and a reduction in monopoly power of firms along the lines of Chapter 8 and Section 12.2. Between Mexico and its partners, efficiency gains should emerge from increased specialization and a reallocation of resources along the lines of comparative advantage outlined in Chapter 4.

Table 12.7 NAFTA and income: static models with CRS[1]

NAFTA country	Tariffs and NTBs	Tariffs, NTBs and Mexican capital inflow[2]	Tariffs, NTBs, Mexican capital inflow and endogenous migration
Mexico			
Wage[3] R	−0.2	9.2	4.7
UW	−0.2	9.2	4.7
S	1.0	7.4	7.7
WC	1.0	8.8	9.1
Rent	1.1	−1.2	−0.9
Real income	0.3	6.4	6.8
USA			
Wage[3] R	0.3	−0.4	1.8
UW	0.4	0.7	1.8
S	0	0.1	0.0
WC	0	0.3	0.2
Rent	0	1.2	1.1
Real income	0	0.1	0.1

[1] Percentage change with respect to no integration.
[2] A7.6 percent increase in Mexican capital stock.
[3] R = rural; UW = urban unskilled; S = skilled; WC = white collar.
Source: Robinson (1991), cited in Brown (1992).

Tables 12.7 and 12.8 list some of the results generated by these models. Table 12.7 reports the results of three scenarios based on a static model with constant returns to scale (CRS). Column (1) depicts NAFTA simply as a removal of tariffs and NTBs. The estimated welfare changes are therefore the result of intersectoral specialization and the removal of consumption distortions. These results reflect the concepts of trade creation and trade diversion of Section 12.1, a difference being that AGE models take explicit account of resource constraints. The results support a general consensus on the static trade effects of the NAFTA, namely that the effects are small for both Mexico and the US. One reason for this outcome is that restrictions on trade between the US and Mexico were already low except in sensitive sectors (textile). Column (2) and column (3) allow for, respectively, international capital mobility and for international capital and labor mobility. In essence, these two columns are a quantification of the theoretical analysis of Section 6.3 and Section 12.4. The capital inflow into Mexico promises to raise its income. The consequences of migration are less obvious, except for certain types of labor. The results suggest that capital was a major constraining factor in the Mexican economy.

Table 12.8 considers the first two scenarios but assumes increasing returns to scale (IRS) and imperfectly competitive market structures. The essential feature of the model is monopolistic competition with free entry of firms and downward sloping average cost curves. Column (1) of Table 12.8 indicates that non-competitive market structures considerably raise the gains from the NAFTA for Mexico (1.6 percent). Compared with Table 12.7, this extra gain is essentially the result of increased scale economies due to the larger market.[17] Column (2) of Table 12.8 corroborates the powerful effects of foreign direct investment on the Mexican economy shown by the perfectly competitive model.

Table 12.8 NAFTA and income: static models with IRS[1]

NAFTA Country	Tariffs and NTBs	Tariffs, NTBs and Mexican capital inflow[2]
Canada		
Real wage	0.4	0.5
Rent	0.4	0.5
Real income	0.7	0.7
Terms of trade	−0.5	−0.5
Mexico		
Real wage	0.7	9.3
Rent	0.6	3.3
Real income	1.6	5.0
Terms of trade	−0.1	−2.5
USA		
Real wage	0.2	0.2
Rent	0.2	0.2
Real income	0.1	0.3
Terms of trade	0.2	0.0

[1] Percentage change with respect to no integration.
[2] 10 percent increase in Mexican capital stock.
Source: Brown *et al.* (1992, cited in Brown, 1992).

12.6 Concluding remarks

How much is a country willing to pay in order to enjoy free trade with a specified group of countries? Each member state of an integrated area has asked itself this question and evaluated the benefits a country expects to reap from integration. The customs union theory presents a number of arguments in favor of or against economic integration within the framework of economic theory but does not, however, provide clear cut answers. It is mostly an empirical question.

A difficulty with traditional customs union theory and with its extensions to include scale economies is that the field is too broad, with too many particular conclusions to different specifications to be comprehensively treated in a consistent manner. Another criticism is the small number of results. Several reasons have been advanced to explain this lack of progress. First, a difficulty with the customs union theory is that it starts from a distorted initial situation and struggles with the complexity of welfare comparisons inherent in second best analyses. Second, the focus of economic integration is on the customs union. But no convincing argument has been advanced for the superiority of this form of integration compared with, for example, a multilateral reduction of trade barriers. Moreover, it remains unclear whether free trade areas represent a net movement towards freer trade since they adopt rules of origin that govern trade within the area. Third, the focus of the theory has been on the static concepts of trade creation/diversion while the bulk of the effects of economic integration seem to come instead from economies of scale and factor mobility. Lastly, unlike other branches of economics, the customs union theory has not evolved enough in response to empirical research. So, the theory keeps emphasizing the effects of trade diversion whereas little empirical support has been found for this concept. In the light of theoretical uncertainty in connection with the welfare effects, there is a clear need for improved links between theory and data and for renewed empirical investigation of the questions raised by economic integration.

Problems

12.1 Consider a non-preferential tariff reduction such that the tariff inclusive domestic price equals p_p in Figure 12.2. Show that this multilateral tariff reduction is superior to the formation of a CU between H and P.

12.2 Assume instead that P is the only producer of the good. Using Figure 12.4, determine the welfare gains or losses arising from a CU and compare your results with those given in the text. Identify trade diversion in this context.

12.3 Characterize the welfare consequences of a CU for each participating country if only the home firm produces. Identify trade suppression and its welfare effects.

12.4 Consider the production function of the domestic economy (subscript h) and of the foreign economy (subscript p): $Q_h = K_h^{\alpha_h} L_h^{1-\alpha_h}$ and $Q_p = K_p^{\alpha_p} L_p^{1-\alpha_p}$. Before capital market integration between H and P, the national capital–labor ratios are assumed similar. However, the capital shares are different. Hence: $K_h/L_h = K_p/L_p = 1$. Take $L_h = L_p = 1$ and $\alpha_h = 0.4, \alpha_p = 0.3$. Given this information: (1) Give the marginal products of capital in the two countries under autarky. Quantify these with the parameter values given above; (2) If one allows for perfect capital mobility, how much capital will flow from one country to the other? Give a number (three decimals); (3) Verify that the marginal products of capital under capital mobility are similar; (4) Determine the groups of primary factors in both countries that oppose and favor full capital mobility between these two regions.

12.5 Consider the production function of the domestic economy (subscript h) and of the foreign economy (subscript p): $Q_h = K_h^{\alpha} L_h^{1-\alpha}$ and $Q_p = K_p^{\alpha} L_p^{1-\alpha}$. Before capital market integration between h and p, the national capital–labor ratios are assumed different, with h being more capital abundant than p that is: $K_h/L_h = 2 > K_p/L_p = 1$. Take $L_h = L_p = 1$ and $\alpha = 0.4$; (1) Give the marginal products of capital in the two countries under autarky. Quantify these with the parameter values given above. (2) If one allows for perfect capital mobility, how much capital will flow from one country to the other? Give a number. (3) Compute the distribution of economic activity (output, labor, capital) between the two countries after integration. (4) Assume now that country p introduces a corporate income tax rate τ_p. Give the tax rate that re-establishes the pre-mobility allocation of physical capital ($K_h = 2; K_p = 1$).

Notes

1. The NAFTA also liberalizes, to some degree, investment among members.
2. See the WTO website for an update of current and planned free trade initiatives.
3. The formation of a CU attracted great attention among economic theorists, and several books and interpretive survey articles appeared on the subject. See e.g. Michaely (1977).

4. The terminology is from Viner (1950). The concepts used here derive, however, from Johnson (1962) who includes both production and consumption effects whereas Viner focuses on the former only.

5. The terminology is from Ethier and Horn (1984).

6. Equation 12.4 also suggests that the ideal partners for the home country to form a CU should be those whose production efficiency approaches that of the outside world. This suggests that the CU should contain a large number of countries since it is more likely to find a partner whose price is close to the world price.

7. Greece had almost no trade with Spain over the sample period and was therefore excluded from the list of EU member countries.

8. The analyses of this section involve scenarios where only trade barriers change, in contrast to Chapter 10 which also considers market segmentation and its counterfactual, full market integration.

9. See Kemp and Wan (1976) for a detailed list of assumptions and the proof of the proposition.

10. Miller and Spencer (1977) and Viaene (1982) are two other studies on joining the EU. Both assume perfect competition and model the transfer payments explicitly. However, terms of trade changes with third countries are ignored and hence also are potential gains from increased market power. Both studies confirm Grinols' result that joining the EU involved a loss in national income. This negative conclusion is also shared by most models of integration that were constructed in the late 1970s and early 1980s under the paradigm of perfect competition.

11. The Hawley-Smoot Tariff Act of 1930 sparked a trade war among trading nations that reduced the US exports and imports by more than half. The measure raised US tariffs to record levels on over 20,000 goods and in response led to immediate retaliation by US trading partners.

12. The material of this section depends upon Krugman (1991) and Van Marrewijk (2007, pp. 288–289).

13. The literature on economic geography uses many of the ingredients of this model: regions, trading blocs, optimal tariffs, iceberg transport costs and love-of-variety utility functions. As in Figure 12.7 many of the results are obtained and/or illustrated using computer simulations. For example, see Brakman et al. (2009), Combes et al. (2008), Fujita et al. (1999) and Van Marrewijk (2007, ch. 14).

14. The terminology is from Bhagwati (1991).

15. See Ruffin (1984) for a detailed review of the MacDougall-Kemp model. It contains extensions to two-good framework and models international migration simultaneously.

16. See Chapter 5 for a primer on multi-country multi-factor multi-good general equilibrium models. See also Lustig et al. (1992) for a collection of papers on several areas of NAFTA. In this collection, Brown (1992) provides a detailed survey of the structure of the AGE models that have been used to assess the impact of NAFTA. See also Srinivasan et al. (1993) and Francois and Shiells (1994).

17. Harris (1984), Harris and Cox (1984) were the first to show that AGE models with a non-competitive market structure and scale economies generate much larger gains from trade liberalization policy than earlier AGE models with perfect competition and constant returns to scale. Harris (1984) shows also that, at the industry level, both models yield dramatically different results. The hypothesis of no correlation between industry effects of both models is accepted at the 99% level of significance.

References and additional reading

Customs union theory

Bhagwati, J.N. (1971), "Trade-Diverting Customs Unions and Welfare Improvement: A Clarification," *Economic Journal*, 81 (323), 580–587.

Bliss, A. (1994), *Economic Theory and Policy for Trading Blocks* (Manchester: Manchester University Press).

Chisik, R. (2003), "Gradualism in Free Trade Agreements: A Theoretical Justification," *Journal of International Economics*, 59, 367–397.

Cooper, C.A. and Massell, B.F. (1965), "Towards a General Theory of Customs Unions for Developing Countries," *Journal of Political Economy*, 73, 461–476.

Corden, W.M. (1972), "Economies of Scale and Customs Union Theory," *Journal of Political Economy*, 80 (3), 465–475.

Ethier, W.J. and Horn, H. (1984), "A New Look at Economic Integration," in H. Kierzkowski (Ed.), *Monopolistic Competition and International Trade* (Oxford: Clarendon Press), 207–229.

Facchini, G. and Testa, C. (2009), "Who is against a Common Market?" *Journal of the European Economic Association*, 7 (5), 1068–1100.

Grossman, G. and Helpman, H. (1995a), "The Politics of Free Trade Agreements," *American Economic Review*, 85 (4), 667–690.

Hadjiyiannis, C. (2004), "Common Markets and Trade Liberalization," *Canadian Journal of Economics.* 37 (2), 484–508.

Hine, R.C. (1994), "International Economic Integration," in D. Greenaway and L.A. Winters (Eds.), *Survey in International Trade* (Oxford: Basil Blackwell), 234–272.

Johnson, H. (1962), "The Economic Theory of Customs Union," in H. Johnson (Ed.), *Money, Trade and Economic Growth* (London: George Allen & Unwin).

Kemp, M.C. and Wan, H.Y. (1976), "An Elementary Proposition Concerning the Formation of Customs Unions," *Journal of International Economics*, 6, 95–97.

McMillan, J. (1993), "Does Regional Integration Foster Open Trade? Economic Theory and GATT's Article XXIV," in K. Anderson and R. Blackhurst (Eds.), *Regional Integration and the Global Trading System* (New York: Harvester Wheatsheaf), 292–310.

Michaely, M. (1977), *Theory of Commercial Policy* (Chicago: University of Chicago Press).

Richardson, M. (1993), "Endogenous Protection and Trade Diversion," *Journal of International Economics*, 34 (3/4), 309–324.

Viner, J. (1950), *The Customs Union Issue* (New York: Stevens & Sons).

Wonnacott, P. and Wonnacott, R. (1981), "Is Unilateral Tariff Reduction Preferable to a Customs Union? The Curious Case of the Missing Foreign Tariffs," *American Economic Review*, 71, 704–713.

Wooton, I. (1986), "Preferential Trading Arrangements: An Investigation," *Journal of International Economics*, 21, 81–97.

Empirics of trade agreements

Baier, S.L. and Bergstrand, J.L. (2007), "Do Free Trade Agreements Actually Increase Members' International Trade?" *Journal of International Economics*, 71 (1), 72–95.

Baldwin, R.E., Begg, D., Danthine, J.-P., Grilli, V., Haaland, J., Neumann, M., Norman, V., Venables, A. and Winters, A. (1992), *Is Bigger Better? The Economics of EC Enlargement* (London: Centre for Economic Policy Research).

Bohara, A.K., Gawande, K., and Sanguinetti, P. (2004), "Trade Diversion and Declining Tariffs: Evidence from Mercosur," *Journal of International Economics*, 64 (1), 65–88.

Bowen, H.P., Munandar, H., and Viaene, J.-M. (2010), "How Integrated is the World Economy?" *Review of World Economics (Weltwirtschaftliches Archiv)*, 146 (3), 389–414.

Bowen, H.P., Munandar, H., and Viaene, J.-M. (2011), "Are EU Countries less Integrated than US States? Theory and Evidence," *Journal of Regional Science*, 51 (4), 653–677.

Brada, J.C. and Méndez, J.A. (1988), "An Estimate of the Dynamic Effects of Economic Integration," *Review of Economics and Statistics*, 70 (1), 163–168.

Broda, C., Limão, N., and Weinstein, D.E. (2008), "Optimal Tariffs and Market Power: The Evidence," *American Economic Review*, 98 (5), 2032–2065.

Brouwer, J., Paap, R., and Viaene, J.-M. (2008), "Trade and FDI Effects of EMU Enlargement," *Journal of International Money and Finance*, 27 (2), 188–208.

Flam, H. (1992), "Product Markets and 1992: Full Integration, Large Gains?" *Journal of Economic Perspectives*, 6 (4), 7–30.

Grinols, E.J. (1984), "A Thorn in the Lion's Paw: Has Britain Paid Too Much for Common Market Membership?" *Journal of International Economics*, 16, 271–293.

Jacquemin, A. and Sapir, A. (1988), "European or World Integration?" *Weltwirtschaftliches Archiv*, 124 (1), 127–138.

Johnson, H.G. (1958), "The Gains from Freer Trade with Europe: An Estimate," *Manchester School*, 26, 247–255.

Miller, M.H. and Spencer, J.E. (1977), "The Static Economic Effects of the UK Joining the EEC: A General Equilibrium Approach," *Review of Economic Studies*, 136, 71–94.

Rose, A. (2000), "One Money, One Market: Estimating the Effect of Common Currencies on Trade," *Economic Policy*, 30, 9–45.

Smith, A. and Venables, A.J. (1988), "Completing the Internal Market in the European Community: Some Industry Simulations," *European Economic Review*, 32, 1501–1525.

Viaene, J.-M. (1982), "A Customs Union between Spain and the EEC," *European Economic Review*, 18, 345–368.

Willenboekel, D. (1994), *Applied General Equilibrium Modelling: Imperfect Competition and European Integration* (Chichester: John Wiley).

Winters, L.A. and Venables, A.J. (1991), *European Integration: Trade and Industry* (Cambridge: Cambridge University Press).

World Bank (2005), *Global Economic Prospects: Trade, Regionalism and Development* (Washington, DC: The World Bank).

International factor mobility

Alfaro, L., Kalemli-Ozcan, S., and Volosovych, V. (2008), "Why Doesn't Capital Flow from Rich to Poor Countries? An Empirical Investigation," *Review of Economics and Statistics*, 90 (2), 347–368.

Bhagwati, J.N. and Srinivasan, T.N. (1983), "On the Choice between Capital and Labour Mobility," *Journal of International Economics*, 14, 209–221.

Calvo, G. and Wellisz, S. (1983), "International Factor Mobility and National Advantage," *Journal of International Economics*, 14, 103–114.

Cheng, L.K. and Wong, K.Y. (1990), "On the Strategic Choice between Capital and Labor Mobility," *Journal of International Economics*, 28, 291–314.

Findlay, R. and Kierzkowski, H. (1983), "International Trade and Human Capital: A Simple General Equilibrium Model," *Journal of Political Economy*, 91, 957–978.

Helpman, E. and Razin, A. (1983), "Increasing Returns, Monopolistic Competition, and Factor Movements: A Welfare Analysis," *Journal of International Economics*, 14, 263–276.

Kemp, M.C. (1964), *The Pure Theory of International Trade* (Englewood Cliffs: Prentice Hall).

Lucas, R.E. (1990), "Why Doesn't Capital Flow from Rich to Poor Countries?" *American Economic Review*, 80 (2), 92–96.

MacDougall, G.D.A. (1960), "The Benefits and Costs of Private Investment from Abroad: A Theoretical Approach," *Economic Record*, 36, 13–35.

Ruffin, R.J. (1984), "International Factor Movements," in R.W. Jones and P.B. Kenen (Eds.), *Handbook of International Economics*, Vol. 1 (Amsterdam: North-Holland), 237–288.

Wong, K.Y. (1983), "On Choosing among Trade in Goods and International Capital and Labor Mobility: A Theoretical Analysis," *Journal of International Economics*, 14 (3/4), 223–250.

Wong, K.Y. (1995), *International Trade in Goods and Factor Mobility* (Cambridge, MA: MIT Press).

Free trade agreements

Brown, D.K. (1992), "The Impact of a North American Free Trade Area: Applied General Equilibrium Models," in N. Lustig, B.P. Bosworth and R.Z. Lawrence (Eds.), *North American Free Trade: Assessing the Impact* (Washington, DC: Brookings Institution), 26–68.

Brown, D.K., Deardorff, A.V. and Stem, R.M. (1992), "A North American Free Trade Agreement: Analytical Issues and a Computational Assessment," *The World Economy*, 15, 11–30.

Francois, J.F. and Shiells, C.R. (1994), *Modelling Trade Policy: Applied General Equilibrium Assessments of NAFTA* (Cambridge: Cambridge University Press).

Harris, R. (1984), "Applied General Equilibrium Analysis of Small Open Economies with Scale Economies and Imperfect Competition," *American Economic Review*, 74 (5), 1016–1032.

Hinojosa-Ojeda, R., and Robinson, S. (1991), "Alternative Scenarios of US-Mexico Integration: A Computable General Equilibrium Approach," *Working Paper*, 609 (University of California, Berkeley).

Lustig, N., Bosworth, B.P., and Lawrence, R.Z. (1992), *North American Free Trade: Assessing the Impact* (Washington, DC: Brookings Institution).

Srinivasan, T.N., Whalley, J., and Wooton, I. (1993), "Measuring the Effects of Regionalism on Trade and Welfare," in K. Anderson and R. Blackhurst (Eds.), *Regional Integration and the Global Trading System* (New York: Harvester Wheatsheaf), 52–79.

Retaliation and trade warfare

Bhagwati, J.N. (2002), *Free Trade Today* (Princeton, NJ: Princeton University Press).

Coneybeare, J.A.C. (1987), *Trade Wars: The Theory and Practice of International Commercial Rivalry* (New York: Columbia University Press).

Dixit, A. (1987), "Strategic Aspects of Trade Policy," in T.F. Bewley (Ed.), *Advances in Economic Theory: Fifth World Congress* (Cambridge: Cambridge University Press), 329–362.

Grossman, G.M. and Helpman, E. (1995b), "Trade Wars and Trade Talks," *Journal of Political Economy*, 103 (4), 675–708.

Johnson, H.G. (1954), "Optimum Tariffs and Retaliation," *Review of Economic Studies*, 21 (2), 142–153.

Kennan, J. and Riezman, R. (1990), "Optimal Tariff Equilibrium with Customs Unions," *Canadian Journal of Economics*, 23 (1), 70–83.

Perroni, C. and Whalley, J. (1996), "How Severe is Global Retaliation Risk under Increasing Regionalism?" *American Economic Review Papers and Proceedings*, 86 (2), 57–61.

Riezman, R. (1982), "Tariff Retaliation from a Strategic Viewpoint," *Southern Economic Journal*, 48, 583–593.

Riezman, R. (1985), "Customs Unions and the Core," *Journal of International Economics*, 19, 355–365.

Riezman, R. (1991), "Dynamic Tariffs with Asymmetric Information," *Journal of International Economics*, 30 (3/4), 267–283.

Regionalism versus multilateralism

Aghion, P., Antràs, P., and Helpman, E. (2007), "Negotiating Free Trade," *Journal of International Economics*, 73 (1), 1–30.

Bagwell, K. and Staiger, R.W. (1998), "Regionalism and Multilateral Tariff Cooperation," in J. Pigott and A. Woodland (Eds.), *International Trade Policy and the Pacific Rim* (London: Macmillan).

Bhagwati, J.N. (1991), *The World Trading System at Risk* (Princeton, NJ: Princeton University Press).

Bond, E. and Syropoulos, C. (1996), "The Size of Trading Blocs: Market Power and World Welfare Effects," *Journal of International Economics*, 64 (1), 65–88.

Ethier, W.J. (1996), "Regionalism in a Multilateral World," Working Paper, International Economics Research Center, University of Pennsylvania.

Karacaovali, B. and Limão, N. (2008), "The Clash of Liberalizations: Preferential vs. Multilateral Trade Liberalization in the European Union," *Journal of International Economics*, 74, 299–327.

Krishna, P. (1998), "Regionalism and Multilateralism: A Political Economy Approach," *Quarterly Journal of Economics*, 113 (1), 227–251.

Krishna, P. (2003), "Are Regional Trading Partners Natural?" *Journal of Political Economy*, 111 (1), 202–226.

Krugman, P.R. (1991), "Is Bilateralism Bad?" in E. Helpman and A. Razin (Eds.), *International Trade and Trade Policy* (Cambridge, MA: MIT Press), 9–23.

Levy, P.I. (1997), "A Political-Economic Analysis of Free-Trade Agreements," *American Economic Review*, 87 (4), 506–519.

Limão, N. (2006), "Preferential Trade Agreements as Stumbling Blocks for Multilateral Trade Liberalization: Evidence for the United States," *American Economic Review*, 96 (3), 896–914.

Panagariya, A. (1996), "The Regionalism Debate: An Overview," *The World Economy*, 22 (4), 477–511.

Saggi, K. (2006), "Preferential Trade Agreements and Multilateral Tariff Cooperation," *International Economic Review*, 47 (1), 29–57.

Sampson, G.P. (1996), "Compatibility of Regional and Multilateral Trading Agreements: Reforming the WTO Process," *American Economic Review Papers and Proceedings*, 86 (2), 88–92.

Wonnacott, R. (1990), *US Hub-and-Spoke Bilaterals and the Multilateral Trading System* (Toronto: Howe Institute).

Integration and economic geography

Brakman, S., Garretsen, H., and Van Marrewijk, C. (2009), *The New Introduction to Geographical Economics*, 2nd ed. (Cambridge: Cambridge University Press).

Combes, P.-P., Mayer, T. and Thisse, J.F. (2008), *Economic Geography: The Integration of Regions and Nations* (Princeton, NJ: Princeton University Press).

Fujita, M., Krugman, P. and Venables, A.J. (1999), *The Spatial Economy* (Boston, MA: MIT Press).

Van Marrewijk, C. (2007), *International Economics: Theory, Application, and Policy* (Oxford: Oxford University Press).

Econometric methods

Zar, J.H. (1972), "Significance Testing of the Spearman Rank Correlation Coefficient," *Journal of the American Statistical Association* 67(339), 578–580.

13

Exchange rates and international trade

The collapse of the Bretton Woods system of fixed exchange rates in 1973 raised theoretical and empirical issues about the consequences of flexible exchange rates for international trade. International trade theory has little say about such effects since it traditionally restricts itself to models in which no nominal exchange rate is defined.[1] On the other hand, models of the international monetary theory rarely address issues of trade patterns. Recent research attempts to connect these two fields by incorporating the nominal exchange rate in trade models. These research efforts can be viewed as a step taken by the international trade literature to reconsider its assumptions about imperfect competition, capital and exchange rate markets.

An important factor affecting firms' foreign trade and investment decisions is the volatility in the major currencies of the world as illustrated by the behavior of the US dollar in the last three decades. This is exemplified in Figure 13.1 where the euro/dollar exchange rate and its volatility (approximated by the coefficient of variation) are displayed for the period January 1999 to February 2011. The figure shows large swings in the level of the euro/dollar rate but also in the volatility of the currency, in particular during the financial crisis of 2008–09. Fluctuations in the currency matter for international trade because of the forward-looking behavior of firms as a result of the time gap between the production date and the payment date for goods. These fluctuations give rise to both "level" and "risk" effects of exchange rates. Of specific interest is the effect that increased exchange rate volatility may have on the level of trade and the role of the forward exchange market in this context. Central to the issue is the popular conjecture that the floating exchange rate regime has led to a decrease in the volume of trade.

This chapter examines topics that attempt to link the exchange rate to international trade. We consider four issues. Section 13.1 considers the role of exchange rates in a partial equilibrium framework and derives the two major results in the field, namely the so-called separation proposition and the full hedging proposition. Section 13.2 looks at the choice of invoice

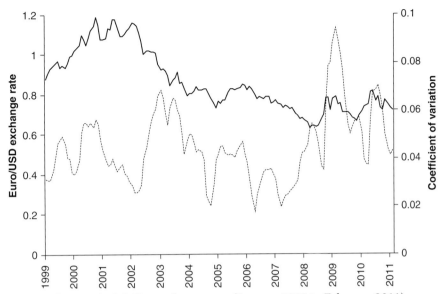

Figure 13.1 The euro/US dollar exchange rate (January 1999 to February 2011)

Notes: (i) The continuous line displays the monthly euro/US dollar exchange rate over the period January 1999 to February 2011 (end of month observations). (ii) The broken line shows the rolling coefficient of variation of the euro/US dollar (standard deviation over the mean exchange rate). It is computed over a rolling window of 12 months starting in January 1998.

currency. Section 13.3 analyzes the factors affecting the pass-through from exchange rates to import prices. Finally, Section 13.4 treats the concept of hysteresis.

13.1 Trade and exchange rate volatility

The exporter's risk-bearing optimum

Consider the problem of a risk-averse domestic firm that produces a single product for export. A production level q entails a cost $C(q)$ where the cost function $C(\cdot)$ is assumed to be strictly convex, increasing and twice differentiable, that is, $C' = \partial C / \partial q > 0, C'' = \partial^2 C / \partial q^2 > 0$ and $C(0) = 0$, primes denoting partial differentiation. Markets are assumed competitive and the world price of the product, expressed in foreign currency, is p^*.

A characteristic of international trade is the practice of extending trade credit. Once goods are delivered, the exporter allows the foreign buyer to defer payment until a fixed future date. Thus, there are two dates: one on which goods are produced and delivered, and one on which they are paid for. The exporter's receipts in domestic currency are given by $\tilde{e}p^*q$ where $\tilde{e}$ is the unknown future spot exchange rate. The exchange rate is defined as the domestic currency price of the foreign currency and the tilde refers to the random nature of the future spot rate. The exporter can cover the exchange rate uncertainty arising from his foreign currency exposure by selling an amount k of foreign currency forward at the known forward exchange rate e_f. This forward transaction will add $(e_f - \tilde{e})k$ to his local currency profits. Given this, the exporter's profit function on the date at which payment is received can be written:

$$\tilde{\Pi} = \tilde{e}p^*q - C(q) + (e_f - \tilde{e})k \tag{13.1}$$

The exporter will choose q and k so as to maximize the expected utility of profits $EU(\tilde{\Pi})$, where E is the expectations operator. $U(\cdot)$ is a strictly concave, increasing and differentiable

Von Neumann-Morgenstern utility function defined over the exporter's profits $\tilde{\Pi}$. The first-order conditions for this maximization problem are:

For q: $EU'(\tilde{\Pi})[\tilde{e}p^* - C'(q)] = 0,$ (13.2)

For k: $EU'(\tilde{\Pi})[e_f - \tilde{e}] = 0,$ (13.3)

where $U'(\cdot)$ is the marginal utility and $EU'(\tilde{\Pi}) > 0$. Using (13.3) to substitute for $\tilde{e}$ in (13.2) gives the solution for the optimal level of export:

$$e_f p^* = C'(q) \qquad\qquad (13.4)$$

The optimal level of export is chosen so as to equate the marginal cost of production to the domestic currency price of q. It is clear from (13.4) that the optimal level of q is independent of exchange rate uncertainty. This result is known as the "separation proposition."

Proposition 13.1 (Separation): When there is access to a forward exchange market, the optimal level of exports is independent of both the distribution of the exchange rate $\tilde{e}$ and the exporter's attitude towards risk.

An implication is that any two firms with the same cost function but with different attitudes toward risk, and with different probability beliefs about the future exchange rate, will produce the same quantities of output. This is the important contribution of a forward market.[2] A second key result in this literature determines the optimal level of k and is known as the "full hedging proposition":

Proposition 13.2 (Full hedge): If the forward exchange market is unbiased, namely $E\tilde{e} = e_f$, then the value of the optimal forward contract is $k = p^*q$.

To demonstrate this result, note that strict concavity of $U(\cdot)$ implies $\text{cov}[\tilde{\Pi}, EU'(\tilde{\Pi})] \leq 0$, with equality holding when profits $\tilde{\Pi}$ are not random. Making use of $(13.1) - (13.3)$ we have:

$$\text{cov}[\tilde{\Pi}, EU'(\tilde{\Pi})] = -EU'(\tilde{\Pi})[(p^*q - k)(E\tilde{e} - e_f)] \leq 0 \qquad\qquad (13.5)$$

(13.5) implies:

$$(p^*q - k)(E\tilde{e} - e_f) \geq 0. \qquad\qquad (13.6)$$

The difference $(E\tilde{e} - e_f)$ is the risk premium and indicates the extent to which the exporter's expectation of the future exchange rate deviates from the market forward rate. When $(E\tilde{e} - e_f)$ is positive, the difference is called a normal backwardation. When negative, this expression is a cotango, when zero, an unbiased forward market. In the latter case, that is, $E\tilde{e} = e_f$, (13.6) is zero and profits $\tilde{\Pi}$ are no longer random. From (13.1), the necessary condition for profits to be non-random is:

$$k = p^*q, \qquad\qquad (13.7)$$

which states that the exporter hedges his export transaction completely. If $E\tilde{e}Le_f$ then from (13.6) it follows p^*qLk, that is, the exporter sells a smaller or greater amount of foreign exchange than his foreign currency receipts. If the forward market is biased, it is optimal for the exporter to speculate on the forward exchange market by taking a short or long position depending on whether the risk premium is negative or positive, respectively.

An example

Assume a trading house that buys commodities on the domestic market and resells them abroad. Further assume that the trading house faces the following inverse supply function for domestic goods: $p = d + q/2$, where d is a constant and q is the quantity purchased at home and sold abroad. The value of domestic purchases is then $dq + q^2/2$. The trading house receives a price p^* in foreign currency on each unit exported and hence earns a total of $\tilde{e}p^*q$ in domestic currency. The profit function of the trading house is then:

$$\tilde{\Pi} = \tilde{e}p^*q - dq - q^2/2 + (e_f - \tilde{e})k \tag{13.8}$$

where k is the amount of forward foreign currency sold at the forward rate e_f.

For analytical convenience, let this exporter's *ex ante* probability beliefs about the value of $\tilde{e}$ be described by a normal probability density function. The distribution has mean $E\tilde{e}$ and variance σ^2, where these values are conditional on the exporter's information set on the decision date. Since $\tilde{e}$ is normally distributed, profits are also normally distributed with mean $E\tilde{\Pi}$ and variance $\mathrm{var}\tilde{\Pi}$. Suppose that $U(\tilde{\Pi}) = -e^{-\alpha\tilde{\Pi}}$ where $\alpha = -U''(\tilde{\Pi})/U'(\tilde{\Pi})$ is the measure of (constant) absolute risk aversion.[3] Expected utility can then be written as $EU(\tilde{\Pi}) = -e^{\alpha(E\tilde{\Pi}-(\alpha/2)\mathrm{var}\tilde{\Pi})}$ given our assumption of normality.[4] Hence, maximizing $EU(\tilde{\Pi})$ is equivalent to maximizing:

$$EV = E\tilde{\Pi} - \frac{\alpha}{2}\mathrm{var}\tilde{\Pi} \tag{13.9}$$

(13.9) is the traditional mean-variance utility function. Using the above profit function, expected profits, the variance of profits and the expected utility of profits take the following form:

$$E\tilde{\Pi} = p^*qE\tilde{e} - dq - \frac{q^2}{2} + (e_f - E\tilde{e})k$$

$$Var\tilde{\Pi} = E\left[\tilde{\Pi} - E\tilde{\Pi}\right]^2 = E\left[\tilde{e} - E(\tilde{e})\right]^2 \left[p^*q - k\right]^2 = \sigma^2 \left[p^*q - k\right]^2$$

$$EV = p^*qE\tilde{e} - dq - \frac{q^2}{2} + (e_f - E\tilde{e})k - \frac{\alpha}{2}\sigma^2(p^*q - k)^2 \tag{13.9'}$$

Maximizing (13.9′) with respect to q and k gives the following optimal solutions:

$$q = p^*e_f - d \tag{13.10}$$

$$k = p^*q - \frac{E\tilde{e} - e_f}{\alpha\sigma^2} \tag{13.11}$$

In (13.10) q does not depend on α or σ^2 which corroborates the separation result (13.4). A change in the forward rate, however, will affect the trade level of q according to the conventional terms of trade analysis. The optimal hedge in (13.11) has two components: a speculation term and the sale of forward currency for trade purposes. The former component, $(E\tilde{e} - e_f)/\alpha\sigma^2$, adds or subtracts from the trade component depending on the sign of the risk premium, that is, $(E\tilde{e} - e_f)$. Contrary to popular belief, it does not take risk-loving agents to get speculative positions. The amount of speculation is decreasing in α and σ^2 but increasing in the risk premium. If the risk premium is zero, the full hedge result, that is, $k = p^*q$, obtains.

Inserting (13.10) and (13.11) in (13.8) and then computing (13.9) gives the level of expected utility at the optimum:

$$EV = \frac{q^2}{2} + \frac{(E\tilde{e} - e_f)^2}{2\alpha\sigma^2} \qquad (13.12)$$

The first term in (13.12) is the expected utility attached to international trade, while the second is the expected utility from speculation. The speculation term vanishes if the forward market is unbiased. If, in addition, the separation result holds, the exporter avoids exchange risk altogether and is indifferent between a fixed or flexible exchange rate regime.

This last conclusion is counter to the popular conjecture that increased exchange rate volatility reduces the volume of trade. However, there are situations in which this conjecture is obtained, two of which are pursued here. The first considers the absence of a forward market; the second questions the exogeneity of the forward rate (Viaene and de Vries, 1992).

No forward market

This situation relates to the case when the trading firm has no access to a forward exchange market. This applies to many developing and transitional economies where well-developed foreign markets do not exist and to industrial countries where access to the market is too costly. If the firm does not have access to a forward market then k in (13.8) is zero. Maximizing (13.9) with respect to q only gives:

$$q = \frac{p^* E\tilde{e} - d}{1 + \alpha p^{*2}\sigma^2} \qquad (13.13)$$

which compares to (13.10). Consider a mean-preserving spread change – that is, a higher volatility of the exchange rate (a higher σ^2) while maintaining the mean $E\tilde{e}$ constant. By (13.13), this change lowers the level of trade and the exporter's expected utility.

A general equilibrium analysis

The separation proposition derived in (13.4) is a partial equilibrium outcome and does not always hold in the general equilibrium sense that the aggregate net supply of forward currency determines e_f. To see this, consider the market clearing condition on the forward market and assume that the number of exporters, importers and speculators is n, m and s, respectively. All agents are assumed to have the same degree of risk aversion $\alpha > 0$. Adding the amounts of forward foreign currency sales by exporters (see (13.11)), importers (see Problem 13.1) and speculators (see Problem 13.2) and solving for the equilibrium forward rate gives:

$$e_f = E\tilde{e} - \Omega\sigma^2(TB + F) \qquad (13.14)$$

where $\Omega = \alpha/(m + n + s)$ measures aggregate risk aversion, TB is the trade balance and F is an exogenous term that represents net forward sales of foreign currency by the central bank.[5] The solution in (13.14) expresses the forward rate in terms of the expected exchange rate, the risk aversion parameter, the conditional variance of $\tilde{e}$ (σ^2) and the net foreign currency exposure of the economy ($TB + F$). A striking implication of this framework is that a change in the volatility will have opposite effects on imports and exports. The intuition behind this result is that importers and exporters are on opposite sides of the forward market. An increase in σ^2 in (13.14) causes, *ceteris paribus*, the forward rate to increase (assuming $(TB + F) < 0$) which increases exports (see (13.10)) and decreases imports (see Problem 13.1). Who gains

Table 13.1 Effect of exchange rate volatility on US bilateral trade flows

US trading partner	US exports to	US imports from
UK	−0.086 (−4.27)	−0.132 (−2.54)
Netherlands	−0.040 (−1.31)	−0.099 (−2.98)
France	−0.043 (−0.75)	−0.091 (−2.46)
Germany	−0.034 (−1.16)	0.086 (1.78)
Canada	−0.055 (−2.44)	−0.125 (−2.40)
Japan	0.064 (2.01)	−0.086 (−2.24)

Note: Elasticities (and *t*-ratios) of US bilateral trade flows with six countries with
respect to bilateral exchange rate volatility (1974–83).
Source: Cushman (1988).

or loses from this increase in exchange risk therefore depends on the net aggregate foreign currency exposure $(TB + F)$: if negative, exporters gain and importers lose and vice versa.[6]

Empirical results

Several empirical studies have examined the hypothesis that increases in exchange rate volatility reduce trade. The results differ depending on whether the analysis assumes the existence of a well-developed forward market. Studies of developing countries in which forward markets are absent generally find a negative relationship between trade and exchange rate volatility (Coes, 1981). For countries with forward markets, no consistent link between volatility and trade has been found. Table 13.1 exemplifies these mixed results by showing the elasticity of US bilateral trade flows to exchange rate volatility. This elasticity is obtained by regressing US bilateral trade flows on a measure of volatility of the bilateral exchange rate with each partner country.[7] Estimates are of either sign and are not always significantly different from zero. In particular, positive elasticities are observed for US exports to Japan and imports from Germany.[8] In contrast, most studies confirm that an increase in the mean level of the exchange rate (a depreciation) does increase exports (not shown).

Consider now a more recent dataset that consists of 29 industrial countries' bilateral trade flows over the period 1980–04. The objective is to test relationship (13.14) using gravity models of Chapter 6. Gravity models consider both bilateral exports and imports to a single country and are therefore the ideal setup to test (13.14). To that end, let us assume F = 0 and proxy TB by the natural logarithm of bilateral exports over bilateral imports and multiply it by the natural logarithm of volatility (TB*ln volatility). Hence, the sign and absolute value of the elasticity of exchange rate volatility are now allowed to vary across time and across all bilateral trade flows in the sample. Table 13.2 reports the estimates of our measure of volatility corrected by the trade balance on trade flows. The negative sign that is expected from the theory is also obtained in Table 13.2. Estimates are significant but small in magnitude indicating small effects of exchange rate volatility on trade flows. However, the absolute value of elasticity estimates increases with the extent of trade unbalance between any two countries.

13.2 The choice of the invoice currency

Apart from the product price and the forward rate, the currency used in an invoice has an important influence on the conduct of international trade. In choosing the currency of invoice

Table 13.2 **Effect of exchange rate volatility on bilateral trade flows of 29 countries**

Variable	Country FE	Country pair FE	Country FE + time FE	Country pair FE + time FE
TB* ln Volatility	−0.084 (0.00)	−0.060 (0.00)	−0.085 (0.00)	−0.063 (0.00)

Notes: (i) Elasticities of bilateral trade flows between 29 countries (Canada, Japan, Switzerland, the US and 25 countries that were EU members in 2004) with respect to bilateral exchange rate volatility. (ii) Volatility is defined as the standard deviation of the monthly percentage changes in the real exchange rate within a year. (iii) Panel least squares over the period (1980–2004) where FE = fixed effects. (iv) p-values in parentheses.
Source: Brouwer *et al.* (2008).

one also chooses which of the two parties to the transaction bears the risk of the exchange rate fluctuations – namely the party whose receipts and costs are not labeled in the same currency. For example, in (13.1), the exporter's receipts are denominated in foreign currency while his costs are denominated in local currency. Hence it is optimal for the exporter to hedge against exchange rate risk.

An empirical regularity relating to the choice of invoice currency is Grassman's (1973) empirical observation that trade is usually invoiced in the exporter's currency. More recent data are given in Table 13.3. This empirical finding has been revisited by several authors (e.g., Goldberg and Tille, 2009). Deviations from this finding are also well recorded (Basevi *et al.*, 1985).

Explanations as to why invoicing is predominantly in the exporter's currency has not received much attention. Bilson (1983) offers a macroeconomic explanation; Giovannini (1988) derives a result that depends on whether profits of a risk-neutral exporter are a concave or a convex function of the exchange rate; Fukuda and Cong (1994) argue that demand conditions in the foreign markets explain the choice of invoice currency by Japanese exporters; Viaene and de Vries (1992) advance as an explanation the strategic non-cooperative bargaining between exporters and importers; Goldberg and Tille (2009) focus on the contribution of macroeconomic variability relative to that of industry-specific features in the selection of an invoice currency.

The hedge decision

Friberg and Wilander (2008) report survey results regarding the currency choice of Swedish exporters. One of the many results is that negotiations matter for prices and the choice of invoice currency. Given this, the bargaining approach by Viaene and de Vries (1992) seems a suitable framework to examine the issues involved. Consider a situation where a domestic exporter and a foreign importer have agreed to trade one unit of a commodity. The exporter charges the price p in his or her currency and charges p^* in foreign currency. Assuming that the domestic currency is the exporter's currency in which his profits are expressed and maximized, the expression for the exporter's profit is:

$$\tilde{\Pi} = \lambda p + (1-\lambda)\tilde{e}p^* - c + (e_f - \tilde{e})k \tag{13.15}$$

where $\tilde{e}$ is the future domestic price of foreign currency, e_f is the forward rate, k is the net supply of forward foreign currency, and c is the per unit production cost in domestic currency. Due to trade credit, the exporter will receive $\lambda p + (1-\lambda)\tilde{e}p^*$ in the future, where λ is the invoice parameter indicating the proportion of domestic currency receipts. To shield himself

Table 13.3 Share of trade contracts denominated in domestic and foreign currency (% of total)

Country	Year of observation	Exports of goods			Imports of goods		
		EUR	US$	HOME	EUR	US$	HOME
USA	2003	–	95	95	2.0	90.3	90.3
Australia	2003	1.4	67.5	27.8	9.4	47.9	32.6
Indonesia	2004	1.2	93.6	0.0	5.7	82.5	0.4
Japan	2003	9.6	48.0	38.4	4.5	68.7	24.6
Thailand	2003	2.7	84.4	5.0	4.3	76.0	5.6
Belgium	2004	57.7	29.6	57.7	55.5	35.1	55.5
France	2003	52.7	33.6	52.7	45.3	46.9	45.3
Germany	2004	61.1	24.1	61.1	52.8	35.9	52.8
Greece	2004	44.3	51.2	44.3	40.6	55.3	40.6
Netherlands	2002	52.0	35.2	52.0	48.0	43.8	48.0
Portugal	2004	57.6	27.4	57.6	58.8	32.6	58.8
Spain	2004	62.6	29.1	62.6	61.1	35.5	61.1
UK	2002	21.0	26.0	51.0	27.0	37.0	33.0
Czech Republic	2003	70.3	13.5	9.6	67.6	18.3	9.3
Hungary	2004	84.8	9.6	2.3	70.8	18.8	6.3
Lithuania	2005	54.8	40.8	1.4	61.0	34.2	1.3
Poland	2004	69.3	21.4	5.1	61.7	26.1	8.5
Ukraine	2004	7.6	78.0	0.4	14.1	76.9	0.4
OPEC	1976	0.0	95.0	0.0	0.0	–	0.0

Notes: EUR = share of trade invoiced in euros; US$ = share of trade invoiced in US dollars; Home = share of trade invoiced in domestic currency; – = not available; selection of countries and period is based on data availability.
Source: Scharrer (1979, cited in Black, 1985), Kamps (2006), Goldberg and Tille (2009).

from the uncertain future spot rate, the merchant can take a hedge k by buying or selling foreign currency forward.

Denote the mean and variance of $\tilde{e}$ as $E\tilde{e}$ and σ^2, respectively, and assume further that the exporter maximizes the mean-variance utility function (13.9) with respect to k. The optimal hedge is then:

$$k = [e_f - E\tilde{e}]/\alpha\sigma^2 + (1-\lambda)p^* \qquad (13.16)$$

and the level of expected utility is:

$$EV = \frac{1}{2}[e_f - E\tilde{e}]^2/\alpha\sigma^2 - c + \lambda p + (1-\lambda)e_f p^* \qquad (13.17)$$

Note that the exporter hedges only a part of his exposure unless the risk premium is zero, that is, $e_f = E\tilde{e}$ when the exporter hedges completely. Even without foreign currency risk, that is, $\lambda = 1$, a risk-averse exporter will still undertake a favorable bet: $k = (e_f - E\tilde{e})/\alpha\sigma^2$. Now consider the case in which the invoice parameter is not exogenous but can instead be determined by the exporter. Since expected utility (13.17) is now a function in λ, differentiation gives:

$$\frac{\partial EV}{\partial \lambda} = p - e_f p^*$$

It is clear that exporters' preferences regarding invoicing do not depend on σ^2 since forward markets are used but depend upon the level of the exchange rate e_f as it transforms the foreign price in home currency. Since EV is linear in λ, EV increases (decreases) with λ as p exceeds (is less than) $e_f p^*$. Since the relevant domain of λ is restricted to the interval $[0, 1]$, three solutions to the above equation may prevail.

First, if $p = e_f p^*$, then any $0 \le \lambda \le 1$ generates the same expected utility and the choice of the invoice currency is irrelevant. Second, if $p > e_f p^*$, then $\partial EV/\partial \lambda > 0$ for $0 \le \lambda \le 1$ and expected utility attains its maximum at the corner solution $\lambda = 1$. Third, if $p < e_f p^*$, then $\partial EV/\partial \lambda < 0$ and expected utility attains its maximum at $\lambda = 0$. If we exclude the case $p = e_f p^*$ and focus on $p < e_f p^*$ or $p > e_f p^*$ (when $\lambda = 0$ or 1) then we need to ask which case, $\lambda = 0$ or $\lambda = 1$, will be the observed outcome. To answer this, we must introduce the preferences of the importer. If the foreign importer sells the imported product in his or her local market at a price expressed in his or her own currency, then it can be shown (see Problem 13.3) that when $p > e_f p^*$, it is optimal for the importer to set $\lambda = 0$ – that is, the importer would prefer to pay in his own currency. However, this conflicts with the exporter's preferences and it is possible by a similar reasoning to show that the conflict holds when $p < e_f p^*$. Hence, how can we resolve the conflict over the invoice parameter between the importer and exporter? One way is to apply models of non-cooperative bargaining that discuss the partition of a melting cake between two parties (Rubinstein, 1982; Sutton, 1986; Rubinstein, 1987).

Sequential bargaining

Imagine that both parties bargain over the value of an invoice parameter by alternating bids until an agreement is reached. Depending on the specifics of the commodity being traded we distinguish between two cases. The first case presumes that the bargaining over λ can be studied in isolation from market considerations. For example, this could arise in the case of trade in non-standardized commodities such as capital goods where the option of finding another importer or exporter is very costly. However, for trade in standardized commodities, market considerations have to be taken into account, because each party can opt out and contact a new partner.

In the first case, assume that each party, in turn, makes an offer in terms of λ and the other party may agree to the offer or reject it. If the other party accepts, the game ends; if the offer is rejected, a counteroffer is made at the next stage; and so on, with no limit on the number of repetitions of the process. As time is an important factor in international trade, each party discounts the final agreement by a discount factor, δ_x and δ_m for the exporter and importer respectively $(\delta_x, \delta_m < 1)$.[9] The discount factors provide an incentive for the players to reach an agreement.

It was shown by Rubinstein (1982) that, in this game, the agreement is immediate and that there is a unique partition which can be supported as a subgame perfect equilibrium.[10] To show this,[11] consider the subgame beginning with an offer made by the exporter at time $t = 2$. Let $\hat{\lambda}$ be this offer, which represents the supremum of the invoice parameter the exporter can expect in this game. Then, $\delta_x \hat{\lambda}$ is the discounted value of this parameter to the exporter at time $t = 1$. Hence, any offer at time $t = 1$ by the importer which gives the exporter a share less than $\delta_x \hat{\lambda}$ will certainly be rejected by him at period 2. So the invoice parameter the importer can obtain cannot be more than $(1 - \delta_x \hat{\lambda})$. This discounted at time $t = 0$ gives $\delta_m(1 - \delta_x \hat{\lambda})$. At time $t = 0$, any offer by the exporter that gives the importer a share of the trade contract in his or her currency less than $\delta_m(1 - \delta_x \hat{\lambda})$ will certainly be rejected by him at period 1. Hence, the exporter will obtain at most a share in own currency equal to $(1 - \delta_m(1 - \delta_x \hat{\lambda}))$. However, this must equal $\hat{\lambda}$ which solves for the equilibrium value of $\hat{\lambda} = (1 - \delta_m)/(1 - \delta_m \delta_x)$. The importer receives $(1 - \hat{\lambda})$. This is the solution reported in Table 13.4.

The result has the feature that the more patient a player, the greater his share in own currency. As δ_x approaches 1 the agreement reaches $\hat{\lambda} = 1$ and the importer faces the full exchange rate risk (vice versa with $\delta_m \rightarrow 1$). There is also a first-mover advantage: for example, when $\delta_x = \delta_m = \delta$, then $\hat{\lambda} = 1/(1 + \delta)$. The party that goes first will therefore have an advantage over the party that goes second since more than half of the trade transaction will be invoiced in the first party's currency. The case in which δ_m is actually equal to 0 leads also to the agreement $\hat{\lambda} = 1$. This characterizes markets for standard homogeneous commodities like primary inputs and precious metals that are quoted in a single currency. In these markets where there is no time to bargain for the invoice currency, transactions are invoiced in a single currency, mostly in US dollars. To avoid a bias towards US dollars the recent empirical literature controls for the degree of product differentiation (e.g., Kamps, 2006; Goldberg and Tille, 2009). A typical example is to use Rauch's (1999) classification that divides commodities into three broad categories: differentiated goods, standard homogeneous goods and non-standard homogeneous goods.

When market considerations matter, it can be shown that the currency of exporters dominates if importers outnumber exporters, since exporters will have some monopoly power. A concrete example helps to illustrate the bargaining power of exporters. The Netherlands had 7701 registered exporters and 9406 registered importers in 1987. Of these, 2923 firms produced and exported manufactured goods directly, while 723 firms produced and imported manufactured goods directly. The rest of the firms were trading houses, focusing either on exports or on imports. Production of manufactures is therefore concentrated, while trading

Table 13.4 The invoice parameter

Discount factors	$\hat{\lambda}$	$1 - \hat{\lambda}$
$0 < \delta_x, \delta_m < 1$	$\dfrac{1 - \delta_m}{1 - \delta_x \delta_m}$	$\dfrac{\delta_m(1 - \delta_x)}{1 - \delta_x \delta_m}$
$\delta_x \rightarrow 1$	1	0
$\delta_m \rightarrow 1$	0	1
$\delta_m \rightarrow 0$	1	0
$\delta_x = \delta_m = \delta$	$\dfrac{1}{1 + \delta}$	$\dfrac{\delta}{1 + \delta}$

Notes: (i) Table 13.4 presents the equilibrium solution $\hat{\lambda}$ conditional upon $p > p^* e_f$ and the exporter having the advantage of making the first offer. The exporter receives $\hat{\lambda}$ and the importer $1 - \hat{\lambda}$. If the importer is the first proposer, the two outcomes have to be interchanged. (ii) δ_x, δ_m represent the discount factors of the exporter and importer, respectively.

activities are spread across a larger number of distributors, and hence importers. Producers that export have a bargaining advantage over the importer since they have a better chance of finding another partner if a deal cannot be made. This analysis is consistent with Grassman's (1973) finding on the use of exporters' currency.

13.3 Prices and exchange rates

The large fluctuations of exchange rates in the last two decades have drawn attention to the pricing policies of international firms. To remain competitive, exporting firms are thought to respond incompletely to exchange rate movements by adjusting their export prices and their mark-up over marginal cost. This phenomenon is termed "exchange rate pass-through" (EPT). Considerable theoretical and empirical research has examined the pricing policies by firms and the differences in the behavior of US and foreign firms. The results have often been used to explain the persistent US trade deficit in spite of the large depreciation of the US dollar starting in the mid-1980s. The argument is that prices and trade volumes of imperfectly competitive industries react less to exchange rate movements than would competitive ones.[12]

Concepts and definitions

The concept of EPT can be best seen by focusing on the pricing behavior of firms which produce both for export and the domestic market. Firms sell in the domestic market at the price p_d and in the export market at the foreign currency price p^*. Firms are assumed to be interested in their domestic currency profits. The relevant price is then the domestic currency price of exports, that is, $p = ep^*$ where the exchange rate e is the domestic currency price of foreign currency. Expressing $p = ep^*$ in relative changes and dividing by $\hat{e}$ gives two related measures of EPT:

$$\varepsilon = 1 + \varepsilon^* \tag{13.18}$$

The first, $\varepsilon = \hat{p}/\hat{e}$, is the elasticity of the domestic currency export price with respect to the exchange rate. The second, $\varepsilon^* = \hat{p}^*/\hat{e}$, is the elasticity of the foreign currency export price with respect to the exchange rate. EPT can be measured by either ε or ε^* (13.18) indicating the relationship between them.[13]

   EPT is complete, incomplete or perverse if a depreciation of the exporter's currency ($\hat{e} > 0$) causes the domestic currency price of exports to be unchanged ($\varepsilon = 0$), to increase ($\varepsilon > 0$) or to decrease ($\varepsilon < 0$). Complete EPT implies that firms maintain own-currency prices and profit margins on their foreign sales constant and mechanically pass any exchange rate change through to buyers. Incomplete EPT implies that exporters absorb some portion of an exchange rate change in their mark-up of price over marginal cost. When the exchange rate depreciates ($\hat{e} > 0$) firms experience rising margins and when the exchange rate appreciates ($\hat{e} < 0$) falling margins. A perverse EPT is theoretically justified when firms seek to increase their market share abroad (Froot and Klemperer, 1989).

   The concept of "pricing to market" (PTM) refers to the case in which exporting firms charge a different price in home and foreign markets.[14] In terms of the above framework, this implies that p and p_d need not be the same. While some natural dispersion in prices is expected when there are transport costs, if prices still differ after correcting for these, then the residual can reflect (i) ineffective spatial commodity arbitrage[15] or (ii) segmented markets where firms are able to discriminate between countries – that is, they are able to set different prices and different mark-ups in different countries.[16]

The exchange rate pass-through under oligopoly

To understand the analytics of EPT, we consider a model of oligopoly of firms in a foreign market due to Dornbusch (1987). This model assumes a single homogeneous commodity and a linear demand for this good:

$$d^* = a^* - p^* \tag{13.19}$$

where d^* is foreign market demand, p^* the price denominated in the currency of the foreign market, a^* a constant capturing the non-price determinants of demand. The foreign market is supplied by n^* foreign firms (indexed i), selling the quantity q_i^* in their local market and by n domestic firms (indexed j) exporting the quantity x_j. It is assumed that: (1) all firms adopt a Cournot quantity strategy; (2) there are barriers to entry so that the number of firms is fixed; and (3) markets are segmented so that we need only focus on prices and quantities in the foreign market.

A foreign firm seeks to maximize its foreign currency profits:

$$\Pi_i^* = (p^* - c^*)q_i^* \quad i = 1, \ldots, n^*$$

where c^* is the foreign firm's constant marginal cost of production. In contrast, a domestic exporting firm maximizes domestic currency profits:

$$\Pi_j = (ep^* - c)x_j \quad j = 1, \ldots, n$$

where c is the domestic firm's constant marginal cost. Since aggregate sales across firms sum to market demand, profit maximization by foreign firm i and domestic firm j with respect to output gives rise to the following reaction functions:

$$a^* - (n^* + 1)q^* - nx - c^* = 0 \tag{13.20}$$

$$a^* - n^*q^* - (n+1)x - \frac{c}{e} = 0 \tag{13.21}$$

where symmetry within each group of firms $(x_j = x, \forall j; q_i^* = q^*, \forall i)$ is assumed. Given this, the reaction functions give the optimal behavior of the representative firm of each group. These functions are depicted in Figure 13.1, the domestic firm's reaction curve being RC, the foreign being R^*C^*.

Solving (13.20) and (13.21) yields the Cournot-Nash equilibrium solution for domestic exports and foreign production:

$$q^* = \frac{1}{(n+n^*+1)}\left[a^* - (n+1)c^* + n\frac{c}{e}\right] \tag{13.22}$$

$$x = \frac{1}{(n+n^*+1)}\left[a^* + n^*c^* - (n^*+1)\frac{c}{e}\right] \tag{13.23}$$

The output supplies depend on the marginal costs in foreign currency. By (13.19), the equilibrium price in the foreign market is:

$$p^* = \frac{1}{(n+n^*+1)}\left[a^* + n^*c^* + n\frac{c}{e}\right] \tag{13.24}$$

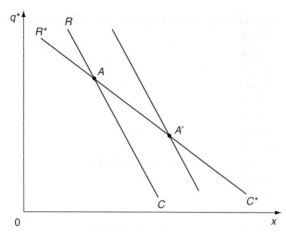

Figure 13.2 The Cournot equilibrium

The industry price depends on a (weighted) sum of the marginal costs in foreign currency of all firms in the market. Given (13.24) and the definition of profits, it is straightforward to show that $\Pi^* = q^2$ and $\Pi = ex^2$.

A devaluation of the exporters' currency (or equivalently an appreciation of the foreign currency, $\hat{e} > 0$) will shift the exporters' reaction curve RC to the right in Figure 13.2. The new Cournot-Nash equilibrium is A', which implies an increase in the market share of exporting firms and a decrease in the market share of foreign firms. The industry price declines, as is seen from (13.24) since an increase in the supply of exports more than offsets the reduction in foreign supply. This depreciation causes also domestic profits to increase because of (i) a level effect of the exchange rate for given quantities and (ii) a relative price effect leading to an increase in exports.

Another key result of this analysis is to show the equivalence between trade policy and exchange rate movements. Equivalence is measured here in terms of output (and profits) and trade policy is assumed to be either a foreign import tariff or a domestic export subsidy. A devaluation has therefore an interpretation similar to that of a domestic export subsidy as both shift RC to the right in Figure 13.2. In contrast, an appreciation has an interpretation similar to that of a foreign tariff on imports since both shift the domestic reaction curve to the left.[17]

Proposition 13.3 (Equivalence): In oligopoly models with Cournot competition an appreciation of the exporter's currency is equivalent to a foreign tariff on imports; a depreciation of exporter's currency is equivalent to a domestic export subsidy.

It is clear that exchange rate fluctuations that are currently observed on exchange markets are far larger than most bound tariffs. Proposition 13.3 is therefore important because it shows how these changes in exchange rates feed into oligopoly models and affect market equilibria.

The last result of this analysis is an expression for the EPT measure. Take the definition of ε in (13.18) and apply it to the reduced form expression for the market price obtained in (13.24) then the EPT measure is:

$$\varepsilon = 1 - \frac{n}{(n + n^* + 1)} \frac{c}{ep^*} \tag{13.25}$$

This indicates that the EPT has two determinants in this model: the relative number of exporting firms and the ratio of marginal cost to the domestic currency price of exports. Noting that $\partial\varepsilon/\partial n < 0$ and $\partial\varepsilon/\partial n^* > 0$ (13.25) allows a comparison of EPT expressions for different assumptions about market structure. A limiting case is when the number of foreign firms relative to the number of home exporting firms is low ($n \to \infty$): EPT is then complete ($\varepsilon = 0$) since price is equal to the marginal cost in the same currency ($p^* = c/e$). If the number of foreign firms is large instead ($n^* \to \infty$) then domestic exporters are price takers and $\varepsilon = 1$. The cases $n^* = 0$ and $n = 1$ correspond to the case of a monopoly and imply $\varepsilon = 1 - c/2ep^*$ so that EPT is incomplete ($\varepsilon > 0$).

Assuming forms of imperfect competition different from those assumed here yields other expressions for EPT than (13.25). These expressions imply that, besides the role of market structure contained in (13.25), the theoretical value of ε depends on (1) the functional form of demand (Dornbusch, 1987; Feenstra, 1989); (2) the functional form for costs (Cheffert, 1994) and (3) the degree of product substitutability in foreign markets (Dornbusch, 1987).

Empirical studies of EPT have, however, not been able to devise tests that can discriminate between these alternative determinants of the value of ε. In particular, a testing of the significance of ε is not a proper test of which theory underlies any particular value of ε. Since one cannot test the theory underlying ε, studies instead focus on the sign of ε and whether it significantly differs from zero. A positive and significant ε indicates incomplete EPT while an insignificant ε is indicative of complete EPT.

Testing of the PTM hypothesis

Analyses of the PTM hypothesis focus on how the ratio of own-currency export price relative to domestic price compares across industries and countries, how it evolves over time, and how it responds to changes in the exchange rate. Marston (1990) undertakes such a test using data on pricing by Japanese manufacturing firms in export and domestic markets.[18] In particular, he looks at the relative price (ep^*/p_d) for 17 Japanese final products over the period from February 1980 to December 1987 and relates this ratio to changes in real exchange rates, real wages and other factors like market structure and industrial production.

The parameter of interest is the PTM elasticity which measures the sustained effect of a rise in the real exchange rate (a depreciation) on the ratio of export to domestic prices. The estimates obtained ranged in size from 0.406 (trucks) to 1.03 (tyres and tubes) for eight products consisting of transport and tractor equipment and from 0.278 (microwave ovens) to 1.11 (amplifiers) for nine consumer products; two coefficients were not significantly different from zero (small trucks, cameras). All elasticities were positive, indicating that a yen depreciation (appreciation) leads Japanese firms to raise (lower) their domestic currency export price relative to their domestic price, evidence of pricing to market. For example, the PTM elasticity of 0.406 for trucks indicates that a rise in the real exchange rate by 1 percent raises the export-domestic price ratio by 0.406 percent.

13.4 Hysteresis

The preceding analysis has focused on the short-run effects of exchange rate changes. However, it is conceivable that entry and exit of firms in response to sufficiently large real exchange shocks can have lasting effects on the market structure, prices and trade volumes.

Models that explore the longer-term effects of exchange rate changes use the concept of hysteresis. Hysteresis is defined as:

> ...an effect that persists after the cause that brought it about has been removed. The argument is that firms must incur sunk costs to enter new markets, and cannot recoup these costs if they exit.
>
> (Dixit, 1989b, p. 205)

The possibility of hysteresis arising from exchange rate shocks was put forward by Baldwin (1988). Baldwin and Krugman (1989) expand this analysis while Dixit (1989a, 1989b) examines hysteresis using the theory of option pricing to analyze investment decisions.[19] These models examine entry and exit decisions of domestic firms in a foreign market. Specifically, firms are assumed to incur a sunk capital cost to enter the market and a fixed maintenance cost to stay active in the market. Sunk costs include the costs of adapting the product to local market conditions (e.g., health and safety regulations, product launching through advertising, and setting up a distribution, sales and service network). Maintenance costs are necessary to prevent sunk assets from disappearing and, hence, the firm from exiting.[20]

Entry and exit conditions

To illustrate hysteresis, consider the model of the previous section, characterized by the solutions (13.22) to (13.25). Recall that the equilibrium profit of each domestic firm is $\Pi = ex^2$ when denominated in domestic currency and $\Pi/e = x^2$ when denominated in foreign currency. Assume for simplicity that firms have static expectations about the exchange rate. Let F be the cost to enter the foreign market and X be the maintenance cost, both being measured in foreign currency. Given this, we consider the export decision of domestic firms under alternative outcomes of profits (and, hence, about the exchange rate):

$$\begin{cases} \text{If } x^2 > F, \text{ enter the foreign market} \\ \text{If } x^2 < X, \text{ abandon the foreign market if already entered} \end{cases} \qquad (13.26)$$

The optimal decision rule (13.26) involves two trigger values of profits, F and X with $F > X$. A domestic firm should enter the foreign market if x^2 rises above F and should abandon the market if x^2 falls below X. Hence, it must be the case that in equilibrium:

$$F \geq x^2 \geq X \qquad (13.27)$$

This relation establishes a range of profits and exchange rates within which the number of firms in the foreign market is constant. Within this range, it is optimal for firms to maintain their current position. Assume that the solution given by (13.22) to (13.24) satisfies (13.27), with inequalities holding strictly. Also, assume that n^* is constant, but that the number of domestic firms may change in response to profits to be earned. A period-by- period Cournot-Nash equilibrium can then be computed.

Figure 13.3 depicts the decision rules given by (13.27). The curves FF and XX give the combinations of e and n such that $x^2 = F$ and $x^2 = X$ respectively. Making use of (13.23), one obtains:

$$n = \frac{1}{\sqrt{F}}\left[a^* + n^*c^* - (n^* + 1)\frac{c}{e}\right] - n^* - 1 \quad FF \text{ curve}$$

$$n = \frac{1}{\sqrt{X}}\left[a^* + n^*c^* - (n^* + 1)\frac{c}{e}\right] - n^* - 1 \quad XX \text{ curve}$$

The XX curve lies to the right of the FF curve because, for a given exchange rate, a lower level of profit can only be achieved by a higher number of domestic firms. Between these two curves is the zone of inaction.[21] Both curves are increasing (at a decreasing rate). Starting from any point on FF, a rise in profits following a depreciation of the domestic currency (an increase in e) has to be offset by entry in order to maintain profits at F. Alternatively, starting from any point on XX, an appreciation leads to a decline in profits below X and leads firms to exit the market until the equality of profits with X is re-established.

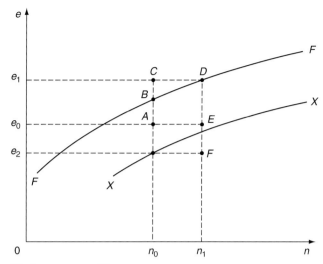

Figure 13.3 Equilibrium range of firms

Extensive and intensive margins of trade

Exports in this framework and world trade in general evolve at two margins: the intensive margin and the extensive margin. The intensive margin refers to variations through time of the amount of trade of exporting firms that have already entered the foreign market. But exports may also increase because new firms that did not export before now decide to enter the foreign market and establish a new trade relationship: this is the extensive margin. In Figure 13.3 we consider a sequence of unexpected changes in the exchange rate and analyze their effects on the market structure in the foreign country. The corresponding changes in the two margins are reproduced in Table 13.5. To understand the sequence of events let us recall the following partial derivatives of the preceding section:

$$\frac{\delta x}{\delta e}\Big|_n > 0, \ \frac{\delta x}{\delta n}\Big|_e < 0 \quad \text{and} \quad \frac{\delta nx}{\delta n}\Big|_e > 0$$

Starting from point A in Figure 13.3, a small exchange rate depreciation that brings the exchange rate, let us say, to B does not affect market structure. The level of exports of existing domestic firms increases and the foreign price p^* falls as a consequence of the reduction in the

Table 13.5 Extensive and intensive margins of exports

Path of changes	Intensive margin of trade (1)	Extensive margin of trade (2)	Total exports (3) = (1) + (2)
$A \to B$	+	0	+
$B \to C$	+	0	+
$C \to D$	−	+	+
$D \to E$	−	−	−
$A \to D$	+	+	+
$A \to E$	−	+	+

Note: The path of changes in the first column corresponds to that of Figure 13.3.

domestic marginal cost measured in foreign currency. In contrast, at a larger exchange rate depreciation like C, profits rise above entry costs and the new equilibrium moves to point D. At D, $(n_1 - n_0)$ new domestic firms have entered the foreign market. If the shock subsequently reverses itself (point E) the initial market structure is not restored. The number of firms remains higher than before since the exchange rate appreciation is not large enough to induce the exit of firms. The initial market structure will only be restored if the exchange rate were e_2. If E is compared with A, the new equilibrium E is characterized by an increase in the market share of exporting firms and a decrease in the market share of foreign firms. Domestic firms export less per firm but the total volume of exports has increased: trade at the extensive margin has increased, that at the intensive margin has decreased. Foreign firms sell less in their local market, both individually and in the aggregate. Industry price declines since the increase in exports more than offsets the reduction in foreign supply. The measure of value of EPT is also smaller.[22]

Empirical results

Models producing hysteresis have been put forward to explain the puzzling observations about the US trade balance. From 1980 to the end of 1984, the real value of the US dollar appreciated sharply but the volume of imports began to rise after a long lag, only at the start of 1983. Starting from the first quarter of 1985, two years of continuous depreciation reduced the real value of the dollar back to its 1978 level. During these two years, there was only a slight increase in real import prices and import volumes did not decrease. Hence, the US trade balance did not improve. Schematically, in our context, if one considers the US as the foreign market, the cycle of the US dollar could be represented in Figure 13.3 by the move of the exchange rate from e_0 to e_1 and back.

Several approaches to empirically test for hysteresis have been undertaken. The first involves the search for structural breaks in the EPT measures. The preceding model implies that the EPT elasticity changes over time but that large exchange rate movements would cause structural breaks in the relationship, like those observed by the passing of trigger values (in Figure 13.3, movement from A to C, D and E). Baldwin (1988) presents evidence that the EPT relationship shifted in the 1980s although no structural break could be found for import volumes. A second test looks at whether entry and exit sunk costs matter in export markets. Tests of this conjecture using Spanish manufacturing firms do support this hypothesis. Over the interval 1990–97, Campa (2004) finds sunk costs F and X to be important factors in determining export market participation. Moreover he finds $F > X$, which supports hysteresis and the model outlined in this section. Over the interval 1990–2002, Blanes-Cristóbal et al. (2008) add the empirical finding that sunk exporting costs differ across destination markets. For example, costs to enter are higher in developed markets than in the rest of the world. A third test derives from Figure 13.3 and Table 13.5: as hysteresis exists, how important is the increase in the number of exporting firms $(n_1 - n_0)$ resulting from a depreciation? According to Campa (2004), about 82 percent of the change in export volumes is due to the intensive margin; the remaining 18 percent is the extensive margin. Also, his estimate of the exchange rate elasticity of Spanish exports is about 0.77. Hence if the currency depreciates by 10 percent, total exports increase by 7.7 percent, 18 percent of which is due to the increase in the number of exporting firms.

13.5 Concluding remarks

This chapter has discussed some of the issues linking exchange rates and international trade. This area of study departs from traditional trade theory by relying on assumptions about imperfect competition and biased and unbiased exchange rate markets.

The central points to be drawn from this analysis are first that there are behavioral differences between importers and exporters. Importers are traditionally understood as the mirror image of exporters for reasons based on the conventional terms of trade analysis. But this chapter has shown that differences in the behavior of exporters and importers go beyond the differentiated response of trade flows to exchange rate changes. The effects of a change in volatility on importers and exporters, for example, are opposite to each other. If the choice of the exchange rate regime (fixed versus flexible) is a political issue, importers and exporters will support different political candidates. Also, exporters and importers can have very different exchange rate expectations.

Second, empirical examination has not kept pace with the theoretical developments. The topic is also marked by conflicting empirical findings. Given this, the results to date suggest a sizable agenda for further research. In particular, there is a general need for the standard results of the literature to be reinterpreted and nested in a unifying framework. This would facilitate the task of empirically formulating nested hypotheses and the identification of those parts of the theory that are at stake.

Problems

13.1 Consider the case of a trading house that imports commodities from abroad and retails them locally. The trading house faces the domestic demand function $p_m = a - q_m/2$. Assume further each unit of the imported commodity costs a fixed foreign currency price p_m^*. Assuming a mean-variance utility function for the importer, derive the optimal solution for the level of imports q_m and for the hedge k_m. Discuss the implications of the separation and full hedging results for the importer's level of expected utility.

13.2 Consider the case of a speculator who has initial wealth W_s. The speculator allocates this wealth among domestic assets, which earn the interest rate r (covered interest parity is assumed to hold), and by open positions in exchange markets with a view to profiting from the discrepancy between the current forward rate and his expected future spot rate. The speculator's future wealth is then:

$$\widetilde{W}_s = (1+r)W_s + (e_f - \tilde{e})k_s$$

Assuming a mean-variance utility function, derive the optimal amount of forward sales k_s so as to maximize the speculator's expected utility of future wealth. Check that the second-order condition for an interior maximum is not violated for risk loving speculators.

13.3 Consider a foreign importer who retails imports on his local market at a price v^*. The importer has the following profit function:

$$\tilde{\Pi} = v^* - \lambda\frac{p}{\tilde{e}} - (1-\lambda)p^* + \left(\frac{1}{\tilde{e}} - \frac{1}{e_f}\right)k^*$$

where the '*' denotes variables denominated in the importer's currency. Maximize (13.9) to find the importer's optimal hedge k^*, and level of expected utility. Show that the importer and exporter disagree about the value of λ.

13.4 Consider the oligopoly situation in the foreign market as sketched in the main text, except now replace the n domestic exporting firms by n foreign affiliates of home-based multinationals. Foreign affiliates have costs that consist of inputs purchased from the parent company at home (intra-firm trade) and of costs in foreign currency terms incurred in the foreign country. Assuming constant marginal costs, how does an exchange rate change affect the equilibrium quantity allocation between foreign firms and foreign affiliates? What is the effect of an exchange rate change on the industry price p^*?

13.5 Consider the entry costs F and maintenance costs X. Indicate whether there is hysteresis if (a) $F = X$; (b) $F<X$; (c) $X = 0$. Outline your reasoning using a graph and considering an appreciation of e.

Notes

1. A major exception is Dornbusch *et al.* (1977).
2. The separation result has been derived by Danthine (1978), Holthausen (1979) and Feder *et al.* (1980) in a closed-economy model of the firm under price uncertainty. Ethier (1973), Baron (1976) and Kawai (1981) derived the same result in an open-economy model, Kawai and Zilcha (1986) under price and exchange rate uncertainty.
3. The condition $\alpha > 0$ implies risk aversion; $\alpha = 0$ risk neutrality and $\alpha < 0$ risk loving.
4. See Hirschleifer and Riley (1992, Chapter 2) for the precise conditions that allow a conversion of $EU(\tilde{\Pi})$ into a function only of $E(\tilde{\Pi})$ and $var\tilde{\Pi}$ and for the errors that are made by the approximation.
5. It is assumed for expository purposes that $E\tilde{e}$ and σ^2 in (13.14) are the same across agents. In practice, market participants are, however, heterogeneous. In an analysis of panel data of bi-weekly surveys on the yen/dollar exchange rate expectations, Ito (1990) finds that traders are characterized by wishful expectations: exporters expect a yen depreciation (relative to others) and importers expect a yen appreciation (relative to others).
6. This result has implications for the political choice of exchange rate regimes since there is a conflict of interest among exporters, importers and speculators over the desired degree of exchange rate flexibility (Ruland and Viaene, 1993).
7. Empirical results are sensitive to the measure that proxies the conditional variance of $\tilde{e}$. Cushman (1988) uses five risk measures based on the idea that past deviations around past expectations provide an estimate of the future standard deviation. See Clark *et al.* (2004) for a comparison of proxies of exchange rate uncertainty.
8. See also Clark *et al.* (2004), Klaassen (2004), Bahmani-Oskooee and Hegerty (2007), Baum and Caglayan (2010) for a review of the recent literature and for new empirical findings.
9. Discounting is measured by the discount rate (the r notation) or the discount factor (the δ notation). The discount rate is analogous to the rate of time preference, r, and the discount factor is $\delta = 1/(1+r)$. No discounting is equivalent to $r=0$ and $\delta = 1$.
10. A subgame perfect equilibrium is a Nash equilibrium for the whole game and its restriction to any subgame must also be a Nash equilibrium (see Osborne and Rubinstein, 1990).
11. The proof is that of Sutton (1986).
12. See Goldberg and Knetter (1997) for an updated review of the theoretical and empirical literature.
13. If the exchange rate e is instead defined as the units of foreign currency per unit of domestic currency (so a domestic devaluation is a decrease in e), then the relationship between export prices in domestic and foreign currency becomes $p=p^*/e$. Taking relative changes and dividing by $\hat{e}$ gives alternative measures of EPT: $\eta+1=\eta^*$, where $\eta=\hat{p}/\hat{e}$ and $\eta^* = \hat{p}^*/\hat{e}$. The latter expressions and (13.18) give four ways to measure EPT altogether. One difference between these alternative measures is that ε^* will generally be non-positive

while η^* is non-negative ($\eta^* = -\varepsilon^*$). The literature has indiscriminately discussed these four measures as characterizing the same thing – the pricing behavior of trading firms – and this has led to some confusion in the interpretation and comparison of theoretical and empirical results. In what follows we consider (13.18) only.

14. See Krugman (1987).

15. For a large number of countries, there are usually official and unofficial barriers to international arbitrage in many commodities. Krugman (1987) cites the example of German automobiles.

16. See Chapters 8 and 10, and Atkeson and Burstein (2007).

17. This proposition is supported by empirical studies. For example, Feenstra's (1989) empirical study is unable to reject the hypothesis that there is a symmetric response of import prices to a change in exchange rate and to a change in import tariff. Hence, research on EPT turns out to be also useful in estimating industry effects associated with trade policy.

18. See Knetter (1992) for an international comparison of PTM behavior.

19. For a review of the recent literature on the analysis of investment decisions under uncertainty, see Dixit (1992) and Dixit and Pindyck (1994).

20. The oligopoly model of this section explains the main features of hysteresis but it is too simple in several ways. First, it is static in that firms take a period-by-period decision to enter or to exit. Recent models examine, in contrast, the intertemporal decision making by firms. Decisions are then forward-looking, with firms rationally computing equilibria in future periods and using this to infer their current period entry or exit decisions. These models convey a broader meaning to exit costs which then include the severance pay that is often part of wage settlements on labor markets.

21. Dixit (1989a) has shown that the zone of inaction, that is, the vertical difference between the FF and XX curves, is increasing with the degree of exchange rate uncertainty.

22. This result follows directly from the partial derivatives of (13.22) to (13.25) with respect to n, assuming $c^* = c/e$ and $a^* - c/e > 0$, the last condition guaranteeing a positive profit margin for a domestic firm in oligopoly.

References and additional reading

International trade and exchange rates: theory

Baron, D.P. (1976), "Flexible Exchange Rates, Forward Markets and the Level of Trade," *American Economic Review*, 66, 253–266.

Danthine, J.-P. (1978), "Information, Futures Prices and Stabilizing Speculation," *Journal of Economic Theory*, 17, 79–98.

Dornbusch, R., Fischer, S., and Samuelson, P.A. (1977), "Comparative Advantage, Trade, and Payments in a Ricardian Model with a Continuum of Goods," *American Economic Review*, 47 (5), 823–839.

Ethier, W. (1973), "International Trade and the Forward Exchange Market," *American Economic Review*, 63, 494–503.

Feder, G., Just, R.E., and Schmitz, A. (1980), "Futures Markets and the Theory of the Firm under Price Uncertainty," *Quarterly Journal of Economics*, 95, 317–328.

Holthausen, D.M. (1979), "Hedging and the Competitive Firm under Price Uncertainty," *American Economic Review*, 69, 989–995.

Kawai, M. (1981), "The Behaviour of an Open Economy Firm under Flexible Exchange Rates," *Economica*, 48, 45–60.

Kawai, M. and Zilcha, I. (1986), "International Trade with Forward-Futures Markets under Exchange Rate and Price Uncertainty," *Journal of International Economics*, 20, 83–98.

Ruland, L.J. and Viaene, J.-M. (1993), "The Political Choice of the Exchange Rate Regime," *Economics and Politics*, 5, 271–283.

Viaene, J.-M. and de Vries, C.G. (1992), "International Trade and Exchange Rate Volatility," *European Economic Review*, 36, 1311–1321.

Viaene, J.-M. and Zilcha, I. (1998), "The Behavior of the Competitive Exporting Firm under Multiple Uncertainty," *International Economic Review*, 39 (3), 591–609.

International trade and exchange rate volatility: empirical studies

Bahmani-Oskooee, M. and Hegerty, S.W. (2007), "Exchange Rate Volatility and Trade Flows: A Review Article," *Journal of Economic Studies*, 34 (3), 211–255.

Baum, C.F. and Caglayan, M. (2010), "On the Sensitivity of the Volume and Volatility of Bilateral Trade Flows to Exchange Rate Uncertainty," *Journal of International Money and Finance*, 29 (1), 79–93.

Brouwer, J., Paap, R., and Viaene, J.-M. (2008), "Trade and FDI Effects of EMU Enlargement," *Journal of International Money and Finance*, 27 (2), 188–208.

Clark, P., Tamirisa, N., Wei S.-J., Sadilov, A., and Zeng, L. (2004), "Exchange Rate Volatility and Trade Flows: Some New Evidence," International Monetary Fund, May.

Coes, D. (1981), "The Crawling Peg and Exchange Rate Uncertainty," in J. Williamson (Ed.), *Exchange Rate Rules: The Theory, Performance and Prospects of the Crawling Peg* (New York: St. Martin's Press), 113–136.

Cushman, D.O. (1988), "US Bilateral Trade Flows and Exchange Risk during the Floating Period," *Journal of International Economics*, 24, 317–330.

Ito, T. (1990), "Foreign Exchange Rate Expectations: Micro Survey Data," *American Economic Review*, 80 (3), 434–449.

Klaassen, F. (2004), "Why is it so Difficult to find an Effect of Exchange Rate Risk on Trade?" *Journal of International Money and Finance*, 28, 817–839.

The invoice currency

Basevi, G., Cocchi, D., and Lischi, P.L. (1985), "The Choice of Currency in the Foreign Trade of Italy," Research Paper, 17 (University of Bologna).

Bilson, J.F.O. (1983), "The Choice of an Invoice Currency in International Transactions," in J.S. Bhandari and B.H. Putnam (Eds.), *Economic Interdependence and Flexible Exchange Rates* (Cambridge, MA: MIT Press), 384–402.

Black, S.W. (1985), "International Money and International Monetary Arrangements," in R.W. Jones and P.B. Kenen (Eds.), *Handbook of International Economics*, Vol. 2 (Amsterdam: North-Holland), 1153–1194.

Friberg, R. and Wilander, F. (2008), "The Currency Denomination of Exports: A Question-naire Study," *Journal of International Economics*, 75, 54–69.

Fukuda, S.-I. and Cong, J. (1994), "On the Choice of Invoice Currency by Japanese Exporters: The PTM Approach," *Journal of the Japanese and International Economies*, 8, 511–529.

Giovannini, A. (1988), "Exchange Rates and Traded Goods Prices," *Journal of International Economics*, 24, 45–68.

Goldberg, L.S. and Tille, C. (2009), "Vehicle Currency Use in International Trade," *Journal of International Economics*, 76 (2), 177–192.

Grassman, S. (1973), "A Fundamental Symmetry in International Payment Patterns," *Journal of International Economics*, 3, 105–116.

Kamps, A. (2006), "The Euro as Invoicing Currency in International Trade," European Central Bank, Working Paper Series, No. 665.

Rauch, J.E. (1999), "Networks versus Markets in International Trade," *Journal of International Economics*, 48 (1), 7–35.

Scharrer, H.E. (1979), "Die Wahrungsstruktuur im Welthandel," Wirtschaftsdienst.

Viaene, J.-M. and de Vries, C.G. (1992), "On the Design of Invoicing Practices in International Trade," *Open Economies Review*, 3, 133–42.

Exchange rate pass-through

Atkeson, A. and Burstein, A. (2007), "Pricing-to-Market in a Ricardian Model of International Trade," *American Economic Review*, 97 (2), 362–367.

Cheffert, J.-M. (1994), *Exchange Rate and Prices in Models of Imperfect Competition*, PhD thesis (University of Namur, Belgium).

Dornbusch, R. (1987), "Exchange Rates and Prices," *American Economic Review*, 77 (1), 93–106.

Feenstra, R. (1989), "Symmetric Pass-Through of Tariffs and Exchange Rates under Imperfect Competition: An Empirical Test," *Journal of International Economics*, 27, 25–45.

Fisher, E. (1989), "A Model of Exchange Rate Pass-Through," *Journal of International Economics*, 26, 119–137.

Froot, K. and Klemperer, P. (1989), "Exchange Rate Pass-Through When Market Share Matters," *American Economic Review*, 79 (4), 637–654.

Goldberg, P.K. and Knetter, M.M. (1997), "Goods Prices and Exchange Rates: What Have We Learned?" *Journal of Economic Literature*, 35 (3), 1243–1272.

Hooper, P. and Mann, C. (1989), "Exchange Rate Pass-Through in the 1980s: The Case of US Imports of Manufactures," *Brookings Papers on Economic Activity*, 1, 297–337.

Knetter, M.M. (1989), "Price Discrimination by US and German Exporters," *American Economic Review*, 79 (1), 198–210.

Knetter, M.M. (1992), "International Comparisons of Pricing-to-Market Behavior," *American Economic Review*, 83 (3), 473–486.

Krugman, P.R. (1987), "Pricing to Market When the Exchange Rate Changes," in S.W. Arndt and J.D. Richardson (Eds.), *Real-Financial Linkages Among Open Economies* (Cambridge, MA: MIT Press), 49–70.

Marston, R. (1990), "Pricing to Market in Japanese Manufacturing," *Journal of International Economics*, 29, 217–236.

Rangan, S. and Lawrence, R.Z. (1993), "The Responses of US Firms to Exchange Rate Fluctuations: Piercing the Corporate Veil," *Brookings Papers on Economic Activity*, 2, 341–379.

Hysteresis

Baldwin, R. (1988), "Hysteresis in Import Prices: The Beachhead Effect," *American Economic Review*, 78 (4), 773–785.

Baldwin, R. and Krugman, P.R. (1989), "Persistent Trade Effects of Large Exchange Rate Shocks," *Quarterly Journal of Economics*, 104 (4), 633–654.

Blanes-Cristóbal, J.V., Dovis, D., Milgram-Baleix, J. and Moro-Egido, A.I. (2008), "Do Sunk Exporting Costs Differ among Markets? Evidence from Spanish Manufacturing Firms," *Economics Letters*, 101, 110–112.

Campa, J.M. (2004), "Exchange Rates and Trade: How Important is Hysteresis in Trade?" *European Economic Review*, 48, 527–548.

Dixit, A. (1989a), "Entry and Exit Decisions under Uncertainty," *Journal of Political Economy*, 97 (3), 620–638.

Dixit, A. (1989b), "Hysteresis, Import Penetration and Exchange Rate Pass- Through," *Quarterly Journal of Economics*, 104 (2), 205–228.

Dixit, A. (1992), "Investment and Hysteresis," *Journal of Economic Perspectives*, 6 (1), 107–132.

Dixit, A. and Pindyck, R.S. (1994), *Investment under Uncertainty* (Princeton: Princeton University Press).

Krugman, P.R. and Baldwin, R. (1987), "The Persistence of the US Trade Deficit," *Brookings Paper on Economic Activity*, 1, 1–55.

Venables, A.J. (1990), "Microeconomic Implications of Exchange Rate Variations," *Oxford Review of Economic Policy*, 6 (3), 18–27.

Non-cooperative bargaining models

Rubinstein, A. (1982), "Perfect Equilibrium in a Bargaining Model," *Econometrica*, 50, 97–110.

Rubinstein, A. (1987), "Perfect Equilibrium in a Market with Decentralized Trade and Strategic Behaviour: An Introduction," London School of Economics, Theoretical Economics Discussion Paper Series, 87/147.

Rubinstein, A. and Wolinsky, A. (1985), "Equilibrium in a Market with Sequential Bargaining," *Econometrica*, 53, 1133–1150.

Sutton, J. (1986), "Non-Cooperative Bargaining Theory: An Introduction," *Review of Economic Studies*, 53, 709–724.

Game theory and information

Hirschleifer, J. and Riley, J.G. (1992), *The Analytics of Uncertainty and Information* (Cambridge: Cambridge University Press).

Osborne, M.J. and Rubinstein, A. (1990), *Bargaining and Markets* (San Diego, CA: Academic Press).

14

Growth and international trade

The achievement of sustained economic growth has been one of the principal objectives of economic policies of the post-war years. Economic growth is seen as a solution to a variety of economic problems, and it is therefore not surprising that the analysis of its determinants has been one of the dominant topics in economic theory.

The study of economic growth was nevertheless dormant for about two decades until it was revived in the mid-1980s. Since then there has been an explosion of interest in this field of research; a scholarly journal has been created to serve as the main outlet for new developments (*Journal of Economic Growth*, Springer) and entire books are necessary to discuss the field thoroughly (see, e.g., Grossman and Helpman, 1991; Barro and Sala-i-Martin, 1995; Aghion and Howitt, 1998, 2009; Jones, 2006; Acemoglu, 2008; Rodrik and Rosenzweig, 2009).

During the past decades, the economic growth of the developed, but mainly the developing, world has been remarkable, as evidenced by the rising trend of per capita income and consumption. Against this background of achievement, many have emphasized the costs of economic growth in terms of its effects upon the environment and the availability of exhaustible resources (World Bank, 2009) and have also pointed that more than 2 billion people in the developing world live on less than 2 dollars a day (World Bank, 2007).

The process of constructing theory usually starts with a summary of stylized facts that are regarded as relevant to the problem of economic growth, and the theoretical model is then made consistent with these facts. The emphasis is on real income per capita. This income measure is important since it is the variable of choice of neoclassical production functions. Also it is an approximation of individual well-being since if total income is distributed equally among individuals in a nation it measures the amount of goods and services that each can afford in a given year. Growth rates of per capita incomes matter as well because they indicate whether the GDP growth of, for example, a developing country more than offsets its faster population growth. For the purpose of illustration, let us consider the 2010 World Bank ranking of 215 countries based on (PPP corrected) gross national incomes per capita. Number one in the list of reported countries is Luxembourg with a per capita income of 63,850 (international) dollars, 206 times larger than that of the Democratic Republic of the Congo (DRC), the lowest-ranked country. Thus, if Luxembourg's per capita income were to remain constant, DRC would have to experience a geometric growth rate of 5.5 percent during 100 years to catch up with Luxembourg. This example illustrates many of the important questions raised by the field: Why is the current distribution of per capita incomes among countries of the world so uneven? Why do some countries grow more rapidly than others? Is it possible to design a growth policy such that poor countries catch up with the rich? Is choosing to globalize an economy part of the policy agenda?

This chapter examines the models that form the basis for much of the intuition economists have about growth. However, our focus will be on those issues that relate specifically to international trade. Although national policies and institutions are often the essential ingredients of a strategy for improving growth, international factors are generally assigned an important role. Section 14.1 prepares for the analysis by deriving the fundamental law of motion of capital intensities. This equation is then applied in Section 14.2 to the Harrod-Domar framework and its open economy extension, the two-gap model. Section 14.3 addresses the neoclassical model of growth and the issue of income convergence. Section 14.4 extends the analysis to the more complex two-sector models of the literature. These latter models incorporate features such as relative prices (often absent in the simpler models) which enable us to discuss the triangular relationship between growth, welfare and the terms of trade. In Section 14.5 we examine the endogenous growth literature. Section 14.6 surveys the empirical tests to which growth models has been subjected.

14.1 Preliminaries

The isolated economy version of traditional growth theories describes essentially a simple one-good economy. The economy's ratio of capital to labor employed is defined as $k(t) = K(t)/L(t)$, where $K(t)$ denotes the stock of capital and $L(t)$ the labor force available at time t. The rate of growth of $k(t)$ equals the difference between the rate of growth of capital and of labor:

$$\frac{\dot{k}(t)}{k(t)} = \frac{\dot{K}(t)}{K(t)} - \frac{\dot{L}(t)}{L(t)} \tag{14.1}$$

where the dot over a variable signifies the instantaneous change of that variable with respect to an infinitesimal increase in time, that is, $\dot{k}(t) = dk(t)/dt$. Henceforth the time subscript is dropped unless needed for clarity.

Gross investment is net capital accumulation plus depreciation:

$$I = \dot{K} + \mu K \tag{14.2}$$

where $\mu > 0$ is the depreciation rate. Dividing both sides of (14.2) by K gives:

$$\frac{\dot{K}}{K} = \frac{I}{K} - \mu \tag{14.3}$$

Equilibrium in a closed economy with no government expenditure requires equality between saving and investment. The saving function determines the division of total output Y

between output to be consumed and output for accumulation. Assuming a constant fraction s ($0 < s < 1$) of total output is saved for investment purposes, (14.3) can be written:

$$\frac{\dot{K}}{K} = \frac{sY}{K} - \mu \tag{14.4}$$

The labor force is assumed to grow at the constant exogenous growth rate n:

$$\frac{\dot{L}}{L} = n \tag{14.5}$$

After substitution of (14.4) and (14.5), (14.1) can be rewritten:

$$\dot{k} = sy - (\mu + n)k \tag{14.6}$$

where $y = Y/L$ is output per worker. (14.6) is the fundamental law of motion for the capital intensity which describes the accumulation of capital per worker available after equipping the new labor and providing for depreciation.

Traditional theories of economic growth are similar in that they start from (14.6) but differ in their assumptions regarding the technology of the economy. The formalized body of work stemming from Harrod (1939) and Domar (1946) rely on a fixed coefficient production function for Y. In contrast, the neoclassical model of growth that stems from Solow (1956) and Swan (1956) allows substitution between capital and labor in the aggregate production function and more importantly assumes decreasing marginal returns to capital.[1]

14.2 The Harrod-Domar model

Multiple equilibria

The Harrod-Domar (H-D) theory of exogenous growth contains the crucial idea that economic growth relates to the determinants of aggregate saving and investment. Though simple, the H-D theory contains a structure whose insights will serve as useful background when more sophisticated issues are addressed.

The technology of the economy is assumed to take the fixed coefficient form:

$$Y = \min\left[\frac{K}{a}, \frac{L}{b}\right] \tag{14.7}$$

where a and b are the capital–output and labor–output ratios, respectively. This technology implies the absence of substitution between capital and labor: total output is either $Y = K/a$ or L/b. This specification implies some unemployment of either capital or labor in the economy. For example, if $Y = K/a$, then some labor is redundant since employment bK/a is less than the endowment L. This implies that, unlike the neoclassical model of growth, the steady state is not independent of initial conditions. The per worker form of (14.7) can be simply written as:

$$y = \min\left[\frac{k}{a}, \frac{1}{b}\right] \tag{14.8}$$

Given this, and assuming $k < a/b$, (14.6) becomes:

$$\dot{k} = \frac{s}{a}k - \lambda k \tag{14.9}$$

where $\lambda = \mu + n$. To obtain the rate of output growth, consider total output which is $Y = K/a$ since $K < aL/b$ by assumption. Applying the rate of change notation gives $\dot{Y}/Y = \dot{K}/K$. Using this and (14.4) one obtains:

$$\frac{\dot{Y}}{Y} = \frac{\dot{K}}{K} = \frac{s}{a} - \mu \tag{14.10}$$

As (14.10) indicates, the growth rate of output and capital must equal the ratio of the saving propensity to the capital–output ratio (s/a) net of the depreciation rate μ. Since the parameters s, a and μ are fixed, growth is exogenous in this model.

The steady-state solution to (14.9) requires that $\dot{k} = 0$ and hence involves the comparison between $(s/a - \mu)$ and n. If $(s/a - \mu) = n$, a razor's edge condition, the capital stock and labor supply grow at a common rate. An entire range of equilibria is then possible, each involving full employment of both factors. However, the likelihood of such a case is low since the parameters involved in the comparison are exogenous and unrelated. However, two more interesting cases emerge, each showing the co-existence of output growth and unused resources in the economy (either labor or capital but not both). If $(s/a - \mu) < n$, labor grows faster than the capital stock which implies unemployment in the economy. As the extent of this redundancy grows, the capital–labor ratio decreases and becomes zero in the limit. If $(s/a - \mu) > n$, the capital stock grows faster than the labor force, implying $K > aL/b$ and $Y = L/b$. Though capital is now the redundant factor, there exists a unique and stable steady state $\bar{k} = s/(n + \mu)b$ that is obtained by substituting $y = 1/b$ in (14.6).

The two-gap model

The H-D theory emphasizes domestic savings as the major constraint on the growth rate of an economy. If the constraint is somewhat relaxed by raising the propensity to save, the result will be a rise in the growth rate of both capital and output. The experience of the developing countries in the 1980s, and of transition economies in the 1990s, suggests a different emphasis, however. In these cases, growth was also constrained by a limited supply of foreign exchange. The open economy version of the H-D theory – the so-called two-gap model – incorporates this foreign exchange constraint and enables one to identify whether growth is limited by a domestic savings gap or a foreign exchange gap. As the two-gap model has been applied to more countries than any other model it seems natural to concentrate on its main ideas and implications.[2]

Consider a small open economy and assume that, at the given terms of trade, the economy is completely specialized (a corner solution on the production possibility curve) in the production of a single commodity. This commodity is both consumed and exported in exchange for an imported capital good. Technology is of the fixed coefficient form (14.7) and it is assumed that $K < aL/b$. Hence, labor is redundant and domestic output depends only on the capital stock. Given this, output and the capital stock grow at the same rate, the latter given by the ratio of investment over the capital stock as in (14.3), assuming $\mu = 0$ for simplicity. Domestic investment comprises capital imports as well as domestic output which must be combined in fixed proportion.

Panel (a) of Figure 14.1 depicts this economy. The vertical axis measures imports of capital goods while the horizontal axis measures the supply of domestic output and its distribution among end-uses. Total output OY is allocated to consumption OC and savings CY according to a constant average propensity to save. The downward-sloping line VY gives the terms of trade, the price of domestic ouput relative to imports. The slope of the ray from C through point V gives the ratio of imported inputs to domestic goods needed to achieve a level of

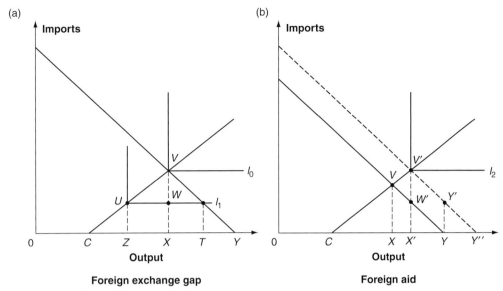

Figure 14.1   The two-gap model

domestic investment. Any point along this ray gives a different level of investment (and there-fore of future output growth), the level increasing as one moves away from C. The economy depicted in panel (a) can sustain a level of investment I_o which requires CX of domestic goods for investment and an amount XY of exported domestic goods to finance the imports VX.

Suppose that, because of a lack of foreign exchange reserves, imports of capital goods are limited to UZ. This can arise if exports are limited to TY (as a result of, for example, a reduction in foreign demand for this economy's product or of a loss of domestic resources in exporting the commodity, for example spoilage, inefficiency). Lower imports imply a decrease in the domestic component of investment to CZ, a lower level I_1 of domestic investment and, hence, an excess supply of savings equal to ZT. The foreign exchange gap is VW.

Now consider panel (b) of Figure 14.1 which assumes that the economy has a target growth rate that corresponds to the investment level I_2. What would be the *ex ante* capital require-ments implied by this targeted growth? The domestic component of investment would be CX' and the amount of imported inputs $V'X'$. An amount $X'Y''$ of exported domestic goods is therefore required to pay for these imports. Since the supply of output is OY, this econ-omy would have a domestic savings gap of YY'' or, equivalently, a foreign exchange gap of $V'W'$. Therefore, the economy cannot achieve the targeted rate of growth unless the propen-sity to save is increased by shifting a proportion YY'' of domestic output from consumption to exports. Another solution would be foreign aid or a foreign loan equal to the amount $V'W'$. Such aid would imply a decrease in exports to $X'Y$ as the proportion XX' of domestic output shifts from exports to the domestic component of investment.

Empirical implementation

Gersovitz (1982) estimated the two-gap model for Argentina, Columbia, Ecuador, Guatemala and Peru using yearly observations over the period 1950–78. Testing the two-gap model involves estimating the physical quantity of investment under two different specifications: the savings-constrained regime and the import-constrained regime. However, only one *ex post* observation on investment is available and in addition, it is not known *a priori* which regime generated this observation. An identification problem therefore arises and consists of determining which constraint holds at different times. Estimation amounts to computing the probability that any observation comes from a particular regime. The results of estimation indicate that for approximately 55 percent of all observations, the probability of a savings-constrained regime exceeded 0.5. This seems to suggest that investment in those countries was less likely to be constrained by imports than by domestic savings. Nevertheless, import-constrained regimes are frequently observed. The case of Ecuador is interesting in that it was the only country in the sample with important oil exports. As expected, the estimation results show evidence of import constrained growth that is followed, after the major oil shocks, by saving constrained growth.

So far terms of trade effects have been ignored and to see their importance, focus on panel (a) of Figure 14.1. Let us consider an increase in the relative price of exports which means an upward rotation of the price line YV around point Y. More capital goods are imported than before for the same volume of exports, implying a higher level of domestic investment and, hence, a higher future growth. If our economy produces raw materials and other primary commodities instead, its terms of trade are more likely to decrease, in which case a lower growth is expected. Hence the analysis of relative prices indicates that what a country exports matters because it affects the time path of a country's terms of trade. A number of empirical studies, reviewed by Harrison and Rodriguez-Clare (2009), suggest that indeed the growth effects of trade depend very much on the composition of exports. Exports are more likely to lead to growth if they are in non-traditional sectors.

14.3 The neoclassical model

The fundamental equation

Specifically retaining equations (14.1) to (14.6), the neoclassical model of growth replaces the technology of the economy of (14.7) by:

$$Y = F(K,L) \tag{14.11}$$

which is a neoclassical production function whose properties are discussed in Chapter 4. The per worker form of (14.11) is:

$$y = f(k) \tag{14.12}$$

Given this, the law of motion of the capital–labor ratio (14.6) can be rewritten as:

$$\dot{k} = sf(k) - \lambda k \tag{14.13}$$

where $\lambda = \mu + n$. (14.13) is called the fundamental differential equation of neoclassical economic growth, a representation of which is shown in Figure 14.2. From (14.13) there exists a steady-state (balanced growth) solution for capital intensity $\bar{k}$ at which the economy will be at rest – that is, at $\dot{k} = 0$. Existence of this equilibrium is ensured by the following conditions, known as the Inada conditions:

$$\begin{cases} f(0) = 0 & f(\infty) = \infty \\ f'(0) = \infty & f'(\infty) = 0 \end{cases} \tag{14.14}$$

Uniqueness and global stability are guaranteed by:

$$f'(k) > 0 \quad f''(k) < 0 \quad \text{for} \quad 0 < k < \infty \tag{14.15}$$

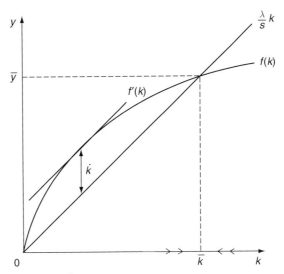

Figure 14.2 Neoclassical growth

At $\bar{k}$, capital and labor grow at the same rate n and, by the assumption of constant returns to scale, real output also grows at this rate. Output per worker and the capital-to-income ratio are therefore constant. However, starting from an early development stage, a country can grow at a rate different from n in the transition towards the balanced growth path.

Exogenous technical progress

The neoclassical model of growth is suitable for extension in a number of different directions. An important extension is the inclusion of technical progress which the literature has examined at great length. This produced the well-known Harrod, Hicks and Solow taxonomic classifications of technical progress (Jones, 1975). An important conclusion of this literature is that technical progress must be labor-augmenting for the neoclassical model to have a steady state with constant growth rates. The model in this form is also able to duplicate a number of stylized facts of growth.

To obtain a simple representation of technical progress in the neoclassical model, retain (14.1) to (14.6) but replace the aggregate production function (14.11) by:

$$Y = F(K, A(t)L) \tag{14.16}$$

with

$$\dot{A}(t)/A(t) = m$$

Technical progress is represented by the term $A(t)$, which transforms natural labor L into measures of effective labor units $A(t)L$. This last term can be interpreted as human capital that accumulates as a result of labor growth and the acquisition of skills through schooling. If m, the relative rate of change of $A(t)$, is positive then technical change is said to be labor-augmenting and advances at the constant exogenous rate m.

If we redefine output per effective unit of labor as $y = Y/A(t)L$ and the capital intensity as $k = K/A(t)L$, the analysis will follow exactly the same lines as the model without technical progress with $A(t)L$ replacing L throughout:

$$\frac{\dot{k}}{k} = \frac{\dot{K}}{K} - \frac{\dot{L}}{L} - \frac{\dot{A}}{A} = \frac{sY}{K} - (\mu + n + m) \tag{14.17}$$

and the fundamental equation (14.13) becomes:

$$\dot{k} = sf(k) - (\mu + n + m)k \tag{14.18}$$

The new steady-state value $\bar{k}$ is found by setting $\dot{k}$ in (14.18) equal to zero to obtain:

$$f(\bar{k}) = \frac{(\mu + n + m)}{s}\bar{k} \tag{14.19}$$

Hence, the neoclassical growth model implies the existence of automatic forces that will lead an economy to its steady state, determined by the parameters n, m, s and μ. Note that initial conditions are immaterial in determining either the steady-state capital intensity or the steady-state growth rate, but these conditions are nevertheless important for the transition to the steady state. This latter point is readily reflected by dividing both sides of (14.18) by k, and then taking the derivative with respect to k:

$$\frac{\partial(\dot{k}/k)}{\partial k} = \frac{s}{k}\left[f'(k) - \frac{f(k)}{k}\right] < 0 \tag{14.20}$$

This derivative is negative by the adding-up property of neoclassical production functions. Hence, the growth rate $(\dot{k}/k)$ is unambiguously larger for lower values of the initial capital–labor ratio. A similar result obtains for the growth rate of output per unit of effective labor $(\dot{y}/y)$. To show this, consider first the following approximation:

$$\dot{y} = f'(k)\dot{k} \tag{14.21}$$

Expression (14.21) implies:

$$\frac{\dot{y}}{y} = \frac{kf'(k)}{f(k)}\frac{\dot{k}}{k} = \Omega\frac{\dot{k}}{k} \tag{14.22}$$

where $\Omega = kf'(k)/f(k)$ is capital's share of national income (provided that capital earns its marginal product). If the production function took the Cobb-Douglas form, then Ω would be constant and thus independent of k. The growth path of y then mimics that of k and the derivative of $\dot{y}/y$ with respect to k is, as in (14.20), negative.

Speed of convergence

Another characteristic of the neoclassical growth model is the so-called speed of convergence, which is the speed at which the economy approaches its steady state. To develop this concept, begin by taking the first-order Taylor expansion of (14.18) around $\bar{k}$:

$$\dot{k} = \left[sf'(\bar{k}) - (\mu + n + m)\right](k - \bar{k})$$

Substitute for s using the steady state condition (14.19):

$$\dot{k} = -\beta(k - \bar{k}) \tag{14.23}$$

where $\beta = (1 - \bar{\Omega})(\mu + n + m)$ and $\bar{\Omega}$ is the steady-state capital share. Parameter β is the speed of convergence and indicates how rapidly the stock of capital per effective worker approaches its steady-state value. Analogous to (14.22), income per effective worker (y) also converges to its steady state ($\bar{y}$) at the rate β. To see this, consider the following approximation to the change in per capita output:

$$y - \bar{y} = f'(\bar{k})(k - \bar{k})$$

which, using (14.21) and (14.23), leads to:

$$\dot{y} = -\beta(y - \bar{y}) \tag{14.24}$$

It is clear from (14.23) and (14.24) that the convergence coefficient β is independent of the production function and of the saving rate. The latter nevertheless affects $\bar{k}$ and $\bar{y}$.

The inclusion of labor-augmenting technical progress does not greatly affect the analytical complexity of the model but does produce conclusions that are often in line with stylized facts that summarize growth experiences (see, e.g. Romer, 1989; Mankiw, 1995). Though some are already known, it is worth summarizing the eight predictions of the model. These predictions constitute hypotheses that can be evaluated using time series and cross-section data:

(1) An economy with a population growth rate n and a labor-augmenting technical improvement that proceeds at the exogenous rate m converges towards a steady growth path where the growth rates of output and capital are equal to $(n + m)$ and the capital–output ratio is constant.

(2) The ratio of capital to labor in natural units grows at the rate m.

(3) The real return to capital is constant and the real wage grows at the rate m, which is also the rate of growth of labor productivity.

(4) The shares of labor and of capital in national income are constant.

(5) Consumption per capita grows at the rate m.

(6) The steady-state level of income depends positively on the rate of saving and negatively on the rate of population growth and the depreciation rate.

(7) The rate of output growth is independent of the rate of saving.

(8) In the long run the economy approaches a steady state that is independent of initial conditions.

The empirical evidence indicates that only hypotheses (1) to (6) pass the test of the data, the remaining two being questionable. Contrary to prediction (7), the data show a strong correlation between growth rates and saving rates across countries. The theorists nonetheless maintain prediction (7) by making the claim that most observations are recorded off the steady state and therefore describe the transitional dynamics of a growing economy.

Result (8) is related to the broader topic of convergence. Consider a group of isolated economies which are assumed to differ in terms of their initial capital intensity but are structurally similar in the sense that production functions and underlying parameters of the neoclassical growth model are the same. Given this, we can infer three predictions about the growth performance of these economies. First, from (14.19), these economies will have the same steady-state capital intensity and the same growth rate. Second, reinterpreting (14.20), the more backward economies with a relatively lower capital intensity will have to grow faster than rich ones in order to converge to those with higher capital intensities. Finally, from (14.23) and (14.24), the economies will have the same speed of convergence β. This last inference is the essence of what is called the absolute convergence hypothesis.

This hypothesis has been extensively tested. The main finding is that absolute convergence is generally accepted for a group of homogeneous countries. However, in a large cross-section of countries, characteristics of countries are too heterogeneous for absolute convergence to hold. Instead a conditional form of convergence is applied controlling for the heterogeneity of countries or regions, as we discuss next.

Conditional convergence

There are two tests of conditional convergence applied to a given set of heterogeneous countries. The first test, called β-convergence, consists of estimating, as in (14.24), the parameter β. There is β-convergence within an economic group if poorer economies tend to grow faster than richer ones to reach a similar steady state. The second but weaker test of convergence is σ-convergence. Convergence occurs in this case if the cross-sectional dispersion of countries, measured by the standard deviation of the logarithm of real per capita income across the group, declines over time.[3] While β-convergence has been investigated in cross-section, panel and time-series approaches, σ-convergence focuses on the cross-section income distribution of these countries.

In an attempt to estimate σ-convergence, consider the natural logarithm of real GNI per capita y_{it} of N economies. The sample standard deviation of log-incomes at date t is given by:

$$\sigma_t = \left\{ \frac{1}{N} \sum_{i=1}^{N} (\ln y_{it} - \mu_t)^2 \right\}^{\frac{1}{2}} \quad t = 0, 1, \ldots T$$

where μ_t is the sample mean of $\ln y_{it}$'s. So sigma-convergence is obtained if σ_t decreases over time within interval T. This concept is illustrated in Figure 14.3 for 18 countries of the Middle East. This is a group of seemingly unrelated economies, known for large labor flows but low trade volumes. Quite expectedly, the starting value is $\sigma_{1991} = 0.49$, a relatively low level comparable to the US in 1900 and Japan in 1930.[4] However, the region has experienced a steady decline in the income dispersion of real per capita incomes.

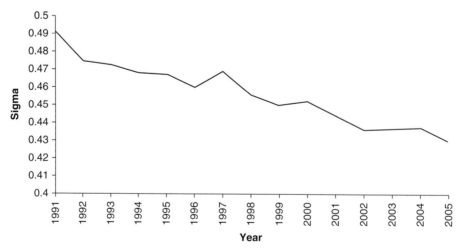

Figure 14.3 σ-convergence in the Middle East

Notes: Computation of σ-convergence for 18 countries of the Middle East using the log of real gross national income (GNI) per capita in international dollars.

Source: Huisman (2010).

Table 14.1 β-convergence

Convergence	47 US States 1880–1990	47 Japanese Prefectures 1930–1990	Equation (14.24)
β	0.0174 (0.0026)[1]	0.0279 (0.0033)	0.042[2]

Notes: (1) Standard error of estimates in parentheses. (2) Constructed value of β in (14.24) using $\overline{\Omega} = 0.30$, $n = 0.01$, $m = 0.02$, $\mu = 0.03$.
Sources: Barro and Sala-i-Martin (1995) and own calculations.

Estimates of β-convergence are commonly obtained from a specification of the form:

$$\frac{1}{T} \ln \left(\frac{y_{iT}}{y_{i0}} \right) = \alpha - \frac{(1 - e^{-\beta T})}{T} \ln y_{i0} + \gamma x_{iT} + u_{i0,T} \quad i = 1, 2, \ldots N \qquad (14.25)$$

where y_{i0}, y_{iT} represent the per capita income in economic unit i at time 0 and T respectively; T is the length of interval; N is the number of cross-sectional observations in a sample that could include countries, counties, regions, and so on; β is the speed of convergence and $u_{i0,T}$ is the error term. γ is the vector of parameters that measures the impact of structural variables x_{iT} on the dependent variable to account for the heterogeneity of economic units.[5]

Using non-linear estimation techniques, Barro and Sala-i-Martin (1995) provide estimates of β for US states for the period 1880–1990 (and for a number of sub-periods) and Japanese prefectures for the period 1930–1990. Table 14.1 reports these estimates. For US states, the point estimate of β for the whole sample is 0.0174; for the period 1960–70, it is 0.0246 (not shown). For Japanese prefectures, the estimated speed of convergence is 0.0279 for the whole sample. From Table 14.1 the conclusion is that as in (14.20) and (14.22) there is a negative correlation between the initial level of income and the following growth experience. In addition, states within the US tend to converge to their steady states at a speed of about 2 percent per year; for Japan, the speed of convergence is slightly higher.

A last question that involves tests of convergence is whether the observed process of convergence is adequately described by the neoclassical growth model of this section. To examine this issue, the theoretical definition of β in (14.23) is used to construct a theoretical estimate and the latter is then compared with regression estimates. The third column of Table 14.1 reports the constructed value of β for the following plausible parameter values: $\overline{\Omega} = 0.30$, $n = 0.01$, $m = 0.02$ and $\mu = 0.03$. As a result, the constructed β is 0.042, which is twice as high as the estimated β of roughly 0.02. Hence, the neoclassical growth model in its present form predicts a speed of convergence that is twice that obtained from the data. This divergence has led the theoretical literature to include, besides physical capital, factors like human capital which increase the value of $\overline{\Omega}$ and hence decrease that of constructed β (Mankiw, 1995).

Welfare: The Ramsey problem

The discussion thus far has focused on the production technology and ignored household behavior except for the exogenously given saving rate s. However, for different values of the saving rate the neoclassical model will approach different steady-state values for the levels of the variables even though the steady-state rate of growth will remain the same. Among the various saving rates, there will exist one rate for which steady-state per capita consumption achieves a maximum. To determine this welfare maximizing rate of savings we need an explicit analysis of household behavior in which the saving rate (s) is treated as endogenous.

This is the problem of a central planner who wants at time $t=0$ to maximize the discounted sum of utility from current and future consumption of an infinitely lived representative agent (e.g., a dynasty):[6]

$$\max_{d(t)} W_0 = \int_0^\infty e^{-\rho t} U(d(t))dt \tag{14.26}$$

subject to

$$\dot{k}=f(k)-d-nk$$
$$0 \le d(t) \le f(k(t)) \quad k(t),\, d(t) \ge 0 \tag{14.27}$$
$$k(0)=k_0$$

Here, one assumes $\mu = m = 0$ for simplicity so that k and d are, respectively, capital and consumption per unit of natural labor ($k = K/L, d = D/L$). Parameter ρ is the rate of time preference. When $\rho > 0$, the consumer gives less weight to future consumption relative to current consumption in terms of utility. Finally, constraint (14.27) states that output is divided between investment, consumption and equipping new labor.

The maximization problem (14.26) involves a choice at each point in time of how national output should be split between consumption and investment (savings), the latter going to produce more output in the future. This control problem is solved by using the maximum principle technique.[7] In this regard, the present value Hamiltonian is:

$$H(t)=e^{-\rho t}\{U(d(t))+v(t)[f(k(t))-d(t)-nk(t)]\} \tag{14.28}$$

where $v(t)$ is the costate variable associated with the state variable k.[8] The necessary and sufficient conditions for an interior maximum under general assumptions on the utility and production functions imply:

$$\frac{\partial H(t)}{\partial d(t)}=0$$

$$\frac{de^{-\rho t}v(t)}{dt}=-\frac{\partial H(t)}{\partial k(t)}$$

$$\lim_{t\to\infty} k(t)v(t)e^{-\rho t}=0$$

Given (14.28), the first two conditions imply:

$$v=U'(d) \tag{14.29}$$

$$\frac{\dot{v}}{v}=-[f'(k)-(n+\rho)] \tag{14.30}$$

From (14.29), we have:

$$\frac{\dot{v}}{v}=\frac{dU''(d)}{U'(d)}\frac{\dot{d}}{d} \tag{14.31}$$

where $dU''(d)/U'(d)$ is the contemporaneous elasticity of marginal utility with respect to consumption. Hence, the differential equation for the costate variable (v) can be written as a function of the differential equation in the control variable (d).

A conventional assumption is that utility has the iso-elastic form:

$$U(d) = \frac{d^{1-\theta}}{(1-\theta)} \quad \text{for } \theta > 0,\ \theta \neq 1$$
$$= \ln d \quad \text{for } \theta = 1 \tag{14.32}$$

so that the elasticity of $U'(d)$ with respect to d is a constant, $-\theta\,(\theta \neq 1)$ This utility function implies also a constant intertemporal elasticity of substitution $1/\theta$.

Rewriting (14.31) taking (14.32) into account and substituting in (14.30) gives:

$$\frac{\dot{d}}{d} = \frac{f'(k) - (n + \rho)}{\theta} \tag{14.33}$$

By the maximum principle, if the paths $\{\bar{d}(t)\}$ and $\{\bar{k}(t)\}$ are optimal, they must satisfy the differential equations (14.27) and (14.33). The latter, with $\dot{d}$ equal to zero, gives the value of $\bar{k}_m$ in the steady state:

$$f'(\bar{k}_m) = n + \rho \tag{14.34}$$

Hence, among all paths of balanced growth, the one yielding the highest consumption per worker is achieved by the path on which the marginal product of capital equals the sum of the growth of labor and the rate of time preference. The corresponding consumption per capita is obtained from (14.27):

$$\bar{d}_m = f(\bar{k}_m) - n\bar{k}_m$$

There are two last points. First, the solution $\bar{k}_m$ is called the "Modified Golden Rule" capital intensity. The "Golden Rule" condition is $f'(\bar{k}_g) = n$.[9] (14.34) therefore modifies the "Golden Rule" by allowing for a non-zero rate of time preference ($\rho \neq 0$). We have $(\bar{k}_g - \bar{k}_m) > 0$ for $\rho \geq 0$ and the difference increases with the rate of time preference. Second, it has been shown that, under certain conditions, the optimal path for a decentralized economy is also that of the centralized economy (Blanchard and Fischer, 1989, Chapter 2). The condition on capital intensity that maximizes steady-state per capita consumption is then obtained from the equality between the interest rate and the sum of n and ρ. Given this equivalence result, the literature interchanges the interest rate and marginal product of capital.

14.4 Two-sector models

Two-sector models of economic growth are viewed as a natural extension of the simpler one-sector models examined above. Two-sector models incorporate features such as relative commodity prices which are often absent in single-sector models but are important to international trade.[10] Below we first consider the comparative statics of growth by showing the so-called immiserizing growth result. We then illustrate some of the difficulties encountered in progressing from single-sector models to more complex dynamic two-sector, two-country models.

Immiserizing growth

A major result deriving from the comparative statics of growth in a two-sector model is the Rybczynski theorem. This basic proposition compares production equilibria at constant commodity prices after factor supplies have changed.[11] When commodity prices are allowed to change a striking result emerges: an open economy experiencing growth can be "immiserized," that is, worse off. The possibility of immiserizing growth was first demonstrated by Bhagwati (1958). Here we first illustrate the conditions for immiserizing growth in the context of the standard $2 \times 2 \times 2$ model of Chapter 4 and then discuss a few empirical findings regarding this proposition.

The necessary condition

Consider the condition for international trade equilibrium prior to growth of one of primary factors. By Walras's Law, it suffices to consider the market clearing condition for one of the two goods of this model. Let us consider the market for commodity 2 which is assumed to be the labor-intensive commodity and to be imported by the capital-rich domestic economy. The market clearing condition in this case is:

$$x_2^*(p_w) + q_2(p_w, h) - h_2(p_w, u_0) = 0 \qquad (14.35)$$

where x_2^*, q_2, and h_2 are the foreign export, the domestic supply and the domestic (compensated) demand for good 2, respectively; the parameter h is an index of primary factors, that is, $h = K, L$; u_0 is the utility level achieved prior to growth and p_w is the international price of good 2 relative to good 1 or the inverse of the domestic country's terms of trade. Total differentiation of (14.35) gives Bhagwati's expression for immiserization:

$$\left(a_1 \frac{q_2}{h_2} \hat{h} + a_2 \frac{q_2}{h_2} \hat{p}_w + a_3 \hat{p}_w \right) + f^* \frac{x_2^*}{h_2} \hat{p}_w \qquad (14.36)$$

where $\hat{z} = dz/z$ denotes the percentage change in any variable starting from the initial situation; $a_1 = (h/q_2)(\partial q_2/\partial h) \gtrless 0$ is the output elasticity of a change in factor supply ($h = K, L$); $a_2 = (p_w/q_2)(\partial q_2/\partial p_w) > 0$ is the price elasticity of domestic supply; $a_3 = -(p_w/h_2)(\partial h_2/\partial p_w) > 0$ is the compensated demand elasticity, and $f^* = (p_w/x_2^*)(\partial x_2^*/\partial p_w) \gtrless 0$ is the price elasticity of foreign supply of imports. Immiserizing growth occurs when (14.36) is negative. An important component of (14.36) is $\hat{p}_w$, the so called "zero gain" terms of trade change, which represents the change in the international price that, once growth has occurred, enables consumers to maintain their pre-growth level of utility u_0. Since nothing guarantees that this "zero gain" price will be the market clearing price on world markets, immiserization will occur if there remains a residual excess demand. Indeed, in this case, the relative price of good 2 must increase which is a deterioration of the terms of trade and, hence, a loss in national welfare that outweighs the welfare gain from factor growth.

The term outside parentheses in (14.36) gives the change in imports supplied from abroad as the result of the terms of trade change $\hat{p}_w$. The terms in parentheses in (14.36) represent the total change in the net domestic supply of good 2. This change is composed of three terms: the change in production of good 2 due to growth $\hat{h}$, the change in the production of good 2, and the change in consumption of good 2, both due to the price change $\hat{p}_w$. Given this, consider a "zero gain" decline in the terms of trade, that is, $\hat{p}_w > 0$. Since the elasticities a_2 and a_3 are positive, the necessary condition for (14.36) to be negative is that either f^* or a_1 or both must be negative. A negative f^* indicates that part of the foreign supply curve is backward bending. A negative a_1 is indicative of factor growth that reduces output of competitive imports. This would be the case if, for example, capital were to increase in supply in a capital-rich economy since, by the Rybczynski theorem, output of the labor-intensive industry would decrease.

The immiserizing growth outcome is illustrated in Figure 14.4. Pre-growth production, consumption and welfare are at A, A' and u_0, respectively. The initial terms of trade are given

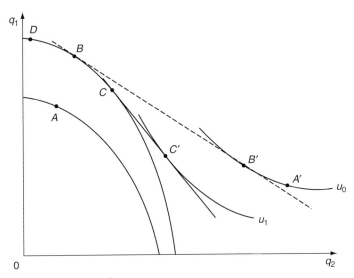

Figure 14.4 Immiserizing growth

by the price line AA' (not drawn). At this price, an increase in capital will cause an outward shift of the production possibility curve with D as the new production point. After growth, the price line BB' gives the zero gain price that maintains consumers on u_0. If, at the price BB', there exists a global excess demand for good 2, the terms of trade will deteriorate further to say CC'. At this post-growth price, production and consumption are at C and C', respectively. The result is a decline in national welfare from u_0 to u_1.

The Prebisch-Singer hypothesis

This Prebisch-Singer hypothesis postulates that LDCs' terms of trade are characterized by a negative long-term trend. This hypothesis, together with the immiserization result, has tantalizing implications for economic growth for some developing economies. If the hypothesis is true, the national income effect of growth is likely to be offset by the deterioration of the terms of trade in which case these economies are "immiserized."

The basis for a negative decline in LDCs' relative export prices is asserted to be due to several factors. A first cause is found in the composition of LDCs' trade with industrialized countries, schematically typified as the exchange of primary commodities for manufactures. Demand for LDCs' products is assumed to be quite inelastic as they are often necessities; supply of these products is assumed inelastic as well, since supply can only be varied after a long time lag. A second cause is seen in the development of new products in industrialized countries that constantly substitute for primary products. In addition, a third cause stems from the less competitive market structure of manufactures, which would be conducive to oligopoly pricing. Given that export supply is inelastic, so runs the argument, a structural decline in demand for primary products causes a large drop in the relative price of these commodities. Likewise, given that import demand is inelastic, any growth that increases LDCs' production of primary products leads to a large decrease in relative prices as well.

The 45-degree rule

While this argument is easy to understand in its own right, it is based on guess estimates of price elasticities of trade and also abstracts from the signals provided by markets in guiding economic activities. In fact, the evidence indicates no pervasive decline in the terms of trade of developing countries. For example, Krugman (1989) develops and tests a formal model that supports the idea that no strong trend in the terms of trade should be expected. The analysis starts by writing the standard trade balance identity of a $2 \times 2 \times 2$ model as:

$$b = m_1^*(Y^*, p) - pm_2(Y, p)$$

where b denotes the domestic trade balance in terms of good 1, m_1^* and m_2 are foreign imports of good 1 and domestic imports of good 2 respectively, Y and Y^* are domestic and foreign national incomes measured in terms of good 1, and p is the price of good 2 in terms of good 1 – that is, the inverse of the domestic terms of trade. It is implicitly assumed that the domestic economy exports good 1 in which it has a comparative advantage in exchange for good 2 in which it has a comparative disadvantage. Differentiating totally and keeping a zero trade balance we obtain:

$$\hat{p} = \frac{\zeta \hat{Y} - \zeta^* \hat{Y}^*}{(\eta + \eta^* - 1)}$$

in which ζ and ζ^* are the income elasticities of demand for good 2 and good 1 respectively, and η and η^* are the (partial equilibrium) price elasticities. The denominator is positive by the Marshall-Lerner stability condition. By the above formula, there will be a trend in the terms of trade unless

$$\frac{\zeta^*}{\zeta} = \frac{\hat{Y}}{\hat{Y}^*}$$

which is referred to as the "45-degree rule." Otherwise, the analysis relates trends in the terms of trade to different income elasticities or to different long-term rates of growth. For example, a more rapidly growing domestic economy is expected to experience, *ceteris paribus*, a deterioration in its terms of trade because it is forced to reduce the price of its exports in order to sell higher quantities. Regressing estimates of income elasticities in world trade on the growth rates of corresponding countries over the period 1955–65, Krugman (1989) obtains the following surprising result:

$$\ln\left(\frac{\zeta^*}{\zeta}\right) = -1.81 + \underset{(0.208)}{1.210} \ln\left(\frac{\hat{Y}}{\hat{Y}^*}\right) \quad R^2 = 0.754 \quad SEE = 0.211$$

This regression result establishes a systematic relation between the ratio of income elasticities in trade and the ratio of rates of growth. The estimated parameter of the ratio of growth rates is positive and not significantly different from unity. The same result seems to persist in more recent periods. Hence, the 45 degree rule that turned out to be unlikely *a priori* becomes an empirical regularity: fast-growing economies tend to face high income elasticities for their exports and low income elasticities for their imports, making trend changes in the terms of trade unnecessary. Krugman appeals to the models of monopolistic competition (see Chapter 8) to show that fast-growing economies expand their share of world markets by expanding the range of goods produced rather than by reducing their export prices. Debaere and Lee (2010) support Krugman's result by showing that fast-expanding nations can avoid adverse terms of trade effects through quality and variety expansion.[12]

14.5 Endogenous growth

The neoclassical model is made consistent with the stylized facts of economic growth by introducing labor-augmenting technical progress into the aggregate production function. Long-run growth of per capita income then corresponds to that of the exogenously given growth rate of the labor-augmenting factor.

However, even the labor-augmenting version of the neoclassical model fails to fully account for the perpetually rising standards of living and the wide cross-country dispersion in both the levels and rates of growth of per capita income. Also, the exogeneity of technical progress must be seen as an analytical convenience rather than a serious representation of reality.

These shortcomings have stimulated the development of endogenous growth models. The models stem from the contributions by Romer (1986) and Lucas (1988). These models share the property that "economic growth is an endogenous outcome of an economic system, not the result of forces that impinge from outside" (Romer, 1994, p. 3).

In these types of model growth can be endogenously driven (1) by growth in human capital that may involve knowledge spillovers (Romer, 1986) or may not (Lucas, 1988; Rebelo, 1991) or (2) by technological innovation (Romer, 1990; Grossman and Helpman, 1991).[13]

Growth driven by human capital accumulation

A common characteristic of endogenous growth models is that growth may be unbounded because the return to investment in broad capital (i.e., both human and physical capital) may not diminish as an economy develops. This fact is illustrated by (14.33). This relationship indicates clearly that the growth in per capita consumption can be sustained ($\dot{d}/d > 0$) only if the marginal product of capital $f'(k)$ stays perpetually above the level given by the sum of n and ρ.

The basic ingredients of endogenous growth models can be illustrated by the following simple representation of technology:

$$y(t) = f(k(t), h(t)) = Ak(t)^\alpha h(t)^{1-\alpha} \quad 0 < \alpha < 1 \tag{14.37}$$

where $y(t)$ is output per worker, $k(t)$ and $h(t)$ are two factors of production (physical and human capital per worker), A is a productivity parameter and α is the share parameter of the k factor. The single commodity is produced either for consumption or for accumulation of the stock of the k factor. Most models specify a law of motion for the h–factor as well.

Given (14.42), the marginal product of the k factor is readily obtained:

$$f'_k = \alpha A \left(\frac{h(t)}{k(t)} \right)^{1-\alpha} \tag{14.38}$$

where $f'_k = \partial f / \partial k$. It is clear from (14.38) that $\partial f'_k / \partial k < 0$ and $\partial f'_k / \partial h > 0$. Hence, whether the marginal product of the k factor in (14.38) decreases as $k(t)$ accumulates depends on the offsetting impact from the accumulation of the h factor. If the h factor is accumulated no slower than the k factor, f'_k will not be decreasing and consequently, long-run growth can be sustained.

Growth driven by knowledge spillover

Consider the following illustration which assumes a competitive equilibrium with external scale economies (Romer, 1986). The motivation for this model is the idea that private knowledge is an intangible capital input in the production of the firm that may have an external spillover effect. Thus, $A(E)F(K_j, L_j, e_j)$ could represent the production technology available to firm j with capital K_j, labor L_j, the private stock of knowledge e_j and the public stock of knowledge E. In the simplest version of the model, E is assumed to increase one-for-one with e_j and the stock of capital is taken to be an index of acquired knowledge ($e_j = K_j$).[14] Assuming identical firms and that $F(.)$ is homogenous of degree 1, aggregation over all firms gives the aggregate production function $A(K)F(K,L)$. If $F(.)$ is Cobb-Douglas, and if the accumulation of public knowledge exhibits diminishing returns, that is, $A(K) = K^\delta$ with $0 < \delta < 1$, aggregate output takes the form $A(K)F(K,L) = K^\delta K^\alpha L^{1-\alpha}$, or in per worker terms:

$$y = f(k,L) = k^{\alpha+\delta} L^\delta \tag{14.39}$$

where $k = K/L$. The marginal product of capital then becomes:

$$f_k' = (\alpha + \delta)\left(\frac{L^\delta}{k^{1-\alpha-\delta}}\right) \tag{14.40}$$

Assume a constant labor force ($n = 0$). If ($\alpha + \delta$) is less than 1, the marginal product f_k' is decreasing in k and as in the neoclassical model, the steady state $\bar{k}$ is given by (14.34). Growth of output will be zero in this case. If ($\alpha + \delta$) is equal to 1, $f_k' = (\alpha + \delta)L^\delta$ in (14.40) and using (14.33), this economy will always be along a constant steady-growth path given by $\dot{d}/d = [(\alpha + \delta)L^\delta - (n + \rho)]/\theta$. If ($\alpha + \delta$) is greater than 1, the marginal product of capital is increasing rather than decreasing in k, so that the per capita capital stock can grow without bound. Per capita output and consumption can grow without bound as well. The level of per capita output in different countries need not converge in this case.[15]

Growth driven by industrial innovation

The innovation approach to endogenous growth theory describes the pace of technological progress as the outcome of deliberate investment decisions by profit seeking firms. Firms undertake research and development (R&D) investments when they see an opportunity to earn profits on their research efforts. The amount of profits earned depends on the market structure. In this context, profit seeking firms will aim their research strategies at three tasks: improving the quality of existing products (Grossman and Helpman, 1991, Chapter 4), improving the methods of production (Aghion and Howitt, 1992), or expanding the variety of goods (Romer, 1990; Grossman and Helpman, 1991, Chapter 3 and Chapter 9). Here we will only discuss the models of product variety.

Define $d(t)$ as the consumption of a single good at time t. In many models, consumption $d(t)$ is modeled as the assembly of $n(t)$ differentiated inputs which are imperfect substitutes for each other:

$$d(t) = \left[\int_0^{n(t)} q_j(t)^\alpha dj\right]^{1/\alpha} \qquad 0 < \alpha < 1 \tag{14.41}$$

where q_j denotes consumption of good j that has been developed and produced by a research firm in the economy and $n(t)$ is the number of input designs available at time t. Specification (14.41) is a reinterpretation of the Dixit-Stiglitz "love for variety" utility function discussed in Chapter 8. The properties of (14.41) are central to this approach of endogenous innovation. The parameter α is a monotone transformation of the (constant) elasticity of substitution, which is $\varepsilon = 1/(1 - \alpha) > 1$. Also, the assembly of $d(t)$ exhibits CRS in the inputs (for given $n(t)$). More importantly, the productivity of primary factors of the economy rises with the number of varieties $n(t)$. To see this, assume all inputs are symmetric, that is, $q_j(t) = q(t)$. Then $d(t) = n(t)^{1/\alpha}q(t)$. It is further assumed that the production of $q(t)$ requires 1 unit of a single primary factor which we take to be labor. Hence, total employment equals $n(t)q(t)$ and the average productivity of labor is $d(t)/n(t)q(t) = n(t)^{-(1-1/\alpha)}$, which increases with $n(t)$ if $\alpha < 1$.

The representative consumer's consumption decision involves a two-stage procedure. In the first stage, the consumer maximizes an instantaneous utility function subject to an instantaneous budget constraint. Assume that the instantaneous utility function is logarithmic as in (14.32), that is, $\ln d(t)$. The first-order conditions for utility maximization subject to the instantaneous budget constraint imply:

$$S(t) = \int_0^{n(t)} p_j(t)q_j(t)dj \tag{14.42}$$

From this, one obtains the set of demand functions:

$$q_j(t) = \frac{S(t)p_j^{-\varepsilon}(t)}{\int_0^{n(t)} p_i(t)^{1-\varepsilon}di} \tag{14.43}$$

With symmetric goods, (14.43) implies that $q(t) = S(t)/p(t)n(t)$ and (14.41) implies that $d(t) = S(t)/p_d(t)$ where $p_d(t) = p(t)n(t)^{(\alpha-1)/\alpha}$.

Substituting the optimal input demands (14.43) into (14.41) and then the obtained result into the utility function, the second stage involves the household maximizing indirect utility over an infinite horizon subject to an intertemporal budget constraint. That is, the problem is to choose the path $S(t)$ that maximizes utility over an infinite horizon:

$$U(\tau) = \int_\tau^\infty e^{-e(t-\tau)}(\ln S(t) - \ln p_d(t))dt \tag{14.44}$$

subject to an intertemporal budget constraint (not shown) that states that the present value of spending is not greater than the sum of households' holding of assets and the present value of labor income. Borrowing and lending are allowed at the nominal interest rate. By normalizing expenditure so that $S(t) = 1$ for all t, the solution to this maximization problem implies that the nominal interest rate $r(t)$ is equal to the subjective discount rate for all t:

$$r(t) = \rho \tag{14.45}$$

This is related to the discussion of the modified golden rule for a decentralized economy in the absence of depreciation and population growth (see (14.34)).

On the production side producers undertake two distinct tasks. They manufacture the known inputs and undertake the development of new designs. It is assumed that each single product design is produced by a single firm. Further, the production of existing products is characterized by CRS and requires one unit of labor per unit of output. Given this and the product demand (14.43), the profit maximization rule for the assumed monopolist amounts to equating marginal revenue and marginal cost, $p_j(t)\alpha = w(t)$ where $w(t)$ is the nominal wage. Consequently, for a unique wage, all suppliers of products charge the same price $p(t) = w(t)/\alpha$ and, by (14.43), sell the same quantity. This pricing strategy yields operating profits per design of:

$$\Pi(t) = p_j(t)q_j(t) - wq_j(t) = \frac{(1-\alpha)}{n(t)} \tag{14.46}$$

after making use of (14.43) and assuming $S(t) = 1$ and symmetric demands. Operating profits are therefore decreasing in the number of designs.

Growth in this economy is driven solely by the increase in the set of available inputs. The development of new input designs takes several forms. Based on the nature of knowledge capital created by research, the following three cases have been considered.

Knowledge capital as private good

To invest in R&D is, in this case, a deliberate decision by the entrepreneur who fully appropriates the returns. The production of new designs follows:

$$\dot{n} = \frac{L_n}{a} \tag{14.47}$$

where L_n is the amount of labor devoted to R&D, a is the labor requirement in the production of one design and the time subscript is omitted. Research activities are assumed perfectly competitive and firms hire research labor until:

$$w = \frac{v}{a}$$

where v is a claim to the stream of profits that accrues to a new design. This relationship expresses the equality between the value marginal product of labor (v/a) and the nominal wage. The variables w and v are in turn determined in general equilibrium.

Asset market equilibrium requires the following arbitrage condition to be satisfied:

$$\Pi + \dot{v} = rv \tag{14.48}$$

The right hand side of (14.48) gives the return to a riskless investment of size v. Alternatively, this amount could be invested in equities so the left-hand side of (14.48) gives the return to owners of the firm that consists of dividends Π and the capital gains $\dot{v}$ equity holders expect to earn on their assets. This arbitrage condition is crucial for explaining why the steady-state relative rate of innovation ($g \equiv \dot{n}/n$) in the economy is zero.[16]

$$g = 0 \tag{14.49}$$

Why? The steady state requires $\dot{v}/v = 0$. As the product variety expands, profit per product declines according to (14.46). The profit rate Π/v is driven to the nominal interest rate, which equals the rate of time preference. The research incentive, and hence growth, is then no longer maintained.

Knowledge capital as national public good

Firms are not always able to fully appropriate the returns to their investments. A reason might be that property rights associated with new designs are not well defined since some of the research results leak out into the pool of public knowledge. This idea is expressed by the following expression for the production of input designs:

$$\dot{n} = \frac{L_n n}{a} \tag{14.50}$$

This indicates that new designs are produced using research labor L_n and the existing stock of knowledge. Here, the total number of existing product designs (n) proxies for the stock of knowledge, the latter having a positive external effect on the production of new designs. Since the positive spillover of n causes the cost of producing new designs to decline, the profit rate is no longer driven to the nominal interest rate and the research incentive is maintained. It can be shown that the relative rate of innovation is in this case:

$$g = (1 - \alpha)\frac{L}{a} - \alpha\rho \qquad (14.51)$$

where L is the total labor supply. Growth of total output in the economy, being proportional to g, is sustained as well.

Knowledge capital as international public good

If the international diffusion of research results is permitted (but not trade) then the stock of knowledge available to firms investing in new product designs is augmented by the stock of foreign knowledge as long as there is no duplication. The production function in this case remains (14.50) but the positive externality from foreign research is now interpreted as $n + \psi n^*$ where n^* stands for the set of available foreign products and Ψ for the fraction of foreign products, unknown to domestic firms ($0 \leq \Psi \leq 1$). In this case, the relative rate of innovation becomes:

$$g = (1 - \alpha)\frac{(L + \Psi L^*)}{a} - \alpha\rho \qquad (14.52)$$

where L^* is the foreign labor force. Comparing (14.51) to (14.52), the latter is not smaller, and is greater for any $\Psi > 0$. With $\Psi = 0$ (that is, a complete duplication of research results in both countries) diffusion would not augment the autarky stock of knowledge.

In the case of both international trade and knowledge diffusion, the following result obtains:

$$g = (1 - \alpha)\frac{(L + L^*)}{a} - \alpha\rho \qquad (14.53)$$

This result is equivalent to (14.52) with $\Psi = 1$, that is, no duplication. National firms that are part of an integrated area avoid duplication of research and the stock of knowledge thereby reaches a maximum.

14.6 Growth empirics

There exists a vast literature that uses cross-country regressions to search for empirical linkages between long-run per capita growth rate and the set of explanatory variables suggested by theory. Besides the initial level of real GDP per capita used to test the convergence hypothesis discussed earlier, the empirical literature suggests that growth rates in income per person depend positively on the investment share of GDP, on various measures of human capital (such as initial secondary school enrolment rates) and depend negatively on the average annual rate of population growth. Altogether, these four variables explain about half of the cross-section variance in growth rates. A first significant portion of the residual is explained by a variety of indicators of economic policy, political and institutional characteristics. For example, countries with political instability (proxied by the number of political upheavals) and market distortions (proxied by, for example, the black market exchange rate premium) tend to have lower growth rates. A second significant portion of the residual is explained by international factors. This section reviews the growth experience of countries with a focus on those issues that relate specifically to international trade.[17]

Trade and growth

Harrison and Rodriguez-Clare (2009) describe 176 studies that use a reduced form relationship between openness and economic growth. They focus on the measures of openness used in the literature but identify the various datasets and the econometric problems linked to identification and causality. Most of the studies they review find a positive relationship between trade volumes and growth.

For example, Dollar and Kraay (2004) test whether openness has systematic effects on economic growth in a cross-section of 101 countries covering the period 1970–90. They start with a standard growth regression like (14.25):

$$\ln y_{it} = \beta_0 + \beta_1 \ln y_{i,t-k} + \gamma x_{it} + \alpha_i + \varepsilon_t + u_{it} \quad i = 1, 2, \ldots N$$

where y_{it} is per capita GDP in country i at date t; $y_{i,t-k}$ is per capita GDP of the same country at date $(t - k)$ with $k = 10$; x_{it} is a vector of control variables that includes trade volumes, that is exports plus imports as a share of GDP; α_i represents country fixed effects and ε_t time fixed effects; N is the number of observations. Taking differences, they estimate the following regression:

$$\frac{1}{k} \ln \frac{y_{it}}{y_{i,t-k}} = \beta_0 + \beta_1 \frac{1}{k} \ln \frac{y_{i,t-k}}{y_{i,t-2k}} + \frac{1}{k} \gamma (x_{it} - x_{it-k}) + (\alpha_i - \alpha_i)$$
$$+ (\varepsilon_t - \varepsilon_{t-k}) + (u_{it} - u_{i,t-k}) \quad i = 1, 2, \ldots N$$

This is the regression of the average growth rate over the $k = 10$ years on average lagged growth and on, among others, average changes in trade volumes. The interest of this specification is that country fixed effects like geography, institutions, legal systems, language and culture captured by α_i cancel since these variables do not vary much within an interval of ten years. Differencing therefore addresses the issue of multicollinearity since country effects are likely to explain trade volumes as well. The main finding is that changes in growth rates are highly correlated with changes in trade. The point estimates indicate that a 100 percent increase in trade volumes raises incomes over a decade by a percentage that varies between 25 and 48 percent.

Besides the multicollinearity among explanatory variables serious shortcomings regarding the specification of the growth equation have been pointed out by the so-called "sceptics" of the growth literature (see, e.g., Rodriguez and Rodrik, 2001; Hallak and Levinsohn, 2009). A first issue relates to the usefulness of the empirical exercise. Even if trade does enhance growth, it is difficult to derive the policy relevance of the result since the mechanisms that lead to such an outcome are not uncovered. A second issue is the possibility of an endogeneity bias in the above regressions: is it openness that explains growth or vice versa? Since output growth, trade, trade policy, and so on in a particular period are likely to be jointly determined, the direction of causality is not obvious. Although the various theories of this chapter implicitly assume that openness explains growth, causality is a testable hypothesis that should be subjected to the data. A third specification issue is an omitted variable bias that arises since openness is always summarized by a single indicator whereas trade and trade policy are multi-dimensional concepts. In Dollar and Kraay (2004) for example, openness is proxied by trade volumes but other studies use tariff protection instead. Much of the intuition regarding the difficulty in using a uni-dimensional index is illustrated in Table 14.2 which reproduces a number of potential openness variables for a number of emerging economies. Because of import price substitution, no relation seems to exist between revenue tariffs in the first column and average tariffs in the third. Except for South Africa, most countries have experienced large

Table 14.2 Measures of trade openness

Country	Revenue tariffs[1]	Tariffs[2]		Change in tariffs[3]	Trade volumes[4]	Antidumping initiations[5]
	2004	1985	2008	1985–2008	2009	1995–2008
Argentina	5.04	27.0	12.43	−14.57	43.90	241
Brazil	4.20	55.6	13.08	−42.52	28.83	170
China	1.93	39.5	14.19	−25.31	57.70	151
India	10.8	98.8	13.82	−84.98	48.81	564
South Korea	2.28	23.0	12.19	−10.81	91.02	108
Mexico	1.00	30.0	9.57	−20.43	64.37	95
South Africa	4.47	6.0	6.82	0.82	72.30	206
Turkey	1.18	26.6	6.99	−19.61	52.51	137

Notes: (1) Revenue tariffs are customs and other import duties divided by total imports of a country evaluated in current US dollars. (2) Tariff is the unweighted average of the applied tariff rates including preferential rates. (3) Difference between 2008 and 1985 tariffs. (4) Trade volume is the sum of exports and imports in goods and services expressed as a percent of GDP in current US dollars. (5) Cumulative sum of initiations over the period 1995–2008.
Sources: World Bank (World Trade Indicators 2009/10 Database) and WTO.

drop in tariffs, the largest decrease being observed for India. However, this trend is offset by a large number of anti-dumping initiations as those countries have enacted anti-dumping laws and made anti-dumping their trade policy of choice. Also, although tariffs have decreased they remain high compared with developed economies. Altogether it is not surprising to observe that empirical results using different proxies for openness may lead to different and often inconclusive results (Harrison and Rodriguez-Clare, 2009).

Estimates of R&D spillovers

Several papers reviewed in Keller (2004) assess the national and international spillovers required to generate endogenous growth. For example, Coe *et al.* (1997) provide estimates of these effects for a group of 77 developing countries from Africa, Asia, Latin America and the Middle East. More recently, Coe *et al.* (2009) studied the relationship between R&D and productivity between 1971 and 2004 using 24 countries as representative of the industrial North. Both studies start with an aggregate production of the type $Y_{it} = A_{it}F(K_{it}, L_{it})$ with A_{it} being a measure of Hicks-neutral technological progress. They assume further $F(K_{it}, L_{it}) = K_{it}^{\alpha_{it}} L_{it}^{(1-\alpha_{it})}$. Total factor productivity (TFP) is defined as:

$$TFP_{it} = A_{it} = \frac{Y_{it}}{K_{it}^{\alpha_{it}} L_{it}^{1-\alpha_{it}}} \qquad i = 1, 2 \dots N \quad t = 1, 2 \dots T \qquad (14.54)$$

TFP gives a measure of the gains in output which cannot be attributed to labor or capital. It varies through time and across countries and is often called the "residual." From the preceding section we know that the residual is largely explained by the assortment of intermediate inputs that expand as a result of R&D investment. The empirical work is therefore performed by linking TFP to measures of own and foreign R&D stocks and a set of other variables.

Table 14.3 Total factor productivity

Countries	Change in TFP: TFP_{2004}/TFP_{1971}	Rate of technological progress (%)
Finland	2.16	2.29
Ireland	3.72	3.94
Israel	1.18	0.49
Korea	3.39	3.65
Netherlands	1.57	1.33
Norway	2.42	2.63
Switzerland	1.10	0.28
United States	1.32	0.82

Sources: Coe *et al.* (2009) and own calculations.

The difficulty in evaluating (14.54) lies in obtaining values for α_i, the other variables being readily available. If we assume perfect competition, the marginal products equal $\alpha_i Y_i/K_i = r_i/p_i$ and $(1-\alpha_i)Y_i/L_i = w_i/p_i$. Hence, under CRS and perfect competition only, α_i and $(1-\alpha_i)$ are the income shares of capital and labor that can be measured directly.

Table 14.3 reports the ratio of TFP in 2004 to TFP in 1971 for a number of countries in the sample. In the second column we compute the TFP growth rates which by (14.54) equal the rates of technological progress ($\dot{A}/A$). In Table 14.3 growth rates are computed as geometric averages, that is:

$$g_{t,t+T}^{TFP} = \left(\frac{TFP_{t+T}}{TFP_t}\right)^{1/T} - 1$$

where $t = 1971, t+T = 2004$ and $T = 34$. In a number of countries like Ireland and Korea, TFP more than tripled over the 34 years showing yearly rates of technological progress in excess of 3.5 percent. By contrast, in some other countries like Israel and Switzerland, TFP rose by only 10–18 percent over the same period, implying yearly rates of technological progress of less than 0.5 percent.

Table 14.4 reports the estimated equations of a country's TFP as a function of the country's R&D capital stock, the foreign R&D capital stock and the domestic human capital as another explanatory variable. The estimates obtained suggest that industrial countries enjoy substantial benefits from R&D carried out within their national boundaries and from R&D carried out by their trade partners. In 1971–2004, a 10 percent rise in own R&D stock increases own TFP by almost 1 percent. This last figure becomes 2.13 percent if the foreign R&D stock increases by 10 percent in the first specification, but 0.35 percent in the specification with human capital. The second specification stresses the important role of domestic human capital on own TFP, the elasticity being 0.725.

How can one country's R&D benefit foreigners? Coe *et al.* suggest international trade as a main transmission channel. International trade stimulates cross-border learning of production methods, product designs and organizational methods. Furthermore, international trade enables countries to acquire technology embodied in intermediate and capital goods and, eventually, to copy foreign technologies that then make their own industries more efficient.

Table 14.4 Panel estimates of technological spillovers (1971–2004)

Explanatory variables[1]	ln TFP	ln TFP
ln S^d	0.095 (17.88)[2]	0.098 (6.13)
ln S^f	0.213 (15.68)	0.035 (3.14)
ln H		0.725 (8.33)
Adjusted R^2	0.80	0.76
Annual observations	34	34
Number of countries	24	24
Pooled observations	816	816
Fixed effects	yes	yes

Notes: (1) S^d represents the domestic R&D capital stock in the business sector, calculated using the perpetual inventory rule (depreciation rate = 0.05); S^f represents the foreign R&D capital stock, constructed as the weighted average of 23 countries R&D stocks with bilateral imports as weights; H is domestic human capital proxied by the average years of schooling.
(2) *t*-statistics in parentheses.
Source: Coe *et al.* (2009).

Another hypothesized channel through which this happens is via human capital which then increases domestic TFP.

Learning rates

In a different setting, the aim of Irwin and Klenow (1994) is to estimate learning rates, for example the rates at which costs fall with each doubling of cumulative output. They use quarterly, firm-level data on seven generations of dynamic random access memory (DRAM) semiconductors over 1974–92 to find such evidence. They show that, on average, unit production costs fall by 20 percent every time cumulative output doubles. They reckon also that when a firm (US or Japanese) makes an extra semiconductor, the spin-offs for other firms are worth about one-third of the first firm's gains. Learning spillovers are found to be just as much between firms in different countries as between firms within a given country. Equally important is the finding that the transmission of learning from one generation of semiconductors to the next is very weak. This last evidence raises questions regarding industrial policies since their effects, which are initially aimed at stimulating a particular generation of semiconductors, would likely be short-lived.

Trade liberalization and markups

Another mechanism for understanding the linkages between openness to trade and growth are the gains that are derived from increased competition.[18] To establish such a link consider the Cobb-Douglas specification of the preceding section: $Y_j = A_j F(K_j, L_j) = A_j K_j^{\alpha_j} L_j^{\beta_j}$, knowing that a general production function would lead to a similar regression equation. Subscript t is ignored for simplicity and a subscript j is introduced to indicate that empirical analyses of this section use firm-level or sector-level data, not country data. Differentiate the production function totally and use the "^" notation (e.g., $\hat{A}_j = dA_j/A_j$) to obtain:

$$\hat{Y}_j = \hat{A}_j + \alpha_j \hat{K}_j + \beta_j \hat{L}_j$$

Though the assumptions of perfect competition and CRS are plausible at the aggregate level, they are ruled out at the firm level. Therefore, let λ_j define the degree of homogeneity of the firm's production function:

$$\lambda_j = \alpha_j + \beta_j$$

Hence:

$$\hat{Y}_j = \hat{A}_j + \beta_j\left(\hat{L}_j - \hat{K}_j\right) + \lambda_j\hat{K}_j \tag{14.55}$$

With imperfect competition on the goods market, the equality between the value marginal product and the nominal wage is:

$$p_j\left(\frac{\eta_j - 1}{\eta_j}\right)A_j\beta_j K_j^{\alpha_j}L_j^{\beta_j - 1} = w$$

where η_j is the positive elasticity of demand faced by the individual firm j (see equation (8.17)). The price-cost mark-up is therefore:

$$\frac{p_j}{w} = \left(A_j\beta_j K_j^{\alpha_j}L_j^{\beta_j - 1}\right)^{-1}\left(\frac{\eta_j}{\eta_j - 1}\right)$$

The ratio of price to marginal cost is proportional to $\eta_j/(\eta_j - 1)$ so that any change in this ratio will be indicative of a change in the mark-up. Next, it is useful to compute the factor share earned by labor:

$$\theta_{Lj} = \frac{wL_j}{p_jY_j} = \left(\frac{\eta_j - 1}{\eta_j}\right)\beta_j < \beta_j$$

Hence, $\theta_{Lj} = \beta_j$ only if $\eta_j = \infty$. Substituting β_j in (14.55), we obtain an expression for output growth that is a sum of three terms:

$$\hat{Y}_j = \hat{A}_j + \left(\frac{\eta_j}{\eta_j - 1}\right)\theta_{Lj}\left(\hat{L}_j - \hat{K}_j\right) + \lambda_j\hat{K}_j \tag{14.56}$$

This is the basic growth equation that has been applied to several environments. For example, using firm-level data, (14.56) is the basic equation that is used to estimate the scale parameter and changes in the mark-up ratio during trade policy episodes.

Harrison (1994) has applied this technique to firm-level data for the Ivory Coast and Levinsohn (1993) to firm-level data for Turkey[19], both studies supporting the hypothesis that trade liberalization policies reduce mark-ups. Badinger (2007) uses a sample of ten EU countries and 18 sectors to estimate the potential pro-competitive effect of the Single Market. Results show significant mark-up reductions in manufacturing and in construction, but not in services. In a similar setting, Feenstra and Weinstein (2010) estimate the impact of globalization and show (i) an increase in import shares, (ii) the exit of US firms and (iii) a reduction in mark-ups.

14.7 Concluding remarks

An important contribution of new growth models is the endogenization of technological change. The thinking about how technological change comes about and how it affects a country's productivity is important to this process. Many theoretical results stress the link between a country's growth, its R&D investment and its rate of innovation. Much of the current debate is whether the efforts of research labs are private knowledge to the active firm or whether this knowledge leaks into the pool of domestic and foreign knowledge. Recent empirical evidence suggests the existence of large spillovers within and outside national boundaries.

The evidence that spillovers are international in scope makes national policy recommendations more complex than initially thought. The set of optimal policy rules, if any, aimed at stimulating high-tech industries have to be modified by taking into account the fact that firms in other countries may benefit as well. Though the empirical results are not totally informative about the underlying transmission mechanism of spillovers, the existence of such spillovers is consistent with the recent trends toward improved protection of intellectual property rights.

Problems

14.1 The literature has criticized the two-gap literature for its neglect of relative prices. However, a number of empirical studies, reviewed by Harrison and Rodriguez-Clare (2009), suggest that the growth effects of trade depend very much on the composition of exports. Consider therefore a deterioration in the terms of trade in Figure 14.1. What are the implications for the composition and growth of domestic output?

14.2 Replace (14.16) by the Cobb-Douglas production function $Y_t = K_t^\alpha (A_t L_t)^{1-\alpha}$. Compute the steady-state value $\bar{k}$ obtained in (14.19), $\bar{y}$ which is the steady state output per effective unit of labor and the steady-state output per worker. Show that that the steady-state per capita income of a country depends on the following six elements: s, n, m, μ, α and A_0. Using the comparative statics of long-run per capita income, discuss the likely sources of heterogeneity in steady-state per capita outputs. Based on your new insights compare Luxembourg and the Democratic Republic of the Congo, the example we used in the introduction to illustrate this chapter.

14.3 Derive formally the eight predictions of the neoclassical growth model with labor-augmenting technical improvements that follow equation (14.24).

14.4 Beta-convergence and sigma-convergence are related concepts. Show that beta-convergence is necessary, though not sufficient, for sigma-convergence.

Notes

1. See, e.g., Burmeister (1980) for a detailed review of the literature.
2. The material of this section partly depends on Findlay (1984) which contains both an exposition and a critique of the two-gap model.
3. Next to β- and σ-convergence, there exist tests of convergence applied to time series. See, e.g., Bernard and Durlauf (1995).
4. See Figures 11.4 and 11.7 in Barro and Sala-i-Martin (1995).

5. Barro and Sala-i-Martin (1995) derive this regression equation using differential equations (14.27) and (14.33) of the Ramsey model and log-linearizing this system around steady states values for the case of a Cobb–Douglas production function. See Appendix 2A.

6. See the initial contribution by Ramsey (1928) and the later developments by Cass (1965) and Koopmans (1965).

7. In this control problem, k is called the state variable; d the control variable; (14.27) is the equation of motion and k_o is the boundary condition. See, e.g., Blanchard and Fischer (1989, Chapter 2) or Intriligator (1971, Chapter 4) for more details.

8. The costate variable is interpreted as the shadow price of additional capital per worker measured in utility units.

9. With depreciation $(\mu \neq 0)$, (14.34) would become $f'(\overline{k}_m) = n + \rho + \mu$ and the Golden Rule condition $f'(\overline{k}_g) = n + \mu$.

10. Relative prices matter as well in single-sector models with borrowing and lending between countries. In this framework, intertemporal trade arises on the basis of differences in autarkic relative prices of present goods in terms of future goods, or 1 plus the autarkic rate of interest. See Blanchard and Fischer (1989) for applications on issues of saving and current account deficit/surplus.

11. This proposition has been shown in the two-good, two-factor context of Chapter 4 and extended to arbitrary numbers of goods and factors in Chapter 7.

12. An extension of the current framework is to consider dynamic two-sector models. They provide additional realism by allowing relative prices to feature explicitly, but there is added complexity because existence, uniqueness and stability of balanced growth paths of economies in isolation cannot be proved for all combinations of assumptions. Even more serious difficulties arise once international trade is introduced. To show the existence of a world steady-state equilibrium one needs to consider two laws of motion like (14.18), one for each country, together with the international market clearing condition that implies trade balance equilibrium. Oniki and Uzawa (1965), Bardhan (1965) and Atsumi (1971) have characterized the existence result and the sufficient conditions for stability. For example, Bardhan (1965) has shown that, when both countries are incompletely specialized, the sufficient conditions for stability are that either consumer goods are more capital-intensive than capital goods or the elasticities of factor substitution are equal to or greater than unity in both sectors in both countries.

13. There exist other classes of endogenous growth models dealing with, for example, public infrastructure (Barro, 1990) and taxation.

14. The model describes a process of knowledge accumulation by investing: learning by investing. Next to this, a strand of the literature, starting with Arrow (1961), places emphasis on on-the-job accumulation of human capital: learning by doing. Lucas (1993) uses learning rates in connection with international trade to explain episodes of very rapid income growth.

15. This model brings out a way in which government intervention affects an economy's growth rate. Because of the external spillover effects of the public stock of knowledge, a firm making investments raises the productivity of other investments, but these revenues cannot be appropriated by the active firm. A subsidy on the private use of capital would enable the economy to achieve the social optimum.

16. See Grossman and Helpman (1991, Chapter 3, Chapter 9) for the formal derivation of this and subsequent results.

17. Equally important is the abundance of studies, compiled by Harrison and Rodriguez-Clare (2009), which test for the role of FDI on a country's growth. An equally large literature,

reviewed by Obstfeld (2009), documents the impact of financial opening on the economic welfare level or growth rate of developing countries. The econometric difficulties that characterize the literature on trade openness and growth are similar and equally severe in the case of FDI flows and financial integration.
18. The material of this section has been inspired by Feenstra (2003, ch. 10, pp. 338–343) and Feenstra and Weinstein (2010).
19. Section 8.1 of Chapter 8 contains a detailed description of Levinsohn's (1993) empirical study.

References and additional reading

The foundation of economic growth

Arrow, K.J. (1961), "The Economic Implications of Learning by Doing," *Review of Economic Studies*, 29, 155–173.

Atsumi, H. (1971), "The Long-Run Offer Function and a Dynamic Theory of International Trade," *Journal of International Economics*, 1, 267–299.

Bardhan, P.K. (1965), "Equilibrium Growth in the International Economy," *Quarterly Journal of Economics*, 79, 455–464.

Bhagwati, J. (1958), "Immizerising Growth: A Geometric Note," *Review of Economic Studies*, 25, 201–205.

Blanchard, O.J. and Fischer, S. (1989), *Lectures on Macroeconomics* (Cambridge, MA: MIT Press).

Burmeister, E. (1980), *Mathematical Theories of Economic Growth* (New York: Macmillan).

Cass, D. (1965), "Optimal Growth in an Aggregative Model of Capital Accumulation," *Review of Economic Studies*, 32, 233–240.

Domar, E.D. (1946), "Capital Expansion, Rate of Growth and Employment," *Econometrica*, 14, 137–147.

Harrod, R.F. (1939), "An Essay in Dynamic Theory," *Economic Journal*, 49, 14–33.

Intriligator, M.D. (1971), *Mathematical Optimization and Economic Theory* (Englewood Cliffs, NJ: Prentice Hall).

Jones, H.G. (1975), *An Introduction to Modern Theories of Economic Growth* (London: Nelson).

Koopmans, T.C. (1965), "On the Concept of Optimal Economic Growth," in *The Econometric Approach to Development Planning* (Amsterdam: North-Holland), reissue of *Pontificae Academiae Scientiarum Scripta Varia*, 28 (1965), 225–230.

Oniki, H. and Uzawa, H. (1965), "Patterns of Trade and Investment in a Dynamic Model of International Trade," *Review of Economic Studies*, 32, 15–38.

Ramsey, F.P. (1928), "A Mathematical Theory of Saving," *Economic Journal*, 38, 543–559.

Solow, R.M. (1956), "A Contribution to the Theory of Economic Growth," *Quarterly Journal of Economics*, 70, 65–94.

Swan, T.W. (1956), "Economic Growth and Capital Accumulation," *Economic Record*, 334–361.

Uzawa, H. (1961), "On a Two-Sector Model of Economic Growth," *Review of Economic Studies*, 29, 40–47.

Ventura, J. (1997), "Growth and Interdependence," *Quarterly Journal of Economics*, February, 57–84.

Endogenous growth

Aghion, P. and Howitt, P. (1992), "A Model of Growth through Creative Destruction," *Econometrica*, 60 (2), 323–351.

Aghion, P. and Howitt, P. (1998), *Endogenous Growth Theory* (Cambridge, MA: MIT Press).

Barro, R.J. (1990), "Government Spending in a Simple Model of Endogenous Growth," *Journal of Political Economy*, 98, S103–125.

Grossman, G.M. and Helpman, E. (1991), *Innovation and Growth in the Global Economy* (Cambridge, MA: MIT Press).

Lucas, R.E. (1988), "On the Mechanics of Economic Development," *Journal of Monetary Economics*, 22, 3–42.

Lucas, R.E. (1993), "Making a Miracle," *Econometrica*, 61, 251–272.

Rebelo, S. (1991), "Long-Run Policy Analysis and Long-Run Growth," *Journal of Political Economy*, 99, 500–521.

Romer, P.M. (1986), "Increasing Returns and Long-Run Growth," *Journal of Political Economy*, 94, 1002–1037.

Romer, P.M. (1989), "Capital Accumulation in the Theory of Long-Run Growth," in R.J. Barro (Ed.), *Modern Business Cycle Theory* (Cambridge, MA: Harvard University Press).

Romer, P.M. (1990), "Endogenous Technological Change," *Journal of Political Economy*, 98, S71–102.

Romer, P.M. (1994), "The Origins of Endogenous Growth," *The Journal of Economic Perspectives*, 8, 3–22.

Sener, F. and Zhao, L. (2009), "Globalization, R&D and the iPod Cycle," *Journal of International Economics* 77, 101–108.

Empirical studies

Badinger, H. (2007), "Has the EU's Single Market Programme Fostered Competition? Testing for a Decrease in Markup Ratios in EU Industries," *Oxford Bulletin of Economics and Statistics*, 69 (4), 497–519.

Barro, R.J. and Sala-i-Martin, X. (1992), "Convergence," *Journal of Political Economy*, 100, 223–251.

Barro, R.J. and Lee, J.-W. (1994), "Losers and Winners in Economic Growth," *The World Bank Economic Review*, (Supplement), 267–314.

Bernard, A.B. and Durlauf, S.N. (1995), "Convergence in International Output," *Journal of Applied Econometrics*, 10, 97–108.

Coe, D.T., Helpman, E., and Hoffmaister, A.W. (1997), "North-South R&D Spillovers," *Economic Journal*, 107, 134–149.

Coe, D.T., Helpman, E., and Hoffmaister, A.W. (2009), "International R&D Spillovers and Institutions," *European Economic Review*, 53, 723–741.

Debaere, P. and Lee, H. (2010), "The Real-Side Determinants of Countries' Terms of Trade: A Panel Data Analysis," Working Paper, Darden School of Business, University of Virginia.

Dollar, D. and Kraay, A. (2004), "Trade, Growth and Poverty," *Economic Journal*, 114 (493), F22–F49.

Feenstra, R.C. and Weinstein, D.E. (2010), "Globalization, Markups, and the US Price Level," NBER Working Paper No. 15749 (Cambridge, MA: NBER).

Hallak, J.C. and Levinsohn, J. (2009), "Fooling Ourselves: Evaluating the Globalization and Growth Debate," in E. Zedillo (Ed.), *The Future of Globalization* (London and New York: Routledge).

Harrison, A.E. (1994), "Productivity, Imperfect Competition and Trade Reform: Theory and Evidence," *Journal of International Economics*, 36 (1/2), 53–73.

Harrison, E.A. and Rodriguez-Clare, A. (2009), "Trade, Foreign Investment and Industrial Policy," in D. Rodrick and M.R. Rosenzweig (Eds.), *Handbook of Development Economics*, Vol. 5 (Amsterdam: North-Holland), ch. 63.

Huisman, F. (2010), *The Middle East: Measuring Economic Integration and Labor Migration*, MSc thesis, Erasmus University Rotterdam.

Irwin, D.A. and Klenow, P.J. (1994), "Learning-by-Doing Spillovers in the Semiconductor Industry," *Journal of Political Economy*, 102 (6), 1200–1227.

Keller, W. (2004), "International Technology Diffusion," *Journal of Economic Literature*, 42 (3), 752–782.

Krugman, P.R. (1989), "Differences in Income Elasticities and Trends in Real Exchange Rates," *European Economic Review*, 33, 1031–1054.

Lee, D.W. and Lee, T.H. (1995), "Human Capital and Economic Growth: Tests Based on the International Evaluation of Educational Achievements," *Economics Letters*, 47, 219–225.

Levine, R. and Renelt, D. (1992), "A Sensitivity Analysis of Cross-Country Growth Regressions," *American Economic Review*, 82, 942–963.

Levine, R. and Zervos, S.J. (1993), "What We Have Learned about Policy and Growth from Cross-Country Regressions," *American Economic Review, Papers and Proceedings*, 83, 426–430.

Levinsohn, J. (1993), "Testing the Imports-As-Market-Discipline Hypothesis," *Journal of International Economics*, 35 (1/2), 1–22.

Obstfeld, M. (2009), "International Finance and Growth in Developing Countries: What Have We Learned?" NBER Working Paper No. 14691 (Cambridge, MA: NBER).

Rodriguez, F. and Rodrik, D. (2001), "Trade Policy and Economic Growth: A Skeptic's Guide to Cross-national Evidence," in B. Bernanke and K. Rogoff (Eds.), *NBER Macroeconomics Annual 2000* (Cambridge, MA: MIT Press).

Wolf, H.C. (1994), "Growth Convergence Reconsidered," *Weltwirtschaftliches Archiv*, 130, 747–759.

World Bank (2007), *World Development Report 2008: Agriculture for Development* (Washington: The World Bank).

World Bank (2009), *World Development Report 2010: Development and Climate Change* (Washington: The World Bank).

Two-gap model

Findlay, R. (1984), "Growth and Development in Trade Models," in R.W. Jones and P.B. Kenen (Eds.), *Handbook of International Economics*, Vol. 1 (Amsterdam: North-Holland), 185–236.

Gersovitz, M. (1982), "The Estimation of the Two-Gap Model," *Journal of International Economics*, 12, 111–124.

Van Wijnbergen, S. (1986), "Macroeconomic Aspects of the Effectiveness of Foreign Aid: On the Two-Gap Model, Home Goods Disequilibrium and Real Exchange Rate Misalignment," *Journal of International Economics*, 21, 123–136.

Other

Acemoglu, D. (2008), *Introduction to Modern Economic Growth* (Princeton: Princeton University Press).

Aghion, P. and Howitt, P. (2009), *The Economics of Growth* (Cambridge, MA: MIT Press).

Barro, R.J. and Sala-i-Martin, X. (1995), *Economic Growth* (New York: McGraw-Hill).

Feenstra, R.C. (2003), *Advanced International Trade: Theory and Evidence* (Princeton: Princeton University Press).

Islam, N. (2003), "What have we Learned from the Convergence Debate?" *Journal of Economic Surveys*, 17, 309–362.

Jones, C.I. (2006), *Introduction to Economic Growth*, 2nd ed. (New York: W.W. Norton & Company).

Mankiw, N.G. (1995), "The Growth of Nations," *Brookings Papers on Economic Activity*, 1, 275–326.

Rodrik, D. and Rosenzweig, M.R. (2009), *Handbook of Development Economics*, Vol. 5 (Amsterdam: North-Holland).

Appendix

Data methods and sources

This appendix gives an overview of the data commonly used in applied analyses of trade and indicates sources for these data.[1] Over the last 15 years internationally comparable data have become widely available on the Internet. The website of any given organization will have a "statistics" link that provides available data. Often, a telephone call to the relevant statistical or research division of an organization can turn up unadvertised databases. While locating unique databases is not always easy, a little effort can prove rewarding. Below, we provide an overview of the nature of trade data and then discuss the nature and sources of the most frequently used international data. The list of World Wide Web links given in the text is not exhaustive, but it does provide a good starting point.

A.1 Trade flow data

The principal source of internationally comparable trade data is the United Nations (UN) *Comtrade* database (http://comtrade.un.org/). These data derive from UN member countries which submit their trade flow data to the United Nations Statistical Office (http://www.un.org/Depts/unsd/). The UN processes and maintains these data. In recent years they have been classified using a system known as the Harmonized System (HS). Before the introduction of the HS in 1988, the trade data were organized according to the Standard International Trade Classification (SITC) system. Due to the change in the system of classification, developing a long time series of trade flows for several countries can require a concordance (translation table) that links one classification system to the other. In part, the ability to translate one classification system to another will depend on the level of detail (disaggregation) desired. In general, the more detailed the level of disaggregation the less precise will be the link between different classification systems.

The harmonized system

The HS is an internationally agreed and comparable six-digit code system for classifying goods/products. It is maintained by the World Customs Organization (http://www.wcoomd.org/home_hsoverviewboxes.htm). The HS comprises approximately 5300 article/product descriptions, arranged in 99 chapters grouped in 21 sections (see Table A.1). The six-digit codes comprise three parts. The first two digits identify the chapter, for example 09 = Coffee, Tea, Maté and Spices. The next two digits identify groupings within the given chapter, for example 09.02 = Tea, whether it is flavored or not. The final two digits are more specific regarding the product, for example 09.02.10 Green tea (not fermented). Down to the HS six-digit level, all countries classify products the same way (a few exceptions exist where some countries apply old versions of the HS). Countries are then free to add additional codes below the six-digit level depending on their needs. For example, the Harmonized Tariff System

Table A.1 Major sections of the Harmonized System (HS), 2007 version

I	Live animals; animal products
II	Vegetable products
III	Animal or vegetable fats and oils and their cleavage products; prepared edible fats; animal or vegetable waxes
IV	Prepared foodstuffs; beverages, spirits and vinegar; tobacco and manufactured tobacco substitutes
V	Mineral products
VI	Products of the chemical or allied industries
VII	Plastics and articles thereof; rubber and articles thereof
IX	Wood and articles of wood; wood charcoal; cork and articles of cork; manufactures of straw, of esparto or of other plaiting materials; basketware and wickerwork
X	Pulp of wood or of other fibrous cellulosic material; recovered (waste and scrap) paper or paperboard; paper and paperboard and articles thereof
XI	Textiles and textile articles
XII	Footwear, headgear, umbrellas, sun umbrellas, walking-sticks, seat-sticks, whips, riding-crops and parts thereof; prepared feathers and articles made therewith; artificial flowers; articles of human hair
XIII	Articles of stone, plaster, cement, asbestos, mica or similar materials; ceramic products; glass and glassware
XIV	Natural or cultured pearls, precious or semi-precious stones, precious metals, metals clad with precious metal and articles thereof; imitation jewelry; coin
XV	Base metals and articles of base metal
XVI	Machinery and mechanical appliances; electrical equipment; parts thereof; sound recorders and reproducers, television image and sound recorders and reproducers, and parts and accessories of such articles
XVII	Vehicles, aircraft, vessels and associated transport equipment
XVIII	Optical, photographic, cinematographic, measuring, checking, precision, medical or surgical instruments and apparatus; clocks and watches; musical instruments; parts and accessories thereof
XIX	Arms and ammunition; parts and accessories thereof
XX	Miscellaneous manufactured articles
XXI	Works of art, collectors' pieces and antiques

(HTS) used by the US goes down to a 10-digit level. However, such detailed categories below the six-digit level are often not internationally comparable.[2]

The Standard International Classification System (SITC)

The SITC system was the main system for classifying trade flow data prior to the introduction of the HS, and it is still widely encountered. Like the HS, the SITC system consists of increasingly disaggregated levels of product categories, beginning from the one-digit *section* level down to the five digit *item* level. The final version, SITC Revision 4 (http://unstats.un.org/unsd/trade/sitcrev4.htm), consists of nine one-digit *sections*, 67 two-digit *divisions*, 262 three-digit *groups*, 1023 four digit *sub-groups* and 2970 five-digit *items*. Table A.2 shows the

Table A.2 Product category headings at the section level of the SITC

Section	Description
0	Food and live animals
1	Beverages and tobacco
2	Crude materials, excluding fuels
3	Mineral fuels, lubricants and related materials
4	Animal and vegetable oils, fats and waxes
5	Chemicals
6	Manufactured goods
7	Machinery and transport equipment
8	Miscellaneous manufactured goods
9	Goods not classified by kind

product category headings at the one-digit *section* level of the SITC. Sections 0–4 comprise agricultural products and raw material while 5–8 are considered to be semi-finished and finished manufactured goods. Section 9 refers to special transactions such as movements of non-monetary gold, and also "hidden" transactions typically related to the sale of military weaponry. A full listing of the SITC (in all its revisions) is available at the UN's comtrade website (http://comtrade.un.org/); a portable document format (pdf) version is available at http://unstats.un.org/unsd/trade/SITC%20Rev%204%20FINAL.pdf.

In principle, the value of transactions recorded at higher levels of aggregation of either the HS or the SITC should equal the sum of transactions at lower levels of aggregation. In reality, the total at higher levels may exceed the sum of lower level items since transactions below US $1,000 are usually not reported. In addition, a UN member country has complete discretion as to the data it reports to the UN. For example, a country may choose not to report sums at lower levels of aggregation for reasons of disclosure or lack of funds (common for developing countries).

For applied work, it is important to recognize that the HS and SITC are a product-based and not industry-based classifications. Hence, each HS or SITC category necessarily involves some aggregation of products produced by different industries. This can create problems when one attempts to develop empirical measures that conform to the industry construct hypothesized by trade theory. More generally, any analysis that seeks to link trade flows to their industry of origin or that attempts to organize trade flows thought to emanate from industries with particular characteristics (e.g., labor-intensive versus capital-intensive, see Leamer, 1984) will require a concordance between the HS or SITC systems and the relevant industrial classification (see Section A.2 below).

Trade reporting systems

Countries use one of two systems for recording trade flows: either the *general trade system* or the *special trade system*. The difference between these systems is the definition of the statistical boundary. Under the *general trade system,* any commodity that crosses the national frontier of the country is recorded. Under the *special trade system,* any commodity that crosses the customs boundary is recorded. Neither system reports "direct transit trade" which refers to the movement of commodities across national frontiers solely for transport.

Recorded exports under the general trade system consist of:

(1) exports of national products;

(2) exports from customs-bonded manufacturing plants;

(3) nationalized exports;

(4) exports from customs-bonded warehouses and free areas.

Most countries aggregate these four categories into two categories when reporting their trade data: national exports and re-exports. National exports consist of items (1) and (2) above, while re-exports consist of items (3) and (4). National exports therefore consist both of goods that are produced domestically and goods that imported but which undergo some physical transformation. Re-exports consist of commodities that are imported and then exported in essentially the same physical condition. However, re-exports can contribute to a country's GDP since activities such as warehousing, repackaging, blending and other simple processing of goods (not involving a transformation of the commodity) represent value added by domestic factors of production.

Recorded imports under the general trade system consist of:

(1) imports entering directly for home consumption or use;

(2) imports into customs-bonded manufacturing plants;

(3) imports into customs-bonded warehouses and free areas.

Exports from, and imports into, customs-bonded warehouses and free trade areas are what is commonly called entrepôt trade. As noted in Chapter 1, entrepôt trade can represent a sizable fraction of a country's total exports.

The primary difference between the *general trade system* and the *special trade system* is that the latter excludes entrepôt trade. Thus, exports recorded under the *special trade system* consist of:

(1) exports of national produce;

(2) exports from customs-bonded manufacturing plants;

(3) nationalized exports.

Recorded imports under the special trade system are:

(1) imports entering directly for home consumption or use;

(2) imports into customs-bonded manufacturing plants;

(3) imports withdrawn (inward) from customs-bonded warehouses and free areas.

The exclusion of entrepôt trade implies that a country's recorded exports and imports are less than they would be if recorded under the general trade system. Hence, export and import volumes can differ across counties due to differences in their system of trade reporting. A further issue is that some countries that report under the general trade system report their national exports but not their re-exports. Hence, the country's total exports are underreported whereas its total imports include the value of any goods ultimately re-exported. This difference can bias measures such as net exports or revealed comparative indexes that use ratios of exports and imports.

Aside from differences in reporting systems, trade figures can be biased for a number of reasons. For example, at one time the US did not record as imports goods produced in Mexico under the *maquiladora* program. In addition, for political reasons, Taiwan's trade is not openly reported in the UN data. In such cases, analysts often resort to "backing-out" the data by using the mirror image data of partner countries. For example, (estimated) data on Taiwanese exports can be obtained by adding the data on partner country imports from Taiwan. Note that the use of partner country data contains a bias since exports are usually measured free-on-board (*fob*) while imports are measured cost-insurance-freight (*cif*), and the latter values normally exceed the former.

Sources

As noted previously, the main online source of trade data is the UN's *Comtrade* data portal (http://comtrade.un.org/db/). The following are some other useful sites of trade (and other international) data:

▲ http://cid.econ.ucdavis.edu/. This site at UC Davis was developed by Robert Feenstra. It contains detailed data on US imports and tariffs as well as long time series on countries' exports and imports around the world.

▲ http://www.macalester.edu/research/economics/page/haveman/trade.resources/tradedata. html. This site was created by Jon Havemen at McCalaster University.

▲ http://www.imf.org. This is the link to the International Monetary Fund whose *Direction of Trade* reports aggregate bilateral trade flows of its member countries.

▲ http://lysander.sourceoecd.org. This is the link to the Organisation for Economic Co-operation and Development (OECD, http://www.oecd.org) main statistics portal. The site contains detailed trade data of OECD countries with individual partner countries.

▲ http://europa.eu.int/en/comm/eurostat. This is the link to the European Statistical Agency (EuroStat). Like the IMF and OECD, EuroStat data usually only cover the trade of its member countries.

A.2   Industry characteristics

Internationally comparable data on industry characteristics is published according to the International Standard Industry Classification (ISIC). Table A.3 shows the industry categories at the three-digit level of the ISIC. The four-digit level of the ISIC roughly matches the three-digit level of the HS and the SITC. UN publications that describe the SITC or ISIC indicate the relationship between these systems of classification. However, the mapping is not one-to-one; that is, a given HS or SITC category may contain products produced by several ISIC industries. Empirical studies routinely adopt the three-digit HS or SITC level as equivalent to the ISIC industry definitions.

Production and inputs

The United Nations Industrial Development Organization (UNIDO, http://www.unido.org) publishes data on production and expenditures on factor inputs in its annual publication *International Yearbook of Industrial Statistics*. These data cover industry variables such as value added, output, wages and salaries, gross fixed capital formation (all in current prices), number of establishments, employment, females employed and production indexes for the 29 three-digit ISIC manufacturing sectors. UNIDO makes these data available online at http://www.unido.org/index.php?id=1000327. The OECD's STAN (STructural ANalysis) database (www.oecd.org/sti/stan/) contains similar data for OECD member countries and covers ISIC-related sectors from 1972. The STAN database includes export and import data for each sector and is cheaper than its UNIDO counterpart, but covers fewer countries. The

Table A.3 International Standard Industrial Classification, three-digit level

ISIC	Description
300	Total manufacturing
311	Food products
313	Beverages
314	Tobacco
321	Textiles
322	Wearing apparel, except footwear
323	Leather products
324	Footwear, except rubber or plastic
331	Wood products, except furniture
332	Furniture, except metal
341	Paper and products
342	Printing and publishing
351	Industrial chemicals
352	Other chemicals
353	Petroleum refineries
354	Miscellaneous petroleum and coal products
355	Rubber products
356	Plastic products
361	Pottery, china, earthenware
362	Glass and products
369	Other non-metallic mineral products
371	Iron and steel
372	Non-ferrous metals
381	Fabricated metal products
382	Machinery, except electrical
383	Machinery, electric
384	Transport equipment
385	Professional and scientific equipment
390	Other manufactured products

STAN database can be found at http://www.oecd-ilibrary.org/industry-and-services/data/stan-oecd-structural-analysis-statistics_stan-data-en.

Input–output data

Calculations of the factor content of trade used in tests of the factor abundance theory (see Chapter 7) require data organized in the form of national input–output (I–O) tables. The international comparability of I–O tables is often hampered as the tables are constructed using national systems of industry classification. Except as noted below, no supranational agency has yet begun to maintain detailed national I–O tables on a consistent basis (or at least make them publicly available). Hence, the main source of detailed I–O tables must remain the national statistical agency responsible for their construction.

In the US, input–output tables are available from the Bureau of Economic Analysis, US Department of Commerce (http://www.bea.gov) and are also published in its *Survey of Current Business*.

The OECD STAN *Input–output Database* (http://www.oecd-ilibrary.org/industry-and-services/data/stan-oecd-structural-analysis-statistics/stan-input–output_data-00169-en) provides comparable I–O tables in both current and constant prices for OECD countries. Similar tables are available from the Global Trade and Analysis Project (GTAP) at Purdue University (https://www.gtap.agecon.purdue.edu/databases/default.asp/). GTAP is primarily concerned with the development and maintenance of Applied General Equilibrium models and data.

Concordances

A concordance (translation table) provides a link between different classification systems. As noted previously, the UN publishes concordances between the HS, SITC and the ISIC. However, these concordances do not contain weights that indicate, for example, the fraction of a given HS category that should be allocated to a given ISIC category or vice versa. The national statistical agency responsible for submitting its country's trade or industry data to the UN maintains (unweighted) concordances between the national systems of commodity or industry classification and the relevant international systems. For example, EuroStat has concordances between the NACE[3] and the ISIC while the US Bureau of the Census (http://www.census.gov) has concordances between the US SIC (Standard Industrial Classification, the North American Industry Classification System (NAICS) and the ISIC (as well as the SITC and HS). These concordances can be obtained by visiting the website of the appropriate statistical agency.

Linked trade and production data

Some international agencies have sought to provide trade and production data classified by the ISIC. The UNIDO *Industrial Demand-Supply Database* reports exports, imports and apparent consumption (production plus imports minus exports) for commodities defined at the six-digit level of the ISIC (http://www.unido.org/index.php?id=1000311). As already noted, the OECD STAN database contains export and import data for 49 ISIC related sectors. Full information for these databases is available at the World Wide Web site of each organization.

A.3 Country characteristics

Data on country characteristics are available from a wide variety of sources. For "raw" data, the principle sources are the "Yearbooks" and similar annual publications of the various UN agencies. These include the UN *Yearbook of National Accounts Statistics*, the International Labour Office's *Yearbook of International Labor Statistics*, and the Food and Agricultural Organization's *Production Yearbook*. Other important sources of country data are the World Bank's *World Tables* and the IMF's *International Financial Statistics*. Most of these publications are available in electronic form at relatively low cost. The following briefly discusses the construction of some country characteristics that are commonly used in the analysis of trade patterns.

Physical capital stock

The calculation of national capital stocks is typically made by summing a country's Gross Domestic Investment (GDI) flows over time while applying deflation and depreciation factors. GDI flows measure expenditures for the addition of reproducible capital goods by the private and public sector. Excluded are increases in natural resources and government expenditures for construction and durable goods for military purposes. There is considerable latitude in choosing a rate of depreciation. If disaggregated data on investment flows are available then allowance can be made for asset lives for different classes of assets (for example structures versus equipment). However, most studies adopt an average asset life of 15 years, which corresponds to an annual depreciation rate of 13.3 percent using the double declining balance method of depreciation. An exception to this is the capital stock calculations made for the Penn World Tables (http://pwt.econ.upenn.edu/). For example, the capital stock estimated contained in version 5.6 used the following depreciation rates: 15% for producer durables, 24% for transport equipment, 3.5% for nonresidential construction, residential construction and other construction.

Another issue to be confronted in computing national capital stocks is the conversion of national currency values into a common unit of account, typically the US dollar. Three alternative methods are discussed below.[4] Let:

I_t = nominal GDI flow in units of home currency in year t;

P_t^b = implicit GDI deflator at time t with base year b, $P_b^b = 1.0$;

e_t = exchange rate at time t, dollars per unit of domestic currency;

δ = rate of depreciation.

The first formula below sums a country's GDI flows measured in domestic currency and then converts this value into dollars using the current exchange rate: The real capital stock at the end of year t measured in year b domestic currency is:

$$K_t^b = \sum_{j=0}^{t} (1-\delta)^{t-j} \left(I_j / P_j^b \right)$$

Multiplying this year t capital stock by the year t GDI deflator in domestic currency units and then the exchange rate in year t gives the current dollar value capital stock:

$$K_{1t}^\$ = K_t^b P_t^b e_t.$$

A defect of this method is that exchange rate changes not offset by domestic price changes can lead to large changes in the measured value of the capital stock. A second method uses the US implicit GDI deflator $(P(\$)_t^b)$ instead of the national currency GDI deflator and then convert the domestic current values at the exchange rate of the base year:

$$K_{2t}^\$ = K_t^b P(\$)_t^b e_b.$$

With purchasing power parity, differences in the exchange rates over time would exactly match the changes in price levels (i.e., $P_t^b e_t = P(\$)_t^b e_b$) and the two measures would be the same.

A final possibility is to convert the investment flows year by year into dollars and then use the US GDI deflator to convert the capital stocks to constant dollar figures which are then summed and convert to current year t dollars:

$$K_{3t}^{\$} = P(\$)_t^b \sum_{j=0}^{t} (1 - \delta)^{t-j} \left(I_j e_j / P(\$)_j^b\right)$$

This last method effectively uses purchasing power parity (PPP) adjusted exchange rates and therefore implicitly assumes that the composition of investment goods in each country is the same. The second and third capital stock measures (K_{2t}^b and K_{3t}^b) are less sensitive to changes in the exchange rate.

In recent years a number of sources for country capital stock data have become available. One common source is the Penn World Tables available at http://pwt.econ.upenn.edu/. The capital stock data are disaggregated by major asset category and the capital stocks have been computed using PPP corrected exchange rates. The OECD database *Flows and Stocks of Fixed Capital* contain annual data on the flows and stocks of fixed capital for individual OECD countries. Some series begin in 1950 but the complete set of data for all series begins in 1968.

Labor force and human capital

The International Labour Office maintains internationally comparable data on countries' labor force which is operationally defined as the Economically Active Population (EAP). The ILO (www.ilo.org) maintains breakdowns of countries' EAP by sex, industry and occupation (see Table A.4).

A country's supply of human capital or "labor skills" is measured by occupational categories, wage differentials or educational attainment. The ILO maintains internationally comparable data on employment by occupation. These data are classified according to the International Standard Classification of Occupations (ISCO). Table A.4 shows the one-digit level of the ISCO. Studies using these occupational data typically measure "high skilled workers" by ISCO 0/1 plus ISCO 2 or ISCO 0/1 alone. To avoid the possibility of simultaneity bias when conducting regression analyses, analysts frequently measure other categories of "labor skills" by subtracting ISCO 0/1 from a country's EAP and then classifying the remaining workers using some other criteria. For example, Leamer (1984) divides a country's EAP into three groups: workers belonging to ISCO 0/1, literate workers not belonging to ISCO 0/1 workers and illiterate workers.

Wage differential measures of human capital are usually calculated on an industry by industry basis rather that at the national level. A common measure is an industry's average wage minus the national wage of persons with less than 12 years of education. The calculation of wage differentials supposes that higher wages reflect higher levels of human capital.

Table A.4 International Standard Classification of Occupations (ISCO) (one-digit level)

ISCO	Description
0/1	Professional, technical and related workers
2	Administrative and managerial workers
3	Clerical workers
4	Sales workers
5	Service workers
6	Agriculture, fishing, and forestry workers
7–9	Production and related workers

Although, as noted, not normally calculated at the national level, one could in principle add the calculated wage differences across sectors.

Measures of educational attainment, that is, the percentage of the population that has attained a given level of education, are also used to capture differences across countries in levels of human capital.[5] A related set of measures are primary and secondary school enrollment ratios. Barro and Lee (2010) have assembled a number of these education-based measures into one comprehensive data set covering 138 countries at various points in time between 1960 and 1989. These data are available for free from the NBER (http://www.nber.org).

One item to note about occupational and educational attainment data is that the base information comes from ten-year population censuses or five-year labor force sample surveys. Hence, observations for years other than census or sample years must be estimated by interpolation or extrapolation. The lack of annual data therefore precludes the use of such data for time series analysis (in the sense that no additional information is gained by having additional non-census year observations).

Land

Measures of land or, more properly, the economic importance of land, derive from the data on land use maintained by the UN Food and Agricultural Organization (http://www.fao.org) and published in its *Production Yearbook*. Several studies use the FAO's measures of a country's land under cultivation and permanent crops, forest land and pasture and grazing land to respectively denote arable land, forest land and pasture land. Again, to remove the possibility of simultaneity bias that can arise in a regression framework, analysts often use hybrid measures of the economic importance of land. For example, Leamer (1984) uses land area differentiated by climate.

A.4 Other international data and sources

A general purpose database is the World Bank's *World Development Indicators*, available at http://data.worldbank.org/data-catalog/world-development-indicators. Similarly, the OECD maintains its "A to Z" list of its various databases (including international labor migration data) at http://www.oecd.org/document/0,3746,en_2649_201185_46462759_1_1_1_1,00.html. The World Bank also maintains data on the ease or difficulty of doing business in different countries located at http://www.doingbusiness.org.

The French Center for Research and Studies on the World Economy (CEPII) maintains a variety of databases that include variables such as economic distance, common language, country boundary contiguity and so on. (http://www.cepii.fr/anglaisgraph/bdd/bdd.htm). Data such as size of governments, legal structure, regulatory trade barriers, as well as the Fraser Institute's *Economic Freedom of the World Index*, can be found at http://www.freetheworld.com.

International data on bound and applied tariff rates as well as measures of non-tariff barriers (NTBs) are compiled by the World Trade Organization (http://www.wto.org) and are available online at http://www.wto.org/english/tratop_e/tariffs_e/tariff_data_e.htm. The World Bank also maintains a portal site to tariff and NTB data at http://wits.worldbank.org/wits/.

Data on import and export prices are available from the US Bureau of Labor Statistics (http://stats.bls.gov). The OECD *International Trade and Competitiveness Indicators* database contains price deflators for broad SITC commodity groups (basic materials, food, fuels and manufactures) of OECD member countries from 1975 onwards.

Data on Foreign Direct Investment (FDI) stocks and flows by country is available from UNCTAD*stat* at http://unctadstat.unctad.org/ReportFolders/reportFolders.aspx?. OECD FDI data are at http://www.oecd.org/document/53/0,3746,en_21571361_33915056_39108725_1_1_1_1,00.html.

Finally, many universities have access to data sets held by the Inter-University Consortium for Political and Social Research (ICPSR) located at http://www.icpsr.umich.edu/icpsrweb/ICPSR/. Your university librarian can tell you how to gain access to the ICPSR system and point you to many other sources of international data.

Notes

1. An important early discussion of the use of international data in trade analysis is Maskus (1991).
2. Codes below the six-digit level are called "tariff lines" since they are country-specific.
3. Nomenclature des Activities de la Community European.
4. This material derived from Leamer (1984, Appendix B).
5. The data on country levels of educational attainment presented in Chapter 1 used these definitions.

References and additional readings

Barro, R.J. and Lee, J.W. (2010), "A New Data Set of Educational Attainment in the World, 1950-2010," NBER Working Paper No. 15902 (Cambridge, MA: NBER).

Feenstra, R.C., Lipsey, R.E., and Bowen, H.P. (1997), "World Trade Flows, 1970–1992, with Production and Tariff Data," *NBER Working Paper 5910.*

Feenstra, R.C., Lipsey, R.E., Deng, H., Ma, A.C., and Mo, H. (2005), "World Trade Flows: 1962–2000," NBER Working Paper No. W11040 (Cambridge, MA: NBER).

Goldsmith, R. and Saunders, C. (Eds.) (1960), The Measurement of National Wealth, NBER Research in Income and Wealth No. 8 (Chicago: Quadrangle Books).

Katz, L. and Summers, L. (1988), "Can Interindustry Wage Differentials Justify Strategic Trade Policy?" National Bureau of Economic Research Working Paper 2739 (Cambridge, MA: NBER).

Leamer, E.E. (1984), *Sources of International Comparative Advantage: Theory and Evidence* (Cambridge, MA: MIT Press).

Maskus, K.V. (1991), "Comparing International Trade Data and Product and National Characteristics Data for the Analysis of Trade Models," in P. Hooper and J.D. Richardson (Eds.) *International Economic Transactions, Issues in Measurement and Empirical Research* (Chicago: University of Chicago Press).

Bibliography

Abraham, F. (1990), "The Effects on Intra-Community Competition of Export Subsidies to Third Countries: The Case of Export Credits, Export Insurance and Official Development Assistance," Report prepared for the Commission of the European Communities.

Abraham, F., Couwenberg, I., and Dewit, G. (1991), "Towards an EU Policy on Export Financing Subsidies: Lessons from the 1980s and Prospects for Future Reform," International Economics Research Papers, No. 77, Centrum voor Economische Studiën, Katholieke Universiteit Leuven.

Acemoglu, D. (2008), *Introduction to Modern Economic Growth* (Princeton, NJ: Princeton University Press).

Aghion, P. and Howitt, P. (1992), "A Model of Growth through Creative Destruction," *Econometrica*, 60 (2), 323–351.

Aghion, P. and Howitt, P. (1998), *Endogenous Growth Theory* (Cambridge, MA: MIT Press).

Aghion, P., Antràs, P., and Helpman (2007), "Negotiating Free Trade," *Journal of International Economics*, 73 (1), 1–30.

Aghion, P. and Howitt, P. (2009), *The Economics of Growth* (Cambridge, MA: MIT Press).

Alfaro, L., Kalemli-Ozcan, S., and Volosovych, V. (2008), "Why Doesn't Capital Flow from Rich to Poor Countries? An Empirical Investigation," *Review of Economics and Statistics*, 90 (2), 347–368.

Alfaro, L. and Charlton, A. (2009), "Intra-Industry Foreign Direct Investment," *American Economic Review*, 99 (5), 2096–2119.

Arkolakis, C., Demidova, S., Klenow, P.J., and Rodríguez-Clare, A. (2008), "Endogenous Variety and the Gains from Trade," *American Economic Review*, 98 (2), Papers and Proceedings of the One Hundred Twentieth Annual Meeting of the American Economic Association, 444–450.

Alvarez, R. and Lopez, R.A. (2005), "Exporting and Performance: Evidence from Chilean Plants," *Canadian Journal of Economics*, 38 (4), 1384–1400.

Alvarez, F. and Lucas, R.E. (2007), "General Equilibrium Analysis of the Eaton-Kortum Model of International Trade," *Journal of Monetary Economics*, 54, 1726–1768.

Anderson, J.E. (1979), "A Theoretical Foundation for the Gravity Equation," *American Economic Review*, 69, 106–116.

Anderson, J.E. (1994), "Tariff Index Theory," *Review of International Economics*, 32 (2), 156–173.

Anderson, J.E. and van Wincoop, E. (2003), "Gravity with Gravitas: A Solution to the Border Puzzle," *American Economic Review*, 93, 170–192.

Anderson, J.E. and Neary, J.P. (2005), *Measuring the Restrictiveness of Trade Policy* (Cambridge, MA: MIT Press).

Anderson, J.E. (2010), "The Gravity Model," NBER Working Paper Series, No. 16576.

Anderson, S.P., de Palma, A., and Thisse, J.F. (1990), "Demand for Differentiated Products, Discrete Choice Models, and the Characteristics Approach," *Review of Economic Studies*, 56, 21–35.

Anderson, T. and Zeile, W.J. (2009), "Operations of US Affiliates of Foreign Companies: Preliminary Results from the 2007 Benchmark Survey," *Survey of Current Business*, available at http://www.bea.gov/scb/pdf/2009/11%20November/1109_foreign.pdf (accessed 24 October 2011).

Andersson, M., Gieseck, A., Pierluigi, B., and Vidalis, N. (2008), "Wage Growth Dispersion across the Euro Area Countries: Some Stylised Facts," Occasional Paper Series, No. 90, European Central Bank (Frankfurt: European Central Bank).

Antràs, P. (2003), "Firms, Contracts and Trade Structure," *Quarterly Journal of Economics*, 118, 1375–1418.

Antràs, P. (2005), "Incomplete Contracts and the Product Cycle," *American Economic Review*, 95 (3), 1054–1073.

Antràs, P. and Helpman, E. (2004), "Global Sourcing," *Journal of Political Economy*, 112 (3), 552–580.

Antràs, P. and Helpman, E. (2008), "Contractual Frictions and Global Sourcing," in E. Helpman, D. Marin, and T. Verdier (Eds.), 9–54.

Aquino, A. (1978), "Intra-Industry Trade and Inter-Industry Specialization as Concurrent Sources of International Trade in Manufactures," *Journal of World Economics*, 114, 275–296.

Armington, P.A. (1969) "A Theory of Demand for Products Distinguished by Place of Production," *International Monetary Fund Staff Papers*, 16, 159–176.

Arrow, K.J. (1961), "The Economic Implications of Learning by Doing," *Review of Economic Studies*, 29, 155–173.

Atkeson, A. and Burstein, A. (2007), "Pricing-to-Market in a Ricardian Model of International Trade," *American Economic Review*, 97 (2), 362–367.

Atsumi, H. (1971), "The Long-Run Offer Function and a Dynamic Theory of International Trade," *Journal of International Economics*, 1, 267–299.

Aw, B-Y. and Roberts, M. (1986), "Estimating Quality Change in Quota Constrained Markets: The Case of US Footwear," *Journal of International Economics*, 21, 45–60.

Aw, B-Y. (1983), "The Interpretation of Cross-section Regression Tests of the Heckscher-Ohlin Theorem with Many Goods and Factors," *Journal of International Economics*, 14 (1/2), 163–167.

Badinger, H. (2007), "Has the EU's Single Market Programme Fostered Competition? Testing for a Decrease in Markup Ratios in EU Industries," *Oxford Bulletin of Economics and Statistics*, 69 (4), 497–519.

Bagwell, K. and Staiger, R.W. (1998), "Regionalism and Multilateral Tariff Cooperation," in J. Pigott and A. Woodland (Eds.), *International Trade Policy and the Pacific Rim* (London: Macmillan).

Bahmani-Oskooee, M. and Niroomand, F. (1998), "Long-run Price Elasticities and the Marshall-Lerner Condition Revisited," *Economics Letters*, 61, 101–109.

Bahmani-Oskooee, M. and Hegerty, S.W. (2007), "Exchange Rate Volatility and Trade Flows: A Review Article," *Journal of Economic Studies*, 34 (3), 211–255.

Baier, S.L. and Bergstrand, J.L. (2007), "Do Free Trade Agreements Actually Increase Members' International Trade?" *Journal of International Economics*, 71 (1), 72–95.

Balance, R.H., Forstner, H., and Murray, T. (1987), "Consistency Tests of Alternative Measures of Comparative Advantage," *The Review of Economics and Statistics*, 121, 346–350.

Balassa, B. (1963), "An Empirical Demonstration of Classical Comparative Cost Theory," *Review of Economics and Statistics*, 45, 231–238.

Balassa, B. (1965), "Tariff Protection in Industrial Countries: An Evaluation," *Journal of Political Economy*, 73 (6), 573–594.

Balassa, B. (1966), "Tariff Reductions and Trade in Manufactures among the Industrial Countries," *American Economic Review*, 56, 466–473.

Balassa, B. (1986), "Intra-Industry Trade among Exporters of Manufactured Goods," in D. Greenaway and P.K.M. Tharakan (Eds.), *Imperfect Competition and International Trade: Policy Aspects of Intra-Industry Trade* (Brighton: Wheatsheaf).

Balassa, B. and Balassa, C. (1984), "Industrial Protection in the Developed Countries," *The World Economy*, 7, 179–196.

Balassa, B. and Bauwens, L. (1987), "Intra-Industry Specialization in a Multi-Industry Framework," *Economic Journal*, 97, 923–939.

Baldwin, R. (1988), "Hysteresis in Import Prices: The Beachhead Effect," *American Economic Review*, 78 (4), 773–785.

Baldwin, R. and Krugman, P.R. (1989), "Persistent Trade Effects of Large Exchange Rate Shocks," *Quarterly Journal of Economics*, 104 (4), 633–654.

Baldwin, R.E. (1971), "Determinants of the Commodity Structure of US Trade," *American Economic Review*, 61, 126–146.

Baldwin, R.E. (Ed.) (1988), *Trade Policy Issues and Empirical Analysis* (Chicago: University of Chicago Press and National Bureau of Economic Research).

Baldwin, R.E. (1989), "Measuring Nontariff Trade Policies," NBER Working Paper No. 2978 (May).

Baldwin, R.E. (1995), "An Economic Evaluation of the Uruguay Round Agreements," *Annual Trade Review*, Claremont-McKenna College.

Baldwin, R.E. (2008), *The Development and Testing of Heckscher-Ohlin Trade Models: A Review* (Cambridge, MA: MIT Press).

Baldwin, R.E. and Cain, G. (2000), "Shifts in Relative US Wages: The Role of Trade, Technology, and Factor Endowments," *Review of Economics and Statistics*, 82, 580–595.

Baldwin, R.E. and Forslid, R. (2004), "Trade Liberalization with Heterogeneous Firms," CEPR Discussion Paper No. 4635.

Baldwin, R.E. and Hilton, S. (1983), "A Technique for Indicating Comparative Costs and Predicting Changes in Trade Ratios," *Review of Economics and Statistics*, 65 (1), 105–110.

Baldwin, R.E., Begg, D., Danthine, J.-P., Grilli, V., Haaland, J., Neumann, M., Norman, V., Venables, A., and Winters, A. (1992), *Is Bigger Better? The Economics of EC Enlargement* (London: Centre for Economic Policy Research).

Ballard, C.L., Fullerton, D., Shoven, J., and Whalley, J. (1985), *A General Equilibrium Model for Tax Policy Evaluation* (Chicago: University of Chicago Press).

Baltagi, B.H. (2005), *Econometric Analysis of Panel Data*, third edition (Chichester: John Wiley and Sons).

Baltagi, B.H., Egger, P., and Pfaffermayr, M. (2007), "Estimating Models of Complex FDI: Are There Third-Country Effects?" *Journal of Econometrics*, 140, 260–281.

Baltagi, B.H., Egger, P., and Pfaffermayr, M. (2003), "A Generalized Design for Bilateral Trade Flow Models," *Economics Letters*, 80 (3), 391–397.

Barba Navaretti, G. and Venables, A.J. (2004), *"Multinational Firms in the World Economy,"* (Princeton, NJ: Princeton University Press).

Bardhan, A. (2009), "A Note of Intra-Firm Trade and Offshoring in Manufacturing and Services," available at http://www.atdforum.org/IMG/pdf_FTA_on_intra_firm_Sufian.pdf (accessed 24 October 2011).

Bardhan, P.K. (1965), "Equilibrium Growth in the International Economy," *Quarterly Journal of Economics*, 79, 455–464.

Barefoot, K.B. and Mataloni Jr., R.J. (2009), "US Multinational Companies: Operations in the United States and Abroad in 2007," *Survey of Current Business*, available at http://www.bea.gov/scb/pdf/2009/08%20August/0809_mnc.pdf (accessed 24 October 2011).

Baron, D.P. (1976), "Flexible Exchange Rates, Forward Markets and the Level of Trade," *American Economic Review*, 66, 253–266.

Barrett, S. (1994), "Strategic Environmental Policy and International Trade," *Journal of Public Economics*, 54, 325–338.

Barro, R.J. (1990), "Government Spending in a Simple Model of Endogenous Growth," *Journal of Political Economy*, 98, S103–S125.

Barro, R.J. and Lee, J.W. (1994), "Losers and Winners in Economic Growth," *The World Bank Economic Review* (Supplement), 267–314.

Barro, R.J. and Lee, J.W. (2000), "International Data on Educational Attainment: Updates and Implications," Center for International Development Working Paper No. 42 (Cambridge: Harvard University Press).

Barro, R.J. and Lee, J.W. (2010), "A New Data Set of Educational Attainment in the World, 1950–2010," NBER Working Paper No. 15902.

Barro, R.J. and Sala-i-Martin, X. (1992), "Convergence," *Journal of Political Economy*, 100, 223–251.

Barro, R.J. and Sala-i-Martin, X. (1995), *Economic Growth* (New York: McGraw-Hill).

Basevi, G., Cocchi, D., and Lischi, P.L. (1985), "The Choice of Currency in the Foreign Trade of Italy," Research Paper, 17, University of Bologna.

Baum, C.F. and Caglayan, M. (2010), "On the Sensitivity of the Volume and Volatility of Bilateral Trade Flows to Exchange Rate Uncertainty," *Journal of International Money and Finance*, 29 (1), 79–93.

Baylis, K. (2007), "Countervailing Duties," in J.D. Gaisford and W.A. Kerr (Eds.), *Handbook of International Trade Policy* (London: Edward Elgar Publishing).

Beghin, J.C. and Knox Lovell, C.A. (1993), "Trade and Efficiency Effects of Domestic Content Protection: The Australian Tobacco and Cigarette Industries," *Review of Economics and Statistics*, 75, 623–669.

Belderbos, R. and Sleuwaegen, L. (1996), "Japanese Firms and the Decision to Invest Abroad: Business Groups and Regional Core Networks," *Review of Economics and Statistics*, 28 (2), 214–221.

Bellis, J.-F. (1990), "The EEC Antidumping System," in J.H. Jackson and E.A. Vermulst (Eds.), *Antidumping Law in Practice: A Comparative Study* (London: Harvester Wheatsheaf).

Bergsten, C.F., Horst, T., and Moran, T. (1978), *American Multinationals and American Interest* (Washington, DC: Brookings Institution).

Bergstrand, J.H. (1983), "Measurement and Determinants of Intra-Industry International Trade," in P.K.M. Tharakan (Ed.), *Intra-Industry Trade: Empirical and Methodological Aspects* (Amsterdam: North-Holland), 201–262.

Bergstrand, J.H. (1989), "The Generalized Gravity Equation, Monopolistic Competition, and the Factor-Proportions Theory in International Trade," *Review of Economics and Statistics*, 71 (1), 143–153.

Bergstrand, J.H. (1990), "The Heckscher-Ohlin-Samuelson Model, the Linder Hypothesis, and the Determinants of Bilateral Intra-Industry Trade," *Economic Journal*, 100, 1216–1229.

Bergstrand, J.H. and Egger, P. (2007), "A Knowledge- and Physical-Capital Model of International Trade Flows, Foreign Direct Investment and Multinational Enterprises," *Journal of International Economics*, 73, 278–308.

Bergstrand, J.H. and Egger, P. (2011), "Gravity Equations and Trade Frictions," in D. Bernhofen, R. Falvey, D. Greenaway, and U. Kreickemeier (Eds.), *Palgrave Handbook of International Trade* (Basingstoke: Palgrave-Macmillan), ch. 17.

Bernard, A.B. and Jensen J.B. (2004), "Why Some Firms Export," *The Review of Economics and Statistics*, 86 (2), 561–569.

Bernard, A.B., Jensen, J.B., Redding, S.J., and Schott, P.K. (2007), "Firms in International Trade," *Journal of Economic Perspectives*, 21 (3), 105–130.

Bernard, A.B., Jensen, J., and Schott, P. (2005), "Importers, Exporters and Multinationals: A Portrait of Firms in the US That Trade Goods," NBER Working Paper No. 11404.

Bernard, A.B., Jensen, J.B., and Schott, P.K. (2006), "Trade Costs, Firms and Productivity," *Journal of Monetary Economics*, 53, 917–937.

Bernard, A.B., Redding, S.J., and Schott, P.K. (2007), "Comparative Advantage and Heterogeneous Firms," *Review of Economic Studies*, 74, 31–66.

Bernard, A.B. and Durlauf, S.N. (1995), "Convergence in International Output," *Journal of Applied Econometrics*, 10, 97–108.

Bernard, A.B., Eaton, J., Jensen, J.B., and Kortum, S. (2003), "Plants and Productivity in International Trade," *American Economic Review*, 93 (4), 1268–1290.

Bernhofen, D.M. (1999), "Intra-Industry Trade and Strategic Interaction: Theory and Evidence," *Journal of International Economics*, 47, 225–244.

Bernhofen, D.M. (2010), "The Empirics of General Equilibrium Trade Theory: What Have We Learned?" Münchener Gesellschaft zur Förderung der Wirtschaftswissenschaft (CESifo) Working Paper No. 3242 (Munich: Münchener Gesellschaft zur Förderung der Wirtschaftswissenschaft, CESifo GmbH).

Bernhofen, D.M. and Brown, J.C. (2004), "A Direct Test of the Theory of Comparative Advantage: The Case of Japan," *Journal of Political Economy*, 112 (1), 48–67.

Bhagwati, J.N. (1958), "Immizerising Growth: A Geometric Note," *Review of Economic Studies*, 25, 201–205.

Bhagwati, J.N. (1964), "The Pure Theory of International Trade: A Survey," *Economic Journal*, 74, 1–84.

Bhagwati, J.N. (1965), "On the Equivalence of Tariffs and Quotas," in R.E. Baldwin *et al.* (Eds.), *Trade Growth and the Balance of Payments – Essays in Honor of Gottfried Haberler* (Chicago: Rand McNally), 53–67.

Bhagwati, J.N. (1968), "More on the Equivalence of Tariffs and Quotas," *American Economic Review*, 58, 481–485.

Bhagwati, J.N. (1971), "Trade-Diverting Customs Unions and Welfare Improvement: A Clarification," *Economic Journal*, 81 (323), 580–587.

Bhagwati, J.N. (1991), *The World Trading System at Risk* (Princeton, NJ: Princeton University Press).

Bhagwati, J.N. (2002), *Free Trade Today* (Princeton, NJ: Princeton University Press).

Bhagwati, J.N and Srinivasan, T.N. (1983), *Lectures on International Trade* (Cambridge, MA: MIT Press), chs 5 and 6, 50–81; appendix B, 384–396.

Bhagwati, J.N. and Srinivasan, T.N. (1983), "On the Choice between Capital and Labour Mobility," *Journal of International Economics*, 14, 209–221.

Bhagwati, J.N. and Srinivasan, T.N. (1983), *Lectures on International Trade* (Cambridge, MA: MIT Press), chs 2–4.

Bilson, J.F.O. (1983), "The Choice of an Invoice Currency in International Transactions," in J.S. Bhandari and B.H. Putnam (Eds.), *Economic Interdependence and Flexible Exchange Rates* (Cambridge, MA: MIT Press), 384–402.

Black, S.W. (1985), "International Money and International Monetary Arrangements," in R.W. Jones and P.B. Kenen (Eds.), *Handbook of International Economics*, Vol. 2 (Amsterdam: North-Holland), 1153–1194.

Blanchard, O.J. and Fischer, S. (1989), *Lectures on Macroeconomics* (Cambridge, MA: MIT Press).

Blanes-Cristóbal, J.V., Dovis, D., Milgram-Baleix, J., and Moro-Egido, A.I. (2008), "Do Sunk Exporting Costs Differ among Markets? Evidence from Spanish Manufacturing Firms," *Economics Letters*, 101, 110–112.

Bliss, A. (1994), *Economic Theory and Policy for Trading Blocks* (Manchester: Manchester University Press).

Blonigen, B.A. (1997), "Firm-Specific Assets and the Link between Exchange Rates and Foreign Direct Investment," *American Economic Review*, 87, 447–466.

Blonigen, B.A. and Bown, C.P. (2003), "Antidumping and Retaliation Threats," *Journal of International Economics*, 60, 243–279.

Blonigen, B.A., Davies, R.B., Waddell, G.R., and Naughton, H.T. (2007), "FDI in Space: Spatial Autoregressive Relationships in Foreign Direct Investment," *European Economic Review*, 51, 1303–1325.

Boadway, R.W. and Bruce, N. (1984), *The Pure Theory of Welfare Economics* (Oxford: Basil Blackwell).

Bohara, A. K., Gawande, K., and Sanguinetti, P. (2004), "Trade Diversion and Declining Tariffs: Evidence from Mercosur," *Journal of International Economics*, 64 (1), 65–88.

Boltuck, R. and Litan, R.L. (Eds.) (1991), *Down in the Dumps: Administration of the Unfair Trade Laws* (Washington, DC: Brookings Institution).

Bond, E. and Syropoulos, C. (1996), "The Size of Trading Blocs: Market Power and World Welfare Effects," *Journal of International Economics*, 64 (1), 65–88.

Boorstein, R. and Feenstra, R.C. (1987). "Quality Upgrading and Its Welfare Cost in US Steel Imports, 1969–74," NBER Working Paper No. 2452 (Cambridge, MA: National Bureau of Economic Research).

Boorstein, R. and Feenstra, R.C. (1991), "Quality Upgrading and Its Welfare Cost in US Steel Imports, 1969–1974," in E. Helpman and A. Razin (Eds.), *International Trade and Trade Policy* (Cambridge, MA: MIT Press), 167–186.

Borjas, G.J. and Bratsberg, B. (1996), "Who Leaves? The Emigration of the Foreign-born," *Review of Economics and Statistics*, 78 (1), 165–167.

Bowen, H.P. (1983), "Changes in the International Distribution of Resources and Their Impact on US Comparative Advantage," *Review of Economics and Statistics*, 65, 402–417.

Bowen, H.P. (1983), "On the Theoretical Interpretation of Indices of Trade Intensity and Revealed Comparative Advantage," *The Review of World Economics*, 119 (3), 464–472.

Bowen, H.P., Leamer, E.E., and Sveikauskas, L. (1987), "Multicountry, Multifactor Tests of the Factor Abundance Theory," *American Economic Review*, 77 (5), 791–809.

Bowen, H.P., Munandar, H., and Viaene, J.-M. (2010), "How Integrated Is the World Economy?" *Review of World Economics* (*Weltwirtschaftliches Archiv*), 146 (3), 389–414.

Bowen, H.P., Munandar, H., and Viaene, J.-M. (2011), "Are EU Countries Less Integrated than US States? Theory and Evidence," *Journal of Regional Science*, 51 (4), 653–677.

Bowen, H.P. and Sleuwaegen, L. (2007), "European Integration: The Third Step," *Journal of International Economics and Policy*, 4 (3), 241–262.

Bowen, H.P. and Sveikauskas, L. (1992), "Judging Factor Abundance," *Quarterly Journal of Economics*, 107 (2), 599–620.

Bowen, H.P. and Wiersema, M.F. (2005), "Foreign-based Competition and Corporate Diversification Strategy," *Strategic Management Journal*, 26 (12), 1153–1171.

Bowen, H.P. and Wiersema, M.F. (2009), "Firm Performance, International Diversification and Product Diversification: Their Interrelationships and Determinants," Queens University of Charlotte McColl School of Business Discussion Paper 2009–4.

Bowen, H.P. and Wu, J-P. (2011), "Immigrant Specificity and the Relationship between Trade and Immigration: Theory and Evidence," Queens University of Charlotte McColl School of Business Discussion Paper 2011–01.

Bown, C.O. and Crowley, M.A. (2007), "Trade Deflection and Trade Depression," *Journal of International Economics*, 72, 176–201.

Braconier, H., Norbäck, P.J., and Urban, D. (2005), "Reconciling the Evidence on the Knowledge-Capital Model," *Review of International Economics*, 13 (4), 770–786.

Brada, J.C. and Méndez, J.A. (1988), "An Estimate of the Dynamic Effects of Economic Integration," *Review of Economics and Statistics*, 70 (1), 163–168.

Brainard, S.L. (1997), "An Empirical Assessment of the Proximity-Concentration Trade-Off between Multinational Sales and Trade," *American Economic Review*, 87 (4), 520–544.

Brakman, S., Garretsen, H., and Van Marrewijk, C. (2009), *The New Introduction to Geographical Economics*, second edition (Cambridge: Cambridge University Press).

Brander, J.A. (1981), "Intra-Industry Trade in Identical Commodities," *Journal of International Economics*, 1, 1–14.

Brander, J.A. (1986), "Rationales for Strategic Trade and Industrial Policy," in P.R. Krugman (Ed.), *Strategic Trade Policy and the New International Economics* (Cambridge, MA: MIT Press), 213–246.

Brander, J.A. (1995), "Strategic Trade Policy," in G. Grossman and K. Rogoff (Eds.), *Handbook of International Economics*, Vol. 3 (Amsterdam: North-Holland), 1395–1455.

Brander, J.A. and Krugman, P. (1983), "A 'Reciprocal Dumping' Model of International Trade," *Journal of International Economics*, 15 (3/4), 313–321.

Brander, J.A. and Spencer, B.J. (1984), "Tariff Protection and Imperfect Competition," in H. Kierzkowski (Ed.), *Monopolistic Competition and International Trade* (Oxford: Oxford University Press).

Brecher, R.A. and Choudhri, E. (1982), "The Leontief Paradox, Continued," *Journal of Political Economy*, 90, 820–823.

Brecher, R.A. (1974), "Minimum Wage Rates and the Pure Theory of International Trade," *Quarterly Journal of Economics*, 98–116.

Brecher, R.A. (1980), "Increased Unemployment from Capital Accumulation in a Minimum-Wage Model of an Open Economy," *Canadian Journal of Economics*, 13, 152–158.

Brecher, R. and Choudhri, E. (1988), "The Factor Content of Consumption in Canada and the United States: A Two Country Test of the Heckscher-Ohlin-Vanek Model," in R.C. Feenstra (Ed.), *Empirical Methods for International Trade* (Cambridge, MA: MIT Press), 5–17.

Bresnahan, T.F. (1989), "Empirical Studies of Industries with Market Power," in R. Schmalensee and R.D. Willig (Eds.), *Handbook of Industrial Organization*, Vol. 3 (Amsterdam: North-Holland), ch. 8.

Broda, C., Limão, N., and Weinstein, D.E. (2008), "Optimal Tariffs and Market Power: The Evidence," *American Economic Review*, 98 (5), 2032–2065.

Broda, C. and Weinstein, D.E. (2006), Globalization and the Gains from Variety, *Quarterly Journal of Economics*, 121, 541–585.

Brooke, A., Kendrick, D., and Meeraus A. (1988), *GAMS: A User's Guide* (Redwood City, CA: The Scientific Press).

Brouwer, J., Paap, R., and Viaene, J.-M. (2008), "Trade and FDI Effects of EMU Enlargement," *Journal of International Money and Finance*, 27 (2), 188–208.

Brown, D.K. (1987), "Tariff, the Terms of Trade, and National Product Differentiation," *Journal of Policy Modeling*, 9 (4), 503–526.

Brown, D.K. (1992), "The Impact of a North American Free Trade Area: Applied General Equilibrium Models," in N. Lustig, B.P. Bosworth, and R.Z. Lawrence (Eds.), *North American Free Trade: Assessing the Impact* (Washington, DC: Brookings Institution), 26–68.

Brown, D.K., Deardorff, A.V., and Stem, R.M. (1992), "A North American Free Trade Agreement: Analytical Issues and a Computational Assessment," *The World Economy*, 15, 11–30.

Burgess, D.F. (1978), "On the Distributional Effects of Direct Foreign Investment," *International Economic Review*, 19, 647–664.

Burmeister, E. (1980), *Mathematical Theories of Economic Growth* (New York: Macmillan).

Burns, M.E. (1973), "A Note on the Concept and Measure of Consumer's Surplus," *American Economic Review*, 63, 335–344.

Calvo, G. and Wellisz, S. (1983), "International Factor Mobility and National Advantage," *Journal of International Economics*, 14, 103–114.

Campa, J.M. (2004), "Exchange Rates and Trade: How Important is Hysteresis in Trade?" *European Economic Review*, 48, 527–548.

Canada, Foreign Affairs and International Trade (2009), "Canada's State of Trade and Investment Update 2008 – including a special feature on Canadian Direct Investment Abroad," available at http://www.international.gc.ca/economist-economiste/performance/state-point/2008.aspx?lang=eng#a1 (accessed 24 October 2011).

Cantwell, J. (1989), *Technical Innovation in Multinational Corporations* (Oxford: Basil Blackwell).

Card, D. and Krueger, A.B. (1995), *Myth and Measurement: the New Economics of the Minimum Wage* (Princeton, NJ: Princeton University Press).

Carlton, D.W. and Perloff, J.M. (2005), *Modern Industrial Organization* (Boston, MA: Pearson-Addison Wesley).

Carr, D., Markusen, J.R., and Maskus, K. E. (2001), "Estimating the Capital-Knowledge Model of the Multinational Enterprise," *American Economic Review*, 91, 693–708.

Casas, F. and Choi, E. (1985), "The Leontief Paradox, Continued or Resolved?" *Journal of Political Economy*, 93, 610–615.

Cass, D. (1965), "Optimal Growth in an Aggregative Model of Capital Accumulation," *Review of Economic Studies*, 32, 233–240.

Caves, R.E. (1971), "International Corporations: The Industrial Economics of Foreign Investment," *Economica*, 38 (149), 1–27.

Caves, R.E. (1974), "Causes of Direct Investment: Foreign Firm's Shares in Canadian and United Kingdom Manufacturing Industries," *The Review of Economics and Statistics*, 56 (3), 279–290.

Caves, R.E. (1985), "International Trade and Industrial Organization: Problems, Solved and Unsolved," *European Economic Review*, 28, 377–395.

Chacholiades, M. (1973), *The Pure Theory of International Trade* (London: Macmillan).

Cheffert, J.-M. (1994), "Exchange Rate and Prices in Models of Imperfect Competition," PhD thesis, University of Namur, Belgium.

Chen, N., Imbs, J., and Scott, A. (2009), "The Dynamics of Trade and Competition," *Journal of International Economics*, 77, 50–62.

Chen, K.-M. and Lin, C.-C. (2007), "The Impact of Exchange Rate Movements on Dumping Activity: Theory and Evidence," paper presented at the Third Annual APEA Conference, Hong Kong University of Science and Technology, Hong Kong, China, 25–26 July.

Cheng, L.K. and Wong, K.Y. (1990), "On the Strategic Choice between Capital and Labor Mobility," *Journal of International Economics*, 28, 291–314.

Chipman, J.S. (1965), "A Survey of International Trade: Part I – The Classical Theory," *Econometrica*, 33, 477–519.

Chisik, R. (2003), "Gradualism in Free Trade Agreements: A Theoretical Justification," *Journal of International Economics*, 59, 367–397.

Chiswick, B.R. (1999), "Are Immigrants Favorably Self-Selected?" *American Economic Review*, 89 (2), 181–185.

Choi, J.P. and Davidson, C. (2006), "Strategic Second Sourcing by Multinationals," *International Economic Review*, 45 (2), 579–600.

Church, J. and Ware, R. (2000), *Industrial Organization: A Strategic Approach* (Boston, MA: Irwin-McGraw Hill).

Clarida, R. (1993), "Entry, Dumping and Shakeout," *American Economic Review*, 83, 180–202.

Clark, P., Tamirisa, N., Wei, S.-J., Sadilov, A., and Zeng, L. (2004), "Exchange Rate Volatility and Trade Flows: Some New Evidence," International Monetary Fund Occasional Paper No. 235 (May).

Clerides, S., Lack S., and Tybout, J.R. (1998), "Is Learning by Exporting Important Micro-Dynamic Evidence from Colombia, Mexico and Morocco?" *Quarterly Journal of Economics*, 113 (3), 903–948.

Coe, D.T., Helpman, E., and Hoffmaister, A.W. (1997), "North-South R&D Spillovers," *Economic Journal*, 107, 134–149.

Coe, D.T., Helpman, E., and Hoffmaister, A.W. (2009), "International R&D Spillovers and Institutions," *European Economic Review*, 53, 723–741.

Coes, D. (1981), "The Crawling Peg and Exchange Rate Uncertainty," in J. Williamson (Ed.), *Exchange Rate Rules: The Theory, Performance and Prospects of the Crawling Peg* (New York: St. Martin's Press), 113–136.

Collie, D. (1991), "Export Subsidies and Countervailing Tariffs," *Journal of International Economics*, 31, 309–324.

Collie, D. (1994), "Strategic Trade Policy and Retaliation," *Japan and the World Economy*, 6, 75–88.

Combes, P.-P., Mayer, T., and Thisse, J.F. (2008), *Economic Geography: The Integration of Regions and Nations* (Princeton, NJ: Princeton University Press).

Coneybeare, J.A.C. (1987), *Trade Wars: The Theory and Practice of International Commercial Rivalry* (New York: Columbia University Press).

Coniglio, N.D., De Arcangelis, G., and Serlenga, L. (2009), "Clandestine Migrants: Do the High-Skilled Return Home First?" Sapienza University, Rome, mimeo.

Cooper, C.A. and Massell, B.F. (1965), "Towards a General Theory of Customs Unions for Developing Countries," *Journal of Political Economy*, 73, 461–476.

Cooper, R. and John, A. (1988), "Coordinating Coordination Failures in Keynesian Models," *Quarterly Journal of Economics*, 103, 441–464.

Corcos, G., Irac, D.M., Mion G., and Verdier, T. (2008), "The Determinants of Intra-Firm Trade," Centra Studi d'Agliano Development Studies Working Papers, No. 267.

Corden, W.M. (1971), *The Theory of Protection* (London: Allen and Unwin).

Corden, W.M. (1972), "Economies of Scale and Customs Union Theory," *Journal of Political Economy*, 80 (3), 465–475.

Cornes, R. (1992), *Duality and Modern Economics* (Cambridge: Cambridge University Press).

Costinot, A. (2009), "On the Origins of Comparative Advantage," *Journal of International Economics*, 77 (2), 255–264.

Costinot, A., Donaldson, D., and Komunjer, I. (2012), "What Goods do Countries Trade? A Quantitative Exploration of Ricardo's Ideas," *Review of Economic Studies*, forthcoming.

Coughlin, C.C. (2010), "Measuring International Trade Policy: A Primer on Trade Restrictiveness Indices," *Federal Reserve Bank of St. Louis*, 92 (5), 381–394.

Criscuolo, C. and Martin, R. (2009), "Global Engagement and the Innovation Activities of Firms," *International Journal of Industrial Organization*, 28 (2), 191–202.

Criscuolo, C. and Martin, R. (2009), "Multinationals and US Productivity: Evidence from Great Britain," *The Review of Economics and Statistics*, 91 (2), 263–281.

Culem, C. and Lundberg, L. (1986), "The Product Pattern of Intra-Industry Trade: Stability among Countries and over Time," *The Review of World Economics*, 122, 113–130.

Cuñat, A. and Melitz, M. (2011a), "Volatility, Labor Market Flexibility, and the Pattern of Comparative Advantage," *Journal of the European Economic Association*, forthcoming.

Cuñat, A. and Melitz, M. (2011b), "A Many-Country, Many-Good Model of Labor Market Rigidities as a Source of Comparative Advantage," *Journal of the European Economic Association, Papers and Proceedings*, forthcoming.

Cushman, D.O. (1988), "US Bilateral Trade Flows and Exchange Risk during the Floating Period," *Journal of International Economics*, 24, 317–330.

Danthine, J.-P. (1978), "Information, Futures Prices and Stabilizing Speculation," *Journal of Economic Theory*, 17, 79–98.

Das, S.R. and Donnenfeld, S. (1987), "Trade Policy and Its Impact on Quality of Imports," *Journal of International Economics*, 23, 77–95.

Das, S. and Donnenfeld, S. (1989), "Competition and International Trade: Quantity and Quality Restrictions," *Journal of International Economics*, 27 (4), 299–318.

Davis, D.R. (1998), "The Home Market, Trade, and Industrial Structure," *American Economic Review*, 88 (5), 1264–1276.

Davis, D.R. and Weinstein, D. (2001), "An Account of Global Factor Trade," *American Economic Review*, 91 (5), 1423–1453.

Davis, D.R. and Weinstein, D. (2003), "The Factor Content of Trade," in E. Kwan Choi and L. Harrigan (Eds.), *Handbook of International Trade* (Malden, MA: Blackwell).

De Benedictis, L. and Tajoli, L. (2011), "The World Trade Network," *The World Economy*, forthcoming.

de Melo, J. and Messerlin, P.A. (1988), "Price, Quality and Welfare Effects of European VERs on Japanese Autos," *European Economic Review*, 32, 1527–1546.

de Melo, J. and Tarr, D. (1992), *A General Equilibrium Analysis of US Foreign Trade Policy* (Cambridge, MA: The MIT Press).

de Melo, J. and Winters, L.A. (1993), "Price and Quality Effects of VERs Revisited: A Case Study of Korean Footwear Exports," *Journal of Economic Integration*, 8 (1), 33–57.

de Meza, D. (1986), "Export Subsidies and High Productivity: Cause or Effects," *Canadian Journal of Economics*, 19, 347–350.

Deardorff, A. (1979), "Weak Links in the Chain of Comparative Advantage," *Journal of International Economics*, 9 (2), 197–209.

Deardorff, A. (1980), "The General Validity of the Law of Comparative Advantage," *Journal of Political Economy*, 88 (5), 941–957.

Deardorff, A. (1982), "The General Validity of the Heckscher-Ohlin Theorem," *American Economic Review*, 72, 683–694.

Deardorff, A. (1990), "Economic Perspectives on Antidumping Law," in J.K. Jackson and E.A Vermulst (Eds.), *Antidumping Law and Practice: A Comparative Study* (Ann Arbor, MI: Harvester Wheatsheaf).

Deardorff, A. (1998), "Determinants of Bilateral Trade: Does Gravity Work in a Neoclassical World?" in J.A. Frankel (Ed.), *The Regionalism of the World Economy* (Chicago: University of Chicago Press), 7–28.

Deardorff, A. and Stern, R.M. (1986), *The Michigan Model of World Production and Trade* (Cambridge, MA: The MIT Press).

Deardorff, A. and Stern, R.M. (1990), *Computation Analysis of Global Trading Arrangements* (Ann Arbor: The University of Michigan Press).

Deardorff, A. and Stern, R.M. (Eds.) (1994), *Analytical and Negotiating Issues in the Global Trading System* (Ann Arbor: University of Michigan Press).

Deardorff, A. and Stern, RM. (1998), *Measurement of Nontariff Barriers: Studies in International Economics* (Ann Arbor: University of Michigan Press).

Deaton, A. and Muellbauer, J. (1980), *Economics and Consumer Behavior* (Cambridge: Cambridge University Press).

Debaere, P. (2003), "Relative Factor Abundance and Trade," *Journal of Political Economy*, 111 (3), 589–610.

Debaere, P. (2005), "Monopolistic Competition and Trade Revisited: Testing the Model Without Testing For Gravity," *Journal of International Economics*, 66, 249–266.

Debaere, P. and Demiroglu, U. (2003), "On the Similarity of Country Endowments," *Journal of International Economics*, 59, 101–136.

Debaere, P. and Lee, H. (2010), "The Real-Side Determinants of Countries' Terms of Trade: A Panel Data Analysis," Working Paper, Darden School of Business, University of Virginia.

Defever, F. and Toubal, F. (2007), "Productivity and the Sourcing Modes of Multinational Firm: Evidence from French Firm-Level Data," CEP Discussion Paper No. 842.

Del Gatto, M., Mion, G., and Ottaviano, G. (2006), "Trade Integration, Firm Selection and the Costs of Non-Europe," CEPR Discussion Paper No. 5730.

Demidova, S. (2008), "Productivity Improvements and Falling Trade Cost: Boon or Bane?" *International Economic Review*, 49 (4), 1437–1462.

Diamond, P. (1982), "Aggregate Demand Management in Search Equilibrium," *Journal of Political Economy*, 90, 881–894.

Dick, A.R. (1993), "Strategic Trade Policy and Welfare," *Journal of International Economics,* 35, 227–249.

Diewert, W.E. (1982), "Duality Approaches to Microeconomic Theory," in K.J. Arrow and M.D. Intrilligator (Eds.), *Handbook of Mathematical Economics* (Amsterdam: North-Holland), 535–599.

Dinwiddy, C.L. and Tal, F.J. (1988), *The Two-Sector Equilibrium Model: A New Approach* (Oxford: Philip Allan).

Disdier, A.-C. and Head, K. (2008), "The Puzzling Persistence of the Distance Effect on Bilateral Trade," *Review of Economics and Statistics,* 90 (1), 37–48.

Dixit, A. (1984), "International Trade Policy for Oligopolistic Industries," *Economic Journal Conference Papers,* 94, 1–16.

Dixit, A. (1987), "Strategic Aspects of Trade Policy," in T.F. Bewley (Ed.), *Advances in Economic Theory: Fifth World Congress* (Cambridge: Cambridge University Press), 329–362.

Dixit, A. (1988), "Anti-Dumping and Countervailing Duties under Oligopoly," *European Economic Review,* 32, 55–68.

Dixit, A. (1989a), "Entry and Exit Decisions under Uncertainty," *Journal of Political Economy,* 97(3), 620–638.

Dixit, A. (1989b), "Hysteresis, Import Penetration and Exchange Rate Pass-Through," *Quarterly Journal of Economics,* 104 (2), 205–228.

Dixit, A. (1992), "Investment and Hysteresis," *Journal of Economic Perspectives,* 6 (1), 107–132.

Dixit, A. and Norman, V. (1980), *Theory of International Trade: A Dual, General Equilibrium Approach* (Cambridge: Cambridge University Press).

Dixit, A. and Pindyck, R.S. (1994), *Investment under Uncertainty* (Princeton, NJ: Princeton University Press).

Dixit, A. and Grossman, G.M. (1986), "Targeted Export Promotion with Several Oligopolistic Industries," *Journal of International Economics,* 21, 233–250.

Dixit, A. and Kyle, A.S. (1985), "The Use of Protection and Subsidies for Entry Promotion and Deterrence," *American Economic Review,* 75, 139–152.

Dixit, A. and Stiglitz, J.E. (1977), "Monopolistic Competition and Optimum Product Diversity," *American Economics Review,* 67, 297–308.

Dixon, P., Parmenter, B., Sutton, J., and Vincent, D. (1982), *ORANI: A Multi-Sector Model of the Australian Economy* (Amsterdam: North-Holland).

Dollar, D. and Kraay, A. (2004), "Trade, Growth and Poverty," *Economic Journal,* 114 (493), F22–F49.

Domar, E.D. (1946), "Capital Expansion, Rate of Growth and Employment," *Econometrica,* 14, 137–147.

Doms, M.E. and Jensen, J. (1998), "Comparing Wages, Skills, and Productivity between Domestically and Foreign-Owned Manufacturing Establishments in the United States," in R.E. Baldwin, R.E. Lipsey, and J.D. Richardson (Eds.), *Geography and Ownership as Bases for Economic Accounting* (Chicago: University of Chicago Press).

Dornbusch, R. (1987), "Exchange Rates and Prices," *American Economic Review,* 77 (1), 93–106.

Dornbusch, R., Fischer, S., and Samuelson, P.A. (1977), "Comparative Advantage, Trade, and Payments in a Ricardian Model with a Continuum of Goods," *American Economic Review,* 47 (5), 823–839.

Dunning, J. H. (1993), *Multinational Enterprises and the Global Economy* (New York: Addison Wesley and Longman)

Dunning, J. and Lundan, S.M. (2008), *Multinational Enterprises and the Global Economy,* second edition (Cheltenham: Edward Elgar).

Eaton, J. and Grossman, G.M. (1986), "Optimal Trade and Industrial Policy under Oligopoly," *Quarterly Journal of Economics,* 101, 383–406.

Eaton, J. and Kortum, S. (2002), "Technology, Geography and Trade," *Econometrica,* 70 (5), 1741–1779.

Eaton, J., Kortum, S., and Kramarz, F. (2004), "Dissecting Trade: Firms, Industries, and Export Destinations," *American Economic Review, Papers and Proceedings,* 93, 150–154.

Eaton, J., Kortum, S., Neimanx, B., and Romalis, J. (2010), "Trade and the Global Recession," University of Chicago, mimeo.

Eaton, J. and Mirman, L.J. (1991), "Predatory Dumping as Signal Jamming," in A. Takayama, M. Ohyama, and H. Ohta (Eds.), *Trade, Policy, and International Adjustments* (New York: Academic Press), 60–76.

Economist, The (2010), *Pocket World in Figures,* 2010 Edition.

Eden, L. (1985), "Microeconomics of Transfer Pricing," in A.M. Rugman and L. Eden (Eds.), *Multinationals and Transfer Pricing* (New York: St Martin's Press),13–46.

Ekholm, K., Forslid, R., and Markusen, J.R. (2007), "Export-Platform Foreign Direct Investment," *Journal of the European Economic Association*, 5 (4), 776–795.

Ethier, W. (1973), "International Trade and the Forward Exchange Market," *American Economic Review*, 63, 494–503.

Ethier, W. (1979), "Internationally Decreasing Costs and World Trade," *Journal of International Economics*, 9, 1–24.

Ethier, W. (1982), "Dumping," *Journal of Political Economy*, 90 (3), 487–506.

Ethier, W. (1984), "Higher Dimensional Issues in Trade Theory," in R. Jones and P. Kenen (Eds.), *Handbook of International Economics*, Vol. 1 (Amsterdam: North-Holland), ch. 3.

Ethier, W. (1982a), "National and International Returns to Scale in the Modern Theory of International Trade," *American Economic Review*, 72, 388–405.

Ethier, W. (1982b), "Decreasing Costs in International Trade and Frank Graham's Argument for Protection," *Econometrica*, 50 (5), 1243–1267.

Ethier, W. (1983), *Modern International Economics* (New York: Norton), Appendix I, 511–556.

Ethier, W. (1987), "The Theory of International Trade," in L.M. Officer (Ed.), *International Economics* (Boston, MA: Kluwer Academic), 1–57.

Ethier, W. (1996), "Regionalism in a Multilateral World," Working Paper, International Economics Research Center, University of Pennsylvania.

Ethier, W. (2011), "Political Economy of Protection," in D. Bernhofen, R. Falvey, D. Greenaway, and U. Kreickemeier (Eds.), *Palgrave Handbook of International Trade* (Basingstoke: Palgrave-Macmillan), ch. 10.

Ethier, W. and Fisher, R.D. (1987), "The New Protectionism," *Journal of Economic Integration*, 2 (2), 1–11.

Ethier, W. and Horn, H. (1984), "A New Look at Economic Integration," in H. Kierzkowski. (Ed.), *Monopolistic Competition and International Trade* (Oxford: Clarendon Press), 207–229.

Faber, R.P. and Stokman, A.C.J. (2009), "A Short History of Price Level Convergence in Europe," *Journal of Money, Credit and Banking*, 41 (2/3), 461–477.

Facchini, G. and Mayda, A.M. (2008), "From Individual Attitudes towards Migrants to Migration Policy Outcomes: Theory and Evidence," *Economic Policy*, 56, 653–713.

Facchini, G. and Mayda, A.M. (2009), "Does the Welfare State Affect Individual Attitudes towards Immigrants? Evidence across Countries," *Review of Economics and Statistics*, 91 (2), 295–314.

Facchini, G. and Testa, C. (2009), "Who is against a Common Market?" *Journal of the European Economic Association*, 7 (5), 1068–1100.

Faini, R. and Heimler, A. (1991), "The Quality of Production of Textiles and Clothing and the Completion of the Internal Market," in L.A. Winters and A. Venables (Eds.), *European Integration: Trade and Industry* (Cambridge: Cambridge University Press).

Falvey, R., Greenaway, D., and Yu, Z. (2006), "Extending the Melitz Model to Asymmetric Countries," The University of Nottingham research paper.

Falvey, R. (1979), "The Comparison of Trade within Export-Restricted Categories," *Journal of Political Economy*, 87 (5), 1142–1165.

Falvey, R. and Nelson D. (2006), "Introduction: Special Issue on 100 Years of Antidumping," *European Journal of Political Economy*, 545–553.

Feder, G., Just, R.E., and Schmitz, A. (1980), "Futures Markets and the Theory of the Firm under Price Uncertainty," *Quarterly Journal of Economics*, 95, 317–328.

Feenstra, R.C. (1985), "Automobile Prices and Protection: The US–Japan Trade Restraint," *Journal of Policy Modeling*, 7 (1), 49–68.

Feenstra, R.C. (Ed.) (1988a), *Empirical Methods for International Trade* (Cambridge, MA: MIT Press).

Feenstra, R.C. (1988b), "Quality Change under Trade Restraints in Japanese Autos," *Quarterly Journal of Economics*, 33 (1), 131–146.

Feenstra, R.C. (1989a) *Trade Policies for International Competitiveness* (Chicago, IL: University of Chicago Press and National Bureau of Economic Research).

Feenstra, R.C. (1989b), "Symmetric Pass-Through of Tariffs and Exchange Rates under Imperfect Competition: An Empirical Test," *Journal of International Economics*, 27, 25–45.

Feenstra, R.C. (1995), "Estimating the Effects of Trade Policy," in G. Grossman and K. Rogoff (Eds.), *Handbook of International Economics*, Vol. 3 (Amsterdam: North-Holland), ch. 30.

Feenstra, R.C. (2003), *Advanced International Trade: Theory and Evidence* (Princeton, NJ: Princeton University Press).

Feenstra, R.C. and Hanson, G.H. (2003), "Global Production Sharing and Rising Inequality: A Survey of Trade and Wages," in E.K. Choi and J. Harrigan (Eds.), *Handbook of International Trade* (Oxford: Blackwell).

Feenstra, R.C. (1994), "New Product Varieties and the Measurement of International Prices," *American Economic Review*, 84 (1), 157–177.

Feenstra, R.C., Lipsey, R.E., and Bowen, H.P. (1997), "World Trade Flows, 1970–1992, with Production and Tariff Data," NBER Working Paper No. 5910.

Feenstra, R.C., Lipsey, R.E., Deng, H., Ma, A.C., and Mo, H. (2005), "World Trade Flows: 1962–2000," NBER Working Paper No. W11040.

Feenstra, R.C., Romalis, J., and Schott, P.K. (2002), "US Imports, Exports, and Tariff Data, 1989–2001," NBER Working Paper No. 9387.

Feenstra, R.C. and Weinstein, D.E. (2010), "Globalization, Markups, and the US Price Level," NBER Working Paper No. 15749.

Feenstra, R.E. (2002), "Border Effects and the Gravity Equation: Consistent Methods for Estimation," *Scottish Journal of Political Economy*, 49, 491–506.

Feinberg, R.M. (1989), "Exchange Rates and 'Unfair Trade,'" *Review of Economics and Statistics*, 71, 704–707.

Feinberg, R.M. and Reynolds, K.M. (2006), "The Spread of Antidumping Regimes and the Role of Retaliation in Filings," *Southern Journal of Economics*, 72 (4), 877–890.

Fels, J. and Gundlach, E. (1990), "More Evidence on the Puzzle of Interindustry Wage Differentials: The Case of West Germany," *Weltwirtschaftliches Archiv*, 3, 544–560.

Findlay, R. (1984), "Growth and Development in Trade Models," in R.W. Jones and P.B. Kenen (Eds.), *Handbook of International Economics*, Vol. 1 (Amsterdam: North-Holland), 185–236

Findlay, R. (1988), "Comparative Advantage," in J. Eatwell, M. Milgate, and P. Newman (Eds.), *The New Palgrave: A Dictionary of Economics* (London: Macmillan), 514–517.

Findlay, R. and Kierzkowski, H. (1983), "International Trade and Human Capital: A Simple General Equilibrium Model," *Journal of Political Economy*, 91, 957–978.

Finger, J.M. (1993), *Antidumping: How it Works and Who Gets Hurt* (Ann Arbor: University of Michigan Press).

Finger, J.M. (1993), "The Origins and Evolution of Antidumping Regulation," in J.M. Finger (Ed.), *Antidumping: How It Works and Who Gets Hurt* (Ann Arbor: University of Michigan Press).

Finger, J.M. and Olechowski, A. (1987), "Trade Barriers: Who Does What to Whom," in H. Giersch (Ed.), *Free Trade in the World Economy* (Tübingen: J.C.B. Mohr), 37–71.

Fisher, E. (1989), "A Model of Exchange Rate Pass-Through," *Journal of International Economics*, 26, 119–137.

Fischer, R.D. (1992), "Endogenous Probability of Protection and Firm Behavior," *Journal of International Economics*, 32, 149–163.

Flam, H. (1987), "Reverse Dumping," *European Economic Review*, 31, 82–88.

Flam, H. (1992), "Product Markets and 1992: Full Integration, Large Gains?" *Journal of Economic Perspectives*, 6 (4), 7–30.

Francois, J.F. McDonald, B.J., and Nordström, H. (1995), "Assessing the Uruguay Round," in W. Martin and L.A. Winters (Eds.), *The Uruguay Round and the Developing Economies* (Washington, DC: World Bank).

Francois, J.F. and Reinert, K.A. (Eds.) (1997), *Applied Methods for Trade Policy Analysis: A Handbook* (Cambridge: Cambridge University Press).

Francois, J.F. and Shiells, C.R. (1994), *Modelling Trade Policy: Applied General Equilibrium Assessments of NAFTA* (Cambridge: Cambridge University Press).

Friberg, R. and Wilander, F. (2008), "The Currency Denomination of Exports: A Questionnaire Study," *Journal of International Economics*, 75, 54–69.

Froot, K. and Klemperer, P. (1989), "Exchange Rate Pass-Through When Market Share Matters," *American Economic Review*, 79 (4), 637–654.

Fujita, M., Krugman, P., and Venables, A.J. (1999), *The Spatial Economy: Cities, Regions, and International Trade* (Cambridge, MA: MIT Press).

Fukuda, S.-I. and Cong, J. (1994), "On the Choice of Invoice Currency by Japanese Exporters: The PTM Approach," *Journal of the Japanese and International Economies*, 8, 511–529.

Gale, D. and Nikaido, H. (1965), "The Jacobian Matrix and the Global Univalence of Mappings," *Mathematische Annalen*, 159, 81–93.

GATT (General Agreement on Tariffs and Trade) (1990), *International Trade* (Geneva: GATT).

GATT (1994), *The Results of the Uruguay Round of Multilateral Trade Negotiations* (Geneva: GATT).

GATT (various years), *Trade Policy Review Mechanism* (Geneva: GATT).

Gersovitz, M. (1982), "The Estimation of the Two-Gap Model," *Journal of International Economics*, 12, 111–124.

Ginsburgh, V. and Keyzer, M. (1997), *The Structure of Applied General Equilibrium Models* (Cambridge, MA: MIT Press).

Giovannini, A. (1988), "Exchange Rates and Traded Goods Prices," *Journal of International Economics*, 24, 45–68.

Globerman, S., Ries J., and Vertinsky, I. (1994), "The Economic Performances of Foreign-Owned Subsidiaries in Canada," *Canadian Journal of Economics*, 27 (1) 143–156.

Goldberg, L.S. and Tille, C. (2009), "Vehicle Currency Use in International Trade," *Journal of International Economics*, 76 (2), 177–192.

Goldberg, P.K. and Knetter, M.M. (1997), "Goods Prices and Exchange Rates: What Have We Learned?" *Journal of Economic Literature*, 35 (3), 1243–1272.

Goldsmith, R. and Saunders, C. (Eds.) (1960), *The Measurement of National Wealth, NBER Research in Income and Wealth No. 8* (Chicago: Quadrangle Books).

Goldstein, M. and Khan, M.S. (1978), "The Supply and Demand for Exports: A Simultaneous Approach," *Review of Economics and Statistics*, 60, 275–286.

Goldstein, M. and Khan, M.S. (1985), "Income and Price Effects in Foreign Trade," in R.W. Jones and P.B. Kenen (Eds.), *Handbook of International Economics*, Vol. 2 (Amsterdam: North- Holland), ch. 20, 1041–1105.

Golub, S.S. and Hsieh, C.-T. (2000), "Classical Ricardian Theory of Comparative Advantage Revisited," *Review of International Economics*, 8 (2), 221–234.

Graham, F. (1923), "Some Aspects of Protection Further Considered," *Quarterly Journal of Economics*, 37, 199–227.

Grassman, S. (1973), "A Fundamental Symmetry in International Payment Patterns," *Journal of International Economics*, 3, 105–116.

Greenaway, D., Hine, R., and Milner, C. (1995), "Vertical and Horizontal Intra-Industry Trade: A Cross Industry Analysis for the United Kingdom," *Economic Journal*, 105, 1505–1518.

Greenaway, D. and Milner, C. (1983), "On the Measurement of Intra-Industry Trade," *The Economic Journal*, 93, 900–908.

Greenaway, D. and Milner, C. (1986), *The Economics of Intra-Industry Trade* (Oxford: Basil Blackwell).

Greenaway, D. and Tharakan, P.K.M. (1986), *Imperfect Competition and International Trade: Policy Aspects of Intra-Industry Trade* (Brighton: Wheatsheaf).

Grinols, E.J. (1984), "A Thorn in the Lion's Paw: Has Britain Paid Too Much for Common Market Membership?" *Journal of International Economics*, 16, 271–293.

Grossman, G.M. (1981), "The Theory of Domestic Content Protection and Content Preference," *Quarterly Journal of Economics*, 96 (4), 583–603.

Grossman, G.M. (1986), "Imports as a Cause of Injury: The Case of the US Steel Industry," *Journal of International Economics*, 20, 201–223.

Grossman, G.M. (1987), "Strategic Export Promotion: A Critique," in P.R. Krugman (Ed.), *Strategic Trade Policy and the New International Economics* (Cambridge, MA: MIT Press), 213–246.

Grossman, G.M. and Helpman, E. (1991), *Innovation and Growth in the Global Economy* (Cambridge, MA: MIT Press).

Grossman, G.M. and Helpman, E. (1995a), "The Politics of Free Trade Agreements," *American Economic Review*, 85 (4), 667–690.

Grossman, G.M. and Helpman, E. (1995b), "Trade Wars and Trade Talks," *Journal of Political Economy*, 103 (4), 675–708.

Grossman, G.M. and Helpman, E. (2002), *Interest Groups and Trade Policy* (Princeton, NJ: Princeton University Press).

Grossman, G.M. and Helpman, E. (2003), "Outsourcing versus FDI in Industry Equilibrium," *Journal of the European Economic Association*, 1 (2/3), 317–327.

Grossman, G.M. and Helpman, E. (2005), "Outsourcing in a Global Economy," *Review of Economic Studies*, 72, 135–159.

Grossman, G.M. and Levinsohn, J.A. (1989), "Import Competition and the Stock Market Return to Capital," *American Economic Review*, 79 (5), 1065–1087.

Grossman, G.M., Helpman, E., and Szeidl, A. (2006), "Optimal Integration Strategies for the Multinational Firm," *Journal of International Economics*, 70, 216–238.

Grossman, S.J. and Hart, O.D. (1986), "The Costs and Benefits of Ownership: A Theory of Vertical and Lateral Integration," *Journal of Political Economy*, 94 (4), 691–719.

Grubaugh, S.G. (1987), "Determinants of Foreign Direct Investment, *Review of Economics and Statistics*," 69, 149–152.

Grubel, H.G. and Lee, H.-H. (2002), *Frontiers of Research on Intra-Industry Trade* (London: Palgrave).

Grubel, H.G. and Lloyd, P.J. (1975), *Intra-Industry Trade* (London: Macmillan).

Grubert, H. and Mutti, J. (1991), "Taxes, Tariffs, and Transfer Pricing in Multinational Corporate Decision Making," *Review of Economics and Statistics*, 79, 285–293.

Gruenspecht, H.K. (1988), "Dumping and Dynamic Competition," *Journal of International Economics*, 25, 225–248.

Gupta, V.K. (1983), "A Simultaneous Determination of Structure, Conduct and Performance in Canadian Manufacturing," *Oxford Economic Papers*, 35 (2), 281–301.

Haberler, G. (1936), *The Theory of International Trade* (London: W. Hodge).

Hadjiyiannis, C. (2004), "Common Markets and Trade Liberalization," *Canadian Journal of Economics*, 37 (2), 484–508.

Hakura, D. (2001). "Why Does HOV Fail? The Role of Technological Differences within the EC," *Journal of International Economics*, 54 (2), 361–382.

Hallak, J.C. and Levinsohn, J. (2009), "Fooling Ourselves: Evaluating the Globalization and Growth Debate," in E. Zedillo (Ed.), *The Future of Globalization* (London and New York: Routledge).

Hamilton, C. and Svensson, L.E.O. (1983), "Should Direct or Total Factor Intensities Be Used in Tests of the Factor Proportions Hypothesis?" *Weltwirtschaftliches Archiv*, 119 (3), 453–463.

Hamilton, J.D. (1994), *Time Series Analysis* (Princeton, NJ: Princeton University Press).

Hanson, G.H., Mataloni, R.J., and Slaughter, M.J. (2001), "Expansion Strategies of US Multinational Firms," *Brookings Trade Forum*, 245–295.

Hanson, H.H. and Xiang, C. (2004), "The Home-Market Effect and Bilateral Trade Patterns," *American Economic Review*, 94 (4), 1108–1129.

Harrigan, J. (1995), "Factor Endowments and the International Location of Production: Econometric evidence for the OECD, 1970–1985," *Journal of International Economics*, 39, 123–141.

Harrigan, J. (1997), "Technology, Factor Supplies and International Specialization: Estimating the Neoclassical Model," *American Economic Review*, 87, 475–494.

Harrigan, J. and Balaban, R. (1999), "US Wage Effects in General Equilibrium: The Effects of Prices, Technology and Factor Supplies, 1963–1991," NBER Working Paper No. 6981 (Cambridge, MA: NBER).

Harris, R. (1984), "Applied General Equilibrium Analysis of Small Open Economies with Scale Economies and Imperfect Competition," *American Economic Review*, 74 (5), 1016–1032.

Harris, R. (1985), "Why Voluntary Export Restraints Are 'Voluntary'," *Canadian Journal of Economics*, 18 (4), 799–809.

Harrison, E.A. (1994), "Productivity, Imperfect Competition and Trade Reform: Theory and Evidence," *Journal of International Economics*, 36 (1/2), 53–73.

Harrison, E.A. and Rodriguez-Clare, A. (2009), "Trade, Foreign Investment and Industrial Policy," in D. Rodrick and M.R. Rosenzweig (Eds.), *Handbook of Development Economics*, Vol. 5 (Amsterdam: North-Holland), ch. 63.

Harrod, R.F. (1939), "An Essay in Dynamic Theory," *Economic Journal*, 49, 14–33.

Hartigan, J.C. (1996), "Predatory Dumping," *Canadian Journal of Economics*, 29 (1), 228–239.

Hatton, T. (1995), "A Model of UK Emigration, 1870–1913," *Review of Economics and Statistics*, 77 (3), 407–415.

Hatzipanayotou, P., Lahiri, S., and Michael, S.M. (2002), "Can Cross-Border Pollution Reduce Pollution?" *Canadian Journal of Economics*, 35 (4), 805–818.

Hazari, B.R. (1978), *The Pure Theory of International Trade and Distortions* (London: Croom Helm), ch. 1, 7–29.

Head, K., Mayer, T., and Ries, J. (2002), "On the Pervasiveness of Home Market Effects," *Economica*, 69, 371–390.

Heller, W.P. (1988), "Coordination Failure with Complete Markets in a Simple Model of Effective Demand," in W.P. Heller, R.M. Starr, and D.A. Starrett (Eds.), *Equilibrium Analysis: Essays in Honor of K.J. Arrow*, vol. 2 (Cambridge: Cambridge University Press).

Helpman, E. (1981), "International Trade in the Presence of Product Differentiation, Economies of Scale, and Monopolistic Competition: A Chamberlin-Heckscher-Ohlin Approach," *Journal of International Economics*, 11, 305–340.

Helpman, E. (1984), "A Simple Theory of International Trade with Multinational Corporations," *The Journal of Political Economy*, 92 (3), 451–471.

Helpman, E. (1987), "Imperfect Competition and International Trade: Evidence from Fourteen Industrial Countries," *Journal of the Japanese and International Economies*, 1, 62–81.

Helpman, E. and Krugman, P.R. (1985), *Market Structure and Foreign Trade, Increasing Returns, Imperfect Competition, and the International Economy* (Cambridge, MA, and London: MIT Press).

Helpman, E. and Krugman, P.R. (1989), *Trade Policy and Market Structure* (Cambridge, MA: MIT Press).

Helpman, E. and Krugman P.R. (1985), *Market Structure and Foreign Trade: Increasing Returns, Imperfect Competition, and the International Economy* (Cambridge, MA, and London: MIT press).

Helpman, E., Marin, D., and Verdier, T. (Eds.) (2008), *The Organization of Firms in a Global Economy* (Cambridge, MA: Harvard University Press).

Helpman, E., Melitz M., and Yeaple, S.R. (2004), "Export versus FDI with Heterogeneous Firms," *American Economics Review*, 94 (1), 300–316.

Helpman, E. and Razin, A. (1983), "Increasing Returns, Monopolistic Competition, and Factor Movements: A Welfare Analysis," *Journal of International Economics*, 14, 263–276.

Heston, A. and Summers, R. (1991), "Penn World Table Version 5.6," Center for International Comparisons at the University of Pennsylvania.

Heston, A., Summers R., and Aten, B. (2009), "Penn World Table Version 6.3," Center for International Comparisons of Production, Income and Prices at the University of Pennsylvania (August).

Hicks, J. (1939), "Foundations of Welfare Economics," *Economic Journal*, 49, 696–712.

Hillman, A. (1980), "Observations on the Relation between 'Revealed Comparative Advantage' and Comparative Advantage as Indicated by Pre-Trade Relative Prices," *The Review of World Economics*, 116, 314–321.

Hindley, B. (1994). "Safeguards, VERs and antidumping actions," in *The New World Trading System* (Paris: OECD), 91–103.

Hine, R.C. (1994), "International Economic Integration," in D. Greenaway and L.A. Winters (Eds.), *Survey in International Trade* (Oxford: Basil Blackwell), 234–272.

Hinojosa-Ojeda, R. and Robinson, S. (1991), "Alternative Scenarios of US–Mexico Integration: A Computable General Equilibrium Approach," Working Paper No. 609 (Berkeley: University of California).

Hirschleifer, J. and Riley, J.G. (1992), *The Analytics of Uncertainty and Information* (Cambridge: Cambridge University Press).

Hoekman, B. 1996. "Trade Laws and Institutions: Good Practices and the World Trade Organization," World Bank Discussion Paper No. 282.

Hollander, A. (1987), "Content Protection and Transnational Monopoly," *Journal of International Economics*, 23, 283–297.

Holthausen, D.M. (1979), "Hedging and the Competitive Firm under Price Uncertainty," *American Economic Review*, 69, 989–995.

Hooper, P. and Mann, C. (1989), "Exchange Rate Pass-Through in the 1980s: The Case of US Imports of Manufactures," *Brookings Papers on Economic Activity*, 1, 297–337.

Horst, T. (1971), "The Theory of the Multinational Firm: Optimal Behavior under Different Tariff and Tax Rates," *Journal of Political Economy*, 79, 1059–1072.

Horst, T. (1972a), "Firm and Industry Determinants of the Decision to Invest Abroad: An Empirical Study," *Review of Economics and Statistics*, 54, 258–266.

Horst, T. (1972b), "The Industrial Composition of US Exports and Subsidiary Sales to the Canadian Market," *American Economic Review*, 62 (1), 37–45.

Horstmann, I.J. and Markusen, J.R. (1987), "Strategic Investments and the Development of Multinationals," *International Economic Review*, 28 (1), 109–121.

Horstmann, I.J. and Markusen, J.R. (1987), "Licensing versus Direct Investment: A Model of Internalisation of the MNE," *Canadian Journal of Economics*, 20, 464–481.

Hufbauer, G., Berliner, D., and Elliott, K.A. (1986), *Trade Protection in the United States: 31 Case Studies* (Washington, DC: Institute for International Economics).

Huisman, F. (2010), *The Middle East: Measuring Economic Integration and Labor Migration*, MSc thesis, Erasmus University Rotterdam.

Hummels, D. (2007), "Transportation Costs and International Trade in the Second Era of Globalization," *Journal of Economic Perspectives*, 21 (3), 131–154.

Hummels, D., Ishii, J., and Yi, K. (2001), "The Nature and Growth of Vertical Specialization in World Trade," *Journal of International Economics*, 54 (1), 75–96.

Hummels, D.L. and Levinsohn, J. (1995), "Monopolistic Competition and International Trade: Reconsidering the Evidence," *Quarterly Journal of Economics*, 110, 799–835.

Hummels, D. and Lugosvskyy, V. (2006), "Are Matched Partner Trade Statistics a Usable Measure of Transportation Costs?" *Review of International Economics*, 14 (1), 69–86.

Hunter, L. and Markusen, J. (1988), "Per-Capita Income as a Determinant of Trade," in R.C. Feenstra (Ed.), *Empirical Methods for International Trade* (Cambridge, MA: MIT Press).

Hwang, H. and Mai, C.-C. (1988), "On the Equivalence of Tariffs and Quotas under Duopoly: A Conjectural Variations Approach," *Journal of International Economics*, 24, 373–380.

Hymer, S. (1976), *The International Operations of National Firms: A Study of Foreign Direct Investment*, PhD dissertation (Cambridge, MA: MIT Press).

Irwin, D.A. (1992), "Strategic Trade Policy and Mercantilist Trade Rivalries," *The American Economic Review, Papers and Proceedings*, 82 (2), 134–139.

Irwin, D.A. and Klenow, P.J. (1994), "Learning-by-Doing Spillovers in the Semiconductor Industry," *Journal of Political Economy*, 102 (6), 1200–1227.

Ishikawa, J. and Komoriya, Y. (2007), "Subsidies and Countervailing Duties with Firm Heterogeneity," *Asia-Pacific Journal of Accounting and Economics*, 14, 279–291.

Islam, N. (2003), "What Have We Learned from the Convergence Debate?" *Journal of Economic Surveys*, 17, 309–362.

Ito, T. (1990), "Foreign Exchange Rate Expectations: Micro Survey Data," *American Economic Review*, 80 (3), 434–449.

Intriligator, M.D. (1971), *Mathematical Optimization and Economic Theory* (Englewood Cliffs, NJ: Prentice Hall).

Jackson, J.H. (1989), *The World Trading System: Law and Policy of International Economic Relations* (Cambridge, MA, and London, UK: MIT Press).

Jackson, J.H. and Vermulst, E.A. (Eds.) (1990), *Antidumping Law and Practice: A Comparative Study* (London: Harvester Wheatsheaf).

Jacquemin, A. and Sapir, A. (1988), "European or World Integration?" *Weltwirtschaftliches Archiv*, 124 (1), 127–138.

Johansen, L. (1960), *A Multi-Sectoral Study of Economic Growth* (Amsterdam: North-Holland).

Johnson, H.G. (1954), "Optimum Tariffs and Retaliation," *Review of Economic Studies*, 21 (2), 142–153.

Johnson, H.G. (1958), "The Gains from Freer Trade with Europe: An Estimate," *Manchester School*, 26, 247–255.

Johnson, H.G. (1962), "The Economic Theory of Customs Union," in H.G. Johnson (Ed.), *Money, Trade and Economic Growth* (London: George Allen and Unwin).

Johnson, H.G. (1970), "The Efficiency and Welfare Implications of the International Corporation," in C.P. Kindleberger (Ed.), *The International Corporation* (Cambridge, MA: MIT Press).

Johnson, H.G. (1971), *Aspects of the Theory of Tariffs* (London: Allen and Unwin).

Jones, C.I. (2006), *Introduction to Economic Growth*, second edition (New York: W.W. Norton & Company).

Jones, H.G. (1975), *An Introduction to Modern Theories of Economic Growth* (London: Nelson).

Jones, R.W. (1965), "The Structure of Simple General Equilibrium Models," *Journal of Political Economy*, 73, 557–572.

Jones, R.W. (1969), "Tariffs and Trade in General Equilibrium: Comment," *American Economic Review*, 59, 418–424.

Jones, R.W., Neary, J.P., and Ruane, F.P. (1983), "Two-Way Capital Flows," *Journal of International Economics*, 14, 357–366.

Jones, R.W. and Scheinkman, J. (1977), "The Relevance of the Two-Sector Production Model in Trade Theory," *Journal of Political Economy*, 85, 909–935.

Kamata, I. (2010), "Revisiting the Revisited: An Alternative Test of the Monopolistic Competition Model of International Trade," La Follette School of Public Affairs, Working Paper No. 2010–007.

Kambourov, G.T. and Manovskii, I. (2008), "Rising Occupational and Industry Mobility in the United States: 1968–1997," *International Economic Review*, 49 (1), 41–79.

Kambourov, G.T. and Manovskii, I. (2009), "Occupational Specificity of Human Capital," *International Economic Review*, 50 (1), 63–115.

Kamps, A. (2006), "The Euro as Invoicing Currency in International Trade," European Central Bank, Working Paper Series, No. 665.

Kant, C.(1988), "Endogenous Transfer Pricing and the Effects of Uncertain Regulation, *Journal of International Economics*, 24, 147–157.

Karacaovali, B. and Limão, N. (2008), "The Clash of Liberalizations: Preferential vs. Multilateral Trade Liberalization in the European Union," *Journal of International Economics*, 74, 299–327.

Katz, L. and Summers, L. (1988), "Can Inter-Industry Wage Differentials Justify Strategic Trade Policy?" National Bureau of Economic Research Working Paper No. 2739.

Katz, L.F. and Summers, L.H. (1989), "Industry Rents: Evidence and Implications," in M.N. Baily and C. Winston (Eds.), *Brookings Papers on Economic Activity: Microeconomics* (Washington, DC: Brookings Institution), 208–275.

Kaufman, D., Kraay A., and Mastruzzi, M. (2003), "Governance Matters: Governance Indicators for 1996–2005," World Bank Working Paper No. 3106.

Kawai, M. (1981), "The Behaviour of an Open Economy Firm under Flexible Exchange Rates," *Economica*, 48, 45–60.

Kawai, M. and Zilcha, I. (1986), "International Trade with Forward-Futures Markets under Exchange Rate and Price Uncertainty," *Journal of International Economics*, 20, 83–98.

Keller, W. (2004), "International Technology Diffusion," *Journal of Economic Literature*, 42 (3), 752–782.

Kee, H., Nicita, A., and Olarreaga, M. (2009), "Estimating Trade Restrictiveness Indices," *Economic Journal*, 119 (534), 172–199.

Kemp, M.C. (1964), *The Pure Theory of International Trade* (Englewood Cliffs, NJ: Prentice Hall).

Kemp, M.C. (1969), *The Pure Theory of International Trade and Investment* (Englewood Cliffs, NJ: Prentice Hall).

Kemp, M.C. and Wan, H.Y. (1976), "An Elementary Proposition Concerning the Formation of Customs Unions," *Journal of International Economics*, 6, 95–97.

Kennan, J. and Riezman, R. (1990), "Optimal Tariff Equilibrium with Customs Unions," *Canadian Journal of Economics*, 23 (1), 70–83.

Kim, S. (1995), "Expansion of Markets and the Geographic Distribution of Economic Activities: The Trends in US Regional Manufacturing Structure, 1860–1987," *Quarterly Journal of Economics*, 110, 881–908.

Kiyota, K. and Urata S. (2008), "The Role of Multinational Firms in International Trade: The Case of Japan," *Japan and the World Economy*, 20(3), 338–352.

Klaassen, F. (2004), "Why Is It So Difficult to Find an Effect of Exchange Rate Risk on Trade?" *Journal of International Money and Finance*, 28, 817–839.

Klein, L.R. (1983), *Lectures in Econometrics* (Amsterdam: North-Holland), 21–36.

Knetter, M.M. (1989), "Price Discrimination by US and German Exporters," *American Economic Review*, 79 (1), 198–210.

Knetter, M.M. (1992), "International Comparisons of Pricing-to-Market Behavior," *American Economic Review*, 83 (3), 473–486.

Kogut, B. and Chang, S.J. (1991), "Technological Capabilities and Japanese Foreign Direct Investment in the United States," *The Review of Economics and Statistics*, 73 (10), 401–413.

Kogut, B. and Kulatilaka, N. (1994), "Operating Flexibility, Global Manufacturing, and the Option Value of a Multinational Network," *Management Science*, 40, 123–139.

Kohler, W. (1988), "Modeling Heckscher-Ohlin Comparative Advantage in Regression Equations: A Critical Survey," *Empirica*, 15 (2), 263–293.

Kohler, W. (1991), "How Robust Are Sign and Rank Order Tests of the Heckscher-Ohlin-Vanek Theorem," *Oxford Economic Papers*, 43 (1), 158–171.

Kohli, U. (1990), "Price and Quantity Elasticities in International Trade," *Economic Letters*, 33, 277–281.

Kohli, U. (1991), *Technology, Duality, and Foreign Trade: The GNP Function Approach to Modeling Imports and Exports* (Ann Arbor and London: University of Michigan Press and Harvester Wheatsheaf).

Kohli, U. (1993), "US Technology and the Specific-Factors Model," *Journal of International Economics*, 34, 115–136.

Koopmans, T.C. (1965), "On the Concept of Optimal Economic Growth," *Pontificae Academiae Scientiarum Scripta Varia*, 28, 225–230.

Krauss, M.B., Johnson, H.G., and Skouras, T. (1973), "On the Shape and Location of the Production Possibility Curve," *Economica*, 40 (159), 305–310.

Kreps, D.A. and Scheinkman, J.A. (1983), "Quantity Precommitment and Bertrand Competition Yield Cournot Outcomes," *Bell Journal of Economics*, 4, 326–337.

Krishna, K. (1987), "Tariffs versus Quotas with Endogenous Quality," *Journal of International Economics*, 23, 97–122.

Krishna, K. (1990a), "The Case of Vanishing Revenue: Auction Quotas with Monopoly," *American Economic Review*, 80 (4), 828–837.

Krishna, K. (1990b), "Protection and the Product Line," *International Economic Review*, 31 (1), 87–102.

Krishna, K. and Itoh, M. (1988), "Content Protection and Oligopolistic Interactions," *Review of Economic Studies*, 55, 107–125.

Krishna, K. and Krueger, A.O. (1994), "Implementing Free Trade Areas: Rules of Origin and Hidden Protection," in A. Deardorff, J. Levinsohn, and R. Stern (Eds.), *New Directions in Trade Theory* (Ann Arbor: University of Michigan Press).

Krishna, P. (1998), "Regionalism and Multilateralism: A Political Economy Approach," *Quarterly Journal of Economics*, 113 (1), 227–251.

Krishna, P. (2003), "Are Regional Trading Partners Natural?" *Journal of Political Economy*, 111 (1), 202–226.

Krueger, A.B. and Summers, L.H. (1988), "Efficiency Wages and the Inter-Industry Wage Structure," *Econometrica*, 56, 259–293.

Krugman, P.R. (1979), "Increasing Returns, Monopolistic Competition and International Trade," *Journal of International Economics*, 9 (4), 469–479.

Krugman, P.R. (1980), "Scale Economies, Product Differentiation and the Pattern of Trade," *American Economic Review*, 70 (5), 950–959.

Krugman, P.R. (1987), "Pricing to Market When the Exchange Rate Changes," in S.W. Arndt and J.D. Richardson (Eds.), *Real-Financial Linkages Among Open Economies* (Cambridge, MA: MIT Press), 49–70.

Krugman, P.R. (1989), "Differences in Income Elasticities and Trends in Real Exchange Rates," *European Economic Review*, 33, 1031–1054.

Krugman, P.R. (1991), "Is Bilateralism Bad?" in E. Helpman and A. Razin (Eds.), *International Trade and Trade Policy* (Cambridge, MA: MIT Press), 9–23.

Krugman, P.R. (1993), "The Narrow and Broad Arguments for Free Trade," *American Economic Review*, 83 (2), 362–366.

Krugman, P.R. and Baldwin, R.E. (1987), "The Persistence of the US Trade Deficit," *Brookings Paper on Economic Activity*, 1, 1–55.

Krugman, P.R. and Obstfeld, M. (1988), *International Economics: Theory and Policy* (Glenview: Scott Foresman), appendix to ch. 2, 36–41.

Krugman, P.R. and Smith, A. (Eds.) (1994), *Empirical Studies of Strategic Trade Policies* (Chicago, and London: University of Chicago Press).

Krugman, P.R. and Venables, A.J. (1995), "Globalization and the Inequality of Nations," *Quarterly Journal of Economics*, 110, 857–880.

Krugman, P.R. and Venables, A.J. (1999), "How Robust Is the Home Market Effect?" MIT and LSE, mimeo.

Kumar, N. (1998), "Multinational Enterprises, Regional Economic Integration, and Export-Platform Production: An Empirical Analysis for the US and Japanese Corporations," *Weltwirtschaftliches Archiv*, 134 (3), 450–483.

Laird, S. and Yeats, A. (1990), *Quantitative Methods for Trade-Barrier Analysis* (New York: New York University Press).

Lall, S. (1980), "Monopolistic Advantages and Foreign Involvement by US Manufacturing Industry," *Oxford Economic Papers*, 32, 102–122.

Lall, S. and Siddharthan, N.S. (1982) "The Monopolistic Advantages of Multinationals: Lessons from Foreign Investment in the US," *Economic Journal*, 92 (367), 668–683.

Lancaster, K. (1966), "A New Approach to Consumer Theory," *Journal of Political Economy*, 31, 1–26.

Lancaster, K. (1979), *Variety, Equity and Efficiency* (New York: Columbia University Press).

Lawrence, R.Z. (2000), "Does a Kick in the Pants Get You Going or Does It Just Hurt? The Impact of International Competition on Technological Change in US Manufacturing," in R.C. Feenstra (Ed.), *The Impact of International Trade on Wages* (Chicago: University of Chicago Press), 197–224.

Lawrence, R.Z. and Slaughter, M. (1993) "International Trade and American Wages in the 1980s: Giant Sucking Sound or Small Hiccup?" *Brookings Papers on Economic Activity: Microeconomics*, 2, 161–226.

Leamer, E.E. (1974), "Nominal Tariff Averages with Estimated Weights," *Southern Economic Journal*, 41, 34–46.

Leamer, E.E. (1980), "The Leontief Paradox Reconsidered," *Journal of Political Economy*, 88 (3), 495–503.

Leamer, E.E. (1981), "Is It a Demand Curve or Is It a Supply Curve? Partial Identification through Inequality Constraints," *Review of Economics and Statistics*, 63, 319–327.

Leamer, E.E. (1984), *Sources of International Comparative Advantage: Theory and Evidence* (Cambridge, MA: MIT Press).

Leamer, E.E. (1988), "In Search of Stolper–Samuelson Linkages between International Trade and Lower Wages," in S.M. Collins (Ed.), *Imports, Exports, and the American Worker*. (Washington, DC: Brookings Institution Press).

Leamer, E.E. (1988), "Measures of Openness," in R.E. Baldwin (Ed.), *Trade Policy Issues and Empirical Analysis* (Chicago: University of Chicago Press and National Bureau of Economic Research).

Leamer, E.E. and Bowen, H.P. (1981), "Cross-Section Tests of the Heckscher-Ohlin Theorem: Comment," *American Economic Review*, 71 (4), 1040–1043.

Leamer, E.E. and Levinsohn, J. (1995), "International Trade Theory: The Evidence," in G. Grossman and K. Rogoff (Eds.), *Handbook of International Economics*, Vol. 3 (Amsterdam: North-Holland), ch. 26.

Lee, D.W. and Lee, T.H. (1995), "Human Capital and Economic Growth: Tests Based on the International Evaluation of Educational Achievements," *Economics Letters*, 47, 219–225.

Leidy, M.P. and Hoekman, B.M. (1988), "Production Effects of Price- and Cost-Based Anti-Dumping Laws under Flexible Exchange Rates," Discussion Paper No. 224, Research Seminar in International Economics, University of Michigan.

Leontief, W. (1953), "Domestic Production and Foreign Trade: The American Capital Position Re-Examined," *Proceeding of the American Philosophical Society*, 97, 332–349.

Leontief, W. (1954), "Domestic Production and Foreign Trade: The American Position Re-examined," *Economica Internazionale*, 7, 3–32.

Lerner, A. (1936), "The Symmetry between Import and Export Taxes," *Economica*, 3, 306–313.

Levchenko, A. (2004), "Institutional Quality and International Trade," *Review of Economic Studies* 74 (3), 791–819.

Levchenko, A., Lewis, L., and Tesar, L. (2011), "The Collapse in Quality Hypothesis," *American Economic Review Papers and Proceedings*, 101 (3), 293–297.

Levine, R. and Renelt, D. (1992), "A Sensitivity Analysis of Cross-Country Growth Regressions," *American Economic Review*, 82, 942–963.

Levine, R. and Zervos, S.J. (1993), "What We Have Learned about Policy and Growth from Cross-Country Regressions," *American Economic Review, Papers and Proceedings*, 83, 426–430.

Levinsohn, J. (1993), "Testing the Imports-as-Market-Discipline Hypothesis," *Journal of International Economics*, 35(1/2), 1–22.

Levy, P.I. (1997), "A Political-Economic Analysis of Free-Trade Agreements," *American Economic Review*, 87 (4), 506–519.

Liesner, H.H. (1958), "The European Common Market and British industry," *Economic Journal*, 68, 302–316.

Limão, N. (2006), "Preferential Trade Agreements as Stumbling Blocks for Multilateral Trade Liberalization: Evidence for the United States," *American Economic Review*, 96 (3), 896–914.

Linder, S. (1961), *An Essay on Trade and Transformation* (New York: Wiley).

Lloyd, P.J. (1982), "3 x 3 Theory of Customs Unions," *Journal of International Economics*, 12, 41–63.

Loertscher, R. and Wolter, F. (1980), "Determinants of Intra-Industry Trade: Among Countries and Across Industries," *The Review of World Economics*, 116, 280–293.

Lucas, R.E. (1988), "On the Mechanics of Economic Development," *Journal of Monetary Economics*, 22, 3–42.

Lucas, R.E. (1990), "Why Doesn't Capital Flow from Rich to Poor Countries?" *American Economic Review*, 80 (2), 92–96.

Lucas, R.E. (1993), "Making a Miracle," *Econometrica*, 61, 251–272.

Lustig, N., Bosworth, B.P., and Lawrence, R.Z. (1992), *North American Free Trade: Assessing the Impact* (Washington, DC: Brookings Institution).

McCulloch, R. (1993), "The Optimality of Free Trade: Science or Religion?" *American Economic Review*, 83 (2), 367–371.

MacDonald, M.J. (1994), "Does Import Competition Force Efficient Production?" *Review of Economics and Statistics*," 76 (4), 721–727.

MacDougall, G.D.A. (1951), "British and American Exports: A Study Suggested by the Theory of Comparative Costs, Part I," *Economic Journal*, 61, 487–521.

MacDougall, G.D.A. (1960), "The Benefits and Costs of Private Investment from Abroad: A Theoretical Approach," *Economic Record*, 36, 13–35.

MacDougall, G.D.A., Dowley, M., Fox, P., and Pugh, S. (1962), "British and American Productivity, Prices and Exports: An Addendum," *Oxford Economic Papers*, 14 (3), 297–304.

McGilvray, J. and Simpson, D. (1973), "The Commodity Structure of Anglo-Irish Trade," *Review of Economics and Statistics*, 55, 451–458.

McLaren, J. (2000), "Globalization and Vertical Structure," *American Economic Review*, 90 (5), 1239–1254.

McMillan, J. (1993), "Does Regional Integration Foster Open Trade? Economic Theory and GATT's Article XXIV," in K. Anderson and R. Blackhurst (Eds.), *Regional Integration and the Global Trading System* (New York: HarvesterWheatsheaf), 292–310.

Magee, S.P. (1980), "Three Simple Tests of the Stolper–Samuelson Theorem," in P. Oppenheimer (Ed.), *Issues in International Economics* (London: Oriel Press), 138–153.

Malueg, D.A. and Schwartz, M. (1994), "Parallel Imports, Demand Dispersion, and International Price Discrimination," *Journal of International Economics*, 37, 167–195.

Mankiw, N.G. (1995), "The Growth of Nations," *Brookings Papers on Economic Activity*, 1, 275–326.

Marchese, S. and De Simone, F.N. (1989), "Monotonicity of Indices of 'Revealed' Comparative Advantage: Empirical Evidence on Hillman's Condition," *The Review of World Economics*, 125, 158–167.

Markusen, J.R. (1983), "Factor Movements and Commodity Trade as Complements," *Journal of International Economics*, 14, 341–356.

Markusen, J.R. (2002), *Multinational Firms and the Theory of International Trade* (Cambridge, MA: The MIT Press).

Markusen, J.R. and Venables, A.J. (1988), "Trade Policy with Increasing Returns and Imperfect Competition: Contradictory Results from Competing Assumptions," *Journal of International Economics*, 24, 299–316.

Markusen, J.R. and Maskus, K.E. (2001), "Multinational Firms: Reconciling Theory and Evidence," in M. Blomstrom and L.S. Goldberg (Eds.), *Topics in Empirical International Economics: A Festschrift in Honor of Robert E. Lipsey* (Chicago: University of Chicago Press for National Bureau of Economic Research).

Markusen, J.R. and Maskus, K.E. (2002), "Discriminating among Alterative Theories of the Multinational Enterprise," *Review of International Economics*, 10 (4), 694–707.

Markusen, J.R. and Venables, A.J. (1998), "Multinational Firms and the New Trade Theory," *Journal of International Economics*, 46, 183–203.

Markusen, J.R. and Venables, A.J. (2000), "The Theory of Endowment, Intra-Industry and Multinational Trade," *Journal of International Economics*, 52, 209–235.

Markusen, J.R., Venables A. J., Eby Konan, D., and Zhang, K.H. (1996), "A Unified Treatment of Horizontal Direct Investment, Vertical Direct Investment, and the Pattern of Trade in Goods and Services," NBER Working Paper No. 5696.

Marquez, J. (1990), "Bilateral Trade Elasticities," *Review of Economics and Statistics* 72, 75–86.

Marshall, A. (1890), *Principles of Economics* (London: Macmillan).

Marston, R. (1990), "Pricing to Market in Japanese Manufacturing," *Journal of International Economics*, 29, 217–236.

Martin, J.P. (1976), "Variable Factor Supplies and the HOS Model," *Economic Journal*, 820–831.

Martin, P. and Rey, H. (2004), "Financial Super-markets: Size Matters for Asset Trade," *Journal of International Economics*, 64, 335–361.

Marvel, H.P. and Ray, E.J. (1995), "Countervailing Duties," *The Economic Journal*, 105, 1576–1593.

Maskus, K. (1991), "Comparing International Trade Data and Product and National Characteristics Data for the Analysis of Trade Models," in P. Hooper and J.D. Richardson (Eds.), *International Economic Transactions, Issues in Measurement and Empirical Research* (Chicago: University of Chicago Press).

Mataloni, R.J. (2008), "US Multinational Companies: Operations in 2006," *Survey of Current Business*, available at http://www.bea.gov/scb/pdf/2008/11%20November/1108_mnc.pdf (accessed 24 October 2011).

Mattoo, A., Neagu, I.C., and Ozden, C. (2008), "Brain Waste? Educated Immigrants in the US Labor Market," *Journal of Development Economics*, 87, 255–269.

Mavroidis, P.C. (2007), *Trade in Goods: The GATT and the Other Agreements Regulating Trade in Goods* (Oxford: Oxford University Press).

Melitz, M. (2003), "The Impact of Trade on Intra-Industry Reallocations and Aggregate Industry Productivity," *Econometrica*, 71 (6), 1695–1725.

Melitz, M. and Ottaviano, G. (2008), "Market Size, Trade and Productivity" *Review of Economics Studies*, 75, 295–316.

Melvin, J.R. (1970), "Commodity Taxation as a Determinant of Trade," *Canadian Journal of Economics*, 3, 62–78.

Melvin, J.R. (1971), "On the Derivation of the Production Possibility Curve," *Economica*, 38 (151), 281–294.

Memedovic, O. (1994), *On the Theory and Measurement of Comparative Advantage, Book No. 65* (Rotterdam: Tinbergen Institute Research Series).

Messerlin, P. (1990), "Anti-Dumping Regulation or Pro-Cartel Law? The EC Chemical Cases," *World Economy,* 13 (4), 465–492.

Messerlin, P. and Reed, G. (1995), "Antidumping Policies in the United States and the European Community," *Economic Journal,* 105, 1565–1575.

Metzler, L.A. (1949), "Tariffs, the Terms of Trade, and the Distribution of National Income," *Journal of Political Economy,* 57, 1–29.

Michael, S.M. (2003), "International Migration, Income Taxes and Transfers: A Welfare Analysis," *Journal of Development Economics,* 72, 401–411.

Michaely, M. (1977), *Theory of Commercial Policy* (Chicago: University of Chicago Press).

Milgrom, P. and Roberts, J. (1992), *Economics, Organization and Management* (Englewood Cliffs, NJ: Prentice Hall).

Miller, M.H. and Spencer, J.E. (1977), "The Static Economic Effects of the UK Joining the EEC: A General Equilibrium Approach," *Review of Economic Studies,* 136, 71–94.

Mills, T.C. (1990), *Time Series Techniques for Economists* (Cambridge: Cambridge University Press)

Moraga-Gonzalez, J.L. and Viaene, J.-M. (2004), "Anti-dumping, Intra-Industry Trade and Quality Reversals," Tinbergen Institute Discussion Paper No. 04-124/2.

Mundell, R. (1957), "International Trade and Factor Mobility," *American Economic Review,* 47, 321–335.

Mussa, M. (1979), "The Two-Sector Model in Terms of Dual: A Geometric Exposition," *Journal of International Economics,* 9, 513–526.

Mussa, M. (1984), "The Economics of Content Protection," NBER Working Paper No. 1457.

Neary, J.P. (1978), "Short-Run Capital Specificity and the Pure Theory of International Trade," *Economic Journal,* 88, 488–510.

Neary, P.J. (2006), "International Trade and the Environment: Theoretical and Policy Linkages," *Environmental and Resource Economics,* 33, 95–118.

Neven, D. and Siotis, G. (1996), "Technology Sourcing and FDI in the EC: An Empirical Evaluation," *International Journal of Industrial Organization,* 14, 543–560.

Nogués, J.J., Olechowski, A., and Winters, L.A. (1986), "The Extent of Non-Tariff Barriers to Industrial Countries' Imports," *The World Bank Economic Review,* 1, 181–199.

Norman, G. and Dunning, J.M. (1984). "Intra-Industry Foreign Direct Investment," *The Review of World Economics,* 120, 522–539.

Nunn, N. (2007), "Relationship-Specificity, Incomplete Contracts and the Pattern of Trade," *Quarterly Journal of Economics,* 122, 569–600.

Nunn, N. and Trefler, D. (2008), "The Boundaries of the Multinational Firm: An Empirical Analysis," in E. Helpman, D. Marin, and T. Verdier (Eds.), *The Organization of Firms in a Global Economy* (Cambridge, MA: Harvard University Press).

Obstfeld, M. (2009), "International Finance and Growth in Developing Countries: What Have We Learned?" NBER Working Paper No. 14691.

OECD (2002), *OECD Economic Outlook,* 2002 (1), 309–320.

OECD (2005), *Measuring Globalisation: OECD Economic Globalisation Indicators.*

OECD (2010), *OECD.Stat,* available at http://www.oecd-ilibrary.org/economics/data/oecd-stat_data-00285-en (accessed 24 October 2011).

Ohlin, B. (1933), *Interregional and International Trade* (Cambridge, MA: Harvard University Press).

Okuno-Fujiwara, M. (1988), "Interdependence of Industries, Coordination Failure and Strategic Promotion of an Industry," *Journal of International Economics,* 25, 25–43.

Oniki, H. and Uzawa, H. (1965), "Patterns of Trade and Investment in a Dynamic Model of International Trade," *Review of Economic Studies,* 32, 15–38.

Osborne, M.J. and Rubinstein, A. (1990), *Bargaining and Markets* (San Diego, CA: Academic Press).

Ottaviano G., Tabushi T., and Thisse J.-F. (2002), "Agglomeration and Trade Revisited," *International Economic Review,* 43, 409–436.

Panagariya, A. (1981), "Variable Returns to Scale in Production and Patterns of Specialization," *American Economic Review,* 71, 221–230.

Panagariya, A. (1996), "The Regionalism Debate: An Overview," *The World Economy,* 22 (4), 477–511.

Pavcnik N. (2002), "Trade Liberalization, Exit, and Productivity Improvement: Evidence from Chilean Plants," *Review of Economics Studies*, 69 (1), 245–276.

Pelzman, J. (1986). "The Tariff Equivalents of the Existing Quotas under the Multifiber Arrangement," paper presented at the Southern Economic Association meetings, 23–25 November.

Perroni, C. and Whalley, J. (1996), "How Severe Is Global Retaliation Risk under Increasing Regionalism?" *American Economic Review Papers and Proceedings*, 86 (2), 57–61.

Prusa, T.J. (1992), "Why Are So Many Antidumping Petitions Withdrawn?" *Journal of International Economics*, 33, 1–20.

Prusa, T.J. (1994), "Pricing Behavior in the Presence of Antidumping Law," *Journal of Economic Integration*, 9 (2), 260–289.

Prusa, T.J. (2001), "On the Spread and Impact of Anti-Dumping," *Canadian Journal of Economics*, 34 (3), 591–611.

Prusa, T.J. and Skeath, S. (2002), "The Economics and Strategic Motives for Antidumping Filings," *Weltwirtschaftliches Archiv*, 138, 389–413.

Pugel, T.A. (1978), *International Market Linkages and US Manufacturing: Prices, Profits, and Patterns* (Cambridge, MA: Ballinger).

Pugel, T.A., Krages, E.S., and Kimura, Y. (1996), "Further Evidence of Japanese Direct Investment in US Manufacturing," *Review of Economics and Statistics*, 78 (2), 208–213.

Qiu, L.D. (1995), "Why Can't Countervailing Duties Deter Export Subsidization?" *Journal of International Economics*, 39, 249–272.

Radelet, S. and Sachs, J. (1998), "Shipping Costs, Manufactured Exports, and Economic Growth," AEA Meetings, Harvard University, mimeo.

Ramsey, F.P. (1928), "A Mathematical Theory of Saving," *Economic Journal*, 38, 543–559.

Rangan, S. and Lawrence, R.Z. (1993), "The Responses of US Firms to Exchange Rate Fluctuations: Piercing the Corporate Veil," *Brookings Papers on Economic Activity*, 2, 341–379.

Rauch, J.E. (1999), "Networks versus Markets in International Trade," *Journal of International Economics*, 48 (1), 7–35.

Rebelo, S. (1991), "Long-Run Policy Analysis and Long-Run Growth," *Journal of Political Economy*, 99, 500–521.

Reimer, J. (2006), Global Production Sharing and Trade in the Services of Factors. *Journal of International Economics*, 68 (2), 384–408.

Reitzes, J.D. (1993), "Antidumping Policy," *International Economic Review*, 34 (4), 745–763.

Ricardo, D. (1821), *The Principles of Political Economy and Taxation* (London: J. Murray).

Richardson, M. (1991), "The Effects of a Content Requirement on a Foreign Duopsonist," *Journal of International Economics*, 31, 143–155.

Richardson, M. (1993), "Endogenous Protection and Trade Diversion," *Journal of International Economics*, 34 (3/4), 309–324.

Riezman, R. (1982), "Tariff Retaliation from a Strategic Viewpoint," *Southern Economic Journal*, 48, 583–593.

Riezman, R. (1985), "Customs Unions and the Core," *Journal of International Economics*, 19, 355–365.

Riezman, R. (1991), "Dynamic Tariffs with Asymmetric Information," *Journal of International Economics*, 30 (3/4), 267–283.

Rob, R. and Vettas, N. (2003), "Foreign Direct Investment and Exports with Growing Demand," *Review of Economic Studies*, 70, 629–648.

Roberts M.J. and Tybout, J. (1997), "The Decision to Export in Columbia: An Empirical Model of Entry with Sunk Cost," *American Economic Review*, 87 (4), 545–564.

Rodriguez, C. (1979), "The Quality of Import and the Differential Welfare Effects of Tariffs, and Quality Controls as Protective Devices," *Canadian Journal of Economics*, 22 (3), 439–449.

Rodriguez, F. and Rodrik, D. (2001), "Trade Policy and Economic Growth: A Skeptic's Guide to Cross-national Evidence," in B. Bernanke and K. Rogoff (Eds.), *NBER Macroeconomics Annual 2000* (Cambridge, MA: MIT Press).

Rodrik, D. (1988), "Imperfect Competition, Scale Economies, and Trade Policy in Developing Countries," in R.E. Baldwin (Ed.), *Trade Policy Issues and Empirical Analysis* (Chicago: University of Chicago Press).

Rodrik, D. and Rosenzweig, M.R. (2009), *Handbook of Development Economics*, Vol. 5 (Amsterdam: North-Holland).

Romer, P.M. (1986), "Increasing Returns and Long-Run Growth," *Journal of Political Economy*, 94, 1002–1037.

Romer, P.M. (1989), "Capital Accumulation in the Theory of Long-Run Growth," in R.J. Barro, (Ed.), *Modern Business Cycle Theory* (Cambridge, MA: Harvard University Press).

Romer, P.M. (1990), "Endogenous Technological Change," *Journal of Political Economy*, 98, 71–102.

Romer, P.M. (1994), "The Origins of Endogenous Growth," *The Journal of Economic Perspectives*, 8, 3–22.

Romer, P. (1994), "New Goods, Old Theory, and the Welfare Cost of Trade Restrictions," *Journal of Development Economics*, 43, 5–38.

Rose, A. (2000), "One Money, One Market: Estimating the Effect of Common Currencies on Trade," *Economic Policy*, 30, 9–45.

Roussland, D. and Soumela, J. (1985), "Calculating the Consumer and Net Welfare Costs of Import Relief," United States International Trade Commission Staff Research Study No.15.

Rubinstein, A. (1982), "Perfect Equilibrium in a Bargaining Model," *Econometrica*, 50, 97–110.

Rubinstein, A. (1987), "Perfect Equilibrium in a Market with Decentralized Trade and Strategic Behaviour: An Introduction," London School of Economics Theoretical Economics Discussion Paper Series, No. 87/147.

Rubinstein, A. and Wolinsky, A. (1985), "Equilibrium in a Market with Sequential Bargaining," *Econometrica*, 53, 1133–1150.

Ruffin, R.J. (1984), "International Factor Movements," in R.W. Jones and P.B. Kenen (Eds.), *Handbook of International Economics*, Vol. 1 (Amsterdam: North-Holland), 237–288.

Ruffin, R.J. and Jones, R.W. (1977), "Protection and Real Wages: The Neo-Classical Ambiguity," *Journal of Economic Theory*, 14, 337–348.

Ruland, L.J. and Viaene, J.-M. (1993), "The Political Choice of the Exchange Rate Regime," *Economics and Politics*, 5, 271–283.

Saggi, K. (2006), "Preferential Trade Agreements and Multilateral Tariff Cooperation," *International Economic Review*, 47 (1), 29–57.

Sampson, G.P. (1996), "Compatibility of Regional and Multilateral Trading Agreements: Reforming the WTO Process," *American Economic Review Papers and Proceedings*, 86 (2), 88–92.

Samuelson, P.A. (1953), "Prices of Factor and Goods in General Equilibrium," *Review of Economic Studies*, 21, 1–20.

Samuelson, L. (1982), "The Multinational Firm with Arm's Length Transfer Price Limits," *Journal of International Economics*, 13, 365–374

Savosnick, K.M. (1958), "The Box Diagram and the Production Possibility Curve," *Ekonomisk Tidsskrift*, 60 (3), 183–197.

Saxonhouse, G. R. (1989), "Differentiated Products, Economies of Scale and Access to the Japanese Market," in R.C. Feenstra (Ed.), *Trade Policies for International Competitiveness* (Chicago: University of Chicago Press and National Bureau of Economic Research).

Scharrer, H.E. (1979), "Die Währung Struktur im Welthandel," Wirtschaftsdienst.

Schott, P.K. (2003). "One Size Fits All? Heckscher-Ohlin Specialization in Global Production," *American Economic Review*, 93 (3), 686–708.

Schuknecht, L. (1992), *Trade Protection in the European Community* (Chur, Switzerland: Harwood Academic Press).

Seade, J. (1978), "Consumer's Surplus and Linearity of Engel Curves," *Economic Journal*, 88, 511–523.

Seade, J. (1980), "On the Effects of Entry," *Econometrica*, 48, 479–489.

Sener, F. and Zhao, L. (2009), "Globalization, R&D and the iPod Cycle," *Journal of International Economics* 77, 101–108.

Shephard, R.W. (1953), *Cost and Production Functions* (Princeton, NJ: Princeton University Press).

Shibata, H. (1968), "A Note on the Equivalence of Tariffs and Quotas," *American Economic Review*, 58, 137–142.

Shoven, J. and Whalley, J. (1984), "Applied General-Equilibrium Models of Taxation and International Trade: An Introduction and Survey," *Journal of Economic Literature*, 22 (3), 1007–1051.

Shoven, J. and Whalley, J. (1992), *Applying General Equilibrium* (New York: Cambridge University Press).

Smith, A. (1776), *An Inquiry into the Wealth of Nations* (London: W. Straham and T. Cadwell).

Smith, A. (1987), "Strategic Investment, Multinational Corporations and Trade Policy," *European Economic Review*, 31, 89–96.

Smith, A. and Venables, A.J. (1988), "Completing the Internal Market in the European Community: Some Industry Simulations," *European Economic Review*, 32, 1501–1525.

Solow, R.M. (1956), "A Contribution to the Theory of Economic Growth," *Quarterly Journal of Economics*, 70, 65–94.

Spencer, B.J. (1993), "Capital Subsidies and Countervailing Duties in Oligopolistic Industries," *Journal of International Economics*, 24, 45–69.

Srinivasan, T.N., Whalley, J., and Wooton, I. (1993), "Measuring the Effects of Regionalism on Trade and Welfare," in K. Anderson and R. Blackhurst (Eds.), *Regional Integration and the Global Trading System* (New York: Harvester Wheatsheaf), 52–79.

Staiger, R.W. (1986), "Measurement of the Factor Content of Foreign Trade with Traded Intermediate Goods," *Journal of International Economics* 21 (3/4), 361–368.

Staiger, R.W. and Wolak, F.A. (1989), "Strategic Use of Antidumping Law to Enforce Tacit International Collusion," NBER Working Paper No.3016.

Stark, O. (1992), *The Migration of Labor* (Oxford: Blackwell).

Stern, R.M. (1962), "British and American Productivity and Comparative Costs in International Trade," *Oxford Economic Papers*, 14 (3), 275–296.

Stern, R.M. (Ed.) (1993), *The Multilateral Trading System: Analysis and Options for Change* (Ann Arbor: University of Michigan Press).

Stern, R.M. and Maskus, K.V. (1981), "Determinants of US Foreign Trade, 1958–76," *Journal of International Economics*, 11 (2), 207–224.

Straubhaar, T. (1988), "International Labour Migration with a Common Market: Some Aspects of EC Experience," *Journal of Common Market Studies*, 27 (1), 45–62.

Sutton, J. (1986), "Non-Cooperative Bargaining Theory: An Introduction," *Review of Economic Studies*, 53, 709–724.

Swan, T.W. (1956), "Economic Growth and Capital Accumulation," *Economic Record*, 334–361.

Swedenborg, B. (1979), "The Multinational Operations of Swedish Firms," Stockholm Industrial Institute for Economic and Social Research.

Taylor, C.T. (2004), "The Economic Effects of Withdrawn Antidumping Investigations: Is there Evidence of Collusive Settlement?" *Journal of International Economics*, 62, 295–312.

Taylor, M.S. (1993), "Quality Ladders and Ricardian Trade," *Journal of International Economics*, 34, 225–243.

Teece, D.J. (1977), "Technology Transfer by Multinational Enterprise: An Assessment," *Economics Journal*, 87, 242–261.

Tharakan, P.K.M. (1983), *Intra-Industry Trade: Empirical and Methodological Aspects* (Amsterdam: North-Holland).

Tirole, J. (1988), *The Theory of Industrial Organization* (Cambridge, MA, and London: MIT Press).

Tomiura, D. (2007), "Foreign Outsourcing, Exporting and FDI: A Productivity Comparison at the Firm Level," *Journal of International Economics*, 72, 113–127.

Tornell, A. (1991), "On the Ineffectiveness of Made-to-Measure Protectionist Programs," in E. Helpman and A. Razin (Eds.). *International Trade and Trade Policy* (Cambridge, MA, and London: MIT Press), 66–79.

Trebilcock, M.J. and Howse, R. (2005), *The Regulation of International Trade*, third edition (London: Routledge).

Trefler, D. (1993a) "Trade Liberalization and the Theory of Endogenous Protection: An Econometric Study of US Import Policy," *Journal of Political Economy*, 101, 138–160.

Trefler, D. (1993b), "International Factor Price Differences: Leontief was Right!" *Journal of Political Economy*, 101 (6), 961–987.

Trefler, D. (1995), "The Case of the Missing Trade and Other Mysteries," *American Economic Review*, 85 (5), 1029–1046.

Trefler, D. (2004), "The Long and Short of the Canada–US Free Trade Agreement," *American Economic Review*, 94 (4), 870–895.

Trefler, D. and Zhu, S. (2010), "The Structure of Factor Content Predictions," *Journal of International Economics*, 82, 195–207.

Tybout, J.R. (2003), "Plant- and Firm Level Evidence on the 'New' Trade Theories," in E.K. Choi and L. Harrigan (Eds.), *Handbook of International Trade* (Oxford: Basil Blackwell).

Tybout, J.R. (2006), "Comments on: Trade Costs, Firms and Productivity," *Journal of Monetary Economics*, 53, 939–942.

US Bureau of Economic Analysis (1990a), *Foreign Direct Investment in the US: Operations of US Affiliates, Revised 1989 Estimates* (Washington, DC: US Bureau of Economic Analysis).

US Bureau of Economic Analysis (1990b), *US Direct Investment Abroad, Revised 1989 Estimates* (Washington, DC: US Bureau of Economic Analysis).

US Bureau of the Census, Annual Survey of Manufactures (1989), *Statistics for Industry Groups and Industries* (Washington, DC: US Bureau of the Census).

US Department of Commerce (2010), *Survey of Current Business* (Washington, DC: US Government Printing Office), 20–35 July.

UNCTAD (United Nations Conference on Trade and Development) (2002), *Trade and Development Report 2002: Developing Countries in World Trade* (Geneva: United Nations).

UNCTAD (2005), *Methodologies, Classifications, Quantification and Development Impacts of Non-Tariff Barriers: Note by the UNCTAD Secretariat* (Geneva: United Nations).

UNCTAD (2009), *World Investment Report* (Geneva: United Nations), available at http://unctad.org/en/docs/wir2009_en.pdf (accessed 25 October 2011).

UNCTAD (2010), *World Investment Report* (Geneva: United Nations).

United Nations, Centre for Transnational Corporations (1992), *The Determinants of Foreign Direct Investment: A Survey of the Evidence* (New York: United Nations).

United Nations (2010), *Millennium Development Goals*, available at http://www.mdg-trade.org (accessed 25 October 2011).

USITC (US International Trade Commission) (1989), "The Economic Effects of Significant US Import Restraints," USITC Publication 2222 (Washington, DC: US International Trade Commission) (October).

Uzawa, H. (1961), "On a Two-Sector Model of Economic Growth," *Review of Economic Studies*, 29, 40–47.

Van Biesebroeck, J. (2005), "Exporting Raises Productivity in Sub-Saharan African Manufacturing Plants," *Journal of International Economics*, 67 (2), 373–391.

Van Marrewijk, C. (2007), *International Economics: Theory, Application, and Policy* (Oxford: Oxford University Press).

Van Wijnbergen, S. (1986), "Macroeconomic Aspects of the Effectiveness of Foreign Aid: On the Two-Gap Model, Home Goods Disequilibrium and Real Exchange Rate Misalignment," *Journal of International Economics*, 21, 123–136.

Vandenbussche, H. and Zanardi, S. (2010), "The Chilling Trade Effects of Antidumping Proliferation," *European Economic Review*, 54 (6), 760–777.

Varian, H. R. (1992), *Microeconomic Analysis*, third edition (W.W. Norton: New York).

Vartia, Y. (1983), "Efficient Methods of Measuring Welfare Change and Compensated Income in Terms of Ordinary Demand Functions," *Econometrica*, 51, 79–98.

Venables, A.J. (1985), "Trade and Trade Policy with Imperfect Competition: The Case of Identical Products and Free Entry," *Journal of International Economics*, 19, 1–19.

Venables, A.J. (1990), "Microeconomic Implications of Exchange Rate Variations," *Oxford Review of Economic Policy*, 6 (3), 18–27.

Venables, A.J. (2004), "Vertical Foreign Direct Investment: Input Costs and Factor Prices," in G. Barba Navaretti and A.J. Venables (Eds.), *Multinational Firms in the World Economy* (Princeton, NJ: Princeton University Press).

Venables, A.J., Rice, P.G., and Stewart, M. (2003), "The Geography of Intra-Industry Trade: Empirics," *Topics in Economic Analysis and Policy*, 3(1), article 11.

Ventura, J. (1997), "Growth and Interdependence," *Quarterly Journal of Economics*, February, 57–84.

Vernon, R. (1966), "International Investment and International Traded in the Product Cycle," *Quarterly Journal of Economics*, 80 (2), 190–207.

Viaene, J.-M. (1982), "A Customs Union between Spain and the EEC," *European Economic Review*, 18, 345–368.

Viaene, J.-M. (1987), "Factor Accumulation in a Minimum-Wage Economy," *European Economic Review*, 31, 1313–1328.

Viaene, J.-M. (1993), "The Harrod-Johnson Diagram and the International Equilibrium," *International Economic Journal*, 7 (1), 83–93.

Viaene, J.-M. and de Vries, C.G. (1992a), "International Trade and Exchange Rate Volatility," *European Economic Review*, 36, 1311–1321.

Viaene, J.-M. and de Vries, C.G. (1992b), "On the Design of Invoicing Practices in International Trade," *Open Economies Review*, 3, 133–142.

Viaene, J.-M. and Zilcha, I. (1998), "The Behavior of the Competitive Exporting Firm under Multiple Uncertainty," *International Economic Review*, 39 (3), 591–609.

Viner, J. (1923), *Dumping: A Problem in International Trade* (Chicago: University of Chicago Press).

Viner, J. (1937), *Studies in the Theory of International Trade* (New York: Harper).

Viner, J. (1950), *The Customs Union Issue* (New York: Stevens & Sons).

Vousden, N. (1987), "Content Protection and Tariffs under Monopoly and Competition," *Journal of International Economics*, 23, 263–282.

Vousden, N. (1990), *The Economics of Trade Protection* (Cambridge: Cambridge University Press).

Weinstein, D. (1989), "Competition, Unilateral Dumping and Firm Profitability," University of Michigan Seminar Discussion Paper No. 249.

Weitzman, M. (1982), "Increasing Returns and the Foundations of Unemployment Theory," *Economic Journal*, 787–804.

Wiersema, M.F. and Bowen, H.P. (2008), "Corporate International Diversification: The Impact of Foreign Competition, Industry Globalization and Firm Diversification," *Strategic Management Journal*, 2 (29), 115–132.

Wiersema, M.F. and Bowen, H.P. (2011), "The Relationship between International Diversification and Firm Performance: Why It Remains a Puzzle," *Global Strategy Journal*, 1(1/2), 152–170.

Willenboekel, D. (1994), *Applied General Equilibrium Modelling: Imperfect Competition and European Integration* (Chichester: John Wiley).

Willig, R. (1998), "Economic Effects of Antidumping Policy," in R.Z. Lawrence (Ed.) *Brookings Trade Forum 1998* (Washington, DC: Brookings Institution).

Willig, R.D. (1976), "Consumer's Surplus without Apology," *American Economic Review*, 66, 589–597.

Winters, L.A. and Venables, A.J. (1991), *European Integration: Trade and Industry* (Cambridge: Cambridge University Press).

Wolf, H.C. (1994), "Growth Convergence Reconsidered," *Weltwirtschaftliches Archiv*, 130, 747–759.

Wong, K. Y. (1983), "On Choosing among Trade in Goods and International Capital and Labor Mobility: A Theoretical Analysis," *Journal of International Economics*, 14 (3/4), 223–250.

Wong, K.Y. (1988), "International Factor Mobility and the Volume of Trade: An Empirical Study," in R.C. Feenstra (Ed.), *Empirical Methods for International Trade*, (Cambridge, MA: MIT Press), 231–250.

Wong, K.Y. (1995), *International Trade in Goods and Factor Mobility* (Cambridge, MA: MIT Press).

Wonnacott, R. (1990), *US Hub-and-Spoke Bilaterals and the Multilateral Trading System* (Toronto: Howe Institute).

Wonnacott, P. and Wonnacott, R. (1981), "Is Unilateral Tariff Reduction Preferable to a Customs Union? The Curious Case of the Missing Foreign Tariffs," *American Economic Review*, 71, 704–713.

Woodland, A.D. (1977), "A Dual Approach to Equilibrium in the Production Sector in International Trade Theory," *Canadian Journal of Economics*, 10 (1), 50–68.

Woodland, A.D. (1980), "Direct and Indirect Trade Utility Functions," *Review of Economic Studies*, 47, 907–926.

Woodland, A.D. (1982), *International Trade and Resource Allocation* (New York: North-Holland).

Wooton, I. (1986), "Preferential Trading Arrangements: An Investigation," *Journal of International Economics*, 21, 81–97.

World Bank (2005), *Global Economic Prospects: Trade, Regionalism and Development* (Washington, DC: The World Bank).

World Bank (2007), *World Development Report 2008: Agriculture for Development* (Washington, DC: The World Bank).

World Bank (2009), *World Development Report 2010: Development and Climate Change* (Washington, DC: The World Bank).

World Economic Forum (1992), *World Competitiveness Report* (International Institute for Management Development).

World Integrated Trade Solution (2010), available at http://wits.worldbank.org/WITS/WITS/ (accessed 25 October 2011).

WTO (World Trade Organization) (various years), *World Trade Report* (Geneva: WTO).

WTO Eds. (1995), *International Trade, Trends and Statistics* (Geneva: WTO).

WTO Eds. (2010), *International Trade Statistics* (Geneva: WTO).

Yang, X. and Heijdra, B.J. (1993), "Monopolistic Competition and Optimum Product Diversity: Comment," *American Economic Review*, 83, 295–301.

Yeaple, S.R. (2003), "The Complex Integration Strategies of Multinationals and Cross Country Dependencies in the Structure of Foreign Direct Investment," *Journal of International Economics*, 60, 293–314.

Yeaple, S.R. (2006), "Offshoring, Foreign Direct Investment, and the Structure of US Trade," *Journal of the European Economic Association*, 6, 602–611.

Zanardi, M. (2000), "Antidumping Law as a Collusive Device," *Canadian Journal of Economics*, 37, 95–112.

Zar, J.H. (1972), "Significance Testing of the Spearman Rank Correlation Coefficient," *Journal of the American Statistical Association*, 67 (339), 578–580.

Zhang, K.H. and Markusen, J.R. (1999), "Vertical Multinationals and Host Country Characteristics," *Journal of Development Economics*, 59, 233–252.

Index